CHRISTIANITY AND FREEDOM

VOLUME 2: CONTEMPORARY PERSPECTIVES

Christianity and Freedom, Volume 2, illuminates how Christian minorities and transnational Christian networks contribute to the freedom and flourishing of societies across the globe, even amid pressure and violent persecution. Featuring unprecedented field research by some of the world's most distinguished scholars, it documents the outsized role of Christians in promoting human rights and religious freedom; fighting injustice; stimulating economic equality; providing education, social services, and health care; and nurturing democratic civil society. Readers will come away surprised and sobered to learn how this very Christian link to freedom often invites persecution. What are the dimensions of persecution and how are Christians responding to that pressure? What resources – theological, social, or transnational – do they marshal in leavening their societies? What will be lost if the Christian presence is marginalized? The answers to these questions are of crucial relevance in a world awash with religious extremism and deepening instability.

Allen D. Hertzke is an internationally recognized scholar of religion and politics. He is author of *Freeing God's Children: The Unlikely Alliance for Global Human Rights* and editor of *The Future of Religious Freedom: Global Challenges.* A past fellow for the Pew Research Center, he directed the study "Lobbying for the Faithful: Religious Advocacy Groups in Washington DC." He is a member of the Pontifical Academy of Social Sciences.

Timothy Samuel Shah is the Associate Director of the Religious Freedom Project at the Berkley Center for Religion, Peace, and World Affairs, and Visiting Assistant Professor in the Government Department, Georgetown University. He is the author most recently of *Religious Freedom: Why Now? Defending an Embattled Human Right* and *God's Century: Resurgent Religion and Global Politics* (with Monica Duffy Toft and Daniel Philpott).

The Religious Freedom Research Project

This volume is the fruit of research conceived and supported by the Religious Freedom Research Project (RFRP) of the Berkley Center for Religion, Peace, and World Affairs at Georgetown University. Under the leadership of Director Thomas Farr and Associate Director Timothy Samuel Shah, the Religious Freedom Research Project is the world's only university-based program devoted exclusively to the analysis of religious freedom, a basic human right restricted in many parts of the globe. The RFRP is made possible by significant grants from the John Templeton Foundation, a partnership with Baylor University's Institute for Studies of Religion, and the generous support of numerous other individuals and foundations.

The goal of the RFRP is to deepen scholarly understanding, inform policy deliberation, and educate the wider public concerning the meaning and value of religious freedom. It achieves this goal through publications such as this one, as well as conferences, workshops, media appearances, a vigorous web presence, and a blog, *Cornerstone: A Conversation on Religious Freedom and Its Social Implications*. Find out more at www.berkleycenter.georgetown.edu/rfp.

Contents

Contributing Authors

Zainal Abidin Bagir is Director of the Center for Religious and Cross-Cultural Studies at the Graduate School of Gadjah Mada University. He was Coprincipal Investigator for a two year research project on Pentecostalism in Indonesia and the Indonesian Coordinator for an international collaboration, the Pluralism Knowledge Programme.

Matthew Barber is a Ph.D. student in the Department of Near Eastern Languages and Civilizations at the University of Chicago, where he studies Islamic thought.

Chad M. Bauman is Associate Professor of Religion and Chair of the Department of Philosophy and Religion and of the Classical Studies Program at Butler University. He is also President of the Society for Hindu-Christian Studies.

Mark Brockway is a doctoral student in political science at the University of Notre Dame. His research focuses on religion in American and transnational politics.

Richard Burgess is Senior Lecturer in Theology at the University of Roehampton, London. He was formerly a lecturer at the Theological College of Northern Nigeria, Jos.

Robert W. Hefner is Professor of Anthropology and Director of the Institute on Culture, Religion, and World Affairs (CURA) at Boston University. He has directed nineteen research projects and is the author or editor of twenty books, including *Shari'a Politics: Islamic Law and Society in the Modern World*.

Allen D. Hertzke is David Ross Boyd Professor of Political Science and Faculty Fellow in Religious Freedom at the University of Oklahoma. He is editor of two recent books: *The Future of Religious Freedom: Global Challenges* and *Religious Freedom in America: Constitutional Roots and Contemporary Challenges*.

Michael Hoffman is a Ph.D. candidate at Princeton University. His work focuses on religion and political behavior.

Amaney A. Jamal is Edwards S. Sanford Professor of Politics at Princeton University and Director of the Mamdouha S. Bobst Center for Peace and Justice. Jamal also directs the Workshop on Arab Political Development. She currently is President of the Association of Middle East Women's Studies (AMEWS).

Todd M. Johnson is Associate Professor of Global Christianity and Director of the Center for the Study of Global Christianity at Gordon-Conwell Theological Seminary. Johnson is Visiting Research Fellow at Boston University's Institute for Culture, Religion and World Affairs, leading a research project on international religious demography.

Paul Marshall is Senior Fellow at the Hudson Institute's Center for Religious Freedom, Washington, D.C.; Distinguished Senior Fellow of the Institute for the Study of Religion at Baylor University; Senior Fellow at the Leimena Institute, Jakarta; and Visiting Professor at the Graduate School of Syarif Hidayatullah State Islamic University (UIN), Jakarta, Indonesia. He is the author and editor of more than twenty books on religion and politics, especially religious freedom, and his writings have been translated into twenty-two languages.

Danny McCain is Professor of Biblical Theology in the Department or Religion and Philosophy of the University of Jos, Jos, Nigeria. As an American who has lived in Nigeria since 1988, he has been an observer of much of the ethnoreligious conflict in Nigeria and actively involved in researching and promoting peace.

Donald E. Miller is Professor of Religion at the University of Southern California and Executive Director of the Center for Religion and Civic Culture at USC. He is the coauthor of *Global Pentecostalism: The New Face of Christian Social Engagements* (University of California Press, 2007) and was the Director of the Pentecostal and Charismatic Research Initiative project funded by the John Templeton Foundation.

Duane Alexander Miller is Lecturer in Church History and Theology for Nazareth Evangelical Theological Seminary (Israel) and Adjunct Professor of Theology at St Mary's University, San Antonio, Texas. He is also Mission Partner with the World Missions Department of the Episcopal Diocese of West Texas.

James Ponniah is Assistant Professor in the Department of Christian Studies at the University of Madras. He holds an M.A. and Ph.D. from the University of Madras.

Reg Reimer, with World Evangelical Alliance, began missionary service in Vietnam in 1966. Through numerous visits to Communist Vietnam since 1980, he has forged close ties with that country's burgeoning Evangelical movement, and advocated strongly for religious freedom. He is the author of an acclaimed book on the movement, *Vietnam's Christians: A Century of Growth in Adversity* (2011).

Rebecca S. Shah is Research Fellow at the Berkley Center for Religion, Peace, and World Affairs, Georgetown University, and Associate Scholar with the Berkley Center's Religious Freedom Project. An economist by training, Shah has been the Project Leader and Principal Investigator for two research initiatives on religion, entrepreneurship, and economic development in the modern world. Her work has been published in a number of scholarly anthologies.

Timothy Samuel Shah is Associate Director of the Religious Freedom Project at the Berkley Center for Religion, Peace, and World Affairs and Visiting Assistant Professor in the Government Department, Georgetown University. He is the author most recently of *Religious Freedom: Why Now? Defending an Embattled Human Right* and *God's Century: Resurgent Religion and Global Politics* (with Monica Duffy Toft and Daniel Philpott).

Sara Singha received her Ph.D. in theological and religious studies from Georgetown University. Her research interests include Muslim-Christian relations and religion and caste in North India and Pakistan.

Philip Sumpter received his Ph.D. in Old Testament at the University of Gloucestershire, United Kingdom. He was Lecturer at Nazareth Evangelical Theological Seminary in Israel and is currently Visiting Lecturer at the European School of Culture and Theology in Stuttgart, Germany.

Mariz Tadros is Fellow and Coleader of the Power and Popular Politics Cluster at the Institute of Development Studies, University of Sussex, United Kingdom.

Daphne Tsimhoni, Ph.D., is retired Professor of Modern Middle East History at the Department of Humanities and Arts, The Technion – Israel Institute of Technology and the Harry S. Truman Research Institute for the Advancement of Peace, the Hebrew University of Jerusalem; her research focuses on Palestinian Christians since the nineteenth century.

Fenggang Yang is Professor of Sociology and Director of the Center on Religion and Chinese Society. He is the Founding Editor of *Review of Religion and Chinese Society* and is the President of the Society for the Scientific Study of Religion (2014–2015).

Acknowledgments

This book is *Volume 2* of a two-volume project, *Christianity and Freedom: Historical and Contemporary Perspectives*. The volumes emerged from a two-year cooperative research initiative conceived and supported by the Religious Freedom Research Project (RFRP) of the Berkley Center for Religion, Peace, & World Affairs at Georgetown University. Founded in 2011, the RFRP has been made possible by significant grants from the John Templeton Foundation, a partnership with Baylor University's Institute for Studies of Religion, and the generous support of numerous other individuals and foundations. At the same time, the opinions expressed in this volume are those of the author(s) and do not necessarily reflect the views of the Templeton Foundation or any other supporting foundations or individuals.

The *Christianity and Freedom* initiative was set in motion by an initial, catalytic grant from the Lynde and Harry Bradley Foundation in 2011. For his crucial role in helping us to conceptualize the project and then inviting us to seek Bradley support, we gratefully acknowledge Daniel Schmidt, Bradley's Vice President for Program. Serendipitously and almost simultaneously, in September 2011, Donald Yerxa and Wilfred McClay went out of their way to encourage us to seek major funding from the Historical Society's Religion and Innovation in Human Affairs Program (RIHA), an initiative they had just launched with the support of the Templeton Foundation. Don Yerxa in particular has proven a constant source of warm encouragement, not least through his gracious invitation to one of the editors (Timothy Shah) to deliver the Donald A. Yerxa Lecture in History on *Christianity and Freedom* at Eastern Nazarene University in April 2014. At a crucial point, before it was clear how much support the project would ultimately secure, Matthew Franck and the Witherspoon Institute stepped in to provide generous bridge funding that enabled us to organize and hold the first planning meeting with our Steering Committee of distinguished scholar-advisers and thus get our work under way in the spring of 2012.

We are delighted to have enjoyed the support of Baylor University, whose investment in this project has blossomed into an ongoing partnership with

Georgetown University's Religious Freedom Research Project. It is a pleasure to single out Ken Starr, President and Chancellor of Baylor University and a contributor to *Volume 1*, and Byron Johnson, Director of Baylor's Institute for Studies of Religion (ISR) and a member of our Steering Committee, for the depth and constancy of their personal and institutional commitment to this project and its goal of advancing scholarship in the cause of human freedom. We also gratefully acknowledge the enthusiasm and wisdom of Carey Newman, Director of Baylor University Press. Carey joined us for the conference in Rome that previewed the project findings and gave us singularly generous and profound counsel concerning the process of taking the fruit of our work to publication. He has also worked closely with us to develop a monograph encapsulating the findings of the *Christianity and Freedom* initiative, making heavy investments of his time (and that of his staff) along the way.

The contributors to the *Christianity and Freedom* volumes presented their initial research at a global conference in Rome on December 13–14, 2013. We are especially grateful to the representatives of the Acton Institute for the Study of Religion and Liberty in Rome – particularly Kishore Jayabalan and Michael Severance – for their counsel and indefatigable assistance in conference organization and planning over many months. We also gratefully acknowledge the Pontificia Università Urbaniana (Pontifical Urban University) and its Secretary General, Father Roberto Cherubini, for their generosity in throwing open the university's beautiful facilities for our use throughout the conference. And we warmly thank the Honorable Kenneth Hackett, United States Ambassador to the Holy See, for hosting a welcome reception in the ambassadorial residence on the eve of the conference for participants and special guests.

Three additional people deserve special mention for their memorable contributions to our Rome gathering. A most dramatic moment was the keynote address of His Beatitude, Louis Raphaël I Sako, Chaldean Catholic Patriarch of Iraq, who challenged us to raise our voices on behalf of Christians imperiled in their ancient lands. His ongoing fight to salvage and restore the pluralist fabric of Middle Eastern societies – now under existential threat – personifies and dramatizes the aims and themes of this project. We were also humbled and buoyed to receive the blessing of the Holy Father, Pope Francis, in a personal audience on the morning of the final day of the conference. With his zest for close ecumenical cooperation, nurtured over many years of friendship with evangelical and other non-Catholic religious leaders in Argentina, he took particular delight that our project and our conference represented a "Baptist-Catholic" collaboration between Georgetown University, America's oldest Catholic university, and Baylor University, the world's largest Baptist university. We interpreted his decision to meet with us – less than a year into his pontificate – as a concrete sign of his passionate concern for religious liberty as well as the growing plight of persecuted Christians worldwide. On both of these issues he has spoken with ever-greater poignancy and clarity over the last two years. Finally, we gratefully acknowledge the role of then-Archbishop Dominique Mamberti, at that time the Vatican Secretary for Relations with States (since made a cardinal by Pope Francis), in launching our conference with a compelling keynote address interweaving the historic significance of the Edict of Milan and the contemporary importance of religious freedom. We also thank Cardinal Mamberti for his role in facilitating our personal audience with Pope Francis.

The success of this endeavor hinged in large measure on the foundational work of the distinguished members of our Steering Committee. These members identified contributing scholars, honed the themes and research questions of the volumes, and diligently reviewed and provided detailed feedback on draft chapters. Furthermore, their own scholarship served as an inspiration and model for many of the contributors to these volumes. Our thanks go out to these outstanding individuals: Thomas Farr, Matthew Franck, Yvonne Haddad, Amaney Jamal, Byron Johnson, David Little, Paul Marshall, and Robert Wilken. We especially want to acknowledge our colleague Thomas Farr, Director of the Religious Freedom Project at Georgetown, for his sage counsel and assiduous work at every stage of this initiative. Robert Wilken also deserves special thanks. In sharing his own pivotal research on the roots of religious freedom in the early church fathers, he proved an indispensable inspiration for this entire project. His close involvement ever since has guaranteed that we have never been without his infectious intellectual enthusiasm.

This project could not have been fulfilled without the vital support of Georgetown University, and particularly the leadership and staff of the Berkley Center for Religion, Peace, and World Affairs. We are profoundly grateful to Thomas Banchoff, Director of the Berkley Center and Georgetown's Vice-President for Global Engagement, as well as Michael Kessler, the Berkley Center's Managing Director. From the very beginning, they have generously contributed their support and encouragement, both intellectual and administrative. Other Berkley Center colleagues who provided essential support include Erin Taylor, Amy Vander Vliet, Melody Fox Ahmed, and Randolph Pelzer.

If the multipronged efforts leading up to the publication of these volumes had a single headquarters, however, it was the Religious Freedom Research Project and its dedicated staff and team of student assistants. More than anyone, these friends and colleagues managed the successful execution of every aspect of this project, down to the last detail, with unfailing cheerfulness and consummate professionalism. We are particularly grateful to the Senior Project Associate, Claudia Winkler, who in effect played the role of managing editor of both of the project volumes, and the former Senior Project Associate Kyle Vander Meulen, who more than any other single person worked to ensure the success of the Rome conference. We are also thankful for the many contributions of the Project Associate Nicholas Fedyk and the former

Project Associate A. J. Nolte. In addition, we acknowledge the many Georgetown students who contributed outstanding research and editorial assistance, especially Louis Cona, Justin Pinkerman, Matthew Quallen, Kevin Sullivan, Timothy Yin, and Harry Green.

Allen Hertzke's work as coeditor of these volumes was supported by the University of Oklahoma's Religious Freedom Project, which he directs under the auspices of the Institute for the American Constitutional Heritage. That program funded two energetic undergraduate research assistants, Gabriella Skillings and Erin Byrne, who helped us manage this complex endeavor. It also funded the work of our talented and assiduous indexer, Alexa Selph.

We are deeply grateful to John Witte Jr., Series Editor of the Cambridge Studies in Law and Christianity, for his enthusiastic backing of this project. We are honored and delighted to be included in his series. We also laud the superb work of Cambridge University Press in publishing these volumes, and we are particularly grateful to Senior Editor John Berger, Managing Editor Stephen Acerra, and the entire team involved in copyediting, production, and marketing.

The John Templeton Foundation deserves a special note of thanks. Without the Templeton Foundation's generous funding in 2011, there would have been no Rome conference and no volume of outstanding essays. In fact, there would have been no Religious Freedom Project at all. The decision to bet on the Religious Freedom Project with a major start-up grant ultimately rested with Dr. Jack Templeton, President of the John Templeton Foundation. It was thus a blow to us and to the visionary philanthropy the Templeton Foundation uniquely embodies that he passed away on May 19, 2015 as this volume was being completed. We take this opportunity to record our unpayable debt of gratitude to Dr. Jack Templeton. And we take this opportunity to pray: Eternal rest grant unto him.... Long may his work continue.

For both of us this project is more than an academic exercise, as we have been inspired and challenged by the faithful witness of our many brothers and sisters in Christ around the world who live under conditions of persecution, yet whose very struggle sows the seeds of a more hopeful future. We pay homage to their inestimable gifts, both to global Christianity and to human freedom. More than anything, these volumes acknowledge and honor the fact that they are not mere victims, passive and mute, but stirring witnesses and incomparably powerful agents of world-historical change.

The process of expressing thanks (however inadequate) to the many people who inspired, supported, and carried this initiative to fruition takes us to a place of deeper gratitude – for our very lives, our liberties, our families, and the many blessings of God's love we experience. To all of this we can only pray: *Deo Gratias.*

Allen D. Hertzke and Timothy Samuel Shah
November 22, 2015, The Solemnity of Christ the King

Introduction

Christianity and Freedom in the Contemporary World

Allen D. Hertzke

The seizure of Mosul, Iraq's second largest city, by Islamic State militants in the summer of 2014 stunned the world. Especially shocking was their brutal efficiency in killing or expelling the entire, and ancient, Christian population from the city. But for those following developments in the region over the past decade this was, sad to say, less of a shock. Since the fall of the Saddam Hussein regime in Iraq, Western advocates such as Nina Shea and local leaders including Chaldean Patriarch Louis Raphaël I Sako of Baghdad have sounded the alarm about the catastrophic assault on Christian minorities, which accelerated with the civil war in Syria and the rise of ISIS. But what has also become evident is that the fate of other vulnerable religious minorities, not to mention the pluralist fabric of these societies, rides on the fate of Christians. Thus the scenario playing out in the Middle East underscores the importance of assessing the role and fate of Christian communities around the globe.

As the historical volume demonstrates, Christianity, with all of its human frailties, nonetheless carries in its DNA a transcendent conception of human dignity and equality conducive to free institutions and societies. Because the experiences of Christian minorities today mirror those that spawned earlier churches' historic innovations, the contemporary situation offers an unprecedented opportunity – a kind of vast global laboratory – to probe how diverse Christian communities are replicating the historical findings of *Volume 1* of this project.

But how do Christian communities under various forms of pressure or hardship instantiate the faith's transcendent vision? In what ways, or where, are they advancing freedom, building civil society, or providing economic uplift in diverse societies around the world? What are the causes and dimensions of the persecution they face and how are they responding to that pressure? What resources – theological, social, or transnational – do they marshal in leavening their societies? And what will be lost if the Christian presence is marginalized or, in the case of parts of the Middle East, vanishes?

These questions are of enormous relevance to understanding contemporary religious persecution and to devising adequate policy responses to it. To answer them the Christianity and Freedom Project commissioned original field research guided by common questions, along with global demographic overviews, thematic investigations, and surveys by leading scholars, to understand how Christian minorities and transnational institutions contribute to societies across the globe. The result is an unprecedented portrait of the contemporary role and response of Christian communities under diverse conditions of struggle, hardship, and oppression.

We begin with the context. Christianity faces a global crisis of persecution, as believers in many places around the world suffer harassment, marginalization, and violence – in more countries and under more diverse settings than any other faith group. A number of recent studies document the contours of this trend. For example, Rupert Shortt, religion editor of the *London Times Literary Supplement*, investigated the shocking treatment of Christians on several continents, often with official collusion, and exposes the indifferent western response. In his 2012 book, *Christianophobia: A Faith under Attack*, he argues that this story is underreported because Christian believers do not become radicalized and tend to resist nonviolently, enabling politicians and the media to play down the problem.[1]

John Allen, senior correspondent for the *National Catholic Reporter*, contends that the persecution of Christians is the most dramatic religion story in the early twenty-first century, yet one that many in the West have little idea is even happening. In his 2013 book, *The Global War on Christians: Dispatches from the Front Lines of Anti-Christian Persecution*, he laments that the new martyrs often suffer in silence.[2] Most recently, a contributor to the present volume, Paul Marshall, along with coauthors Lela Gilbert and Nina Shea, document the scope and trends of this crisis in *Persecuted: The Global Assault on Christians* (2013). Because this work so nicely catalogs the diverse origins and settings of persecution, we commissioned Marshall to team up with the demographer Todd M. Johnson to map the terrain of anti-Christian persecution and its diverse motivations. One of the key findings of that exploration, as Marshall documents in this volume, is that the very association of Christianity with freedom sparks repression by totalitarians, autocrats, and theocratic regimes threatened by Christians' independence, transcendent allegiances, and cultivation of civil society.[3]

Despite the mounting evidence of this crisis, skeptics remain in the academy and commentariate. Candida Moss, who claims that ancient Christians invented the story of martyrdom to propagandize the faith, sees the same phenomenon in stories of anti-Christian persecution today.[4] This seems like willful ignorance. In a span of less than a year we have witnessed the rapid liquidation of Christianity in the Nineveh Plain, the methodical demolition of church buildings in eastern China, massive atrocities against Christians by Boko Haram in Nigeria, the bombing of Christian churches in Pakistan, the heartrending beheadings of Coptic Christians in Libya, and the slaughter of Christian students in Kenya.[5]

Systematic documentation, moreover, demonstrates the widespread nature of assaults on Christian communities. The nonpartisan Pew Research Center's meticulous studies reveal global patterns of harassment of specific religious peoples by governments and dominant social groups – including killings, physical assaults, arrests, desecration of holy sites, mob violence, intimidation, and discrimination in employment, education, and housing. During the six years covered (2007–2013) Christians suffered harassment at some point in a total of 151 countries, more than that of any other religious group.[6] Muslims, the next group facing harassment (in a total of 136 countries over the period), suffer both in non-Muslim societies and Muslim-majority countries – the latter often for being the wrong kind of Muslims. Christians, on the other hand, suffer in more diverse settings and across a wider geographic span.

Beyond the humanitarian and human rights dimensions of this crisis, why does this matter? As the contributors to this volume show, it matters because Christianity plays a distinct and often outsized role in promoting ideas and practices of freedom globally and in their particular communities. Votaries of liberty, whether religious or not, thus have a stake in the fate of this global religious community.

To be clear, we do not suggest that Christian churches always or everywhere promote human freedom in the world today. As in history, contemporary Christian communities can be deeply compromised by political interests, swept up in ethnic violence, or complicit in exploitation. The failure, even complicity, of churches during the Rwanda genocide reminds us of this. More recently, Christian militias and mobs have engaged in widespread violence against Muslims in the Central African Republic. But both of these cases sparked soul searching by Christian leaders and subsequent initiatives of peacemaking and reconciliation.[7] Christianity's DNA, combined with its robust global humanitarian networks, serves as a potential – if not inevitable – corrective of universal human failures.

With this context in mind, we now turn to a review of the contributions in this volume, beginning with several chapters that survey the global scene. Todd M. Johnson, the world's most eminent scholar of religious demography, launches this assessment with a new and comprehensive analysis of the demographics of persecution. He concludes that more than one of every five Christians in the world live in states where they are likely to face persecution. This amounts to some 500 million Christians. By 2020, Johnson predicts, this figure will rise to 600 million, or nearly a quarter (23.5 percent) of the world's Christian population. Indeed, persecution against Christians persists in more nations and affects more people than it does any other religious community. Some of the fastest-growing traditions in global Christianity – such as Pentecostal and independent churches – find themselves under increasing risk of persecution.

Working with patterns identified by Dr. Johnson, Paul Marshall presents a taxonomy of the sources of anti-Christian persecution. In his chapter, "Patterns and Purposes of Contemporary Anti-Christian Persecution," Marshall finds that persecution against Christians is massive, widespread, increasing, and underreported. In probing the patterns of this persecution, he finds four principal sources: 1) the Communist remnant (China, Vietnam, Laos, North Korea, and Cuba); 2) South Asian religious nationalism (India, Nepal, Sri Lanka, and Bhutan); 3) the Muslim-majority world; and 4) authoritarian and national security states. Marshall also examines a fifth threat to Christian freedom: Western secularism. While milder than the other categories, restrictions and hostilities in a number of countries in the West are growing and cause for alarm, particularly because they undercut the ability of the West to uphold international norms and law on religious freedom. Marshall offers a penetrating theological explanation that unites the disparate sources of persecution. Because Christianity denies that the state is the ultimate arbiter of human life, it challenges all attempts – whether Communist, theocratic, ethnic nationalist, or authoritarian – to impose a single authority in state and society. Thus a key driver in the contemporary persecution of Christians is the very association of Christianity with freedom and pluralism – a finding with profound policy implications.

Donald E. Miller next synthesizes the cutting-edge findings of a massive study he directed of global Pentecostalism. His chapter demonstrates the energy, vitality, and entrepreneurial resourcefulness of Pentecostal and charismatic congregations. With one-quarter of the world's Christians, this movement represents a pivotal renewal force within global Christianity, fueled by religious zeal, bold vision, adaptability to local context, rapid indigenization, and nonhierarchical organization. Miller documents the widely varied initiatives of Pentecostal and Charismatic Christians in numerous communities of Latin America, Africa, and Asia. These initiatives include the provision of food and clothing for the impoverished, youth programs, high-quality schools in slums, medical clinics, blood banks, alcohol and drug rehabilitation, and mental health programs. Miller finds that those who embrace the conservative moral ethic of Pentecostalism experience upward mobility and the sense of agency that flows from it. While often facing discrimination or persecution, Pentecostals are learning how to work creatively with government officials in pressing for their right to religious freedom and in that way opening spaces for others in civil society.

Miller's chapter also underscores a crucial finding about conditions for Christianity in Latin America. As he demonstrates, the explosive growth of Pentecostalism there initially sparked animosity with the Catholic majority. But as Pentecostal communities planted deep roots in many Latin American countries, healthy competition and dialogue ensued. Indeed, as Anthony Gill has documented,

Pentecostal competition invigorated Catholicism in the continent and spurred broad protections of religious liberty and resulting norms of interreligious amity.[8]

Rebecca S. Shah's chapter, "Empowering Poor Women," elaborates on Miller's findings about the Christian contribution to personal agency and upward mobility. Based on more than a thousand new interviews on three continents, Shah's fine-grained analysis documents the empowering role Christian faith can play in the lives of poor women in developing countries. With a special focus on female converts to Christianity from "untouchable" backgrounds in India, Shah finds that the new faith of these women often enhances their dignity, agency, and hope for the future. She also finds that participation in small, face-to-face Christian communities gives them access to networks of support and accountability that yield significant economic and social benefits. For example, Shah demonstrates that women who participate in these faith-based networks are more successful in microfinance projects; more able to save money for the needs of their families, including their children's education; and more likely to report cases of domestic abuse and enlist community leaders to combat it.

Rounding out our global overviews, Mark Brockway and Allen D. Hertzke explore what they term global Christian networks for human dignity. The Christian idea of the surpassing worth of all persons made in the image of God – which drove Christian contributions to freedom in antiquity – can serve as a powerful challenge for Christians to address affronts to human dignity in the contemporary world. As Brockway and Hertzke show, the globalization of Christianity marries this idea of dignity with the growing capacities of transnational Christian networks. Their chapter illustrates how Christian dignity is instantiated in overlapping networks focused on global poverty, AIDS, human trafficking, religious persecution, displacement, and war. These Christian networks play an invaluable if unheralded role on the global stage in human rights advocacy, humanitarian succor, and peacemaking.

We now turn our attention to field research findings on the role and status of Christian minorities in different nations around the globe. Fenggang Yang launches this exploration with his stunning chapter "The Growth and Dynamism of Chinese Christianity." Drawing on the unprecedented access of a large team of field research scholars in China, Yang documents the accelerating growth of Christianity in the face of state repression. Today at least 5 percent of China's vast populace is Christian, and, with compounding growth rates, that percentage will rise exponentially. Remarkably, Yang predicts that by 2030, China may well pass the United States as having the world's largest Christian population. As Yang demonstrates, Christianity's growth has moved from rural to urban areas, from the marginalized to middle-class professionals, and toward greater diversification and indigenization.

Yang finds close parallels between Christianity in China today and its position in the Roman Empire on the eve of the Edict of Milan, nicely capturing the value of examining the faith across time and place. Just as Christianity spread through the networks of the Roman Empire, today's Christians capitalize on China's robust infrastructure for travel, communication, and global commerce to share and entrench the faith. Similarly, Christianity provides appealing sources of morality and meaning that propel its growth, just as it did in ancient Rome. Finally, compounding growth rates in China today parallel those that took Christianity from 5–10 percent of the Roman Empire in 300 A.D. to 50 percent by 350, leading Yang to see a similar trajectory as possible in China.

What makes this dynamic growth fateful is Christianity's outsized role in promoting human rights, religious freedom, civil society, and social welfare. Indeed, Yang demonstrates how Christians are at the front lines of practicing and promoting individual freedoms, rule of law, civic engagement, and charitable enterprise. Buoying this engagement have been the rise of Christian entrepreneurs and business networks; the conversion of exiled leaders of the 1989 democracy movement and the ongoing conversion of Chinese students; and the prominence of Christian lawyers in the defense of human rights. Moreover, Yang's own initiatives suggest a growing boldness of these advocates. As recounted in the chapter, Yang convened a group of prominent Chinese Christian lawyers, pastors, and academics at Purdue University in May 2014. Those advocates signed a strong declaration, "The Purdue Consensus on Religious Freedom," that called upon the regime to live up to international standards on religious liberty.

From China we turn to Indonesia, the world's largest Muslim-majority nation. Robert W. Hefner and Zainal Abidin Bagir assembled an international team of Muslim and Christian scholars to assess Christianity and religious freedom in Indonesia. Bagir and Hefner find that Christians are making constructive political contributions despite rising threats to their freedom and security. Christians constitute nearly 10 percent of Indonesia's population, and they have made crucial contributions to its culture, education, and independence struggle. However, major Christian leaders interviewed in 2013 argue that conditions for Christians have deteriorated since Suharto's fall fifteen years ago. Christians report more frequent attacks on churches and schools as well as efforts to marginalize them socially and politically. In this challenging climate, Christians continue to participate in Indonesia's formal framework of cooperation between the government and religious institutions, but they are also pressing authorities to do more to guarantee their freedom and security.

Another international team, Chad M. Bauman in the United States and James Ponniah in India, chart the growth and challenges for Christianity in India. In a groundbreaking study based on extensive new field research, Bauman and Ponniah provide an up-to-date account of the status and role of Christianity in the world's largest democracy, Hindu-majority India. Constituting only about 4 percent of the population, the Christian community has made substantial and disproportionate contributions to Indian civil society, especially in education, health care, poverty amelioration, and human rights activism. However, Bauman and Ponniah show that Christianity's appeal to low-caste and tribal peoples has provoked fear among the guardians of traditional Indian society, resulting in attempts – sometimes violent – to limit the freedom of Christians. And yet the Christian community's growing experience of harassment and violence has not led it to withdraw from civil society. On the contrary, Bauman and Ponniah conclude that Christians have increased their investment in the people of India. They are forming partnerships not only with other minority communities experiencing oppression, including Muslims, but also with secular-minded Hindus and human rights activists.

Next, Reg Reimer draws upon a rich network of local contacts to explore the contributions of Christians to freedom amid adversity in Vietnam. Though marginalized and perennially suspect in the Communist state, Christians represent growing and productive communities deeply embedded in the national cultures of Vietnam. Reimer shows that Christianity contributed to Vietnam's modernization, including the universally used writing script that enabled high literacy rates. While composing 10 percent of the population, Christians play an outsized role in education, health, aid to the poor and vulnerable, and upholding of human rights. With particular appeal to stigmatized ethnic minorities, the Christian "good news" that every person is created in God's image acts as a liberating force for oppressed peoples. Christian conversion also provides a documented economic uplift by promoting education, agency, industry, and thrift. Reimer finds that social hostility against Christians is often tolerated or instigated by local governmental authorities, but that Christians are increasingly protesting that treatment, standing up for human rights, and acting as a liberalizing force in society. Christian communities, particularly Protestants, also model democracy with free and regular elections for pastors, elders, and denominational church officials.

Blending deep personal experience and months of targeted field investigation, Sara Singha explores the challenge and leaven of Christian communities in Pakistan. Singha begins by recounting how Christians played a vital role in the formation of Pakistan by pivotally backing the effort of Pakistan's founder, Muhammad Ali Jinnah, to establish the country as a pluralistic democracy. Today Christians run orphanages, hospitals, clinics, women's centers, and social work agencies across the nation. Their educational system is the most highly rated in the country, attracting the children of many elite Muslim families. Unfortunately, over time Pakistan's governments have embraced exclusionary policies that undermine Jinnah's vision and threaten the ability of Christians to contribute constructively to Pakistani society. Apostasy and blasphemy laws have created a chilling environment for Christians, in which the mere accusation can unleash vigilante attacks against vulnerable religious minorities. Since these tools of intimidation are also employed against Ahmadis, Muslim reformers, and women's rights advocates, we see again how the fate of Christians is twinned with the maintenance and expansion of freedom. While Christians are increasingly fearful – for good reason in light of church bombings, mob violence, and state harassment – Singha shows that they are also increasingly active and assertive players in public life.

Turning to a crucial fault line of ethnoreligious clashes, Richard Burgess and Danny McCain chart the challenge to Christianity of religious violence in Nigeria. Burgess and McCain focus primarily on the role of Christian communities in central and northern Nigeria in the face of violence and discrimination. In the core northern states where Shari'a law is enforced, Christians face severe restrictions on religious practice and vigilante violence. In the border region, they confront widespread destruction of church property and extensive killings at the hands of the brutal Boko Haram insurgency, which in 2015 proclaimed its allegiance to the Islamic State in the Middle East. While these attacks have led some Christian youth to lash out in reprisals against Muslims, Christian leaders have undertaken creative initiatives of conflict prevention, interfaith dialogue, and peacemaking. In addition, churches remain extensively involved in ministries of assistance to widows and orphans, health care, development projects, skills training, and microenterprises. Repression and violence have generally sparked increasing political engagement by Christians, though in some contexts insecurity has led to evacuation and a diminished Christian presence. While Boko Haram atrocities have received international attention, Burgess and McCain delve beneath the headlines to recount the often-courageous Christian responses, which deserve wider recognition and support.

We round this contemporary volume with several chapters on the role of Christians increasingly under siege in the Middle East. We begin with the timely chapter by Mariz Tadros, "Copts of Egypt: Defiance, Compliance, and Continuity." On the basis of extensive participant observation, along with dozens of interviews with Christians and Muslims who have been directly involved in Egypt's dramatic political upheavals over the past three years, Mariz Tadros provides a firsthand account of Coptic contributions to civil and religious freedom in the largest and most influential Arab country. For more than one thousand years, the Copts have contributed to Egypt's political thought, enriched its culture, and strengthened its economy. Copts played a pioneering role in developing indigenous secular thinking and participated en masse in emancipatory revolutions from 1919 to the present day. However, between January 2011, with the onset of the revolutionary protests against Mubarak, and today, in the aftermath of the ouster of President Morsi, Egypt has witnessed the worst anti-Coptic backlash in modern history. At the same time, it has also experienced some of the highest levels of interreligious solidarity. Tadros marshals original qualitative and quantitative research to clarify the rising challenges Copts have faced, as well as how they are likely to shape Egypt's future.

Next we feature two chapters on the distinct challenges of Christians in the Holy Land. In the first chapter, Duane Alexander Miller and Philip Sumpter show that Palestinian Christians live a precarious existence, caught between the constrictions of Israeli policies (and a poor economy) in the West Bank and rising Islamist social pressures within Palestinian society. Emigration is a crucial problem, as adaptable young people seek better economic opportunities abroad. Christian leaders and churches have responded to this challenge of sustaining the next generation by providing housing for young families and promoting economic development, often drawing upon transnational denominational support. Another strategy of survival has been the operation of high-quality Christian schools that appeal to Muslim youth, offering the opportunity to inculcate notions of tolerance and charity and thus leaven Palestinian society as a counterweight to militancy. Field research in the West Bank uncovered how believers navigate the fierce challenges of their dual identity as Christians and Palestinians through a two-level discourse that affirms Palestinian solidarity on the public level but in private insists that growing Islamist antagonism threatens their presence and freedom.

In the next chapter the Israeli scholar Daphne Tsimhoni examines Christians in the state of Israel. Tsimhoni begins with a comprehensive portrait of the demographic presence, status, and role of Christian communities in Israel and East Jerusalem. She charts the distinct characteristics of the different centers of Christians in Israel, the state discrimination and social pressure they face, and tensions between integration and emigration. While representing a small minority, Christians have played a prominent role as spokespersons of the Arab minority in the Knesset and providers of educational and welfare services. The chapter explores how they might help promote peace and understanding between Jews and Palestinian Arabs.

Though political turmoil in the Middle East threatens ancient Christian communities, Amaney Jamal and Michael Hoffman provide a glimmer of hope in their chapter on Arab Muslim attitudes toward religious minorities. Using new and unique data from the second wave of the Arab Barometer survey, Jamal and Hoffman examine perceptions toward religious minorities in ten Arab countries. They find that in this region – often a hotbed of politically driven religious conflict – tolerance of religious minorities is actually quite high. While considerable differences exist both within and across countries, citizens of the Arab world are, for the most part, highly supportive of political and religious rights for non-Muslims, including Christians, and believe that religious minorities should be welcome in Muslim states. Majorities of Muslims in every country included in this survey support equal political rights for non-Muslims, would be willing to have a non-Muslim as a neighbor, and believe that religious differences are not a reason to doubt a fellow citizen's patriotism. These hopeful findings cast doubt on common claims that religion – and particularly, Islam – is an intractable source of intolerance in the Middle East.

Finally, we are pleased to have the tremendously timely contribution by Matthew Barber on the crisis facing Christians in Iraq and Syria. Barber, who has lived and conducted extensive field research in the region over the past several years, was studying in Syria when the civil war erupted and, momentously, was in northern Iraq in the summer of 2014 when Islamic State militants expelled Christians from Mosul and assaulted Yazidis in the Sinjar Mountains. He was one of the first outside observers to interview Christian families and Yazidi refugees fleeing from the ISIS reign of terror.

Barber begins by providing a lens into the historical roots of the various Chaldean and Assyrian Christian communities in the region, and how they faced successive shocks in the twentieth century – the Ottoman collapse, colonial exploitation, and the emergence of Baathist regimes. This historical context helps the reader understand the precarious position of these communities, which left them uniquely vulnerable when social order collapsed in the wake of the Iraq war and the Syrian conflict. Barber's historically informed ethnography illuminates the on-the-ground experience of Christians in the face of chaos, brutal atrocities, and religious cleansing. Portentously, he finds that, in the absence of outside intervention, self-defense may be the best hope for remnants of these ancient communities. Indeed, Christians have begun forming self-defense militias, an entirely understandable response to the existential peril they face. Let us hope that more vigorous international responses will provide alternatives to this bleak scenario.

SUMMARY THEMES

Three broad themes emerge from this volume's rich scholarship. First, in assaying global Christianity we are struck by the tremendous diversity of its contexts, challenges, and responses. Nested amid Dalit women in India, business networks of Southeast Asia, teeming Chinese cities, African villages, Latin American favelas, or refugee camps in Turkey, it spans the globe and adapts to diverse cultural and political environments. It faces a parlous existence in the Middle East but dynamic growth in China and Africa. Confronting varying forms of pressure, Christians respond in multifold ways. They form coalitions to protect their rights; they engage in interfaith initiatives of peacemaking; they cultivate civil society and pledge their loyalty as citizens. Sad to say, Christians sometimes lash out in reprisals, as in the Central African Republic; sometimes their heroic efforts are undermined by failing states, as in South Sudan; or sometimes they simply flee peril, as in Syria and Iraq.

Second, the advance and maintenance of freedom around the globe are tied to the fate of Christianity. Careful field research demonstrates the outsized role of Christian communities in defending religious freedom and human rights, empowering the marginalized, and providing education, health care, and social services. Pledging fealty to an authority higher than the state, Christians strive to carve spaces for autonomous civil society and conscience rights that underpin democratic governance. Moreover, wide-ranging indigenous initiatives are vitally linked to global Christian humanitarian networks and human rights advocacy, magnifying policy impact. Associated with freedom or, in the minds of autocrats and theocrats, with the West, Christians often serve as the "canaries in the coal mine," signaling looming threats to liberties in diverse societies. As we see in the Middle East, the destiny of other religious minorities, and of women and Muslim reformers, is often twinned with the fate of Christianity. Something vital will be lost if this presence is marginalized or vanishes.

Third, the crisis facing Christian minorities around the world, along with growing awareness of their leavening role in diverse societies, may propel new forms of ecumenism and solidarity in the global Christian family. The scandal of disunity that afflicts the faith, and its enormous cultural variety in diverse settings, can leave the persecuted feeling forsaken by their more comfortable brothers and sisters. This sentiment was eloquently expressed by Patriarch Sako, head of Iraq's Chaldean Catholic community, in a 2103 keynote speech at the Rome conference that launched this project. "We feel forgotten and isolated," he remarked. "We sometimes wonder, if they kill us all, what would be the reaction of Christians in the West? Would they do something then?"[9]

As dramatic assaults against Christians have unfolded since Sako's forsaken cry, we discern growing signs of profound ecumenism and solidarity. Matthew Barber recounts in this volume that when ISIS seized Mosul its personnel began spray painting Christian properties with the Arabic letter *nūn* (ن) for "Nazarene." After Christians fled, the *nūn* served to designate properties that ISIS could appropriate. After these events "the *nūn* became an international symbol of solidarity with Iraq's Christian community and was widely displayed in demonstrations and social media as a show of support." Similarly, the shocking beheading of the Egyptian Copts in Libya aroused widespread pledges of Christian solidarity, led by Pope Francis's heartfelt prayers for "our brother Copts" and all others of Christianity's disparate branches whose "blood is mixed" in martyrdom. This consciousness of an *ecumenism of blood*,[10] indeed, may usher a new chapter in the history of Christianity, one that transcends division and offers a more cohesive vision of the faith to the world. We pray this volume will contribute to that worthy aim.

NOTES

1   Rupert Shortt, *Christianophobia: A Faith under Attack* (London: Ebury, 2012; Grand Rapids, MI: Eerdmans, 2013).

2   John Allen, *The Global War on Christians: Dispatches from the Front Lines of Anti-Christian Persecution* (New York: Penguin Random House, 2013).

3   Paul Marshall, *Persecuted: The Global Assault on Christians* (Nashville: Thomas Nelson, 2013).

4   Candida Moss, *The Myth of Persecution: How Early Christians Invented a Story of Martyrdom* (New York: HarperCollins, 2013).

5   Bracketing these incidents the Islamic State liquidated Christians from Mosul in June 2014 and Shabab slaughtered 147 students in Kenya. On the demolition of some four hundred churches in Zhejiang province of China see Tom Phillips, "China Ends Anti-Church Demolition Campaign," *Telegraph*, March 20, 2015; on the latest incident see Jeffrey Gettleman, Isma'ill Kushkush, and Rukmini Calimachi, "Somali Militants Kill 147 at Kenyan University," *New York Times*, April 3, 2015, which describes how the militants separated Christian and Muslim students before killing the Christians; on Pakistani church bombings see Mubasher Bukhari, "Twin Bombings at Churches in Pakistan Kill 14, Wound 78," *Reuters*, March 15, 2015. Atrocities by Boko Haram throughout this period have been widely documented and are reported in this volume by Burgess and McCain.

6   The Pew Research Center's successive reports on global restrictions on religion document yearly summaries of harassment of particular religious groups, as well as periodic summary tabulations over time. The most recent report is "Latest Trends in Religious Restrictions and Hostilities," Pew Research Center, February 26, 2015. The longitudinal summary is provided by the previous report, "Religious Hostilities Reach Six-Year High," Pew Research Center, January 14, 2014.

7   Jennifer Bryson, "When Christians Kill and Destroy but Also Make Peace, CAR Today," *Arc of the University* Blog, March 20,2015, http://arcoftheuniverse.info/when-christians-kill-and-destroy-but-also-make-peace-car-today

8   Anthony Gill, *The Political Origins of Religious Liberty* (New York: Cambridge, 2008).

9   Sako gave his address on December 14, 2013, in Rome, as reported by John Allen, "Iraqi Catholic Leader Asks West: 'If They Kill Us All, Will You Do Something Then?'" *National Catholic Reporter*, December 15, 2013.

10 Pope John Paul II employed the term "ecumenism of martyrdom" in his Apostolic Letter "Tertio Millenio Adveniente," November 10, 1994. This idea has been picked up by John L. Allen Jr., *The Global War on Christians* (New York: Image, 2013). Responding to the beheadings of Copts Pope Francis employed even more evocative theological language in stressing that the "ecumenism of blood" – of Catholic, Orthodox, Protestant, Anglican, and all others who confess Christ – is mixed in modern martyrdom. See "Pope Francis and the Copts: Blood and Ecumenism," *Economist*, February 17, 2015.

1

Persecution in the Context of Religious and Christian Demography, 1970–2020

Todd M. Johnson

EXECUTIVE SUMMARY

This paper presents estimates of the number of Christians facing persecution around the world from 1970 to 2020. The purpose of this analysis is to provide a religious demographic context for discussions about Christianity and religious freedom in the twenty-first century. The paper includes demographic analysis of both the Christians living under persecution and the persecutors.

Paul Marshall's taxonomy of persecution is used to produce estimates of the numbers of Christians living under various kinds of restrictions. Persecution is viewed in the context of the five different kinds of states (Self-Professing Communist States, National Security States, South Asian Religious Nationalist States, Muslim-Majority States, and Western Secularist States), divided into key persecuting countries. Tables track the religious demographics of these states over time (1970–2020) with a special focus on Christian demographics, including blocs and movements (e.g., Roman Catholics, Protestants, Evangelicals, Renewalists) and Christian traditions (e.g., Lutherans, Presbyterians, Baptists).

If one excludes Western secularism as a special but not comparable kind of persecution, then it can be said that about 500 million Christians (22 percent of the global total in 2010) are living in states in which they are subject to persecution. An additional 208 million live in Western Secularist States, where they might face discrimination. Altogether 708 million Christians (31 percent of the global total in 2010) live in the fifty-four countries identified in Marshall's taxonomy. The number of Christians living under persecution appears to be increasing. It should be noted that in 1970 more than 152 million Christians lived in the forty-six states where they were subject to persecution. This represented more than 26 percent of all Christians at the time, a higher percentage than that of 2000, when 405 million living in these states represented just above 20 percent of all Christians. By 2020 this is expected to rise to 600 million, or 23.5 percent of all Christians. This shows that persecution, measured by the countries in the taxonomy, is affecting an increasing proportion of the Christian community in the period 2000 to 2020.

Orthodox Christians have experienced a disproportionate amount of persecution. This was especially true for much of the twentieth century, when the rise of communism in the former Soviet Union subjected millions of Orthodox believers to severe persecution. Today, some of the fastest-growing segments of global Christianity (such as Independents and Renewalists) are increasingly in contexts in which they are subject to persecution.

RELIGIOUS DEMOGRAPHY AND PERSECUTION

The study of religious demography is essential to understanding persecution of Christians. Determining how many Christians are persecuted requires knowledge of the number of Christians in a given region or country. In addition, the persecutor acts in the context of a particular religious or nonreligious majority (often in control) in a region or country. Religious demography thus offers crucial information about the *persecuted* and the *persecutor*.

TWO TAXONOMIES NEEDED TO ANALYZE TRENDS

Consequently, in order to assess the global status of Christians in relation to persecution (or freedom), two separate inquiries are needed. One first has to determine who is a Christian and how many there are in every country of the world. A detailed taxonomy has been developed for this purpose, appearing in a series of publications beginning with the *World Christian Encyclopedia*.[1] One also has to determine which Christians are persecuted and which are not. For this paper, we utilize Paul Marshall's definition of persecution (see later discussion) and his taxonomy of countries where Christians are subject to persecution, first developed in his book *Persecuted*.[2] With these two taxonomies it is possible to determine how many Christians live in countries where religious freedom is limited or where Christians are persecuted.

ORGANIZATION OF THE PAPER

To achieve our goal of quantifying Christian persecution around the world we follow a series of steps. First, we give a brief overview of major changes in Christian demographics from the time of Christ to the present. Studying data from 100 years (1910–2010), we examine how the five major Christian traditions (Anglicans, Independents, Orthodox, Protestants, and Roman Catholics) have grown numerically.

Second, we use Paul Marshall's taxonomy of persecution to produce estimates of the numbers of Christians living under various kinds of restrictions. In this way, we are able to see persecution in the context of the different kinds of states into which Marshall has divided key persecuting countries (communist and post-communist, national security states, South Asian religious nationalist, the Muslim world, and Western secularist). Using tables, we track the religious demographics of these states over time (1970–2020), with a special focus on Christian demographics.

Third, we study major Christian traditions (e.g., Roman Catholics, Protestants, Orthodox) and minor Christian traditions (e.g., Lutherans, Presbyterians, Baptists) in light of Marshall's persecution taxonomy in order to make comparisons between groups. We then present a global assessment of persecution for major and select minor Christian traditions across the world's 232 countries.

PART I

Changing Demographics of Christianity from Christ to Present

Christianity has grown from a small contingent of disciples in Palestine in the first century to, by mid-2013, a global family of more than 2.3 billion people. Throughout the entire history of Christianity, followers of Christ have faced opposition and persecution. It is possible to investigate, for any given point in Christian history, who is doing the persecution and who is being persecuted. One of the ways to consider the demographic story is to map Christianity's statistical center of gravity – the geographic point at which there are equal numbers of Christians to the north, south, east, and west.[3] The changing location of this point reveals the relative movement of Christianity over time. The line connecting these points is the "trajectory" of global Christianity (see Map 1). In the early centuries the trajectory moved irregularly around the eastern Mediterranean, but after 600 it settled into a very consistent pattern. As the religion took hold in Europe, the trajectory moved steadily north and west until around 1500, when 92 percent of all Christians were European. As Europeans rediscovered the rest of the world, however, Christianity began a slow but sustained progress back toward the Global South.[4] In the eighteenth and nineteenth centuries the movement was more west than south, as the Christian population in Northern America swelled; by 1970 Northern America would be home to more Christians than any other United Nations region. After 1900, however, the pace of movement southward accelerated, the result of missionary activity and indigenous evangelism in the Global South during the preceding centuries.[5]

The church in the Global South continued to expand rapidly throughout the twentieth century. Africa saw the most robust growth, from 10 million Christians in 1900 to 360 million in 2000. In the second half of the century, however, the

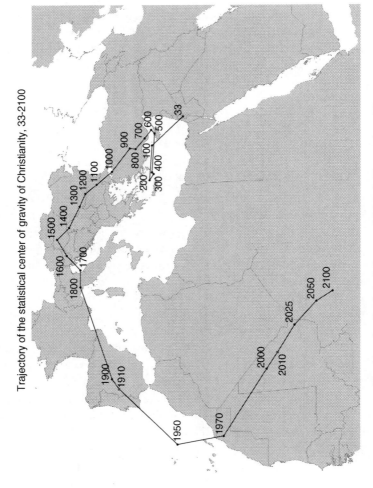

Trajectory of the statistical center of gravity of Christianity, 33-2100

MAP 1 Tracking the Statistical Center of Global Christianity, AD 33–2100.

fastest-growing portion of the global church was in Asia. For the first time in more than thirteen hundred years the center of global Christianity was again moving toward the east. The growth in the Global South shows no indication of slowing during the twenty-first century; the church continues to expand in Latin America, Africa, Asia, and Oceania. Continued southeasterly movement is likely to carry the statistical center of gravity of Christianity from Mali to northern Nigeria in the twenty-second century. Christianity truly has become a global movement, expressing itself in a majority of the languages and cultures in the world.

Christians by Global North/South, AD 33–2010

Another way to consider Christian demographic history is to understand the distribution of Christians by continent and then to translate that distribution into the current understanding of Global North (Northern America and Europe)[6] and Global South (Africa, Asia, Latin America, and Oceania). Figure 1.1 illustrates the steady decline and then more recent growth in the percentage of Christians in the Global South, from the time of Christ to the present. Note that Christians in the Global South (Africa and Asia) represented at least 50 percent of all Christians from the beginning of Christianity until the year 923. For more than one thousand years after that, the Global North dominated Christian demographics. In the twentieth century as a result of a dramatic turnaround the majority of Christians (since 1981) once again live in the Global South. Note as well that the current percentage of Christians in the Global South more closely matches the proportion of the world's total population living in the Global South.

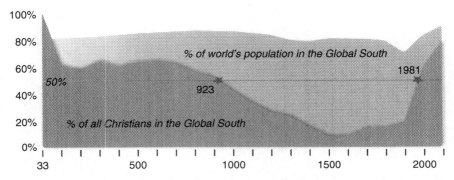

FIGURE 1.1. Percentage of all Christians in the Global South, AD 33–2100. Used by permission of the Centre for the Study of Global Christianity.

Changing Demographics of Religions, 1910–2010

The persecution of Christians can also be understood in the context of the changing demographics of religion over the past 100 years. Table 1.1 is a quick reference for comparing the global strength of each religion as a percentage of the world's population in 1910 and 2010, as well as a way to compare a religion's growth rate with that of other religions and with the world's population as a whole.[7] In addition, one can compare growth rates over the century (1910–2010) or over the ten-year period from 2000 to 2010. Four trends for the 100-year period are immediately apparent. First, Christianity, as a percentage of the world's population, has declined slightly (from 34.8 percent to 32.9 percent). Second, Islam has grown from 12.6 percent to 22.5 percent of the world's population, the most significant change in proportion for any of the large religions. Third, Buddhists and Chinese folk religionists have together shrunk from more than 30 percent of the world's population to less than 14 percent. Fourth, agnostics and atheists together grew from less than 1 percent of the world's population to nearly 12 percent.

One-hundred-year growth rates (expressed as average annual growth rates)[8] in Table 1.1 put these changes in context. World population grew at about 1.38 percent per year from 1910 to 2010. Atheists (6.54 percent p.a.) and agnostics (5.46 percent p.a.) grew more than four times faster than the world's population while Jains grew at 1.31 percent p.a., or at about the same rate as the world's population. A different situation is described by the ten-year growth rates between 2000 and 2010. During that period, world population grew at 1.22 percent annually. Among the larger religions, Islam was the fastest growing in this short period, at 1.92 percent p.a., while Christianity lagged behind at 1.35 percent p.a.[9] Note that both agnostics (0.36 percent p.a.) and atheists (0.08 percent p.a.) are now growing much more slowly than the world's population. This is due largely to the resurgence of religion in China.

Religionists versus Nonreligionists

Despite attempts by sociologists and historians to depict the twentieth century as a "secular" century, most people have, in fact, been religious. In 1910, well more than 99 percent of the world's population was religious. By 2010 this had fallen to 88 percent. But this 100-year snapshot does not reflect the fact that the high point for the nonreligious was around 1970, when almost 20 percent of the world's population was either agnostic or atheist (see Table 1.2). The collapse of Communism in the late twentieth century was accompanied by a resurgence of religion, making the world more religious in 2010 than in 1970. This continues in the present even though the number of atheists and agnostics continues to rise in the Western world, while the

TABLE 1.1. *World religions by adherents, 1910–2010*

Religion	Adherents 1910	% 1910	Adherents 2010	% 2010	100-year 1910–2010 % p.a.	10-year 2000–2010 % p.a.
Christians	611,810,000	34.8	2,272,715,000	32.9	1.32	1.35
Muslims	221,748,000	12.6	1,558,183,000	22.5	1.97	1.92
Hindus	223,383,000	12.7	933,176,000	13.5	1.44	1.35
Agnostics	3,369,000	0.2	684,555,000	9.9	5.46	0.36
Buddhists	138,064,000	7.9	499,030,000	7.2	1.29	0.98
Chinese folk religionists	390,254,000	22.2	439,921,000	6.4	0.12	0.20
Ethnoreligionists	135,074,000	7.7	243,862,000	3.5	0.59	1.14
Atheists	243,000	0.0	137,819,000	2.0	6.54	0.08
New religionists	6,865,000	0.4	63,436,000	0.9	2.25	0.34
Sikhs	3,232,000	0.2	23,719,000	0.3	2.01	1.51
Jews	13,194,000	0.8	13,748,000	0.2	0.04	0.37
Spiritists	324,000	0.0	13,727,000	0.2	3.82	0.95
Taoists	437,000	0.0	8,490,000	0.1	3.01	1.76
Confucianists	1,010,000	0.1	8,233,000	0.1	2.12	0.45
Baha'is	225,000	0.0	7,297,000	0.1	3.54	1.73
Jains	1,446,000	0.1	5,299,000	0.1	1.31	1.49
Shintoists	7,613,000	0.4	2,779,000	0.0	-1.00	0.15
Zoroastrians	119,000	0.0	196,000	0.0	0.50	0.72
Total population	**1,758,412,000**	**100.0**	**6,916,183,000**	**100.0**	**1.38**	**1.22**

Source: Todd M. Johnson and Brian J. Grim, eds., *World Religion Database* (Leiden and Boston: Brill, accessed October 2013).

TABLE 1.2. *Percentage of the world's population belonging to no religion or religion, 1910–2010*

	1910	1950	1970	2000	2010
No Religion	0.2	6.7	19.2	13.0	11.9
Agnostics	0.2	5.1	14.7	10.8	9.9
Atheists	0.0	1.6	4.5	2.2	2.0
Religion	99.8	93.3	80.8	87.0	88.1
Christians	34.8	34.4	33.3	32.4	32.9
Muslims	12.6	13.5	15.5	21.0	22.5
Hindus	12.7	12.8	12.6	13.3	13.5
Buddhists	7.9	6.9	6.4	7.4	7.2
Other religionists	31.8	25.7	13.1	12.8	12.0

Source: Todd M. Johnson and Brian J. Grim, eds., *World Religion Database* (Leiden and Boston: Brill, accessed October 2013).

current growth of religions of all kinds in China (where the vast majority of the nonreligious live today) makes it likely that the percentage of people globally who are religious will continue to grow for many more decades. Thus, from this alternate point of view (1970–2010), there has been a global religious resurgence.

Changing Demographics of Christianity, 1910–2010

As observed in Table 1.2, Christians have constituted approximately one-third of the world's population over the past 100 years. Yet, in this same period, Christianity has experienced a profound shift in its ethnic and linguistic composition, revealed by Table 1.3. In 1910 more than 80 percent of all Christians lived in Europe and Northern America (the Global North). By 2010 this figure had fallen to less than 40 percent, with the majority of Christians located in Africa, Asia, and Latin America. The Global North was 95 percent Christian in 1910. Five regions in the Global South, all the focus of intense Christian missionary activity over the preceding centuries, were also at least 90 percent Christian in 1910. The twenty-one UN regions are listed in Table 1.3, illustrating the North/South dichotomy.[10] This dichotomy is especially significant today for Christians because the term "Southern Christians" or "Christians of the Global South" is increasingly replacing the synonymous term "non-Western Christians."[11] By 2100, more than three-fourths of all Christians will likely be living in the South.[12] This represents a return to the demographic makeup of Christianity at the time of Christ (predominantly southern) but also depicts a vast expansion of Christianity into all countries as well as thousands of peoples, languages, and cultures.

By 2010 only three of the regions with the highest percentage of Christians in 1910 (Central America, South America, and Polynesia) were still at least 90 percent Christian, and each is in the Global South. They were joined by Micronesia and Melanesia (the latter seeing the Christian portion of its population rise from 15.4 percent in 1910 to 91.5 percent in 2010). In an additional seven regions the Christian population exceeded 80 percent, but both Australia/New Zealand and Western Europe had fallen below that level by 2010. Middle Africa also saw phenomenal growth in its Christian population, from 1.1 percent in 1910 to 81.8 percent in 2010. The continent of Africa grew from 9.3 percent Christian in 1910 to 48.2 percent in 2010. Although three of the other four regions that were less than 10 percent Christian in 1910 remained below that level in 2010, the Christian percentages increased over the century, except in Northern Africa. Western Asia also saw its Christian percentage drop to 6.2 percent in 2010 from 22.8 percent in 1910.

In 1910 nine of the ten countries with the most Christians were in the North (see Table 1.4). The shift of Christianity southward over the following century left the United States, Russia, and Germany as the only Northern countries on the list for 2010. The Christian percentage of the population in the "top ten" countries by Christian percentage also declined between 1910 and 2010 (see Table 1.5). Of the countries with the fastest Christian growth between 1910 and 2010, seven were in Africa and three in Asia (see Table 1.6). In the period 2000–2010, the fastest growth is found in Asia (seven countries) and Africa (three countries).

Of the four major traditions within Christianity, Roman Catholics represent just more than half of all Christians, growing from 47.6 percent in 1910 to 51.6 percent in 2010 (see Table 1.7). Their percentage of the global population grew slightly as well, from 16.6 percent in 1910 to 17.0 percent in 2010. This, however, masks a steep decline in adherents in Europe, with a simultaneous rise in Africa, Asia, and Latin America. Both the Orthodox and Anglicans have lost percentage shares within Christianity, as well as among the global population. Orthodoxy, decimated by the rise of Communism, dropped from 20.4 percent of the global population in 1910 to 12.2 percent in 2010. At the same time, the Orthodox fell from 7.1 percent of all Christians in 1910 to 4.0 percent in 2010. Protestants (here including Anglicans) also experienced slight losses, going from 24.4 percent to 22.2 percent of all Christians from 1910 to 2010. Their share of the global population also decreased, from 8.4 percent to 7.3 percent in the same period. Independents,[13] on the other hand, increased their shares of the total Christian community and the global population. Independents, especially in Africa and Asia, represented only 1.7 percent of all Christians in 1910,

TABLE 1.3. *Christianity (C) by United Nations continents and regions, 1910–2010*

Region	Population 1910	C 1910	% 1910	Population 2010	C 2010	% 2010	Population 1910–2010 % p.a.	C 1910–2010 % p.a.	Population 2000–2010 % p.a.	C 2000–2010 % p.a.
Africa	124,541,000	11,636,000	9.3	1,031,084,000	497,318,000	48.2	2.14	3.83	2.46	2.71
Eastern	34,658,000	5,267,000	15.2	342,595,000	225,603,000	65.9	2.32	3.83	2.80	2.96
Middle	19,445,000	207,000	1.1	124,978,000	102,239,000	81.8	1.88	6.40	2.92	3.00
Northern	30,322,000	3,080,000	10.2	199,620,000	10,076,000	5.0	1.90	1.19	1.66	0.90
Southern	6,819,000	2,526,000	37.0	58,803,000	48,427,000	82.4	2.18	3.00	1.35	1.36
Western	33,296,000	557,000	1.7	305,088,000	110,973,000	36.4	2.24	5.44	2.70	2.75
Asia	1,026,693,000	25,086,000	2.4	4,165,440,000	344,142,000	8.3	1.41	2.65	1.14	2.27
Eastern	554,135,000	2,251,000	0.4	1,593,571,000	129,170,000	8.1	1.06	4.13	0.56	3.01
South-central	345,718,000	5,182,000	1.5	1,743,101,000	69,111,000	4.0	1.63	2.62	1.49	2.05
South-eastern	93,859,000	10,124,000	10.8	597,097,000	131,494,000	22.0	1.87	2.60	1.31	1.81
Western	32,982,000	7,529,000	22.8	231,671,000	14,367,000	6.2	1.97	0.65	2.36	1.24
Europe	427,044,000	403,546,000	94.5	740,308,000	580,656,000	78.4	0.55	0.36	0.15	0.26
Eastern	178,184,000	159,695,000	89.6	296,183,000	248,257,000	83.8	0.51	0.44	-0.28	0.38
Northern	61,473,000	60,324,000	98.1	98,795,000	73,809,000	74.7	0.48	0.20	0.45	0.20

Region										
Southern	76,828,000	74,391,000	96.8	154,712,000	127,347,000	82.3	0.70	0.54	0.61	0.55
Western	110,558,000	109,136,000	98.7	190,618,000	131,243,000	68.9	0.55	0.18	0.32	-0.19
Latin America	78,254,000	74,462,000	95.2	596,191,000	550,744,000	92.4	2.05	2.02	1.26	1.24
Caribbean	8,173,000	7,986,000	97.7	41,625,000	34,746,000	83.5	1.64	1.48	0.80	1.08
Central	20,806,000	20,595,000	99.0	160,546,000	153,999,000	95.9	2.06	2.03	1.41	1.38
South	49,276,000	45,881,000	93.1	394,021,000	361,999,000	91.9	2.10	2.09	1.24	1.20
N America	94,689,000	91,429,000	96.6	346,501,000	272,563,000	78.7	1.31	1.10	0.94	0.64
Oceania	7,192,000	5,651,000	78.6	36,059,000	27,291,000	74.4	1.64	1.59	1.62	1.14
Australia/NZ	5,375,000	5,207,000	96.9	26,773,000	18,208,000	68.0	1.62	1.26	1.48	0.71
Melanesia	1,596,000	245,000	15.4	8,729,000	7,985,000	91.5	1.71	3.55	2.23	2.29
Micronesia	89,400	68,600	76.7	498,000	463,000	93.1	1.73	1.93	0.04	0.09
Polynesia	131,000	130,000	99.4	660,000	635,000	96.2	1.63	1.60	0.75	0.73
Global total	1,758,412,000	611,810,000	34.8	6,916,183,000	2,272,715,000	32.9	1.38	1.32	1.22	1.35

Source: Todd M. Johnson and Brian J. Grim, eds., *World Religion Database* (Leiden and Boston: Brill, accessed October 2013).

TABLE 1.4. *Top 10 countries by largest Christian population, 1910 and 2010*

Country	Christians 1910	Country	Christians 2010
United States	84,801,000	United States	248,783,000
Russia	65,757,000	Brazil	177,577,000
Germany	45,755,000	Russia	115,942,000
France	40,895,000	Mexico	113,110,000
United Kingdom	39,298,000	China	107,956,000
Italy	35,219,000	Philippines	84,909,000
Ukraine	29,904,000	Nigeria	73,632,000
Poland	22,102,000	Congo DR	59,086,000
Brazil	21,576,000	Germany	58,091,000
Spain	20,354,000	India	56,383,000

Source: Todd M. Johnson and Brian J. Grim, eds., *World Religion Database* (Leiden and Boston: Brill, accessed October 2013).

TABLE 1.5. *Top 10 countries by percentage Christian, 1910 and 2010*

Country	% Christian 1910	Country	% Christian 2010
Finland	100.0	Samoa	98.8
Slovenia	100.0	Romania	98.5
Barbados	100.0	Malta	98.0
Spain	100.0	Guatemala	97.4
Portugal	100.0	Moldova	96.7
Malta	100.0	Grenada	96.6
Haiti	99.9	El Salvador	96.5
Ireland	99.9	Martinique	96.5
Puerto Rico	99.9	Peru	96.5
Martinique	99.8	Aruba	96.4

Source: Todd M. Johnson and Brian J. Grim, eds., *World Religion Database* (Leiden and Boston: Brill, accessed October 2013).

but rose to 16.6 percent by 2010. Their share of the global population also increased, from 0.6 percent to 5.5 percent.

Movements within Christianity also experienced changes in size and percentage over the 100-year period (see Table 1.7). Evangelicals[14] and Renewalists[15] are

TABLE 1.6. *Top 10 countries by annual growth of Christians, 1910–2010 and 2000–2010*

Country	% 1910–2010 p.a.	Country	% 2000–2010 p.a.
Chad	12.46	Afghanistan	18.00
Burkina Faso	12.30	United Arab Emirates	10.81
Nepal	10.93	Qatar	9.26
Rwanda	10.84	Cambodia	9.26
Burundi	10.69	Burkina Faso	5.71
Central African Republic	10.46	Bahrain	5.55
Saudi Arabia	9.60	Kuwait	5.14
South Sudan	8.58	South Sudan	5.12
Cote d'Ivoire	8.56	Western Sahara	4.89
Oman	8.24	Singapore	4.81

Source: Todd M. Johnson and Brian J. Grim, eds., *World Religion Database* (Leiden and Boston: Brill, accessed October 2013).

considered movements because their members are found in the four traditions listed in the following. Evangelicals are mainly found in the Protestant and Independent traditions while Renewalists are found among Catholics, Protestants, and Independents. In both movements, there are very few Orthodox. In 1910, Evangelicals, mainly Protestants in the Global North, represented 14.8 percent of all Christians and 5.2 percent of the global population. By 2010 Evangelicals had dropped to 13.1 percent and 4.3 percent, respectively. Renewalists (Pentecostals and Charismatics), on the other hand, grew rapidly, from just 0.1 percent of the global population and 0.2 percent of all Christians in 1910 to 8.5 percent and 25.7 percent, respectively, by 2010.

Another important indicator of Christian demographics, the most common mother tongues of Christianity, is shown in Table 1.8. Note that Spanish is in the first position and has been since at least 1970. English is a distant second, followed by Portuguese and then Russian. The surprise is the next position. With the recent growth of Christianity in China, Mandarin Chinese is now the fifth-largest Christian mother tongue, surpassing traditionally "Christian" languages such as French, German, Polish, and Ukrainian. Languages of the Global South are moving up the list, with Amharic, Igbo, Yoruba, and Korean poised to push European languages out of the top ten.

The changing demographics of global Christianity and global religious communities show that any study of persecution of Christians is dynamic, not

TABLE 1.7. *Christian (C) traditions and movements, 1910–2010*

	Name	Adherents 1910	% 1910	% of all Cs 1910	Adherents 2010	% 2010	% of all Cs 2010
Traditions	Independents	10,338,000	0.6	1.7	378,279,000	5.5	16.6
	Orthodox	124,871,000	7.1	20.4	277,035,000	4.0	12.2
	Protestants	147,908,000	8.4	24.2	504,010,000	7.3	22.2
	Catholics	291,291,000	16.6	47.6	1,172,889,000	17.0	51.6
Movements	Evangelicals	90,769,000	5.2	14.8	297,937,000	4.3	13.1
	Renewalists	1,203,000	0.1	0.2	585,143,000	8.5	25.7

Source: Todd M. Johnson, ed., *World Christian Database* (Leiden and Boston: Brill, accessed October 2013).

TABLE 1.8. *Christianity (C) by mother tongue, mid–2010*

Language	Largest population	Countries	Speakers	Christians	% Christian
Spanish	Mexico	78	397,338,000	373,377,000	94.0
English	United States	195	325,051,000	252,126,000	77.6
Portuguese	Brazil	58	207,527,000	189,750,000	91.4
Russian	Russia	76	135,508,000	121,102,000	89.4
Chinese, Mandarin	China	116	892,149,000	90,771,000	10.2
French	France	140	61,227,000	43,185,000	70.5
German, Standard	Germany	91	59,520,000	42,122,000	70.8
Polish	Poland	46	41,058,000	38,618,000	94.1
Ukrainian	Ukraine	40	40,525,000	36,026,000	88.9
Tagalog	Philippines	54	34,366,000	33,699,000	98.1
Amharic	Ethiopia	12	24,992,000	24,580,000	98.4
Italian	Italy	64	29,594,000	24,262,000	82.0
Romanian	Romania	47	25,127,000	24,148,000	96.1
Igbo	Nigeria	5	19,475,000	19,236,000	98.8
Yoruba	Nigeria	15	32,797,000	19,126,000	58.3
Korean	South Korea	41	77,507,000	18,578,000	24.0
Cebuano	Philippines	1	18,499,000	18,210,000	98.4
Malayalam	India	18	44,664,000	15,232,000	34.1
Tamil	India	29	84,023,000	12,817,000	15.3
Catalán	Spain	8	13,415,000	12,489,000	93.1
Greek	Greece	84	12,473,000	12,071,000	96.8
Hungarian	Hungary	30	12,945,000	11,249,000	86.9
Dutch	Netherlands	30	17,137,000	11,239,000	65.6
Haitian	Haiti	10	11,241,000	10,609,000	94.4
Bavarian	Austria	15	13,715,000	10,593,000	77.2

Source: Todd M. Johnson, ed., *World Christian Database* (Leiden and Boston: Brill, accessed October 2013).

static. In fact, the compositions of both Christian communities around the world and those that persecute them have been shifting constantly. This directly impacts any estimates of the number of Christians under duress. Careful attention to these dynamics ensures that citations of the numbers of Christians under persecution have meaning.

PART II

The next step in determining the number of Christians under persecution is to define persecution and to identify countries in which they might be persecuted on the basis of that definition. While, in general, studies of religious freedom provide some context for Christian persecution, different religious communities are denied freedom from one country to the next. In other words, in some countries it is difficult to be a Hindu; in others, a Christian; and in still others, a Baha'i. The Pew Research Center reports on the limits to religious freedom in most countries in the world, with Christians as the most widely persecuted religious group (139 countries).[16] While most advocates of religious freedom have seen the wisdom of advocating freedom for all groups, it is possible to try to isolate countries where persecution of a particular religious community is a problem. This paper focuses on persecution of Christians but recognizes that denial of religious freedom and persecution is a problem facing many religious communities (and nonreligious communities).

Defining Persecution

Paul Marshall, Lela Gilbert, and Nina Shea offer a definition of persecution in their book *Persecuted*. They state that the U.S. International Religious Freedom Act of 1998 (IRFA) contains a useful description of persecution in the context of religious freedom. It defines violations of religious freedom (persecution) to include arbitrary prohibitions on, restrictions of, or punishment for

- Assembling for peaceful religious activities such as worship, preaching, and prayer;
- Speaking freely about one's religious beliefs;
- Changing one's religious beliefs and affiliation;
- Possession and distribution of religious literature, including Bibles;
- Raising one's children in the religious teaching and practices of one's choice;
- Arbitrary registration requirements;
- Any of the following acts if committed on account of an individual's religious belief or practice: detention, interrogation, imposition of an onerous financial penalty, forced labor, forced mass resettlement, imprisonment, forced religious conversion, beating, torture, mutilation, rape, enslavement, murder, and execution.[17]

These form the basis of factors that determine whether or not Christians, in particular, are persecuted. These could be applied to any other religious (or nonreligious) community.

Marshall's Taxonomy

Next, Marshall et al. offer a taxonomy of countries where Christians are subject to persecution, matching the preceding definition. They designate five different kinds of countries that are involved in persecution of Christians: (1) Communist countries, (2) post-Communist countries, (3) national security countries, (4) South Asian nationalist countries, and (5) Muslim countries. In recent correspondence,[18] Marshall adjusted his taxonomy by combining his post-communist states and national security states and by adding a new type: Western secularist states. Thus he proposes five categories of grounds (or motives) for persecution and the countries most associated with them. In each case, Marshall selected countries from a potentially longer list because he felt that they represented a more significant threat to Christian populations living there. The five are

1. Self-Professed Communist States (five countries)

   This category includes five Communist countries (China, Vietnam, Laos, North Korea, and Cuba). These are all still controlled by past regimes that seized power around the middle of the twentieth century.

2. National Security States (thirteen countries)

   This category includes ten post-Communist countries (Russia, Uzbekistan, Turkmenistan, Azerbaijan, Tajikistan, Belarus, Kazakhstan, Kyrgyzstan, Armenia, and Georgia). These are grouped together because the post-Communist countries often maintain the policies regarding religion that they had when they were officially Communist. Here, the state is the usual persecutor. In addition, Myanmar (Burma), Ethiopia, and Eritrea are included as states that are driven less by ideology or religion and more by regimes that repress others simply to maintain their own power.

3. South Asian Religious Nationalist States (four countries)

   This category includes India, Nepal, Sri Lanka, and Bhutan. In these states, Hindu or Buddhist reactionary forces attack religious minorities. The violence is usually societal rather than state-sponsored, but states (Sri Lanka, Nepal) or local governments (parts of India) can be complicit by not providing adequate protection, by not prosecuting attackers, or by charging those who have been attacked.

4. Select Muslim-Majority States (twenty-four countries)

   This category includes Malaysia, Turkey, Turkish-controlled Cyprus, Morocco, Algeria, Jordan, Yemen, the Palestinian Territories, Saudi Arabia, Iran, Egypt, Pakistan, Afghanistan, Iraq, Nigeria, Indonesia, Bangladesh, Somalia, Syria, Brunei, Libya, Maldives, Sudan, and Comoros. Many different patterns of persecution are found in these states. In Iran the repression is from the state, while there is comparatively little societal repression. In Indonesia the repression is societal, but the state is weak and does not protect its religious minorities. In other cases (Iraq, Somalia, Nigeria), the country is fragmented and persecution is often regionalized.

5. Select Western Secularist States (eight countries)

While Marshall has not defined this category precisely, for the purposes of our analysis we are including countries that are 20 percent or more nonreligious (including both atheists and agnostics) in Western Europe, Northern Europe, Southern Europe, Northern America, and Oceania (post-Communist Eastern Europe and New Zealand are excluded by Marshall). As of mid-2010 this included Germany, France, the United Kingdom, Canada, Australia, the Netherlands, Belgium, and Sweden. Christians living in secular states find themselves discriminated against in numerous ways, but Marshall did not include this category in *Persecuted* since the difficulties faced by Christians in these countries were not as severe as those in the other categories. Nonetheless, Marshall feels that the discrimination against Christians is worsening and so must be addressed.

With Marshall's taxonomy, the following caveats are important to consider:

1. The categories are not very precise. Neither countries nor political and religious motives fall into clearly discrete categories. For example, Marshall lists Myanmar (Burma) under national security states, along with Ethiopia and Eritrea. As noted, these states are driven less by ideology or religion and more by regimes that repress others simply to maintain their own power (Zimbabwe would be similar). Ten years ago, however, he would have classified Burma more under religious nationalism since, although it repressed Buddhists as well, it used a rationale of defending Buddhism in its repression of Christian and other religious minorities.

2. The general categories describe grounds/motives of persecution rather than countries. Not all similarly placed countries are repressive. For example, compared to others in their categories, both Lithuania and the Islamic state of Senegal are relatively free of violence toward religious communities. In addition, there are variations within countries – northern Nigeria is more dangerous then southern Nigeria. Finally, different Christian traditions might face different levels of persecution. For example, the Pentecostal minority in Russia is more likely to be persecuted than the Orthodox majority.

3. Similarly, amounts of persecution vary within categories. Among the Muslim countries, living as a Christian in Morocco is not the same as in Saudi Arabia; among post-Communist countries, religious freedom in Georgia is much better than that in Uzbekistan. Marshall has focused on the more egregious cases and called them "persecution," a classification that usually yields a list of about forty-six countries (not including Western secularism).

Having established a "list" of countries where one finds persecution of Christians, we can now examine the religious and Christian demographics of these countries.

Self-Professed Communist States

Table 1.9 shows the religious demographic makeup of Communist states in 2010. One (Cuba) has a Christian majority, one (North Korea) an agnostic majority, and two (Laos and Vietnam) have Buddhist majorities. China has no absolute majority of a single religion and is the most diverse.

Table 1.10 shows that the number of Christians living in self-professed Communist states has been on the rise since 1970, when it was approximately 8 million. In 2010 it was 123 million (5.4 percent of all Christians globally). In 1970 more than 58 percent of people in these states were agnostics or atheists, but this figure had fallen to 39 percent in 2010 and continues to fall. By 2020 45 percent will be either Chinese folk religionist (CFR) or Buddhist. This changing religious demographic scene is largely due to religious resurgence in China.

National Security States

Table 1.11 shows that the religious demographic makeup of national security states in 2010 is quite varied. Five of the states have Christian majorities, while only one (Belarus) has a large numbers of agnostics (atheists are reported separately). In addition, seven have Muslim majorities and one has a Buddhist majority. Consequently, as Marshall states in his descriptions, persecution of Christians in these countries is perpetrated less by religious communities and more by the state, whether national, provincial, or local.

Table 1.12 shows that the number of Christians living in national security states (NSS) has been on the rise since 1970, when it was approximately 79 million. In 2010 it was 194 million (8.5 percent of all Christians globally). In 1970 more than 38 percent of people in NSSs were agnostics or atheists, but this had fallen to 4.2 percent in 2010 and continues to fall. By 2020 83.5 percent will be either Christians or Muslims. This changing religious demographic scene is largely due to the collapse of the Soviet Union.

TABLE 1.9. *The religious composition of 5 Self-Professed Communist States, by country, 2010*

Country	Population 2010	Christians	Christian %	Muslim %	Agnostic %	Buddhist %	Hindu %	Tribal %*	CFR %*
China	1,359,821,000	107,956,000	7.9%	1.6%	32.5%	15.4%	0.0%	4.3%	30.3%
Vietnam	89,047,000	7,532,000	8.5%	0.2%	12.6%	49.2%	0.1%	10.4%	1.0%
North Korea	24,501,000	205,000	0.8%	0.0%	56.8%	1.5%	0.0%	12.3%	0.1%
Cuba	11,282,000	6,681,000	59.2%	0.1%	18.0%	0.1%	0.2%	0.0%	0.2%
Laos	6,396,000	187,000	2.9%	0.1%	0.9%	52.2%	0.1%	42.8%	0.4%

* *Religion note:* Tribal is also known as ethnoreligionist; CFR stands for Chinese folk religionist.

Source: Todd M. Johnson and Brian J. Grim, eds., *World Religion Database* (Leiden and Boston: Brill, accessed October 2013).

TABLE 1.10. *Combined religious composition of all 5 Self-Professed Communist States, 1970–2020*

Religion	Population 1970	% 1970	Population 2000	% 2000	Population 2010	% 2010	Population 2020	% 2020
Agnostics	414,087,000	46.8%	461,660,000	33.0%	469,547,000	31.5%	465,534,000	29.6%
Chinese folk religionists	211,628,000	23.9%	407,266,000	29.1%	413,619,000	27.7%	422,842,000	26.9%
Buddhists	83,063,000	9.4%	225,609,000	16.1%	257,096,000	17.2%	289,759,000	18.4%
Christians	8,333,000	0.9%	89,448,000	6.4%	122,561,000	8.2%	163,775,000	10.4%
Atheists	98,851,000	11.2%	106,956,000	7.6%	109,126,000	7.3%	106,921,000	6.8%
Ethnoreligionists	46,281,000	5.2%	68,767,000	4.9%	73,663,000	4.9%	75,551,000	4.8%
Muslims	12,396,000	1.4%	20,457,000	1.5%	22,480,000	1.5%	25,692,000	1.6%
New religionists	6,389,000	0.7%	12,082,000	0.9%	13,221,000	0.9%	14,123,000	0.9%
Taoists	200,000	0.0%	4,430,000	0.3%	5,553,000	0.4%	6,001,000	0.4%
Spiritists	1,516,000	0.2%	1,913,000	0.1%	1,938,000	0.1%	1,920,000	0.1%
Confucianists	1,000,000	0.1%	1,605,000	0.1%	1,704,000	0.1%	1,800,000	0.1%
Baha'is	201,000	0.0%	374,000	0.0%	415,000	0.0%	456,000	0.0%
Hindus	15,500	0.0%	93,000	0.0%	100,000	0.0%	106,000	0.0%
Sikhs	8,000	0.0%	18,200	0.0%	19,400	0.0%	20,500	0.0%
Jews	2,700	0.0%	3,700	0.0%	3,900	0.0%	4,100	0.0%
Shintoists	0	0.0%	160	0.0%	180	0.0%	190	0.0%
Zoroastrians	50	0.0%	64	0.0%	68	0.0%	70	0.0%
Total population	883,971,000	100.0%	1,400,683,000	100.0%	1,491,047,000	100.0%	1,574,503,000	100.0%

Source: Todd M. Johnson and Brian J. Grim, eds., *World Religion Database* (Leiden and Boston: Brill, accessed October 2013).

TABLE 1.11. *The religious composition of 13 National Security States, by country, 2010*

Country	Population 2010	Christians	Christian %	Muslim %	Agnostic %	Buddhist %	Hindu %	Tribal %*	CFR %*
Russia	143,618,000	115,942,000	80.7%	11.4%	5.6%	0.4%	0.0%	0.7%	0.0%
Ethiopia	87,095,000	52,153,000	59.9%	33.9%	0.1%	0.0%	0.0%	6.0%	0.0%
Myanmar	51,931,000	4,063,000	7.8%	3.8%	0.4%	74.7%	1.7%	9.6%	0.3%
Uzbekistan	27,769,000	348,000	1.3%	94.0%	3.4%	0.1%	0.0%	0.2%	0.0%
Kazakhstan	15,921,000	4,222,000	26.5%	67.9%	4.1%	0.1%	0.0%	0.2%	0.0%
Belarus	9,491,000	7,012,000	73.9%	0.3%	22.2%	0.0%	0.0%	0.0%	0.0%
Azerbaijan	9,095,000	301,000	3.3%	94.8%	1.7%	0.0%	0.0%	0.0%	0.0%
Tajikistan	7,627,000	97,100	1.3%	95.9%	2.1%	0.1%	0.0%	0.1%	0.0%
Eritrea	5,741,000	2,667,000	46.5%	51.5%	1.4%	0.0%	0.0%	0.6%	0.0%
Kyrgyzstan	5,334,000	412,000	7.7%	81.5%	8.1%	0.5%	0.0%	0.4%	0.0%
Turkmenistan	5,042,000	77,400	1.5%	94.7%	3.0%	0.0%	0.0%	0.0%	0.0%
Georgia	4,389,000	3,734,000	85.1%	10.5%	3.6%	0.0%	0.0%	0.0%	0.0%
Armenia	2,963,000	2,770,000	93.5%	0.2%	3.8%	0.0%	0.0%	0.0%	0.0%

Note: Tribal is also known as ethnoreligionist, CFR stands for Chinese folk-religionist.

Source: Todd M. Johnson and Brian J. Grim, eds., *World Religion Database* (Leiden and Boston: Brill, accessed October 2013).

TABLE 1.12. *Combined religious composition of all 13 National Security States, 1970–2020*

Religion	Population 1970	% 1970	Population 2000	% 2000	Population 2010	% 2010	Population 2020	% 2020
Christians	79,226,000	32.7%	167,348,000	48.3%	193,798,000	51.5%	209,345,000	50.8%
Muslims	38,243,000	15.8%	94,734,000	27.4%	113,259,000	30.1%	134,686,000	32.7%
Buddhists	21,693,000	9.0%	36,821,000	10.6%	39,421,000	10.5%	43,721,000	10.6%
Ethnoreligionists	8,232,000	3.4%	10,421,000	3.0%	11,410,000	3.0%	11,215,000	2.7%
Agnostics	51,552,000	21.3%	28,979,000	8.4%	13,350,000	3.6%	9,522,000	2.3%
Atheists	40,131,000	16.6%	5,542,000	1.6%	2,439,000	0.6%	1,368,000	0.3%
Hindus	451,000	0.2%	878,000	0.3%	939,000	0.2%	921,000	0.2%
Confucianists	0	0.0%	718,000	0.2%	770,000	0.2%	770,000	0.2%
Jews	2,337,000	1.0%	372,000	0.1%	275,000	0.1%	186,000	0.0%
Baha'is	21,700	0.0%	133,000	0.0%	149,000	0.0%	154,000	0.0%
Chinese folk religionists	80,000	0.0%	127,000	0.0%	136,000	0.0%	135,000	0.0%
New religionists	10,500	0.0%	55,900	0.0%	55,300	0.0%	59,300	0.0%
Zoroastrians	200	0.0%	6,800	0.0%	7,700	0.0%	7,600	0.0%
Sikhs	5,000	0.0%	5,800	0.0%	5,200	0.0%	5,200	0.0%
Jains	500	0.0%	2,400	0.0%	2,600	0.0%	2,500	0.0%
Total population	**241,982,000**	**100.0%**	**346,145,000**	**100.0%**	**376,017,000**	**100.0%**	**412,098,000**	**100.0%**

Source: Todd M. Johnson and Brian J. Grim, eds., *World Religion Database* (Leiden and Boston: Brill, accessed October 2013).

South Asian Religious Nationalist States

Table 1.13 offers a religious demographic profile of South Asian religious nationalist states in mid-2010. Hinduism is the dominant religion and Muslims are the second-largest group in the taxonomy. While persecution can emerge from the religious communities, the state can also be a significant persecutor of religious minorities, as indicated by the example of Hindu nationalist–led governments in India.

Table 1.14 shows that about 59 million Christians (2.6 percent of all Christians) lived in South Asian Religious Nationalist States in mid-2010. Hindus and Muslims together numbered more than 85 percent of the population. Christian communities are growing in these states and are projected to rise to exceed 70 million by 2020.

Select Muslim Majority States

Table 1.15 shows that the Christian populations range in size in select Muslim Majority States. Despite its large Christian population, Nigeria is included by Marshall in this list because almost all persecution of Christians takes place in its Muslim majority northern states. Persecution of Christians in some of these countries is the result of Islamic Shari'a law or Islamist influence. In others, the pressure is more societal than governmental (e.g., Indonesia).

Table 1.16 shows that Christians are growing as a percentage of the combined population in the select Muslim Majority States, from 8.9 percent in 1970 to 11 percent (projected) in 2020. In 2010, 121 million Christians lived in these states. Ethnoreligionists are declining as a percentage (usually converting to either Islam or Christianity). Agnostics and atheists numbered less than 1 percent in 2010. About two-thirds of all Muslims live in these states.

Western Secularist States

Western Secularist States are defined as those 20 percent or more nonreligious in 2010, excluding Estonia, Latvia, and New Zealand. Christians constitute more than 60 percent of the population in all of these states (see Table 1.17). While Christians might face discrimination in these states, their presence as a majority puts them in a different context. In all totals of "Christians under persecution" we have excluded Christians living in these states to distinguish between persecution and discrimination.

Table 1.18 shows that while the percentage of Christians in Western Secularist States is declining (88 percent in 1970 to a projected 65.5 percent in 2020), Christians

TABLE 1.13. *The religious composition of 4 South Asian Religious Nationalist States, by country, 2010*

Country	Population 2010	Christians	Christian %	Muslim %	Agnostic %	Buddhist %	Hindu %	Tribal %	CFR %
India	1,205,625,000	56,383,000	4.7%	14.2%	1.2%	0.7%	73.0%	3.7%	0.0%
Nepal	26,846,000	906,000	3.4%	4.2%	0.3%	11.5%	67.4%	13.1%	0.1%
Sri Lanka	20,759,000	1,832,000	8.8%	8.5%	0.5%	68.9%	13.0%	0.0%	0.0%
Bhutan	717,000	6,700	0.9%	0.2%	0.0%	84.0%	11.4%	3.4%	0.0%

Source: Todd M. Johnson and Brian J. Grim, eds., *World Religion Database* (Leiden and Boston: Brill, accessed October 2013).

TABLE 1.14. *Religious composition of all four South Asian Religious Nationalist States, 1970–2020*

Religion	Population 1970	% 1970	Population 2000	% 2000	Population 2010	% 2010	Population 2020	% 2020
Hindus	442,752,000	76.4%	787,262,000	72.6%	900,589,000	71.8%	995,830,000	70.8%
Muslims	64,128,000	11.1%	144,560,000	13.3%	173,590,000	13.8%	203,212,000	14.4%
Christians	21,694,000	3.7%	47,021,000	4.3%	59,128,000	4.7%	70,737,000	5.0%
Ethnoreligionists	20,598,000	3.6%	43,513,000	4.0%	48,719,000	3.9%	53,929,000	3.8%
Buddhists	13,770,000	2.4%	23,349,000	2.2%	26,630,000	2.1%	29,924,000	2.1%
Sikhs	10,312,000	1.8%	18,995,000	1.8%	21,970,000	1.8%	25,516,000	1.8%
Agnostics	2,070,000	0.4%	12,212,000	1.1%	14,142,000	1.1%	16,693,000	1.2%
Jains	2,585,000	0.4%	4,386,000	0.4%	5,073,000	0.4%	5,859,000	0.4%
Atheists	726,000	0.1%	1,688,000	0.2%	1,954,000	0.2%	2,301,000	0.2%
Baha'is	740,000	0.1%	1,633,000	0.2%	1,888,000	0.2%	2,173,000	0.2%
Chinese folk-religionists	60,500	0.0%	154,000	0.0%	178,000	0.0%	214,000	0.0%
Zoroastrians	91,800	0.0%	75,200	0.0%	74,800	0.0%	67,500	0.0%
Jews	9,200	0.0%	9,500	0.0%	10,900	0.0%	11,100	0.0%
New religionists	0	0.0%	920	0.0%	1,000	0.0%	1,200	0.0%
Shintoists	0	0.0%	150	0.0%	170	0.0%	190	0.0%
Total population	579,536,000	100.0%	1,084,857,000	100.0%	1,253,946,000	100.0%	1,406,467,000	100.0%

Source: Todd M. Johnson and Brian J. Grim, eds., *World Religion Database* (Leiden and Boston: Brill, accessed October 2013).

TABLE 1.15. *Religious composition of 24 Muslim Majority States, by country, 2010*

Country	Population 2010	Christians	Christian %	Muslim %	Agnostic %	Buddhist %	Hindu %	Tribal %	CFR %
Indonesia	240,676,000	29,186,000	12.1%	79.1%	1.3%	0.8%	1.6%	2.3%	0.9%
Pakistan	173,149,000	3,774,000	2.2%	96.2%	0.1%	0.1%	1.3%	0.1%	0.0%
Nigeria	159,708,000	73,632,000	46.1%	45.9%	0.3%	0.0%	0.0%	7.7%	0.0%
Bangladesh	151,125,000	751,000	0.5%	88.8%	0.1%	0.6%	9.5%	0.4%	0.0%
Egypt	78,076,000	7,876,000	10.1%	89.3%	0.5%	0.0%	0.0%	0.0%	0.0%
Iran	74,462,000	272,000	0.4%	98.8%	0.3%	0.0%	0.0%	0.0%	0.0%
Turkey	72,138,000	194,000	0.3%	98.3%	1.0%	0.0%	0.0%	0.0%	0.0%
Algeria	37,063,000	64,600	0.2%	98.5%	1.2%	0.0%	0.0%	0.0%	0.0%
Sudan	35,652,000	1,916,000	5.4%	90.7%	0.9%	0.0%	0.0%	2.8%	0.0%
Morocco	31,642,000	31,300	0.1%	99.7%	0.1%	0.0%	0.0%	0.0%	0.0%
Iraq	30,962,000	478,000	1.5%	97.5%	0.5%	0.0%	0.0%	0.0%	0.0%
Afghanistan	28,398,000	29,300	0.1%	99.7%	0.0%	0.0%	0.0%	0.0%	0.0%
Malaysia	28,276,000	2,517,000	8.9%	56.5%	0.4%	5.3%	6.3%	3.5%	18.4%
Saudi Arabia	27,258,000	1,193,000	4.4%	92.1%	0.6%	0.3%	2.0%	0.2%	0.1%
Yemen	22,763,000	39,200	0.2%	99.1%	0.1%	0.0%	0.6%	0.0%	0.0%

(continued)

TABLE 1.15 (cont.)

Country	Population 2010	Christians	Christian %	Muslim %	Agnostic %	Buddhist %	Hindu %	Tribal %	CFR %
Syria	21,533,000	1,119,000	5.2%	92.8%	1.9%	0.0%	0.0%	0.0%	0.0%
Somalia	9,636,000	4,500	0.0%	99.8%	0.0%	0.0%	0.1%	0.1%	0.0%
Jordan	6,455,000	172,000	2.7%	94.0%	2.5%	0.0%	0.0%	0.0%	0.0%
Libya	6,041,000	163,000	2.7%	96.6%	0.2%	0.3%	0.1%	0.0%	0.0%
Palestine	4,013,000	74,600	1.9%	80.6%	5.6%	0.0%	0.0%	0.0%	0.0%
Cyprus[a]	1,104,000	793,000	71.8%	21.9%	3.6%	0.6%	0.3%	0.0%	0.0%
Comoros	683,000	3,300	0.5%	98.3%	0.1%	0.0%	0.0%	1.0%	0.0%
Brunei	401,000	55,000	13.7%	57.0%	1.1%	9.7%	0.9%	10.1%	5.2%
Maldives	326,000	1,500	0.4%	98.4%	0.1%	0.6%	0.3%	0.0%	0.0%

[a] Marshall refers to Turkish-controlled Cyprus while this table reports the United Nations estimate of the population of all of Cyprus.

Source: Todd M. Johnson and Brian J. Grim, eds., *World Religion Database* (Leiden and Boston: Brill, accessed October 2013).

TABLE 1.16. Combined religious composition of select 24 Muslim Majority States, 1970–2020

Religion	Population 1970	% 1970	Population 2000	% 2000	Population 2010	% 2010	Population 2020	% 2020
Muslims	383,701,000	80.5%	828,305,000	84.1%	988,054,000	84.0%	1,158,220,000	83.6%
Christians	42,518,000	8.9%	98,472,000	10.0%	121,081,000	10.3%	151,724,000	11.0%
Hindus	18,627,000	3.9%	20,629,000	2.1%	23,073,000	2.0%	25,636,000	1.9%
Ethnoreligionists	17,446,000	3.7%	16,524,000	1.7%	19,718,000	1.7%	21,162,000	1.5%
Chinese folk religionists	3,677,000	0.8%	6,212,000	0.6%	7,393,000	0.6%	8,474,000	0.6%
Agnostics	1,346,000	0.3%	5,300,000	0.5%	6,580,000	0.6%	7,903,000	0.6%
Buddhists	2,255,000	0.5%	3,972,000	0.4%	4,641,000	0.4%	5,242,000	0.4%
New religionists	6,160,000	1.3%	4,278,000	0.4%	4,307,000	0.4%	4,302,000	0.3%
Atheists	307,000	0.1%	527,000	0.1%	631,000	0.1%	738,000	0.1%
Jews	153,000	0.0%	441,000	0.0%	525,000	0.0%	647,000	0.0%
Baha'is	346,000	0.1%	546,000	0.1%	589,000	0.1%	617,000	0.0%
Sikhs	51,100	0.0%	185,000	0.0%	227,000	0.0%	276,000	0.0%
Zoroastrians	31,500	0.0%	73,000	0.0%	82,900	0.0%	85,000	0.0%
Jains	1,200	0.0%	2,500	0.0%	3,100	0.0%	4,800	0.0%
Total population	**476,620,000**	**100.0%**	**985,468,000**	**100.0%**	**1,176,905,000**	**100.0%**	**1,385,030,000**	**100.0%**

Source: Todd M. Johnson and Brian J. Grim, eds., World Religion Database (Leiden and Boston: Brill, accessed October 2013).

TABLE 1.17. *Religious composition of 8 Western Secularist States, by country, 2010*

Country	Population 2010	Christians	Christian %	Muslim %	Agnostic %	Buddhist %	Hindu %	Tribal %	CFR %
Germany	83,017,000	58,091,000	70.0%	4.9%	22.2%	0.1%	0.1%	0.0%	0.0%
France	63,231,000	41,685,000	65.9%	8.6%	18.9%	0.8%	0.1%	0.2%	0.4%
United Kingdom	62,066,000	44,886,000	72.3%	3.9%	19.5%	0.3%	0.9%	0.0%	0.1%
Canada	34,126,000	23,662,000	69.3%	2.4%	18.2%	1.5%	1.1%	0.4%	2.0%
Australia	22,404,000	15,542,000	69.4%	2.0%	21.8%	2.1%	0.8%	0.3%	0.3%
Netherlands	16,615,000	10,516,000	63.3%	6.2%	26.4%	1.2%	0.6%	0.0%	0.0%
Belgium	10,941,000	7,667,000	70.1%	5.5%	21.5%	0.2%	0.1%	0.0%	0.1%
Sweden	9,382,000	5,952,000	63.4%	3.8%	19.8%	0.4%	0.1%	0.1%	0.0%

Source: Todd M. Johnson and Brian J. Grim, eds., *World Religion Database* (Leiden and Boston: Brill, accessed October 2013).

TABLE 1.18. *Combined religious composition of all 8 Western Secularist States, 1970–2020*

Religion	Population 1970	% 1970	Population 2000	% 2000	Population 2010	% 2010	Population 2020	% 2020
Christians	221,806,000	88.5%	207,365,000	72.3%	208,001,000	68.9%	206,831,000	65.5%
Agnostics	18,609,000	7.4%	51,401,000	17.9%	62,193,000	20.6%	71,568,000	22.7%
Muslims	2,657,000	1.1%	13,474,000	4.7%	15,144,000	5.0%	18,712,000	5.9%
Atheists	5,051,000	2.0%	7,292,000	2.5%	8,449,000	2.8%	9,476,000	3.0%
Buddhists	98,300	0.0%	1,772,000	0.6%	1,998,000	0.7%	2,230,000	0.7%
Hindus	266,000	0.1%	1,173,000	0.4%	1,417,000	0.5%	1,764,000	0.6%
Jews	1,436,000	0.6%	1,417,000	0.5%	1,452,000	0.5%	1,422,000	0.5%
Chinese folk religionists	96,000	0.0%	933,000	0.3%	1,060,000	0.4%	1,180,000	0.4%
Sikhs	225,000	0.1%	690,000	0.2%	838,000	0.3%	959,000	0.3%
New religionists	223,000	0.1%	445,000	0.2%	484,000	0.2%	524,000	0.2%
Ethnoreligionists	67,500	0.0%	318,000	0.1%	353,000	0.1%	382,000	0.1%
Baha'is	65,200	0.0%	116,000	0.0%	128,000	0.0%	178,000	0.1%
Spiritists	39,800	0.0%	142,000	0.0%	151,000	0.1%	161,000	0.1%
Confucianists	1,000	0.0%	53,400	0.0%	63,600	0.0%	85,200	0.0%
Jains	5,000	0.0%	27,800	0.0%	34,800	0.0%	44,300	0.0%
Zoroastrians	410	0.0%	10,400	0.0%	11,700	0.0%	12,300	0.0%
Taoists	0	0.0%	4,000	0.0%	4,600	0.0%	4,700	0.0%
Total population	**250,647,000**	**100.0%**	**286,634,000**	**100.0%**	**301,784,000**	**100.0%**	**315,534,000**	**100.0%**

Source: Todd M. Johnson and Brian J. Grim, eds., *World Religion Database* (Leiden and Boston: Brill, accessed October 2013).

form the majority in states where they are considered victims of discrimination. At 208 million in 2010, they represent just below 10 percent of all Christians in the world.

All States in Taxonomy

Table 1.19 summarizes the demographic profiles of the five categories of states in the taxonomy. If one excludes Western secularism from the list, as a special but not comparable kind of discrimination, then it can be said that about 500 million Christians (22 percent of the global total in 2010) are living in states where they are subject to persecution. An additional 208 million live in states where they might be discriminated against (Western Secularism). Altogether, 708 million Christians (31 percent of the global total in 2010) live in the fifty-four countries identified in the taxonomy by Paul Marshall. It should be noted that in 1970 (Table 1.20) more than 152 million Christians were living in the forty-six states where they were subject to persecution. This represented more than 26 percent of all Christians at the time, a higher percentage than that of 2010. By 2000, the 405 million living in the forty-six states represented a little more than 20 percent of all Christians. By 2020 this is expected to rise to 600 million, or 23.5 percent of all Christians. This shows that persecution, measured for the forty-six countries in the taxonomy, is affecting an increasing number of Christians, even when the absolute percentage is falling. Moreover, the proportion of the Christian community living in persecutory states rose during the first decade of the twenty-first century and can be expected to continue to grow during the 2010s.

Table 1.20 presents the religious profile of the forty-six states identified by Marshall as Self-Professed Communist States, National Security States, South Asian Nationalist States, and Muslim Majority states. Christians have been growing as a percentage of the population of these forty-six states, increasing from only 7 percent in 1970 to a projected 12.3 percent by 2020. Muslims have also been growing (from 23.4 percent in 1970 to 32.8 percent by 2020). Hindus have remained about the same, while agnostics have been declining (21.3 percent in 1970 to 10.3 percent by 2020).

Table 1.21 shows a different profile than Table 1.20. When Western Secularist states are included, then Christianity has remained approximately the same percentage (~15 percent) since 1970. Muslims have grown as a percentage from 21.1 percent in 1970 to 30 percent by 2020. Agnostics shrank from 20 percent in 1970 to 12 percent by 2010. Atheists also decreased from 6.0 percent to 2.6 percent in the same period.

TABLE 1.19. *Combined religious compositions of states in the taxonomy, by country, 2010*

Country	Population 2010	Christians	Christian %	Muslim %	Agnostic %	Buddhist %	Hindu %	Tribal %	CFR %
Self-Professed Communist States	1,491,047,000	122,561,000	8.2%	1.5%	31.5%	17.2%	0.0%	4.9%	27.7%
National Security States	376,017,000	193,798,000	51.5%	30.1%	3.6%	10.5%	0.2%	3.0%	0.0%
South Asian Religious Nationalist	1,253,946,000	59,128,000	4.7%	13.8%	1.1%	2.1%	71.8%	3.9%	0.0%
Select Muslim Majority States	1,241,539,000	124,339,000	10.0%	84.4%	0.6%	0.4%	1.9%	1.7%	0.6%
Total excluding Western Secularist States	4,362,550,000	499,826,000	11.5%	31.1%	11.6%	7.5%	21.2%	3.5%	9.7%
Select Western Secularist States	301,784,000	208,001,000	68.9%	5.0%	20.6%	0.7%	0.5%	0.1%	0.4%
Total of 54 countries	4,664,334,000	707,827,000	15.2%	29.4%	12.1%	7.1%	19.9%	3.3%	9.1%

Source: Todd M. Johnson and Brian J. Grim, eds., *World Religion Database* (Leiden and Boston: Brill, accessed October 2013).

TABLE 1.20. *Combined religious composition of 46 states in taxonomy (minus Western secularism), 1970–2020*

Religion	Population 1970	% 1970	Population 2000	% 2000	Population 2010	% 2010	Population 2020	% 2020
Muslims	515,580,000	23.4%	1,134,089,000	29.3%	1,356,761,000	31.1%	1,595,086,000	32.8%
Hindus	461,846,000	21.0%	808,873,000	20.9%	924,713,000	21.2%	1,022,508,000	21.1%
Christians	152,773,000	6.9%	405,135,000	10.5%	499,826,000	11.5%	598,703,000	12.3%
Agnostics	469,207,000	21.3%	508,690,000	13.2%	504,368,000	11.6%	500,532,000	10.3%
Chinese folk religionists	215,456,000	9.8%	413,779,000	10.7%	421,350,000	9.7%	431,693,000	8.9%
Buddhists	120,798,000	5.5%	289,802,000	7.5%	327,849,000	7.5%	368,717,000	7.6%
Ethnoreligionists	93,377,000	4.2%	140,057,000	3.6%	154,564,000	3.5%	163,060,000	3.4%
Atheists	140,057,000	6.4%	114,776,000	3.0%	114,230,000	2.6%	111,414,000	2.3%
Sikhs	10,376,000	0.5%	19,207,000	0.5%	22,225,000	0.5%	25,821,000	0.5%
New religionists	12,559,000	0.6%	16,418,000	0.4%	17,585,000	0.4%	18,485,000	0.4%
Taoists	200,000	0.0%	4,430,000	0.1%	5,553,000	0.1%	6,001,000	0.1%
Jains	2,586,000	0.1%	4,391,000	0.1%	5,078,000	0.1%	5,866,000	0.1%
Baha'is	1,310,000	0.1%	2,690,000	0.1%	3,045,000	0.1%	3,405,000	0.1%
Confucianists	1,000,000	0.0%	2,330,000	0.1%	2,481,000	0.1%	2,579,000	0.1%
Spiritists	1,516,000	0.1%	1,913,000	0.0%	1,938,000	0.0%	1,920,000	0.0%
Jews	2,506,000	0.1%	828,000	0.0%	817,000	0.0%	850,000	0.0%
Zoroastrians	124,000	0.0%	155,000	0.0%	166,000	0.0%	160,000	0.0%
Shintoists	0	0.0%	310	0.0%	340	0.0%	380	0.0%
Total population	2,201,271,000	100.0%	3,867,563,000	100.0%	4,362,550,000	100.0%	4,856,801,000	100.0%

Source: Todd M. Johnson and Brian J. Grim, eds., *World Religion Database* (Leiden and Boston: Brill, accessed October 2013).

TABLE 1.21. *Combined religious composition of all 54 states in taxonomy, 1970–2020*

Religion	Population 1970	% 1970	Population 2000	% 2000	Population 2010	% 2010	Population 2020	% 2020
Muslims	518,238,000	21.1%	1,147,563,000	27.6%	1,371,995,000	29.4%	1,613,798,000	31.2%
Hindus	462,112,000	18.8%	810,046,000	19.5%	926,130,000	19.9%	1,024,272,000	19.8%
Christians	374,579,000	15.3%	612,500,000	14.7%	707,827,000	15.2%	805,534,000	15.6%
Agnostics	487,816,000	19.9%	560,091,000	13.5%	566,561,000	12.1%	572,099,000	11.1%
Chinese folk religionists	215,552,000	8.8%	414,712,000	10.0%	422,410,000	9.1%	432,873,000	8.4%
Buddhists	120,897,000	4.9%	291,574,000	7.0%	329,847,000	7.1%	370,948,000	7.2%
Ethnoreligionists	93,445,000	3.8%	140,375,000	3.4%	154,918,000	3.3%	163,443,000	3.2%
Atheists	145,108,000	5.9%	122,068,000	2.9%	122,679,000	2.6%	120,890,000	2.3%
Sikhs	10,601,000	0.4%	19,897,000	0.5%	23,063,000	0.5%	26,779,000	0.5%
New religionists	12,782,000	0.5%	16,862,000	0.4%	18,069,000	0.4%	19,009,000	0.4%
Taoists	200,000	0.0%	4,434,000	0.1%	5,558,000	0.1%	6,005,000	0.1%
Jains	2,591,000	0.1%	4,418,000	0.1%	5,113,000	0.1%	5,911,000	0.1%
Baha'is	1,375,000	0.1%	2,866,000	0.1%	3,173,000	0.1%	3,583,000	0.1%
Confucianists	1,001,000	0.0%	2,383,000	0.1%	2,545,000	0.1%	2,664,000	0.1%
Jews	3,942,000	0.2%	2,245,000	0.1%	2,260,000	0.0%	2,271,000	0.0%
Spiritists	1,556,000	0.1%	2,055,000	0.0%	2,089,000	0.0%	2,081,000	0.0%
Zoroastrians	124,000	0.0%	166,000	0.0%	177,000	0.0%	173,000	0.0%
Shintoists	0	0.0%	310	0.0%	340	0.0%	380	0.0%
Total population	2,451,918,000	100.0%	4,154,197,000	100.0%	4,664,334,000	100.0%	5,172,335,000	100.0%

Source: Todd M. Johnson and Brian J. Grim, eds., *World Religion Database* (Leiden and Boston: Brill, accessed October 2013).

PART III

Christian Blocs and Movements in Marshall's Taxonomy

Table 1.22 allows us to examine the impact of persecution on the four major Christian blocs (Independents, Orthodox, Protestants/Anglicans, and Roman Catholics) and the two movements (Evangelicals and Renewalists). What is surprising about these results is the great variation from one bloc or movement to the next. In Table 1.19 we concluded that 22 percent of all Christians in 2010 lived under the threat of persecution (in the forty-six countries identified by Marshall). A close reading of Table 1.22 allows us to conclude the following about different Christian blocs and movements:

1. The number (and percentage) of Independents under persecution has also grown since 1970, when about 12.3 percent lived in the forty-six countries (to 36 percent in 2010, well above the 22 percent average for all Christians). This is partly due to the growth of Independents in self-professed Communist states, especially the house church movement in China.
2. A disproportionate percentage of the Orthodox global community in 1970 was under persecution (48.8 percent). While the proportion had increased to 65 percent in 2010, most of the persecution in these states is now experienced by non-Orthodox Christian groups. This highlights a significant limitation of the taxonomy.
3. Protestants (including Anglicans) have experienced a growth in persecution since 1970, rising from 10 percent to nearly 27 percent of the community by 2010. Some of this can be attributed to the growth of this bloc in tense religious climates in Africa (such as Nigeria).
4. Roman Catholics, by far the largest Christian tradition, have experienced the least persecution (by Marshall's taxonomy), though it grew from 3.9 percent of the persecuted community in 1970 to 7.3 percent in 2010. The largest Catholic majority countries in the world are those with little or no persecution of Christians (Brazil, Mexico, Philippines, United States, Italy).
5. The percentage of Evangelicals living in countries where they are subject to persecution grew from 12.1 percent in 1970 to 28.4 percent by 2010. This is far greater than the average for the Christian community and can be attributed to the growth of Evangelicalism in Africa, Asia, and Latin America.
6. Renewalists also live in countries where they are subject to persecution. In 1970, 18.6 percent lived in these countries. By 2010, this proportion had grown to 25.6 percent. This is true, despite the fact that Catholic Charismatics, a significant segment of Renewalists, tend to live in countries where there is less persecution.

TABLE 1.22. *Christian blocs and movements under persecution, 1970 and 2010*

Bloc	Group name	Population 1970	Population 2010	% Globe 1970	% Globe 2010
Independents	Self-Professed Communist States	297,000	76,337,000	0.3%	20.2%
	National Security States	2,152,000	5,587,000	2.2%	1.5%
	South Asian Religious Nationalist States	3,435,000	17,404,000	3.6%	4.6%
	Select Muslim Majority States	5,944,000	36,900,000	6.2%	9.8%
	Persecution Grounds (excluding Western Secularism)	11,828,000	136,227,000	12.3%	36.0%
	Select Western Secularist States	4,627,000	8,659,000	4.8%	2.3%
	Persecution Grounds total	16,454,000	144,886,000	17.1%	38.3%
Independents	Globe	96,408,000	378,279,000	100.0%	100.0%
Orthodox	Self-Professed Communist States	7,000	55,300	0.0%	0.0%
	National Security States	61,238,000	166,005,000	42.4%	59.9%
	South Asian Religious Nationalist States	1,818,000	4,803,000	1.3%	1.7%
	Select Muslim Majority States	7,379,000	9,785,000	5.1%	3.5%
	Persecution Grounds (excluding Western Secularism)	70,442,000	180,648,000	48.8%	65.2%
	Select Western Secularist States	2,328,000	4,807,000	1.6%	1.7%
	Persecution Grounds total	72,770,000	185,455,000	50.4%	66.9%
Orthodox	Globe	144,367,000	277,035,000	100.0%	100.0%
Protestant/ Anglican	Self-Professed Communist States	645,000	26,454,000	0.3%	5.2%
	National Security States	3,057,000	18,534,000	1.2%	3.7%
	South Asian Religious Nationalist States	7,140,000	19,616,000	2.8%	3.9%

(continued)

TABLE 1.22 (cont.)

Bloc	Group name	Population 1970	Population 2010	% Globe 1970	% Globe 2010
	Select Muslim Majority States	14,470,000	69,893,000	5.7%	13.9%
	Persecution Grounds (excluding Western Secularism)	25,312,000	134,498,000	9.9%	26.7%
	Select Western Secularist States	96,790,000	77,918,000	38.0%	15.5%
	Persecution Grounds total	122,101,000	212,415,000	47.9%	42.1%
Protestant/ Anglican	Globe	255,017,000	504,010,000	100.0%	100.0%
Roman Catholics	Self-Professed Communist states	7,175,000	27,235,000	1.1%	2.3%
	National Security States	1,254,000	3,918,000	0.2%	0.3%
	South Asian Religious Nationalist States	9,387,000	20,049,000	1.4%	1.7%
	Select Muslim Majority States	8,231,000	34,108,000	1.2%	2.9%
	Persecution Grounds (excluding Western Secularism)	26,047,000	85,301,000	3.9%	7.3%
	Select Western Secularist States	104,236,000	109,250,000	15.7%	9.3%
	Persecution Grounds total	130,283,000	194,550,000	19.6%	16.6%
Roman Catholics	Globe	664,928,000	1,172,889,000	100.0%	100.0%
Evangelicals	Self-Professed Communist States	302,000	16,985,000	0.3%	5.7%
	National Security States	1,863,000	14,819,000	1.8%	5.0%
	South Asian Religious Nationalist States	2,813,000	9,927,000	2.7%	3.3%
	Select Muslim Majority States	7,819,000	42,937,000	7.4%	14.4%
	Persecution Grounds (excluding Western Secularism)	12,798,000	84,668,000	12.1%	28.4%
	Select Western Secularist States	22,651,000	19,949,000	21.4%	6.7%
	Persecution Grounds total	35,449,000	104,617,000	33.5%	35.1%

Evangelicals	Globe	105,958,000	297,938,000	100.0%	100.0%
Renewalists	Self-Professed Communist States	226,000	53,988,000	0.4%	9.2%
	National Security States	2,318,000	14,173,000	3.7%	2.4%
	South Asian Religious Nationalist States	2,869,000	20,701,000	4.6%	3.5%
	Select Muslim Majority States	6,238,000	60,687,000	10.0%	10.4%
	Persecution Grounds (excluding Western Secularism)	11,652,000	149,549,000	18.6%	25.6%
	Select Western Secularist States	3,181,000	13,142,000	5.1%	2.2%
	Persecution Grounds total	14,832,000	162,691,000	23.7%	27.8%
Renewalists	Globe	62,674,000	585,144,000	100.0%	100.0%
Total population	Self-Professed Communist States	883,971,000	1,491,047,000	23.9%	21.6%
	National Security States	241,982,000	376,017,000	6.6%	5.4%
	South Asian Religious Nationalist States	579,536,000	1,253,946,000	15.7%	18.1%
	Select Muslim Majority States	495,783,000	1,244,539,000	13.4%	18.0%
	Persecution Grounds (excluding Western Secularism)	2,201,271,000	4,362,550,000	59.6%	63.1%
	Select Western Secularist States	250,647,000	301,784,000	6.8%	4.4%
	Persecution Grounds total	2,451,918,000	4,664,334,000	66.4%	67.4%
Total population	Globe	3,691,173,000	6,916,183,000	100.0%	100.0%

Source: Todd M. Johnson, ed., *World Christian Database* (Leiden and Boston: Brill, accessed October 2013).

Select Christian Traditions under Persecution

Table 1.23 allows us to examine the impact of persecution on select traditions (each part of the larger blocs listed). Again, considering that 22 percent of all Christians live in the forty-six countries where Christians are subject to persecution, we can conclude the following:

1. Anglicans are increasingly likely to face persecution. While only 6.8 percent lived in these forty-six countries in 1970, by 2010 24.9 percent did (greater than the average for all Christians). This is due primarily to the growth of the Anglican Church in the Muslim Majority States, with Nigeria as the main area of growth. Anglicans in the northern provinces of Nigeria are the most likely to be persecuted there.
2. Baptists have increasingly been under persecution, rising from 9.3 percent in 1970 to 25.9 percent in 2010.
3. Mormons are generally not found in situations where they are subject to persecution. Their percentage was only 0.6 percent in 1970, rising to 1.1 percent by 2010.
4. Lutherans are increasingly found in situations of persecution, rising from 7.6 percent to 14.6 percent between 1970 and 2010. Note that much higher percentages of Lutherans live under Western Secularism, though this percentage has fallen since 1970 (22.1 percent to 16.4 percent in 2010).
5. Methodists have also seen a dramatic rise in their numbers under persecution, from 5.4 percent to 16.2 percent between 1970 and 2010.
6. Reformed and Presbyterian churches are increasingly under persecution, rising from 13.3 percent to 17.5 percent between 1970 and 2010. They too have experienced significant growth in the Muslim Majority States.

Christians are experiencing an upsurge in persecution around the world. Approximately 500 million Christians (22 percent of the global total) in 2010 were living in forty-six countries that have been identified by Paul Marshall as states where Christians are subject to persecution. While a higher percentage of Christians lived in these forty-six countries in 1970 (26 percent), by 2000 this percentage had fallen to just above 20 percent. By 2020 this is expected to rise to 600 million people, or 23.5 percent of all Christians. This shows that persecution, measured in terms of the 46 countries in the taxonomy, is affecting an increasing proportion of the Christian community from the period 2000 to 2020.

Another major finding is that Orthodox Christians have continued to bear a disproportionate share of persecution. Unfortunately this was also true for much of the twentieth century, when the rise of communism in the former Soviet Union put millions of Orthodox believers under intense persecution. As noted earlier, today,

TABLE 1.23. *Christian traditions by persecution grounds, 1970 and 2010*

Tradition	Group name	Population 1970	Population 2010	% Globe 1970	% Globe 2010
Anglicans	Self-Professed Communist States	14,600	8,200	0.0%	0.0%
	National Security States	39,500	70,100	0.1%	0.1%
	South Asian Religious Nationalist States	46,200	54,200	0.1%	0.1%
	Select Muslim Majority States	3,128,000	21,489,000	6.6%	24.8%
	Persecution Grounds (excluding Western Secularism)	3,220,000	21,621,000	6.8%	24.9%
	Select Western Secularist States	34,070,000	30,566,000	71.9%	35.2%
	Persecution Grounds total	37,291,000	52,188,000	78.7%	60.2%
Anglicans	Globe	47,408,000	86,746,000	100.0%	100.0%
Baptists	Self-Professed Communist States	41,300	116,000	0.1%	0.2%
	National Security States	1,699,000	9,824,000	4.2%	12.7%
	South Asian Religious Nationalist States	1,545,000	4,124,000	3.8%	5.3%
	Select Muslim Majority States	507,000	5,881,000	1.2%	7.6%
	Persecution Grounds (excluding Western Secularism)	3,791,000	19,945,000	9.3%	25.9%
	Select Western Secularist States	1,932,000	883,000	4.7%	1.1%
	Persecution Grounds total	5,723,000	20,828,000	14.0%	27.0%
Baptists	Globe	40,806,000	77,54,000	100.0%	100.0%
Mormons	Self-Professed Communist States	7,000	400	0.2%	0.0%
	National Security States	50	26,400	0.0%	0.2%
	South Asian Religious Nationalist States	0	10,300	0.0%	0.1%
	Select Muslim Majority States	11,200	121,000	0.4%	0.8%

(continued)

TABLE 1.23 (cont.)

Tradition	Group name	Population 1970	Population 2010	% Globe 1970	% Globe 2010
	Persecution Grounds (excluding Western Secularism)	18,300	159,000	0.6%	1.1%
	Select Western Secularist States	238,000	616,000	7.7%	4.3%
	Persecution Grounds total	256,000	774,000	8.2%	5.4%
Mormons	**Globe**	**3,107,000**	**14,339,000**	**100.0%**	**100.0%**
Lutherans	Self-Professed Communist States	210	1,200	0.0%	0.0%
	National Security States	277,000	143,000	0.7%	0.3%
	South Asian Religious Nationalist States	793,000	1,891,000	2.0%	3.7%
	Select Muslim Majority States	2,000,000	5,329,000	5.0%	10.6%
	Persecution Grounds (excluding Western Secularism)	3,070,000	7,364,000	7.6%	14.6%
	Select Western Secularist States	8,888,000	8,293,000	22.1%	16.4%
	Persecution Grounds total	11,958,000	15,656,000	29.8%	31.0%
Lutherans	**Globe**	**40,158,000**	**50,483,000**	**100.0%**	**100.0%**
Methodists	Self-Professed Communist States	15,000	65,700	0.1%	0.2%
	National Security States	29,100	204,000	0.1%	0.7%
	South Asian Religious Nationalist States	957,000	1,126,000	3.6%	3.7%
	Select Muslim Majority States	449,000	3,477,000	1.7%	11.5%
	Persecution Grounds (excluding Western Secularism)	1,450,000	4,872,000	5.4%	16.2%
	Select Western Secularist States	2,348,000	1,149,000	8.8%	3.8%
	Persecution Grounds total	3,799,000	6,021,000	14.2%	20.0%

Methodists	Globe	26,680,000	30,148,000	100.0%	100.0%
Reformed/ Presbyterians	Self-Professed Communist States	126,000	63,000	0.4%	0.1%
	National Security States	18,700	111,000	0.1%	0.2%
	South Asian Religious Nationalist States	351,000	1,097,000	1.0%	1.8%
	Select Muslim Majority States	4,238,000	9,341,000	11.9%	15.4%
	Persecution Grounds (excluding Western Secularism)	4,734,000	10,611,000	13.3%	17.5%
	Select Western Secularist States	9,157,000	5,154,000	25.8%	8.5%
	Persecution Grounds total	13,892,000	15,764,000	39.2%	26.0%
Reformed/ Presbyterians	Globe	35,474,000	60,708,000	100.0%	100.0%

Source: Todd M. Johnson, ed., *World Christian Database* (Leiden and Boston: Brill, accessed October 2013).

while large numbers of Orthodox Christians live in these countries, they are no longer the victims. At the same time, some of the fastest-growing segments of global Christianity (e.g., Independents, Evangelicals, Renewalists) are increasingly found in contexts in which they are subject to persecution.

NOTES

1 For a detailed enumeration of Christians past, present, and future in every country of the world, see *World Christian Encyclopedia: A Comparative Survey of Churches and Religions in the Modern World*, 2nd ed., ed. David B. Barrett, George T. Kurian, and Todd M. Johnson (New York: Oxford University Press, 2001). A detailed examination of the methods and sources of religious demography has been published in Todd M. Johnson and Brian J. Grim, *The World's Religions in Figures: An Introduction to International Religious Demography* (Oxford: Wiley-Blackwell, 2013). Data in this paper are drawn from the *World Christian Database* and *World Religion Database*, both published by Brill in the Netherlands. The *World Christian Database* contains details on various Christian traditions, with estimates of adherents in each denomination by country for the years 1970, 2000, and 2010.

2 Paul Marshall, Lela Gilbert, and Nina Shea, *Persecuted: The Global Assault on Christians* (Nashville: Thomas Nelson, 2013).

3 See Todd M. Johnson and Sun Young Chung's "Christianity's Centre of Gravity, AD 33–2100" in *Atlas of Global Christianity*, ed. Todd M. Johnson and Kenneth R. Ross (Edinburgh: Edinburgh University Press, 2009), 50–53.

4 "South" is defined as the remaining 16 current UN regions (comprising 185 countries): Eastern Africa, Middle Africa, Northern Africa, Southern Africa, Western Africa, Eastern Asia, South-central Asia, South-eastern Asia, Western Asia, Caribbean, Central America, South America, Australia/New Zealand, Melanesia, Micronesia, and Polynesia.

5 Documented in *Atlas of Global Christianity*, ed. Todd M. Johnson and Kenneth R. Ross (Edinburgh: Edinburgh University Press, 2009).

6 Here, "North" is defined in geopolitical terms by 5 current United Nations regions (comprising 53 countries): Eastern Europe (including Russia), Northern Europe, Southern Europe, Western Europe, and Northern America. The United Nations definition also includes Australia and New Zealand.

7 For a more comprehensive treatment of these statistics, see Todd M. Johnson and Brian J. Grim, *The World's Religions in Figures: An Introduction to International Religious Demography* (Oxford: Wiley-Blackwell, 2013).

8 Calculated with the formula $\{[(\text{Adherents 2010}/\text{Adherents 1910})^{(1/100)}]-1\} * 100$.

9 Note that although Christian growth has slowed slightly (1.32% p.a. to 1.31% p.a.), it is now outpacing world population growth and is therefore gaining a small percentage of the world's population every year.

10 A United Nations Development Program document, "Forging a Global South" (New York: May 2003), states, "The use of the term 'South' to refer to developing countries collectively has been part of the shorthand of international relations since the 1970s. It rests on the fact that all of the world's industrially developed countries (with the exception

of Australia and New Zealand) lie to the north of its developing countries" (inside front cover).

11 For example, Anglicans in the Global South spoke out under the leadership of Nigerian Primate Peter Akinola in the document "Statement of the Primates of the Global South in the Anglican Communion in Response to the Consecration of Gene Robinson on 2 November 2003," accessed October 2013, www.anglican-nig.org/glbsouthst.htm

12 Increasingly, "Northern" Christians are Southern Christians who have immigrated to the North. For example, some of the largest single congregations in Europe are led by and composed of Africans.

13 Independents are defined as "churches or individual Christians separated from, uninterested in and independent of historic denominationalist Christianity." Examples include African Independent Churches, house churches in China, and networks such as the Vineyard churches.

14 Evangelicals are defined as "a sub-division mainly of Protestants and Independents consisting of all affiliated church members calling themselves Evangelicals, or all persons belonging to Evangelical congregations, churches or denominations; characterized by commitment to personal religion (including new birth or personal conversion experience), reliance on Holy Scripture as the only basis for faith and Christian living, emphasis on preaching and evangelism, and usually on conservatism in theology."

15 "Renewalists" is a cover term referring to three types of Pentecostals and Charismatics: (1) members of Pentecostal denominations such as the Assemblies of God; (2) members of non-Pentecostal churches who have been filled with the Holy Spirit such as Catholic Charismatics; and (3) members of Independent Charismatic churches, such as African Independent Churches, experiencing the same gifts of the Holy Spirit but without accepting the same terminology or polity.

16 "Rising Tide of Restrictions on Religion," Pew Research Center (September 2012): 23, accessed October 2013, http://www.pewforum.org/files/2012/09/RisingTideofRestrictions-fullreport.pdf

17 Marshall et al., *Persecuted*, 6–7.

18 Paul Marshall, e-mail to Todd M. Johnson, March 9, 2013.

2

Patterns and Purposes of Contemporary Anti-Christian Persecution

Paul Marshall

EXECUTIVE SUMMARY

The contemporary Christian church exists in every country; in most it is growing, and in many it is persecuted. Currently, Christians are the most widely persecuted religious group in the world, suffering discrimination, harassment, repression, and violence in approximately 133 countries, and, in some areas, particularly in the Muslim majority world, this is increasing. This persecution is also often underreported or downplayed.

There are currently four major patterns of anti-Christian persecution; while these do not include all instances, they cover more than 90 percent of them. These patterns are (1) the remaining self-professed Communist countries – China, Vietnam, Laos, North Korea, and Cuba – where the state is the usual persecutor; (2) South Asian religious nationalism – in India, Nepal, Sri Lanka, and Bhutan – where reactionary Hindu and Buddhist elements attack religious minorities and persecution is primarily societal rather than state-directed, though states or local governments can be complicit; (3) the Muslim majority world, where although it does not involve the most Christians, it is the site of the most widespread persecution and is the area where persecution is increasing; (4) post-Communist, national security, and other authoritarian states, including Burma, Ethiopia, Eritrea, Uzbekistan, Turkmenistan, and Belarus.

While they do not rise to the level of persecution, there are also increasing restrictions on religious freedom in the West caused by newer forms of secularism, which I also briefly describe.

These categories are not precise, since countries themselves do not reduce to simple patterns – for example, Burma has combined a national security state with religious nationalism – but they do indicate the major trends.

The reasons for persecution are varied and do not constitute a unitary "war" on Christians. But one common feature is that in the modern age, the traditional

Christian belief that *sacerdotium* (church) and *regnum* (state) were two distinct bodies manifests itself practically in a denial that the state is all-encompassing or the ultimate arbiter of human life. Hence, this belief is a foundation for social and political pluralism. Accordingly, Christians are often subject to persecution by those who have a monistic conception of the social order and the state – that there is one order of authority in society whose reach applies to every person and institution and to which all must submit. Contemporary monisms include communism, other authoritarianisms, radical Islamist conceptions, religious nationalisms, and several contemporary secularisms.

Other factors in the persecution of Christians include the claim that Christians are foreigners, often coupled with opposition to conversion to Christianity, which is often seen as a threat to the political and social order. Finally, the common Christian stress on a new spiritual birth often challenges traditional orders in which social position is ascriptive and inherited from birth.

While there are still repressive and reactionary forms of Christianity, one of the major contemporary factors in the persecution of Christians is the association of Christianity with freedom.

PATTERNS OF CONTEMPORARY ANTI-CHRISTIAN PERSECUTION

In Syria in October 2013, the Islamist rebel militias Al Nusra Front and Daash (now usually referred to as ISIS) occupied Sadad, an ancient Christian town of some 15,000 people between Damascus and Homs, for over a week. Archbishop Selwanos Boutros Alnemeh, Syriac Orthodox Metropolitan of Homs and Hama reports that "What happened in Sadad is the most serious and biggest massacre of Christians in Syria in the past two years and a half.... 45 innocent civilians were martyred for no reason, and among them several women and children, many thrown into mass graves. Other civilians were threatened and terrorized. 30 were wounded and 10 are still missing. For one week, 1,500 families were held as hostages and human shields. Among them children, the elderly, the young, men and women.... All the houses of Sadad were robbed and property looted. The churches are damaged and desecrated, deprived of old books and precious furniture.... What happened in Sadad is the largest massacre of Christians in Syria and the second in the Middle East, after the one in the Church of Our Lady of Salvation in Iraq, in 2010."[1]

The killings in Sadad, which included torture, were preceded the previous month by attacks on another ancient Christian region, Ma'loula, where the churches were bombarded and plundered and the inhabitants forced to convert to Islam: those who did not were killed.

INTRODUCTION

I will attempt to give a brief overview of contemporary anti-Christian persecution – that is, persecution prompted at least in part by the fact that those persecuted are Christians, or are thought to be Christians.[2] It should be noted that many of the governments, societies, and groups that persecute Christians also persecute other religious groups, and persecute additional groups for reasons that have little relation to religion.

People of all religions or none also suffer persecution for their faith or religious identity. Many are persecuted by the same people who persecute Christians. For some, such as Mandeans and Yizidis in Iraq, Baha'is and Jews in Iran, Ahmadis and Hindus in Pakistan, Tibetan Buddhists and Falun Gong in China, Independent Buddhists in Vietnam, Rohingya Muslims in Burma, the persecution is particularly intense and cruel.[3]

Despite the prevalence of religious persecution, there are at least three reasons why the contemporary persecution of Christians merits close attention – it is massive, it is relatively underreported, and in several parts of the world it is growing.

Christians the Most Widely Persecuted

The Pew Forum on Religion and Public Life, a highly respected source of data on religion, reports that in recent years Christians have suffered harassment by the state and/or society in 133 countries – two-thirds of the world's states – and suffer in more places than any other religious group.[4] Similar findings are reported by sources as diverse as the Vatican, Open Doors, *Commentary*, *Newsweek*, and the *Economist*. Indeed, one estimate, by the Catholic Bishops' Conferences of the European Community, maintains that 75 percent of acts of contemporary religious intolerance are directed against Christians.[5] Metropolitan Hilarion, chairman of the Russian Orthodox Church's Department for External Church Relations, recently stated that "over 100 million Christians are subject to persecution today."[6]

Some of these claims are disputed, and in this paper I will simply claim, along with the Pew Forum, that Christians are the most widely persecuted religious group in the world. Metropolitan Hilarion also asserts this, as has German Chancellor Merkel, and Pope Benedict XVI, who stated: "At present, Christians are the religious group which suffers most from persecution on account of its faith."[7] Together with Pope Benedict, I would affirm, "This situation is unacceptable," because it is "an insult to God and to human dignity; furthermore, it is a threat to security and peace, and an obstacle to the achievement of authentic and integral human development."[8]

The repression falls on every type of Christian – Protestants and Catholics, Eastern Orthodox and Oriental Orthodox, Methodists and Mennonites, Charismatics and

Calvinists, sacramental and simple, old churches and new, those who worship in cathedrals and churches steeped in millennia of history, or house churches meeting in secret, Christians in groups or alone and isolated. This broad panorama of abuse has prompted Cardinal Kurt Koch, president of the Vatican's Pontifical Council for Promoting Christian Unity, to describe today's increasing persecution as the "Ecumenism of the Martyrs."[9]

Contrary to the contemporary Western postcolonial construct of Christianity as a Western, white man's religion, some three-quarters of the world's 2.2 billion nominal Christians live outside the developed West, as do perhaps four-fifths of the world's active Christians.[10] Of the world's ten largest Christian communities, only two, the United States and Germany, are in the developed West. China may soon be the country with the largest Christian population,[11] Latin America is the largest Christian region, and Africa is on its way to becoming the continent with the largest Christian population. The average Christian on the planet, if there could be such a one, would likely be a Brazilian or Nigerian woman or a Chinese youth.

The very scale, scope, and variety of the persecution of Christians make it difficult to put it into focus. This is one reason why it is often not reported, or not reported well.[12]

The Persecution of Christians Is Often Downplayed

In order to illustrate how the persecution of Christians is downplayed, I will consider some recent statements by U.S. government officials.

American foreign policy officials have seemed to believe that it would be "special pleading" to do anything specific to highlight and help persecuted Christians. When twenty thousand Christian families were being violently driven from Baghdad's Dora neighborhood in 2006–2007, Secretary of State Condoleezza Rice maintained that the administration could not take effective action to protect them from being murdered and kidnapped because it did not want American policy to be seen as "sectarian."[13] But the United States was already deeply involved in sectarian considerations; Secretary Rice made her statement at the very time the United States was waging a military surge against Islamic Sunni extremists and was engaged in intensive efforts to ensure that nonviolent Sunnis gained positions in the Iraqi government, which, thanks to the overthrow of Saddam Hussein, was run largely by Shias, whom the administration had helped politically strengthen and unify. U.S. policy in Iraq had many sectarian considerations – except with regard to Christians and other non-Muslims, such as Mandaeans and Yazidis, who, because they were peaceful, were consistently overlooked and who now form a disproportionate number of Iraqi refugees.

On November 1, 2010, Islamist extremists assaulted Baghdad's Our Lady of Perpetual Help Catholic Church during a Sunday Mass, killing or wounding virtually all of the congregation. This atrocity occurred at a pivotal moment, when violence and the Baghdad government's failure to protect non-Muslims were leading to their eradication from Iraq. The White House condemned "this senseless act of hostage-taking and violence by terrorists linked to Al-Qaeda in Iraq that occurred Sunday in Baghdad killing so many innocent Iraqis."[14] But it did not mention who the victims were, nor that were they were massacred in church during Sunday worship. In contrast, on October 4, 2011, and on January 11, 2012, for example, when two mosques were vandalized in Israel, the Department of State was specific about the victims and motives, condemning "the dangerous and provocative attacks on a mosque in the northern Israeli town of Tuba-Zangariyye, which took place on October 3. Such hateful sectarian actions are never justified."[15]

On Easter morning in 2012, a Protestant church in Kaduna, Nigeria, was targeted by a suicide car bombing that killed thirty-nine and wounded dozens, apparently the handiwork of Boko Haram, an ISIS–linked terrorist network. The previous Christmas, Boko Haram had bombed St. Theresa's Catholic Church outside the capital, Abuja, killing forty-four worshipers, and the group also attacked Christian churches in the towns of Jos, Kano, Gadaka, and Damaturu. There was no official comment from the Obama administration about this massacre of Christians on Christians' most holy day. However, on Easter day, Secretary Clinton issued a press release celebrating the Romani people and demanding that Europe become more inclusive of them.[16] No doubt there is need for such inclusivity, but why was this the sole message at Easter when there had been a slaughter of Nigerian Christians?

Sometimes this downplaying is accompanied by the sentiment "Why focus on what is happening to Christians; many other groups are also persecuted." The U.S. State Department's 2013 report on international religious freedom appears to take this position. The report very properly highlights growing anti-Semitism worldwide, and Secretary of State John Kerry used the opportunity to announce the appointment of Ira Forman as the new special envoy to monitor and combat anti-Semitism. However, there was no systematic attention to massive persecution of Christians worldwide. This persecution is mentioned in the executive summary, but only in such a way as to downplay, and even to slight, the point. The report states, "While Christians were a leading target of societal discrimination, abuse, and violence in some parts of the world, members of other religions, particularly Muslims, suffered as well." This is obviously true – I know no one who would deny it – but the wording elides the fact that Christians are indeed "a leading target" (in fact *the* leading target). On these grounds, Secretary Kerry could equally have mentioned anti-Semitism only in passing and then quickly added that, of course, others suffer as well. This rationale could obviate mentioning the persecution of any group at all on the grounds that others were also persecuted. Thus, the rampant persecution of Christians is not highlighted but sidestepped and ignored.[17]

The Persecution of Christians Is Increasing

The sections that follow, describing persecutory trends in the world, will illustrate the growth of recent persecution, especially in the Muslim majority world. The essays in this volume also illustrate widespread growth in persecution. Metropolitan Hilarion aptly summarizes the situation:

> Regrettably, the problem of discrimination against Christians acquires ever larger scales to become one of the important issues on the international agenda. This situation is connected to a large extent to the situation in the Middle East and North Africa, where the so-called Arab Spring has become the cause of the mass exodus of Christians. The number of the Christian community in Iraq has decreased many times. Christians are subjected to severe persecution and violence in Egypt, Libya, Afghanistan, Pakistan, North Sudan and a number of other countries. In connection with this situation, representatives of the Russian Orthodox Church draw the public attention to the need to set up special mechanisms for protecting the rights of Christians in the world. Speaking at the UN General Assembly last autumn, I called upon the world community to take urgent measures to protect Christians.[18]

We should not ignore the persecution of others, nor seek any special privileges for Christians, but currently we face the opposite problem that many of our political leaders and media often neglect the persecution of Christians.

WHAT ARE VIOLATIONS OF RELIGIOUS FREEDOM AND WHAT IS PERSECUTION?

Many terms, such as *persecution, serious or egregious violations, religious cleansing,* and *genocide,* are ill defined and controversial. As in all human rights reporting, the accuracy, precision, and meaning of the numbers of those persecuted are often as uncertain and contested as key terminology.

I will follow the U.S. International Religious Freedom Act (IRFA) of 1998, which defines violations of religious freedom to include arbitrary prohibitions on, restrictions of, or punishment for

- assembling for peaceful religious activities such as worship, preaching, and prayer;
- speaking freely about one's religious beliefs;
- changing one's religious beliefs and affiliation;
- possession and distribution of religious literature;
- raising one's children in the religious teachings and practices of one's choice.

Other violations of religious freedom specified by IRFA include

- arbitrary registration requirements;
- any of the following acts if committed on account of an individual's religious belief or practice: detention, interrogation, imposition of an onerous financial penalty, forced labor, forced mass resettlement, imprisonment, forced religious conversion, beating, torture, mutilation, rape, enslavement, murder, and execution.[19]

Of course, Christians, like all human beings, may suffer for reasons other than faith. They may suffer persecution not because they are Christians per se but instead on the grounds of language, race, or ethnicity. Or, they may simply be in the wrong place at the wrong time. We do not cover these instances, since they are not necessarily tied to Christians' faith. Instead we will focus on the suffering inflicted on people at least in part *because they are Christians* – suffering they would not have had to endure otherwise.

Certainly, the dividing line is not clear and precise. Christians, especially pastors, are often brutally attacked in Colombia, Peru, Mexico, Zimbabwe, the Philippines, and many other places. They are killed because they have stood against repressive regimes, against corrupt local officials, against guerrillas that may be even more repressive than the regimes they would replace, and against vicious drug cartels. But others who are not Christian suffer in the same circumstances. The issues are complex, since many believe it is their Christian duty to stand against any form of oppression; for this they suffer and die. I do not pretend to say definitively that this is not religious persecution, but I will not include these courageous cases in this discussion

PATTERNS OF PERSECUTION

The Categories

There are currently four major patterns of anti-Christian persecution; while these do not include all instances of conflict and persecution, such as in the contemporary Central African Republic, or in Mexico, they cover the great majority of them. These patterns, together with the countries and areas most associated with them, are the following.

Self-Professed Communist Countries

The remaining self-professed Communist countries are China, Vietnam, Laos, North Korea, and Cuba. While we can dispute the degree to which they continue to be Communist in any real sense, nevertheless they still claim to be motivated by ideology, and that ideology is antireligious. Here the state is the usual persecutor.

South Asian Religious Nationalism

In India, Nepal, Sri Lanka, and Bhutan, reactionary Hindu and Buddhist elements attack religious minorities. The persecution here is primarily societal rather than state directed, but states (Sri Lanka, Nepal) or local governments (parts of India) can be complicit in not providing adequate protection, and/or not prosecuting attackers, and/or instead pressing charges against those who have been attacked,

The Muslim Majority World

While it does not involve the most Christians, the Muslim majority world is the site of the most widespread persecution, and it is an area where the persecution of Christians is increasing. There is tremendous variation in the type and extent of persecution from country to country. In Malaysia, Turkey, Algeria, and Brunei there are restriction and regulation. In Saudi Arabia, Sudan, Afghanistan, Iran, and the Maldives, there is government repression. In Syria, Iraq, Nigeria, Indonesia, Bangladesh, Yemen, Libya, and the Palestinian Territories there have been terrorist, militia, and societal violence and a weak state. In Pakistan and Egypt, there are all of these, and in areas of Iraq and Syria invaded by ISIS, and in parts of Somalia, there is systematic eradication of Christians and other minorities. Even in comparatively open countries such as Morocco, Jordan, and Mali, there are growing problems.

Post-Communist, National Security, and Other Authoritarian States

The post-Communist, national security, and other authoritarian states include Burma/Myanmar, Ethiopia, Eritrea, as well as post-Communist states – including Russia, Uzbekistan, Turkmenistan, Azerbaijan, Tajikistan, Belarus, Kazakhstan, Kyrgyzstan, Armenia, and Georgia. Again, the abuses of religious freedom vary dramatically among these countries. Eritrea is one of the world's most vicious religious persecutors, whereas Russia, Georgia, and Armenia are comparatively open. Some post-Communist countries simply maintain the policies regarding religion that they had when they were officially Communist. Since the dynamics are similar from regime to regime, I have chosen to group them together.

Persecution in these states is usually less driven by ideology or religion than by an authoritarian regime that represses others simply because it wishes to maintain power and privilege and so crush other centers of allegiance and authority. This is the most porous category since, of course, in most of the other countries I cover, whatever else they might want to do, the regimes also want to maintain their power and privilege. However, in these other instances, the power is (also) sought ostensibly in support of a policy, ideology, or religion rather than for the mere purpose of self-aggrandizement. Here I am suggesting that self-aggrandizement is the primary motive. Some states in this category are not static within my typology or may fit under multiple classifications. Burma moves between general authoritarianism and religious nationalism. Ethiopia also faces great problems, especially in the East, from Wahhabi-influenced radical Islam, so Ethiopia has two marked trends.

Western Secularism

There is little persecution, as defined previously, in Western Europe, North America, and Australasia, and the situation is vastly different from the violent attacks that take place elsewhere. Hence, I have not included it as one of the categories of persecution. However, the state of religious freedom in these regions is worsening, and so I will briefly outline some of these. In much of the Western world, the concept of the secular, a term derived from Christian theology, has transformed from the idea of a nonconfessional state and opposition to religious discrimination to the idea that religion should be excluded from public life itself, including societal life, leading to extreme forms of secularism such as *laïcité* and Kemalism.

Limits of These Categories

Clearly, these categories are not very precise. Neither countries nor political and religious motives fall into clearly distinct and discrete categories. For example, I list Burma as a "national security state," whereas ten years ago I would have classified it under "religious nationalism" (and might do so again) since, although it also repressed Buddhists, it used a rationale of defending Buddhism in its repression of Christian and other religious minorities. And, of course, the situation in Burma is now rapidly changing, with increased religious-nationalist and ethnic persecution of Muslims. There can be many overlapping dynamics within a single country or region. Also, while I will refer to countries, there is often regional variation within countries.[20]

The categories also focus on *grounds* and *motives* of persecution, not on the particular pattern of persecution in individual countries per se. The typology used and the labels assigned to various categories do not indicate that all similarly placed countries or areas are equally repressive. For example, the Baltic States are surely "post-communist" countries – the progeny of the collapse of the Soviet Union – and Senegal is a Muslim majority state. However, all of these countries are free of severe religious persecution. Amounts of persecution vary greatly within these categories and patterns. Among Muslim countries, Morocco is not Saudi Arabia; among post-Communist countries Georgia is not Uzbekistan. There is also variation within countries: Christians are persecuted in North-East Kenya, but not in Kenya as a whole; and in Zanzibar, but not in Tanzania as a whole.

These patterns also include Christian on Christian persecution or, more commonly, discrimination and harassment. This is particularly true with post-Communist and other authoritarian states. In the post-Communist states there is often a de jure or de facto privileged position for Orthodox churches, and other Christians may face discrimination and harassment, as in Georgia, Armenia, and Russia, and sometimes worse, as in Belarus and Central Asia. A similar pattern occurs in parts of Ethiopia. In southern Mexico there is a hard-to-classify phenomenon of nominal Catholics, usually opposed by the church, persecuting Protestants who refuse to participate in village ceremonies.[21]

COUNTRIES

Self-Professed Communist Regimes

A forty-something woman, who lived in a city of North Pyongan Province, North Korea, was caught with a Bible in her home. She was seized, dragged from her house, and publicly shot to death. Her execution took place on the threshing floor of a farm. Government officials demanded that there be one witness to the execution, who later said. "I was curious why she was to be shot. Somebody told me she had kept a Bible at her home. Guards tied her head, her chest, and her legs to a post, and shot her dead."[22]

China, Vietnam, Laos, Cuba, and North Korea are all still controlled by party regimes that seized power around the middle of the twentieth century. Over the last two decades – with the notable exception of North Korea – the ideological rigidity of Stalin, Mao, and Ho Chi Minh has been tempered by openings to the larger world and an interest in global trade. But these regimes remain highly repressive, and they are still the largest source of Christian persecution, simply because of the sheer number of Christians living within their borders – especially in China.

Today, China is emerging as a global economic powerhouse and an assertive regional force poised to eclipse the Asian-Pacific democracies both militarily and economically. Vietnam, Laos, and Cuba remain poor and slower to enter global markets, but they too are reaching out for investment, trade, and tourism. North Korea, in a class by itself, remains closed, openly hostile to the West, and devoted to Soviet-inspired totalitarianism.

These countries' ideologies initially viewed Christianity, like all religions, as an impediment to progress, its moral codes as mere superstition, and its spiritual consolation and message of hope as an opiate. They, and their ideological allies in the Soviet bloc, sought to eradicate all religions. They did so brutally. Over decades, churches were devastated as Christians were martyred for their faith by the thousands in merciless prison and labor camps and by firing squads and assassins' bullets. North Korea still practices this vicious style of persecution.

By 1991, the Soviet Union had collapsed and splintered. Vietnam, Laos, and Cuba were left without a patron and with little choice but to court Western trade and aid. China had already begun to shed its stagnating Marxist economic policies. With greater global engagement, these states needed to soften their reputations and internal policies.

This internal loosening, though it falls far short of real religious freedom, has meant that Christianity has begun to rise. Catholic and Protestant churches are rebuilding. Christian faith is spreading, and, gradually, Christian public worship and practice are widening. In China in particular, Christianity is experiencing spectacular and unprecedented growth. In China, there are probably at least 70 million Christians, and the number may be much higher.[23]

However, none of these states has made reforms in civil and political rights comparable to their economic liberalization. The Communist Party in these countries seeks to control all political and nearly all civic activity, including religious activity. More subtle forms of repression are replacing mass killings and penal camps; Christian practice is now surveilled, registered, regulated, and restricted.

Unauthorized or independent religious activity is still treated as a crime, and brutality against and imprisonment of Christians still continue. In Vietnam and Laos, authorities may force unregistered Christians in remote ethnic areas to recant their faith. North Korea has made no substantial reforms regarding religious freedom since its founding more than half a century ago.

In general, this state repression is proving to be a losing proposition – there are likely now more Christians than Communist Party members in China. In Vietnam, Laos, and Cuba, despite continued oppression, the numbers of Christians and churches – including house churches – are rising, and governments must adjust.[24]

South Asian Religious Nationalism

In Kannur village in Karnataka State in India, Pastor Samuel Kim of Jerusalem Prayer House was beaten unconscious by Hindu extremists on October 11, 2012. He was admitted to R. L. Jallappa Hospital with a broken rib, severe injuries to his head and neck, and bruises on the rest of his body. Early the next morning, assailants came to his private ward to kill him. "Five extremists came near my bed, started to strangle me and brought a razor to slit my throat," he said, but the attackers fled when they heard people nearby. The local superintendent of police gave him protection for the week he was in the hospital, and registered a case against the extremists, but no arrests were made. Police warned him not to lead worship again or there might be "dire consequences." In Karnataka, Christians are attacked on religious grounds about three times per week.[25]

In South Asia, while there are often widespread freedom and peaceful religious coexistence among stunningly varied neighbors, there are extremist Hindu and Buddhist religious movements that not only correctly connect their countries' culture to their religion but go further to equate their religion with the nature and meaning of the country itself. Because of this equation, they feel threatened by other religions and may persecute minority tribes and religions, often including Christians. The majority of Hindus and Buddhists are peaceful followers of their religion. However, it is important to realize that factions of these groups also have strong militant traditions and do not always abjure violence – something we see, for example, in recent Buddhist attacks on Muslims in Burma, attacks often led by monks.

Religious persecution regularly occurs in India, Sri Lanka, Nepal, and Bhutan. These countries are strikingly different – for one thing, India has more than one thousand times as many people as Bhutan – but there are common patterns in repression. One pattern is that groups within the majority religion maintain that they are the only indigenous, authentic, and legitimate religion in the country, so that the country in some sense belongs to them. Other groups and other religions are perceived as foreign. The dominant religious group then denigrates and may even physically attack members of other religions. In India, most of the violence is between Muslims and Hindus, but there is also extensive violence by extremist Hindus aimed at the Christian minorities. There have also been attacks by Muslims on Christians, especially in Kashmir.

Christianity is sometimes treated as a foreign faith, although in South Asia it has roots that go back further than in most of Europe. Sometimes the Christian faith is pilloried as a British colonial import, even though Christianity in India is older than it is in Britain. In India, the most ancient churches trace their founding to the ministry of the apostle Thomas, the "doubting Thomas" who was skeptical of Jesus's resurrection and who is believed to have arrived in Kerala in Southwest India around AD 52.

Christians are also attacked because many of them believe that they have a duty to evangelize, urging others to trust in Jesus. For religions that believe that their people and land are necessarily tied to a particular faith, evangelism may be treated as invasion, imperialism, and usurpation, even when the evangelists are their longtime neighbors. In such contexts, much of the violence is related to conversion to Christianity. Often the violence has political overtones, as when local strongmen try to preserve positions of power rooted in local customs. Abusive incidents often spike during election periods as vying political candidates try to gather nationalist and chauvinist support by vilifying supposed outsiders. Even political leaders of the majority faith – for example, Mohandas Gandhi in India and S. W. R. D. Bandaranaike in Sri Lanka – have been assassinated by radicals who thought them too conciliatory to minorities.

Again, it must be emphasized that this is not the majority pattern within these religious cultures or in these countries. The results of these attitudes, however, are pervasive insults, discrimination, harassment, and hundreds of episodes of religious violence.

Each of these countries is undergoing momentous changes. India has been experiencing sustained economic growth that may make it one of the world's great powers. Sri Lanka's civil war effectively ended in 2009. In 2008, Nepal's conflict with Maoists largely ended, the Hindu monarchy was abolished, and the country was declared a secular republic. That same year, Bhutan held its first democratic elections and became a constitutional monarchy, and the new constitution promised "freedom of thought, conscience, and religion."[26]

So far these changes have not often produced increased freedom from persecution for Christians or other religious minorities. In India, conversion to Christianity is frequently restricted – de facto if not de jure – especially at the provincial level by radical elements within the majority religion. Harassment by several state governments, coupled with endemic violent local attacks, continues. The end of Sri Lanka's war led not to harmony but to an upsurge of violence against Christians and others. In Nepal, Christianity is still not legally recognized, while reactionary Hindu militias such as the Nepal Defense Army threaten to bomb every Christian household. Similarly, in Bhutan, Christians cannot yet have church buildings or cemeteries since Christianity is not legally recognized.

The Muslim Majority World

A fifty-five-year-old Somali, Musa Mohammed Yusuf, was the leader of an underground church in Yonday village, located twenty miles from Kismayo. In February 2009, Musa was questioned in his home by a group of radicals from the notorious Al-Shabab. Well aware that he was in grave danger, Yusuf fled to Kismayo.

When the radicals returned to Musa's home the following day, they were enraged to find that he had run away. As his wife, Batula Ali Arbow, watched, they roughly gathered up the couple's three sons: twelve-year-old Hussein Musa Yusuf, eleven-year-old Abdi Rahaman Musa Yusuf, and Abdulahi Musa Yusuf, age seven.

Batula fainted. She said later, "I knew they were going to be slaughtered. Just after some few minutes I heard a wailing cry from Abdulahi (who was) running towards the house...." When she regained consciousness, Batula learned that Abdulahi had escaped the terrorists and survived the attack. But the Al-Shabab terrorists had beheaded her other two boys.[27]

Even though the remaining self-professed Communist countries persecute the most Christians, it is in the Muslim majority world where persecution of Christians is now most intense and involves the greatest number of countries. Ominously, persecution in these areas is increasing. Extremist Muslims are expanding their repression and sometimes even directing it at their coreligionists, the majority of Muslims who reject the radicals' program.

The range, type, and intensity of persecution vary widely. Malaysia, Turkey, the area administered by Turkish Cypriots or Turkish Military in Cyprus (as it is officially known), Morocco, Algeria, Jordan, and the Palestinian Territories are not as dangerous for Christians as Saudi Arabia and Iran. Nonetheless, in varying degrees, they discriminate against Christians, and at times, Christians are subject to acts of persecution, which serve to restrict Christian practice.

In principle, Saudi Arabia forbids any Christian, or other non-Muslim, worship, and no Saudi is allowed to be Christian. The millions of Christians in Saudi Arabia must hide their faith and seek the protection and secrecy of foreign worker or embassy compounds in order to pray in community. This option is more available to Westerners than to the larger groups of Christians from Egypt, Lebanon, the Philippines, Pakistan, and Bangladesh. Saudi Arabia's grand mufti, an authoritative religious figure who is appointed by the king and supported by the state, has recently declared that it is "necessary to destroy all the churches of the region."[28]

Iran is imprisoning, and sometimes killing, members of its growing Farsi-speaking churches, largely because the members of these churches have a Muslim background. Strikingly, in Iran the persecution is almost entirely by the state and its organs – there is little persecution by the society at large.

Egypt, Pakistan, Afghanistan, and Sudan vary widely in geography, culture, and degree of Christian presence. Egypt is still home to the largest, and one of the most ancient, Christian communities in the greater Middle East, whereas not a single church (building) now remains in Afghanistan; its tiny Christian population consists of relatively recent converts, who must live in hiding. Christians, who count for fractions of the populations of Pakistan and North Sudan, can, while subject to attack, for the most part openly operate churches. But while their circumstances differ, the Christians in these four countries constitute severely persecuted minorities whose survival depends on a constant struggle in the face of ever-increasing Islamic extremism.

In the Muslim majority areas we have described so far, the main source of repression and persecution has either been Islamist governments, as in Saudi Arabia and Iran, or a vicious mixture of governments, mobs, and vigilantes, often acting in concert, as in Afghanistan and Pakistan. There is another set of countries where the persecution of Christians is not usually committed directly by the government – at least not the central government – but rather by extremists in society, including militias and terrorists. The problem with these countries' governments is that they cannot, or at least do not, control or stop this violence.

In some cases, such as Indonesia and Bangladesh, the central government is not strong enough to maintain security, or it is simply unwilling to risk political unpopularity by effectively countering extremists. In Egypt, whatever the reasons, the government has not adequately protected the Copts from attacks, nor punished their attackers. U.S. government agencies and international and Egyptian human rights groups speak of a climate of "impunity" in relation to attacks on Copts.

Somalia is still in the midst of a brutal civil war and has been without an effective central government since 1991. The Al Qaeda–linked Al-Shabab militia is engaged in a systematic campaign to kill all Somali Christians on the grounds that they are apostate. The world paid some attention with the vicious attack on people in the shopping mall in Nairobi in 2013, when the terrorists released Muslims and focused on killing non-Muslims – predominantly Christians in that context – but the ongoing killings in Somalia itself have drawn little attention.

In Iraq and Nigeria, militias and terrorist groups in large parts of the country are comparatively undeterred when they target religious minorities. In recent years, Nigeria probably has had the largest number of Christians killed on the grounds that they are Christian. The numbers in the last few years are in the thousands, and in recent decades, perhaps tens of thousands. Most of the recent killings are at the hands of Boko Haram.

Syria is currently in the middle of a multisided civil war in which people of every religion suffer, along with those of no religion at all. But as in Iraq after 2003, the non-Muslim minorities, the majority of whom are Christian, suffer disproportionately. They usually do not have their own militias; thus they are easier targets, and radical Islamist movements attack them as infidels. Maronite Archbishop Samir Nassar of Damascus has stated that the only project the Maronite Church in Syria has is to "build a bigger cemetery."[29]

And recently in Iraq as well as Syria, the self-proclaimed "Islamic State," ISIS, has set new standards of evil in persecution as it has practiced forced conversion, abduction, sexual slavery, crucifixion, and beheading of those who refuse to submit to its religious dictates.

Currently, Christians are fleeing the Palestinian areas, Lebanon, Iraq, Syria, and Egypt. In 2003 in Iraq, Christians were some 4 percent of the population, but they make up a much larger percentage of the refugees; perhaps two-thirds of Christians have fled in the last decade, and now, with ISIS, many more will flee. Many Egyptian Copts fear that the Arab Spring has become an Islamist winter for them, especially since the pogroms of August 14–16, 2013 – perhaps the worst attacks in Egypt since 1321 – and they wonder whether they too must flee. Many have already done so.

Post-Communist, National Security, and Other Authoritarian States

Shortly after releasing a cassette tape of gospel songs in May 2004, singer Helen Berhane was arrested in Asmara, Eritrea, and imprisoned at the Mai Serwa prison camp outside the city. She spent much of her two and a half years of captivity in a metal shipping container and was routinely tortured in efforts to make her recant her faith. She was subjected to "the helicopter" – in which detainees are contorted into an excruciating position with their feet and hands tied together behind their backs – to force her to renounce her faith. She was also beaten repeatedly over the course of her imprisonment. By October 2006, she had been tortured so badly that prison authorities allowed her to be admitted to a local hospital. After being released from prison shortly thereafter, Berhane was confined to a wheelchair due to extensive damage to her feet and legs from beatings.[30]

Wehazit Berhane Debesai, who was in her 30s, died of pneumonia in Eritrea during the week of October 14, 2013, following a year of imprisonment in harsh conditions, where she was denied access to medical treatment because she refused to denounce her Christian beliefs. Her death coincided with the arrest of about 70 Christians at a prayer gathering in Asmara, the capital. These arrests bring to nearly 300 the number of Christians known to have been taken into custody during what local Christians have called the most serious campaign against the Eritrean Church yet.[31]

Among the post-Communist states originating after the breakup of the former Soviet Union, some states, such as Lithuania, Latvia, and Estonia, have become free and functional, and most of the rest have given up official Communism. However, many still follow the repressive tactics of registration and control practiced by their predecessor regimes. Some are still under the authority of the very same ruling cliques, their economies remain controlled, and they apply the same repressive measures as before. Belarus, Turkmenistan, and Uzbekistan remain among the most restrictive countries in the world. As with the leaders of former Communist regimes, these rulers are usually fanatically secular (at least those who are not compromised by back-room dealings with religious factions) and seek to control all religious activity. In these countries, "post-Communist" means something like "still largely Communist but unwilling to admit it."

Although the intensity of control varies, the tactics are remarkably similar. Religious groups are required to register, but the terms of registration can cripple both small and large communities of believers. Sometimes these requirements are impossible to meet, and, even if achieved, lead to increased surveillance and control. Religious communities that try to register are often required to have a minimum number of members, and to have already been in existence for years, sometimes decades – a very difficult requirement for a group that is still desperately trying to gain a legal existence. The restrictive requirements function as a catch-22: In order to meet, you must be registered; in order to register, you must prove that you have been meeting for years. Those who refuse to register, or whose applications are refused, may be harassed, intimidated, and potentially hounded out of existence.

In these countries, one usually does not witness the widespread deaths and endemic violence that occur elsewhere. Nevertheless, there is a pervasive and repetitive pattern of suffocating and contradictory restrictions designed to grind down those who seek to worship God according to their conscience. Government policies are intended specifically to erode all free expressions of faith.

Apart from the post-Communist countries, there are other authoritarian regimes that, while without a developed justifying ideology, severely repress their religious believers. Some, such as Burma and Eritrea, have been among the worst persecutors in the world. Their common feature is that they are, or have been, heavily militarized states with rulers determined to stamp out any kind of opposition or center of power other than their own. In Burma this repression has been exacerbated by the presence of Christians in many of the non-Burmese ethnic groups, who, because they seek autonomy, have been persecuted as non-Burmese as well as non-Buddhist. Ethiopia can be repressive of other Christians in defending the place of the Ethiopian Orthodox Church, and the country is also experiencing increasing violence against Christians from growing Wahhabism in the eastern areas.

WESTERN SECULARISM

As noted, Western Europe, North America, and Australasia do not have persecution as defined here, and their situation is vastly different from the vicious repression that we have described in other places. Nevertheless, while these areas remain largely free, religious restrictions there are now increasing, an especially troubling trend in countries that have recently been very free. Also, the erosion of religious freedom in the West itself might be one reason why opinion formers there now tend to downplay religious freedom issues in general, and to pay comparatively less attention to the religious persecution of Christians (and others) worldwide.

These changes in the West are tied to the growth of newer interpretations of what it means to be "secular." The term "secular," along with its cognates, has a range of meanings and has often carried a positive religious meaning – emerging as it did from within Christian thought. The words "secularism" and "secularization" were derived from the Latin *saeculum:* The vocation of the priests who withdrew from the world was religious, and the vocation of the priest who took an active role in society was secular.[32] In such usage, "secular" did not mean the absence of religion but the lack of direct control by the church. One could be religious in the secular realm – the area where most Christians and others live out most of their lives. Hence, religion and its influences could be pervasive in secular society and often were.

The related idea of a plural, secular society of free religious and secular influences, with opposition to religious discrimination, has been changing into what Charles Taylor describes as a public arena that has "been allegedly emptied of God, or of any reference to ultimate reality," resulting in extreme *laïcité* and virtual Kemalism.[33] In much current Western jargon, the secular arena is no longer treated as a companion to the religious sphere but as its opposite. Parallel to this, as Bishop Tartaglia has pointed out, much of modern liberalism now tends "to imply that institutions like the family, the church, and other associations exist only with the permission of the state, and to exist lawfully they must abide by the dictates and the norms of the state ... which is intolerant of anyone who questions it.[34]

Hence, politicians and policy makers, among others, often reduce freedom of religion to freedom of worship, which limits the freedom to practice, express, teach, criticize, or leave a religion publicly, or to introduce religion into the societal and public arena. The freedom to worship is defended only as an essentially private activity, with few civic or public policy implications. There is also a widespread, uncritical assumption that secular societies are tolerant and free, when in fact many of the world's most repressive regimes, including the worst, North Korea, are highly secular. This truncation of religion is combined with growing hostility to religion. The Pew Research Center's 2012 "Rising Tide of Restrictions on Religion" reports that such restrictions have now risen in many countries that previously had low or moderate restrictions or hostilities, such as Switzerland and the United States. Simultaneously, countries such as the United Kingdom, Germany, and France experienced a substantial rise in social hostilities involving religion; in fact, those countries scored higher on the Pew Forum's Social Hostilities Index than Iran, Sudan, and Lebanon.[35]

This leads to an increasingly restrictive view of religion and religious freedom. In one case, a nurse, Shirley Chaplin, was asked by her hospital not to wear her cross on her necklace, a cross that she had worn on wards for thirty years, and in 2013 the European Court of Human Rights (ECHR) ruled that she had not suffered religious discrimination. During the review at the ECHR, the lawyer representing the British government told the court that the refusal to allow Mrs. Chaplin to wear her cross visibly at work "did not prevent . . . [her] practicing religion in private."[36] This narrow conception of religious freedom, that religion is something to be protected only in private activities, is in contrast to article 18 of the Universal Declaration of Human Rights, which stipulates, "Everyone has the right to freedom of thought, conscience and religion; [including] freedom, either alone or in community with others and *in public or private*, to manifest his religion or belief in teaching, practice, worship and observance" (emphasis added).[37]

Other examples include restrictions of religious expression. In France and Belgium religious dress is restricted, mainly affecting Muslims but also other religious groups including Christians.[38] In Sweden the National Union of Teachers, one of the largest unions, maintains that religious schools are antiscience and religious dogmas are dangerous.[39] Sweden's former minister for health and social affairs has called on scientists and politicians to "fight against religious dogmas."[40] In addition to anticult statutes that can be employed against certain Christian sects, France even passed a law that banned public prayer in Paris.[41]

The nexus of family law and education increasingly demonstrates the harsh impact of new forms of secularism. The governments of Sweden and Germany forbid home schooling, which some parents view as central to imparting Christian faith to their children. In 2009 Swedish authorities seized custody of seven-year-old Dominic Johansson from his home schooling parents as they were boarding a plane for mission work in India. Five years later Dominic is still in custody of the state and the parents only receive visitation rights for sixty minutes every fifth week.[42] In Germany the Wunderlich family has been fined and their children forced to attend public school,[43] while the home schooling Remeikes fled and are seeking asylum in America.[44]

While home schooling is protected in the United States, religious institutions face increasing pressure to violate religious tenets or close. In Massachusetts, Washington, D.C., and Illinois long-standing Catholic adoption programs have been forced to close because authorities insisted that they violate church teachings about where children can best be raised.[45] Across the country religious student groups have been denied status as recognized clubs by universities because their requirement that leaders be faithful to the groups' commitments in belief and conduct is said to be illegal discrimination.[46] Christian colleges have been threatened with the loss of accreditation for adhering to traditional Christian sexual ethics,[47] while numerous other religious educational institutions and charities face heavy fines for not including abortifacients in their health plans.[48]

While these restrictions do not compare with massacres in Iraq and Nigeria or government repression in China, they represent a shriveling of protection of religious belief and conscience that should not be ignored.

REASONS FOR PERSECUTION

"Subversives" and Nonconformists

The contemporary persecution of Christians is not a unitary phenomenon – it is not a single "war on Christians." The motives and dynamics are different in each of the five patterns we have discussed, and in the cases that fall outside these patterns. Nevertheless, there are some common themes.

One of these is Christian understandings of religion and state, often now expressed in shorthand as the relation of God and Caesar. While there has always been confusion, and often conflict, and sometimes even war over what we now often mislabel the relation between "church and state," one of the distinctive features of Christianity since its earliest years has been its insistence on the necessary temporal existence of two authorities instead of the one sole authority that has been a feature of most cultures and regimes. Even when Christianity became the official religion of the Roman Empire, it was still understood that *sacerdotium* ("church") and *regnum* ("state") were two distinct bodies. There were henceforth *two* centers of authority in society, and neither could be reduced to the Other: Both were believed to be divine institutions, but they were understood to have quite distinct roles so that one could not usurp the role of the other. As George Sabine wrote,

> The rise of the Christian Church, as a distinct institution entitled to govern the spiritual concerns of mankind in independence of the state, may not unreasonably be described as the most revolutionary event in the history of Western Europe, in respect both to politics and to political thought.[49]

Henry Kissinger similarly observed:

> Restraints on government derived from custom, not constitutions, and from the universal Catholic Church, which preserved its own autonomy, thereby laying the basis – quite unintentionally – for the pluralism and democratic restraints on state power that evolved centuries later.[50]

Even if, as the other essays in these volumes show, it was not quite as unintentional as Kissinger implies, clearly the practice of the church and of Christians often did not meet this standard. Most Christians believe in original sin; hence it is a standard Christian belief that Christians will fail at living out their beliefs, and most have so failed. Jews and heretics were still persecuted, and inquisitions and wars were still defended. These are pervasive, tragic, and bloody historical facts.

But people still always believed that there should be boundaries between these institutions, and they struggled over centuries to define them. This meant that the church, whatever its lust for power and civil control, always had to acknowledge that there were forms of political power that it could not and should not exercise. And the political orders, whatever their fervent and continuing drive to subsume all of human life under their control, always had to acknowledge that there were areas of human life that were necessarily and properly beyond their reach. However much the boundaries were continually muddled, muddied, and bloodied, there was an abiding sense that the political order could not be identified with the order of ultimate human concern; that the spiritual core of human life, and the authority this embodied, was a realm beyond civil control. As with Pontius Pilate, the political ruler always faced "another king."[51]

The key ingredient in this stress on the limits of political power was not, in the first place, a doctrine of or an explicit call for human rights and freedom, although these were, as the essays in these volumes show, also a major part of Christian history.[52] Rather, it was a view of the distinct roles of different institutions. This view, in turn, permeated the culture with the belief that political and ecclesiastical jurisdictions were distinct and limited in their authority, and should always remain so.

Nor was the defense of the freedom of the church a purely parochial concern. The church was the single most pervasive institution in society – one with much more influence than the often weak state, which had a head and arms, but little body. In modern terms, the church composed the "media," since if any news was spread, it did so via announcements from the pulpit in the only place where people gathered – the church. The church also ran universities and the rest of the educational system. Canon law was also more pervasive than the dictates of kings. It usually governed marriage and therefore shaped what people did with inheritance and property. The church also ran whatever welfare arrangements there might be. It was *this* institution, the one that shaped most of society, and its pervasive relation to the political order with which early theorists of church-state relations were concerned.[53] Defending a free church meant defending a society free from imperial and monarchical control.

This division of authority remains pervasive in the teachings, and usually the practice, of Christians in the modern age. In China, for example, Christians are a high proportion of human rights and democracy advocates.[54] On May 10, 2011, the Beijing-based Shouwang church, one of the largest and most influential illegal 'house churches,' together with others petitioned the Chinese government for its independence, declaring that "freedom of religious belief is the paramount freedom.... It is also the cornerstone of other political rights and property rights." One signatory to the petition, Wang Wenfeng, general secretary of Wenzhou China Theology Forum, argued that "issues related to supervising a church are basically issues of faith. State religious affairs agencies are agencies for implementing government policies, and there are insurmountable differences as far as function between them and issues of faith."[5]

The conception of a distinction between ecclesiastical and political authority has meant that Christians often say, with Peter, that they must obey God rather than man and are obliged to serve "another king." This confession, however primitive, denies that the state is the all-encompassing or ultimate arbiter of human life. As such, it can provide a foundation of social and political pluralism. The claim that *Caesar is not God* challenges authoritarian regimes, ancient Romans and modern totalitarians and authoritarians alike, and draws an angry and often bloody response.[56]

Since they deny absolute authority to the political regime, Christians are often subject to persecution by those who have a monistic conception of the social order and the state – that there is one order of authority in society to which all must submit. Contemporary monisms include communism, other authoritarianisms, radical Islamist conceptions, religious nationalisms, and contemporary secularisms that believe that the state has the authority and duty to regulate the conduct of every societal institution. Tension between a Christian understanding of authority and a monistic understanding underlies much contemporary persecution of Christians. North Korea and Saudi Arabia are two very different countries, yet they share a common characteristic: In both, all nationals must follow the state's official religion, a Kim dynasty personality cult in the former and Wahhabi Islam in the latter.

"Foreigners"

Another reason for persecution is the perception of Christians as foreigners. When the subject of Christian persecution is raised, it is often associated with violence directed against missionaries. That certainly occurs, and many brave and dedicated Christian expatriates suffer. But overwhelmingly, those who suffer most are indigenous Christians, who outnumber missionaries by about ten thousand to one. In fact, the single largest destination for Christian missionaries is now the United States, to which churches throughout the world send pastors to help their growing immigrant flocks adjust to a new world.

In Egypt, Turkey, China, India, Iran, Afghanistan, and elsewhere, although Christians are indigenous, they are often associated with the West and suspected as a fifth column. But Christianity is far older in these countries than is Communism or Islam; Christianity is older in Africa than in Europe, in India than in England, in China than in America.

"Converts"

Much violence is visited on those who choose to become Christians; they are often labeled as apostates or weak-minded people subjected to "fraudulent" conversion. Conversion can be punished in places as diverse as Iran and India. In the Muslim world, converts can be punished, even killed, for leaving Islam.[57] The *Economist* has concluded that "there is a specific problem with Islam" in persecuting converts. It urges, "More Muslim leaders need to accept that changing creed is a legal right. On that one point, the West should not back down. Otherwise believers, whether Christian or not, remain in peril."[58] Even in generally moderate countries, conversion may be forbidden. In Malaysia, converts have been sent to reeducation camps. Even Morocco expelled dozens of expatriate Christians after accusations that they had discussed their faith with Muslims.

Turkey's converts have greater rights than in Saudi Arabia and Iran but, as one Turkish Christian leader put it:

> [converts] have to contest for every inch of legal territory. They are constantly surveilled by national security agencies. They have been threatened, attacked, hauled into court on bogus charges, and even brutally murdered by ultra-nationalists linked to a nationwide plot to destabilize the Turkish government.... Although many Turkish congregations meet quietly and safely on a Sunday, no group anywhere in the country meets without carefully taking the measure of each new person who walks through the door.[59]

There is a particular relation of converts and modernity – they both emphasize choice. Traditional societies have a tendency to be ascriptive – in economy, social position, and religion – you are what you were born to be; you will normally be what your parents were. With globalization, there is much more of an emphasis on choice; now you might, within limits, decide to do and be and believe something else. What you were born as is important, but you can be born again. Religions that emphasize freedom to change have an elective affinity (to use Weber's term) with the choices offered by modernity. Hence, Christians may be persecuted as threats to traditional social orders.

CLOSING

There is no single war against Christians; anti-Christian persecution has many instigators and intents. It is also true that other religious minorities suffer grievous persecution in many of these same countries, and we believe that all people, regardless of religious affiliation, should be equally concerned with the persecution of people of any or no religion. But, since Christians are the world's most widely persecuted group, their situation deserves particular attention and action.

There is a church building in the city of Nusaybin, in southeastern Turkey, where a famous Christian community dates back to the second century.[60] In the fourth century, this church nurtured Ephrem, perhaps the greatest of the Syrian theologians, who is venerated as a saint in Eastern Christianity. The ancient building was locked and abandoned after World War I when the congregants, fleeing the Ottoman slaughter of Eastern Christians, escaped into Syria. For almost eighty years there were no Christians in the city, but now the diocese has sent a Christian family from a local village to live in a small apartment behind the church in order to prevent the sacred space from falling apart.

Ten years ago, Tom Oden and I had the opportunity to enter the deserted, rock and dust-laden crypt to see the tomb of Jacob of Nisibis, for whom the Jacobite church is named. While we contemplated his sarcophagus, our local driver, unprompted, began to sing an ancient hymn. His strong voice filled the tomb with almost unearthly resonance. We listened in silent awe. Afterward, we asked him what the words meant. He told us that the lyrics were from Ephrem himself. His words remain:

> *Listen, my chicks have flown,*
> *left their nest, alarmed*
> *By the eagle. Look,*
> *where they hide in dread!*
> *Bring them back in peace!*

NOTES

1 "Syriac Orthodox Archbishop Alnemeh: 'In Sadad, the Largest Massacre of Christians in Syria,'" *Agenzia Fides*, October 31, 2013, http://www.fides.org/en/news/34602-ASIA_SYRIA_Syriac_Orthodox_Archbishop_Alnemeh_In_Sadad_the_largest_massacre_of_Christians_in_Syria#.UpJDheLUcs4

2 Parts of this paper are adapted from Paul Marshall, Lela Gilbert, and Nina Shea, *Persecuted: The Global Assault on Christians* (Nashville: Thomas Nelson, 2013).

3 Paul Marshall, ed., *Religious Freedom in the World* (Lanham, MD: Rowman & Littlefield, 2007). For overviews of religious freedom and religious persecution in general, see the Global Restrictions on Religion reports produced by the Pew Forum on Religion and Public Life (http://www.pewforum.org/); the annual reports on religious minorities produced by the First Freedom Center, http://www.firstfreedom.org/content/New2012Report.pdf; and the annual religious freedom reports produced by the Department of State and the United States Commission on International Religious Freedom.

4 "Rising Restrictions on Religion – One-Third of the World's Population Experiences an Increase," *Pew Forum on Religion and Public Life*, August 9, 2011, http://www.pewforum.org/2011/08/09/rising-restrictions-on-religion2/

5 John Pontifex and John Newton, eds., *Persecuted and Forgotten? A Report on Christians Oppressed for Their Faith, 2011 Edition* (Sutton, UK: Aid to the Church in Need, 2011), 11, http://www.holyseemission.org/pdf/Persecuted_&_Forgotten_2011.pdf; Paul Marshall, "Vatican to the U.N.: 100,000 Christians Killed for Their Faith Each Year," *National Review Online*, May 29, 2013, http://www.nationalreview.com/corner/349530/vatican-united-nations-100000-christians-killed-faith-each-year; "Christians and Lions,"

Economist, December 31, 2011, http://www.economist.com/node/21542195. See also the reports in the essays in this volume, especially that by Todd M. Johnson.

6 *"Religious Factor in International Relations*: The Metropolitan Hilarion's lecture at the Moscow State Institute of International Relations," *Interfax*, October 24, 2013, http://www.interfax-religion.com/?act=documents&div=232. On the number of Christians currently persecuted, see Todd M. Johnson's paper in this volume, "Persecution in the Context of Religious and Christian Demography, 1970–2020."

7 Benedict XVI, "Message of His Holiness Pope Benedict XVI for the Celebration of the World Day of Peace," Vatican Website, January 1, 2011, http://www.vatican.va/holy_father/benedict_xvi/messages/peace/documents/hf_ben-xvi_mes_20101208_xliv-world-day-peace_en.html

8 Ibid.

9 Marine Soreau, " 'Ecumenism of Martyrs' Presented as Path to Unity," *Zenit*, September 16, 2011, http://www.zenit.org/article-33454?l=english

10 Pew Forum on Religion and Public Life, *Global Christianity: A Report on the Size and Distribution of the World's Christian Population* (Washington, DC: Pew Research Center, 2011), http://www.pewforum.org/Christian/Global-Christianity-worlds-christian-population.aspx

11 On the number of Christians in China, see Fenggang Yang's paper in these volumes, "The Growth and Dynamism of Chinese Christianity."

12 The year 2013 saw the publication of several books on the contemporary persecution of Christians. Apart from Marshall et al., see John Allen, *The Global War on Christians: Dispatches from the Front Lines of Anti-Christian Persecution* (New York: Image, 2013); Rupert Shortt, *Christianophobia: A Faith under Attack* (Grand Rapids, MI: Eerdmans, 2013); and Raymond Ibrahim's *Crucified Again: Exposing Islam's New War on Christians* (Washington, DC: Regnery, 2013). Other works include Ron Boyd-MacMillan, *Faith That Endures: The Essential Guide to the Persecuted Church* (Grand Rapids, MI: Revell, 2006); Carl Moeller and David W. Hegg, *The Privilege of Persecution* (Chicago: Moody, 2011); Baroness Cox and Benedict Rogers, *The Very Stones Cry Out: The Persecuted Church: Pain, Passion and Praise* (London: Continuum, 2011). The annual *Operation World: The Definitive Prayer Guide to Every Nation* (Colorado Springs, CO: Biblica Publishing) also contains much useful information. Open Doors publishes a very valuable annual index of the persecution of Christians. Paul Marshall and Nina Shea's *Silenced: How Apostasy and Blasphemy Codes Are Choking Freedom Worldwide* (New York: Oxford University Press, 2011) describes, among many other things, the treatment of converts to Christianity in the Muslim world and beyond. Eliza Grizwold's *The Tenth Parallel: Dispatches from the Fault Line between Christianity and Islam* (New York: Farrar, Straus & Giroux, 2010) outlines conflict of Muslims and Christians from the Atlantic to the western Pacific. See also Lela Gilbert, *Baroness Cox: Eyewitness to a Broken World* (Grand Rapids, MI: Monarch Books, 2007) and the International Institute for Religious Freedom's bi-yearly *International Journal for Religious Freedom*. Since many of the attacks on Christians and much of the antipathy toward Christians stem from bigoted understandings of conversion, see also Elmer John Theissen, *The Ethics of Evangelism: A Philosophical Defense of Proselytizing and Persuasion* (Downers Grove, IL: IVP Academic, 2011), which defends evangelism as ethical and its absence as unethical. Charles L. Tieszen's *Re-Examining Religious Persecution: Constructing a*

Theological Framework for Understanding Persecution (Johannesburg: AcadSA, 2008) discusses many related theological issues.

13 Michael Youash, "Iraq's Minority Crisis and U.S. National Security: Protecting Minority Rights in Iraq," *American University Law Review* 24, no. 2 (2008): 347, http://digitalcommons.wcl.american.edu/cgi/viewcontent.cgi?article=1090&context=auilr

14 Nina Shea, "The White House's Generic Response to an Act of Anti-Christian Terrorism," *National Review Online*, November 2, 2010, http://www.nationalreview.com/blogs/print/251901

15 Office of the U.S. Department of State Spokesperson, "Mosque Attack in Northern Israel," U.S. Department of State Press Statement, October 4, 2011, http://www.state.gov/r/pa/prs/ps/2011/10/175020.htm; Michael Youash, "Iraq's Minority Crisis and U.S. National Security," *American University International Law Review* 24, no. 2 (2008): 341–375.

16 Office of the U.S. Department of State Secretary, "International Roma Day," Department of State Press Statement, April 8, 2012, http://www.state.gov/secretary/rm/2012/04/187589.htm

17 Paul Marshall, "The Bad News about the New State Department International Religious Freedom Report," *National Review Online*, May 22, 2013, http://www.nationalreview.com/corner/349068/bad-news-about-new-state-department-international-religious-freedom-report-paul

18 "Religious Factor in International Relations," *Interfax.*

19 For all of the bulleted points, see International Religious Freedom Act of 1998, Public Law 105–292, *U.S. Statutes at Large* 115 (1998), http://www.state.gov/documents/organization/2297.pdf

20 I will usually refer to countries, but in several cases, persecution is not countrywide but is concentrated in specific areas – for example, in Nigeria or Kenya. In India, patterns of persecution are different in different states, and countries as diverse as China and Indonesia show regional variations.

21 On religious freedom in Belarus, see Olga Grace, "BELARUS: Religious Freedom Survey, September 2014," *Forum 18 News Service*, September 16, 2014, http://www.forum18.org/archive.php?article_id=1997; on Russia, see Geraldine Fagan, "RUSSIA: Religious Freedom Survey, July 2012," *Forum 18 News Service*, July 19, 2012, http://www.forum18.org/archive.php?article_id=1722; on Armenia, see "Attacks on the members of the Evangelical Church of Yerevan after Archimandrite Komitas's statements," *Religions in Armenia*, September 9, 2013, http://www.religions.am/eng/news/attacks-on-the-members-of-the-evangelical-church-of-yerevan-after-archimandrite-komitas%E2%80%99s-statements/; on Georgia, see Felix Corley, "Little Justice Yet for Persecution's Victims," *Forum 18 News Service*, November 10, 2006, http://www.forum18.org/archive.php?article_id=867; on Mexico, see "Head of Town in Mexico Sends Mob to Beat, Abduct Christians," *Morningstar News*, November 11, 2013, http://morningstarnews.org/2013/11/head-of-town-in-mexico-sends-mob-to-beat-abduct-christians/, and other Morningstar reports; on Ethiopia, see Rebecca Seiler, "Christian Prisoner Soka Araro to Be Released," *International Christian Concern*, February 3, 2015.

22 Yeo-sang Yoon and Sun-young Han, *2009 White Paper on Religious Freedom in North Korea* (Seoul: Database Center for North Korean Human Rights, March 20, 2009), 145, http://www.uscirf.gov/images/2009%20report%20on%20religious%20freedom%20in%20north%20korea_final.pdf. Used with permission.

23 The Pew Forum on Religion and Public Life, *Global Christianity.*

24 United States Commission on International Religious Freedom (USCIRF), *Annual Report 2011*, 208, http://www.uscirf.gov/images/book%20with%20cover%20for%20web.pdf

25 "Attackers in India's Most Violent State Follow Christians Even to Hospitals," *Morning Star News*, November 23, 2012, http://morningstarnews.org/2012/11/attackers-in-indias-most-violent-state-follow-christians-even-to-hospitals/

26 "Official Recognition Eludes Christian Groups in Bhutan," *World Watch Monitor*, February 2, 2011, http://www.compassdirect.org/english/country/12469/32148

27 "Islamists in Somalia Behead Two Sons of Christian Leader," *World Wide Monitor*, July 1, 2009, https://www.worldwatchmonitor.org/news/2009/07-July/4474

28 Joseph Mayton, "Christians Angry as Saudi Grand Mufti Calls for Churches to Be Destroyed," *Bikyamasr*, March 16, 2012.

29 "Maronite Prelate in Syria: Only Project We Have Is Building a Bigger Cemetery," *Zenit*, November 22, 2013, http://www.zenit.org/en/articles/maronite-prelate-in-syria-only-project-we-have-is-building-a-bigger-cemetery

30 "Asylum for Eritrean Gospel Singer," *BBC*, October 22, 2007, http://news.bbc.co.uk/2/hi/7056120.stm; "Update: Good News," November 3, 2006, Amnesty International, http://www.amnesty.org.uk/actions_details.asp?ActionID=10

31 "Christian Woman Dies in Eritrean Jail as Prisoner of Conscience," *CharismaNews*, November 4, 2013, http://www.charismanews.com/world/41626-christian-woman-dies-in-eritrean-jail-as-prisoner-of-conscience

32 Elisabeth Shakman Hurd, *The Politics of Secularism in International Relations* (Princeton, NJ: Princeton University Press, 2008).

33 Charles Taylor, *A Secular Age* (Cambridge, MA: Harvard University Press, 2007).

34 "Report of the Georgetown Symposium on Religious Freedom and Equality: Emerging Conflicts in North America and Europe, April 11–12, 2012," Religious Freedom Project, Berkley Center for Religion, Peace and World Affairs, Georgetown University, April 2012, http://repository.berkleycenter.georgetown.edu/101018RFPGeorgetownSymposiumReligiousFreedomEqualityEmergingConflictsNorthAmericaEurope.pdf

35 Pew Research Religion and Public Life Project, *Rising Tide of Restrictions on Religion* (Washington, DC: Pew Research Center, 2011), http://www.pewforum.org/2012/09/20/rising-tide-of-restrictions-on-religion-findings

36 Bruno Waterfield, "Christians Should Leave Their Beliefs at Home or Get Another Job," *Telegraph*, September 4, 2012, http://www.telegraph.co.uk/news/religion/9520026/Christians-should-leave-their-beliefs-at-home-or-get-another-job.html

37 The Universal Declaration of Human Rights. *The United Nations*. http://www.alliancedefendingfreedom.org/News/PRDetail/8727

38 "Annual Report of the U.S. Commission on International Religious Freedom April 2013," 281–282, http://www.uscirf.gov/sites/default/files/resources/2013%20USCIRF%20Annual%20Report%20%282%29.pdf

39 "Prohibit Schools Standing on Religious Basis," *Debatt*, April 16, 2006, http://www.dn.se/debatt/forbjud-friskolor-som-star-pa-religios-grund/ (in Swedish).

40 "Dogmas Danger to the World," *Svenska Dagbladet*, April 20, 2005, http://www.svd.se/opinion/brannpunkt/dogmer-fara-for-varlden_414297.svd (in Swedish).

41 Rachael Curtis, "Religious Freedom and the French Law Banning Prayer in Paris' Public Streets," *Human Rights Brief*, October 25, 2011. http://hrbrief.org/2011/10/religious-freedom-and-the-french-law-banning-prayer-in-paris%E2%80%99-public-streets/

42 Johansson v. Gotland Social Services resource page, *Alliance Defending Freedom*, April 22, 2013. http://www.adfmedia.org/News/PRDetail/3607

43 "Free to Leave, but Family Vows to Stay and Fight," *Home School Legal Defense Association*, December 9, 2014. http://www.hslda.org/landingpages/Wunderlich/default.asp#article

44 Romeike v. Holder. *Alliance Defending Freedom*, December 20, 2013. http://www.alliancedefendingfreedom.org/News/PRDetail/8727

45 Michael Terheyden, "Catholic Charities Forced to Shut Down Services around the Country," *Catholic Online*, June 7, 2011. http://www.catholic.org/news/national/story.php?id=41680

46 Stanley Carlson-Thies, "Protecting Religious Freedom," *Outcomes Magazine*, https://ym.christianleadershipalliance.org/?ProtectingReligious

47 David French, "The Persecution of Gordon College: Traditional Christian Education Is under Attack," *National Review*, January 26, 2015, 21–22.

48 For a catalog of these growing restrictions see Allen D. Hertzke, "A Madisonian Framework for Applying Constitutional Principles on Religion," in *Religious Freedom in America: Constitutional Roots and Contemporary Challenges* (Norman: University of Oklahoma Press, 2015).

49 George Holland Sabine and Thomas Landon Thorson, *History of Political Theory* (New York: Holt, Rinehart & Winston, 1961), 180. David Little adds, "I would underscore that statement several times" in his *Religion, Order and Law* (New York: Harper, 1969), 36.

50 Henry Kissinger, *Does America Need a Foreign Policy?* (New York: Simon & Schuster, 2001), 20–21. For background that suggests that this was not "quite unintentional," see Brian Tierney, *Religion, Law and the Growth of Constitutional Thought, 1150–1650* (Cambridge: Cambridge University Press, 1982).

51 This is drawn from Paul Marshall, *God and the Constitution: Christianity and American Politics* (Lanham, MD: Rowman & Littlefield, 2002), 117.

52 See the essays in the historical volume, especially Robert Louis Wilken, "The Christian Roots of Religious Freedom," Ian Christopher Levy, "Tolerance and Freedom among the Late Medieval Theologians and Canonists," John Witte, "Calvinist Contributions to Freedom I Early Modern Europe," David Little, "Constitutional Protections of the Freedom of Conscience in Colonial America: The Rhode Island and Pennsylvania Experiments," Matthew J. Franck, "Christianity and Freedom in the American Founding," Daniel Philpott, "Christianity: A Straggler on the Road to Liberty?," and Robert Woodberry, "Protestant Missionaries & the Priority of Conversion Attempts in the Spread of Education, Printing, Colonial Reform, and Political Democracy." Many of these authors also stress the importance of Christianity's struggle for the independence of the church.

53 Marshall, *God and the Constitution*, 117–118.

54 See Fenggang Yang's paper in these volumes, "The Growth and Dynamism of Chinese Christianity."

55 "We Stand Up for Our Faith – A Petition to the National People's Congress Concerning the Conflict between Church and State," *China Aid*, May 10, 2011, http://www.chinaaid .org/2011/05/we-stand-up-for-our-faith-petition-to.html; "No Response a Half-Month after 17 Christian Church Pastors in China Submit a Joint Petition," Zhang Min, Journey of the Soul, *Radio Free Asia*, May 28, 2011, http://www.chinaaid.org/2011/06/no-response-to-pastors-joint-petition.html

56 Paul Marshall and Lela Gilbert, *Their Blood Cries Out* (Dallas: Word, 1997), 9. See also Nina Shea, *In the Lion's Den* (Nashville: Broadman and Holman, 1997).

57 Elmer John Thiessen, *The Ethics of Evangelism*.

58 "Christians and Lions," *Economist*, December 31, 2011, http://www.economist.com/ node/21542195

59 Letter provided to Nina Shea through the U.S. Commission on International Religious Freedom, March 15, 2012; for fear of reprisal, the author requested anonymity.

60 The following section is taken from Marshall et al., *Persecuted*, 20.

3

Where the Spirit Leads: Global Pentecostalism and Freedom

Donald E. Miller

Religions that do not experience organizational, theological, and ritual renewal tend to decline, losing market share to competing religious groups that are more creative and adaptable to contemporary culture and political realities. Currently, Christianity is the world's largest religion, with approximately 2.2 billon adherents, followed by Islam with 1.6 billion, Hinduism with 1 billion, and Buddhism with fewer than a 0.5 billion. Christianity, however, would not be in this place of dominance without renewal movements throughout its history. Most recently, an example of a renewal movement is Pentecostalism, which was ignited by the Azusa Street revival in 1906 and rapidly began exporting missionaries around the world, followed by what became known as the charismatic renewal among Catholics and some mainline Protestants beginning in the 1960s.

Defining Pentecostalism is complex because of its many permutations. Theologically, Pentecostals trace their history back to the early Christian church when, fifty days after Jesus's reported resurrection, the Holy Spirit descended on his disciples and followers, enabling them to "speak in tongues" and empowering them to heal those who were sick, as well as giving them the gift of prophecy and appropriate other "gifts" of the Spirit. In the intervening two thousand years, there are various instances when ecstatic religious experiences were manifested, but the contemporary origins of Pentecostalism are typically traced to the recurrence of speaking in tongues in 1901, when students at Bethel Bible School in Topeka, Kansas, were moved by the Spirit under the tutelage of Charles F. Parham. A few years later, Parham took his message regarding Spirit baptism to Houston, Texas, where William J. Seymour, a black Holiness preacher, became convinced that the Holy Spirit was still in the business of working supernatural miracles. Seymour then began preaching the same message to a small gathering of people in 1906 in Los Angeles, igniting what became known as the Azusa Street revival, attended by thousands of people and named after the street where an interracial gathering began to replicate the acts of the first-century apostles: speaking in tongues, healing the infirm, and prophesying.

According to Allan Anderson, a simultaneous expression of the gifts of the Spirit was manifest in India (1905–1907) in the Mukti ("Salvation") revival, led by a woman, Pandita Ramabai.[1] But Anderson does not dispute the importance of the events in Los Angeles, because it launched a massive missionary movement in which individuals experienced their "call" to spread the gospel around the world, many believing that their gift of tongues would serve them well in foreign countries. Also, they went in faith, without return tickets home, believing that the return of Christ was imminent. Cecil Roebeck says that "between April 1906 and the end of the year, the Azusa Street Mission commissioned 19 first-time missionaries.[2] They went to India, Sweden, Palestine, Angola, and Liberia, an indication of the range of their vision. And according to Anderson, by 1915, there were 150 expatriate Pentecostal missionaries in such faraway locations as China.[3]

While there were a number of Pentecostal denominations of U.S. and European origin that emerged in the aftermath of the Azusa Street revivals, many of these denominations have routinized, and currently their growth is primarily outside their country of origin. Furthermore, there have been numerous local denominations that have formed, especially in the Global South, and many of these groups are now sending missionaries around the world. South Korea, Nigeria, Brazil, and India are prime examples of what is sometimes referred to as the "reverse missionary movement." But one of the most dynamic expressions of Pentecostalism is found in churches that have broken away from the "classical" Pentecostal denominations, feeling that they had become too controlling, bureaucratic, and staid – especially in terms of manifestations of the "gifts" of the Holy Spirit – and instead have formed their own renegade churches, many of which have birthed numerous "daughter" churches and may be on the way to creating their own quasi-denominations. These neo-Pentecostal churches tend to be driven by a charismatic leader who does not have seminary education, but experienced a dramatic life-change conversion, and now applies his business savvy to creating innovative ways of propagating the Christian gospel.

Today, many Protestant congregations have been "Pentecostalized," and hundreds of indigenous denominations with Pentecostal and charismatic characteristics have emerged in Latin America, Africa, and Asia. The result is that religious monopolies have been challenged around the world, both within Christianity – for example, where Roman Catholicism or Orthodoxy was the primary religious option – as well as in regions of the world where Christianity was virtually nonexistent. This expansion of Christianity through missionary activity and the dramatic growth of Pentecostal-style religion has created religious conflicts, has contributed to religious persecution, and, at the same time, has stimulated religious pluralism, allowing for religious choice that previously did not exist.

Pentecostals and charismatic Christians, both Protestant and Catholic, may currently number more than 500 million people, or about one-quarter of all Christians. Many of the largest congregations in the world are Pentecostal or charismatic – some with tens of thousands of members. Also, many of the most creative, innovative, and entrepreneurial congregations are Pentecostal. And many of the most missionary-minded individuals are also Pentecostal, seeking to spread the "good news" around the globe.

According to Todd Johnson, in 1910 there were five thousand Christian denominations in the world.[4] By 1970, this number had increased to twenty thousand. Currently, there are more than forty thousand denominations, and the vast majority of these new denominations are Protestant independent groups, many with a Pentecostal or charismatic flavor. What is striking, however, is not just the growth of different Christian groups, but their geographical location. According to Johnson, in 1910, more than 80 percent of all Christians were located in Europe or North America. Today, fewer than 40 percent of Christians are in these two regions of the Western world. Instead, the center of gravity of Christianity has moved to the Global South, with the fastest growth occurring in Africa and Asia.

Furthermore, in areas such as Latin America, which traditionally have been Roman Catholic, there is a substantial shift occurring in the religious identification of Christians, with increasing numbers changing to some form of Protestantism and especially Pentecostalism. According to Paul Freston, "Latin America is now the global heartland of Pentecostalism," and he says that there are more Pentecostals in Brazil than in any other country.[5] In the 2000 census in Brazil, 10 percent of the population identified with Pentecostal churches. Today, Freston thinks the number is closer to 12 percent, and he guesses that another 2 percent of the population attends charismatic Protestant churches that are not explicitly Pentecostal. He says that currently about 12 percent of Latin America as a whole is Protestant, 70–75 percent of these individuals Pentecostal.

Andrew Chestnut places these numbers in historical perspective, saying that 1 percent or less of Latin America was Protestant in 1940.[6] The game changer has been Pentecostalism, which introduced a new style of worship music, less bureaucratic forms of social organization, and an emphasis on the supernatural. These elements appealed to millions of nominal Roman Catholics who converted to Protestantism. Freston, for example, cites a survey[7] done about ten years ago in Rio de Janeiro that indicated that only 30 percent of Pentecostals had been born into the religion – the rest were converts.[8] Similar findings were found in the Pew Forum surveys, discussed later.

Inevitably, the success of Pentecostalism in Latin America has led to charges of "sheep stealing" by Roman Catholic bishops and clergy in Latin America, creating animosity between these two factions of Christianity. However, in the last decade or so, some Roman Catholic clergy have begun to compete with Pentecostals, emphasizing healing and more dynamic forms of worship. Also, in some areas of Latin America there are Pentecostal–Roman Catholic dialogue groups forming, a healthy development for the unity of Christianity, since previously many Pentecostals refused to acknowledge that Catholics were even Christians – saying that they worshipped "idols" and were not "born again."

In 2006, the Pew Forum did a ten-nation survey of Pentecostalism, which led to some important generalizations. For these surveys, they developed two categories – Pentecostals, which referred to respondents who identified with a Pentecostal denomination, such as the Assemblies of God or the Church of God in Christ or the Brazil-based Universal Church of the Kingdom of God – and "charismatics" who did not belong to a Pentecostal denomination but who nevertheless identified themselves as a "charismatic Christian" or "Pentecostal Christian," or who reported speaking in tongues at least several times a year. Combining these two categories, the Pew Forum developed a more general category that they called "renewalist," which included Catholics who were part of the Charismatic Renewal movement.

According to the Pew Forum surveys, Guatemala has the highest percentage of renewalists in Latin America, with 60 percent (20 percent Pentecostals and 40 percent charismatics).[9] In Africa, Kenya had the highest percentage of renewalists, at 56 percent (33 percent Pentecostals and 23 percent charismatics). And in Asia, the Philippines was highest at 44 percent renewalists, with 40 percent being classified as charismatic. When one analyzes only Protestants, the picture is somewhat dismal for mainline, non-Pentecostal denominations. For example, here are the statistics for percentages of Protestants who were *neither* Pentecostal *nor* charismatic: Brazil: 22 percent, Chile: 22 percent, Guatemala: 15 percent, Kenya: 27 percent, Nigeria: 40 percent, South Africa: 57 percent, and Philippines: 33 percent.[10] Of the ten countries surveyed, only South Africa had more than 50 percent of Protestants from non-Pentecostal or noncharismatic orientations.

Perhaps most striking across the ten countries surveyed is that renewalists were not necessarily disproportionately drawn from the lower socioeconomic sectors of society when compared with their fellow countrymen. Furthermore, they were not disproportionately women. And, third, although renewalists are conservative on sexuality related issues (e.g., opposed to abortion and premarital sex), they were quite progressive on social welfare issues, including their affirmation of democracy, belief that the church should speak out on social issues, and affirmation of free-market economics. And, somewhat surprisingly, renewalists were more inclined to have experienced or observed some form of supernatural healing than to speak in tongues on a regular basis. Each of these generalizations warrants a brief comment and contextualization.

The roots of Pentecostalism are among the poorer classes of society. Theoretically this makes sense, fitting nicely with deprivation models of religion whereby religious ecstasy and the promise of supernatural healing are compensation for living on the margins of society without health care and financial stability. However, an odd thing happened, contradicting Marxist theories of religion as an "opiate" of the people: Namely, many people who embraced the conservative moral ethic of Pentecostalism began to experience upward social mobility. Men, in particular, quit drinking, gambling, and womanizing, reforms that then led to surplus capital that was invested in the education of their children as well as better health care for the entire family. Young women were less promiscuous, delaying sexual debut, pregnancy, and marriage – gaining more opportunities for education and employment outside the home. Pentecostal men were viewed as morally upright, and employers started to move them into middle management positions. And perhaps even more fundamental, people living on the margins began to have hope for the future, inspired by their religion – which sometimes took the form of the "prosperity gospel." Within a generation or two, and sometime less, many Pentecostals started to experience upward economic mobility, a finding that explains, at least in part, why the Pew Forum study found that renewalists are not disproportionately from the lower sectors of society.

More surprising is the finding by the Pew Forum that renewalists are not disproportionately women. In my own observations of Pentecostalism, it is not unusual for two-thirds of the seats in worship services to be occupied by women. And it is also my experience that women are very often the first to convert within a family, taking their children to church, which they view as a safe environment and a good place to learn moral values. Within Pentecostal churches, women – and particularly lower-class women – find the support and social roles that are not available in larger society. They have a new dignity as they participate in church activities. And eventually, their husbands are often wooed into the church, pressured by their wives, or else they go out of respect for the transformation that they observe among family members. Although the top leadership are men, new women converts strike a patriarchal bargain based on the personal benefit they derive as their menfolk tend to be less abusive, better fathers to their children, and more responsible wage earners after their conversion. Also, there are multiple roles for women within Pentecostal churches – even if they are not the senior pastor. Pentecostalism has historically been more open to women than many mainline Christian denominations. Aimee Semple McPherson is just one example; several authors who have written chapters in a recent book I coedited provide numerous other examples.[11]

The stereotype that Pentecostals are so "heavenly minded" that they are no earthly good has a partial ring of truth, since they are very focused on prayer, worship, and personal purity. However, from the very beginning of the movement, Pentecostals have been involved in charitable activities, oftentimes at informal levels, and in the last fifteen years or so, many large Pentecostal churches have developed significant social ministries related to education, health care, counseling, and other issues. Although sometimes these ministries are primarily for church members, increasingly Pentecostals are focused on the wider community, seeing such ministries as an expression of Jesus's commitment to feed the hungry, minister to those who are sick, and care for the needy. Typically, these social ministries are not political or policy focused, but I have observed Pentecostal gatherings of clergy in places such as Uganda and Kenya that are addressing the issue of political corruption. Also, increasingly Pentecostal churches are partnering with Christian NGOs, such as World Vision and Food for the Hungry, on large-scale rural development projects and even social issues related to AIDS, female genital mutilation, and more. Hence, it is not surprising that the Pew Forum found Pentecostals to have political and social welfare attitudes that were not very different from those of their fellow countrymen.

Finally, what is somewhat more surprising is the generalization from the Pew Forum surveys that healing is more prominent than speaking in tongues, since glossolalia was an early earmark of Pentecostalism. In part, this observation may derive from the fact that Catholic charismatics were included in their survey, and speaking in tongues is not emphasized within the Catholic Charismatic Renewal movement to the same degree as it is within Pentecostal circles. However, I have noticed in my own experience of attending Pentecostal churches, and especially neo-Pentecostal megachurches, that speaking in tongues has become highly ritualized and confined to a few minutes of collective "prayer language," lacking the steps of "interpretation" that were instructed by the apostle Paul. In short, tongues speaking seems to have become routinized in many congregations. This is also somewhat true of healing, which previously was often quite dramatic, with crutches being cast aside after individuals moved to the front of the church for prayer. Nevertheless, among the hundreds of people whom I have interviewed over the past two decades, many individuals point to an experience of personal healing, or the healing of a friend or relative, as the turning point in their own conversion. Whether these healings are due to a placebo effect is not for me to judge; experientially, they are real to the participants in these churches, as are miraculous stories of people being raised from the dead.

In spite of some domestication of Pentecostal experience, there are a number of elements of Pentecostal and charismatic churches that have a bearing on the issue of religious freedom. It is my view that Christianity would be in global decline without the emergence of the Pentecostal movement and its various offshoots a hundred years ago. Furthermore, there is every reason to believe that Pentecostalism has some life left to it, since various neo-Pentecostal churches continue to renew the mother movement. Also, Pentecostalism has become thoroughly indigenized; that means that new sources of creative innovation are emerging that are culturally and politically resonant with the local context.

Trying to identify the DNA of a movement as broad as Pentecostalism is a challenge; one distinguishing feature is the way in which Pentecostalism democratizes the Christian faith. Rejecting hierarchical expressions of Christianity, Pentecostalism affirms the priesthood of all believers. Everyone is equal in God's eyes; the important point is that one affirms the calling of the Holy Spirit on you're his or her life, potentially as a pastor, or as a businessperson, a carpenter, or a maid. Because the ministry is given to the people, members of Pentecostal churches are empowered to be God's agents in the world and in the church. In practice, some pastors – especially dynamic, charismatic leaders – may play an important role in casting the vision for the church. But the actual work of ministry is done by the people. In the most successful churches, including those with large staffs, the role of the pastor is to equip the people for ministry, training them, but not doing the ministering himself or herself. This is clearly seen in churches with cell-based organizational structures. Every member is part of a cell group of a half-dozen to fifteen people. The cell group is led by a layperson. Clergy seldom attend, if ever, although they typically have a role in training cell group leaders. When the cell group grows larger than a dozen or fifteen, it is divided, and a new leader is given the opportunity to exercise his or her "gifts" by leading Bible study, prayers, and so on. In fact, even the gift of healing is available to laypersons, as are prophecy, baptism, and other opportunities.

One consequence of democratizing the sacred is that it is much more difficult for a repressive state to control renewal-style religion than to manage hierarchical religions, where one can arrest the leadership and the movement falls apart. I encountered a good example of this in the Republic of Armenia, which is dominated by the Armenian Apostolic Church. In a confrontation several years ago, the leader of a ten-thousand-member Pentecostal church told the government, which was a surrogate for the Orthodox (Apostolic) Church, that it could either work with the leadership of their church or deal with one thousand cell groups. The government selected the former option, and the result is that this Word of Life church is successfully moving forward on many fronts, including building a large church that will seat several thousand people at one time.

A second element of Pentecostal DNA is the focus on religious experience, which acknowledges that the Holy Spirit may speak directly to individual believers. This can occur through dreams, an audible voice, or reflection on scripture whereby one receives a strong calling or "feeling" that he or she should do a specific thing.

Sometimes this calling is starting a new ministry; other times it may be leaving the comfort of one's country and being a missionary in a new land or developing a new "gift" that has not previously been exercised. I have heard numerous accounts from people who said that they resisted the Spirit for a while, but the "voice" or "leading" persisted until they acted on it. These powerful spiritual encounters do not respect traditional authority, either of government, family, or even church leadership. Individuals responding to their "call" may undergo substantial hardship, but in retrospect they see this as God's way of pruning their ego, building personal strength, and equipping them for the task. This model of leadership is quite different from what the sociologist Max Weber called legal-rational styles of authority or, alternatively, traditional models of leadership, in which one respects custom and hierarchy.

A third element of Pentecostal DNA is its adaptability to different cultural contexts and circumstances. Renewal movements inevitably point back in time to the origins of the religion, when conditions were organizationally simple and religious experience was prized over ensconced authority. In the case of Christianity, this means that two thousand years of tradition can be dismissed or even viewed as corrupt – especially in terms of institutional forms. Rather, one appeals to the model of the early Christian church, the example of Jesus, and the power of the Holy Spirit after Jesus's resurrection. This appeal to the primitive church enables one to critique existing religious institutions – much as Jesus did – and view the authority of the state as an earthly institution that may persecute but cannot restrict one as he or she pursues the leading of the Holy Spirit. Such religious zeal is nearly uncontrollable, because prison, restrictions, and even death are not sufficient deterrents to the work that God, through the Holy Spirit, has ordained.

Fourth, Pentecostals believe that they have the truth – with a capital _T_. Therefore, they have an obligation to share it with the world. This may lead to demonizing other religious traditions, including those within Christianity. In the viewpoint of outsiders, Pentecostals may appear to be unsophisticated, dogmatic, uncompromising, and even arrogant. On the other hand, it is precisely their certainty about the faith – or their particular brand of it – that contributes to their zeal and makes them committed missionaries and dedicated, almost beyond comprehension, to their church and spreading the good news as they perceive it. Indeed, risk taking seems to be wrapped up in the Pentecostal DNA and is reinforced from the pulpit and in publications.

Fifth, not only are Pentecostals risk takers, but they tend to be visionaries, with what might even be perceived as completely unrealistic goals and ambitions. Compared to typical mainline Protestant pastors, the charismatic leaders of large Pentecostal megachurches tend to thrive on "big ideas" related to building projects, saving "unreached" peoples, and planting new churches. Particularly in neo-Pentecostal churches, where they do not have to follow bureaucratic procedures, visionary ideas draw the congregation to new levels of giving, self-sacrifice, and personal piety – such as round-the-clock prayers, and so on. Sometimes outside prophets are invited into the congregation for special meetings, and radical new ideas are planted. Often members of the congregation go out and pursue these ambitious ideas with some degree of success, and thus the idea of "self-fulfilling" prophecy takes on a whole new meaning within the Pentecostal context.

Sixth, in recent times, Pentecostalism has had a great boost from modern technology and advanced forms of travel. Unlike many denominations, which tend to operate within the confines of their own institution, many Pentecostal churches, and especially neo-Pentecostal churches, are part of international networks that operate independently of denominational ties and country boundaries. Senior pastors and church leaders connect through international conferences; they communicate by e-mail; they share songs, sermons, organizational insights, and ideas for new ministries. Hence, in a matter of seconds, new ideas are flowing around the world, and that is one reason that so many of these churches are creative and innovative. They are picking up the latest ideas from global thought leaders and practitioners, and they are trying them out in their own local context.

Seventh, Pentecostal churches and especially large neo-Pentecostal churches tend to have culturally current worship music that appeals to a younger generation of members. Worship is joy-filled. People are on their feet dancing, swaying, singing. Oftentimes the musicians are highly professional, sometimes having entertained in clubs and secular venues prior to their conversion. They take the musical idiom of contemporary culture into the church, but change the words – not the style. Young people are attracted to this music. Gone are the organs and choirs, replaced by guitars, drums, saxophones, and singers – each in front of an individual microphone. And the worship leader knows how to modulate the mood of the audience, taking them into the quiet space of prayer and worship and by the end of the service into the triumph of living out the Christian life in secular society.

Eighth, many of the megachurches are run like corporate businesses, with efficiency and direction. I visited a large Pentecostal church in Malaysia and interviewed a member who worked for an international consulting firm. After his conversion, he had tried some non-Pentecostal churches, but he yearned for a fast-paced, CEO-led church that paralleled his business experience. He found it in the church he now attends. Several weeks later, I visited a church in Indonesia and heard the same story as we sat around a corporate-type boardroom table. The pastor had a degree in business, and the church ran with the efficiency of a major corporation, an attribute that, in turn, attracted staff members with the same competencies as well as members who wanted a church that was contemporary in substance and form.

Ninth, many Pentecostal churches do not have the look and feel of a traditional church. Gone are the steeples, stained glass, and pews. These churches often meet in former movie theaters or transformed warehouses. The Malaysian church mentioned previously constructed their structure to look like an industrial building, in part because it is located in an industrial park, and the area is not zoned for a church. They purposely set up a corporation that owns the building and land, which then leases to the church. And the Indonesian church that I previously mentioned has constructed a large building that doubles as a school and has an auditorium that they frequently rent to other groups, including Muslim groups. The vast majority of Pentecostal churches, of course, are relatively small. They tend to meet in storefronts; if they grow larger they can easily upgrade to larger facilities since they are rented and not owned.

Mainline churches often look sleepy in comparison to these fast-moving, creative, adaptable churches. Furthermore, mainline Protestant churches are often promoting moral principles that are red-hot in a Western setting, such as the United States, but in fact are divisive in the Global South. I am, of course, thinking of issues related to homosexuality, the blessing of same-sex unions, and high-flung ideas about religious freedom and pluralism. In contrast, Pentecostal churches tend to be rooted in the concrete reality of everyday life in their local context. They know local government leaders as well as the mentality of their own people, and they know when to push and when to accommodate. And they know the immediate needs of their people, which may have little relation to certain Western values related to individual freedom and rights.

Over the past several decades I have had the opportunity to observe Pentecostal churches in a variety of different cultural settings. Much of what I have described in the preceding section applies to "open-market" countries with a considerable degree of religious freedom. But I have also had the opportunity to travel in countries with a more regulated religious marketplace, and that travel has allowed me to observe some ways in which the churches manage their religious freedom. And to a lesser degree I have traveled in highly regulated religious marketplaces. While not definitive, I have some observations regarding coping strategies utilized by Pentecostals in these various contexts.

Recently my colleague Tetsunao Yamamori and I were in Shanghai and Beijing for several weeks, talking with house church leaders. Contrary to some stereotypes, urban house churches are no longer "underground." There are thousands of them in large cities. Government authorities are aware of many, if not most of them, and they meet for tea or informal conversation with house church leaders on a regular basis. So long as foreigners are not involved with the church, house churches remain relatively small, and if they do not engage in any sort of political activity, they are allowed to exist. Pentecostal churches are somewhat more problematic because they are "too noisy," and if they have connections to Taiwan, South Korea, or even Hong Kong, questions may be raised. Also, it is important to note that many urban house church leaders are not particularly well disposed to Pentecostal churches, in part because they do not fit with the mentality of educated professionals who are upwardly mobile, as they are.

One of the negative effects of state oversight in China is that house churches must practice a rather truncated view of the Christian gospel, not engaging issues related to social justice, human rights, or even social welfare, except on a very informal level. Any sort of formal social ministry would need to be registered, and house church members resist registration, which would put them under the authority of the government rather than Christ. In contrast, registered Three-Self Patriotic Churches appear to be flourishing. Bibles are readily available through Three-Self churches, as is Christian literature. On a Sunday morning when I attended services at the Haidian Christian Church in Beijing, I spotted a Josh McDowell book on apologetics on a display table; there was a free medical clinic set up outside the church; a video was shown during the service of a half-dozen young adults who had been baptized the previous week; and the style of worship and preaching would have fit anywhere in a megachurch in the United States. The auditorium, seating nearly a thousand people, was packed, including the overflow meeting room.

Yamamori and I also visited a number of large churches in both Malaysia and Indonesia. In every case we found the leadership of these Pentecostal churches to be very respectful of government regulations. For example, in Malaysia, they only sought converts among the Chinese, not among the Malay, who are Muslim by birth. For this reason, church leaders said that it is questionable whether Christians will increase over their current figure of 9 percent, in part because many economically successful Chinese are leaving Malaysia. I have already mentioned that one of the churches we visited in Malaysia met in an industrial style building, which had been designed with a large auditorium, Sunday school meeting rooms, and offices for the staff. On the Sunday that we were there, they baptized about twenty people, and as each one was introduced, he or she was identified by name, occupation, and school grade – showing evident pride in the successful nature of those who were joining the church. This church has also started ninety-two other churches, including in Nepal and India. Also, we visited a substantial new four-story building they had just built that was a block from the church. It was just ready to open with a dialysis center on one floor, a gymnasium on another, plus a coffee shop, a space for physical therapy, and a huge room for youth programs. Church members viewed this building as their contribution to the civic welfare of the community.

This church in Malaysia does not take political stances, although it does host forums for candidates to express their views. The pastor recognizes that members of his congregation vote for multiple candidates, and he says that the church has the obligation for members to be well informed prior to their vote. All he says from the pulpit is that people should vote for "righteousness." Recently they had hosted a candidate forum in which the daughter of the opposition leader expressed the view that Malay should have the right to choose their religion, which is technically possible but nearly impossible to do. This caused a huge controversy, not directed against the church, but about the fact that a Muslim woman would articulate such a point of view. Also stirring in the courts at the time was an appeal by the Catholic Church that Christians should have the right to use the word "Allah" for God, as they had for many years, whereas that right now was in question. Very recently an appeals court decided against the Catholic Church's petition and there will undoubtedly be an appeal to their Supreme Court.

We also visited a Pentecostal church in Malaysia that was much less affluent, but it was clearly a very vital religious community. They sponsor a home for mentally challenged children who are a financial drain on the congregation, but they are committed to caring for these children. They also give rice and oil to impoverished families, and they have publicly honored the police department as a way of demonstrating their civic engagement. This independent Pentecostal church was in stark contrast to a rather depressing interview that we had with several leaders from a "classic" Pentecostal denomination. We were told that rules and regulations within this denomination stifle innovation. Seminary students do not want to pioneer new churches, but instead want a comfortable job in one of the denomination's megachurches. A seminary professor told us that speaking in tongues is minimized in many of their churches, and he wondered whether this had any relation to the fact that students were reading the theologian Rudolf Bultmann on demythologizing the New Testament. In contrast, the pastor of the previously mentioned church said that speaking in tongues is an important part of his prayer life. He said that there are things we do not know how to pray for and so this is done with tongues, uttering things that come from the Holy Spirit, not from ourselves. He also attributed the fresh quality of their worship and church life to the Holy Spirit, saying that the Spirit is "creative," and to have too many rules is to quench the activity of the Holy Spirit.

In Indonesia we visited a church that went under the name ROCK, which stands for "Representatives of Christ's Kingdom." The auditorium and office space for this church are located in a multistory malllike building with shops of various sorts. A senior pastor told us that the role of Christians is to be a "blessing" to all people, including Muslims. Collectively, their goal is to make Indonesia a better country. He said, "We pray for the best president, not a Christian president." Their values, he said, are captured in the acronym "LIGHT," which stands for love/loyalty, integrity, generosity, humility, and truth. One way that they act out these values is to sponsor some of the best schools in the slum area, where they also have an active medical program. They deliberately counter the image of the senior pastor as the "big boss."

Instead, they think that every vocation has worth, whether one is a government employee, an educator, or in the arts, sports, business, or technology. Members of this church focus on the "incarnational Jesus," in which people see Jesus through them as they seek to be the "salt of the earth." They are not interested in labels; in fact, they say that they do not even put their "ROCK" symbol on their posters that advertise events. Like many neo-Pentecostal churches, they are part of a network of churches and are related to about 175 churches globally, and they also have 7 satellite churches, but they seem to have very little interest in being formalized into a denomination.

In both Indonesia and Malaysia, Pentecostal churches seem to flourish so long as they honor the principle of pluralism in their country and do not proselytize outside the specified boundaries. Also, Pentecostal churches gain credibility within the eyes of the government and general population when they provide social services to people in need. However, I did not sense that they were engaged in compassion ministries with an ulterior motive; rather, they see such programs and acts as a reflection of the Christian gospel. Indirectly, however, programs such as high-quality education are a means of communicating the principles of Christianity to Muslims who attend their schools because of their excellence. Organizationally, social ministries are operated under separate nonprofit status, preventing the problem of overlap with the legal status of the church. The churches that seemed to be flourishing were not bogged down in denominational structures and tradition, but had a fresh, corporate feel to them –in terms of both buildings and leadership style. During a visit in Jakarta, leaders of an umbrella organization of non-Pentecostal churches were struggling to come to grips with their declining status, seeking to understand why Pentecostal churches were growing, but they were also defensive – regarding Pentecostals as sheep stealers. In a roundtable discussion with members of this organization, one person confessed that mainline churches may be operating with an agrarian mentality – singing their eighteenth-century songs – while Pentecostal churches understand urban culture, as reflected in their worship, buildings, and organizational structure.

In Kerala, India, I encountered a definite contrast between older, established Pentecostal churches and what were described as "New Generation" churches. For example, we visited the seminary and office buildings of a very established group, the India Pentecostal Church (IPC), which has about seven thousand congregations. In a roundtable discussion with seminary faculty, they showcased their very formalized organizational structure. We met in a beautiful dining hall and were served an elaborate meal. Short, disciplined presentations were made by faculty members, some using PowerPoint. This meeting was in sharp contrast to our informal discussion with two pastors from a rapidly growing church called Heavenly Feast, whom we met on the stage of an open-air building that seated several thousand people. Sitting on plastic chairs, we were served coconuts with a straw, which we sipped during their descriptions of their own testimonies and the ministry of the church.

The Heavenly Feast church had not been able to meet in their building for the past three weeks because of persecution by Hindu extremists. In response, they were renting five auditoriums around the city where they could accommodate smaller crowds. In spite of this challenge, they seemed to be flourishing. They were regularly broadcasting on two major secular channels and one religious radio channel. They had one thousand cell groups, which they called "care" cells.

Members of Heavenly Feast are genuinely concerned about the poor. They challenge people to put aside one handful of rice every day, which they then collect at the church, feeding up to two thousand people at a time. They are also helping one thousand children with food, clothing, and tuition. And they have given away a thousand wheelchairs, plus they have an active program for people who are drug and alcohol addicted. In spite of the current persecution, they have a plan to build a church seating fifteen thousand people – but in a new location.

I also visited a "New Generation" church in the southwestern part of India, although the pastor was indifferent to the label. They appropriately called themselves the "Blessing Center" and view their role as blessing the society around them. Sixty percent of their members were born Hindu. Many people are attracted to the church through their TV programs, a demonstration of the power of media to communicate without engaging in direct evangelization of people from another faith. During their thirty-minute TV programs, they focus directly on people's needs. Hence, during exam time for students, they offer study tips and try to blunt the pressure that sometimes leads to suicide by young people who are competing to be at the top of their class. They also distribute hundreds of school bags to students, along with notebooks, which have the church phone number on them so that students can call and talk to someone if they are distressed. Additionally, they operate free medical camps every third Sunday, plus they have a blood bank and clothing program. The senior pastor said that he makes a point of never criticizing other religions. Several thousand people were at the service that I attended, which included a very well developed Sunday school program for children. They have eight hundred lay leaders and fourteen other Blessing Centers in India. They find that the greatest opposition occurs in rural areas of India where Hinduism is very strong. There seems to be greater tolerance in the city, a theme that I also heard in Malaysia.

In my three trips to India, several points stand out in my mind. One is the extreme devotion and pietism of members of Pentecostal churches. I talked to several seminary students at Doulos College. A young woman told me that she wakes at 2 a.m. every day to pray and then again at 4 a.m. and she continues to pray multiple times during the day. A young man who is a convert with a Sikh background reiterated the same pattern, waking at 5 a.m. to pray on the rooftop of his building. He said that when he first converted to Christianity, he was beaten by his parents, but now twenty people in his village, including family members, have become Christians. I also recall waking up early in Chennai to attend a 6 a.m. prayer meeting. I expected there might be a few dozen people. Instead, there probably were fifteen hundred – each with a Bible and notepad, with men sitting on one side and women on the other of a large open-air building. This monastic-type practice is clearly conditioning the hearts of these people to hear God's calling.

I also clearly remember visiting with a group of young pastors in Hyderabad when one of them casually mentioned that a woman had been raised from the dead. Later in the week, Yamamori and I were taken to a few of the fifty small village churches that were part of a network overseen by a young missionary from the Dalit class of untouchables. Upon arriving at the church led by the pastor who had referred to the woman who was raised from the dead, I insisted that we should interview her. And so we drove down the narrow roads of the village to her house, whereupon a crowd gathered when I took out my camera, including an elderly Hindu who appeared to be a village elder. He confirmed the story that this pastor told, which was reiterated by the young woman. The pastor had been passing through the village when he was asked to cast demons out of this girl; he did so and then went on to another village. On his return home, he was accosted by family members, saying that he had killed her and that they were preparing to bury the girl, having already called a village doctor to confirm her death. Perhaps in desperation, the pastor started praying over her and an hour or so later, she returned to life, describing how Jesus had appeared to her while she was dead. I also heard other supernatural accounts of people being raised from the dead in India, but this one seemed the most credible. The bottom line is that healing of various kinds is viewed as evidence of God's power and provides a turning point in conversion and confirmation of the truth of one's faith.

In the case of Malaysia, Indonesia, and India, Christianity is a minority religion within dominant Muslim or Hindu countries. It is also useful to look at Pentecostalism within dominant Christian countries, and specifically where Orthodoxy is favored over Protestantism. I have been to the Republic of Armenia, which is considered to be the first country to convert to Christianity in the fourth century, on many different occasions. Although Christianity was nearly snuffed out during seventy years of communist domination, the Armenian Apostolic Church survived – but under heavy state regulation and with only a few priests and a handful of active members, most of them elderly women. However, when Armenia became independent from the former Soviet Union in the early 1990s, the Orthodox Church sprang back to life. Nearly simultaneously, in the mid-1990s, a Pentecostal Word of Life church was born, currently led by a convert to Christianity, Artur Simonian. This church now has ten thousand members. It has twenty-three daughter churches in Armenia, as well as Georgia, Turkey, Russia, Iran, Syria, Lebanon, and several European countries, as well as one church in the United States.

As one might predict, the numerical success of this Pentecostal church in the Republic of Armenia has angered the hierarchy of the Orthodox Church. At one point their offices were raided and there was an attempt to close them down. But today, the main persecution originates in the media, which label them as a cult. Pastor Artur, however, points to the freedom of people in the church related to dress and personal choice. Artur avoids talking about politics from the pulpit, except for references to corruption. He never criticizes the "mother" church, which is closely aligned with the government. Members try to demonstrate their Christian values by caring for children who are abused; assisting the elderly, who often live very marginal lives; and helping to feed the poor and needy. While the pastor teaches about tithing, he has no idea what people give and there is no tracking of tithes. The worship style of this church differs dramatically from the formal liturgy of the Apostolic Church, and I distinctly remember trying to videotape one of their youth services, except that the microphone on my camera kept going into the red because of the distortion of the volume level. In a recent interview, Artur repeatedly said that they are a family – as a church – and they teach family values, believing that caring for one another is an important value within the Christian faith.

One of their sister Word of Life churches is in Moscow, with about three thousand members. Like the Yerevan church, it is filled with young people, contemporary music, and a dynamic team of pastoral leaders. It is not surprising that leaders of the Orthodox Church, whether in Armenia or Russia, feel threatened. Even though the Orthodox often have beautiful churches, they are weighed down by tradition. The services are interminably long. The liturgy is chanted, and the priests are garbed in clothing styles that are centuries old – sharply contrasting with Pastor Artur in his jeans and sports shirt. Nevertheless, there is some indication that Pentecostalism is having an effect on Orthodoxy. For example, in Egypt there is a growing charismatic element within the Coptic Church that is influenced by various Western Pentecostals. There are also indigenous ministries, such as Stephen's Children, which is led by the saintly "Mama Maggie," who works exclusively with children living in Cairo's worst slums. And even in Armenia there appear to be some reforms within the Orthodox Church that may be linked to the competition that they are experiencing from vibrant Pentecostal churches such as the Word of Life.

Hence, in examining the relationship of Pentecostalism to religious freedom, it is important to contextualize it *within* Christianity, where Pentecostalism is challenging Catholic, Orthodox, and mainline Protestant churches for members, as well as to examine challenges *between* religions, where Pentecostalism may be in tension with Islam or Hinduism. In both of these contexts, it is possible that the aggressive proselytizing of Pentecostals may provoke persecution. And their exclusive claims to truth may hinder them from being good neighbors or participating in interfaith activities. Nevertheless, in the churches that I have observed, there tends to be an attempt to honor the laws of the state, to respect the rights of other religious traditions, and to witness to the Christian faith through charitable acts rather than dogmatic preaching. However, I also recognize that this may be only one slice of Pentecostalism, and there undoubtedly exists a more hard-line, exclusive expression. But it is precisely this expression of the faith that neo-Pentecostals reject, such as being forbidden to wear jewelry and enforcing restrictive dress codes.

In my concluding observations, I will focus on what I have called "progressive Pentecostals," acknowledging that these generalizations may not apply to more traditional forms of Pentecostalism.

First, I believe that religious competition is fundamentally healthy for the creative evolution of religion. Without competition, renewal and reform do not take place and religion gradually becomes irrelevant to the daily needs and aspirations of people. Furthermore, I do not believe that "one size fits all." Human beings are a diverse lot, and consequently it is appropriate that there are many different varieties of religion. Hence, when governments positively sanction a single religious option and repress other religious expressions, over time religion loses its ability to function positively within civic life and to meet the population's needs at personal and communal levels. Although it may seem counterintuitive to say this, monopolistic religions are actually harming themselves when they collaborate with the state to repress competition. Why? Because healthy religion is a constantly evolving phenomenon, and not being challenged by competing alternatives means that the dominant religion is going to fail to evolve at the same speed as cultural change.

The implication of this view of competition is that Pentecostalism potentially fulfills a positive function, not only for the health of Christianity, but also as it provides an alternative to the dominant religion where Christianity occupies a minority status. Having said this, I want to acknowledge quickly that there are charlatans among Pentecostals. It is not unusual to read negative news reports of high-flying Pentecostal and charismatic pastors who are involved in tax evasion, sexual scandals, and conspicuous consumption, including owning private jets, multiple million-dollar residences, and so on. Furthermore, manipulation undoubtedly exists in some of the "health and wealth" prosperity gospel churches, which is difficult to reconcile with the humble lifestyle of the founder of Christianity. Having acknowledged these pathologies – which exist in every institution and religious faith – there are manifold expressions of the variant strains of Pentecostalism that are creatively mediating between the sacred and profane, transforming human life and institutions.

Second, there is a definite fit between the DNA of Pentecostalism and democratic values. Pentecostalism, at root, challenges hierarchical, authoritarian structures, empowering the laity and the priesthood of all believers. All religious callings are equal in God's sight, and everyone has the right to have direct access to God, the "king" of the universe. It is a small leap from this religious perception to saying that everyone should have a vote, that all votes are equal, and that all people are of equal value, regardless of wealth or power. In empirical studies of the correlation between Pentecostalism and democracy, Robert Woodberry argues that "Pentecostalism has a moderate positive impact on the spread and stability of democracy."[12] What is increasingly evident is that the stereotype of Pentecostalism as being politically right-wing and repressive simply does not hold in a number of cases, as argued by Timothy Wadkins on the basis of his research in El Salvador.[13] Furthermore, there need not be an antinomy between progressive expressions of Pentecostalism and the prosperity gospel, since giving people hope can become a self-fulfilling prophecy, especially when it is matched with proscriptions against alcohol, gambling, womanizing, and so forth.

Third, in spite of the perceptions of many mainline Protestants that Pentecostals are "primitive" because of their embrace of tongues, healing, and the supernatural, in actual practice Pentecostalism often has a modernizing influence on society. Especially in animistic cultures, Pentecostalism offers a monotheistic God, or one Spirit, in place of the multiple spirits of traditional religion, which war within the individual and are a disruptive force in society. Furthermore, Pentecostal worship is actually more in sync with contemporary culture than the liturgy of many mainline, Catholic, and Orthodox churches. Pentecostals know how to use technology in their worship services, as well as how to connect with one another through various networks via the Internet, and so on. It is also common to see books on the shelves of Pentecostal pastors by the latest Western leadership and business gurus. In short, these pastors and their churches are not bound by traditionalism which; that is why they are a challenging renewal force within Christianity.

Fourth, Pentecostalism is providing a response to postmodern culture in a way that mainline religions clearly are not, or else they would not be in decline. Within our disenchanted world – to use Max Weber's term – Pentecostals are offering an expansive sense of joy, mixed with a degree of supernaturalism that reenchants the material (and materialistic) world of many people. Harvey Cox says that Pentecostalism fills the "ecstasy deficit" of people living in a capitalistic world environment. Or framed in another way, during the Enlightenment, the mind was separated from the body, and what Pentecostalism does is reconnect the body through religious experience with the mind and religious beliefs.

By making this judgment, I am not necessarily spiritualizing Pentecostalism. It is an open question as to whether the Holy Spirit exists independently of one's consciousness. An enormous amount of research related to the brain and its incredible capacity is occurring. Some of this research is summarized in the book *Hallucinations* by Oliver Sacks, which elaborates the multiple ways in which the mind can "see" and create various realities – voices, fantastic beings, and so on. And the Stanford anthropologist Tanya Luhrman has made similar arguments based on her close observation of a Vineyard church filled with middle-class Americans. In her view, religion is a matter of practice, and through prayer and worship people experience "realities" that nonpracticing people do not experience or have no affinity.

And when it comes to healing, studies show that the placebo effect is remarkably strong, although less is known about how the mind controls various biological and neurological agents that deal with pain, contract tumors, and actually eliminate certain pathogens. Hence, there is something arrogant and actually narrow-minded for religiously nonpracticing people to say that these realities do not exist or are not experienced as "real." It is quite possible that Pentecostals are having visions, hearing voices, and making prophecies that are not mere ego projections, but arise from the deepest sources of human inspiration – what for lack of a better term might be called the Spirit. At minimum, Pentecostals demonstrate that religion is not simply a phenomenon based on reason.

Finally, it is appropriate to speculate about the future of Pentecostalism, since this has implications for its role related to religious freedom and the religious marketplace more generally. One possibility is that Pentecostalism will lose its uniqueness. First, as does any institutional form it will routinize over time, becoming progressively more bureaucratized, choking out the freshness and creativity of the Spirit at work. Second, it appears that many expressions of Christianity are becoming Pentecostalized, a trend that may dilute the uniqueness of the original movement as it emerged from the Azusa Street revivals. A third possibility is that the spiritual zeal associated with Pentecostalism will become domesticated as members become increasingly middle-class and well educated. And a fourth possibility is that Pentecostalism may be a significant force that continues to energize the Christian faith for decades. After all, its DNA is a rather powerful amalgamation of elements, which should strike fear in the heart of any competitor. Because of the religious zeal of the participants, who are buttressed in their commitment and self-confidence by powerful religious experiences, Pentecostals are able to propose agendas that do not respect political power, cultural obstacles, or personal difficulties. Like invasive viruses, Pentecostals worm their way into the most inhospitable locations and then reproduce with remarkable proficiency, supported by a global network of coconspirators.

NOTES

1 Allan H. Anderson, "The Emergence of a Multidimensional Global Missionary Movement: Trends, Patterns, and Expressions," in *Spirit and Power: The Growth and Global Impact of Pentecostalism*, ed. Donald Miller, Kimon Sargeant, and Richard Flory (New York: Oxford University Press, 2013), 31.
2 Cecil M. Robeck, Jr. "Launching a Global Movement: The Role of Azusa Street in Pentecostalism's Growth and Expansion," in *Spirit and Power*, 54.
3 Anderson, "The Emergence of a Multidimensional Global Missionary Movement," 33.
4 Todd M. Johnson, "Global Pentecostal Demographics" in *Spirit and Power*, 319.
5 Paul Freston, "Pentecostals and Politics in Latin America: Compromise or Prophetic Witness?," in *Spirit and Power*, 104.
6 Andrew Chesnut, "Spirited Competition: Pentecostal Success in Latin America's New Religious Marketplace," in *Spirit and Power*, 65.
7 The Pew Research Center, Pew Forum on Religion and Public Life. *Spirit and Power: A 10-Country Survey of Pentecostals*, pp. 34, 75–78.
8 Freston, "Pentecostals and Politics in Latin America," 104.
9 John C. Green, "Pentecostal Growth and Impact in Latin America, Africa, and Asia: Findings from a Ten-Country Survey," in *Spirit and Power*, 332.
10 Ibid., 333.
11 Estrelda Alexander, "Beautiful Feet: Women Leaders and the Shaping of Global Pentecostalism," in *Spirit and Power*, 225–241; Katherine Attanasi, "Constructing Gender within Global Pentecostalism: Contrasting Case Studies in Colombia and South Africa," in *Spirit and Power*, 242–256.
12 Robert D. Woodberry, "Pentecostalism and Democracy: Is There a Relationship?" in *Spirit and Power*, 135.
13 Timothy H. Wadkins, "Pentecostals and the New World Order in El Salvador: Separating, Consuming, and Engaging," in *Spirit and Power*, 143–159.

4

Christianity among the Marginalized: Empowering Poor Women in India

Rebecca S. Shah

Christ gave me a pagri [a turban, which is a symbol of respect], in place of dust.

Lal Begri, Dalit convert in Pasrur, 1933[1]

I tried to kill myself three times. A sister took me to church. I met Jesus. I am here today.

Maliga, Dalit convert in Baglur Slum, Bangalore, 2013

One cannot help but notice the extent to which terms such as "hope," "self-control," and "dignity" – words with an unmistakable religious resonance and valence – have moved to the center of discussion on economic development and poverty alleviation. With the rise in behavioral economics and broader notions of human development and deprivation, it is no longer unusual for major economists to address these topics in their lectures, books, and leading economics journals. It is equally striking, however, that these concepts appear to float freely of any reference to or grounding in religious tradition or community. Indeed, while there is a growing openness to the economic importance of issues of identity, dignity, hope, and self-control, there has *not* been a parallel openness to the economic importance of religion per se or of specifically religious beliefs, practices, and communities.

For many of the world's poor the indignity and stigma that they face may be a result of their outcaste status and religious identity. Poverty can mean more than being simply materially or physically deprived; it can also mean being deprived of self-respect, dignity, and self-worth in ways and for reasons that are not reducible to material factors. Therefore, indicators that primarily assess material and physical dimensions of deprivation are woefully inadequate to gauge the complete emotional, psychological, and spiritual impoverishment the poor in various parts of the world deal with every day.

For these reasons, the economist Glenn Loury emphasizes social ties and relationships are integrally and constitutively important for development. He argues that orthodox models of human capital were too individualistic and focused on an individual's human capital accumulation,[2] and do not take into account the spiritual and social context in which that individual was embedded. Loury maintains that any understanding of human capital development – and of human and economic development more broadly – must be viewed in *relational* terms. What is the relationship of parents to their children, such that they are willing to invest in their education? What is the relationship of people to the institutions and networks who may be willing to invest in them? How do people view themselves? How do people view each other? Since all human development is socially mediated, occurring within social contexts and institutions, it follows that a lack of strong and intimate connections to communities and social networks is an intrinsic dimension of deprivation the poor often suffer.

The potential of religious perspectives to provide an expansive and more realistic notion of the human person and human development is best articulated in the work of the economist and development ethicist Denis Goulet. "Authentic development," writes Goulet, occurs when all human needs including "societal openness to the deepest levels of mystery and transcendence" are embraced and satisfied. According to Goulet, it may be valuable and laudable that development economists look beyond the bounds of rational choice and have pushed economics to situate economic behavior within human communities. It is also valuable that welfare economics and behavioral economics have introduced more realistic assumptions about human behavior, choices, and relationships. But according to Goulet, this does not go far enough. In his view, economics must find a way to recognize the religious yearnings and aspirations of human beings. If modern economics continues to yield an understanding of human development that ignores the role of religion, governments and development institutions will persist in acting as "one-eyed giants" who "analyze, prescribe, and act *as if* man could live by bread alone, *as if* human destiny could be stripped to its material dimensions alone."[3] According to Goulet, development is more human and more developed when people are called to "*be* more" rather than simply "*have* more." The goal of development should be to satisfy the needs of "all in man and all of men."

We see echoes of this vision in Catholic social teaching, which links freedom and development. According to *Gaudium et Spes*,[4] "Human freedom is often crippled when a man encounters extreme poverty, just as it withers when he indulges in too many of life's comforts and imprisons himself in a kind of splendid isolation. Freedom acquires new strength, by contrast, when a man consents to the unavoidable requirements of social life, takes on the manifold demands of human partnership, and commits himself to the service of the human community." And in the 1967 papal encyclical *Populorum Progressio*[5] ("On the Development of Peoples"), Pope

Paul VI explicitly states that "man is truly human only if he is the master of his own actions and the judge of their worth, only if he is the architect of his own progress."

Anchored in this richer understanding of human development, I present here a coherent and compelling picture of the role of religious faith in the lives of converts to Christianity in India. Specifically, this chapter clarifies how such conversions among Dalits (the "broken," referring to "untouchables" or "outcastes") in India have both historically and in recent years contributed essential value to the lives of the poor and are enhancing their economic and social outcomes. To identify the beneficial economic and social results that conversion may generate, the chapter will observe what happens when very poor individuals and communities in entirely non-Christian contexts such as India convert to Christianity.

I begin this chapter by reviewing the historical context of preindependence India, when Dalits (untouchables) began to convert to Christianity in such large numbers that these "mass conversion" movements were responsible for reshaping the religious demography of the Indian subcontinent. I then present striking new research findings on the contemporary impact of Christian conversions on the social and economic uplift of the very poor, especially marginalized women. Significant numbers of outcastes in the poorest Indian communities are converting to indigenous expressions of revivalistic and converstionistic Christianity. My research shows that such conversions uniquely propel life transformations.

At a time of growing global dissension about conversionary religion, the volume and pace of outcaste and tribal conversions to revivalist Christianity are generating intense controversy and even violent conflict in parts of India. Furthermore, in a context where religious freedom for converts to Christianity is severely under threat such as in India, this chapter demonstrates that in certain cases, conversion to Christianity can give individuals (especially the most marginalized women) a new sense of self and a new relationship to the wider world – all of which can be conducive to forms of individual empowerment, social liberation, and economic improvement.

The clearest way to identify the beneficial economic and social outcomes that conversion can generate is to observe what happens when individuals and communities in entirely non-Christian contexts such as India convert to Christianity. The research presented here builds upon and deepens prior research into the role of conversions on economic progress and social uplift.[6] In particular, this new research features the results of a large recent survey of poor women that fortuitously captured a significant sample of revivalist converts, enabling me to provide a fine-grained comparison of these women to their peers in the same slums. Such conversions are often ignored, for three reasons. First, it is assumed that they are a highly marginal and infrequent phenomenon. In part this is because of high regulatory barriers to

Dalit conversions (Dalits and tribal members who convert to Christianity lose an array of government benefits for which they would otherwise be eligible as members of "scheduled castes") and because of the recent level of intense persecution of Christians by a Hindu nationalist group, the Rashtriya Swayamsevak Sangh (RSS). Second, it is assumed that what few conversions that do occur are artificially generated, as it were, by Western-operated and Western-funded missionary activity. In fact, however, by far the largest and most important cases of Evangelical and Pentecostal conversion have occurred – and continue to occur – almost entirely outside the auspices of Western missionary endeavor. Third, it is assumed that whatever conversions do occur are driven by material or instrumental benefits, that converts are merely "rice Christians." As we will see, this image is wholly inaccurate.

My reading of numerous studies of Pentecostalism's impact on the poor throughout the developing world – particularly studies by Emílio Willems, David Martin, Sheldon Annis, David Maxwell, Cornelia Butler Flora, Rowan Ireland, Elizabeth Brusco, and many others – persuades us that the core spiritual dynamic is similar across time and across a variety of cultural contexts. In other words, while the Indian context is distinct, the way spiritual transformation of conversion to Christianity translates into social and economic betterment for the poor may be as applicable to fervent Pentecostal converts in the favelas of Brazil as it is to outcaste converts from small independent churches in southern India.

DALITS AND UNTOUCHABILITY

> The man born in the outcaste village may as soon think of building his house in the other group as a pig may think of going to live in his master's front room.[7]

The poor in India have always suffered from both social isolation and material poverty. The most marginalized and ostracized group in India are the Dalits. "Dalit" is a term literally meaning "broken," and it is used to describe people who are traditionally regarded as "untouchable" or "outcaste" according to the Hindu caste system. One is born a Dalit and will die a Dalit – that is the way matters have stood for centuries in India. Dalit status is a matter of irrevocable, hereditary membership, conferred by birth. Dalits are often employed in jobs that befit their hereditary status, jobs that are seen as ritually polluted and unclean.

An outcaste is, as the name suggests, a person who by birth is denied the privilege of associating with "caste" or "respectable" Hindus. He or she is thus cast out or dismissed from social contact and lives beyond the fringes of respectable society. Caste rules and customs perpetuated by the upper caste groups assured that social contact with "outcastes" – out of caste groups – were minimized. These included customs relating to marriage, food, residence, occupation, and dress.

"Untouchability," based on Hindus laws of ritual purity and impurity, was applied to prevent contact with outcaste groups. Untouchables were relegated to occupations that exacerbated feelings of disgust because their traditional occupations involved "unclean" work – with dead animals as leather workers or as sweepers working with human refuse, for example. Untouchability, once proclaimed against a particular caste, continues for generations.

Sanctioned by Hinduism in its most important religious texts (the Vedas and the Manusmruti), untouchability is also practiced by other major religions in India. However, surveys show that Hindus were more likely than other religion to admit to practicing untouchability.[8] Moreover, studies find that religious discrimination against Dalits is "incredibly widespread." Religious discrimination, which includes the restriction of Dalits from entering the village temple and from touching religious articles that are in use for worship by non-Dalits, is almost uniformly reported across most of the villages.[9]

Thus Dalit communities are among the most marginalized populations on earth, making them a unique laboratory to examine the dynamics of religious conversion on self-concept and agency.

HISTORICAL CONTEXT: RELIGION AND EMPOWERMENT IN PREINDEPENDENCE INDIA

The distinguishing features of Christian mass movements are a group decision favorable to Christianity and the consequent preservation of the convert's social integration. Whenever a group larger than a family, accustomed to exercise a measure of control over the social and religious life of the individuals that compose it, accepts the Christian religion (or a large proportion accept it with the encouragement of the group), the essential principle of mass movement is manifest.[10]

In order to understand the potential impact of spiritual capital on the economic and social well-being of the poor, and particularly the most deprived population in India, outcastes or Dalits, it is helpful to review historical research on mass conversion to Christianity in India in the past. In 1928, Dr. John Mott, chair of the International Missionary Council, suggested that the Methodist bishop and missionary to India J. Waskom Pickett conduct a rigorous study of conversion movements then occurring among thousands of outcastes. Mott envisioned a study that would employ rigorous scientific methods to assess the quality and impact of the mass conversion movements sweeping the country.

Pickett conducted his study between 1930 and 1931. His mass movement survey was the earliest example of a household survey designed to collect detailed data on the religious, social, and economic status of people in India. The survey developed separate schedules and was used to collect information from converts as well as from their non-Christian neighbors. Data on the economic and social status of Dalit Christians were collected from the ten main areas where large numbers of Dalits converted to Christianity. These areas included both northern and southern India. By the end of 1931, the survey staff had completed thirty-eight hundred household interviews, making it the most ambitious survey ever conducted outside the West at the time. To date, it remains the single largest database amassed on Dalit Christianity and its social and economic impact.

One finding of Pickett's study was that most Dalits interviewed converted to Christianity for its intrinsic impact on their dignity, identity, and overall well-being. They did not generally convert for short-term material gain, as many Hindu critics of conversion at the time (including the Indian independence leader Mahatma Gandhi) claimed, and as many Christian missionaries feared. Frequently denied a dignified status, Dalits embraced Christianity because they believed it would improve the overall quality of their lives. Pickett and his colleagues found that Dalit converts often experienced a higher quality of life that included better health, education, and material prosperity, but material benefit was not generally the sole or primary motive for conversion ex ante. Rather, in most cases, the motive lay in the Dalit belief that Christianity embodied a life of dignity and hope for a future free of degradation and subservience. Bishop Pickett's household survey of converts revealed that many Dalits hoped that conversion offered them an identity rooted in a personal faith in a loving God rather than in an identity dependent on the recognition of higher castes. In the words of one of the converts, "I wanted to become a Christian so I could be a man. None of us was a man. We were dogs. Only Jesus could make men out of us."

Pickett's study did suggest that conversion to Christianity yielded wide-ranging developmental benefits. One tangible benefit to poor women was that revivalist Christianity laid down a clear imposition of moral restraints. Traditionally, a hardworking man might be a good provider, a good husband, and a good father, and yet his conscientious discharge of family duties might not be inconsistent with sporadic visits to the local brothel. Evangelical Christianity made it clear that such forms of behavior were morally irreconcilable; adultery often resulted in excommunication.[11]

No issue drew more animated discussion from non-Christian informants during the mass movement survey than the treatment of wives, with the vast majority agreeing that Christian husbands were less abusive, more loving, and more likely to take their earnings home than squander them on drink or women. Christian women related to their husbands with greater confidence than their non-Christian counterparts, and couples consulted each other on household matters. Moreover, the survey suggested that family now became a unit, a place where relationships were built and nurtured. No economic incentive or government program could cause a man to change his inner attitude or disposition toward his family, to be less selfish in his spending patterns, to be more respectful of his wife, or to be more involved in his child's development. Conversion to Evangelical Christianity seemed to bring about just these changes. As we will see in the following, more fine-grained contemporary research underscores how this tangible benefit of poor women continues to operate.

CONTEMPORARY RELIGION AND EMPOWERMENT IN INDIA

The findings presented here are part of a broader, multiregional study of the role of religion in developmental uplift for impoverished women, who often constitute the most marginalized poor in developing nations. The research team I direct has conducted in-depth and multiple interviews with hundreds of poor women in Asia, Africa, and Latin America. Our focus on Dalits in India produced one of the most unexpected and stunning opportunities to examine one aspect of empowerment – how conversion unleashes forms of dignity and agency with tangible results for economic and social advancement. We discovered that a significant sample of the women in our study were converts to Pentecostal forms of Christianity, enabling us to test how that choice affected self-concept and traits conducive to social and economic advancement.

DALIT CONVERTS IN BAGLUR SLUM

Just as Bishop Pickett's historical study of the mass-conversion movements in preindependence India challenged conventional skepticism about the motives and consequences of Christian conversion in India, our study of religious behavior and economic change among Dalits in urban-poor Bangalore challenges that skepticism today. Building on previous historical work, the study was designed to investigate the influence of religious change and religious behavior on a poor and marginalized Dalit community and whether similar religious dynamics exercise an important developmental influence today. Whatever the influences of religion in the past, might religious identities, beliefs, practices, and choices exercise an observable and measurable influence on the economic and social well-being of poor individuals and societies in the contemporary world?

The research set out to test the economic and social consequences of specific religious practices and attitudes among Dalit women microentrepreneurs in Baglur slum, which is one of the largest and most notorious slums in urban Bangalore. In particular, I suggest that certain forms of religious behaviors such as religiously motivated giving may be associated with greater self-control, thrift, a sense of agency and empowerment, improved familial relations, and participation in supportive religious networks and communities. As poor Dalit women microentrepreneurs made choices about certain religious behaviors or decided to change religions, that is, convert, we hypothesize that there could be a) a reduction in nondurable consumption and an increase in future-regarding patterns of investment, b) an improvement in overall social well-being through improved self-esteem and agency, and, finally, c) a greater involvement in religious networks and communities that provided social and spiritual support.

While global poverty and inequality, especially among the very poor and marginalized such as the Dalits in India, remain huge problems, any tools for addressing them – including religious change/behavior-related tools – should be explored. Our fine-grained analysis suggests how incremental change at the local level – for example, persuading girls to attend and complete school at the local level, or in our case harnessing the liberating potential of religious faith in enough Dalit women microcredit entrepreneurs – could begin to have a broad impact over time.

We designed our sample to interview three hundred Dalit female microcredit clients from Hindu, Muslim, Mainline Protestant, Evangelical, and Catholic backgrounds. Over three years, we interviewed the same three hundred clients three times. In total we conducted some nine hundred individual face-to-face interviews in Baglur slum of Bangalore, India. During the first of three waves of interviews we unexpectedly discovered that 23 percent of our sample – seventy of three hundred women – had identified themselves as "converts." These women were all converts from Hinduism and belonged to indigenous, independent Pentecostal churches. This fortuitous result provided the opportunity to examine the role of conversion to this vibrant and encompassing form of Christianity. This focus on converts to Pentecostalism was based on our empirical findings, not on a bias toward Pentecostals or rigid imposition of theories on the data. Not only did my research team find far more conversions to Pentecostalism than to other groups. We also found these converts were the most distinct. Thus we only focused on converts to Pentecostal Christianity after realizing that they were distinct from other groups in our sample. There is an extensive literature from Latin America and Africa that suggests that these findings are not implausible or idiosyncratic (see Donald E. Miller's chapter in this volume), but if we had not found such strong differences, we would not have focused on this group.

Baglur slum is situated beneath a busy flyover that whisks passengers from the city's new international airport to the designer-decorated offices of Infosys or Microsoft. Baglur lies on prime property right in the middle of India's IT capital.

In a city where rents are among the highest in the country, Baglur provides an affordable and accessible option to many of its residents who work as maids or chauffeurs for Bangalore's burgeoning middle class. Baglur bears no resemblance to the high-end apartment complexes that surround the slum on all four sides. It is a maze of litter-strewn lanes, open sewers, and numerous cramped huts. After dusk, few auto-rickshaw or taxi drivers are willing to drive beyond the railway lines that divide respectable neighborhoods from Baglur and its surrounding smaller slums.

In 2014 the slum received a drinking water connection, yet very few homes have a direct water line. Many residents have electricity, but few of them have indoor plumbing. There are a few communal toilets but most of them are filthy or broken. Many of the young women in the slum are forbidden to use public toilets because of the risk of being raped after dark. Baglur also has a large number of successful small businesses – butcher shops, garment shops, as well as the ubiquitous liquor stores that are located in three different parts of the slum.

At first glance, Baglur looks like a typical slum. It is crowded and filthy; it is located near a busy highway; the neighborhood is dangerous and most of the "respectable" buildings such as schools and offices are situated on the other sides of the railway tracks. But Baglur is a bit different. Dotted all over the slum are numerous prayer rooms and small independent churches. These independent churches – reminiscent of "storefront" churches in urban America – are self-supporting microcommunities, separate from all mainstream denominations, that unabashedly proclaim the full use and manifestation of the Pentecostal gifts of the spirit. They are situated right in the middle of slum areas that are home largely to Dalits and poor members of the lower castes. Most of the congregants are Dalit converts, and the Pentecostal pastors are also Dalits.

To illustrate the growing influence of these indigenous Pentecostal churches among the urban poor in North Bangalore, where Baglur slum is situated, we conducted a mapping of an area roughly 1.5 miles in June 2012. Within the compact 1.5-square-kilometer area alone, we identified more than 150 churches. An overwhelming majority of these churches (120 or more) were identifiably Pentecostal or charismatic in some sense, as indicated by interviews with pastors, church leaders, and members. All of the five mainline churches, both Protestant (Church of South India) and Roman Catholic, are located beyond the confines of the slum.

It is not unusual for members to be sole supporters of the work of the independent church. Few of the churches were registered to receive foreign exchange or foreign donations from mission organizations or individuals living abroad. Without a Foreign Contribution Regulation Act (FCRA) registration, no organization in India can legally receive foreign contributions. In recent years, Christian organizations including churches have been have been under greater scrutiny by government, and few organizations are willing to risk violating the law. Therefore most of the independent "storefront churches" in Baglur are supported by the members' tithes and donations. A large number of the churches meet in rented storefronts in the slum and on the main road, while others have raised enough capital from their members and from other local middle-class churches to build their own structures.

In addition to the weekly Sunday services, a majority of these independent churches conduct weekly "fasting and prayer" meetings that are well attended and often take place all night and usually on the weekend. While most of the churches have male pastors, there are many women evangelists who live in the community and are actively involved in evangelism in the local slum areas. Many of the female evangelists are Dalit converts from Hinduism. The size of these independent churches ranges from the Agape Church, which had an official membership of two thousand people, to the Gateway Hope Church, which had an official membership of forty, including the pastor and his family of four. The average membership of the smaller churches ranges from around forty members to two hundred members. In some cases, the churches draw members from the surrounding areas such as Lingarajapuram and Williams Town.

The rest of this chapter will identify ways in which certain forms of religious behavior and change, in particular conversion to forms of indigenous Pentecostal Christianity, may enhance economic and social outcomes of the poor Dalit women microentrepreneurs. Our research found that the Dalit microentrepreneurs we interviewed who were women who were active participants in conversionary Protestant communities who were most likely to exhibit this empowering, prodevelopmental package[12] of practices, choices, and beliefs – what we and other scholars have referred to as *spiritual capital* – were converts to various forms of indigenous or independent Pentecostalism. Again, we can speak with some confidence about these women converts because – unexpectedly – they ultimately represented almost one-quarter of our sample (23 percent).

CHRISTIANITY AND FREEDOM FROM FATALISM AND HOPELESSNESS

What we know about poverty is that it depresses and discourages the poor to the extent that they are unable to make rational choices about their future. As human beings we have an innate tendency to undervalue future events by putting off today those tasks that are due in the future but if completed today could earn us a greater return. Instead we favor those goals and tasks that are immediate but less rewarding. Robert Strotz (1956) was the first economist to study what has come to be known as "dynamically inconsistent" consumption patterns – "inconsistent" because a person's behavior will most likely be at odds or inconsistent with what is his optimal behavior. Optimal behavior is choosing a plan of consumption or spending in the present that will maximize one's utility in the future. However, in most cases, instead of seeking to gain a greater reward for her future investment, she chooses to "precommit"[13] her future to satisfy her desires at the present time. Those who continue to behave in

TABLE 4.1. *Who is in control of your life? (2011)*

	Fate (percentage)	Hands of God	In own control	Don't know/ cannot say	N
Hindu	17	63	9	11	109
Muslim	3	79	8	10	51
Catholic	4	84	10	2	58
Mainline Protestant	8	92	0	0	12
Convert	0	96	4	0	70

Source: Study on Tithing and Thrift among the Enterprising Poor in Bangalore, India, 2011–2013.

such an "inconsistent" manner are often termed "spendthrifts," while others who recognize the errors of their ways and begin to change their consumption patterns are termed "thrifty."

Recent work by development economists strongly influenced by behavioral economics, such as the MIT economists Esther Duflo and Abhijit Banerjee and the Harvard economist Sendhil Mullainathan, demonstrates that the poor spend a disproportionate amount of their income on "temptation goods" that satisfy "visceral pleasures" rather than on long-term investments in their future well-being, such as education for their children or health insurance. In their work on poverty and self-control, Duflo and Banerjee show that for a variety of reasons, the poor lack the incentive and *psychological capacity* to make the right choices about their future and thus become trapped in a cycle of lower future investment that leads to greater levels of poverty.[14]

As part of our study in Baglur, Dalit women were asked to respond to the following question: *Some people believe their life is dominated by fate or some power beyond their control; some people believe their life is in the hands of God; and some people believe their life is in their own control. What do you believe?* The question elicited two extreme responses. Most of the women who said that their life is in God's hands said so with a confident tilt of their head and added, "Definitely, it is in God's hands." Those who said their lives are governed by fate, or *"thalai vidhi"* in Tamil, did so shaking their heads and tapping their foreheads. (The Tamil word for "fate" is *thalai vidhi*, which also means "to hit one's (fore)head.") Some of these women also added, "What to do? This is how it is."

In Table 4.1, we see that women in all religious traditions state that their lives are in the "hands of God." However, Hindu women (17 percent) are the most likely to say that their lives are controlled by fate. Converts to Christianity are the most likely say their lives are in the "hands of God," and no convert says that her life is controlled by fate.

Many of the women we interviewed talked about their lives being in the "hands of God." By this we mean that the women may have believed that their lives were in the hands of a personal God whom they can relate to and who is interested in their well-being. Placing one's life in the "hands of God" could offer the women the security of a faith in a loving God who was personal and inclusive. For these women, the knowledge and security of a protective and caring providence may enable investment in their future as they could have a life free of fear and full of possibilities.

Unfortunately, fate can be a dominant feature of a poor Dalit's life. Abject poverty may cause an overwhelming sense of despair and anxiety and may sap a person's morale, potentially leading to a withdrawal from society. Deprivation and poverty may also strength a person's belief that the outcomes of her life are not in her control but rather in the control of powerful people, fate, or luck. Therefore, the lack of progress or of any potential to succeed may lead a person either to succumb to temptation or to give up on investing in the future. After repeated failures and the anticipation of yet another failure, the poor person may be forgiven for not wanting to see what the future has in store because she may not wish to be disappointed *again*. Unfortunately, by avoiding contemplating the future, because of the fear of disappointment, the poor person's inaction may cause him or her to fall victim to the very shocks and bad events he or she is trying to avoid by ignoring the future. For example, when asked why a majority of the clients in our survey did not purchase health insurance for members of their family who had chronic health conditions such as heart problems and diabetes, more than 60 percent of people surveyed said that they had not thought about the possibility of a bad outcome for their family members. It may be the case that those people who are more likely to experience bad outcomes in the future such as failure in their business or a medical shock are the ones who may be the least likely to protect themselves against such outcomes.

In our study we began to understand that a person who has a fatalistic view of the world is linked to her fear of the unknown and in particular to her fear of unknown evil spirits, whose powers could cause illness, turn a husband away from his wife, and even kill. As do many of the poor in India, the residents of Baglur slum fear the danger of evil spirits. It is not uncommon to see mothers and children carrying charms or paying weekly visits to the local *pujari* or fakir to protect them from evil spirits that they believe lurk everywhere. Anxious to protect their family and their children in particular, many of the women in the slum pay for charms and amulets to keep them safe from harm.

A look at some of the most common personal religious practices reveals that women in our sample are most likely to fear the unknown when it means that their children and families could be affected. Table 4.2 shows the percentage of women in the sample who used a black spot on their children to ward off the evil eye (*dristi*).

TABLE 4.2. *Percentage of women who adopted certain practices to ward off evil in the past 12 months (2013)*

	Applied black spot to avoid evil eye (*dristi*)	Visited "holy man, pujari, or fakir"	Used "yellow powder" to cast spells	N
Hindu	49	45	48	109
Muslim	41	12	10	51
Catholic	29	22	10	58
Mainline Protestant	17	5	0	12
Pentecostal Convert	14	4	7	70

Source: Study on Tithing and Thrift among the Enterprising Poor in Bangalore, India, 2011–2013.

We also see the percentage of women who used black magic or in this context "yellow powder," or visited a "holy man, pujari, or fakir,"[15] to help them with a family problem.

These practices suggest a fatalism that might undercut taking practical actions to deal with problems. To illustrate the dangerous hold fatalism has on the poor, we asked Dalit women in our study to identify the various practices they adopted to avoid the evil eye. Converts to Pentecostal Christianity were the least likely to apply black spots on their children's faces to mar the child's beauty in an attempt to dissuade evils spirits from harming them. Table 4.2 identifies 48 percent of Hindu women who used "yellow powder" to cast spells on their errant husbands who were suspected of having affairs with other women in the slum. Interestingly, Roman Catholic women were not immune to the need to get help from a local holy man (not a priest or pastor) to help assuage their fears of the unknown.

Just as hopelessness or fatalism acts as a constraint on a person's agency and empowerment, hope instills confidence about the future. While pervasive fatalism and the dominating power of blind fate lead the poor woman to believe that she has little control over events in her life, hope, and religiously motivated hope in particular, may foster efficacious agency. By hope, we do not mean an inchoate optimism or feeling that situations might turn out well. Hope is also not merely imagining a future that one aspires to be a part of, but that one cannot do anything to realize. We suggest that religiously motivated hope rests on a profound and active belief in the power of the transcendent to influence and empower one's life in the here and now. Although the poor are economically impoverished, we know from ample survey data,[16] as well as our own on-the-ground studies, that they are rich in religiosity and the kinds of religious beliefs that might ground a concrete sense of hope about the future.

Perhaps one of the clearest indications of how hope may help the poor aspire to a more secure future can be seen in our data on housing. Baglur faces an unprecedented property boom and rapidly rising cost of residential land in Bangalore city, so the slum residents are constantly threatened with eviction by developers and corrupt local government officials. In July 2013 the cost of one square foot of land in Baglur slum was thirty thousand rupees, or five hundred U.S. dollars. In the Baglur slum many of the residents acquired de facto rights to their property when they claimed the land as squatters when they arrived in the city fifty years ago as bonded laborers and artisans. However, few residents hold formal, legally enforceable documents or land title, known as a *kartha*, and many have been evicted because they did not have the money to bribe government officials to help secure the documents.

In 2005, the Karnataka Slum Development Association (KSDA) set out to distribute federal funds to build permanent homes for slum dwellers in Bangalore city. To qualify for a government loan, a person must belong to a "Scheduled Caste" or "Scheduled Tribe." KSDA has just started building permanent homes in Baglur, and few respondents in our sample (only seven) received government grants to build a house. All these women are Hindus. The government sanctioned two lakhs of rupees (four thousand dollars) to build each house. In most cases, the government contractors took the money directly from KSDA to build a very basic (and often incomplete) structure. The homeowners were liable to raise additional funds to complete the building.

Neither Christians nor Muslims are eligible for any type of government loans or grants such as a KSDA grant, as a result of the 1950 presidential order in the Indian constitution, which states, "*No person who professes a religion different from the Hindu [Sikh or Buddhist] religion shall be deemed to be a member of a Scheduled Caste.*" Christians and Muslims who owned homes had to finance the entire construction with no help from the state. Furthermore, although religious foundations fund some home construction in the slum, none of the women in our sample had received money from any nongovernmental or religious agency to build her home.

This makes all the more striking our finding regarding homeownership by Pentecostal converts. Table 4.3 presents results of our survey on homeownership. Muslims in the study were the least likely to own a home. Data for three years, from 2011 until 2013, show that homeownership among Muslim clients ranged from 6 percent to 12 percent. Homeownership among mainline Christians was higher in two of the three years, but this concerned a very small size of the sample of mainline Protestants (N = 12). The much larger sample of Pentecostal converts to Christianity (n = 70) reported homeownership of 57 percent in 2011 to 60 percent in 2013. None of the converts who were interviewed had received any government grant for building her home.

TABLE 4.3. *Percentage of women who own or rent their homes*

	2011		2012		2013		
	Own	Rent	Own	Rent	Own	Rent	N
Hindu	38	62	35	65	29	71	109
Muslim	6	90	12	88	12	88	51
Catholic	51	49	43	57	43	57	58
Mainline Protestant	42	58	75	25	75	25	12
Convert	57	43	60	40	60	40	70

Source: Study on Tithing and Thrift among the Enterprising Poor in Bangalore, India, 2011–2013.

Another example from the study that demonstrates the powerful prodevelopmental power of hope is provided by our data on education. Converts to Pentecostal Christianity are more likely to send their children to private Christian schools or to private nonreligious schools than their Hindu or Muslim counterparts. More than 25 percent of Muslim and Hindu women send their children to government schools compared to only 6 percent of converts. On average, private schools have better educational outcomes than government schools. Private schools are almost always English-medium and children who attend private schools are better able to attend preuniversity and degree colleges. Most private and religious universities accept students who complete high school in English. Private religious schools are some of the most sought after schools in the area. They have a history of teaching in English and the teachers are better trained than those in the average government and nonreligious private schools.

As we see in Table 4.4, 72 percent of converts send their children to English-medium, fee-paying Christian schools compared to 65 percent of Roman Catholics, 40 percent of Hindus, and 14 percent of Muslims. A majority of the Christian fee-paying schools in the area are Roman Catholic, and children whose parents are Roman Catholic receive free or subsidized education. Non-Roman Catholics are required to pay the full fees including an initial installment of about six thousand rupees in special fees.

The average cost of educating a child in a private school is five hundred rupees a month. This does not include the cost of books, transport, or special fees. Thus while rates of private school enrollment are higher for all Christian groups, Pentecostal converts demonstrated unusual agency in taking this action.

The converts to Pentecostal Christianity in our sample display patterns of behavior that indicate that they may be less averse to taking risks than their Hindu, Muslim, Catholic, and even mainline Protestant counterparts. Poverty debilitates the poor

TABLE 4.4. *Percentage of women who educated their children aged four to eighteen in various types of schools*

	Private school nonreligious English-medium	Private school religious Christian English-medium	Government school Kannada-medium (state language)	Private school religious Muslim Urdu-medium	Private school religious Hindi-, English- or Kannada-language	No school	N
Hindu	32	40	26	0	0	3	109
Muslim	39	14	25	18	0	4	51
Catholic	26	65	9	0	0	0	58
Mainline Protestant	0	100	0	0	0	0	12
Convert	22	72	6	0	0	0	70

partly by breeding hopelessness and fear and undermining the capacity to plan for the future, and this trend, in turn, is partly attributable to the poor's vulnerability and isolation in the face of numerous forms of risk. Furthermore, the poor lack a comfortable buffer of finance to enable them to weather sudden economic shocks such as paying for high medical bills that could drag them into years, and perhaps even generations, of financial debt. The poor also lack robust and supportive social networks and institutions that would help them secure good jobs, low rates of interest, decent housing, good health care, and high-quality education – the kinds of things that can help them either avoid major risks or cushion them against important risks or shocks when they happen. However, even in the face of relentless challenges, hope gives the poor a sense of security in a caring and responsive providence to enable them to take risks and make choices that could lift them and their families out of poverty.

CHRISTIANITY AND THE FREEDOM TO PARTICIPATE IN MEANINGFUL RELATIONSHIPS

Glenn Loury emphasizes how identity choice is a "social event." A person's identity is shaped by interacting with people within a community, not merely through the individual assertion of his or her values and experiences. People who interact frequently, who live in close proximity to each other, and who share similar social experiences and engage in similar activities may ultimately embrace similar identities. To the extent, therefore, that a few members of the community may have a negative self-image or a negative identity, other members of the same and relatively closed community are likely to embrace and sustain a negative collective identity as well. Furthermore, people who are pessimistic about themselves and their circumstances and who are socially isolated tend to feel victimized and are less willing or able to take risks to improve their lives and more likely to participate in dysfunctional behavior (such as alcoholism or drug abuse). Such behavior can sustain and reinforce the group's isolation from the mainstream population; that isolation in turn can lead to abandonment and further destructive behavior.

On the basis of our study we find that healthy relationships among poor Dalit women can be undermined and blocked by a socially reinforced sense of "underworth." For centuries, Dalit oppression and isolation from mainstream Hindu society created a dysfunctional collective identity that not only destroyed their sense of worth, but also robbed Dalits of the will to improve their lives and transform their circumstances. The concepts of an individual's will and sense of worth are distinct features, but they can also reinforce each other. The process can be conceptualized in terms of a negative feedback loop in which a person's lack of worth or value reinforces his inability to act to change his life, and that inability in turn lowers his sense of self; thus he spirals downward into a destructive and vicious cycle of psychological and physical debilitation

This is why conversion can exercise such a powerful effect. The Nobel Prize–winning economist George Akerlof believes that one of the most important economic decisions a person can make may be the decision about what kind of person he or she should be. (Recall the outcaste quoted earlier, who said, "I wanted to become a Christian so I could be a man. None of us was a man. We were dogs.") In Akerlof's view, in seeking to maximize their outcomes, individuals make economic decisions that enhances and preserve their dignity and sense of worth as well as maximize their utility. When the poor are excluded from the opportunity to make decisions about their identity, they are prevented from making the most basic choices about the quality of their lives and the lives of their families and communities. Furthermore, decisions that affirm or deny a person's identity also affirm or deny a person's agency.

Access to religious networks and communities may enable the poor to seek reciprocity and demand equity in their relationships rather than passively accept injustice. For example, being a part of protective and caring communities and networks may open a door out of the world of domestic violence. The Indian National Family Health Survey (NFHS), one of the largest surveys of women and children in the country, reported that only one of four women surveyed who had been a victim of domestic violence sought outside help. Table 4.5 provides the results of our survey on this pivotal dimension.

The striking finding here is the dramatic agency of the Pentecostal converts, who were much more likely to take action (telling a pastor) when faced with domestic abuse. Of the converts to Pentecostal Christianity in the study who ever experienced domestic violence, 57 percent reported their abuse to a pastor or a member of a pastoral team. None of the Muslim women in the sample who experienced domestic violence ever talked to anyone, even a family member, about the abuse.

Strikingly, converts were more likely to tell their pastor about instances of domestic violence than members of their own family. I contend that the influence of religious leaders (who are men) may have an empowering impact on women who experience domestic violence because the men who victimize them are more likely to listen to other men than to women counselors or social workers. In the sample area, male pastors from the local Pentecostal churches regularly visited the homes of converts to offer prayer and counseling, and these regular visits may shame some abusive husbands into curbing their violent behavior.

Religious communities and networks could assist women in dealing with violent and dangerous husbands. The benefits of being involved in religious networks and communities go beyond the opportunity to form meaningful social relationships with others – as significant and important as these relationships may be. Being

TABLE 4.5. *Percentage of women who ever experienced domestic violence who sought help*

	Hindu	Muslim	Catholic	Mainline Protestant	Pentecostal convert
Told No One	90	100	73	75	43
Told Family Member(s)	7	0	8	0	0
Told Pastor/Pastoral Team	3	0	0	25	57
Told Priest/Parish Priest (Roman Catholic)	0	0	19	0	0
Told Priest at Temple (Hindu)	0	0	0	0	0
Told Imam	0	0	0	0	0
Number of Women Interviewed	108	58	51	12	70

Source: A Preliminary Study on Tithing and Thrift among the Enterprising Poor in Bangalore, India, 2011–2013.

involved in religious networks and communities gives people a sense of belonging to a wider religious group in which they are embedded. Women who face violence and domestic abuse may be more likely to share their problems with a community of people they trust and with whom they feel connected on a deep level. These communities may include male leaders or members who could assist the abused women by counseling the abusive husband.

In sum, being part of a faith community and network can help launch a woman on a virtuous circle: A woman feels better, works more, and earns more money. The extra money earned and saved encourages the woman to earn more and to save more and to plan for future investment such as building a house or buying a refrigerator. An increase in income enables her to reach a "tipping point" that can propel her out of the poverty trap and into more productive and future-oriented patterns of expenditure and saving.

CHRISTIANITY AND THE FREEDOM TO "BE MORE"

Economists study the world by performing the same experiment over and over again (or running the same model over and over again) until they discover mathematical laws that elegantly predict the future state of a particular object. They seek to discover the "laws" of economics by emulating the style, elegance, and parsimony of physics. As Gerard Debreu[17] notes, it is undeniable that since economists have tended to model their work on natural sciences such as physics that work is relatively inhospitable to moral and spiritual considerations. Furthermore, because of the consequent mathematization and reductionism of economics, economists have sought to approximate reality on the basis of fewer and fewer assumptions. Most economics textbooks, therefore, assume that individuals have a parsimonious set of exogenous preferences, make choices with little or no concern for others, and have no nonmonetary constraints on their choices. Individuals are assumed to choose the best possible combination of goods and services to enable them to achieve the most utility, regardless of noneconomic factors such as family, identity, motivation, or belief.

Over the past few decades, however, there has been an increasing turn among major economists toward highlighting the inconsistency between deterministic models of rational choice and human behavior. The Nobel Prize–winning economist Amartya Sen has challenged the decision-making framework of utility theory by suggesting that any theory of welfare must be based on more than individual utilities and must assume a broader view of the dimensions of human well-being. In his 1979 Tanner Lecture, Sen introduced the concept of human "capabilities," which has revolutionized the conventional assessment of welfare. Sen proposed a shift from a focus on welfare as based primarily on income and on the accumulation of goods and commodities to a focus on welfare as based on the ability and freedom to choose what one values and has reason to value. This is not to say that a person's welfare is entirely independent of "basic goods" such as food, shelter, warmth, and so forth. Instead, Sen maintains that the assessment of human welfare must go beyond the assessment of utility, the fulfillment of basic needs, and the provision of income and must take into account the intrinsic value and importance of individual choice and freedom. In short, human development is coextensive with the expansion of human capabilities. This expansion enables people to enjoy and pursue what they value and have reason to value. Put negatively, according to Sen in his major book *Development as Freedom* (1999), human development can be understood as the "removal of various unfreedoms that leave people with little choice and little opportunity of exercising their reason and agency." Interestingly, Sen more than implies that the "unfreedoms" or constraints that can limit human capabilities – and, therefore, block human development – can be internal to human choices and the psychology and character of human beings as well as a result of external forces beyond people's immediate control.

One of the ways in which individuals demonstrate a deep and enduring engagement with their religion is through voluntary financial giving. Tithing can increase other forms of religious commitment and foster ethical behavior that may influence economic outcomes. It may seem paradoxical that such religious practices as tithing and fasting could spur economic uplift. But what we found is that they do

TABLE 4.6. *Percentage of women reporting regular and intermittent giving*

	Regular	Intermittent	N
Hindu	45	55	109
Muslim	87	13	58
Catholic	55	45	51
Mainline Protestant	71	29	12
Convert	88	12	70

Source: Study on Tithing and Thrift among the Enterprising Poor in Bangalore, India, 2011–2013.

so by helping the poor practice patience by reframing the cost of sacrificial financial giving so that it becomes a reward or a guarantor of future rewards.

All respondents in our survey were asked to state whether they donated money regularly or intermittently. A "regular" giver was defined as someone who tithed or engaged in voluntary religious giving at regular intervals once a week, once a month, twice a year, or once a year. An "intermittent" giver was defined as someone who felt no obligation to give money at regular intervals and only voluntarily contributed money if she was able to do so. As we see in Table 4.6, nearly eight out of ten converts to Christianity engaged in regular voluntary religious contributions. These contributions were made as soon as they received their monthly wage or every Sunday during church. In most cases, converts reported tithing 10 percent of their income. The 45 percent of Hindu women who reported giving financial contributions on a regular basis did not have a set amount of money that they contributed but said that they donated what they had at the time

Further analysis predicted the probability of tithing once a week for women from various religious traditions. The predicted probability of tithing once a week is the highest for converts to Pentecostal Christianity; more than 50 percent of converts were predicted to give voluntary *weekly* financial contributions to their churches. In contrast, the predicted probability of tithing once a week was the lowest among Hindu women in the sample. Catholics and mainline Protestants are most likely to tithe once a month, and majority of the women who belonged to these two religious groups reported paying a fixed monthly subscription to the local church in lieu of tithes or other voluntary financial contributions. No Muslim woman in our sample was predicted to give weekly financial contributions, but a majority (67 percent) were predicted to give yearly contributions, as is consistent with the Islamic tradition of annual Zakat. Hindus in all three years are most likely to give once a year because they go on a yearly pilgrimage to Om Shakti or Tirupathi.

TABLE 4.7. *Percentage of women who fasted by frequency and religious tradition*

	Weekly/ Monthly	Festival times (approximately twice a year)	Once a year	Do not fast	N
Hindu	12	28	7	53	109
Muslim	3	3	91	3	58
Catholic	53	0	0	47	51
Mainline Protestant	42	33	0	25	12
Convert	94	3	3	0	70

Source: Study on Tithing and Thrift among the Enterprising Poor in Bangalore, India, 2011–2013.

The overwhelming majority of converts to Christianity (94 percent) in our study participated in fasting and prayer meetings at least once a month (Table 4.7). In some ways, the pressures on faith are far more acute for the poor than for those with ample resources. For the poor entrepreneurs with very little margin, who are struggling to provide for their families month to month, the pressure to make any profit at any cost can even be greater and leave even less room for the influence of religious faith. No doubt it would have been easier for the women to save the money they tithed to purchase food or medicines or spend more time with their families than in prayer meetings. This makes this commitment all the more remarkable.

Not only did tithing provide development resources for convert communities, but it appears to have instilled habits conducive to personal advancement. In other words, it is not coincidental that the converts who tithe also are more likely to own their own homes and send their children to private schools.

How then did religious conversion to Christianity help the poor women in our study focus on long-term investment and limit their spending to enable them to improve their future and that of their families? How were the converts in our study able to have effective access to and control over their income and invest in a home, which could yield long-term economic betterment?

One possible explanation for the improved economic prosperity is that the women were launched into a virtuous circle. To see how this may be possible is to understand that the poor may be caught in a "poverty trap." A poverty trap occurs whenever there is a steep relationship between income earned today and the possibility of income in the future or over a certain period. The poor become "trapped" because there is a reduction in the overall level of income or assets in the present period and because the rate of return of investing in food or education or housing is so low for the poor, they become more and more impoverished over time. Furthermore, because poverty is inherently depressing and can lead to hopelessness and discouragement, the poor are less likely to practice self-control, and this tendency could plunge a person into even greater debt and poverty.

Initially the access of credit through microfinance can begin to address the balance between assets and self-control. With the availability of credit, the poor at least have an opportunity to begin to seek and invest in goods and behaviors that are focused on the long-term instead of the immediate. Microcredit can act as a stimulus to induce the poor to start saving for their future.

With greater access to credit, however, there is an increased risk of "giving in" to temptation and using the funds to serve immediate needs instead of investing it in those goods and services that will yield results in the future. Therefore, the focus of my Tithing and Thrift Project has been on how faith and its disciplines – particularly tithing and fasting – may help the poor resist this temptation and promote future-regarding behavior. To this end, the project seeks to understand better how faith and future-regarding behavior – including the exercise of self-control – *interact*.

One of the key features of the microfinance contracts binding the members of a *sangam* is joint liability: Each member is liable for the loans of the others. Microentrepreneurs such as the women in Baglur learn the disciplines and skills of prudent money management in the context of a group. If an entrepreneur squanders her resources and fails to make a timely repayment, the group members can exclude her, with the severe consequence that she loses face in the community as well as the opportunity for future loans.

Along with the *involuntary saving* imposed on members of a joint-liability *sangam*, as helpful as it is in promoting basic money management, tithing promotes the habit of *voluntary self-control*. In Tamil, the language spoken by many of the women I interviewed, the word for "tithe" is *kannike*, which also means "make a vow." Once a person commits to tithe a certain amount of money, she has made a solemn vow to God to contribute this money for his purposes, which may include providing relief for people even poorer than they are.

Among other things, the commitment of a significant portion of one's income to God means that less of one's money is available for present-oriented consumption. More deeply, tithing inculcates the habit of seeing all of one's money as a loan from God, and thus to be saved, invested, or spent in ways that please him. Thus, à la Max Weber, tithing (along with fasting) fosters a culture of self-restraint – of "inner-worldly asceticism" – that shields the poor from myopic overconsumption. This overconsumption, in turn, often drives cycles of overindebtedness. Microenterprise development (MED) organizations can even inadvertently exacerbate such cycles by making it possible for the poor to assume even more loans – sometimes at exceedingly high interest rates – to escape debt. Tithing, we observed, can help short-circuit or even reverse the treadmill of overconsumption and overindebtedness.

In a sense, tithing simultaneously widens one's circle of accountability and widens one's circle of security, each of which encourages thrift. Through tithing, the poor enact a view of themselves as accountable not only to their *sangam* or family members but to God. By being accountable *to God*, they feel an inner conviction to use their money wisely. In addition, tithing inculcates the belief that all of one's resources come *from God*, who is a faithful provider. By thus widening the circle of security beyond the *sangam* and the family, tithing encourages the poor to trust in God as their ultimate security, provider, and guarantor of their future. The result is that the poor are more likely to escape the prison of present-oriented consumption, which often results from the anxious belief that they must spend today because they may have little or nothing to spend tomorrow.

Another way in which private religious beliefs may impact economic outcomes of individuals and their families is through the rate at which a person discounts the future. The discount rate measures the opportunity cost of capital. It measures how much interest a person could earn on her money if she invests it for the future. For example, people who hold a strong belief in the existence of life after death may discount the future less. That is, they may invest in doing things today even though there is no immediate return so that they can gain the rewards in the long run. Certain religious beliefs and practices may motivate people to have more patience in the present and to curb spending in the short term and invest their money in goods and services that yield benefits in the long term.

In their article "Religious People Discount the Future Less," in the journal *Evolution and Human Behavior*, the psychologist Evan Carter and his coauthors found that the more religious participants in their study exhibited a "stronger preference for larger later rewards than did their less religious counterparts." Furthermore, the authors found that the association of religious commitment with future-oriented patterns of behavior was partially mediated by the religious participant's tendency to view the future as more salient. This pattern may have a bearing on economic dynamics among the poor.

CONCLUSION

A gross error it is to think that regal power ought to serve for the good of the body and not of the soul, for men's temporal peace and not their eternal safety; as if God had ordained Kings for no other end and purpose but only to fat up men like hogs and to see that they have their mash?

– Richard Hooker, *Laws on Ecclesiastical Polity* VIII, 3.5, 154

Hooker's provocative quotation need only replace the word "Kings" with "development actors," and it will describe how today's development practices and policies often reduce human beings to mere mechanisms. In an effort to engineer, monitor, and measure economic change, development agencies have left out what makes people human; they have left out a person's soul. Consider a true development policy not by the value of production but by ways it enriches human flourishing through giving people spiritual freedom and freedom of religious reform and conversion.

As documented here, religious conversion may activate in the converts powerful new concepts of value and initiative in two main ways: first, through the *attitudes and perceptions* of the converts toward themselves, and mutual attitudes and perceptions toward the family and the wider community, and second, through a combination of an access to credit and a new identity that may allow converts to harness their *agency and capability* into investing in the future to improve their lives, the lives of their families, and the lives of the wider community. Furthermore, attitudes and perceptions and agency and capability are interrelated partly because a higher sense of worth and stronger sense of will reinforce each other.

NOTES

1 John C. B. Webster, *A History of the Dalit Christians in India* (San Francisco: Mellen Research University Press, 1992), 23.
2 Glenn C. Loury, 2005. "The Neumann Lecture." Unpublished lecture given in Budapest, Hungary, on the occasion of receiving the 2005 John von Neumann Award, Rajk László College, Corvinus University of Economic Science and Public Administration, Budapest, Hungary, September 30, 2005.
3 Denis Goulet, "Development Experts: The One-Eyed Giants." *World Development* 8 (1980): 481–489.
4 "Paul VI. Vatican II. Pastoral Constitution on the Church in the Modern World – *Gaudium et Spes.*" *1965*; D. J. O'Brien and Shannon, T. A. *Catholic Social Thought: The Documentary Heritage* (New York: Orbis Books, 1992).
5 "Paul VI. Vatican II. On the Development of Peoples – Populorum Progressio. *1967.*" D. J. O'Brien, and T. A. Shannon, *Catholic Social Thought: the Documentary Heritage* (New York: Orbis Books, 1992).
6 Rebecca Shah and Timothy Shah, "Pentecost amid Pujas: Charismatic Christianity among Dalit Women in 21st Century India," in Robert Hefner, ed., *Pentecostal Modernity in the Global South* (Bloomington: Indiana University Press, 2013).
7 Jarrell Waskom Pickett, *Christian Mass Movements in India: A Study with Recommendations* (New York: Abingdon Press, 1933), 63.
8 S. Desai, R. Vanneman, C. A. E. R. N. D National, and Inter-University Consortium for Political and Social Research, *India Human Development Survey (IHDS), 2015* (Ann Arbor, MI: Inter-University Consortium for Political and Social Research distributor, 2015).
9 *Understanding Untouchability: A Comprehensive Study of Practices and Condition in 1589 Villages* (Robert F. Kennedy Foundation Center for Justice and Human Rights, 2009).

10 Jarrell Waskom Pickett, *Christian Mass Movements in India: A Study with Recommendations* (New York: Abingdon Press, 1933).

11 Susan Billington Harper, *In the Shadow of the Mahatma: Bishop V. S. Azariah and the Travails of Christianity in British India*, Studies in the History of Christian Missions (Grand Rapids, MI: Eerdmans, 2000), 279.

12 By a "prodevelopmental" package of behaviors, choices, and beliefs, we mean beliefs and practices that foster a positive economic and social outcome such as a cessation of alcoholism, saving for the future, an investment in durable goods such as housing, and an investment in health and education. These prodevelopmental behaviors and beneficial social and economic outcomes may be associated with certain types of religious beliefs, practices, and participation.

13 R. H. Strotz, "Myopia and Inconsistency in Dynamic Utility Maximization," *Review of Economic Studies* 23 (1955): 165–180.

14 Abhijit V. Banerjee and Esther Duflo, *Poor Economics: A Radical Rethinking of the Way to Fight Global Poverty* (New York: Public Affairs, 2011).

15 There are many well-known holy men, *pujaries* (Hindu holy men) and fakir (Sufi holy men), who live near the slums. It is very common practice to visit holy men if an individual has a family problem and they will give the women certain food or powders to use. Women are most likely to visit a holy man when they experience problems when their husband has or is suspected of having an affair with another woman.

16 Deepa Narayan-Parker, *Can Anyone Hear Us?* (New York: Published by Oxford University Press for the World Bank, 2000).

17 Debreu, Gerard. "The Mathematization of Economic Theory," *American Economic Review* 81 (1991): 1–7.

5

Transnational Christian Networks for Human Dignity

Mark Brockway and Allen D. Hertzke

Imago Dei is the Christian theological view that all people are made in the image and likeness of God and thus have surpassing equal worth and dignity. It gained prominence in the late Roman Empire when Christianity began to offer a broad critique of common practices that we now see as unjust, cruel, or exploitative – such as slavery, sexual coercion, and indifference to the poor. It was in these arenas that the gulf between Christian dignity and societal practices seemed most glaring. In his chapter on the Christian responses to this gulf in late antiquity (*Volume 1*), Kyle Harper documents how the idea of universal dignity provided the underpinning and fulcrum for the later development of human rights in the modern era. In other words, he shows how the liberal revolutions of the eighteenth century proclaiming the "universal rights of man" are inconceivable without the concept of all humans as beings of incomparable worth and value, made in the image and likeness of God. To be sure, Christian-influenced societies fall short of this ideal, sometimes egregiously so. But as Harper and other contributors to these volumes show, Christianity carries deep in its DNA this radical notion of universal dignity, which serves as a challenge or rebuke to societal conditions and practices of the age.[1]

What we find stunning is the resonance between the concerns raised by Christians in the ancient world and those expressed through global Christian networks in the twenty-first century. Today we see campaigns against human trafficking, sexual coercion, slavery, poverty, illiteracy, religious persecution, exploitation, violence, and war – echoing and expanding on the early social witness of Christians in the ancient world. But today these are global campaigns fueled by the resources of transnational Christian networks. The momentous globalization of Christianity marries the idea of dignity with the striking capacities of transnational Christian networks of communication, solidarity, and assistance. This chapter focuses on the global impact of the Christian ethic by examining some of its most important contemporary initiatives. We will see how the Christian DNA reaches across the globe, magnified by considerable resources and unparalleled transnational linkages.

FRAMEWORK FOR UNDERSTANDING THE ROLE OF GLOBAL
CHRISTIAN NETWORKS

One of the driving factors in the emergence and clout of international Christian networks has been the tectonic shift of the Christian population to the developing nations of the Global South. Whereas in 1900, 80 percent of Christians lived in Europe and North America, now at least 60 percent of all Christians can be found in Asia, Africa, and Latin America.[2] This continuing trend nests the church amid poverty, exploitation, war, persecution, and displacement. International mission and development networks channel awareness of these conditions to lay believers and policy makers in the West.

This phenomenon is nicely illustrated by a single denomination, the Seventh Day Adventist Church. Though born of nineteenth-century revivals in the United States, it is no longer primarily an American institution. Indeed, only 1 million of its 16 million members are Americans,[3] and it is staffed by indigenous leaders around the world. Thus, when the Adventist Relief and Development Agency champions global "food security," it represents both the humanitarian impulse of the church and the experience of its congregations abroad.

Another development is the expansion of global communication and travel, which draw grassroots constituencies into international engagement. Lay Americans meet visiting foreign religious leaders in their churches; they communicate via e-mail with counterparts around the world; and more than a million believers a year travel on mission trips to work on humanitarian projects, often side by side with fellow believers in poor nations.[4] And sometimes this involves more than short-term commitments. *Christianity Today* profiled a nineteen-year-old college student, Carys Parker, who was raised entirely on an African Mercy medical ship that her parents served. The novelty of this upbringing, which impressed upon her the dignity of afflicted persons, only occurred to her when she went off to college and began living a "normal" middle-class American life.[5]

What Western mission travelers discover is that they are not sent to spread the gospel among the heathen but to work alongside fellow Christians, whose depth and vibrancy of faith inspire or "convict" them. Wanting to support their suffering brothers and sisters in Christ, they become advocates for public policy initiatives to address poverty, disease, and exploitation. They become contributors to NGOs, form campus groups to fight trafficking, and write to their representatives in Congress about AIDS funding or debt relief.

With this framework in mind, we now turn to illustrations of how the Christian concept of dignity becomes instantiated through modern global networks.

CHRISTIAN DEVELOPMENT NETWORKS AND GLOBAL POVERTY

Truly I tell you, whatever you did for one of the least of these my brothers and sisters you did for me.[6]

As Kyle Harper observes: "On no other social issue does the Christian gospel provide such complete and unambiguous marching orders" as on the problem of poverty. Jesus begins his ministry by proclaiming good news to the poor and liberty for the oppressed, and his parable of the Good Samaritan demands that his followers see any hurting person as a neighbor they are called upon to love. The Christian mandate reaches its pinnacle in Matthew 25's depiction of the Day of Judgment, in which the blessed inherit the kingdom because they succored the hungry, the thirsty, the naked, the stranger, the prisoner. Indeed, the faithful are called upon to see Christ himself in the faces of the poor, the marginalized, and the exploited.

This mandate breathes with special urgency for those engaged in Christian humanitarian ministries working among people vulnerable to famine, disease, violence, exploitation, and displacement. Indeed, extensive interviews with leaders of Christian nongovernment organizations (NGOs) and indigenous local staff reveal how deeply animated they are by Matthew 25 and the Good Samaritan.[7] The gospel mandate also calls forth the formidable lay generosity that generates multibillion-dollar resources for the growing network of Christian NGOs that support emergency relief, health care, education, agricultural initiatives, and economic advancement. These programs, impressive in scope, sophistication, and on-the-ground reach, fill a crucial niche in global development, as they represent the largest nongovernmental enterprise in the world. Moreover, the major development programs operated by the United Nations, the United States Agency for International Development (USAID), and the European Union routinely contract with Christian NGOs to implement local projects or deliver famine relief.[8]

This strategic position enables Christian NGOs to exercise creative leverage in high-level policy circles. With some of the best indigenous networks in developing nations, they generate valuable information on emerging problems and possible remedies. In turn, their global linkages and elite governmental access equip them to convey information to high-level policy makers. Finally, because of their reach into congregations with numerous lay donors, they can generate grassroots support in the United States and other powerful nations for public policies to address global poverty. These various networks, as we will see, magnify the valuable humanitarian work of Christian NGOs with focused public policy initiatives. What is striking is the range and impact of this advocacy and how it marries credibility of effective programs with the passionate grassroots concern for people in far corners of the world.

From Mission to Development to Advocacy

The precursors of today's international Christian NGOs were missionary programs to "make disciples of all nations," which took on true global scope with vast American and British endeavors from the nineteenth century onward. As Robert Woodberry shows, Christian missions did far more than evangelize; they set up schools and promoted literacy, especially for girls; built health clinics; organized charitable enterprises; and responded to crises. Because the Christian message especially appealed to marginalized ethnic minorities and social outcasts, missionaries and local pastors found themselves drawn into the role of defenders of these local communities, sometimes against colonial administrators. International Christian missions also put comfortable lay believers in the West in touch with the plight of the destitute in other lands.

In the first decades of the twentieth century we see early stirrings of distinct Christian initiatives in relief and development. With such groups as the Mennonite Central Committee and the American Friends Service Committee, this work was tied to denominations' peacemaking ethic. But it was the devastating wake of the Second World War that launched the major wave of organizational growth, as international church leaders and lay activists built upon existing mission programs to create independent NGOs that addressed poverty, war, famine, disease, and natural disasters. Note the year these major organizations were created: Catholic Relief Services, 1943; Lutheran World Relief, 1945; Church World Service of the National Council of Churches, 1946; World Vision, 1950; Compassion International, 1952; Caritas International, 1954. Over the following several decades these groups were joined by Adventist Relief and Development Agency, Habitat for Humanity, Jesuit Refugee Services, Mercy Corps, Samaritan's Purse, World Concern, World Hope International, and World Relief, among others. In addition, we see a host of specialized initiatives, such as the Mercy medical ships previously mentioned. Collectively these Christian organizations constitute the largest nongovernmental development network in the world today.[9]

While initiated in the United States and Europe, these Christian NGOs have become truly global enterprises, with international boards, operations through regional and national affiliates in a hundred-plus countries, and international staffs of up to ten thousand. Wander the halls of NGO headquarters or country offices and you will see a veritable UN of faces. In addition, these organizations have undergone what Andrew Natsios describes as decolonialization, the process of turning over control of field programs to people in the beneficiary countries.[10] Today the vast majority of personnel in Christian NGOs are indigenous people living amid suffering or exploited people. For example, Jesuit Refugee Services employs staff among the displaced who themselves live and work in refugee camps. Those indigenous personnel gain vital information about refugee flows and conditions, which is readily communicated to policy makers by their Jesuit brethren in the West.

As this example suggests, large relief and development agencies have moved naturally from solely delivering services to engaging in public policy advocacy. With teams on the ground in some of the most forbidding places on earth, these NGOs gain unique insight into Western military, trade, and aid policies, which they share in legislative testimony or meetings with executive agencies. Because of the size of the U.S. government's footprint on the global stage, NGO leaders have especially become aware of how small changes in U.S. policy can magnify their efforts. Global communication enables them to relay policy concerns instantaneously to their Washington representatives and grassroots constituencies, who press high-level government officials to address their concerns. In this sense, international Christian networks foster an advocacy infrastructure for otherwise powerless people. Indeed, the advocacy leaders of large Christian NGOs in Washington, D.C., convey that they see themselves, in effect, as "lobbyists" for refugees in the Congo or trafficked children in Asia or imprisoned pastors in China.[11]

Dramatic Examples of Impact

The global network of Christian NGOs raises awareness around issues previously invisible to the international community. World Vision, for example, noticed that illegal diamond traffic in central Africa was fueling violent militias and exploiting child soldiers. In cooperation with other organizations and business, World Vision succeeded in its effort to establish an international protocol to address the tragic costs of "conflict diamonds" (later exposed in the 2006 movie *Blood Diamond*).[12]

Global Christian networks have been pivotal to the ongoing effort to relieve debts burdening impoverished nations. In 2000, Pope John Paul II joined American religious groups, secular organizations, and such celebrities as Bono in the "Jubilee 2000" campaign for global debt relief. This coalition identified how debt accumulated by deposed governments posed a crushing burden on poor countries, which were unable to fund health, education, and economic development programs. Taking its inspiration from the "Year of Jubilee" in Hebrew scripture in which debts were forgiven, the movement sought debt write-offs by lender nations, the International Monetary Fund, and the World Bank. Critical to the success of this effort was an appropriation of some $400 million by the United States to pay down debts, which would leverage much more from international institutions and other nations. Drawing upon their international development networks, Christian leaders anchored the coalition and were pivotal in persuading conservative legislators normally skeptical of foreign aid to back the congressional appropriation.[13]

The nexus of global Christian networks and U.S. foreign policy is illustrated vividly by the distinct role Christian NGOs played in the development of the President's Emergency Plan for AIDS Relief (PEPFAR), which was launched in 2003. Christian development organizations such as World Vision and Catholic Relief Services saw the devastating impact of HIV/AIDS firsthand, especially in Africa, and had begun developing their own relief programs in the 1990s. In addition, many lay members learned about the AIDS crisis in Africa as a result of the growing number of mission trips sponsored by American congregations. Employing the access they enjoyed with President George W. Bush, evangelical leaders joined with Catholics and Jewish groups to lobby the president on AIDS, and he ultimately made it a signature issue. Since the launch of the PEPFAR initiative in 2004, AIDS funding has more than tripled. Though some AIDS activists criticized its abstinence component, the program succeeded in delivering antiretroviral treatment to more than 2 million HIV-positive Africans by 2008 (up from just 50,000 before PEPFAR), saving many lives and contributing to economic development.[14]

As these examples demonstrate, international Christian NGOs play a leading role both in direct humanitarian work and in the policy advocacy or peacemaking that flows from it.

GLOBAL CHRISTIAN NETWORKS, TRAFFICKING, AND SLAVERY

The spirit of the Lord is upon me ... to proclaim release of the captives.[15]

Modern slavery – the sexual exploitation of trafficked women and children, along with forced labor, debt bondage, chattel birth, and other forms of servitude – is perhaps the most compelling threat to human dignity today. The wide scope of modern slavery and trafficking – encompassing more than 20 million people[16] – is due in part to the involvement of dangerous organized criminal syndicates that specialize in trafficking and labor exploitation. They employ intricate systems to move individuals within countries and across borders and employ violence and intimidation to keep them in bondage.[17]

Because traffickers purposefully take advantage of weak governments and ineffective law enforcement, transnational Christian NGOs have provided some of the most effective documentation, rescue, rehabilitation, and justice advocacy for trafficking victims. Despite their limited resources compared with a $32 billion human trafficking industry,[18] Christian anti-trafficking NGOs implement effective mitigation and prosecution strategies by partnering with and inspiring both governmental and nongovernmental entities. These Christian-based anti-trafficking efforts are the modern incarnation of a long tradition of antislavery movements by

Christian actors and organizations. They are not an anomaly but a continuation of the Christian instantiation of *Imago Dei* through history and across the globe.

Christian anti-trafficking initiatives have proliferated since the 1990s. Some focus on documentation, others on rescue and rehabilitation, others on law enforcement – and all have dramatically raised awareness of the problem, enhancing national and international polices.

One of the most vivid examples of the modern Christian anti-trafficking movement is the work of the International Justice Mission (IJM), founded and led by Gary Haugen. Haugen's searing experience documenting atrocities in Rwanda motivated him to create a Christian organization devoted to the international fight against injustice.[19] Haugen, an evangelical Christian, sees the fight for global justice as a central tenet of the Christian faith.[20] He blends hardheaded expertise with evangelical fervor in advocating for victims of violence and injustice, particularly regarding human trafficking. With a network of investigators and attorneys around the world, IJM directly frees victims, educates law enforcement officials, exposes corruption, and presses for more effective national and international laws and policies. From Russian orphan trafficking to debt bondage in India to child prostitution in Cambodia, the organization tackles a host of abuses. In successfully elevating the problem of trafficking and modeling effective law enforcement strategies to attack it, Haugen was recognized by the U.S. State Department as a Trafficking in Persons "Hero" – the highest honor awarded by the U.S. government for antislavery leadership.

IJM engages in three primary efforts. First, it partners with local law enforcement and government agencies to rescue and protect victims and prosecute crimes. Second, it promotes institutional reforms through educational partnerships with governmental organizations to reform justice systems. Third, IJM offers continued support for the systems it puts into place. The combination of these three efforts creates a powerful reporting, rescue, and reform network.[21] The organization magnifies its impact through collaboration with other international organizations. IJM provided victim identification in Cambodia for the United Nations Office on Drugs and Crime in 2009.[22] In 2014, IJM linked with Noonday Collection, a human rights–conscious fashion brand to offer women sustainable, reliable employment.[23] Despite its Christian roots, the IJM does not take a victim's religion into account when offering aid, and religious conversion is not part of their advocacy; the mission promotes dignity and human rights for their own sake. This narrative resonates deeply in Christian communities, which helped IJM sustain a budget of more than $40 million.[24]

The network-building activity of IJM and other Christian organizations reaches beyond direct humanitarian efforts into policy change.[25] In 2000, this network was able to marshal its forces behind the Trafficking Victims Protection Act, landmark

American legislation that established a new office at the State Department with real enforcement teeth.[26] This legislative victory helped spark greater attention by other governments and the United Nations. This success illustrates the potent combination of international advocacy networks and grassroots political mobilization. This network was extremely effective because it both *witnessed* humanitarian tragedy and *created* legislative change based on those accounts of atrocities. In 2013 the reauthorization of the act enhanced protections for trafficking victims and vigorous prosecution of offenders, demonstrating the enduring transformative impact of this mobilization.

Another organization that demonstrates the link between Christian theology and anti-trafficking efforts is the Catholic women's organization Talitha Kum: The International Network of Consecrated Life Against Trafficking in Persons. Talitha Kum draws inspiration from the biblical stories of Ruth and the Samaritan woman to inspire solidarity with female victims of trafficking.[27] Sponsored by the International Union of Superiors General, Talitha Kum draws on the network of women in Catholic religious orders to respond to human rights abuses globally. It magnifies its impact by partnering with governments and intergovernmental organizations. It has teamed up with the (156-member) International Organization for Migration; received funding from the United States Bureau of Population, Refugees, and Migration; and partnered with the U.S. State Department (the latter to combat human trafficking at the 2014 World Cup).[28]

Such efforts as Talitha Kum tap into the considerable resources of the global Catholic Church, which increasingly addresses trafficking. In May 2013, Pope Francis requested an examination of "human trafficking and modern slavery" from his research academies, in part inspired by his direct contact with these issues through his work in the slums of Buenos Aires. In response, a global workshop was sponsored by the Pontifical Academies of Sciences and Social Sciences, along with the World Federation of the Catholic Medical Associations, which produced detailed recommendations for the church, governments, and global institutions.[29] Guided by this initiative, Pope Francis joined with other Christian leaders in elevating the issue. After a meeting at the Vatican on June 16, 2014, for example, Pope Francis and Justin Welby, the archbishop of Canterbury, launched the Global Freedom Network to fight against "new forms of enslavement."[30] Then in December of 2014 Pope Francis hosted an unprecedented gathering of religious leaders at the Vatican – representing Catholic, Anglican, Orthodox, Muslim, Hindu, Buddhist, and Jewish faiths – who issued a joint declaration to end slavery.[31] Francis also devoted his January 1, 2015, World Peace Day message to human trafficking as a crime against humanity and a "scourge upon the body of Christ," while the Pontifical Academy of Social Sciences Plenary Meeting in April of 2015 convened scholars, law enforcement experts, and activists to highlight successful anti-trafficking strategies.

The combined initiatives of the Holy See and the world Anglican Communion, along with the growing evangelical networks anchored by IJM, could mark a new epoch in the fight against human trafficking. Religious actors and NGOs, indeed, are at the center of the fight against human trafficking and modern slavery. They operate on-the-ground initiatives and exercise international leadership, marshaling significant networks and resources to their cause. While there is a long way to go, their pioneering work has helped spark a much broader global effort. From local governments to the UN, governmental organizations now recognize trafficking as a real threat to human dignity and security. In 2014, President Barack Obama declared January as National Slavery and Human Trafficking Prevention Month, calling trafficking a "global tragedy."[32] Governments around the world have begun to strengthen laws and address corruption – a breeding ground for traffickers. By placing human dignity at the center of their advocacy, religious actors helped catalyze nonreligious actors and organizations to this global cause.

THE UNDERGROUND NETWORK FOR NORTH KOREAN REFUGEES

He has anointed me to preach good news to the poor ... to set at liberty those who are oppressed.[33]

The Christian concept of universal human dignity drives global campaigns against religious persecution, slavery, and exploitation. It also propels initiatives to uplift the poor, provides succor to refugees, and sparks public policies to ameliorate suffering. These impulses have converged to produce a nascent movement on behalf of the oppressed people of North Korea – a transnational underground railroad for refugees.

The human rights and humanitarian nightmare of the hermit kingdom of North Korea has been well documented in the UN report of the Commission of Inquiry on Human Rights in the Democratic People's Republic of Korea (DPRK).[34] Stalinist in its totalitarian control of society and Orwellian in its rituals, the regime's abysmal human rights record includes a vast system of brutal gulags, wide-scale arrests, torture, killings, and engineered starvation in which the authorities literally decide who eats and who does not. North Korean refugees who flee this hell are subject to rampant exploitation in China or are sent back to face concentration camps or execution, especially if they are suspected of being Christians.

Because of their on-the-ground operations among refugees, Christian groups have provided crucial documentation of conditions inside North Korea, and they have highlighted the ideology behind the regime's brutality – a kind of state religion in which leaders are viewed as gods and those who do not pay homage are treated as heretics. Christian solidarity activists also partner with human rights groups in a campaign of political advocacy on behalf of the people inside North Korea and those who flee it.

An extraordinary movement for escapees is now emerging, inspired by the Christian ethic of human dignity. Chinese Christians populate the front lines of this group. They form an underground network *within an underground network* motivated and supported by a larger Christian humanitarian framework. Local Christian communities in China, themselves vulnerable to pressure by the Beijing regime, are providing refuge and being drawn into a nascent underground network. At considerable sacrifice and risk to themselves, Chinese Christians successfully transport North Korean defectors and refugees to safer conditions overseas.

North Korean defectors embody the struggle for basic human dignity – they seek an alternative to oppression, starvation, and dehumanization characteristic of their home country. But the condition of Christians and Christianity in North Korea is even more perilous because it threatens the ideology of the state religion. In March 2014, Kim Jong-un ordered the deaths of thirty-three Christians believed to be working with the South Korean Baptist missionary Kim Jung-wook.[35] Religious believers and missionaries face imprisonment and death on a regular basis.

Considering the intense repression of Christianity in North Korea, refugees' willingness to accept direct aid from explicitly Christian actors is striking. Many refugees, having just crossed into China by the Tumen River, are quickly instructed to "look for the cross," in other words, to seek out Christians to aid in their escape.[36] Often going from church to church, they must find refuge for weeks or months as arrangements are made to transport them out of China to Malaysia or the United States. Their Samaritan saviors represent a movement that is both highly localized and internationally connected through a preexisting Christian plexus. Once North Koreans flee for their safety, the humanitarian nature of local Christians quickly trumps any prejudice refugees might have against Christians.

Once refugees cross the border, a large number convert to Christianity, largely as a result of the intense presence of both Chinese and South Korean Christians in Korean border areas. In her book *Escape from North Korea*, Melanie Kirkpatrick tells the story of refugees' path to escape and asylum. She highlights the myriad disparate paths of North Korean escapees, including North Korean Christian converts such as the late Song Jong-nam who *return* to North Korea to spread their faith.[37] Refugees are influenced to convert by the members of the Christian networks that assist in rescuing them. Moreover, North Koreans do not "jettison" their faith once they reach another country such as South Korea – many form Christian groups of North Korean refugees.

In addition to small-scale exploitation, the Chinese government's policy of repatriation for North Korean escapees is a terrible sentence for any refugee caught by the Chinese government. Captured refugees are subject to torture, imprisonment in labor camps, and even death – sentences that are only increased in severity for Christians. In February, the UN issued a report condemning the practice, indicating that refugees were subject to torture upon repatriation: "In many instances, the violations found by the Commission constitute crimes against humanity."[38] China has since continued to strengthen its borders, causing North Koreans to seek out more and more hazardous paths to freedom.

If these challenges were not enough, Chinese Christians also face prosecution for assisting escaped North Koreans. Tu Airong, a Chinese Christian who assisted North Koreans escaping to Thailand, is facing twenty years in prison for aiding refugees.[39] Chinese Christians are in a unique position; they are threatened by their own government for involvement in humanitarian efforts.

What motivates Chinese Christians to risk arrest and give what little they have to assist these refugees? Their actions must be inspired by a deep underlying faith calling them to value and protect the dignity of the unfortunate. As we see in the chapter by Fenggang Yang, Chinese Christians are well aware of the sacrifices necessary for faith. Because of China's restrictive policies, the cost of discipleship is quite high, galvanizing and emboldening Christians and leading to incredible strength and focus of faith communities. Moreover, the biblical parables of the Good Samaritan and the poor widow in the temple must resonate deeply in the minds of Chinese Christians – they give what little they have to help others.

Escape to a foreign country from China is not a quick or easy process. Partnership with locals and other aid organizations is essential because refugees must stay out of sight to dodge Chinese government officials. The Seoul-based Christian organization Helping Hands Korea provides assistance through shelters in China, as well as aid in leaving China if necessary.[40] This period can last months while foreign embassies are petitioned for asylum on behalf of the escapee. Some desperate refugees have scaled the walls of the U.S. Consulate to gain asylum.[41] Many must remain in China, which holds the largest population of North Koreans outside North Korea itself.[42]

Once refugees escape to foreign countries, they can become powerful advocates for the cause of North Korean freedom. One refugee, Joseph Kim, even gave a TED talk about his experience with underground escape networks.[43] Lee Soon Ok, another North Korean living in the United States, gave a stirring testimony at the Second Summit of Christian Leaders on Religious Persecution in May 2002 in Washington, D.C.[44] As in so many other cases, the best advocates for freedom are those who witnessed atrocities firsthand – they inspire thousands to their cause through talks to church congregations and testimonies in religious news media.

Like many of the other cases in this chapter, these testimonies inspired lobbying in the United States to back up local action overseas. Christian actors and organizations assisted in the passage of the North Korean Human Rights Act of 2004. This act sought to expand protection for refugees, conditioned U.S. humanitarian aid to North Korea on transparent improvements in access for people in need, and called for the inclusion of human rights considerations in all negotiations with the regime.[45] Though not vigorously implemented, it did reflect the way the Christian information networks helped shift the focus of U.S. policy from nuclear weapons to human rights issues. Among other things, the act allowed North Koreans to gain refugee status and permanent residence in the United States.

While the work of Christian freedom networks might only scratch the surface of the North Korean problem, these networks are evidence of an exciting development in global Christian humanitarian efforts. Instead of outside Christian actors, Chinese Christians fill the pivotal and most dangerous roles. Chinese Christians are not instructed by other Christians but are instead inspired to enact the belief in dignity, life, and respect central to Christian theology. They are evidence that the modern shift in Christianity to the Global South has taken on a life of its own. Instead of recipients, these Chinese Christians are propagators of humanitarian succor – despite their limited resources. They form true partnerships with global Christian organizations and networks.

CHRISTIAN PEACEMAKING NETWORKS

Blessed are the peacemakers, for they shall be called the children of God.[46]

Contemporary wars and violence disproportionately afflict the world's poor and call forth Christian peacemaking impulses. Monica Toft, Daniel Philpott, and Timothy Shah in *God's Century* define religious peacemaking efforts as "any activity carried out by a religious actor that is aimed at transforming a condition of violence or deep injustice into one of *shalom*, or 'just peace'."[47] This definition encompasses a host of different efforts, from mediation in active conflicts, to facilitation of peaceful transitions to democracy, to postconflict reconciliation. In nearly every Christian peace effort, a strong emphasis on human dignity shines through as a prerequisite to negotiations, mediations, or reconciliation. Inspired by biblical teachings, such as the preceding injunction from the Sermon on the Mount, Christian actors and organizations tread into many strife-torn nations seeking to end war and begin reconstruction. Unlike such traditional institutions as the UN, religious organizations are often able to espouse true neutrality and cultivate trust-based linkages among all sides of the conflict.

Beyond neutrality and trust, Christian groups employ expansive human networks to promote peacemaking. From the hierarchal Catholic Church to the more decentralized Protestant denominations, Christians of all types use humanitarian and evangelistic connections to respond to conflicts across the globe. International church leaders, academics, and others use these systems to communicate with rebel factions, warlords, governments, and local religious groups. In this way, religious peacemakers employ two of the most important commodities in conflict resolution: communication and information. With access to local actors and international partners, they can move from the front lines of conflict to international councils.

The struggle to end conflicts confronts entrenched governments, ruthless rebel leaders, pervasive grievances, and economic privation, which can easily derail negotiations and reconciliation. Under the right circumstances religious actors are uniquely situated to circumvent these limitations. According to Douglas Johnston and Cynthia Sampson, "their special contributions could not have been achieved by comparable secular efforts."[48] Religious actors take something extra to the negotiating table – a spiritual ethic, trust-based access, and their positions as nongovernmental entities.

Christian organizations are not the only religious groups to engage in peacemaking – Buddhist, Islamic, and Jewish actors also negotiate treaties, call for policy changes, and take active roles in postconflict resolution. But an examination of modern religious peacemaking efforts demonstrates the prevalence of Christian actors in global peacemaking. The authors of *God's Century* provide the most comprehensive and systematic documentation of religious-based mediation over the past three decades.[49] Of the twenty-one disputes they identified in which religious actors played a role, sixteen involved Christian groups exclusively, another Christian and Muslim groups, and another an American statesman and Episcopal priest. The other three disputes involved mediation by Buddhists and Muslims. Moreover, of the conflicts in which religious actors played a strong mediating role, *all involved Christian actors*. Thus Christianity plays a disproportionate role in faith-based conflict mediation. The global size and span of Christianity, its ethic of peacemaking, and its robust international networks combined to produce this striking pattern.

Illustrative of this role is the Community of Sant'Egidio, an organization of peacemakers nested in the larger Catholic world. In the *God's Century* study, this one group engaged in seven of the mediation cases, five of which involved strong mediation. The intensity and scope of the community's involvement in mediation efforts demonstrate the power of focused efforts connected to global Catholic networks. While their extraordinary efforts span activities from prayer to peace conferences, they seem to have an ability to draw disparate violent factions to the table in such diverse nations as Mozambique, Algeria, Uganda, Kosovo, Guatemala, and Liberia.[50] In contrast to traditional methods of engagement, Sant'Egidio stresses multipolar, synergistic efforts that incorporate actors at all levels, from the grass roots to the international. This strategy offers responsiveness to local needs and guarantees of international organizations.

Previous humanitarian work and grassroots social transformation enhance the leverage of the Community of Sant'Egidio. In Uganda it was able to foster relationships with leaders of the Lord's Resistance Army – an effort that helped broker peace talks and the eventual settlement in the Ugandan civil war.[51] Notably, Uganda is more than 40 percent Catholic,[52] underscoring the benefits of a preexisting religious framework for conflict resolution efforts. Shared religious traditions can, in some cases, provide the motivation for mutual understanding.

Within the larger Christian effort, Christian pacifist denominations offer a doctrinal and practical expression of the biblical call to be peacemakers. In particular, Quakers and Mennonites cultivate a focused peace network.[53] They can be extremely effective in conflict resolution strategies because their long histories of pacifism and neutrality allow them to avoid many of the historical liabilities of governmental and even larger religious institutions; they have no history of violence or support of one side or another in a conflict. Pacifist organizations have been active in a number of conflicts, from Nigeria to Nicaragua and Zimbabwe. They also utilize an intense preexisting network to gain access to elite actors on all sides of conflicts.[54]

A remarkable early example involved Quaker mediation of the Nigerian civil war in the late 1960s, which demonstrated the transformative potential of religious neutrality and respect for the dignity of all combatants. A postindependence legacy of corruption, election fraud, and economic disparity set the stage for significant conflict in Nigeria. In response, members of the American Friends Service Committee sponsored a series of working groups as early as 1961 aimed at ameliorating ethnic tensions.[55] When civil war broke out in Nigeria in 1967,[56] Quaker representatives capitalized on this prior work. They reiterated their commitment to conciliation by acting as reliable, unbiased communicators between the rebels and the government.[57] Because they enjoyed the trust of both sides, Quaker intermediaries provided valuable avenues others could not. Indeed, they traveled back and forth between rebel camps and the government capital, transmitting messages and mitigating miscommunication, fear, and reprisals, facilitating postconflict reconciliation.[58]

Mennonites provided another example of religious conciliation, this time in Nicaragua. The Sandinista revolution, which sparked a proxy war with U.S. backed counterrevolutionaries in the 1980s, also spawned a conflict between the regime and the Miskito Indians of the East Coast. With their autonomy threatened by the Marxist thrust of the regime, the Miskitos rebelled. As it turned out, the Moravian Church had deep roots among this tribe and enlisted the efforts of their Mennonite brethren, in particular the well-known peacemaker John Paul Lederach. Drawing deeply from Mennonite spirituality, Lederach and team conducted intense mediation negotiations between Nicaraguan authorities and tribal representatives.

These sessions, which involved prayer and worship as a means to build mutual trust, helped defuse the conflict and ultimately led to the granting of greater autonomy to the tribal people of the region.[59]

Christian humanitarian NGOs, which we emphasized earlier, can also play a crucial role in peacemaking and postconflict reconciliation. They do so indirectly by fostering the kind of development that reduces suffering, grievance, and societal conflict. But their on-the-ground presence can draw them into direct and active mediation initiatives. For example, strife in the Central African Republic (CAR) has spawned violence by Christian militias against Muslims, resulting in the destruction of numerous mosques and a massive exodus of Muslim refugees. In response, the large Christian NGOs working in CAR – especially World Vision and Catholic Relief Services – are collaborating with Muslim groups in peacemaking efforts to quell the violence and promote reconciliation.[60]

The achievements of the community of Sant'Egidio, the peace churches, and Christian NGOs are rooted in an intense and authentic spiritual response to be Christian peacemakers. Despite their institutional, organizational, and practical differences, a similar focus on human dignity and trust building allows them to communicate with parties other institutions cannot. Their reputations as unbiased arbiters afford them access to all sides of a conflict – a most valuable ability in peace negotiations. International, national, and local churches and religious actors around the world take key roles in mediation, conciliation, truth and reconciliation commissions, and other peace efforts. As a consequence, strategies rooted in religious and spiritual ideologies are influencing governmental and international efforts toward conflict resolution. Whether it is the vast connections of the Catholic Church or the intense resolve of Quakers and Mennonites, religious peacemaking facilitates global conflict resolution.

THE SCOPE AND LIMITS OF GLOBAL CHRISTIAN ADVOCACY: THE PAINFUL LESSON OF SOUTH SUDAN

Blessed are those who mourn, for they shall be comforted.[61]

South Sudan represents the stunning case of a new nation born out of transnational advocacy, providing another illustration of the reach of global Christian networks. As recounted in *Freeing God's Children*,[62] Christian solidarity activists and their Jewish allies mounted a formidable international movement on behalf of the African peoples of southern Sudan, who were engulfed in a brutal civil war with the Islamist Arab government in Khartoum. Accounts of religious cleansing and slavery animated passionate responses and creative tactics of the movement, which led to the passage of the Sudan Peace Act in 2002 and subsequent American diplomatic initiatives that induced Khartoum to let the South secede. With much jubilation South Sudan was declared an independent state in July of 2011.

International Christian NGOs invested heavily in the new country, and local Christian leaders engaged in heroic efforts to consolidate and weave the nation together. But the country – afflicted by decades of devastation, bereft of infrastructure, beset by tribal and ethnic divisions, and sapped by poor governing capacity – may be too fragile to hold. Tragically, in December of 2013 a power struggle in the capital city of Juba erupted into widespread tribal violence and armed insurrection, sparking a new round of massive displacement, disease, and looming famine. A Hobbesian nightmare of warlords leading ethnic militias in atrocities and reprisals haunts the once-hopeful land. The painful lesson of South Sudan is that the absence of a functioning state can undermine the best efforts of international Christian advocates or heroic sacrifices of Christian civic society actors. In other words, in a broken world there is no guarantee that formidable advocacy and solidarity will always succeed. But if the nation steps back from the precipice, it will likely owe its rescue to the very Christian networks – indigenous and international – that gave its birth.

For centuries uneasy relations have existed between the dominant Arabic-speaking people of northern Sudan and the ethnically distinct and often marginalized African tribes of the South and Nuba Mountains.[63] Simmering tensions erupted into civil war in 1983 when a militant Islamist regime in Khartoum – the same one that gave refuge to Osama Bin Laden – launched a campaign of forced Islamization on the African Christian and animist populations of the South.

Guided by an ideology of racial and religious superiority, the regime waged its self-declared jihad in scorched earth fashion, burning villages and crops, slaughtering livestock, indiscriminately killing civilians, and abducting women and children into chattel slavery, which often involved concubinage and forced conversions. This two-decade conflict claimed the lives of some 2 million black Africans, displaced another 5 million, and enslaved thousands more. Because Christianity provided the cultural glue for the peoples of the South, the Khartoum regime sought to eradicate its presence by destroying churches, religious schools, and clinics. This combination of massive killing, manufactured famine, and forced conversions aimed at the destruction of a distinct people led international monitors to depict the regime's campaign as genocidal.[64]

Christian networks played a pivotal role in plucking this tragedy from the backwaters of international concern. Courageous local pastors and bishops in southern Sudan long championed the cause of their communities – providing succor, documenting atrocities, and even mediating violent clashes between factions of the Southern People's Liberation Army (SPLA).[65] As the crisis deepened, they formed the Sudan Council of Churches, which became instrumental in fostering transnational relationships between local Christian congregations and international

NGOs and solidarity groups. With unique on-the-ground access to some of the most remote regions in this sprawling land, indigenous Christian leaders conveyed vital information on the crisis to a growing international Christian human rights and solidarity network.

Because of their global denominational linkages, southern Sudanese Catholic and Anglican bishops became especially influential voices for their besieged flocks. They traveled abroad, testified before policy makers, and were feted at congregations and advocacy gatherings in the United States and Europe. For example, the Sudanese Catholic Bishop Macram Gassis acted as a hub of information on the Sudanese crisis by channeling timely accounts to the global Catholic Church. U.S. Catholic bishops in turn sent delegations to Sudan and attracted more attention to the cause in Catholic publications. Gassis himself was the first person to testify to the U.S. Commission on International Religious Freedom.

Churches and aid agencies, especially in the United States, also provided haven for Sudanese refugees and escaped slaves, who became powerful voices for the cause. Such figures as Francis Bok and Abuk Bak spoke frequently at churches and synagogues, testified at congressional hearings, and appeared in Christian magazines. Their voices helped fuel interest in the slave redemption initiatives of John Eibner of the Swiss-based group Christian Solidarity International. These initiatives bought the freedom of thousands of slaves, ignited a broad social movement with creative tactics, and ultimately led to the voluntary manumission of thousands of other slaves when the war ended.

Massive grassroots mobilization, dramatic demonstrations at the Sudanese embassy, and creative lobbying tactics ultimately coalesced around the Sudan Peace Act, legislation condemning Sudanese violence and pressing Sudanese peace talks. The act, passed in October of 2002, threatened economic and military embargoes against the Sudanese government if it failed to engage in good-faith negotiations with the SPLA. The act also directed high-level U.S. diplomatic engagement to facilitate serious negotiations between the two sides, which ultimately led to the signing of the Comprehensive Peace Agreement (CPA) in 2005. A provision of that agreement allowed southern Sudanese the opportunity to vote on independence after an interim period. After an overwhelming referendum vote in January of 2011, the new nation celebrated its independence that summer.

From the signing of the CPA through the fall of 2013 the land enjoyed its first extended respite from war and strife in a generation. Global Christian NGOs invested heavily in the new nation by providing many essential services. Field research in August of 2013, on the eve of the December breakdown, revealed the prominence of such groups as Samaritan's Purse, Catholic Relief Services, World Vision, Adventist Relief and Development Agency, and Caritas International. These groups, working through indigenous church networks and in cooperation with the

UN and USAID, provided a substantial share of the education, health services, and emergency relief that the fledgling government could not.

But a combination of bad luck and parlous circumstances rendered the transition to self-government precarious. Shortly after the CPA was signed in 2005 the leader of the SPLA, John Garang, was killed in a helicopter accident. Though not without flaws, Garang was the most educated and sophisticated of the rebel leaders, and certainly the only figure with the potential capacity to unite the various factions and perhaps establish a nascent functioning government. After independence the absence of effective leadership became glaring, as rampant corruption or ineptitude by government officials – mostly former SPLA commanders with no governing expertise – squandered oil revenue and aid money.

Lagging development is manifest. With few miles of paved roads in a country the size of France, much of the land is inaccessible for months of the rainy season. The capital city of Juba is a jumble of rutted muddy streets and hovels, with no central electrical or water service but with large walled government compounds and mansions for leaders seemingly unconnected to the people.

Observers point to other problems: the lack of inclusion of civil society actors in the peace process, the failure of reconciliation that left tribal factions simmering beneath the surface, premature independence for a traumatized and exhausted people unprepared for self-government, and perhaps some naivety of Christian advocacy groups who thought that independence from Khartoum would unleash a beneficent reign.[66]

Still we hope. Andrew Natsios, former USAID administrator and special envoy to Sudan, described churches as "the most functional indigenous institutions," going so far as to say they will determine Sudan's future.[67] As clashes between government troops and insurgents plunged the country into chaos, local bishops and pastors have provided singular moral voices, chastising the contesting political and tribal factions, striving to mediate the dispute, and offering their help in the long and painful process of reconciliation and recovery. We in the West must pledge our best efforts, of course, but as believers we must also pray for our brothers and sisters in this afflicted land.

CHRISTIAN NETWORKS FOR GLOBAL RELIGIOUS FREEDOM AND HUMAN RIGHTS

> Blessed are those who are persecuted for righteousness' sake, for theirs is the kingdom of heaven.[68]

While religiously motivated Christians serve economically and politically vulnerable populations around the world, they also face widespread harassment, persecution, and violence, as this volume vividly documents. Christians under pressure respond in diverse ways – vigorously fighting for their religious rights, forming coalitions to advance religious freedom, but also, sad to say, fleeing existential peril, as we see in Syria and Iraq. While case studies in this volume illuminate these diverse responses and strategies, our purpose in this section is to map the role of international Christian networks in both championing the rights of fellow believers and advancing religious freedom as a universal right. Unfortunately, this fight is not as simple as providing food aid or antiretroviral medication. Religious persecution is pervasive, ingrained, and institutionalized in many countries – even in the developed world. Undaunted, Christians have taken up this fight at home and abroad, marshaling their global networks to protect not just the rights of Christians but those of all religious believers.

Preservation of religious liberty is not just one of many important rights; it is central to human dignity, a lynchpin of the bundled cluster of liberties.[69] In many countries, especially in the developing world, religion is taking on growing prominence. In China, a country officially atheist, survey respondents increasingly cite religion and religious protection as important in their lives.[70] The story is the same across the Global South from India to Africa – religion and religious adherence are on the rise. However, in many cases, this rise is occurring in the face of intense and sometimes violent restrictions that threaten both individual conscience and institutional expression, undermining the security and flourishing of entire societies.

Christians, informed and motivated by a theology encouraging religious freedom, are key advocates for what Alfred Stepan calls the *twin tolerations* – the institutional arrangement of democratic equality and religious freedom necessary for successful democratic nation building. The call for religious freedom by the majority of Christian denominations and international advocates is a direct reflection of *imago dei* outlined masterfully elsewhere in this volume. As human beings made in the image and likeness of God, Christians call for the preservation of the right to seek God and fulfill transcendent duties of conscience, unmolested by governmental interference. Evangelical and Catholic scholars, in a joint statement entitled *In Defense of Religious Freedom* published in 1994, spell out the spiritual need for religious freedom:

> The God who gave us life gave us liberty. The God who has called us to faith asks that we defend the possibility that others may make similarly free acts of faith. By reaffirming the fundamental character of religious freedom, we contribute to the defense of freedom and to human flourishing, in our countries and throughout the world.[71]

This powerful statement demonstrates the root of religious freedom advocacy in Christian principles characteristic of nearly all Christian sects. While Christians differ significantly in theology and practice, something about their shared biblical basis motivates intense advocacy for religious freedom, and human rights more generally.

In their book *The Price of Freedom Denied*, Brian Grim and Roger Finke link religious freedom to broader liberties and beneficial societal conditions. They find that religious freedom is highly correlated with political freedom, freedom of the press, gender equality, and civil liberties. Even more, religious liberty is connected to interreligious amity, regional peace, economic investment, public health spending, and democracy. While Christians may be uniquely galvanized by modern martyrdom, their efforts for religious freedom serve the broader cause of human rights and democracy.

Christian advocacy for global religious freedom was coterminous with the founding of the international human rights regime after the Second World War. Mainline Protestant leaders capitalized on the networks of the World Council of Churches to press for the adoption of the Universal Declaration of Human Rights. With access to Eleanor Roosevelt, who chaired the drafting committee of the declaration, they played a key role in that foundational document, particularly article 18 on religious freedom, and backed subsequent international covenants.[72]

Evangelical groups gained prominence during the cold war, as diverse Christian solidarity groups – such as Voice of the Martyrs, Open Doors, International Christian Concern, Christian Solidarity International, Christian Solidarity Worldwide, and International Christian Concern – documented persecution against fellow believers, first behind the Iron Curtain and then beyond. Though sometimes competing or sectarian in their focus, they provided valuable documentation and helped lay the groundwork for broader, more ecumenical initiatives.

The most recent incarnation of this approach is the work of the China Aid Association founder Bob Fu. Fu converted to Christianity after an American teaching English in China gave him a biography of a Chinese intellectual who converted to Christianity.[73] Now Fu helps Chinese Christians with legal aid and asylum. He also lobbies politicians directly for increased protection of Chinese Christians, which also encompasses support for the broader human rights advocacy of Christian lawyers in China, who take on the cause of other believers, such as Falun Gong practitioners. As with the teacher who gave Fu the biography that changed his life, global advocacy against religious persecution would not be possible without preexisting international Christian networks.

Denominational networks and associations also play a pivotal role. Notable in the evangelical world are the Baptist World Alliance and the World Evangelical Alliance. The latter group publishes an international journal on religious freedom, illustrating how Christian advocacy for religious freedom reaches beyond advocating for fellow believers.[74]

In the Orthodox world the leading advocate for religious freedom is Patriarch Bartholomew I of Constantinople. As the "first among equals" in the Eastern Orthodox Communion, Bartholomew's tenure is typified by a vigorous defense of religious freedom and human rights, as well as initiatives to enhance interreligious understanding and tolerance. His firsthand experience with the marginalization of religious minorities in Turkey informs his witness. He capitalizes on his global position to remonstrate with political leaders for greater religious rights.

The largest denominational network, of course, is the Catholic Church, with a billion adherents and a unique diplomatic reach. In 1965, Vatican II issued *Dignitatis Humanae*, its declaration on religious freedom. This historic document asserts religious freedom as a core requirement of human dignity and represents a monumental call for all Catholics to promote flourishing societies through expansive religious liberty. Although the inspiration for the doctrine is firmly biblical, the document advocates religious liberty for all, not just Catholics or Christians. As Daniel Philpott shows in *Volume 1*, this document helped inspire the last great, and largely Catholic, wave of global democratization. And the Church continues to be active in its efforts for religious liberty. The United States Conference of Catholic Bishops constantly lobbies Congress for increased attention to religious freedom efforts. They issue reports and statements based on their connections to global Catholic communities of believers who are witnessing persecution. Pope John Paul II frequently promoted religious freedom, and Pope Francis raised the issue with President Barack Obama at a meeting in March 2014. The Holy See also marshals its diplomatic forces behind the cause, creating a powerful force for global religious freedom.

Beyond denominational or sectarian advocacy for Christian rights, we also see the rise of Christian-based groups that advance religious freedom as a universal right. The Institute for Global Engagement (IGE) is one organization taking full advantage of these networks and marshaling them for religious freedom efforts. Anchored in Christian teaching, IGE seeks to establish religious freedom as a cornerstone of international economic, security, and diplomatic interests. To that end the IGE draws together scholars and international and national leaders to discuss and implement religious freedom efforts in China, Southeast Asia, and Africa. In Vietnam, for example, the IGE has signed, and periodically reaffirmed, agreements to help establish religious freedom efforts through regular meetings and certification programs. These relationships are possible because the IGE promotes respect of all parties as a guiding principle in negotiations. Though motivated by Christian conviction, IGE supports religious freedom for all by sponsoring forums on interreligious relations and creating strategic partnerships with members of Islamic governments in Pakistan or atheist officials in China.

IGE illuminates how a Christian NGO works toward religious freedom and human dignity across the globe.

Another notable organization is Advocates International, founded by the late Sam Ericsson. The organization enlists indigenous lawyers in countries around the world to take on pro bono cases defending religious rights. The annual advocates' conference resembles a session of the UN where lawyers from different continents assemble for training and inspiration but also for networking with others for ideas and assistance in their home countries.

No account would be complete without the pioneering work of Nina Shea, founder and director of the Center for Religious Freedom in Washington, D.C. A Catholic trained as a human rights lawyer, Shea became troubled by the lack of attention to religious freedom in the human rights community. She went on to found an organization at the center of documentation of persecution and advocacy for religious freedom. From the beginning of the war in Iraq, through the conflict in Syria, Shea has been a singular voice in challenging American policy makers to address the existential crisis of the ancient Christian communities in those two lands.[75]

The Becket Fund for Religious Liberty takes its name and inspiration from the archbishop of Canterbury who defended the church against interference from the monarch in the twelfth century. Founded by Kevin "Seamus" Hasson, a Catholic, as a legal institute to defend the religious rights of all believers, it has expanded its international advocacy in recent years. After working as an advocate for the Becket Fund, Tina Ramirez went on to found Hardwired, another international religious freedom advocacy group. Ramirez was instrumental in raising the profile of the case of Mariam Ibrahim, the Sudanese Christian woman under a death sentence in Sudan for an apostasy conviction.

Academic institutes also play a crucial role in upholding international law and norms on religious freedom. An excellent example is the International Center for Law and Religious Studies at Brigham Young University, founded by Cole Durham. We often see how unorthodox or minority Christian sects disproportionately add distinct voices to religious freedom advocacy. The Church of Jesus Christ of Latter Day Saints, or the Mormons, experienced severe religious persecution in nineteenth-century America. That experience, along with a strong theological tenet of religious freedom in Mormon doctrine, informs the work of Durham and the center. As an international law expert, Cole Durham witnessed the breakup of the Soviet Union and seized the opportunity to travel to new democracies in Eastern Europe and help draft constitutional provisions on religious freedom. From that foundation he developed a global stature as the leading international law expert on religious liberty. He travels the world to offer expert testimony at international and national tribunals, hosts religious officials of numerous countries for workshops on model religious laws, and has coorganized training sessions at law schools in China and Vietnam with the IGE.[76]

The collective advocacy of diverse Christian actors is nicely illustrated in the campaign for the U.S. International Religious Freedom Act of 1998. The act establishes religious freedom as a central aim of American foreign policy. It also created an ambassador adviser to the president on religious freedom as well as a Commission on International Religious Freedom. The passage of the act was the culmination of an intense lobbying effort by Catholic, Episcopal, evangelical, and Mormon organizations, as well as Jewish, Baha'i, and Tibetan Buddhist allies.

Though initially driven by concern for persecution of Christians overseas, alliances forged in the campaign broadened the legislation to apply to all people. Moreover, the legislation anchored U.S. promotion of religious freedom in article 18 of the Universal Declaration of Human Rights and other international covenants. Understood as a central pillar of human rights, international religious freedom must be promoted as a basic concern of American foreign policy. Again, a lobbying effort born out of global Christian solidarity networks motivated tangible policy change in the United States. Though not vigorously implemented as advocates had hoped, the law's mandated annual report by the State Department provides an invaluable resource of global documentation of barriers to religion freedom around the globe.

Drawing on biblical teaching and religious doctrine, Christian advocates use the intense combination of network communication and political advocacy to fight for religious freedom at home and abroad. In so doing they reaffirm the centrality of religious and spiritual freedom to human dignity and flourishing, while they advance the broader cause of human rights.[77]

That all Christian traditions and communions experience persecution somewhere on the globe, and that all have leaders advancing the idea of religious freedom as a universal right, creates a unique opportunity for genuine ecumenism among believers. This takes its most poignant form in the idea of an *ecumenism of martyrdom* first articulated by Pope John Paul II in his apostolic letter "Toward the Third Millennium"[78] and echoed by subsequent voices.[79]

SUMMARY

Each instantiation of the idea of Christian dignity cataloged in this chapter is notable in its own right. But collectively we see the full scope and weight of this witness in the world. Christian networks, while not always successful, play an expansive and invaluable role on the global stage in human rights advocacy, humanitarian efforts, and peacemaking.

At a more theoretical level, what we observe is the emergence of a genuine global system, in which a theological ideal serves as a central organizing principle. Unlike governmental structures or even UN institutions, this system is more organic and nimble in upholding the dignity of every human person. This system links local actors and congregations with international mission, development, and denominational structures that magnify the collective Christian witness in policy circles. Perhaps we stand at a hinge of Christian history, as the faith's contribution to freedom becomes fully manifest and global.

NOTES

1 Kyle Harper, "Christianity and the Roots of Human Dignity in Late Antiquity," in *Christianity and Freedom: Historical Perspective*, ed. Timothy Samuel Shah and Allen D. Hertzke (New York: Cambridge University Press, 2016).

2 Philip Jenkins, *The Next Christendom: The Coming of Global Christianity*, rev. and expanded ed. (New York: Oxford University Press, 2007).

3 Interview with Charles Sandefur, president, Adventist Relief and Development Agency, June 2009.

4 Robert Wuthnow, *Boundless Faith: The Global Outreach of American Churches* (Berkeley: University of California Press, 2009).

5 Kate Tracy, "Dropping Anchor," *Christianity Today*, July/August 2014, 72–75.

6 Matthew 25:40, NIV Bible.

7 As director of the Pew Research Center's 2011–2012 study "Lobbying for the Faithful," Allen D. Hertzke interviewed a number of the advocacy directors of international relief and development organizations, and during field research in South Sudan in August of 2014 he interviewed country officials and indigenous staff of these organizations. The invocation to see the face of Christ in those they serve arose routinely and naturally in these conversations. See "Lobbying for the Faithful," Pew Research Center, http://www.pewforum.org/2011/11/21/lobbying-for-the-faithful-exec/

8 Stephen V. Monsma, "Faith-based NGOs and the Government Embrace," in *The Influence of Faith: Religious Groups and U.S. Foreign Policy*, ed. Elliott Abrams (Lanham, MD: Rowman & Littlefield, 2001).

9 An excellent account of one aspect of this growing network is Robert Calderisi, *Earthly Mission: The Catholic Church and World Development* (New Haven, CT: Yale University Press, 2013).

10 Andrew S. Nasios, "Faith-Based NGOs and U.S. Foreign Policy," in *The Influence of Faith: Religious Groups and U.S. Foreign Policy*, ed. Elliot Abrams (Lanham, MD: Rowman & Littlefield, 2001).

11 Allen D. Hertzke heard this from his interviews with advocacy directors of international relief development organizations.

12 Interview with Robert Seiple, former head of World Vision, 2006.

13 Joshua William Busby, "Bono Made Jesse Helms Cry: Jubilee 2000, Debt Relief, and Moral Action in International Politics," *International Studies Quarterly* 51 (2007): 247–275; "Religious Leaders Cheer Debt Relief," *Christian Century*, November 2000.

14 Scott Baldauf and Jina Moore, "Bush Sees Results of His AIDS Plan in Africa," *The Christian Science Monitor*, February 20, 2008, 7.

15 Luke 4:18, RSV Bible.

16 This is the figure given by the 2014 State Department's Trafficking in Person's report http://www.state.gov/j/tip/rls/tiprpt/2014/index.htm. Kevin Bales estimates 27 million persons in conditions of slavery. Kevin Bales, *Disposable People: New Slavery in the Global Economy* (Berkeley: University of California Press, 2000).

17 UNODC Global Report on Trafficking in Persons 2014; Bales, *Disposable People.*

18 Jeremy Haken, "Transnational Crime in the Developing World," *Global Financial Integrity*, February 2011.

19 Quentin Hardy, "Hitting Slavery Where It Hurts (Gary Haugen of International Justice Mission)." *Forbes* 172, no. 14 (2004): 76.

20 As Haugen writes, the "good news" about injustice is that God is against it, thereby mandating that believers must fight against it as well. See Gary Haugen, *The Good News about Injustice* (Downers Grove, Il: InterVarsity Press, 1999).

21 See the IJM Web site at IJM.org for a detailed mission and strategy statement.

22 See the UNODC report "Victim Identification Procedures in Cambodia," 2013. Accessed May 27, 2014, http://www.unodc.org/documents/southeastasiaandpacific/Publications/2013/NRM/FINAL_Draft_UNODC_report_Cambodia_NRM.pdf

23 See the Noonday Collection Web site for more information. Accessed June 21, 2014, http://www.noondaycollection.com/styleforjustice

24 See International Justice Mission 2013 annual report, http://www.ijm.org/sites/default/files/download/IJM-2013-Annual-Report_Downloadable.pdf

25 Allen D. Hertzke, *Freeing God's Children: The Unlikely Alliance for Global Human Rights* (Lanham, MD: Rowman & Littlefield, 2006), 316.

26 For text of the act and subsequent reauthorizations see the State Department Web site. Accessed May 28, 2014, http://www.state.gov/j/tip/laws/

27 See Talitha Kum's Web site for more information and mission statement. Accessed May 24, 2014. www.talithakum.info. Also the U.S. Embassy to the Holy See Conference on Building Bridges of Freedom: Public-Private Partnership to End Modern Day Slavery, May 18, 2011.

28 See an account of the event in U.S. Vatican Embassy Web site. Accessed June 16, 2014, http://vatican.usembassy.gov/news-events/launch-talitha-kums-countering-trafficking-in-persons.html. Also Elise Harris, "Anti–Human Trafficking Effort Launched Ahead of World Cup." Accessed June 21, 2014, http://www.catholicnewsagency.com/news/anti-human-trafficking-effort-launched-ahead-of-world-cup/

29 Allen D. Hertzke is a member of the Pontifical Academy of Social Sciences and received the e-mail from the Chancellor of the Academies, which contained a scan of the handwritten note from Pope Francis, dated May 13, 2013, describing his personal interest in addressing human trafficking. The joint statements of the workshop are contained on the Pontifical Web site, http://www.pass.va/content/scienzesociali/en/events/2009–13/trafficking/traffickingstatement.html

30 Nicole Winfield, "Pope Francis and Archbishop of Canterbury Pledge to Fight Human Trafficking Together," *Huffington Post*, June 16, 2014. http://www.huffingtonpost.com/2014/06/16/pope-francis-justin-welby-modern-slavery_n_5499330.html?utm_hp_ref=religion

31 Global Freedom Network, www.globalfreedomnetwork.org, accessed March 28, 2013. This Web site contains the declaration and original signatories.

32 Presidential Proclamation – National Slavery and Human Trafficking Prevention Month, 2014.

33 Luke 4:18, RSV Bible.
34 Accessed at www.ohchr.org June 2014.
35 "Kim Jong-Un Calls for Execution of 33 Christians," *Washington Times*. Accessed May 8, 2014, http://www.washingtontimes.com/news/2014/mar/6/kim-jong-un-calls-execution-33-christians/
36 For an in-depth look at this process at the North Korean border see Melanie Kirkpatrick,: *The Untold Story of Asia's Underground Railroad* (Encounter Books, 2013), chapter 2.
37 Kirkpatrick, *Escape from North Korea*. Chapter 9
38 Report of the Detailed Findings of the Commission of Inquiry on Human Rights in the Democratic People's Republic of Korea, February 17, 2014.
39 Report from Chinaaid.org. Accessed May 7, 2014, http://www.chinaaid.org/2012/11/chinese-christian-who-helped-hundreds.html
40 Information from the Helping Hands Korea Web site and Bryan Kay, "Tim Peters Provides Helping Hands to North Korean Defectors," *Christian Science Monitor*, October 28, 2011, http://www.csmonitor.com/World/Making-a-difference/Change-Agent/2011/1028/Tim-Peters-provides-Helping-Hands-to-North-Korean-defectors
41 Elisabeth Rosenthal, "North Koreans Seek Asylum at Consulates in China." *New York Times*, May 9, 2002, http://www.nytimes.com/2002/05/09/world/north-koreans-seek-asylum-at-consulates-in-china.html
42 Hazel Smith, "Explaining North Korean Migration to China." Accessed June 21, 2014, http://www.wilsoncenter.org/publication/explaining-north-korean-migration-to-china
43 See Joseph Kim's talk on the TED conference Web site. Accessed May 7, 2014, https://www.ted.com/talks/joseph_kim_the_family_i_lost_in_north_korea_and_the_family_i_gained
44 See "Persecution Summit Takes Aim at Sudan, North Korea," *ChristianityToday.com*. Accessed June 21, 2014, http://www.christianitytoday.com/ct/2002/aprilweb-only/4-29-43.0.html Also Simon Tisdall, "Witness Reveals Horror of North Korean Gulag," *Guardian*, July 18, 2002, World News section, http://www.theguardian.com/world/2002/jul/19/northkorea
45 Kirkpatrick, *Escape from North Korea*, 204–205.
46 Matthew 5:9, King James Version of the Bible.
47 Monica Duffy Toft, Daniel Philpott, and Timothy Samuel Shah, *God's Century: Resurgent Religion and Global Politics* (New York: W. W. Norton, 2011), 177.
48 Douglas Johnston, "Review of the Findings," in *Religion, the Missing Dimension of Statecraft*, ed. Douglas Johnston, and Cynthia Sampson (New York: Oxford University Press, 1995), 164.
49 See chapter 7 and the table on p. 190–191 in Toft, Philpott, and Shah, *God's Century*.
50 Scott Appleby, *The Ambivalence of the Sacred: Religion, Violence, and Reconciliation* (Lanham, MD: Rowman & Littlefield, 2000), 291.
51 Monica Duffy Toft, Daniel Philpott, and Timothy Samuel Shah, *God's Century: Resurgent Religion and Global Politics* (New York: W. W. Norton, 2011), 189.
52 Bureau of Democracy, Human Rights, and Labor. "International Religious Freedom Report 2009," October 26, 2009.
53 For a historical and analytical look at Christian pacifist religions see Cecil John Cadoux, *Christian Pacifism Re-Examined* (Oxford: Oxford University Press, 1940).
54 Adam Curle, *True Justice: Quaker Peace Makers and Peace Making* (Philadelphia: Quaker Books, 2007).

55 Michael Norton Yarrow, *Quaker Experiences in International Conciliation* (New Haven, CT: Yale University Press, 1978), 188–196.

56 For a history of the Nigerian Civil War see John De St. Jorre, *The Nigerian Civil War* (London: Hodder & Stoughton, 1972).

57 Cynthia Sampson, "'To Make Real the Bond between Us All': Quaker Conciliation during the Nigerian Civil War," in *Religion, the Missing Dimension of Statecraft* ed. Douglas Johnston and Cynthia Sampson (New York: Oxford University Press, 1995), 94–100.

58 Ibid, 106–110.

59 For a broad account of Mennonite peacemaking, see Cynthia Sampson and John Paul Lederach, *From the Ground Up: Mennonite Contributions to International Peacebuilding* (New York: Oxford University Press, 2000). For the Nicaragua case see Bruce Nichols, "Religious Conciliation between the Sandinistas and East Coast Indians of Nicaragua," in *Religion, the Missing Dimension of Statecraft*, ed. Douglas Johnston and Cynthia Sampson (New York: Oxford University Press, 1995).

60 Jennifer Bryson, "When Christians Kill and Destroy but Also Make Peace, CAR Today," *Arc of the University* Blog, March 20,2015, http://arcoftheuniverse.info/when-christians-kill-and-destroy-but-also-make-peace-car-today

61 Matthew 5:4, RSV Bible.

62 Allen D. Hertzke, *Freeing God's Children: The Unlikely Alliance for Global Human Rights* (Lanham, MD: Rowman & Littlefield, 2004, Chapter 7).

63 Roland Werner, William Anderson, and Andrew Wheeler, *Day of Devastation Day of Contentment: The History of the Sudanese Church across 2000 Years* (Nairobi, Kenya: Paulines Publications Africa, 2000).

64 U.S. Committee on Refugees, "A Working Document: Quantifying Genocide in the Southern Sudan 1983–1993," October 1993, and "Working Document II: Quantifying Genocide in Southern Sudan and the Nuba Mountains, 1993–1998," December 1998; The Committee of Conscience, Holocaust Museum, "Genocide Alert," issued in October 2000.

65 Werner, Anderson, and Wheeler, *Day of Devastation Day of Contentment*, especially chapter 14, "Death Has Come to Reveal the Faith: The Church in the South 1983–2000."

66 See John Young, *The Fate of Sudan: The Origins and Consequences of a Failed Peace Process* (London: Zed Books, 2012). Interviews and field observations by Allen D. Hertzke in August of 2013 suggested some of these concerns.

67 Andrew S. Natsios, *Sudan, South Sudan, and Darfur: What Everyone Needs to Know* (New York: Oxford University Press, 2012).

68 Matthew 5:10, RSV Bible.

69 For the correlation of religious freedom with other freedoms see Brian J. Grim and Roger Finke, *The Price of Freedom Denied* (New York: Cambridge University Press, 2011), 206.

70 Ibid., 203–204.

71 "In Defense of Religious Freedom: A Statement of Evangelicals and Catholics Together," 1994; eighteen years later a successor group published an identically titled statement, in *First Things*, March 2012, http://www.firstthings.com/article/2012/03/in-defense-of-religious-freedom

72 John Nurser, *For All Peoples and All Nations: Christian Churches and Human Rights* (Washington, DC: Georgetown University Press, 2005).

73 Bob Fu, *God's Double Agent: The True Story of a Chinese Christian's Fight for Freedom* (Grand Rapids, MI: Baker Books, 2014); Mary Kissel, "Bob Fu: The Pastor of China's Underground Railroad," *Wall Street Journal*, June 1, 2012, http://online.wsj.com/news/articles/SB10001424052702303640104577438562289689498

74 See *International Journal for Religious Freedom* published by Institute for Religious Freedom of the World Evangelical Alliance.

75 Nina Shea coauthored with Paul Marshall and Lela Gilbert, *Persecuted: The Global Assault on Christians* (Nashville: Thomas Nelson, 2013).

76 See the organization's Web site at iclrs.org

77 The Baptist World Alliance explicitly cites the defense of human rights as a fundamental aim of its 228 conventions in 121 countries comprising 420 million believers. Press Release, "Baptists Gather in Historic City in Turkey," July 3, 2014, communications@bwanet.org

78 "Tertio Millenio Adveniente," Apostolic Letter of Pope John Paul II, November 10, 1994.

79 John L. Allen Jr., *The Global War on Christians* (New York: Image, 2013).

6

The Growth and Dynamism of Chinese Christianity

Fenggang Yang

The history of Christianity in China can be traced back at least to the seventh century, when Nestorian Christians once flourished in the Tang dynasty. However, the continuous presence of Christianity in China did not start until 1582 for Catholics, when the Jesuit Matteo Ricci arrived in China, and not until 1807 for Protestants, when Robert Morrison of the interdenominational London Missionary Society arrived. In the eighteenth and early nineteenth centuries, Christianity was sometimes prohibited under the seclusion policy of the Qing government. Only after the Opium Wars in 1840–1860 was the Qing government forced to abandon the seclusion policy and allow Christian missions throughout the country. This unfortunate history led to the Chinese perception of a connection between Christianity and Western imperialism and colonialism. The Chinese Communist Party continues to call upon this perception in its anti-Christian campaigns.

Today, Christianity remains a minority religion in China, but Christians constitute a growing minority that has made significant contributions to the expansion of freedom in Chinese society. While many other chapters in this book document the persecution and suffering of Christians in various parts of the world, this chapter describes the extraordinary growth of Christianity despite persecution and restrictions in the People's Republic of China (PRC). I will also describe the various contributions of Christians to the expansion of freedom in Chinese society. The dynamism and growth of Chinese Christianity, as I will show, bear striking resemblance to characteristics of faith in the Roman Empire on the eve of the Edict of Milan. The trajectory of Christianity in China, therefore, has momentous global implications.

SOCIAL AND POLITICAL CONTEXTS IN THE TWENTIETH CENTURY

As did many developing countries, China underwent dramatic social and political changes in the twentieth century. Two revolutions radically changed the political system twice: The Republican Revolution in 1911 overthrew the Qing dynasty and established the first republic in Asia; the Communist Revolution in 1949 swept mainland China and drove the republican government to the island of Taiwan. Between the two revolutions were devastating civil wars and the War of Resistance against Japan during World War II. Since the establishment of the PRC under the Chinese Communist Party (CCP) in 1949, frequent political campaigns have resulted in millions of unnatural deaths. Then, in the last three decades or so, fast and continuous economic growth under the new leadership of the CCP resulted in rapid industrialization, urbanization, and hundreds of millions of uprooted migrants floating within and beyond Chinese borders.

In spite of the numerous calamities throughout the twentieth century, China has become substantially modernized in economy, military, technology, education, medicine, and other aspects of social life. However, this modernization was not initiated internally but coerced by external forces that threatened the existence of the Chinese nation. In modern times, China suffered the first defeats in the Opium Wars in the 1840s and 1850s when Britain and France, in the name of protecting free trade, deployed modern gunboats and firearms and knocked down the closed borders of China. Other Western powers, Russia, and Japan followed suit and eventually divided up China for their colonialist interests. It became clear to the Chinese people that the Qing government was too weak to resist the colonialist powers. The external humiliation and internal corruption eventually gave rise to the Republican Revolution in 1911 and the establishment of the Republic of China in 1912. However, the Republican Revolution did not ensure social stability and economic prosperity but opened battlegrounds for warlords and colonialist invasion by Japan.

This coerced modernization process unsettled cultural and religious traditions. For almost two millennia, Confucianism was the dominant moral and ideological system in China. It was politically reinforced through the Imperial Examination System, which selected government officials on the basis of their knowledge of Confucian classics. However, after repeated defeats by the colonialist powers and under pressure from cultural elites, the Qing government eventually abolished the Imperial Examination System in 1905 and began to develop modern schools teaching modern sciences and humanities.

Soon after the Republican Revolution, some military elites from the old regime made attempts to reestablish a dynastic monarchy and tried to rally support by reestablishing Confucianism. In reaction, cultural elites, especially those young intellectuals who had studied in Europe, the United States, and Japan, mounted fierce attacks on Confucianism, characterizing it as the cultural and spiritual culprit of China's feudalist corruption, military humiliation, and social backwardness. Similar to the French Enlightenment and consistent with modernization discourse, the New Culture Movement in the 1910s and 1920s attacked all religions, including Confucianism as a kind of religion, charging that religion was incompatible with modernity. In addition, Christianity was singled out for rejection because of its perceived connection with Western colonialism and imperialism.

The iconoclastic New Culture and antireligion movements prepared the way for the rise of the Chinese Communist Party. Inspired by the Russian Bolshevik Revolution and directed by the Third International, the Comintern, which was under Soviet leadership, the Chinese Communist Party was established in 1921 and grew in strength and popularity amid wars in the 1920s and 1930s. It eventually defeated the Republican government under the Kuomintang, took control of the mainland, and established the PRC in 1949. Under Communist rule, the cultural and religious transformation has continued on the ideological basis of Marxism-Leninism-Maoism.

THE RELIGIOUS POLICY TOWARD CHRISTIANITY UNDER COMMUNIST RULE

Since 1949, the CCP has maintained an atheism-based religious policy, insisting that atheism is an integral part of the orthodox ideology of Marxism-Leninism-Maoism. The Chinese Communist atheism has been expressed in two major forms: The enlightenment atheism follows French Enlightenment discourse and treats religion as a false consciousness, which may be eliminated through education and propaganda; militant atheism follows the Bolshevik discourse and treats religion as an antirevolutionary social force, which must be suppressed with political measures. Support for both forms of atheism may be found in the writings of Marx, Lenin, and Mao. Alternating between the two forms of atheism, CCP religious policy has swung between limited tolerance and violent suppression or applied a mixture of both to different regions or to different religions.

The religious policy of the PRC may be divided into five periods: The First period from 1949 to 1957 is characterized by suppression of some religions and co-option of world religions; the second period from 1957 to 1966 by forceful reduction of religious venues and activities; the third period from 1966 to 1979 by eradication of all religions; the fourth period from 1979 to 1994 by limited tolerance while wishing for reduction of religious believers; and the fifth period from 1994 to 2013 by pragmatic management and containment of religious revivals.

Soon after the founding of the PRC in 1949, the Communist Party launched political campaigns against religious organizations as ideological enemies and subversive political forces. First, the cultic or heterodox sects of Chinese folk religious traditions were banned. Second, the world religions of Christianity, Islam, and Buddhism had too many followers to be eliminated immediately; therefore, the party-state took pragmatic and strategic measures to co-opt and control a few leaders and worked through cooperative leaders to coerce religious groups and individuals to cut off their ties with the outside world and to purge their feudalist elements from within.

The co-option-and-control strategy was first applied to Protestant Christians. The party-state handpicked some cooperative leaders and instructed them to carry out a "patriotic" movement in the name of making Chinese Protestant churches become self-ruling, self-supporting, and self-propagating, which became known as the "Three-Self" principle. Christian churches and organizations were demanded to sever ties with foreign mission boards, denominations, and organizations immediately. Foreign missionaries were driven out of the PRC. Christian schools, universities, and hospitals were either closed down or taken over by the government.

The party-state hoped that Chinese Catholics would adopt the same three-self reforms. When the Catholic clergy met these maneuvers with great resistance, the party-state responded with severe crackdowns on the clergy, expelling the representative of the Vatican, foreign bishops, and foreign leaders of religious orders. Some foreign missionaries and loyal Chinese Catholics were imprisoned and tortured as spies of the United States or as antirevolutionary elements.

Eventually, the party-state succeeded in forming national associations for the five religions, namely, the Buddhist Association of China and the Islamic Association of China in 1953, the Christian Three-Self Patriotic Movement Committee of China in 1954, the Daoist Association of China, and the Catholic Laity Patriotic Association of China in 1957, which was renamed the Catholic Patriotic Association of China in 1962. Thereafter, these "patriotic" associations have served as extended arms integral to the control apparatuses of CCP religious policy.

By 1957, the political threats of religious groups to the new regime were annihilated. Thereafter, along with the Socialist Transformation that collectivized or nationalized the economy for central planning, religious policy shifted to increasing economic production. For Christians, the socialist transformation led to disbanding Protestant denominations, converting clergy and professional ministers to manual laborers, and consolidating and reducing the numbers of churches and worship services. Regardless of the previous denominational backgrounds, all Protestant Christians were amalgamated for joint worship services at the consolidated churches under the supervision of the local Christian Three-Self Patriotic Movement Committee. The resistant leaders of Christian sects and independent churches were imprisoned or sent to labor camps. The Chinese Protestant churches were forced into the so-called postdenominational era. The number of churches and church activities began diminishing in the following years. Some counties, such as those in Wenzhou, Zhejiang, were declared "no-religion counties."

In 1966, the CCP launched the Great Proletarian Cultural Revolution to destroy and sweep away the "Four Olds" – Old Customs, Old Culture, Old Habits, and Old Ideas. All religions fell into the categories of the Four Olds. The Bible and other religious scriptures were burned; religious artifacts were smashed; churches and temples were ransacked, torn apart, or shut down; religious leaders and staunch believers were targeted as personifications of the Four Olds, and many of them were mocked, harassed, imprisoned, tortured, or killed. The remaining believers were forced to make public renunciations and became subject to mass struggle meetings where they were publicly humiliated and persecuted in front of a mass gathering of people. All religions, including Christianity, were eradicated from the public scene in the entire society. This was more extreme than the religious policy of the Soviet Union. The only other Communist country that banned all religions was Albania.

After the death of the CCP Chairman Mao Zedong in 1976, the new CCP leadership under Deng Xiaoping set a new course for the country, focusing on economic development. In order to rally the people of all walks of life around the central task of economic development, the pragmatic CCP leadership began to loosen control over various aspects of social life. Beginning in 1979, a limited number of Protestant and Catholic churches, Buddhist and Daoist temples, and Islamic mosques reopened for religious services. The thirteen-year eradication policy was officially abandoned.

In 1982, the limited religious tolerance was formally inscribed in a new edict, entitled "The Basic Viewpoint and Policy on the Religious Affairs during the Socialist Period of Our Country," which has become better known as "Document No. 19." This central document of the CCP has served as the basis of the religious policy in China since that point. It grants a legal existence to Buddhism, Daoism, Islam, Protestantism, and Catholicism under the government-sanctioned "patriotic" associations, but not to any group outside the five religious associations, nor to any other religions. Furthermore, Document No. 19 proscribes proselytizing outside approved religious premises and directs that atheist propaganda must be carried out unremittingly, just not inside churches, temples, and mosques. The CCP authorities appeared to believe that only the diehard religious believers from the pre-1949 old society would continue to practice religion and they would eventually die out. The new people who were born in the new China and grew up under the CCP rule would never accept the false consciousness of religion.

Since the total ban of religion was lifted in 1979, however, a religious upsurge has outpaced regulatory expansion in spite of accelerated efforts for control. Because economic development remains the central task of the CCP top leadership, many local governments have often used this to justify the pragmatic and tolerant approach to various religions, that is, putting religion to use for economic development, such as building temples for tourism or allowing for more churches in order to attract overseas investments.

By the mid-1990s, it became apparent that many kinds of religions had revived, and many young people had become religious believers. Without revamping the atheist basis, the religious policy evolved from wishing to reduce the number of believers to trying to contain the religious revivals. In 1994, the State Council published two ordinances that required all religious groups to register with the government and prohibited foreigners from proselytizing in China. In 1996, the CCP and the State Council issued a joint decree to curb the building of temples and outdoor Buddha statues and constrict authority to grant new building permits for religious venues to provincial governments. In 1999, Falun Gong was banned as an "evil cult" (*xie jiao*), its core leaders were jailed, and its founder took refuge in the United States. In the following years, provincial governments issued numerous "temporary" or "draft" ordinances and administrative orders aimed at controlling religious and cultic groups. Eventually, these administrative orders were consolidated into the State Council's Regulations of Religious Affairs, which took effect on March 1, 2005.

Recently, instead of equally repressing all religions, the regime has taken cautious steps to tilt the religious policy toward favoring Buddhism, Daoism, and folk and popular religions and reviving Confucianism, in part for the purpose of countering the rapid growth of Christianity. Christianity has been routinely criticized in the official media as a foreign religion and a potential force of subversion to the CCP rule. The recent tilted policy toward Chinese traditional religions does not have a theoretical justification based on Marxism-Leninism-Maoism, which is still nominally the CCP orthodox ideology, but is often justified on the basis of nationalism.

In the PRC, there are multiple party-state apparatuses to control religion, "including the United Front Department, the Religious Affairs Bureau, the Nationalities Affairs Commission, the Political-Legal Commission, the Ministries of Propaganda, Culture, Education, Science and Technology, and Health, and the people's associations of the Workers' Union, the Communist Youth League, and the Women's Union."[1] Per the division of work and responsibility, the major control apparatuses are the United Front Departments of the CCP and the Religious Affairs Bureaus of the government. The United Front Department (UFD) of the CCP Central Committee has a division of religious and ethnic affairs, which is charged both to make religious policies and to rally religious leaders around the CCP. The day-to-day administration of religious affairs lies in the Religious Affairs Bureau (RAB) of the State Council, which was upgraded to become the State Administration of Religious Affairs in 1998. Meanwhile, the Ministry of Public Security (police) deals with all illegal religious activities, including any illegal activities of the five official religions and all activities of all other religions. The

Ministry of State Security (MSS) also watches over some religious groups and active leaders, especially since the early 1990s, when the Chinese authorities intensified the fight against infiltration by foreign religious organizations and foreign political entities using religion. Since the crackdown on Falun Gong and the banning of "evil cults," an anticult ministry has been set up under the secretive name of the "610 Office."[2] The 610 Office reports directly to the CCP Politburo and at the top level has a higher status than the State Administration of Religious Affairs. A 610 Office has been added to provincial, prefecture, and even county-level governments. Besides Falun Gong, many Christian sects or Christianity-inspired cultic groups have been banned as evil cults. Since 1999, more resources have been put into religious control and atheist propaganda, including publishing the new magazine *Science and Atheism* by the Chinese Academy of Social Sciences, organizing atheist and anticult associations at provincial and municipal levels, organizing atheist and anticult exhibitions, and organizing study sessions by the CCP and Communist Youth League branches.

In practice, the UFD and RAB usually rule through the so-called patriotic religious associations. The associations of the five official religions are nongovernmental organizations in name only and function as an extension and delegation of the RAB. For example, in principle, the provincial-level Christian Three-Self Patriotic Movement Committee (TSPM) holds the power of approval to ordain ministers, but no one can be ordained without prior approval by the provincial RAB. The prefecture- or county-level TSPM appoints the senior pastors of local churches, but the appointment must be first approved by the same-level RAB and/or UFD. More importantly, the national, provincial, prefecture, and county TSPM committees are separate organizations independent of each other. That is, the local TSPM committees are not under the leadership of the provincial or national TSPM committees. TSPM committees must report to the RAB on the same level and the one immediately above. When a church plans to organize meetings or activities involving people beyond the local administrative region, it has to apply to the higher-level RAB for approval. That is, if the activity involves people from another county, it has to be approved by the prefecture RAB; if from another prefecture, then from the provincial RAB; if from another province or from another country, then from the State Administration of Religious Affairs (SARA). These rules and mechanisms apply to all five religions.

THE SURVIVAL AND REVIVAL OF CHRISTIANITY UNDER CHINESE COMMUNIST RULE

Despite persecution, suppression, and restriction, however, Christianity has survived and has been reviving and thriving. This is evident against the historical background. By the time of the establishment of the People's Republic of China in 1949, church reports show nearly 3 million Catholics and about 1 million Protestants, who constituted less than 1 percent of the Chinese population of about a half-billion at the time.

First of all, the campaign of suppression and persecution in the first three decades of the PRC, as described in the previous section, failed to eliminate Christianity. In fact, it failed to reduce the number of Christians. The persecutions were severe. According to some Chinese historians, "Between 1950 and 1978, some five hundred thousand Christians, both Catholic and Protestant, died from CCP persecution, half of those during the Cultural Revolution."[3] However, Chinese Christians persisted by going underground before and during the Cultural Revolution. By the end of the eradication period, the Catholics managed to retain their flocks, and the number of Protestants even multiplied by three times. The "Document No. 19" of 1982 acknowledged that there were about 3 million Catholics and about 3 million Protestants in China at the time. In other words, in spite of the a half-million unnatural deaths of Christians in the previous three decades or so, the number of Catholics in 1980 had remained about the same as in 1950, and the number of Protestants had tripled. One of the factors could be the natural population increase in the first thirty years of the PRC, but it is also evident that there were many new converts to Protestant Christianity among people who did not have a Christian family background.

Since 1979, Catholics have maintained a slow but steady growth, and Protestant growth has accelerated. In 1991, the Information Office of the PRC State Council released the *White Paper on the Status of Human Rights in China*, which reported 3.5 million Catholics and 4.5 million Protestants. This is a 50 percent increase in the number of Protestants in less than a decade. In 1995–1996, the State Religious Affairs Bureau and the CCP United Front Department jointly carried out a general survey of religion (*zongjiao pucha*) through up-the-ladder reporting, beginning with officially approved churches, temples, and mosques and moving up the administrative levels of the government agencies. On the basis of this survey, the 1997 *White Paper of Freedom of Religious Belief in China* reported about 4 million Catholics and more than 10 million Protestants. Compared with the previous report, the number of Catholics increased modestly, and the number of Protestants more than doubled. Some of the increase may reflect the fact that more Christians became willing to "come out of the closet" and be active in church attendance. Meanwhile, the active evangelism by Protestants also drew in newly baptized Christians.

In 2009, in a series of articles for the commemoration of the sixtieth anniversary of the PRC, the official Xinhua News Agency reported 5.3 million Catholics and 16 million Protestants. Most recently, the semiofficial 2010 *Blue Book of Religions* by the Chinese Academy of Social Sciences (CASS) reports 23.05 million Protestants, a number that is claimed to be based on a national survey of 63,680 individuals carried out by the Institute of World Religions of the CASS in 2008–2009. This survey was commissioned by the SARA and had not been made available for the academic community beyond the CASS until today, leading people to think that this number is probably no more than the upper limit the SARA is willing to admit. Even if we accept this number, Protestant Christians have increased more than seven times since 1980, or twenty-three times since 1950. This is nothing but extraordinary.

Moreover, the published official numbers of the CCP are commonly believed to be underestimates. On various occasions, such as private conversations outside academic conferences, Chinese officials of religious affairs, religious leaders, and scholars commonly confide that the published official numbers are lower than the actual but no one is sure about how much lower. Part of the problem is due to underreporting in the official estimates, which is in fact an open secret in Chinese bureaucracy. Ye Xiaowen, the former director of the State Religious Affairs Bureau, which was upgraded to the State Administration of Religious Affairs in 1998, openly admitted the problem in a speech given at the CCP Central School in 1997. He said that local officials who reported negative or little growth of religious believers were more likely to be promoted, while conversely those who did not faced demotion. Therefore, government officials of the religious affairs bureau frequently fabricated numbers in reporting to the higher level of authority. But this is not simply a problem limited to lower-rank governments or officials. The State Administration of Religious Affairs itself has maintained in its official statements, from the mid-1990s until now, that "there are about a hundred million believers of all religions in China." No one appears to believe this number even though it is ubiquitous in formal reports and official statements. The repeated utterance of "one hundred million religious believers" by Chinese officials and official publications shows that this has been the upper limit publicly admissible by the CCP.

While the Chinese authorities have underreported the number of Christians in China on public occasions, some Communist officials may have also played up the number internally on occasion. In 2008, an article in the U.S. magazine *Christianity Today* claims, "According to reliable reports, he [Ye Xiaowen] used the 130 million head count [of Christians] at two government briefings in 2006."[4] Many Chinese researchers were also alerted or alarmed by the official talking of the "avalanche growth of Christianity" and asked to carry out research and formulate strategies to control the growth. The higher estimates would make the Christian presence appear to be a bigger threat to the Communist political order; thus more state resources might be steered toward the control apparatus of the religious affairs bureau. Indeed, that apparatus has been increased multiple times in the last two decades.

Interestingly, some Western sources have given higher estimates as well. The missionary organization Asian Harvest asserts that there are 104 million Chinese

Protestant Christians in 2010.[5] The World Christian Database similarly reports 108 million Christians in China in 2010.[6] Some people have even uttered as many as 200 million Chinese Christians.[7] But all of these suggestions are probably higher than the actual.

In this muddled field, some scholars have taken a prudent approach in trying to estimate the number of Christians in the underground or house churches. In the early 1990s, when the official number was 4.5 million Protestants, Allen Hunter and Kim-Kwong Chan concluded that the actual figure of Protestants in China was very likely to be 20 million or more.[8] That is, there were probably three times more Protestants outside the officially approved churches than in them. A decade later, Daniel Bays, following the church researcher Tony Lambert, who examined the numbers of Christians in each of the provinces, cautiously took the number of about 50 million Protestants as a conservative estimate.[9] The highest number of Catholics that has been suggested is about 12 million, and this number has been repeatedly cited for more than a decade by now.[10]

Finally, the report of *Global Christianity* by the Pew Research Center's Forum on Religion and Public Life in 2011, after some careful combing of estimates based on prudent reasoning, concludes, "Based on a review of these estimates, the Pew Forum's demographers think that the 2010 Christian share of China's population is likely in the neighborhood of 5% (or 67 million people of all ages)," which "includes non-adult children of Chinese believers and un-baptized persons who attend Christian worship services." More specifically, it includes 5.7 million Catholics in the state-approved Catholic Patriotic Association, 3.3 million with unregistered Catholic Congregations, 23.05 million Protestants in churches aligned with the state-approved Protestant Three-Self Patriotic Movement Committee, 35 million independent Christians, 20,000 Orthodox Christians, and fewer than 1,000 other Christians such as expatriates living in China.[11]

The various reported or estimated numbers of Protestant Christians are summarized in Table 6.1. It is necessary to note that Table 6.1 includes Protestant Christians in the PRC only. In the Chinese societies of Hong Kong, Macau, and Taiwan, there are also hundreds of thousands of Christians, many of whom migrated from mainland China and maintain ties with Christians in the mainland. In the expansion of freedom in Chinese societies, the roles of Chinese Christians in Taiwan and Hong Kong must be examined along with that of mainland Chinese Christians.

THE DIVERSIFICATION OF CHRISTIAN CONVERTS

Protestant Christianity has grown not only in number but also in diversity in demographic and social backgrounds. The CCP authorities and some Chinese scholars of religious studies habitually characterize Chinese Christianity with the

TABLE 6.1. *Catholic and Protestant Christians in China*
(in parentheses)

Year	Catholics	Protestants
1950	3,000,000	1,000,000
1980	3,000,000	3,000,000
1990	3,500,000	4,500,000
1993		(20,000,000)
1997	4,000,000	10,000,000
2003	(12,000,000)	(50,000,000)
2009	5,300,000	16,000,000
2010		23,050,000
2011	(9,000,000)	(58,000,000)

so-called three more's (*san duo*) or four more's (*si duo*); that is, the majority of Chinese Christians are less educated, old, female, and living in the rural areas. Even if this was so in the 1980s, it is no longer true in the twenty-first century. In the urban areas that I have visited since 2000, there have been clear increases of young and college-educated Christians. At the same time, many of the rural Christians have become urban residents or migrant workers in the cities. I will describe some of the major categories of Christians and their initial rising period in the following.

Rural Christians from the 1950s to the 1980s

Until the 1980s, both the officially sanctioned churches and the underground house churches managed to survive and grow primarily in the rural areas.[12] Several protodenominational networks originated in the central provinces of Henan and Anhui and spread throughout many provinces.[13] This is perhaps due to, in large part, the lack of effective control by the party-state in the countryside.[14] In recent years, along with the rapid industrialization and urbanization, many rural residents have migrated to the urban areas for new opportunities, subsequently forming churches of migrant workers.[15]

Christian Businesspeople in the 1990s

In 1992, the CCP officially set a clear goal of the economic reforms to develop a market economy; thereafter, the private sector of the economy emerged, together with the rise of a new class of entrepreneurs and business in the 1990s. Among them were some Christians. The phenomenon of "Boss-Christians" was especially noticeable in the economically developed Wenzhou area, which has been dubbed China's Jerusalem for the high concentration of Christians in the population.[16] In fact, Christian businesspeople are active in many parts of China.[17] There are also many overseas Chinese Christian entrepreneurs.[18] The rise of Christian businesspeople has been noticed by the media[19] and has helped to change the stereotype of Christianity for many nonbelievers, who began to realize that not all Christians were illiterate, old female peasants. Instead, Christians can be prosperous; that attribute makes Christianity attractive to some non-Christians.

"Cultural Christians" in the 1990s

In spring 1989, there was an exciting prodemocracy movement initiated by college students and intellectuals. However, the movement tragically ended when tanks rolled through the Tiananmen Square on June 4, resulting in the deaths of hundreds, if not thousands, of young people. Interestingly, this tragedy marked a turning point for Chinese intellectuals in their search for spiritual meaning and hope for China. This became noticeable first among the Chinese students and visiting scholars in the United States.[20] In the PRC, after the Tiananmen Square incident, political matters became taboo for research and discussion. Subsequently, some college professors turned their interest to studying Christianity as an element of Western culture. They examined Christian contributions to the humanities; taught courses in philosophy, history, and literature with a focus on Christianity; organized conferences and public forums to discuss Christian theological ideas; and translated books into Chinese.[21] Their activities contributed to the so-called Christianity fever among the college students and college-educated young professionals. The "cultural Christians" in the 1990s were not necessarily committed Christians, but nonetheless they were enthusiastic about the positive contributions of Christianity to modern societies and helped to change further the stereotype of Christianity in the mind of many Chinese people.[22] For many of the "cultural Christians," what began as an interest in the Christian culture ended in accepting the Christian faith and being baptized into the church.

Christian Professionals in the 2000s

In the new century, the college-educated professionals have continued their search in Christianity beyond the college campus. Many new converts are white-collar professionals – engineers, accountants, managers, physicians, teachers, and others. The increase of such Christians has become noticeable both in the newly emerged urban house churches and in the government-sanctioned "Three-Self" churches.[23] Also, since the 1980s, many Chinese have studied abroad in the United States and other countries. Some of them converted to Christianity during their study stay.[24] Some of these overseas converts have returned to China to work as engineers, scientists, and professors, contributing to the growth of Christianity with their overseas experiences and transnational networks.[25]

Christian Artists, Journalists, and Lawyers in the 2000s

Other interesting new categories of Christians include Christian novelists, artists, journalists, and lawyers. Their professions make them influential through cultural activities and mass media. Indeed, some Christian lawyers have become well-known public figures in China because of their relentless defense of civil rights and human rights,[26] which I will describe later.

In sum, Christianity in China has attracted converts from diverse social backgrounds, including middle-class professionals and businesspeople. By now, Christianity in China has shed its image of deprived individuals struggling to survive as marginalized people. Christianity has been winning hearts in the social and cultural mainstream. In fact, even some CCP members and government officials have become Christians as well, even though the CCP officially prohibits its members to become believers of any religion. Evidently, Christianity in China has grown not only in number but also in strength. Christians have made and are making significant contributions to the expansion of freedom in Chinese society.

CHINESE CHRISTIANS AND THE EXPANSION OF FREEDOM IN CHINESE SOCIETY

The contributions of Chinese Christians to the expansion of freedom in Chinese society are great in breadth and depth. Given the continuity of modern Chinese history and transnational links with other Chinese societies, I will first briefly describe Christian contributions before and beyond the PRC. Then I will discuss their multiple contributions in contemporary mainland China.

Before and Beyond the PRC

It would take volumes to document the contributions Christians have made to the expansion of freedom in modern China. These would include improving the physical health from modern/Western medicine and health care to unbinding women's feet and gender equality, to adopting modern printing of books and creating the first magazines and newspapers. As a very brief summary here, we have to mention, at the very least, four spheres: education, the Republican Revolution in 1911, the constitutional protection of religious freedom in the 1910s, and the democratization of the Republic of China on Taiwan since the 1970s.

First is the Christian contribution to modern education. Yung Wing (1828–1912) was the first Chinese student to graduate from an American college. Sponsored by Christian missionaries and families, Yung graduated from Yale in 1854. Instead of entering the Christian ministry as expected by his sponsors, he dedicated himself to helping to strengthen China through education. The most outstanding contribution he made was his initiative of the Chinese Educational Mission (1872–1881), which sent 120 young Chinese students to study in New England. Many of these students became the first engineers and educators in modern China.[27] Following this tradition, many Chinese Christians have dedicated themselves to modern education, establishing hundreds of Christian and independent schools and colleges.[28] In the twenty-first century, education will be one of the major areas used by Chinese Christians to resist the state monopoly.

Second is the Christian contribution to the Republican Revolution. Sun Zhongshan (Sun Yat-sen 1866–1925) was the founding father and the first president of the Republic of China (ROC). He first learned about Christianity in Hawaii in an Anglican school and was later baptized in Hong Kong by an American missionary of the Congregational Church. His revolutionary activities and his blueprint for the new republic are arguably rooted in his Christian faith. Huang Xing (1874–1916), a close friend of Sun, who commanded a number of uprisings against the Qing government and became the first commander-in-chief of the Republic of China, was also a Christian, as were many of the revolutionaries and martyrs in the period leading to the establishment of the Republic of China in 1912.[29] The Christian contribution to the Republican Revolution is understudied and not widely known until now.[30]

Third is the Christian contribution to the protection of religious freedom. Christians campaigned for the constitutional protection of religious freedom in the early years of the ROC. Under President Sun Zhongshan, the Provisional Constitution of the ROC contained a clear statement: "All people of the Republic are equal regardless of race, class and religion. . . . All people have the right to believe in religion." However, some Confucianists advocated establishing Confucianism as the state religion in the constitution. Soon after the founding of the ROC, a Constitution Drafting Committee was organized with thirty elected members from the Congress. But the first constitution was not enacted until 1923, and it remained in effect for only one year before China fell apart in civil wars. A major dispute was about religious freedom during the deliberation process. While Confucianists wanted a clause respecting Confucianism, the Christian members of the Congress strongly opposed it. Christians also mobilized religious believers to uphold religious freedom in the constitution. Protestant Christians first formed the Beijing Association for Religious Freedom and against State Religion in September 1913 and submitted their statement to the Congress. Catholics, Buddhists, and Daoists followed suit in pronouncing the same position. Protestant denominations held a united meeting on October 20, 1913. Then,

> on November 27 [of 1913], the representatives of Buddhism, Daoism, and Islam, along with the Catholic and Protestant representatives in Beijing, held the second united meeting. As a result, the United Petition League of All Religions was finally established. The aim of this league was to "ask for religious freedom and protest against the state religion, as well as to prevent any law that would lead to religious inequality."[31]

In 1916, the Society for Religious Freedom was formally founded. Headquartered in Beijing with well-organized departments, "the society held meetings and speeches, sent letters and telegrams, propagated its ideas, and established local offices."[32] The Christian-led efforts succeeded in preserving the religious freedom clause in the constitution of the early ROC. After the Resistance War against the Japanese Invasion, a new constitution of the ROC was enacted in 1947; it reaffirmed the religious freedom clause and no establishment of Confucianism. This has been the constitution of the ROC to today, even though the ROC retreated to the island of Taiwan in 1949.

Fourth is in Christian contribution to the democratization of the Republic of China on Taiwan. Christians played important and complicated roles in the peaceful democratic transition of the Republic of China on Taiwan. The ROC Constitution of 1947 was suspended in the following year as a result of the escalation of the civil war between the CCP and Kuomintang (the Nationalist Party). When the People's Republic of China was established in 1949 in the mainland, the Republic of China government and Kuomintang under the leadership of Chiang Kai-shek retreated to the island of Taiwan. Martial law was imposed in the ROC on Taiwan and was not lifted until 1987. Beginning in the early 1970s, democratic movements gained momentum in Taiwan and eventually brought about full democratization. Already now there have been several rounds of presidential elections and the alteration of the ruling party.

At first, some Christian churches and other religious groups contended for greater religious freedom.[33] The Taiwan Presbyterian Church, the largest denomination in Taiwan, made declarations for human rights and concerning the future of the country; they openly supported the political dissident movements, and some of the dissidents were even Christians themselves.[34] Meanwhile, within the ROC government there were also Christians among top leaders. In fact, President Chiang Kai-shek and his successor, his son, Chiang Ching-kuo, were Christians. The next successor in the Kuomintang, Lee Teng-hui, who later became the first democratically elected president of the ROC in 1996, was also a Christian. In 2012 I interviewed the Reverend Lien-hwa Chow, who was the preacher at the congregation Chiang Kai-shek attended, and the minister who baptized Chiang Ching-kuo. I also interviewed the Reverend Chun-Ming Kao, the former general secretary of the Presbyterian Church in Taiwan, who was imprisoned in 1980–1984 for his support of the political dissidents. My interviews with these two most prominent Christian leaders in Taiwan made me realize the importance and complexity of the faith factor in the political process and democratic transition of the ROC in Taiwan. Even though some scholars have studied religion and democratization in Taiwan,[35] the faith factor, especially the roles of Christian leaders and organizations, has not been given due credit, waiting for more systematic examination.

Christians Fighting for Their Own Religious Freedom in the PRC

In the PRC under the CCP, Catholics and Protestants have shown the most tenacity in preserving their religious freedom under severe persecution in the first three decades. Some Protestant leaders such as Y. T. Wu (Wu Yaozong), K. H. Ting (Ding Guangxun), and T. C. Chao (Zhao Zichen) cooperated with the CCP closely and eventually were co-opted into the control apparatus of the Christian Three-Self Patriotic Movement Committee. But other Protestant leaders, especially of indigenous denominations and independent churches, such as Wang Mingdao in Beijing, Watchman Nee (Ni Tuosheng) in Shanghai, and Samuel Lamb (Lin Xiangao) in Guangzhou, rejected cooperation in spite of imprisonment for two to three decades. When the "union services" (*lianhe libai*) under the TSPM committee were forced on Protestants, that is, Protestant Christians of different denominations and churches had to join the same worship services organized by the local TSPM committee, in 1957, many Christians stopped attending church and moved underground to hold gatherings at homes or in the wilderness. The house church movement was thus born, preserving the seeds for revivals in the 1970s and 1980s.[36]

The Catholic clergy was even more audacious in resistance, in alignment with the Vatican's opposition to communism. When the CCP authorities were trying to form the Catholic Patriotic Association, for several years they were unable to find any bishop willing to cooperate. Like Protestant leaders, some Catholics were imprisoned for two to three decades. Most prominently, Bishop of Shanghai Ignatius Kung Pin-Mei (Gong Pinmei) was arrested in 1955 and sentenced to life imprisonment for his counterrevolutionary activities.[37] Eventually, the party-state could only manage to form the Catholic Laity Patriotic Association in 1957; it was renamed the Catholic Patriotic Association after some new bishops were selected without Vatican approval. The underground Catholic Church has persisted until today in their resistance in spite of the frequent imprisonment and torture of bishops and priests.

The tenacity of both Protestants and Catholics, along with that of other religions, eventually forced the CCP to abandon the eradication policy. In 1979, when some churches were reopened for religious service, the "patriotic" associations were restored as well. These associations at local and national levels worked to reopen many churches, serving as the middlemen in negotiations with various government agencies and residents to return church properties to Christians and reestablishing Christian seminaries. But many Christians continue to perceive the "patriotic" associations as part of the party-state control apparatus and have refused to join. A well-known case is the house church in Guangzhou that met at the home of Samuel Lamb (Lin Xiangao). From the 1980s, he regularly gathered hundreds of people at his home for Bible study and worship service. The control apparatus disrupted it many times, including taking away the sound system and detaining Lamb, but the weekly gatherings have continued at his home to today. The underground and house churches have persisted, remaining a perennial headache for the control apparatus.

In the twenty-first century, along with formerly rural Christians moving to the urban areas and forming the migrant workers' churches – house churches outside the "patriotic" association – some new types of house churches have emerged in metropolitan areas of Beijing, Shanghai, Wuhan, Chengdu, Guangzhou, Xi'an, and other cities. Many of these church members are college-educated young professionals. As self-identified spiritual heirs of the house church movement, these new professionals' churches refuse to join the "patriotic" association, even though some of them have tried to gain legal status by applying for registration directly with the Religious Affairs Bureau. One example is the Shouwang Church in Beijing.

The founding pastor of Shouwang Church, Jin Tianming, was a student at Tsinghua University when the 1989 democracy movement and Tiananmen Square incident happened. As a new convert to Christianity, he dedicated himself to evangelism and founded a number of small groups that met for Bible study and Sunday worship services at people's homes. In 2003, the small groups were combined as a unified congregation for corporate Sunday worship service at a rented hall in an office building. Armed with the knowledge of the constitution that promises the freedom of religious belief and other laws and ordinances, they submitted an application in 2005 to the Haidian District Religious Affairs Bureau for legal recognition. The bureau responded with a requirement that the Shouwang Church join the Haidian Christian Three-Self Patriotic Movement Committee and have their pastors certified by that committee. The Shouwang Church refused on the basis of both the constitution and the new Regulations of Religious Affairs that took effect on March 1, 2005, which do not include such explicit requirements. After the application was rejected, Shouwang Church submitted a petition to the

Religious Affairs Bureau of the Beijing Municipality, which has not yet responded. In the meantime, the police, joined by the other agencies of the control apparatus, have made several attempts to disrupt and dismiss the Sunday worship service of Shouwang Church. At one such disruption in 2008, the police videotaped all who attended, made records of their identification cards and employment information, and followed up with warnings through their employers and school counselors that they should stop attending. One of the elders of Shouwang Church was an associate professor of philosophy at Renmin University. Facing pressures from the university, instead of giving up attending and serving the church, he submitted a formal letter to withdraw from the CCP. Interestingly, that application was not approved either. Failing to pressure the church members to stop attending, the control apparatus then turned to the real estate owner to cancel the rental contract with the church and to prevent other real estate owners from renting a hall to the church. Shouwang Church responded by mobilizing resources and purchasing halls in an office building, paying in full with cash. After learning about it, the control apparatus pressured the real estate developer into not giving them the keys to the church. Since Easter 2011, the Shouwang Church has been evicted from the rental hall and prevented from entering their purchased property, and the church leaders have been prevented from leaving their homes on the weekend. Senior Pastor Jin Tianming has been, in effect, under house arrest to this day. In spite of such measures of persecution, the Shouwang Church has persisted by bonding together through small groups. Also, the church has called for holding the Sunday worship service at a public square in a commercial plaza. Every Sunday, there are two dozen or more members trying to go to that square with a printed order of worship service, and every Sunday, police have guarded that square and rounded up the worshippers but released them a few hours later. This has continued every Sunday since Easter Sunday of 2011. Since summer 2014, the Sunday temporary detentions have turned to administrative detentions for the most active lay leaders, but some members continue to attempt to go to the plaza for their Sunday worship gathering.

Shouwang's fight for their religious freedom may appear to be unsuccessful because it has not succeeded in holding a Sunday worship service in that public square or at its purchased or rented halls. However, its resistance has probably raised the costs for the party-state authorities to impose strict control, thus serving as a deterrent to the control apparatus for further actions against other house churches, which number in the thousands in Beijing. In short, the Shouwang Church has fought in the front line of resistance so that other house churches can continue to operate with few problems. Indeed, the house churches in Beijing and other cities have been growing, and many of them have been very open about their activities. Many house churches put their worship service photos and video recordings of the 2013 Christmas celebrations on Internet Web sites.

Several house churches in Chengdu in the southwest have formed an alliance – a presbytery. This is a pioneering development. The alliance of the churches has established a library open to the public, a seminary to train ministers, and a day school for school-age children and has its own printing and publishing departments. Even though none of these are considered legal in China today, these house churches nonetheless have been able to operate with few disruptions by the control apparatus. The founding pastor of the Autumn Rain Blessings Church in Chengdu, Wang Yi, converted to Christianity in 2005. He was a professor of jurisprudence before he quit in 2008 to become a full-time minister. He stated at a public forum on January 8, 2013, at Purdue University that despite problems from the authorities, his church is practicing all the freedoms promised by the Chinese constitution: freedom of religious belief, freedom of assembly (church gatherings), freedom of speech (preaching), and freedom of the press (printing and distributing books, booklets, newsletters, and other materials).

Evidently, the tenacious fights of the house churches have been pushing the envelope of restriction and have succeeded in enlarging the free space for their religious practice. Even though every step forward incurs some costs, including financial, material, physical, and psychological costs for house church Christians, their efforts have rendered the containment policy of the party-state ineffective. The number of house churches has apparently increased, both in the form of small groups meeting at people's homes and in large congregations meeting at big sanctuaries.

Christian Lawyers Fighting for Civil and Human Rights

In the new century, there has been the rise of *"weiquan* lawyers," lawyers and professors in law schools who have taken up cases of civil rights and human rights. In December 2005, the *Yazhou Zhoukan (Asia Weekly)* in Hong Kong selected *weiquan* lawyers in the PRC as the "Persons of the Year." This was the first high-profile media coverage of the rising *weiquan* lawyers. *Weiquan* lawyers seek to work within the existing legal system and call on the authorities to honor the protection of rights promised in the constitution and codified in various laws, challenging some laws and ordinances that violate the constitution. There are a series of well-known court cases, two of which are illustrative of the *weiquan* movement.

In 2003, three law school students led the campaign to abolish the "custody and repatriation" regulation, which gave the police the power to detain anyone who did not carry a valid ID card or local resident permit (*hukou*) and return him to his original home region. Moreover, the detainees were often tortured before being repatriated. On March 20, 2003, a college graduate seeking employment in Guangzhou was detained and beaten to death at the detention center. After this was reported in the media, three law students and some senior scholars of jurisprudence sent open letters to the authorities and spoke to the media, claiming the regulation made by the State Council was unconstitutional and that laws should be passed by the People's Congress instead of the administration. Three months later, on June 20, Premier Wen Jiabao of the State Council announced the abolition of the regulation. This victory was encouraging to the *weiquan* movement.

In 2004, a house church minister in Beijing, Mr. Cai Zhuohua, was arrested for printing and distributing Bibles. This was considered a political case of "overseas infiltration of religion" because Mr. Cai used donations from overseas to print and distribute more than 200,000 Bibles and Bible-related books. However, the official allegation in court was "illegal business operation," which is the common charge authorities have used for religious suppression. In 2005, several lawyers and legal scholars joined to defend Mr. Cai Zhuohua and his coworkers at a court in Beijing. Their main argument was that Mr. Cai was not operating a business and did not gain financial profit through the operation. His printing and distributing Bibles were for the purpose of evangelism, which is a right guaranteed by the Chinese constitution. Therefore, this was a case of religious persecution in the name of economic crime. The defense lawyers also pointed out the police's violations of procedural codes during the process of detention and interrogation. However, the court ignored the defense arguments and sentenced Mr. Cai to a three-year prison term for the said economic crime. Afterward, the lawyers released the court arguments through the Internet. The well-made arguments and fearless contests of these lawyers won the respect of the public.

In its special "Persons of the Year" issue, the *Yazhou Zhoukan* profiled fourteen prominent *weiquan* lawyers, including many of those involved in the Cai Zhuohua case. Interestingly, seven of the fourteen lawyers were self-identified Christians, two had Christian family members, and another three expressed strong interest in Christian beliefs. Actually, many of the Christians among the *weiquan* lawyers are recent converts to Christianity, most likely because the Christian faith provides them an anchorage for their life and fight for justice.[38]

The Christian *weiquan* lawyers have defended many cases involving not only Christians, but also other religious groups, including Tibetan Buddhist monks, Falun Gong followers, and followers of the so-called evil cults designated by the Chinese authorities.[39] Those cases have proven to be even more dangerous to the defense lawyers. Many of them have been disbarred, physically threatened, or injured during confrontations with the police, and some even imprisoned. The most well-known person in this regard is Mr. Gao Zhisheng. After defending Mr. Cai Zhuohua, he went on to investigate persecutions reported by followers of Falun Gong and subsequently wrote several open letters to the CCP calling for religious freedom. The Chinese authorities responded with detentions, tortures, and eventually imprisonment in a remote prison in Xinjiang in the far west. Among the fourteen prominent *weiquan* lawyers profiled by the *Yazhou Zhoukan*, almost all have had troubles with the authorities, and some are in prison, in exile, or under house arrest.

In spite of the harsh treatment, the number of Christian *weiquan* lawyers is increasing. Beginning in 2006, some of them have tried to form fellowship associations for mutual support and collaboration. Since 2013, dozens of Christian *weiquan* lawyers have mobilized for the legal battles involving Christian churches in Henan and Shaanxi. One of the cases in the Pingdingshan Municipality of Henan concerns followers of a sect that the authorities regard as a cult. In another case in Nanle County of Henan, the authorities arrested the leader of the Protestant Three-Self Patriotic Movement Committee and several coworkers. This Christian leader in the officially sanctioned church had engaged in a series of *weiquan* activities. The church coworkers also tried to protect the interest of their church against the real estate developer supported by the new CCP secretary of the county. In each of these cases, more than a dozen *weiquan* lawyers from various parts of China joined efforts to defend the rights of the accused.

On May 5–7, 2014, a symposium on religious freedom in Chinese society was held at Purdue University, and the participants included some of the most active *weiquan* lawyers in China (two of the invited lawyers were stopped at the Beijing airport by police and prevented from leaving China for participating in this symposium), Chinese Christian ministers in China and those based in North America who have frequently traveled to China, and academic scholars. The symposium discussed legal cases involving religion in recent years, principles and practices to defend the rights of Chinese citizens of Christian churches in the Three-Self Patriotic Movement Committee system, of Christian house churches in rural and urban areas, of underground and aboveground Catholic bodies, of Christianity-related sectarian and heretical groups, and of non-Christian religions such as the Falun Gong, Tibetan Buddhism, and Islam.

After three-day engaging discussions, some consensus emerged among the participants who had different positions. Consequently, some participants initiated the drafting of a text of consensus for signatures so that the understanding of religious freedom can be spread and greater attention can be paid to the issues of religious freedom in China. The text was finalized after further discussion by the symposium participants. A week later, the text and a list of the fifty-two initial signatories of the Purdue Consensus on Religious Freedom were released to the public on May 14, 2014.[40] Since then, more people have expressed their support for the consensus and have spread the statements of the consensus text through Chinese blogs and social media. As a scholar and a participant and observer of this unprecedented event, I was most impressed by the broadmindedness of the Chinese Christian leaders. While firm in their Christian faith and conservative in their evangelical theology, they are simultaneously ardent modern citizens self-consciously inheriting the universal values as embodied in the United Nations' Charter, Universal Declaration of Human Rights, and several other covenants. In a time when the Chinese Communist party-state has mounted a new round of anti-Christian campaigns by demolishing church buildings and persecuting Christian leaders,[41] the consensus is a timely declaration that gives some hope for a better China in the future.

Christians Fighting for the Political Freedom

After the 1989 democracy movement and the Tiananmen Square massacre, many of the movement leaders fled to the United States and other Western countries. A significant number of the well-known exiled democracy fighters have since converted to Christianity, including Yuan Zhiming, Xiong Yan, Zhou Fengsuo, Zhang Boli, and Chai Ling, who were on the most wanted lists of the Chinese authorities in 1989. Although some of them, such as Yuan Zhiming and Zhang Boli, have become ministers and devoted themselves to saving individual souls through evangelism instead of saving the Chinese nation through direct political activism, they continue to be concerned about and hopeful for China's democratization. Others have continued in their activism. Zhou Fengsuo has led a foundation to provide support for the families of political prisoners in China and, in recent years, has sponsored some veteran dissidents or their children out of China to the United States. Chai Ling established a charity organization for girls and women in China, fighting for their equality and against forced abortion and infanticide. Bob Fu's ChinaAid is a powerful organization campaigning for religious freedom and human rights in China, including rescuing the blind activist Chen Guangcheng and some other political dissidents. Yu Jie, a Christian writer and public critic, has been outspoken in openly criticizing the PRC politicians. In his biography of Liu Xiaobo, the Nobel Prize Laureate in peace who has been imprisoned in China, Yu Jie claims that Liu Xiaobo may have accepted Christian beliefs.

Indeed, a number of veteran political dissidents and prisoners in the PRC, both past and present, are Christians. For example, Wang Bingzhang (b. 1947) was probably the first PRC national who earned a doctorate degree in Western society. Upon receiving his doctorate in pathology in 1982 from McGill University, he started *China Spring*, the first Chinese language prodemocracy magazine edited by the mainland Chinese and published in North America. He traveled to China many times and cofounded political parties to challenge the one-party rule of the CCP. In 2002, he was abducted while traveling in Vietnam and taken into custody in China, later sentenced to life in prison.[42] Another political prisoner is Liu Xianbin (b. 1968), who was an active participant in the 1989 Democracy Movement and has been imprisoned multiple times for his persistent activism, including publishing articles on the Internet calling for democratic reform and organizing the China Democracy

The numerical growth will inevitably lead to social and political changes. However, given the unusual rapidity, which leaves little time for preparation by Christians and non-Christians, it is difficult to predict what kind of social and political changes the Christianization of China will effect in China and the globalizing world. As this book examines Christianity and freedom in historical and global contexts, these questions are particularly pertinent here: Will the Christianization of China continue to introduce greater freedom for everyone in China, or will we see some kind of theocracy, like the Constantine Roman Empire, which led to religious inquisitions, religious wars, and the arguable Dark Ages?

Recently, some Chinese Christian intellectuals have begun to engage in public discussions about church-state relations in Chinese politics, articulating their vision for a pluralistic and democratic China. Moreover, they have taken the initiative to organize conferences for such discussions. Sponsored and organized by Chinese Christians, some of the Chinese public intellectuals in four different ideological streams joined for the first time in August 2013 in Oxford, England. "Remarkably, for a group of people who in Chinese public life are often at each other's throats, they came up with what is now being dubbed the 'Oxford Consensus' – four theses expressing their hopes for a pluralistic, liberal China."[49] This is a hopeful development with great promise. More recently, the Purdue Consensus on Religious Freedom in 2014 gives this author more hope for a future China that might be able to take the historical lessons in the previous Christendom and strive for a better world.

NOTES

1 For a translation and commentary on this CCP circular, see Donald E. MacInnis, *Religion in China Today: Policy and Practice* (Maryknoll, NY: Orbis Books, 1994).
2 It is said that the name was from the CCP directive on June 10, 1999, which established this anticult ministry.
3 Lian, Xi, *Redeemed by Fire: The Rise of Popular Christianity in Modern China*. New Haven, CT: Yale University Press, 2010: 204.
4 Rob Moll, "Great Leap Forward: China Is Changing and So Is Its Church," *Christianity Today*, 52, no. 5 (2008): 22–33.
5 Paul Hattaway, "How Many Christians Are There in China?" *Asia Harvest* (www .asiaharvest.org), http://www.asiaharvest.org/pages/Christians%20in%20China/How%20 Many%20Christians%20are%20There%20in%20China.pdf, 2010.
6 World Christian Database, http://www.worldchristiandatabase.org/wcd/, 2010.
7 Philip Jenkins, "Who's Counting China?" *Christian Century*, August 10, 2010, 45.
8 Allen Hunter and Kim-Kwong Chan, *Protestantism in Contemporary China* (Cambridge: Cambridge University Press, 1993), 66.
9 Daniel Bays, "Chinese Protestant Christianity Today," *China Quarterly* 174, no. 2 (2003): 488–504; Tony Lambert, *China's Christian Millions* (London and Grand Rapids, MI: Monarch Books, 1999).

10 Richard Madsen, "Catholic Revival during the Reform Era." *China Quarterly* 174, no. 2(2003): 468–487. Holy Spirit Study Center, 2009. "Estimated Statistics for Chinese Catholic 2009," http://www.hsstudyc.org.hk/en/china/en_cinfo_china_stat09.html

11 Pew Research Center's Forum on Religion and Public Life, Global Christianity: A Report on the Size and Distribution of the World's Christian Population, 2011: 97–98.

12 Ka Lun Leung, *The Rural Churches of Mainland China since 1978* (Hong Kong: Alliance Bible Seminary, 1990); J. Chao and R. Chong, *A History of Christianity in Socialist China, 1949–1997* (Taipei: China Ministries International Publishing, 1997).

13 David Ackman, *Jesus in Beijing: How Christianity Is Transforming China and Changing the Global Balance of Power* (Washington, DC: Regnery, 2003).

14 Jianbo Huang and Fenggang Yang, "The Cross Faces the Loudspeakers: A Village Church Perseveres under State Power," in *State, Market, and Religions in Chinese Societies*, ed. Fenggang Yang and Josphe Tamney (Leiden and Boston, MA: Brill, 2005), 41–62.

15 Fuk-tsang Ying, Hao Yuan, and Siu-lun Lau, "Striving to Build Civic Communities: Four Types of Protestant Churches in Beijing," *Review of Religion and Chinese Society* 1, no. 1(2014): 78–103.

16 Cunfu Chen and Tianhai Huang, "The Emergence of a New Type of Christians in China Today," *Review of Religious Research* 46, no. 2 (2004): 183–200; Nanlai Cao, *Constructing China's Jerusalem: Christians, Power, and Place in Contemporary Wenzhou* (Stanford, CA: Stanford University Press, 2011).

17 I, along with some collaborators in China, have interviewed many Christian businesspeople and published descriptions and analyses. See Fenggang Yang, "The Chinese Protestant Ethic during the Market Transition in China" (in Chinese), in *Searching for a Path: Christian Faith and Contemporary Chinese Society*, ed. Xiyi Yao (Hong Kong: CGST Press, 2007), 107–139; Xiangping Li and Fenggang Yang, "Christian Ethics and the Construction of Social Trust: Christian Enterprises in Contemporary China" (in Chinese), 287–302 in Gao, Shining and Fenggang Yang, eds. *From the Armchair to the Field: Selected Articles of the Beijing Summit on Chinese Spirituality and Society*, vol. 2 (Beijing: China Social Sciences Press, 2010), 287–302; Gao Shining and Fenggang Yang, "Religious Faith and the Market Economy: A Survey on Faith and Trust of Catholic Entrepreneurs in China," in *Money as God?: The Monetization of the Market and Its Impact on Religion, Politics, Law and Ethics*, ed. Jürgen von Hagen and Michael Welker (Cambridge: Cambridge University Press, 2014), 339–361.

18 Joy Kooi-Chin Tong, *Overseas Chinese Christian Entrepreneurs in Modern China: A Case Study of the Influence of Christian Ethics on Business Life* (London and New York: Anthem Press, 2012).

19 E.g., Carol Huang, "Christianity in a Chinese Workplace? For Some," *Christian Science Monitor*, July 2, 2008, http://www.csmonitor.com/World/Asia-Pacific/2008/0702/p01s05-woap.html; R. Scott Macintosh "China's Prosperity Inspires Rising Spirituality," *Christian Science Monitor*, March 9, 2006, http://www.csmonitor.com/2006/0309/p01s04-woap.html

20 Fenggang Yang, *Chinese Christians in America: Conversion, Assimilation, and Adhesive Identities* (University Park, PA: Penn State University Press, 1999).

21 John W. Kennedy, "Disciplining the Dragon: Christian Publishing Finds Success in China," *Christianity Today*, January 20, 2012, http://www.christianitytoday.com/ct/2012/january/publishing-success-china.html

22 Fredrik Fällman, "Faith, Hope, Love and Modernity Reflections on 'Cultural Christians' in Contemporary China," *Monumenta Serica* 54(2006): 405–415.

23 Ying, Yuan and Lau, "Striving to Build."

24 See Yang, *Chinese Christians in America*; Andrew Abel, "Favor Fishing and Punch-Bowl Christians: Ritual and Conversion in a Chinese Protestant Church," *Sociology of Religion* 67, no. 2 (2006): 161–178; Brian Hall, "Social and Cultural Contexts in Conversion to Christianity Among Chinese American College Students," *Sociology of Religion* 67, no. 2 (2006): 131–147; Yuting Wang and Fenggang Yang, "More than Evangelical and Ethnic: The Ecological Factor in Chinese Conversion to Christianity in the United States," *Sociology of Religion: A Quarterly Review* 67, no. 2 (2006):179–192. See also Yu Miao, "Chinese Students Find Faith, and a Home, in a Foreign Land," Religion News Service," April 17, 2009, http://www.purdue.edu/crcs/itemNews/RNSnews/RNSnews.html; Reshma Kirpalani, "Chinese Students Choosing Christianity," ABC News, March 10, 2011, http://abcnews.go.com/US/chinese-students-choose-christianity/story?id=13086190

25 See Fenggang Yang, "Chinese Christian Transnationalism: Diverse Networks of a Houston Church," in *Religions across Borders: Transnational Religious Networks*, ed. Helen Rose Ebaugh and Janet S. Chafetz (Walnut Creek, CA: AltaMira Press, 2002), 129–148.

26 See Rana Siu Inboden and William Inboden, "Faith and Law in China," *Far Eastern Economic Review* 172, no. 7 (2009): 44–47.

27 Liel Leibovitz and Matthew I. Miller, *Fortunate Sons: The 120 Chinese Boys Who Came to America, Went to School, and Revolutionized an Ancient Civilization.* New York: Norton, 2011. Edward J. M. Rhoads, *Stepping Forth into the World: The Chinese Educational Mission to the United States, 1872–81* (Hong Kong: Hong Kong University Press, 2011).

28 Daniel H. Bays and Ellen Widmer, eds. 2009. *China's Christian Colleges: Cross-Cultural Connections, 1900–1950* (Stanford, CA: Stanford University Press, 2009).

29 Li Jinqiang, Li Zhigang, Lin Zhiping, Zha Shijie, and Wei Waiyang. *A Hundred Christians in the History of the Last A Hundred Years* (Taipei: Cosmic Light, 2011).

30 Lin, Chi-ping, "Centennial Witnesses," *Cosmic Light* 450 (2011.10).

31 Yi Liu, "Confucianism, Christianity, and Religious Freedom: Debates in the Transformation Period of Modern China (1900–1920)," in *Confucianism and Spiritual Traditions in Modern China and Beyond*, ed. Fenggang Yang and Joseph B. Tamney (Leiden and Boston: Brill, 2012), 259–260.

32 Ibid., 263.

33 Pen-hsuan Lin, *A Study of Church-State Conflicts in Taiwan* (Taipei: Daoxiang Press, 1994); Hei-yuan Chiu, *Religion, Magic and Social Change* (Taipei: Guiguan Books, 2006).

34 Lien-Hwa Chow, *Memoir* (Taipei: Lianhe Wenxue Chubanshe [United Literature Press], 1994); Chun-ming Kao, *The Path of the Cross: A Memoir* (Taipei: Wangchunfeng Wenhua Shiye, 2001).

35 E.g., Richard Madsen, *Democracy's Dharma: Religious Renaissance and Political Development in Taiwan* (Berkeley and Los Angeles: University of California Press, 2007); Cheng-tian Kuo, *Religion and Democracy in Taiwan* (Albany: State University of New York Press, 2008).

36 Chao and Chong, *A History of Christianity in Socialist China*,; David Aikman, *Jesus in Beijing: How Christianity is Transforming China and Changing the Global Balance of Power* (Washington, DC: Regnery Publishing, Inc., 2003); Zhiming Yuan, *The Cross: Jesus in China* (A Documentary film, Petaluma, CA: China Soul for Christ Foundation, 2003).

37 Kung was secretly named a *cardinal in pectore* in the consistory of 1979 by Pope John Paul II. He was released in 1985, was exiled to the United States in 1988, and died in 2000.

38 Inboden and Inboden, "Faith and Law in China."

39 Eva Pils, "Asking the Tiger for His Skin: Rights Activism in China," *Fordham International Law Journal* 30, no. 4 (2006):1208–1287. Human Rights Watch, *"Walking on Thin Ice": Control, Intimidation and Harassment of Lawyers in China* (New York: Human Rights Watch, 2008).

40 See "Purdue Consensus on Religious Freedom with Signatories," http://www.purdue .edu/crcs/itemMeetings/purdueSymposium/purdueSymposium2014/consensus.html

41 Ian Johnson, "Church-State Clash in China Coalesces around a Toppled Spire," *New York Times*, A4, May 30, 2014.

42 BBC, "China's Veteran Dissident Wang Bingzhang." 2003, http://news.bbc.co.uk/2/hi/ asia-pacific/2593593.stm, accessed on February 14, 2014.

43 Reuters, "Dissident Gets 'Unusually Harsh' 10 Years' Jail." March 28, 2011.

44 Yang, Jianli, Echoes of Tiananmen Square. *Washington Post*, September 30, 2007.

45 Fenggang Yang, "The Chinese Protestant Ethic."

46 Fenggang Yang, *Religion in China: Survival and Revival under Communist Rule* (New York: Oxford University Press, 2012).

47 Fenggang Yang, "Lost in the Market, Saved at McDonald's: Conversion to Christianity in Urban China," *Journal for the Scientific Study of Religion* 44, no. 4 (2005): 423–441.

48 Rodney Stark, *The Rise of Christianity: A Sociologist Reconsiders History* (Princeton, NJ: Princeton University Press, 1996).

49 Ian Johnson, "Qa. and A.: Yang Fenggang on the 'Oxford Consensus' and Public Trust in China," Ian. 2013. http://sinosphere.blogs.nytimes.com/2013/10/18/q-a-yang-fenggang-on-the-oxford-consensus-and-public-trust-in-china/?_php=true&_type=blogs&_php= true&_type=blogs&_r=2, accessed on February 14, 2014.

7

Christianity and Religious Freedom in Indonesia since 1998

Zainal Abidin Bagir and Robert W. Hefner

EXECUTIVE SUMMARY

With a population of almost 250 million people, 87.2 percent of whom are Muslim, Indonesia is today the largest Muslim majority society in the world. Some 9.9 percent of the population is Christian, 7 percent Protestant; 2.9 percent Catholic. Indonesia is also third largest and one of the younger among the world's democracies, having undergone a transition from authoritarian rule to electoral democracy in May 1998.

Christian leaders interviewed in 2013 for this report were of the opinion that Christians enjoyed a freer and more socially favorable situation prior to the events of 1998 and that the country's transition to a more open political system has heightened social and religious tensions. Christian interviewees pointed to a heightened frequency of attacks on church buildings, greater difficulty in securing permits for the construction of churches and schools, and pressures to restrict the number of Christians in the higher levels of state administration, among other obstacles, as evidence of a relative deterioration in interreligious relations. However, these same Christian officials were unhesitant in affirming that the transition to democracy is necessary and important and that the best way to address current deficiencies is by working with Muslims and others to promote the rule of law and multireligious tolerance. Some officials criticized earlier generations of Christian leaders for being too accommodating to the Indonesian state. Most felt that the resources for pluralist coexistence, including those in the Muslim community, were still strong but had yet to be fully mobilized or backed up by an effective legal system.

The Indonesian case importantly illustrates that although Christians have made signal contributions to Indonesian politics, culture, and education, Dutch colonialism and the mission system it promoted were premised on a corporatist and consociational rather than liberal model of religious freedom. For most of their 350 years in the archipelago, the Dutch prioritized their commercial and political interests and discouraged missionization in all but a few regions. When, at the end of the nineteenth century, the Dutch gave the green light to missionaries, their policies set aside specific territories for individual denominations, encouraging a close identification of region, ethnicity, and denomination rather than religious liberty or individualistic voluntarism.

Since independence, most Indonesian Christians have advocated policies supportive of religious freedom. But they have done so in a framework that accepts the broadly consociational patterns of religious governance inherited from the Dutch. As in the early twentieth-century Netherlands, consociationalism is a political system in which (to quote the political scientist Arend Lijphart) "the centrifugal tendencies in a plural society are counteracted by the cooperative attitudes and behavior of the leaders of the different segments of the population." Contrary to some Anglo-American models of religious governance, in consociational systems the state characteristically works with religious leaders to recognize and demarcate state-authorized religious groupings, so that the state can provide funds for their schools, houses of worship, and social welfare services. Faith communities that do not enjoy state recognition are at a legal and social disadvantage.

It is this variety of religious freedom and governance that today prevails in Indonesia. Rather than rejecting its terms, Indonesian Christians have for the most part welcomed its consociational guarantees – even while pressing the government to abide more faithfully by its terms.

INTRODUCTION

With a population of almost 250 million people, 87.2 percent of whom are Muslim, Indonesia is today the largest Muslim majority society in the world. It is also third largest and one of the younger among the world's democracies. Some 9.9 percent of the population is Christian, 7 percent Protestant; 2.9 percent Catholic.[1] The remaining 3 percent of the population is made up of (in order of declining demographic numbers) Hindus, Buddhists, and Confucians, as well as a few hundred thousand practitioners of local or ethnic religions. The diversity of Indonesian culture and the challenge of religious freedom are compounded by the fact that the country has more than three hundred ethnic groups distributed across three thousand inhabited islands. Indonesia is also distinctive in that, prior to the great wave of Islamization that occurred between the thirteenth and eighteenth centuries, the region's major kingdoms were Hindu or Hindu-Buddhist.

In the modern period, interreligious relations have at times been marked by social tension. Faced with a restless Muslim population, European colonialism promoted a policy not of liberal freedom, but of consociational corporatism, in which state officials sought to manage religious communities and maintain civic order through top-down controls on religious leadership and public expression. During the last eight decades of their rule, Dutch colonial authorities imposed strict controls on Islamic schooling, pilgrimage, and associations. From the late nineteenth century onward, Dutch officials also promoted non-Muslim conversion to Christianity in a few portions of the archipelago, in an effort to counter the spread of Islam into non-Muslim territories. In those regions where missions were allowed, the colonial government allocated specific territories to the representatives of one church, rather than encouraging a liberal pattern of multiconfessional freedom. Different varieties of Christianity came to be associated with specific territories and ethnic groups.

Notwithstanding these policies, native Christians in Indonesia played a positive role in the struggle for national independence. No less significantly, in the first three decades following the declaration of independence in August 1945, Christians exercised influence in the young country's leadership disproportionate to their numbers in society. Less directly as a result of its Christian population than through the influence of modern notions of constitutional democracy, Indonesia after independence also promoted ideas of religious freedom, albeit in a consociational framework different from Anglo-American varieties of Western liberalism. Consociationalism is a political system found in plural societies in which "the centrifugal tendencies in a plural society are counteracted by the cooperative attitudes and behavior of the leaders of the different segments of the population. Elite cooperation is the primary distinguishing feature."[2] In modern Europe, the Netherlands and Belgium are regarded as the two primary examples of consociational governance. Another distinctive feature of consociationalism is that the state works with religious leaders to recognize and demarcate state-authorized religious groupings, so that the state can provide funds for their schools, houses of worship, and social welfare services. As the Dutch sociologist Anton Zijderveld has emphasized, in the Netherlands such vertical structures facilitated "a great social peace," one vital for the development of Dutch democracy, but the system also had qualities that, rather than emphasizing individual freedom, can appear "authoritarian and elitist."[3]

The independent Republic of Indonesia maintained these cautious consociational policies on religion and state, developing administrative policies intended to support religious freedom while also placing limitations on activities seen as threatening civic order or the national interest. Although not based on any single religion, today Indonesia is not a secular state in the Western liberal sense. The first principle of the nation's ideological charter, or *Pancasila* (the "Five Principles"), affirms that the state is based on belief in a single and unitary divine being, referred to in the neutral (rather than explicitly Islamic) terminology of Tuhan Yang Maha Esa ("God the All Powerful and One"). Legally, citizens cannot advocate atheism; a law forbidding religious defamation also restricts critical commentary on any of the state's recognized religions (see later discussion). Through its Ministry of Religion, the government provides support to six state-recognized religions: Islam, Protestant Christianity, Catholicism, Hinduism, Buddhism, and Confucianism. Here again, the model of religious governance is closer in spirit to early twentieth-century Dutch consociationalism than to Anglo-American liberalism.

It is these circumstances – the diversity of religious traditions alongside the numerical predominance of Muslims, and the state's consociational provisions for recognized religions – that make the issue of religious freedom in Indonesia today so complex. The challenge has been compounded since May of 1998, when President Muhammad Soeharto's "New Order" regime (1966–1998) ended, and the country undertook a far-reaching transition to democracy. Today, political scientists regard Indonesia as one of the more successful democratic transitions of the post–cold war era.[4] However, the transition has been accompanied by religious tensions and occasional violence, a significant portion of which has targeted Christians and other religious minorities, including Muslim minorities. Although democratization has greatly enhanced some freedoms, it has challenged the country's religious minorities and raised questions about religious freedom generally.

The present report on Christianity and religious freedom in Indonesia has two main foci: first, to compare and analyze the situation of Indonesian Christians, as well as some other religious communities, before and after the 1998 transition to democracy; and, second, to highlight some of the special challenges faced by Indonesian Christians today, especially in their relation to the state and the country's Sunni Muslim majority. In preparing this report, the authors have relied on interviews conducted with sixteen Christian leaders in early 2013; they have also drawn on their research conducted in separate projects between 2000 and 2010.[5]

There was a consensus among the 2013 interviewees that Christians enjoyed a freer and more favorable social situation prior to the events of 1998, and that the country's transition to a more open political system has heightened tensions. Christian interviewees pointed to several indicators of a general deterioration in their situation: a heightened frequency of attacks on church buildings, often on the grounds that those buildings were erected without government permits; greater difficulty in securing permits for the construction of churches and schools; pressures to restrict the number of Christians in the higher levels of state administration; the implementation of laws said to be inspired by Islamic sharia, laws that most interviewees regard as contravening Indonesia's constitution; and, most generally, efforts on the part of private citizens and state officials to "Islamize" public life, a process from which Christians and other religious minorities feel excluded. In light of these developments, many Christian leaders feel that the post-1998 political opening, combined with a weakening of state law enforcement, has resulted in greater restrictions on religious freedom and greater segregation by religious community.

Nonetheless, the officials interviewed for this report are unanimous in affirming that the transition to democracy is necessary and important, and that the present circumstance of Christians and other minorities may be only transitional. Christian activists and political intellectuals played a prominent role in the prodemocracy mobilization that contributed to the ouster of President Soeharto in May 1998. The reservations expressed by Christian leaders today, then, do not extend to the democratic system itself, but to a perceived failure of state officials to enforce the law, maintain equality for all citizens (including non-Christian minorities), and contain the excesses of exclusivist organizations.

Many leaders point out, however, that the unsettledness of the transition has also encouraged some Christians to engage in introspection and self-critique. Christian leaders and activists interviewed by one of the report's authors in the period from 2000 to 2010 pointed out that segments of the Christian community had a tendency to be exclusive in their dealings with non-Christians. The transition to a more open and democratic political system has led to efforts by many Christian leaders to rethink how a Christian mission should be realized. Many Christian leaders insist that the challenges faced by Indonesian Christians today are not specifically *Christian* but *Indonesian*. Foremost among these challenges is the unwillingness of the state to uphold the law and defend religious pluralism. The Christian interviewees pointed out that the sole answer to this problem is to improve the functioning of democracy by working side by side with Muslims and other Indonesian citizens.

The discussion that follows will begin with a brief history of Christianity and religious plurality in Indonesia, from precolonial times to today. The second section will examine an often overlooked aspect of the situation of Christians in Indonesia, one closely related to the colonial legacy of Dutch consociationalism: the presence and function of the Christian and Catholic Directorates in the Ministry of Religious Affairs. In its final sections, the report looks at several of the unintended consequences of democratization: 1) declining political and bureaucratic representation of Christians, 2) pressures on churches, and 3) the "Islamization" of the public space though sharia bylaws and other mechanisms. The report concludes with a reflection on the challenges to and the future of Christianity and religious freedom in Indonesia.

CHRISTIANITY AND RELIGIOUS PLURALITY IN EARLIER TIMES

When Europeans first made their way to the Indonesian archipelago in the early sixteenth century, the territory they encountered was not one of timeless or isolated populations, but a bustling maritime realm with a thousand-year history of commerce and cultural exchange. In the 1500s, the most important trade routes linked Muslim principalities in the east of the archipelago with larger ports in its west. Earlier, in the first millennium of the Common Era, Buddhism and Hinduism had made their way to court centers throughout the region, becoming the religion of state in most of the west-central archipelago's kingdoms. Although Arab-Muslim traders had sailed across island Southeast Asia since the seventh century, there was little conversion of native peoples to the religion prior to the late thirteenth century. Native conversion began in the latter period on the northern coast of Sumatra and continued eastward over the next centuries along the region's main trade routes. By the seventeenth century, Islam was the religion of most coastal and some interior states. The impetus for this conversion does not appear to have been religious warfare, although there were limited instances of this. The greater influence was that much of the trade linking the archipelago with India and southern China had fallen into Muslim hands by the thirteenth century, and Islam came to occupy a central position in regional politics and culture.[6]

State enforcement of Islamic law was not common in precolonial Southeast Asia, and most kingdoms had a limited system of Islamic courts if any at all. However, conversion to Islam meant that the Muslim faithful were linked through pilgrimage and education to Islamic centers in the Middle East. In the first centuries after conversion, these networks carried more Sufi mystics than sharia-minded jurists, but in the late eighteenth and, especially, the nineteenth centuries the growing traffic in pilgrims led to madrassa education, reformist ideas, and a greater concern for Islamic law. The consolidation of Dutch power over the East Indies in the nineteenth and early twentieth centuries provided an infrastructure that further facilitated these reformist trends. By the end of the nineteenth century, a more self-consciously normative Islamic community had emerged, and over the course of the twentieth century it became actively involved in the growing opposition to Dutch colonialism.

Notwithstanding these developments, large portions of the archipelago remained aloof from the maritime trade and the Islamic faith with which it was associated. In the final decades of the nineteenth century, the Dutch sought to extend their rule to all portions of the archipelago, and as they did so, they sought to convert the practitioners of tribal religions in these isolated regions to Christianity. For most of their 350 years in the archipelago, the Dutch had prioritized their economic interests and discouraged missionization among Muslims, fearing it might jeopardize their commercial interests.[7] In the late nineteenth century, however, the state gave the green light to missionaries, including in portions of south-central Java, where much of the population identified with a syncretic variety of Islam.[8] Rather than encouraging religious freedom and an open mission field, the government set aside specific territories for individual denominations, encouraging a close identification of region, ethnicity, and denomination.[9]

In Java, the most populous of the archipelago's islands, the mission initiative met with little success. However, among the interior and upland animists of Sulawesi,

Kalimantan, and eastern Indonesia, the colonial government worked closely with missionaries, and Christianity took hold. Schooling provided Christians with a comparative cultural advantage that they maintained well into the last quarter of the twentieth century. One of the most lasting legacies of the Christian emphasis on general as well as religious education, however, was that it served as a catalyst for a new variety of Islamic schooling promoted by Muslim reformists, not least of all those associated with the Muhammadiyah organization, the largest movement of Islamic reform in the world.

The most critical area of Dutch intervention in religious affairs, however, was not support for Christian missions or (least of all) the promotion of individual religious freedom, but the effort to contain the spread of Islam. Dutch anxieties about Islam were reinforced by the prominence of Islamic appeals in anticolonial rebel ranks during the Dutch-Java War of 1825–1830, and again in the anticolonial resistance of the Sultanate of Aceh at the end of the nineteenth century.[10] From the mid-nineteenth century onward the Dutch sought to privatize the profession of Islam among native officials (*priyayi*) in government service. Educational programs for children of the native elite attempted to inculcate Western values of progress and secularism in opposition to Islamic ideals.[11] The peace produced by Dutch rule, however, facilitated a great wave of migration by Islamic traders, scholars, and teachers into inland Java, Sumatra, Kalimantan, and Sulawesi, where formal Islamic institutions had previously been weak or nonexistent. As colonial commerce provided new opportunities for natives, the ranks of educated and pious Muslims also increased, as did new movements for Islamic reform.[12]

By the late 1920s, leaders in both the Muslim traditionalist and modernist communities had begun to link their ideas on religious reform to appeals for "freedom" (*kemerdekaan*) from European rule. The Western ideal of national freedom had, and would continue to have, a broader resonance in native society than did liberal notions of economic freedom or freedom of individual conviction. Dutch policies had for the most part reinforced the association of religion (including Christianity) not with individual freedom, but with territory, ethnicity, and consociational controls. The Muslim leadership that emerged in the final decades of Dutch rule hoped to position their organizations at the forefront of the growing movement for political change in the Dutch Indies, advocating the establishment of some form of Islamic state. The new Muslim activists found themselves in competition, however, with a multiconfessional nationalist movement. The movement was largely under Muslim leadership but enjoyed the support of Christians, Hindus, and other minorities. The resulting contest between Islamic and multiconfessional visions of nationhood was to remain a key feature of Indonesian politics, and a major constraint on liberal ideas of religious freedom, for the remainder of the twentieth century.

This contest between these two nationalist movements, each with a different vision of nation and religious coexistence, was particularly intense in Java, where almost half of the country's population lived. The rivalry was exacerbated by the divide between observant or normative-minded Muslims, sometimes referred to as *santri*, and Javanese Muslims of a more nominal or syncretic orientation, referred to as *abangan* (lit., "red"). This competition reached new heights as a result of the sociopolitical dislocations of the Japanese occupation (1942–1945), the war for independence (1945–1949), and the period of parliamentary democracy (1950–1957). In the last of these periods, the country's main political parties "threw themselves into expanding not merely their own memberships but those of affiliated associations of youth, women, students, farmers, workers, intellectuals, and others," who "competed fiercely for influence in every sphere of life and on a round-the-clock basis."[13] The heightened competition caused a marked deterioration in relations across religious and ideological communities, which – again on the model of Dutch consociationalism – came to be known as "pillars" or (in Indonesian) "streams" (Ind., *aliran*). The competition intensified in the early 1960s, as the Indonesian Communist Party became the largest of the country's parties, and Muslim associations were put on the defensive. In this setting, debates over individual religious freedom seemed less urgent than were strategies for party-based mobilizations.

In this same unsettled context, some groups began to train paramilitaries. Many linked to Muslim political organizations went on to play a central role in the mass killings of Communists during 1965–1966, in the aftermath of a failed left-wing officers' coup the night of September 30, 1965. In the months that followed, Muslim political organizations, as well as some Christians and Hindus, joined forces with the conservative wing of the armed forces to launch a campaign for the mass killing of Communists, who were accused of having masterminded the Jakarta coup. Although some Christians participated in the killing, most churches did not – a fact not lost on some families of victims of the violence. Six months into the anti-Communist campaign, about a half-million people had died, and the Communist Party – until then the largest of Indonesia's political parties – lay in ruins.[14]

Even prior to the 1965–1966 killings, the growing politicization of religious identities had led a few nominal Muslims to deny their birth religion and flirt with conversion to non-Islamic religions. In colonial times, conversion to Christianity had been rare among Muslims, even among Java's nominally Muslim *abangan*, because of the Dutch-reinforced identification of Christianity with Europeans. However, after independence, rates of conversion to Christianity among nominally Muslim Javanese increased. The first years of Indonesian independence had seen churches struggling to rid themselves of the stigma of identification with the Dutch by transferring clerical administration to native hands. In the months following the 1965–1966 killings, the new government implemented policies that restricted individual religious freedom while also providing greater support for state-recognized religions. The pattern here was again that of consociational politics, not liberal freedom. On the assumption that religion was the best antidote to Communism, state officials launched "building up" (*pembinaan*) programs that required all citizens to profess a state-authorized religion. Schoolchildren were obliged to receive two hours of instruction in the religion of their choice each week. Those not yet professing a recognized religion were required by school officials to choose one.

In remote provinces such as interior Papua or central Kalimantan, the state turned to Western missionaries to help in the task of national integration. In exchange for their development services, the missionaries were allowed to proselytize among natives who did not yet profess a state-recognized religion. By the standards of the larger Muslim world, the government's outreach to Western missionaries was unusual; it caused deep resentment among pious Muslims. However, the generous government policy eventually changed. Indonesia was swept by the first phases of an Islamic resurgence in the 1970s, and in 1978 the government imposed new restrictions on mission activity. When, in the mid-1990s, the Soeharto regime began to reach out to Islamists in groups such as the conservative Indonesian Council for Islamic Predication (Dewan Dakwah Islamiyah Indonesia, DDII), it reversed its policies, even allowing DDII preachers into regions recently converted to Christianity or Hinduism.[15]

Notwithstanding these policy shifts, Christians and Hindus at first enjoyed greater success at attracting converts than did Muslims. Between 1966 and 1976, some 2 million ethnic Javanese from nominally Islamic backgrounds converted to Christianity. Some 250,000 to 400,000 became Hindu.[16] Although conversion to Hinduism has virtually stopped since this early period and conversion to Christianity has slowed, to this day memories of the post-1966 conversion remain a source of resentment in conservative Muslim circles. The memories have strengthened the determination of some in the Muslim community to restrict Christian proselytization and church building, and to promote a strict interpretation of the state's blasphemy law (see later discussion). The memory also reinforced conservative Muslim skepticism toward Western appeals for a fuller liberalization of state policies on religious freedom.

However, the political views of Indonesia's Muslim majority are highly varied, and a pluralist current emerged in these years as well. Beginning in the late 1970s, the country experienced a far-reaching resurgence of Islamic observance. Far more than in some Middle Eastern Muslim lands, the resurgence included intellectual leaders such as the well-known Nurcholish Madjid, individuals who were openly committed to ideas of democracy, freedom of religion, and women's rights.[17] As illustrated by the involvement of Muslim students in the overthrow of President Soeharto in May 1998, many pious youth also saw Islam as consistent with democratic values.[18] At the same time, however, the resurgence also had a deeply conservative stream. In the aftermath of the overthrow of President Soeharto in May 1998 and the transition to democracy, many conservative Islamists again organized themselves into paramilitary groups. They challenged the proponents of pluralist democracy and rejected efforts to promote a more individualistic understanding of religious freedom. Although the proponents of this antipluralist approach to religious freedom have fared poorly in each of Indonesia's national elections since 1999, their militancy has succeeded in putting Christians and other religious minorities on the defensive.

In the first four years after Soeharto's resignation, Indonesia was plagued by a series of ethnoreligious conflicts, many of which involved Christian-Muslim violence. There was a precedent for such violence even in the final years of the Soeharto regime; more than four hundred churches were destroyed between 1994 and 1999. However, in Kalimantan, central Sulawesi, and, most tragically, the Moluccas (known in Indonesian as Maluku), the period 1999–2003 saw an unprecedented increase in communal violence. The worst violence took place in Ambon and Maluku in northeastern Indonesia, where some ten thousand people died. Since 2003–2004, most of the country's communal violence has been contained. The results of the four national elections held since 1999 have been notable for the moderation of their outcome. Nonetheless, religion in some regions remains a source of discord. The memories of communal violence have led most Christian and Muslim leaders to agree on the wisdom of some variety of consociational accommodation – even as individual leaders disagree on how to balance consociational peace with individual religious freedom.

CHRISTIANITY WITHIN THE STATE: PARTIAL REPRESENTATION AND ACCOMMODATION

Any discussion of Christianity and the state in Indonesia must also mention the distinctive situation of Christianity within the state administration. While the constitution mentions no single religion by name, specific religious groupings are recognized in lower-level regulations. On many occasions, government officials reject the idea that Indonesia has "official religions" or "acknowledged religions," saying that all religions are acknowledged in Indonesia. However, in administrative practice a clear distinction is made between state-recognized religions and other faith-based traditions. The Explanation of the 1965 Law on Prevention of Defamation of Religion portrays an implicit hierarchy of religions, with highest recognition given to the six world religions (Islam, Protestantism, Catholicism, Hinduism, Buddhism, and Confucianism, all acknowledged and provided with state funding), followed by other world religions (acknowledged but with no funding), then local religions and "beliefs," or *kepercayaan* (acknowledged, but not defined as "religions" [*agama*]); atheism is not recognized and thus is effectively illegal. The 2006 Law on Civil Administration stipulates that a citizen's religion must be recorded for administrative purposes. The law also distinguishes state-recognized faiths from those "that have not been acknowledged" or those associated with "beliefs" (*penghayat kepercayaan*).[19] Religious traditions regarded as mere "beliefs" enjoy few of the privileges associated with recognized religions; some risk prosecution under the terms of Indonesia's blasphemy law (discussed later).

Since the early years of the republic, Protestantism and Catholicism have figured among those religions that enjoyed full state recognition; early on they were also represented in the Ministry of Religious Affairs (MORA). MORA was established on January 3, 1946, at first to accommodate the demands of Muslim political organizations while still upholding the multiconfessional nature of the state. The ministry gradually began to develop administrative wings for non-Islamic religions recognized by the state.

In its present organization, there are divisions at the level of General Directorate related to the religions acknowledged by the state. Funding for each of the directorates is provided for two types of activities: "religious affairs" (salaries for some but not all *da'wa* preachers, religious outreach in various public spheres, and maintenance of facilities of worship) and formal religious education (schools, colleges, and universities, including funding for religious teachers' salaries).[20] The pattern is again in keeping with consociational models of religious education in European countries such as the Netherlands and Belgium, where religion teachers and education are publicly funded. In Indonesia, religious education is mandatory in all public and private schools from elementary school through college, and each religion in the Directorates oversees the religious curriculum offered in schools. With regard to Protestant Christians, the state funds support for teachers who provide religious instruction in state schools and, in some areas, in Sunday schools. MORA also provides funding to Protestant seminaries, as well as scholarships to students. At present, there are six State Protestant Colleges (Sekolah Tinggi Agama Kristen Protestan Negeri, or STAKPN).[21] As yet there is no state-funded Catholic College, although the Catholic Directorate continues to entertain the possibility of establishing one.[22]

The directorates also supervise national examinations on religion and oversee accreditation of religious colleges or universities. In the Protestant Directorate, there has been a concern that the quality of some Protestant theological schools has declined in recent years, as a result of the proliferation of new denominations, especially those of Pentecostal orientation. To comply with the national regulation on education, as of 2013 all the theological schools had to be accredited by the state, and those that fail to meet national standards are likely to be closed.

The Protestant Directorate also approves new denominations (known in Indonesia as synods). In the research interview for this report, the then-director of Protestant affairs, Edison Pasaribu, mentioned that since 1998 there has been an explosion of synods, many of them Pentecostal. In response, a moratorium on the creation of new synods has been in effect since 2005. The general director of the Protestant Directorate explained that the new synods often split from their parent synod for theological, political, or economic reasons. The directorate found that after a few years many new synods cease operation. In response to fissiparous tendencies like these, the Protestant division within MORA has encouraged churches to resolve their differences through consultation rather than the creation of new churches or synods.

Among the most important responsibilities with which the Protestant Directorate is charged is to determine whether the state should recognize particular denominations. For example, in 1976, after consulting the Protestant Directorate, the Indonesian attorney general banned the Jehovah's Witnesses on the grounds that their teachings are heterodox. The group had also earned the ire of state authorities as a result of their door-to-door proselytization and refusal to salute the Indonesian flag. However, in 2001, during the presidency of Abdurrahman Wahid – a Muslim leader well known for his liberal views on matters of religious freedom – the ban was revoked.

For religious sects in any faith tradition, not having recognition from the directorate entails substantial social disadvantages; among other obstacles, it makes it difficult to obtain permission to build houses of worship. In addition, a nonauthorized religion runs the risk of being accused of defaming religion if and when its activities are seen as challenging a state-recognized religion.[23] As this example illustrates, the directorate's work is supposed to be administrative, but it is not always easy to separate administration from state involvement in theological matters.

For each of the religions recognized by the ministry, the government designates and chooses to communicate with a religious council that is expected to represent the religious community in dealings with the state. This corporatist pattern of representation had its roots in the Dutch colonial period but was reinforced in the independence era with the establishment of the Ministry of Religion. The government consults each council on matters related to the religious community it represents. In the case of Protestantism, the council in question is the Indonesian Communion of Churches (PGI), established in 1950. For Catholics, the council role is played by the Indonesian Bishops' Conference (KWI, Konferensi Waligereja Indonesia).

At present there are 88 Protestant synods under the PGI.[24] Even though the PGI is regarded as representative of Protestant Christians in Indonesia, there are in fact some 300 Protestant synods registered in the Protestant Directorate. This means that the

PGI formally incorporates only one-third of all synods. However, in addition to the PGI, there are two other large associations of Protestant churches: the Communion of Indonesian Evangelical Churches and Organizations (Persekutuan Gereja-gereja dan Lembaga-lembaga Injili Indonesia, or PGLII), which was established in 1971[25] and currently incorporates 106 synods,[26] and the Communion of Indonesian Pentecostal Churches (Persekutuan Gereja-gereja Pentakosta Indonesia, or PGPI), which was established in 1998 (but has historical roots that reach back to 1955),[27] with 81 synod members.[28]

It is important to point out that a number of evangelical and Pentecostal churches are associated with the PGI; some churches join more than one association.[29] Since the PGI includes the larger synods, it is estimated that its affiliated synods together include some 80 percent of all Protestants. It is for this reason that the government feels justified in regarding the PGI as best qualified to represent the full Protestant community. Nonetheless, to reach out to churches outside the PGI, the PGI has participated in the formation of the Organization for Inter-Church Consultation (Badan Musyawarah Antar Gereja), as well as, more recently, the Indonesian Christian Forum, which is related to the Global Christian Forum. The latter body includes all Christian denominations, including Catholics and Orthodox Christians.

State-church relations are simpler with regard to the (Roman) Catholic Directorate because of the Catholics' lack of denominational diversity and continuing Vatican administrative guidance. The Catholic Directorate has existed since the establishment of MORA in 1946. It envisions itself as a bridge that connects the government to the church and Catholic social organizations.[30] Today Indonesia has ten archdioceses and twenty-seven dioceses, incorporating a total of 1,201 parishes. Unlike the situation with regard to the Protestant Directorate, the Ministry of Religious Affairs is not involved in recognizing different synods, since the Catholic community is denominationally unitary. The ministry's involvement in Catholic education is also less extensive than is the case with Protestantism, since as yet there are no state-supported Catholic colleges or universities. Seminaries too are managed entirely at the diocesan level, without state support (however, as noted earlier, the directorate is entertaining the possibility of establishing a state-supported seminary).[31] The state does provide supplemental salaries for religious teachers in both public and private Catholic schools.

Just as the Ministry of Religion's Catholic Directorate is less extensively involved in church affairs than its Protestant counterpart, the Catholic religious council, the Indonesian Bishops' Conference (KWI), is organized in a more autonomous manner. The KWI's membership is made up of bishops, all of whom serve at the behest of the church. Unlike the PGI, the KWI also does not have branches in the provinces or districts. Also unlike PGI, it does not have rival organizations seeking to represent Catholics. In large part, the KWI's distinctive organization reflects the fact that the organization predates the establishment of the republic. The conference was established in 1924 and acquired its current name in 1987.[32] The conference is also not specifically Indonesian; bishops' conferences exist in many other countries, and they are established with the approval of the Holy See. Organizationally speaking, the KWI is actually more closely tied to the global Catholic communion than it is to the Indonesian state.

It is instructive in this regard to compare the KWI and PGI with other religious councils in Indonesia. Muslims, for example, have the Majelis Ulama Indonesia (Indonesian Council of Ulama, or MUI), which was established in 1975 by the New Order government. At the time of its founding, the MUI grouped several large Muslim organizations and was supposed to function as a moderate, progovernment liaison to the larger Muslim community. Long regarded as relatively pliant in its interactions with the state, the MUI from 1998 onward took a more independent and conservative stance vis-à-vis the government. Although in principle its decisions (fatwa) on religious matters are not binding on Muslims, the council has in recent years sought to secure their enforcement by the state. During this same period, the MUI has also come to play a central role in efforts to define and control Islamic orthodoxy – including the sensitive and often controversial task of identifying who is and who is not Muslim.[33] In this and other respects, many Muslim groupings – and especially conservative groupings – have been more eager than their Christian counterparts to make the state a partner in their public programs.

There is another difference between Protestant Christian and Catholic and Muslim interactions with the state. The general directorates for Catholics and Protestants within the Ministry of Religious Affairs are small and restricted in scope. In several recent disputes involving Christians and Muslims (see later discussion), the directorates do not seem to have voiced distinct positions. The minister of religious affairs in 2009–2014, Suryadharma Ali – a conservative Muslim with ties to one of Indonesia's only two parties that call for state implementation of Islamic law – has derided Protestants and Catholics as "discriminating against themselves."[34] In reality, however, the directorates have served as a moderating influence on the more aggressive wings of their respective religious communities.

PARTICIPATION OF CHRISTIANS IN POLITICS AND THE BUREAUCRACY

Christian representation in the state is not limited to the small General Directorate in the Ministry of Religious Affairs. During the first twenty years of the New Order period (1966–1998), there was a widespread perception that Christians were overrepresented in the Indonesian state and military. In the late 1980s and, especially, the 1990s, President Soeharto encountered growing opposition to his rule, and he responded in part by cultivating support in the Muslim community and distancing himself from Christians. Faced by a growing prodemocracy movement that included many Muslims, in his final years as president, Soeharto reached out, not just to Muslims, but to conservative Islamist groupings, including some that spoke of an international Christian conspiracy against the president because he was Muslim. Christians lamented these developments as a "return to primordialism." Many in the Muslim wing of the prodemocracy and human rights community also regretted the development, even while recognizing that a new accommodation of Muslim religious interests was needed.

With the political transition of 1998, restrictions on party organization were lifted and there was a proliferation of new parties. Unlike the situation in, say, post–Arab Spring Egypt, parties advocating Indonesia's transformation into an Islamic state have fared poorly in national elections; their share of the national vote has declined in most of the elections held since 1999. Not surprisingly, Christian-based parties have for the most part performed even more poorly at the national level, although they have enjoyed some support in Christian majority areas of eastern Indonesia. In general, however, the opening of the political system to democratic wheeling and dealing has not benefited the Christian community. Power sharing in government, including the selection of cabinet ministers, is now done primarily with an eye toward wooing the larger parties. In this situation, minorities such as the Christians are at a distinct disadvantage. A similar process of politically leveraged appointments and deal making has now extended to lower levels of the state administration and even into educational institutions including public universities.

Many conservative Muslims allege that, in the New Order period, Christians did much the same thing, appointing coreligionists to strategic posts. Dr. Eben Nubantimo, former head of the Evangelical Protestant Church of Timor (Gereja Masehi Injili Timur), understands these perceptions and blames them on New Order policies, which forced "harmony" while repressing dissenting voices. Professor John Titaley, the rector of the Satya Wacana Christian University in Salatiga, Central Java, expressed regret over the fact that today this attitude extends to making it more difficult for Christians to win academic promotion. He was of the opinion that opportunities for Christians have shrunk since the end of the New Order. Some young Christians interviewed for this report insisted that, with time, this phenomenon will diminish as Christian-Muslim suspicions recede. The fact remains, however, that most Christian respondents reject any attempt to create a proportional balance in political appointments based on religious representation in society.

In strife-torn territories such as Maluku, the issue of proportional balance often has a different dynamic, a legacy related to the Malino peace accord that ended most conflict in this region after 2003–2004. According to Pastor Agustinus Ulahaiyanan of the Amboina Diocese, people now speak of the position of Ambon mayor as having to have "balance": If during this term the mayor is Muslim, during the next term he or she should be a Christian. For Pastor Ulahaiyanan, this arrangement amounts to a profound misinterpretation of the Malino peace agreement. Jacky Manuputty, a Protestant minister and renowned peace activist in Ambon, also mentions an unwritten convention that candidates who want to compete for the position of governor, mayor, or head of district (*bupati*) have to reflect a similar Christian-Muslim reciprocity. For example, if the governor is a Christian, then the vice-governor has to be Muslim, and vice versa. Christian leaders such as Manuputty regard such turn taking in government positions as too narrow an understanding of democratic power sharing and merely perpetuating religious divides.

Ambon is not the only place where religion plays a role in local politics; local elections in many districts today are colored by religious symbols and concerns. Indeed, in some settings one sees deliberate exploitation of religious symbols and what Indonesians call "black campaigns," in which blatant appeals are made to religious identity.[35] In the 2011 election for the governor and vice-governor of Jakarta, the eventual winning slate paired a Muslim known as relatively casual in his profession of the faith, Joko Widodo, with Basuki Tjahaja Purnama, a Christian of Chinese ethnic background. The two were from multiconfessional parties (the Indonesian Democratic Party of Struggle [PDI-P] and the Great Indonesia Movement Party [Gerindra]). In the course of the campaign, the challengers to Widodo made repeated appeals to conservative Islamic and anti-Chinese sentiment. Nonetheless, the Widodo-led slate prevailed. In the 2014 presidential elections, there were similar efforts to exploit conservative Islamic sentiment, in a campaign that pitted the then-governor of Jakarta, Joko Widodo, against a former army general, Prabowo Subianto. Although the precise balance of forces was extremely complex and, in fact, some Christians supported Prabowo, the Widodo campaign again prevailed. For supporters of religious pluralism in Indonesia, these outcomes are regarded as hopeful signs that the electorate is capable of rejecting divisive religious appeals. In general, in fact, many Christians and pluralist Muslims feel that religious labels are of diminishing importance in national and local elections. They are less certain that this progress in electoral outcomes has been replicated in other realms of public life.

WHEN INTOLERANCE MEETS WEAK LAW ENFORCEMENT: RECENT INCIDENTS OF ANTICHURCH VIOLENCE

When respondents are asked to name the most important problem facing Christians in Indonesia today, most mention attacks on churches and the difficulties involved in securing permits for church construction. Many lament what they describe as the government's "indifference" to such matters. Reports by independent watchdog groups over the past five years also lament government inaction in the face of rights abuses.[36]

Although many observers agree that Indonesia has made progress toward consolidating its democracy, most also point out that the transition to democracy has been accompanied by rising intolerance on the part of some Muslim groups and weak protection of religious freedom, especially for religious minorities – including Muslim minorities. Intolerance is particularly pervasive among small groups of militant Islamists, who, again, have not managed to win support in national elections. However, many people feel that there has been something of a "conservative turn" even among mainstream Muslims, the consequences of which have been felt by Muslims and non-Muslims alike.[37] The Reverend Dr. Andreas Yewangoe, the head of PGI, who was interviewed for this report, strongly believes that there is still a wellspring of what he calls "authentic harmony" between the Muslim and Christian communities. But he also observed that the followers of conservative transnational Islamic groups have increased in numbers in recent years and contributed to rising exclusivity. Dr. Pradjarta Dirdjosanjoto, the head of Percik, a civil society organization in Salatiga (Central Java) focusing on peace building, interfaith dialogue, and "local theology," pointed out that transnational influences of an exclusivistic nature have affected not only Muslims, but also Christian groups.[38]

In the post-1998 era, the growth of intolerance has been exacerbated by the weakening of law enforcement – this despite the adoption of stronger constitutional guarantees of religious freedom in the early years of the post-Soeharto transition. As documented in the series of *Annual Report on Religious Life in Indonesia* issued by the Center for Religious and Cross Cultural Studies (CRCS) although incidents of communal violence and terrorist attacks in the name of Islam have decreased dramatically since the early 2000s, two serious challenges to religious freedom remain.

The first of these challenges concerns the growing recourse to the 1965 law on religious defamation. The law was enacted by President Sukarno in response to Muslim concerns over the proliferation of syncretic, and sometimes explicitly anti-Islamic, new religious movements, especially among ethnic Javanese. Prior to 1998, the defamation law was in fact rather rarely used, having been applied in just ten cases over a thirty-five-year period. Since the transition to democracy, however, the number of prosecutions based on the law has spiraled to forty cases in ten years.[39] Although the language of the law is subject to diverse interpretations, its aim is to criminalize the behavior of anyone who proposes interpretations that deviate from the principles of any of the six religions acknowledged in Indonesia. In recent years, prosecutions under the law have targeted not only new religious movements, but nonorthodox yet long-established groups such as the Ahmadiyah and Shi'i, and even Sufi groups.[40] While the majority of prosecutions target Muslims, there have also been prosecutions attempted within the Christian and Hindu communities. However, most cases target nonconformist believers within a particular religion, rather than alleged defamations across religious lines.

The second challenge to religious freedom concerns restrictions on the building of houses of religious worship. Most of these cases involve conservative Muslim challenges to Christians. However, in parts of Sumatra, Papua, and Nusa Tenggara Timur, where Muslims are in the minority, there have also been occasional protests by Christians against mosque construction. In 2011, for example, there were thirty-six complaints involving the building of houses of worship: Twenty-four of them involved Muslim challenges to Christian churches; three involved Muslim challenges to Ahmadiyah mosques; and one involved a Christian challenge to the construction of a mosque in the Christian majority town of Kupang.[41]

The concern raised by these incidents has been compounded by the fact that national and regional governments have taken few steps to resolve the cases, notwithstanding the appeals of civil society organizations in and outside Indonesia. All Christian leaders interviewed for this report agree that the core of the problem lies in the state's reluctance to enforce existing laws. Weak law enforcement has two deleterious consequences: tolerance of violence done against minority religious groups and nonenforcement of existing regulations when the targeted religious group actually abides by state law.

The second of these issues relates to a 2006 Joint Ministerial Decree, issued by the ministers of religious affairs and of domestic affairs. The decree sought to improve on an earlier regulation, issued in 1969, by stipulating that (local) government is ultimately responsible for providing space for houses of worship, in those instances where a religious community fulfills all permit requirements. According to article 14:3 of the decree, the requirements for building a house of worship are (1) signatures of at least ninety potential users of the house of worship, (2) support from sixty persons in the neighborhood, (3) written approval of the local branch of the Ministry of Religious Affairs, (4) written approval from the Forum for Inter-religious Harmony (Forum Kerukunan Umat Beragama or FKUB).

The FKUB is a state-sponsored multireligious body formed at the provincial, district, and city levels; since 2006, five hundred such entities have been established across Indonesia. All state-acknowledged religions in a particular territory must have at least one representative on the FKUB, and the board's membership must reflect the proportion of adherents of different faith traditions in the local district. An important condition to protect the interests of minority groups is that no decision should be made by simple majority vote. Research conducted by the CRCS indicates that while in some places FKUB boards work well enough to resolve religious conflicts, in other places they do not. Another improvement on the previous regulation is that, once all the requirements are fulfilled, the local government is supposed to respond to the permit proposal in ninety days. However, while there have been cases in which such proposals were processed speedily, some proposals are delayed in the FKUB.

The Joint Decree remains controversial. Its supporters would like to see it elevated to the status of law; its critics insist it provides a pretext for intolerance and should be revoked. Others, including some of the Christian leaders interviewed for this report, insist that good relations are what is important and no regulation is needed. It has been widely documented that opponents of building new houses of worship often invoke the regulation (especially its clauses about neighborhood approval) to block church construction. Others stage demonstrations to pressure the local FKUB not to support the issuing of permits. Interestingly, in majority Christian territories such as Ambon and Kupang, mainline Christian groups have invoked the regulation to block the construction of churches by minority Christian groups, including Pentecostals and the Jehovah's Witnesses.

Two cases that have acquired particular notoriety in recent years involve the GKI Taman Yasmin Church in Bogor and the HKBP Filadelfia Church in Bekasi. In both cases, pressured by militant Islamist groups, mayors in each town revoked church-building permits that had already been approved by other local authorities. The affected church congregations responded by suing in court and went on to win their cases in the Supreme Court. Despite this legal victory, local authorities still refused to allow church construction. Asked to address the issue, Indonesia's president, Susilo Bambang Yudhoyono, responded that according to the constitution he is not supposed to meddle in mayoral affairs.

In the case of GKI Taman Yasmin and HKBP Filadelfia, the solution proposed by local government officials was to move the church to an entirely different neighborhood. The HKBP Filadelfia accepted the offer, but then government officials did not follow through. The GKI Taman Yasmin rejected the offer of relocation. In an effort to publicize their cause, congregants from both churches have regularly gathered to worship in front of the Presidential Palace in Jakarta. Thus far, however, no solution has been reached.

The situation with regard to permits for houses of worship is more potentially destabilizing than even these cases illustrate. As explained by the Reverend Paul Richard Renwarin of Manado, most houses of worship in Indonesia, be they churches or mosques, actually never went through the process of securing legal permits. In most instances, neighbors' approval has been secured through informal channels. Problems occur only when certain actors challenge the arrangement. Unfortunately, such challenges have become more common in the post-Soeharto era, in part because political actors regard them as an effective tool for mobilizing support for electoral candidates. These and other cases reveal a dark side to the decentralization of powers that has taken place since the end of the Soeharto era.

Although until 2012 the CRCS's *Annual Reports* found that the great majority of conflicts over church building were concentrated in West Java, more recently incidents have occurred in other regions. Most dramatically, in the district of Singkilin, the special district of Aceh, sixteen Protestant churches were forcibly closed in 2012. One was burned down when the Christian leaders attempted to negotiate an alternate agreement with the government. This incident took place as the new district head of Aceh Singkil was being inaugurated. The district head had campaigned on a promise of making the securing of building permits for churches easier. The suspicion thus was that the arson attack was carried out by his political opponents, or by members of the Islamic Defenders Front, a hard-line Islamist militia, which had also recently established a local chapter in the region.[42] Although some of the churches that were closed had been built years ago without permits, the church that was burned down had long had a permit. It is noteworthy that the regulations for building a house of worship in Aceh are more stringent than the national regulations: Instead of 90 users, the regulation requires 150 users; instead of support of 60 persons from the neighbourhood, it requires 120.

The central government's lack of resolution on these issues has compounded the problem and encouraged vigilantes to perpetuate similar attacks elsewhere. It is no coincidence that, in regions such as West Java, militants involved in attacks on churches have also taken action against other religious minorities including the Ahmadiyah. In Aceh, in the same period that actions were taken against Christian churches, militants also launched campaigns against supposed Muslim "deviants," most of whom were associated with unorthodox Sufi groupings.

A second way in which government inaction has compounded religious tensions relates to terrorism. Although in recent years the incidence of terrorist attacks has diminished, it is widely suspected that violent militants have turned their attention away from armed attacks toward joining forces with militant but nonterrorist opponents of the Ahmadiyah, Shi'i minority, and Christians. As the International Crisis Group warned, "The threat of extremist violence in Indonesia is not over, even though the last two years have seen major successes in breaking up extremist networks … even with so many strikes against them, extremists have been able to regroup under pressure and plot new operations." The report goes on to warn, "There is some evidence to suggest that once there is positive reinforcement for one kind of violence, it may be easier to move on to another."[43] In 2011 there were attacks on a mosque (in a police complex in Cirebon, West Java) and a church (in Solo, Central Java) that involved suicide bombing. The perpetrators were related, and the Cirebon bomber was also known to be active in anti-Ahmadiyah demonstrations. The actors were thus involved in forms of violence previously seen as distinct.[44]

The ability of local officials to defy court decisions and the lengthy nature of legal proceedings all have led Christian leaders to question the effectiveness of legal solutions to interreligious disputes. Some have concluded that, rather than pursuing legal channels, the priority should be to implement "cultural approaches."[45] Eben Nubantimo, for example, sees that the regulation on the construction of houses of worship has provided a pretext for intolerance and makes communication more difficult. "Nurturing good relations, rather than insisting on regulation, is more natural." Many Christian interviewees agreed on this point.

There is another significant feature to the problem of churches. The religious demography of Indonesia has become more complex and introduced a new dynamic to interreligious conflict. Today, when a church is attacked in Java, many Christians worry that a revenge attack will be launched on Muslims in Christian majority regions. Indeed, in Kupang, for example, during a dialogue session between Muslim and Christian youths following the protest against the building of a mosque in the city, a bitter dispute of just this nature broke out: "Why should we defend Muslims, if they attack Christians in other places?" However, an interfaith coalition was organized and tensions diminished. In other Muslim minority places such as Ambon, Manado, and Jayapura, such arguments about Muslims' attacking Christians in Java are heard frequently at the popular level. However, here too Christian and Muslim leaders have succeeded in quelling tensions. Christian leaders in Manado, in particular, are proud of what they believe is a unique example of Muslim-Christian harmony, exemplified in the fact that Manado established its own interfaith organization (BKSAUA, Badan Kerjasama Antar Umat Beragama) well before the national government launched its program in 2006. In Ambon, too, Christian and Muslim peace activists are today better organized and quick to respond to threats with what they creatively refer to as "peace provocation." The Reverend Jacky Manuputty, who was instrumental in initiating the "peace provocateur" movement, recently received an international peace award for his role in peace building in Ambon.

Another response to the difficulties facing churches takes the form of self-reflection among Christians. While still maintaining that the state should guarantee the rights of all citizens to worship and build places of worship, some Christian leaders have reminded their fellow Christians that building more churches should not be the main goal of mission. For the Reverend Yewangoe, what is more important is that the church be a blessing for everyone, not only Christians.

"ISLAMIZATION" OF PUBLIC SPACE: SHARIA BYLAWS AND OTHER TRENDS

Another trend since 1998 has been the widespread proliferation of bylaws in towns, districts, and provinces said to be inspired (to varying degrees of explicitness) by

Islamic sharia. In 2002 Indonesia's parliament voted down proposals that would have amended article 29 of the constitution to require the state to enforce Islamic law for Muslim citizens. Some Indonesia observers imagined that this settled the question of state-enforced Islamic law once and for all. Over the next four years, however, Muslim activists and political parties – including some parties long regarded as secular nationalist – joined forces in 53 of the country's 470 districts and municipalities to introduce legislation that Indonesians refer to as "sharia-oriented regional regulations" (*peraturan daerah syariah Islam*).

In terms of content, many of these regulations are not specifically Islamic. Claiming to act in the name of public morality rather than sharia, some regulations impose stricter controls on gambling, women's movement at night, and the consumption of alcohol. About one-half of the regional regulations, however, do explicitly reference Islamic norms. These regulations mandate the mastery of basic religious activities, such as reading the Quran or paying religious alms (*zakat*) or wearing Islamic dress in public. With the notable exception of the special province of Aceh, none of the regional regulations seeks to enforce Islamic criminal law; neither does any apply the *hudud* penalties mandated in classical Islamic jurisprudence for theft, highway robbery, adultery, and other "crimes against God."

Notwithstanding their variable content, the bylaws have been regarded by many Christians as one more index of the growing Islamization of Indonesian public life. The Christian leaders interviewed for this report were not opposed to *all* sharia bylaws. Many viewed positively the legislation that had allowed for the mushrooming of Islamic banks. One interviewee, Andreas Yewangoe, even pointed to the fact that taking interest is also forbidden by the Bible, and he saw sharia banks as an understandable form of resistance against the contemporary globalization of Western capitalism. Some Pentecostal Christians also voice support for laws that seek to restrict prostitution and alcohol consumption, restrictions that they see as consistent with their own values.[46]

The majority of Christian leaders, however, worry that the sharia bylaws erect symbolic boundaries between Muslims and non-Muslims, risking the relegation of the latter to second-class citizenship. Such an outcome is seen as a betrayal of the constitution and the ideals of Indonesian nationhood. Although it has been widely observed that the pace of sharia bylaw creation has slowed since 2004, it has not by any means stopped.[47] Indeed, data provided by the National Commission on Women (Komnas Perempuan) indicate that between 2009 and August 2013 the number of regulations (issued since 1999) more than doubled, from 154 to 342.[48] The commission's figures include administrative regulations and circulars in addition to formal bylaws, but they are illustrative of a continuing momentum. Analysts including Michael Buehler have pointed out that some of the most active proponents of sharia bylaws have been secular nationalist politicians attempting to shore up their support in the Muslim community.[49] However, even if that is true, Islamist groups have used the campaign to promote their own agenda, with the result that Christians and other minorities feel that their access to public space is increasingly restricted.

Another important illustration of a similar trend is the effort to Islamize public schools – either officially, through a change in the law on national education and curricula, or through informal channels, such as the organization of religious extracurricular activities in public schools. Recent research on two well-regarded state high schools in Yogyakarta shows how this effort at Islamization is attempted, but the report also shows that many students, including Muslims, resist such initiatives on grounds that they are exclusivist.[50]

Prof. John Titaley of Satya Wacana University has provided another example of what he regards as increasing religious segregation. Today there are fewer multiconfessional public cemeteries and more cemeteries that exclude non-Muslims. Whether with restrictions on church building, diminished opportunities for state employment, sharia bylaws, or Islam in public schools, Titaley concludes that the end of Soeharto's New Order has disadvantaged Christians. For Titaley, all this is evidence of the fact that Indonesian democracy has taken a majoritarian turn, away from the founding ideals of equal citizenship and the protection of minority rights.

MUSLIM-CHRISTIAN "AUTHENTIC HARMONY": SOCIAL CAPITAL FOR DEMOCRACY?

Although most agreed that before 1998 Muslim-Chrsitian relations were more harmonious, interviewees for this report tried to put recent developments in a broader perspective. Prof. Franz Magnis Suseno, a prominent Jesuit and public intellectual, believes that despite the difficulties and violence reported by the media, the fact is that "the vast majority of Indonesia's Christian communities live and worship free from fear and interference in a Muslim majority country, and that religious conversion has never been prohibited."[51] The Reverend Paul Richard Renwarin of the majority Christian district of Manado emphasizes a similar fact: that most recent cases of religious conflict have taken place in a few regions, like West and East Java, and these are not representative of Indonesia as a whole.

Most interviewees also pointed out that religious harmony prior to 1998 was maintained by an authoritarian regime that repressed social differences and imprisoned dissidents. As a minority, Christians had always felt that they needed to have protectors within the state. Throughout the history of Christianity in Indonesia, "The church's relationship to power changed little: a patron-client relationship with the Dutch colonial government, a feudalistic relationship with Soekarno, and opportunism practiced in the New Order era. The reasons varied – theological pietism, sociocultural patterns, survival strategy – but the basic attitude remained constant."[52] After reviewing the history of Christianity in Indonesia over the past two centuries, Jan S. Aritonang concludes, "The experience in this 'Reformation' era, and in all of the periods of the presence of Christianity in this country, also teaches that the Christians should not only develop a good relationship with the government but move on to build a closer involvement and commitment with the people in their struggling for a better life."[53] John Titaley urged his fellow Christians to understand democracy better and have an awareness that colonialism has ended and there can be no special privileges or protections for Christians.

Reverend Yewangoe observed that most of the problems involving religion today are not Christian or Muslim problems, but Indonesian problems, which have to be solved by every citizen regardless of religion. "We [at PGI] do not see issues such as GKI Yasmin as an issue of Christian suffering. This is not an exclusive Christian problem. This is a problem of the nation." Dr. Pradjarta of the Percik Foundation echoed this sentiment, adding that in recent years Ahmadis have suffered far more than have Christians.

Most Christian interviewees agreed that the real problem was not majority-minority relations (a polarity to which many interviewees object), but the challenge of building a spirit of equality and solidarity capable of grounding all interreligious relations. Yewangoe gave the example of remote villages of Central Sulawesi, where, on the occasion of a Protestant synod meeting, Muslim women in hijab helped prepare food for their Christian neighbors. In Papua, he noted, a festival commemorating the introduction of the Bible to the land was also accompanied by a Muslim music group. Dr. Pradjarta of the Percik Institute added that he felt that, as a result of recent incidents, efforts to forge dialogue and cooperation across religious communities have actually intensified. Father Magnis-Suseno voiced a similar sentiment. For him, "the strongest guarantee for the future of religious tolerance and social order in Indonesia" lies in the recent improvement in Christian-Muslim relations. "For some fifteen years now, relations between Christians and the two big mainstream Islamic organizations, Nahdhatul Ulama and Muhammadiyah, have become closer and there exists real friendship among some of their leaders.... When we have real problems, we would not go to the authorities but directly to our Muslim friends. Mainstream Islam resolutely rejects violence."[54] For the Catholic archbishop of Semarang (Central Java), Mgr. Johannes Pujasumarta, "the key to building the future is how to build a sincere dialogue with our fellow Indonesian Muslim brothers and sisters." Notwithstanding recent antipluralist incidents, many interviewees observed that resources for harmonous relations are still abundant at the grassroots level. In the New Order period, interfaith dialogue was the result of government engineering. Today it is the result of the genuine efforts of society-based individuals and groups.

Challenges nonetheless remain. As observed by Jacky Manuputty, the trust built through interfaith cooperation can be depleted in the heat of electoral competition. No less significant, the heightened social and economic mobility of the past forty years has placed Christians and Muslims in new situations, including some in which migrants from one faith displace local peoples from another. Tensions of an ethnoreligious nature have risen to new heights in places such as Manado, Ambon, Kupang, and Jayapura, where native Christians find themselves in competition with hardworking and economically savvy migrants from Java or Makassar. But many locals take pride in pointing out that there are many examples of Christians and Muslim migrants who have developed close ties of grassroots coexistence.

The realization that the difficulties Christians experience are not specifically "Christian problems" is not a perspective restricted to Christian liberals. Budijanto's research on Christian evangelicals in post-1998 Solo found that, in the face of growing religious tensions, Evangelical leaders began to articulate their public identity in terms of Indonesianness and human rights, emphasizing the challenges shared by other religious minorities.[55] In recent years, the younger generation of Pentecostal ministers has also become increasingly involved in activism with other religious groups.[56] There are also many examples of leaders representing PGI and KWI making joint statements with other religious leaders to address issues ranging from corruption to intolerance.[57] Just as Muslim leaders speak out on issues involving churches, Christian leaders are not shy about talking about the plight of nonmainstream Muslim groups such as the Ahmadiyah and the Shi'i. In the latter cases, however, the Christian leaders' insistence on the groups' rights to religious freedom has met with criticism from certain Muslim groups and governmental circles who regard this stance as meddling in Muslim affairs.

In addition to these individual incidents of cross-religious alliance, there are examples of more sustained effort, involving the establishment of interfaith coalitions. A case in point is the 2006 establishment of the National Alliance for Unity in Diversity (Aliansi Nasional Bhineka Tunggal Ika or ANBTI). Emerging from an earlier planning group for a cultural parade and conference, the alliance mobilized in response to growing concerns about the plight of pluralism in Indonesia. Recently the ANBTI has been involved in advocacy in cases of religious freedom impacting Christians, Ahmadi, and Shi'i Muslims, as well as discrimination faced by mystical groups (*aliran kepercayaan*).

While ANBTI has mobilized civil society and religious organizations, another alliance, called Sobat KBB (or "friends of religious freedom and belief"), was forged in 2013 to draw together the victims of religious violence. The group is now led by a Christian priest whose church in Bekasi was forced to move; the group's secretary is an Ahmadi; the treasurer is a follower of Sapta Darma (a mystical group); its coordinators include individuals from the church in Bogor that was denied a license and a Shi'i from Sampang, Madura, whose community was attacked in 2011. Sobat KBB is still formulating its agenda, and it has started to build a network of victims to defend shared interests. All these examples underscore that there is a growing realization, among Christians and non-Christians, that problems faced by particular religious communities are challenges faced by the entire Indonesian nation.

CONCLUSION

The story of religious freedom in Indonesia is not a simple one. The legacy of Dutch colonialism reinforced not a deterritorialized and individualized model of religious freedom, but a consociational framework in which religion was defined in relation to ethnicity, territory, and group rights. The freedom of the individual was balanced by a vigilant concern for maintaining intergroup harmony. Religious governance in the independence era reinforced this consociational legacy. The legacy was compounded by the heightened political competitions of the 1950s and 1960s, which harnessed faith and ideological commitments, not to the cart of religious freedom, but to polarizing political competitions. The repressive controls of the New Order period curbed public outbreaks of ethnoreligious tension. But the regime's selective repression of organized Muslim groupings during its first years and of Christians and Muslim democrats during its later years only deferred the task of constructing a new operating consensus for religious coexistence. Notwithstanding recent incidents of religious violence, Christian leaders and Muslim pluralists today remain hopeful that such a framework is finally being forged.

In the next few years, the resolution of two challenges will likely decide the circumstances of religious freedom for Christians and Indonesians generally: first, the government's indecisiveness in matters of law enforcement, and, second, the contestation between the moderate Muslim groups that historically dominated Indonesian Islam and smaller Islamist groups, which have been able to exercise an influence disproportionate to their actual numbers in society. With regard to the first problem, the government clearly has the capability to enforce law, yet it has not done enough to protect religious freedom. As noted by Father Magnis-Suseno, despite impressive success in fighting terrorism, "the government seems reluctant to take action when minorities are threatened" – including Muslim minorities such as the Ahmadiyah.[58]

With regard to the contestation between moderate and militant Muslim groups, the hope remains that the traditionally moderate, mainstream organizations, especially Muhammadiyah and Nahdhatul Ulama (NU), will exercise a constraining influence on militant radicalism. On most issues, these mainstream groups have struggled to maintain a centrist position, but they are also torn by their own disputes.[59] As the authors of a recent study argue, the full potential of these two groups to promote pluralist coexistence "remains unrealised"; beyond statements by certain individuals, "one has not yet seen either organisation, as institutions, drawing upon that authority in the interests of religious minorities."[60] The example serves as a sobering reminder that Indonesia has a wealth of social resources for pluralist coexistence, and it is in these that pluralist-minded Indonesians of all faiths place their hope. But much work remains to be done.

NOTES

1 Data are from the 2010 Census by the Central Bureau of Statistics, Indonesia, as analyzed in Agus Indiyanto, *Agama di Indonesia dalam Angka: Dinamika Demografis Berdasarkan Sensus Penduduk Tahun 2000 dan 2010* (Yogyakarta: Center for Religious and Cross-cutural Studies, Universitas Gadjah Mada, 2013).

2 See Arend Lijphart, *Democracy in Plural Societies: A Comparative Exploration* (New Haven, CT, and London: Yale University Press, 1977), 1.

3 Anton C. Zijderveld, "Civil Society, Pillarization, and the Welfare State," in *Democratic Civility: The History and Cross-Cultural Possibility of a Modern Political Ideal*, ed. Robert W. Hefner (New Brunswick, NJ, and London: Transaction, 1998), 153–171; quotation is from p. 159.

4 Saiful Mujani and R. William Liddle, "Indonesian Democracy: From Transition to Consolidation," in *Democracy and Islam in Indonesia* ed. Mirjam Kunkler and Alfred Stepan (New York: Columbia University Press, 2013), 24–50.

5 Marthen Tahun and Zainal Abidin Bagir carried out some of the interviews and coordinated the research team in other cities, which included Angie (Manado), Yance Rumahuru (Ambon), and Agnes (Yogyakarta and Salatiga, Central Java). Based in Jakarta and Yogyakarta, Robert W. Hefner carried out interviews with Christian and Muslim leaders on the challenge of plurality in post-Soeharto Indonesia in 1999–2010.

6 Anthony Reid, *Southeast Asia in the Age of Commerce, 1450–1680. Vol. 2. Expansion and Crisis* (New Haven: Yale University Press, 1993), 144.

7 Philip van Akkeren, *Sri and Christ: A Study of the Indigenous Church in East Java* (London: Lutterworth Press, 1969).

8 Robert W. Hefner, "Of Faith and Commitment: Christian Conversion in Muslim Java," in *Conversion to Christianity* ed. Robert W. Hefner (Berkeley: University of California Press, 1993), 102–105.

9 See Rita Smith Kipp, *Dissociated Identities: Ethnicity, Religion, and Class in an Indonesian Society* (Ann Arbor: University of Michigan Press, 1991) and Lorraine Aragon, *Fields of the Lord: Animism, Christian Minorities, and State Development in Indonesia* (Honolulu: University of Hawaii Press, 2000).

10 Merle C. Ricklefs, *A History of Modern Indonesia*, 2nd ed. (Stanford, CA: Stanford University Press, 1993), 135–137.

11 See Heather Sutherland, *The Making of a Bureaucratic Elite: The Colonial Transformation of the Javanese Priyayi* (Singapore: Heinemann Educational Books, 1979).

12 See M. C. Ricklefs, *Islamisation and Its Opponents in Java, c. 1930 to Present* (Singapore: NUS Press, 2012), and Michael Francis Laffan, *Islamic Nationhood and Colonial Indonesia: The Umma below the Winds* (London and New York: Routledge, 2003).

13 Benedict Anderson, "Old State, New Society: Indonesia's New Order in Historical Perspective," *Journal of Asian Studies* 42 (1983): 477–496, citation from p. 487.

14 See Robert Cribb, *The Indonesian Killings 1965–1966: Studies from Java and Bali* (Clayton, Australia: Monash Papers on Southeast Asia, No. 21, Centre of Southeast Asian Studies, Monash University 1990).

15 On the New Order's early agreements with Western missionaries to "build up" remote regions of Kalimantan, Sulawesi, and Irian Jaya, see Lorraine Aragon, *Fields*, and, for West Papua, Charles E. Farhadian, *Christianity, Islam, and Nationalism in Indonesia* (New York: Routledge, 2005).

16 See Robert W. Hefner, *Civil Islam: Muslims and Democratization in Indonesia* (Princeton, NJ: Princeton University Press, 2000), ch. 6.

17 See Greg Barton, "The Emergence of Neomodernism: A Progressive, Liberal Movement of Islamic Thought in Indonesia," *Studia Islamika: Indonesian Journal for Islamic Studies* 2 no. 3 (1995): 1–71.

18 See Masykuri Abdillah, *Responses of Indonesian Muslim Intellectuals to the Concept of Democracy (1966–1993)* (Hamburg: Abera Verlag Meyer, 1997).

19 The Civil Administration Law stipulates that religion is recorded on the identity card, with other than six religions recorded as "Other." Yet ambiguous religious identification in practice may result in later difficulties in registration of marriage, employment as a civil servant, or access to education for children. The law was discussed in the parliament in late 2013 for possible revision. Some MPs, especially from the multiconfessional nationalist party PDI-P, proposed that *kepercayaan* be included among the acknowledged religions, but this proposal was rejected.

20 As an illustration, MORA is among the top five state ministries that received the highest level of funding in the 2013 state budget: USD $4.2 billion, or 2.7 percent of the total state budget. In 2013, the budget for the Catholic Directorate was approximately USD $50 million (1.3 percent of the total), out of which 10 percent is for Catholic education. The budget for the Protestant Directorate is USD $85 million. The Hindu Directorate received 53 million (making up for a budgetary shortfall the prior year: normally the amount is around 38 million). The Buddhist Directorate receives almost 20 million. Beyond general secretariat expenses, there is usually an attempt to divide the budget proportionally – that is, in proportion to the percentage of adherents of the religions. See, http://www.dpr.go.id/complorgans/commission/commission8/risalah/K8_risalah_RDP_Komisi_VIII_DPR_RI_dengan_Dirjen_Bimas_Kristen,_Dirjen_Bimas_Katholik,_Dirjen_Bimas_Hindu,_dan_Dirjen_Bimas_Buddha_Kementerian_Agama_R.I.pdf

21 The six STAKPNs are in Ambon, Tarutung (North Sumatra), Jayapura (Papua), Palangkaraya (Central Kalimantan), Toraja (South Sulawesi), and Manado (North Sulawesi).

22 http://www.kemenag.go.id/index.php?a=berita&id=120015. As a comparison, there are several State Hindu Colleges and one State Hindu University; there are also several State Buddhist Colleges. With regard to Islam, there are six State Islamic Universities (UIN), sixteen State Institutes of Islamic Science (IAIN), and more than thirty State Islamic Colleges.

23 As a comparison, in the case of Islam, one very contentious case is the Ahmadiyah; the group has existed in Indonesia since the early twentieth century and has legally registered with the Ministry of Domestic Affairs. Over the years, however, the semigovernmental Indonesian Council of Ulama (MUI) and other organizations have declared the organization deviant and called for its abolition. In 2008 the government, under pressure from Muslim groups, issued a regulation severely restricting the group's activities, but it stopped short of banning the organization outright.

24 *Buku Almanak Kristen Indonesia*, Persekutuan gereja-Gereja Indonesia (PGI), 2010; see also http://www.pgi.or.id/index.php/id/profil/gereja-gereja-anggota-pgi. The data provided here are official; other sources cite slightly different synod totals.

25 See http://www.pglii.net/

26 See http://www.pglii.net/DATA%20ANGGOTA%20PGLII%202011–2015.htm

27 See http://www.pgpi-news.org/index.php?option=com_content&view=article&id=3:sejarah &catid=5:sejarah-pgpi&Itemid=8

28 See http://www.pgpi-news.org/index.php?option=com_content&view=article&id=10:nama-sinode-gereja-anggota-pgpi&catid=3:organisasi-pgpi&Itemid=3

29 A good enumeration of the synods in the three organizations as well as of the churches that join more than one organization can be found at http://binsarspeaks.net/?p=1983 (updated July 2013).

30 See http://bimaskatolik.kemenag.go.id/index.php?a=artikel&id2=kategori

31 See http://www.kemenag.go.id/index.php?a=berita&id=120015

32 See http://www.kawali.org/viewPage.php?aid=2

33 See Moch Nur Ichwan, "Towards a Puritanical Moderate Islam: The Majelis Ulama Indonesia and the Politics of Religious Orthodoxy," in *Contemporary Developments in Indonesian Islam: Explaining the "Conservative Turn,"* ed. Martin van Bruinessen (Singapore: ISEAS, 2013), 60–104.

34 See http://www.thejakartapost.com/news/2013/04/02/minister-christians-bring-discrimination-themselves.html

35 See CRCS, *Annual Report on Religious Life in Indonesia 2009* (Yogyakarta: Center for Religious and Cross-Cultural Studies, Gadjah Mada University, 2010).

36 There are at least three such national reports and a few more at the provinvial level, published by civil society organizations including the Setara Institute and the Wahid Institute, and by an academic program based at Gadjah Mada University's Center for Religious and Cross-Cultural Studies (CRCS), which is directed by the Indonesian coauthor of this report. These reports found similar problems, though they use different methods and count incidents by different means. The CRCS reports, entitled *Annual Report on Religious Life in Indonesia* (from 2008 until 2012), are available at, http://crcs .ugm.ac.id/annual-report-top; one of the reports is available in English translation.

37 This is the term used in Martin Van Bruinessen, *Contemporary Developments* (2013).

38 See, for example, International Crisis Group, *Indonesia: "Christianisation" and Intolerance*, Asia Briefing no. 114, Jakarta and Brussels, November 24, 2010.

39 Melissa Crouch, "Law and Religion in Indonesia: The Constitutional Court and the Blasphemy Law," *Asian Journal of Comparative Law* 7, no. 1 (2012), 1–46; and Zainal Abidin Bagir, "Bagaimana Merespon 'Perbedaaan,' 'Penyimpangan,' dan 'Penodaan'?" an expert witness paper for the review of the Law on Prevention of Defamation of Religion at the Constitutional Court, January 2013 (unpublished).

40 Zainal Abidin Bagir, "Defamation of Religion Law in Post-Reformasi Indonesia: Is Revision Possible?" *Australian Journal of Asian Law* 13, no. 2 (2013): 1–16.

41 Different reports give higher numbers of incidents because of different methods of counting. CRCS reports tend to use a stricter method for counting incidents. Also, what is counted is the number of houses of worship – not the number of incidents; one house of worship may experience several incidents.

42 CRCS, *Laporan Tahunan Kehidupan Beragama di Indonesia 2012* (Yogyakarta: Center for Religious and Cross Cultural Studies, Gadjah Mada University, 2013), 36–39.

43 International Crisis Group, *How Indonesian Extremist Regroup*, Asia Report no. 228 – 16 July 2012; International Crisis Group, *Indonesia: "Christianisation" and Intolerance*, Asia Briefing no. 114, Jakarta and Brussels, November 24, 2010.

44 CRCS, *Annual Report on Indonesian Religious Life 2011* (Yogyakarta: Center for Religious and Cross Cultural Studies, Gadjah Mada University, 2012), 54–55.

45 CRCS *Annual Report on Religious Life in Indonesia 2012* looked at several attempts at mediation and emphasized the importance of a less formal, or less court-based, approach, one that places greater emphasis on society's capability to solve problems using available social mechanisms and conflict-resolution approaches.

46 This point is discussed further in the forthcoming CRCS volume on Pentecostalism in Indonesia.

47 See Robin Bush, "Regional Sharia Regulations in Indonesia: Anomaly or Sympton?" in *Expressing Islam: Religious Life and Politics in Indonesia*, ed. Greg Fealy and Sally White (Singapore: Institute of Southeast Asian Studies, 2008), 174–191. For a more recent overview of sharia regulations in Indonesia, one that suggests the current is far from over, see Tim Lindsey's, *Islam, Law and the State in Southeast Asia*, Vol. I: Indonesia (London: I. B. Tauris, 2012), 363–400.

48 See Komnas Perempuan Press Release, "Lembar Fakta Kebijakan Daerah terkait Pemenuhan Hak-hak Konstitusional 15 Agustus 2013," reprinted at, http://radarsukabumi .com/?p=80540.

49 Cf. Michael Buehler, "Partainya Sekuler, Aturannya Syariah," *Tempo*, September 4, 2011, 74–75. See also his, "Subnational Islamization through Secular Parties: Comparing Shari'a Politics in Two Indonesian Provinces," *Comparative Politics*, 46, no. 1 (2013): 68–82.

50 Hairus Salim et al., *Ruang Publik Sekolah: Negosiasi dan Resistensi di SMUN di Yogyakarta* (Yogyakarta: CRCS Press, 2010); a summary of the research in English is recounted in Mohammad Iqbal Ahnaf, *Contesting Morality: Youth Piety and Pluralism in Indonesia* (Yogyakarta: CRCS Pluralism Working Paper no. 10, 2012).

51 Franz Magnis-Suseno, S.J., "Will Religious Tolerance in Indonesia Continue?" Accessed November 29, 2011, http://www.commongroundnews.org/article.php?id= 30731&lan=en&sp=0

52 Bambang Budijanto, "Evangelicals and Politics in Indonesia," in *Evangelical Christianity and Democracy in Asia*, ed. David Halloran Lumsdaine (Oxford and New York: Oxford University Press, 2009), 160.

53 Th. van den End and Jan S. Aritonang, "1800–2005: A National Overview," in *A History of Christianity in Indonesia*, ed. Jan S. Aritonang and Karel Steenbrink (Leiden and Boston: Brill, 2008), 137–226.

54 Franz Magnis-Suseno, "Pluralism Challenged: What Is Happening to Religious Freedom in Indonesia?" in *Religious Pluralism and Religious Freedom: Religions, Society and the State in Dialogue*, ed. Stefan Hammer and Fatimah Husein (Yogyakarta: Center for

Religious and Cross-Cultural Studies, Gadjah Mada University and University of Vienna, 2013), 55–60 (citation is from pp. 59–60).

55 Bambang Budijanto, "Evangelicals and Politics in Indonesia: The Case of Surakarta," in *Evangelical Christianity and Democracy in Asia*, ed. David Halloran Lumsdaine (Oxford and New York: Oxford University Press, 2009), 172–178.

56 Zainal Abidin Bagir, "Pentecostal-Muslim Relations in Indonesia: Indifference, Potential for Conflict and Prospects for Harmony," in *Aspirations for Modernity and Prosperity: Symbols and Sources behind Pentecostal/Charismatic Growth in Indonesia*, ed. Christine Gudorf, Zainal Abidin Bagir, and Marthen Tahun, pp. 171–194 (Adelaide: Australasian Theological Forum Press, 2015).

57 One prominent recent example that created headlines was one such joint statement issued in January 2011 on the eighteen "lies" of the government, which include issues of intolerance, treatment of minority groups, as well as government policies on poverty and economic issues. See, CRCS, *Annual Report on Indonesian Religious Life in Indonesia*, 2011 (Yogyakarta: CRCS, Gadjah Mada University, 2012), 68.

58 Magnis Suseno, "Will Religious Tolerance in Indonesia Continue?" *Common Grounds News Service*, November 29, 2011

59 There have also been worries that these mainstream groups have been "infiltrated" by conservative Islamists. See, for example, Ahmad Najib Burhani, "Liberal and Conservative Discourses in Muhammadiyah," 105–144.

60 Robin Bush and Budhy Munawar Rachman, "NU and Muhammadiyah – Majority Views on Religious Minorities in Indonesia," in *Religious Minorities in Muslim-Majority States in Southeast Asia: Areas of Toleration and Conflict*, ed. Bernard Platzdasch and Johan Saravanamuttu (Singapore: ISEAS, 2014), 78–103.

8

Christianity and Freedom in India: Colonialism, Communalism, Caste, and Violence

Chad M. Bauman and James Ponniah

The Christian community in India is relatively small, yet its contribution to civil society has been substantial, at least from the perspective of those who consider Western secular, democratic forms of governance ideal. At the same time, however, the influence of this small community provokes anxiety among the guardians of "traditional" Indian society. For them, the Christian community represents a threat to essentially Indian social structures and cultural norms, and a potential fifth column within the Indian nation (because of Indian Christians' putative "foreign" loyalties and alliances with Western Christians). These anxieties have given rise to attempts to circumscribe Christian freedoms (particularly the freedom to evangelize), political and legal harassment, and even acts of violence.

This chapter explores these issues in four parts. The first provides contextual demographic data on the Indian Christian community, as well as a history of the development of tensions between India's Christians and Hindus. In the second part we look closely at the sources and severity of the social, legal, political, and violent pressures felt by the contemporary Indian Christian community. The third section focuses on the effects of these pressures on Indian Christian life and practice, and on Indian social and political life more generally. Finally, the last section provides a catalog of Christian contributions to Indian civil society, particularly in the form of projects and institutions involved in education, medicine, poverty amelioration, and human rights activism.

The structure of the chapter is not intended to read as a warning about what might be lost if the Christian community continues to be subjected to pressure. It is certainly true that the challenges faced by the contemporary Indian Christian community do present the possibility that their contributions to civil society could be lost or limited in substantial ways. Even so, a simple warning such as this would be inappropriate for at least two reasons. First, for the sake of balance, we must proceed without assuming in an a priori fashion that Christian contributions to Indian society have been useful or positive from all perspectives. There is indeed, as we discuss later, a robust public debate about that very issue in India today. Second, it would be inaccurate to assume that the pressures experienced by Christians in contemporary India have led them to withdraw from the public sphere. In fact, as we detail in the following, in many cases Indian Christians' experiences of harassment and violence have provoked them to become *more* engaged in civil society, and not only in their own interest, but also on behalf of other marginalized, oppressed, and threatened peoples.

We have been indirectly conducting research on the topic of this chapter for more than five years, both through our own ethnographic investigations and by engaging with relevant archival, statistical, and secondary scholarly resources. In recent years, however, our research has had direct bearing on the subject matter of this chapter. From 2011 to 2013, we conducted interviews with more than two hundred people in and around the villages surrounding Delhi, Calcutta, Bombay, Bhubaneswar, Kandhamal, Sambalpur, Pune, Goa, Bangalore, Mangalore, Chennai, Trichy, Madurai, Kanyakumari, Dehra Dun, and Hyderabad.[1]

CONTEXTUAL AND HISTORICAL BACKGROUND

Official Indian census data suggest that Christians constitute approximately 2.4 percent of the Indian population, but many believe that the censuses significantly underestimate the size of the community. There are a number of reasons why this may be true. First, the census questions themselves have, for complicated reasons, occasionally discouraged members of India's lower-caste communities from registering themselves as Christian. Second, many low-caste Christians avoid registering themselves officially as such in order to continue taking advantage of government reservations (in academic institutions, the civil service, legislatures, etc.; see later discussion) for which official conversion to Christianity would make them ineligible. Other Christians profess their faith only secretly, in order to avoid the negative ramifications of doing so more openly in their families or villages. Still others express devotion to Christ, but do not claim exclusive devotion to Christianity. Statisticians who rely upon the reported membership of Indian Christian churches and denominations arrive at much higher numbers than the official count. Johnson and Ross, for example, estimate that India's 58 million Christians constitute 4.8 percent of the population. For a variety of reasons, this figure seems to us the most reasonable.[2] Similarly, statistics on growth vary considerably. Johnson and Ross estimate that the Indian Christian community grew by roughly 2.75 percent annually between 2000 and 2010, a period during which the Hindu community grew only 1.46 percent per year. Mandryk, on the other hand, suggests that the Christian population is growing at an annual rate of 3.7 percent.[3]

With 8 million members, Roman Catholicism remains the largest denomination in India. Boasting 2 million members, the Church of South India is a distant second. The Syro-Malabar Catholic Church, Seventh-Day Adventists, Oriental Orthodox Churches, United Evangelical Lutheran Churches, and Believers Church (associated with the American Mission, Gospel for Asia) each claim between 1 and 2 million members, with the Church of North India just below that mark.[4] Roughly half of India's Christians are now associated with evangelical, charismatic, Pentecostal, and other independent "renewalist" churches and denominations.[5]

The history of Indian Christianity begins with the St. Thomas, or Syrian Christians. These Christians trace their history to the evangelical work of St. Thomas the apostle, who, they believe, arrived in what is today Kerala in 52 CE. Such a trip would have been possible for a first-century Jew, and certain noncanonical Christian scriptures can be read to suggest that Thomas visited India on his missionary journeys. But the myth cannot be historically verified. What is more certain, however, is that settlers and missionaries from the Church of the East (the Nestorian Church), who followed East Syrian liturgical rites, established a Christian presence in southern India by around the third century CE.[6] The ancestors of these Malayalam-speaking St. Thomas Christians had achieved a relatively high status within South Indian society already by the sixth century. They then rose to prominence as a high-ranking warrior and merchant community in the medieval period, when they competed for and received local "honors" (*mariyatai*) from, and the patronage of, petty kings along the southwestern Malabar Coast.[7]

Their high social and religious status was facilitated, in part, by the fact that their religious cult apparatus, which focused on the shrines of charismatic, thaumaturgical saints (many of them from Syria), resembled and was intimately related to that of local Hindus and Muslims. Moreover, the "honors" bestowed on St. Thomas Christians entailed their participation in acts of worship during Hindu ceremonies and festivals sponsored by local rulers. For these reasons, the St. Thomas Christians were relatively well integrated into South Indian society during this period, and they were treated as a community of high social and ritual rank.[8]

After the end of the fifteenth century, however, a number of social and political processes conspired to disintegrate India's Christians from their social, cultural, and religious milieu. The most obvious and important of these processes was colonialism. The Portuguese arrived in South India in 1498 and allied themselves with St. Thomas Christians. The alliance offered certain benefits to India's ancient Christians, but it also associated them forever after, in the minds of other Indians, with the excesses of Portuguese imperialism (e.g., the Inquisition). At the same time, missionaries associated with or protected by Portuguese political authority began converting large numbers of low-caste Hindus to Christianity, with the effect of slowly undermining the high social status the Indian Christian community had previously enjoyed.

These trends continued into the era of British colonialism, which made itself felt on the Malabar Coast when the Hindu states of Travancore and Cochin became British East India Company (BEIC) tributaries in 1795. Economic and political processes set in motion by the BEIC threatened the viability of the St. Thomas Christian community's traditional occupations, eroding its status even further.[9] In the meantime, evangelical BEIC residents and British missionaries had set about reforming what they considered the unacceptably syncretistic nature of St. Thomas Christianity. However, it was the St. Thomas Christians' syncretism and openness to participating in the rites and celebrations of non-Christian local rulers that had preserved their integration and relatively high status within local economies of purity and pollution.[10] In addition, as had their predecessors, Christian missionaries enjoying the protection of the BEIC also converted large numbers of low-caste Hindus to the faith. Consequently, by the halfway point of the nineteenth century upper-caste Hindus along the Malabar Coast began to consider St. Thomas Christians to be a ritually polluting caste and withheld honors from them in local Hindu festivals.[11] Hindu-Christian riots resulting from honors contestations became more and more regular in areas with large St. Thomas Christian and upper-caste Hindu populations.[12]

The association of Christianity with colonialism, the Europeanization of St. Thomas religious belief and practice, and the growing numbers of low-caste converts to Christianity had a profoundly negative effect on the perception of Indian Christianity, and on relationships between Christians and Hindus. The deterioration of Hindu-Christian relations was further accelerated by the rising number of missionaries at work in India after 1813, the related British involvement in colonial education and social reforms (e.g., the banning of widow burning, or suttee, in 1829), and policy changes disfavoring India's traditional landed elites. By the second half of the nineteenth century, then, India's Christians, both ancient and new, had come to be perceived by many as adherents of a "foreign" religion with suspect political loyalties. Not surprisingly, native Indian Christians were regularly targeted in the Great Rebellion of 1857.[13] In the subsequent Hindu revival movements of the late nineteenth century, missionaries and native Indian Christians were frequently attacked, rhetorically *and* physically.[14]

The distinction between Christians and adherents of India's other religions was further reinforced by the British tendency to conceive of and organize India's population according to religious community – a tendency most clearly manifested in decennial censuses collected by the British. In the late nineteenth century, British administrators began to enumerate and thereby politicize religious identity, and in the early twentieth century they decided to grant separate electorates to India's religious minorities.[15] Individually, and in combination, these policies buttressed "the supposedly primordial corporate identity and structures of leadership of castes and religious sects ... thereby rendering rigid what had hitherto been more negotiable entities."[16] Other factors too complex to be covered in these pages compounded the effect, for example, the development of highly politicized associational life (often organized along religious lines) in the rapidly growing urban centers of British India[17] and the "fractured"[18] and at times paradoxically atavistic modernity of India's urban Hindu middle classes, which impeded the development of more inclusive and interreligious countercolonial Indian identities.[19]

Already in the late nineteenth century, Hindus began establishing organizations to undermine or counter the influence of Christianity in India. The most important of these early organizations was the Arya Samaj, founded in 1875 by Swami Dayanand Saraswati (1824–1883).[20] Yet Christianity continued to grow, and conversions even accelerated in the last decades of the nineteenth century, in large part as a result of a series of devastating famines that provoked conversions and sent famine orphans into Christian orphanages (and from there into churches).[21] Observing this trend, authors in the first decades of the twentieth century, such as U. N. Mukherji, predicted the demise of Hinduism. Other Hindus established *sabhas* ("societies"), and eventually, in 1925, the All-India Hindu Mahasabha ("Great Society"), to defend Hinduism against Christian (and Muslim) incursions. Those involved in such movements agreed that the essence and special genius of Indian identity, and the only possible source of the kind of unity that would be required to displace the British, was "Hinduness," or Hindutva, as articulated by V. D. Savarkar's 1923 tract, *Hindutva: Who Is a Hindu?*

In contemporary India, those who most regularly advocate the circumscription of minority religious freedoms (rhetorically or violently) are most often associated with the Sangh Parivar, the "Family of the Sangh," a collection of Hindu nationalist organizations. The constituent bodies of the Sangh Parivar were established by members of the Rashtriya Swayamsevak Sangh (National Volunteer Organization), or RSS, which itself was founded in 1925. The RSS's founder, Maharashtrian Keshav Baliram Hedgewar (1889–1940), was inspired by Savarkar's notion of Hindutva, and his organization grew quickly throughout the 1920s, 1930s, and 1940s. The RSS eventually spawned other religious, cultural, and political organizations intent on defending Hinduism and containing the Muslim and Christian "threat." These included the Akhil Bharatiya Vanvasi Kalyan Ashram, or ABVKA ("All-India Forest-Dweller's Welfare Center," founded in 1952); the Vishwa Hindu Parishad, or VHP ("World Hindu Council," founded in 1964); and what became the Bharatiya Janata Party or BJP ("Indian People's Party") – India's primary opposition political party and perennial opponent of the more secularist Congress Party.[22]

Those affiliated with the Sangh Parivar generally advocate more expansive legal constraints on minority religious freedoms, and more aggressively so, than those not affiliated with the Sangh. However, concerns about the spread and growth of "foreign" faiths such as Islam and Christianity are relatively widespread in contemporary India. Even Gandhi, whose inclusive conception of Indian unity contrasted significantly with the Hindu-oriented nationalism of Savarkar and Golwarkar, regularly accused Indian converts of being denationalized. He criticized missionaries for targeting lower-caste Hindus (whom he controversially considered unintelligent and gullible) and for using social services to lure impecunious Indians to the Christian path.[23] Gandhi also called into question the dominant Christian conception of conversion (as a salvation-inducing shift from one religious affiliation to another) and cast doubt on the desirability and motives of the Christian evangelical project itself.

Gandhi was assassinated by a man with links to the Sangh Parivar months after India gained independence in August 1947 and therefore had little direct effect on the development of its constitution. While still alive, Gandhi famously had given ambiguous replies to questions about whether conversion or evangelism should be banned in an independent India. In a strong statement from which he later backed away, at least to some extent, he said, "If I had power and could legislate I should certainly stop all proselytizing. It is the cause of much avoidable conflict between classes and unnecessary heart-burning among missionaries."[24] In many ways, then, Gandhi mainstreamed criticism of Christian mission work. He reflected an ambivalent attitude toward the liberal idea of freedom of religion, taken to include the practice of religious persuasion and conversion. This attitude remains typical even among Hindus otherwise supportive of secular governance. Such widespread ambivalence about the propriety of religious evangelism and conversion blunts the secularist critique of the Sangh's more chauvinistic and antiminority actions and proposals.

Given this widespread ambivalence about Christian evangelizing, it is perhaps not at all surprising that the Constituent Assembly – the body charged with developing independent India's constitution – entertained the idea of a constitutional ban on conversion when debating India's constitution. In the end, the ban did not pass, in large part because of objections from Christians and more generous and secular-minded Hindus in the assembly. When the Drafting Committee finally forwarded the draft constitution to the Constituent Assembly in February 1948, it included the following statement: "Subject to public order, morality and health ... all persons are equally entitled to freedom of conscience and the right freely to profess, practice and propagate religion." Debate erupted, as it had earlier in the process, over the inclusion of the right to "propagate religion," and many Hindus expressed concern that it would undermine and even threaten the very survival of Hinduism. However, Christians and their non-Christian allies were able to garner enough support for the wording to have it included as article 25 in the constitution.[25] Thus, Christian voices were clearly instrumental in ensuring that robust religious freedoms were enshrined in the Indian constitution. Nevertheless, many Hindus left the debates feeling that Christians had taken advantage of the Hindu majority's generosity, and this feeling undoubtedly tinctured debates about missionaries and conversion in the following decade.

For example, in the decade after independence, Sangh groups and other Hindu *sabhas* prompted several states to conduct inquiries into the tactics and legality of Christian missionaries. The most famous of these resulted in the publication of the influential *Christian Missionary Activities Inquiry Committee Report* (1956), widely known as the Niyogi Committee Report (after the name of the judge who chaired the committee). The Niyogi Committee, which was sponsored by the Madhya Pradesh state government, conducted and transcribed hundreds of interviews with members of all religious communities around Madhya Pradesh and present-day Chhattisgarh. On the basis of these interviews, and on its somewhat prejudiced analysis of an impressive array of missionary literature, the committee concluded that Christianity was growing rapidly (and at the expense of Hinduism). They alleged that foreign Christians sought not only the souls of Hindus, but their political loyalty as well. Furthermore, they claimed that Christians were using their superior access to Western wealth and technological prowess, manifested primarily in their medical and educational facilities, to gain access to non-Christian Indians in order to lure, cajole, or dupe them into converting to Christianity.[26]

The committee recommended that India send home foreign missionaries focused primarily on evangelism and counseled the drafting of laws prohibiting conversion by "force, fraud, or inducement" (or sometimes, "force, fraud, and *allurement*"). This phrase, and its attendant assumptions and implied accusations, have become a touchstone of the antimissionary movement in India, and one finds the phrase used regularly, even today, in public discourse and parliamentary discussion.

The accusation that Christianity spread primarily through force, fraud, and inducement rested on the belief that missionaries frequently leveraged their greater access to Western wealth and power – through, for example, the offers of cash, loans, legal help, medical care, or education (free or at reduced rates for Christians), and so on – to tempt or oblige non-Christians to convert. Such implicit and explicit offers had occasionally been made in earlier eras of missionary work. But the assertion that they were widespread was outdated even in the 1950s and is even more so today (though a "new breed"[27] of well-funded, aggressively evangelistic, mostly independent evangelical and Pentecostal Indian missionaries has returned, to some extent, to missionary tactics long ago abandoned by mainstream Protestants and Catholics).

At the most fundamental level, the phrase expresses concern that the contemporary religious playing field is uneven, and that the superior wealth and power of the Western world tilt the competition in favor of religions, including Christianity, that are popularly associated with it (even if illegitimately so). Such concerns led the Niyogi Committee members to recommend a ban on conversion by force, fraud, and allurement and inspired a series of state laws (most of which are euphemistically called "Freedom of Religion" laws) enacting the proposed ban in Odisha (1967), Madhya Pradesh (1968), Arunachal Pradesh (1978), and elsewhere.[28] Lawmakers proposed similar policies at the national level three times (in 1954, 1960, and 1978) but failed each time to gain the support necessary for passage.[29]

Odisha's "Freedom of Religion Act, 1967," which became the model for others, prohibits "conversion from one religion to another by the use of force or inducement or by fraudulent means and for matters incidental thereto." While the act defined "conversion" in a relatively straightforward manner, it left spacious room for interpretation in its definitions of "force," "fraud," and "inducement." Force, for example, included "threat of divine displeasure or social excommunication." By definition, then, conversions resulting from Christian preaching about the judgment of God on sinners would be illegal. "Fraud" was defined vaguely, and in a circular fashion, as "misrepresentation or any other fraudulent contrivance." Similarly, a broad definition of "inducement," as "the offer of any gift or gratification, either in cash or in kind and shall also include the grant of any benefit, either pecuniary or otherwise," left substantial margin for interpretation. Was the offer of Christian fellowship, for example, an inducement? The promise of life within a community that (rhetorically, at least) proclaimed the equal dignity of all people? Acts of charity for the poor, even if offered to all religious people, and without any explicit strings attached? Other so-called freedom of religion laws suffered from similar ambiguities.

While to our knowledge no one has ever been successfully prosecuted under these laws, they are frequently used to harass the Indian Christian community. In fact, attacks on Christians often end only when their attackers haul them to the police, who book the victims for "forcible conversion" at the instigation of attackers. While the charges are almost inevitably dropped, Christians often are jailed for several hours, days, or even months or are forced to pay bribes or bail to secure their release.[30]

Since the acts include language that was rejected by the Constituent Assembly and did not appear in the constitution, they were challenged almost immediately in court. The High Courts of Odisha struck down that state's law, but its counterpart in Madhya Pradesh upheld its equivalent, and eventually, the Supreme Court of India was called upon to reconcile the verdicts in the case of *Stanislaus vs. The State of Madhya Pradesh*, which was decided in January of 1977. The Supreme Court upheld the ruling of Madhya Pradesh's High Court, and the constitutionality of the acts themselves. While the Christians who argued in favor of the right to propagate before the Constituent Assembly no doubt assumed it included the right to convert others, the Supreme Court distinguished between propagation and conversion. What the constitution's article 25 grants, the Court argued:

> is not the right to convert another person to one's own religion, but to transmit or spread one's religion by an exposition of its tenets ... there is no fundamental right to convert another person to one's own religion because if a person purposely undertakes the conversion of another person to his religion ... that would impinge on the "freedom of conscience" guaranteed to all the citizens of the country alike.[31]

As a result, therefore, there remains in India no nationally guaranteed right to seek the conversion of another person intentionally. Practically, decisions with respect to the constitutional right to "propagate" are made on the ground, by local legislatures. At the very least, the decision returned in *Stanislaus vs. The State of Madhya Pradesh* paved the way for the drafting of new state laws proscribing conversion, which several states have since done.

SOURCES AND SEVERITY OF PRESSURES ON THE INDIAN CHRISTIAN COMMUNITY

As indicated, though these laws have rarely, if ever, been used successfully to prosecute Christian pastors, evangelists, or missionaries, the ambiguous definitions they deploy for terms like "fraud" and "allurement" have allowed for the frequent legal harassment of ordinary Christians. While the Indian constitution therefore appears, prima facie, to enshrine a relatively expansive degree of religious freedom, including the freedom to "propagate" one's religion, the Supreme Court's decision to distinguish the right to *convert another* from the right to propagate has effectively restricted that freedom. (Whether the right to convert another *should* be protected is of course another matter.) The restriction is manifested legally in the Court's refusal to assert that the right to convert another is a fundamental right. It is also apparent socially in the fact that India's history of judicial tergiversation and legal ambiguity has created a good deal of confusion, which, combined with the uneven and sometimes compromised application of the law, makes space for abuse and the use of existing laws to harass Christians.

If the lack of full freedom to proselytize represents one form of pressure on India's Christians (at least on the evangelistic among them), and its "Freedom of Religion" laws represent a second (again, at least on expansionist Christian communities), then India's reservation system supplies yet a third. The Indian constitution allows for positive forms of discrimination akin to affirmative action on behalf of India's minority communities. And since independence, Indian legislatures, both national and at the state level, have preserved reservations for minority communities in legislatures, civil service, and educational institutions. Among the groups favored by the reservation system are members of India's lower castes ("Scheduled Castes," or SC) and tribes ("Scheduled Tribes," or ST). A presidential order in 1950 stipulated that "no person who professes a religion different from Hinduism shall be deemed to be a member of a scheduled caste." And later rulings further clarified that Sikhs and Buddhists were, for these purposes, to be considered "Hindu." (No such stipulations were placed on ST identity.)

The argument in favor of the presidential order has been that officially, at least, Christians do not recognize caste, and, therefore, that low-caste converts to Christianity should no longer be considered low caste. Opponents of the order have pointed out that many SC converts to Christianity continue to suffer prejudice due to their low-caste status, at the hands of both Hindus *and* other Christians, and have argued, therefore, that that SC converts to Christianity deserve continued access to SC reservations. At the root of the issue, of course, lie unresolvable debates about whether caste is a *Hindu* or *Indian* social product.

What this means, in practice, is that SC converts to Christianity lose access to the politically and financially important reservations they enjoy before conversion. The reservation system, then, constitutes a kind of disincentive for SC Hindus to convert to Christianity.[32] No doubt some who might have been inclined to convert refuse to do so for this very reason. For similar reasons, a large number of SC Hindus who do convert to Christianity refuse to acknowledge their conversion formally and continue to register themselves as Hindu in order to protect their access to reservations. This widespread dissimulation has itself been the source of significant tension between India's Christians and Hindus. The anti-Christian violence in Kandhamal, Odisha (on which, more later), was fueled in part by tensions related to the issue.[33]

India's legal system therefore puts direct and indirect pressure on, or disprivileges, its Christian community (or at least its *evangelistic* Christian community) in at least three ways. As indicated, legal harassment often accompanies, or extends and exacerbates, the hardship of physical assault, Thus, to the three forms of pressure exerted on the Indian Christianity community enumerated earlier, we must add a fourth: violent attack. The violence that India's Christians experience falls primarily into two broad categories: 1) what we might call "everyday" attacks and 2) large-scale riot violence. In what follows, we briefly describe each of these in turn.

In the postcolonial era, India's Christians have never experienced the kind of violence that India's Muslims have endured. Indeed, from independence until the late 1990s, attacks on Christians were relatively rare. According to United Christian Forum for Human Rights (UCFHR) estimates, for example, only thirty-two cases of violence against Christians were officially registered between 1964 and 1996. In 1997, though, UCFHR noted fifteen cases, and in 1998, astoundingly, the number jumped to ninety.[34] Between 1998 and 2007, the number of cases reported in the media rose to their current levels of around 250 to 300 attacks a year.[35] Our own fieldwork suggests these figures may even underestimate the frequency of anti-Christian attacks. We call these attacks "everyday" not to diminish their effects or severity, but rather to highlight the fact that they are, in a very literal sense, quite nearly a daily occurrence. Moreover, they are "everyday" in the sense of being routine or unremarkable. They are also *routinized*, even stylized.

Most of the everyday attacks target pastors, preachers, and evangelists (and their followers), sometimes in their own churches but more often while they are at work on the streets, in vacation Bible schools, or in the homes of converts or potential converts. In the usual pattern, a small group or mob of people identified by the victims as "Hindu nationalists," or members of the "Sangh Parivar," "BJP," "RSS," "Bajrang Dal," or "VHP," approaches the victims and accuses them of fraudulent or "forcible" conversion. The hostile group then proceeds to steal, destroy, or dispose of any evangelistic media in the victims' possession (along with the means of transportation – e.g., bikes, motorcycles – that allows them to travel for evangelical purposes). Next, the mob begins slapping, punching, kicking, and dragging the victims, sometimes halfheartedly, and at other times with vigor and reckless violent abandon, even mirth. The everyday attacks are only very rarely fatal, but the victims commonly receive injuries that require hospitalization. Frequently, they are then kidnapped or otherwise transported against their will to another village, or to a police station, where they often find that charges have already been registered against them (charges that almost never lead to prosecution, let alone conviction). The victims who are taken to a police station often find little protection there, and many are interrogated by the police or incarcerated for a few hours or days "for their own protection" (which in some cases may in fact be true but is often nothing more than an excuse for illegal detainment).

Whereas the "everyday" violent attacks on Indian Christians tend to target specific people or communities, the anti-Christian riots tend to be more widespread and generalized. Already in the 1980s there were occasional communal riots involving Christians. The best known and most significant of these originated in Mandaikadu village, in the southernmost coastal district of Kanyakumari (Tamil Nadu). During a popular local Hindu temple festival in 1982, rumors spread that some Christian men had molested Hindu women taking their ritual baths. Tension spread between Christians and Hindus in the location, and police intending to quiet the conflict ended up firing into a crowd and killing at least six Christians. The violence then spread to surrounding villages in the weeks afterward. At least two more persons were killed in subsequent police interventions, and another person died in Hindu-Christian clashes in the village of Kovalam, while hundreds more were injured. Christians and Hindus alike were affected by the violence; churches, temples, schools, and convents were destroyed, and many wells were poisoned. In Pollamthurai village alone the homes of more than six hundred Catholic fisher folk were destroyed, along with valuable fishing equipment. Officially, nine Christians died in the attacks, though many believe the number to be higher. Though official figures include no Hindus among the dead, many witnesses allege that several Hindus were also killed by rioting Christians.[36] The Mandaikadu riots seemed an aberration to many at the time. Indeed, it was not until Christmas in 1998, in the Dangs, Gujarat, that another similar riot occurred. This time, the violence was more one-sided and targeted tribal converts to Christianity. Though none lost their lives in the attacks, rioters destroyed dozens of Christian homes, schools, and places of worship over the span of several days.

Though the "everyday" incidents of anti-Christian violence continued apace in the intervening years, no large-scale riots occurred again until the day before Christmas, in 2007, when violence erupted in Kandhamal, Odisha. Though not the first incident in the violence, an early altercation between Christians and the traveling entourage of Swami Lakshmanananda Saraswati (a beloved but controversial Hindu leader known for his social and religious work among local tribal peoples, his promotion and defense of Hinduism, and his criticism of Christian evangelism) galvanized anti-Christian activists in the region and probably ensured that the riots would spread farther, and last longer, than might have otherwise been the case.

The 2007 Kandhamal violence lasted for a few days, but then broke out again eight months later, in August of 2008, after the swami was assassinated in cold blood while celebrating Krishna's birthday in his ashram, surrounded by followers (several of whom were also killed). Naxalites, the violent Maoist revolutionaries at work in large swaths of rural India, claimed responsibility, but many of the swami's followers believed Christians had carried out the attack, either alone or in league with the Naxalites. As a result, they unleashed a series of devastating assaults on Christians, Christian neighborhoods, and Christian villages. During the two rounds of violence, at least fifty people lost their lives; dozens were beaten, shot, stabbed, molested, and raped; and thousands lost their homes. At the height of the second round of violence, around 30,000 Christians were in refugee camps spread throughout the region, a number that is particularly striking given that the most recent census figures suggest that there are only around 117,000 Christians in the entire district.[37] Afterward, violence occurred in other states, especially in and around Mangalore and Bangalore (both in the state of Karnataka). Though most of the victims were Christian, many Hindus were also attacked and driven out of their homes. Some became refugees themselves; others lost their lives. In one attack in Kandhamal alone, a Christian mob destroyed 120 Hindu homes.

National Sangh spokespersons portrayed the anti-Christian violence as a natural (if regrettable) and therefore, in their view, at least somewhat justifiable response to Christian evangelizing and "conversion activities." On the other hand, local observers more frequently understood the attacks as a result of the sinister and concerted exploitation, by Sangh activists and local Oriya traders,[38] of economic competition between the mostly Christianized, somewhat more financially successful SC Pana community and the largely un-Christianized, less developed ST Kandha community. These observers also attributed the attacks to political tensions arising from the Pana community's attempt to have itself reclassified as an ST, for reasons articulated previously.[39]

It is difficult to account for the rise in anti-Christian violence since the end of the 1990s. Some have linked it to the growing strength of the BJP, which gained greater power at the center, and in many individual states, in the elections of 1998 (but which had by 2004 relinquished many of those same gains).[40] Others have suggested that the Sangh turned its attention to Christians after concluding that its anti-Muslim agenda was no longer reaping the same political rewards.[41] Others have noted that 1998 was the year that Sonia Gandhi, the Italian- and Catholic-born widow of a former Indian prime minister, Rajiv Gandhi, took control of the more secularist Congress Party, making it attractive for the Congress Party's rivals to promote and perpetuate suspicions about the "foreign" religion of Christianity. Still others have suggested the rise in anti-Christian rhetoric and violence might represent an offended response to the quite public targeting of India's Hindus by Christian evangelical and missionary groups (as exhibited, for example, by "AD2000" and the "Joshua Project").[42] We have ourselves have suggested elsewhere that the rise in anti-Christian violence is perhaps at least partially related to the increasing force of globalization in 1990s India, of which Christians are often perceived to be patsies, and for which they seem to stand, in the minds of many, as proxies.[43]

Whatever the immediate causes, what makes it possible that India's Christians could become the focus of antiminority sentiment and violence is the widespread, anxiety-producing perception that Christianity is an ever-expansionist religion with strong political and cultural allegiances to the West. Critics argue that Christianity, if left unchecked, could threaten the current hierarchical social and cultural structures, and even the political integrity of the Indian nation, as it is believed to be doing among the separatist movements in India's Northeast. (The fact that members of these separatist movements have sometimes had Christian roots contributes to the widely held public perception that they operate with the tacit or even direct support of local Christians and Christian institutions.) While few Indians actively advocate restrictions on conversion in contemporary India, and while fewer still participate in violence against India's Christians, the concerns of those who do are quite widely shared. For this reason, public condemnation of anti-Christian rhetoric, activity, and violence is often not as negative or forceful as one might expect, and this muted response contributes to its perpetuation.

If the lack of a forceful public denunciation of anti-Christian activism accounts, at least partly, for its survival and growth, so too does another, less obvious fact: Anti-Christian activism *works*. Criticisms of Christian thought, practice, and especially evangelism have provoked profound transformations in Indian Christian life and practice. Insofar as the criticisms have been civil, we might celebrate these transformations as the positive result of public debate in an open, democratic society. After all, it is through public contestation that societies attempt to achieve consensus about the good and socialize their members in accordance with collective notions of appropriate behavior. But the very uncivil legal harassment of Christians and the violence committed against them have *also* worked, and here neutral observers may have more reason for concern. In what follows, we briefly articulate a number of tangible effects of anti-Christian activism in India, grouped into three major categories: 1) demographic effects; 2) theological, liturgical, and evangelistic effects; and 3) political effects.

Demographic Effects

The primary demographic effect of anti-Christian activism has been the internal migration of Christians from areas where they are a threatened minority to places where they are no longer, or not as acutely, threatened (e.g., larger urban centers, or villages, cities, districts, and states where Christians constitute a majority). While we suspect that the everyday incidents of anti-Christian violence subtly support the out-migration of Christians from hostile regions, it is in the wake of the Kandhamal riots that we see the demographic effects of anti-Christian violence most clearly. Because of continued harassment, lost employment or educational opportunities, and threats of violence after the riots, many Christians who fled to refugee camps during the Kandhamal violence had trouble resettling in their home villages. Because of these challenges, many Christians in Kandhamal decided to resettle outside the region. A good number migrated to Bhubaneswar, the capital and largest city of Odisha, for jobs and security. Others left the state entirely, moving to nearby urban centers such as Bangalore, or to states, like Kerala and Tamil Nadu, more hospitable to Christians. If one of the goals of those who perpetrate anti-Christian harassment and violence is to Hinduize local geographies, then it is clear that the riots worked spectacularly. Kandhamal today is a much more Hindu space than it was in 2007;[44] one report suggests that as many as twenty-five thousand Christians were permanently displaced from the region as a result of the riots.[45]

Theological, Liturgical, and Evangelistic Effects

The effects of anti-Christian activism on Christian life and practice are more complex. Since the colonial period, Christian-Hindu debates have caused at least some European missionaries and Indian Christians to reconsider their prior belief in the exclusive soteriological efficacy of Christianity, whereas interacting with Hindus merely confirmed and entrenched the theological exclusivism of others. Additionally, Indian complaints about the putative "foreignness" of convert culture, worship, and theology were no doubt at least partially responsible for the Christian theological and liturgical innovations (e.g., "indigenization" and "acculturation") that began in earnest in the 1960s.[46] Moreover, it is equally clear that the lack of enthusiasm for direct evangelism shown by contemporary mainstream Indian Protestant, Catholic, and Orthodox Christians is related to their desire to maintain their status as respectable communities in predominantly Hindu India (though in this case the shift in focus from evangelism to social transformation also reflects theological and missiological trends among liberal Christians worldwide).

The same impulse that led some Indian Christians to seek theological connections with their non-Christian neighbors prompted them, after the escalation of anti-Christian violence, to seek more practical connections as well. In the aftermath of the religious violence in Karnataka in 2008, for example, Catholic bishops in the state made friendly visits to Hindu and Muslim places of worship and joined hands with Hindu swamis at Pejawar Matt in a rally against land mining. Other groups, such as the Catholic Sabha in Mangalore, have focused on making Christian celebrations including Christmas more welcoming to non-Christians and now sponsor interfaith meetings highlighting the values that Christians hold in common with non-Christians during the season. Such efforts reflect a significant change in the attitude of many Christians toward non-Christians, a change made explicit by the Catholic archbishop of Bangalore, Bernard Moras, who told us:

> Building up bridges and developing respect for each other is true evangelization. That is the kingdom which the Lord expected us to build. [The] Lord has not said, "convert everyone." [Rather, he said go] and proclaim the kingdom of peace, justice, and solidarity, where all can respect and all can live together. This I personally feel is today's evangelization.... Your relationship is evangelization. Your whole life is evangelization. Removing those barriers that exist among us is evangelization. Barriers do exist among us: barriers with other religions, barriers with other denominations, barriers with the non-believers[47]

Interreligious engagements like these described by the archbishop function not only to build good relationships between different religious communities but also to give visibility to existing interreligious harmony and interaction in India.

Since the 1990s, as a response to negative perceptions of their ministries, many religious communities have also begun to reconceive of their ministerial function. For example, our conversation partners in both Odisha and Karnataka insisted that Christians needed to become more inclusive, particularly in their provision of social service. Because of the violence, said one, "We make sure that every deserving person, irrespective of religion, becomes the beneficiary of our humanitarian aid. We have given aid to everyone for the construction of [homes] so that there is no jealousy on the part of the Hindu Dalits[48] and tribals against Christian Dalits and thus they cannot be easily persuaded to attack Christians by the Hindu radicals."[49] Similarly, we observed in the violence-affected village of Letingia (Kandhamal) that a Christian agency had funded the construction of a community prayer hall in which symbols of different religious traditions were visible, and on the walls of which quotations from non-Christian leaders such as the Dalit rights activist B. R. Ambedkar were inscribed. Archbishop Moras indicated his support for such efforts:

> I always tell priests, "You are parish priests for everyone within the parish – maybe in a different sense but all [of them] are your parishioners, Catholics as well as non-Catholics, Hindus, Muslims and everyone.... We have to build bridges wherever it is possible so that these attacks will stop.... If you don't tackle issues you can't come together ... it can be the cleanliness, water supply, road maintenance, children's education, power supply or poverty. Leave out religion. Form committees [that can] tackle the issues."[50]

The evidence suggests that many Christians, and particularly Catholics in areas where Christians have been attacked, have taken the archbishop's advice to heart.

Since the 1990s, even evangelical and Pentecostal Christians have altered the way they evangelize in response to the increasingly bellicose responses of Hindus. Until the 1990s, open-air preaching in public spaces (including Hindu religious sites), often with megaphones or other amplification systems, was not at all uncommon, and evangelists in an earlier era could expect to have friendly conversations and debates with their interlocutors. But since the 1990s, largely as a result of Hindu agitation, most Christians have adopted a less antagonistic approach. In fact, Richard Howell, general secretary of the Evangelical Fellowship of India, told us that almost nobody engages in public street preaching anymore because of fear of being physically assaulted. Open-air preaching, or what we might refer to as "cold-call" evangelism, has been largely replaced by evangelistic techniques that include "Web evangelism," "friendship evangelism," and "care cell evangelism," which emphasize utilizing networks of friendship and family ties, and evangelizing only to those who have invited the evangelist to do so. Other changes are also apparent. For example, in Karnataka, as elsewhere, the Church of South India now requires converts to sign and register an official affidavit, complete with name, signature or thumbprint, and picture, indicating that they have decided to become Christian without any inducement and of their own free will.

Without exception, Christians with whom we conversed indicated that the growing hostility of those affiliated with the Sangh Parivar was responsible for these and other changes. However, our Christian conversation partners were divided on the question of whether the changes should be considered positive or negative. Some clearly considered the earlier, freer evangelistic era the "good old days." Among those who speak ruefully of the good old days is a small subset that refuses to adjust to the new normal and that continues to engage in more aggressive forms of evangelism. For some, in fact, doing otherwise would be an act of apostasy, a failure to carry out what they construe as their Christian obligation to witness openly, regularly, and broadly. Any decent evangelist, the leader of a large Indian missions association told us, should be "going out and getting some slaps." It is clear, then, that for at least some Indian Christians what others might call "persecution" and "martyrdom" functions as a confirmation that they are acting in accordance with Christ's dictates. Those who understand their Christian duty in this way interpret their experiences as a fulfillment of biblical prophecies foretelling resistance to the spread of the gospel. In short, some Christians have maintained an assertive, public style of evangelism, while others have adapted their evangelistic methods to a more hostile social setting – perhaps even to the point of avoiding evangelism altogether. Disagreements over evangelistic methods have divided the Christian community, and the resultant disunity has left all Indian Christians more vulnerable to attack and marginalization.

Political Effects

Hindu resistance to evangelism and, in some cases, to Indian Christians' free and open worship has forced Christians to fight for their rights of religious freedom. Doing so has transformed them into active political citizens of the Indian nation. Stories told by those we conversed with in both Odisha and Karnataka provide many examples of the ways that Christians have tried, through political means and action in civil society, to overcome their victimhood and to assert their rights as legitimate citizens of India. One of the effects of recent violence against India's Christians in these contexts, therefore, has been to turn them from a state of quiescence into a more active political force.

Christians employed a variety of strategies to put pressure on state governments to act on their behalf in the context of anti-Christian violence. They engaged in demonstrations and strikes, which brought the normal, day-to-day functioning of civil society to a halt. They transformed their church premises into hubs of political activity, and their church altars into podiums for political speeches. They enlisted support from opposition parties (both Odisha and Karnataka were governed, at the time of the violence, by the BJP and its allies/affiliates). They enlisted support from other minorities, and from Muslims in particular. They joined hands with secular-minded Hindus. They used strong language in their dealings with state authorities. They engaged cautiously in dialogue with leaders of the very same Hindu nationalist groups that had attacked them, as well as with those in charge of law and order (some of whom had been complicit in the violence). They used their networks to nationalize and internationalize the issue, in order to bring outside pressure to bear on their state and national governments.

Though India's Christians had never been completely dormant in the political domain, the experience of violence stimulated new activities and catalyzed many of the community's previously unknown or underutilized political capacities. Many of our interlocutors believed that India's Christian leaders had been rather politically inactive and naïve until the 1990s, when they realized that they could no longer afford to be neutral or indifferent in the face of mounting anti-Christian rhetoric and violence. According to the famous Catholic theologian Felix Wilfred:

> Unlike [the] independence struggle [in which they were politically active], Indian Christians in post-independence India … participated less and less in debating and discussing issues that concerned the nation and its people. The kind of debates and discussions that Christians [had previously] engaged in … did not take place any more in Christian communities in post-independence India. This only indicates that "Christians" were becoming more and inward looking.[51]

Since the 1990s, however, Indian Christian behavior has changed, and not just in Karnataka and Odisha.

One of the most obvious, earliest, and concrete Christian political responses to the experience of violence was the formation of interdenominational networks and alliances. A whole range of such networks were founded or – in the case of those created earlier – became more active or proactive after the late 1990s. The United Christian Forum for Human Rights is perhaps the most powerful and best known. But many other similar, smaller state and regional networks or associations emerged around the same time as well. These organizations reflect the perceived need of Christians to be strongly united and supportive of one another in the face of religious violence and in order to withstand the threats and attacks of radical Hindu groups more effectively.

A secondary effect of these organizations has been to increase the ecumenical spirit among India's Christians. In the context of these new organizations, mainline churches, evangelical groups, and individual pastors joined together, began to know one another, and agreed upon certain common strategies and guidelines for their Christian practice and proclamation. In places such as Bangalore, such groups began to meet once a month for workshops or seminars on noncontroversial topics such as the Lord's Prayer, the concept of salvation, and how most appropriately to communicate the Christian message to non-Christians. These groups also deliberated on matters of concern to Christians more generally and submitted memoranda to the Karnataka government on various issues, including a successful demand for the release of a Christian minority fund of around about 500 million rupees to be used for the reconstruction of churches and in the support of struggling Christians in the state.[52]

The Catholic hierarchy has been hesitant to engage in highly political issues, and the Catholic Bishops Conference of India's (CBCI) official appeal, just before the general elections in 2009, for the electorate to vote for a party that would promote secularism was a rare intervention. Nevertheless, the hierarchy has pursued certain strategies to help address the reality of the violence and harassment experienced by Catholics and other Christians. For example, a new portfolio of "public relations officer" (PRO) has been created in the diocesan administration and staffed with priests. The role of the office is to communicate Christian opinions and concerns to the public clearly and accurately and to build rapport with local politicians and law enforcement officers. Such PROs have been established both in Delhi, India's administrative capital, and in areas of conflict, including Bhubaneswar (Odisha), Bangalore, and Mangalore.[53]

If the Catholic hierarchy has been reticent in engaging the structural aspects of anti-Christian violence, the Catholic laity have not, and in this regard the lay-led All India Christian Council (AICC) and All India Catholic Union (AICU) merit special mention. These two organizations have been active not only on political issues of concern to Christians, but also in advocating and supporting secular governance in India more generally. Formed in 1999, the AICC has emerged today as a significant voice in contemporary Indian politics. The AICC alliance cuts across denominational barriers to counter the growing violence and threats against Christians but also speaks out on behalf of other minorities and oppressed castes (regardless of their religious affiliation). The organization seeks "to pursue proactive and not just reactive actions to help the Christian community and other minorities, as well as Dalits, tribals and backward communities." As of early 2006, the AICC membership included more than five thousand associations, federations, denominations, institutions, NGOs, mission agencies, and Christian lay leaders. The AICC frequently cooperates with civil liberties and human rights groups and leaders. It also networks with Indian associations abroad, as well as with international human and Christian rights groups such as the Dalit Freedom Network and Christian Solidarity Worldwide.[54]

Whereas the AICC seeks to be ecumenical in outlook, the AICU is purely Catholic by definition and has a much longer history, having been formed in 1930. The organization's Web site claims that it reflects the aspirations of India's "1.6 crore [16 million] Catholic [l]aity active in more than 160 dioceses spread across the country," and states:

> [The] AICU is the forerunner in all legitimate causes for Catholics in India. Its prime aim is to protect [the] national, political and social interest[s] and rights of the Catholics. [It has fought] against [the] Niyogi Committee Report, O. P. Tyagi Bill in 1978, Kerala Education Bill, [and the Freedom of Religion Act] of Orissa State, which were intended to infringe the rights of the Christians in the [c]ountry.[55]

Gradually, the AICU, as has the AICC, has become more involved in broader political issues, including advocacy on behalf of India's marginalized northeasterners and Muslims.

The local manifestation of the AICU in Mangalore, the Catholic Sabha, played a major role after the violence. The Catholic Sabha was particularly instrumental in unifying and getting out the Christian vote in the 2009 postviolence Karnataka state elections, in which the state's Christians joined with their Muslim neighbors and secular-minded Hindus to defeat the BJP in seven of eight constituencies in the Mangalore region.[56] Catholic clergy in Karnataka also cooperated to ensure the full participation of the Catholics under their care in the elections by suspending all church activities except the daily mass on that day. The local bishop sent a circular to every Karnataka parish, appealing to Catholics to exercise their voting rights. Later, when an official report on the unrest in Karnataka seemed, from a Christian perspective, to absolve those culpable for the violence in Karnataka, the Catholic Sabha organized a massive silent rally and sent a detailed memorandum to the government urging it to disregard the report.

Historically, one of the most effective ways for Christians to register their concerns (as well as their contributions to civil society) has been to unite in closing down their educational institutions in order to pressure social and government actors to meet their demands. This tactic has been deployed particularly in South India, and it was among the most dramatic of the national Indian Christian community's responses to the violence in Kandhamal. The strategy has become somewhat less effective in recent years, however, with the emergence of many high-standard non-Christian private schools. Moreover, shutting down schools has sometimes provoked a backlash, since schoolchildren typically bear no responsibility for the injustices the school closings intend to protest. Thus, the closures appear to punish the innocent.

If Christian political responses to the community's marginalization, harassment, and experiences of violence have been externally controversial at times, they have also not always enjoyed the full support of all Christians. The vast majority of Indian Christians interpret the current situation as a "kairological moment," that is, a moment of opportunity, given by God, for Christians to stand firm for their faith and to be ready even for "martyrdom." Nonetheless, a small minority of Christian intellectuals sees matters differently. While they sympathize with Christians who are the unfortunate victims of religious violence, they regard the rise of anti-Christian sentiment as an occasion for introspection. They perceive the social hostilities as an opportunity for Christians to give up their parochial mind-set in order to engage more wholeheartedly in dialogue with adherents of other religions, civil society groups, and secular forces. These intellectuals would like Christians to focus attention on issues that affect the nation and its people generally (and not merely on those pertaining to Christians and their ostensible "rights").

There are some signs that Christians are becoming less parochial in their political thinking, as in their advocacy for Muslim and not-necessarily-Christian tribal and dalit rights in India, as described previously. Yet even this kind of advocacy can be easily dismissed, by critics, as more evidence of Indian Christians' putatively consistent antimajority and anti-Hindu stance. Though attacks on Christians have generated internal unity and strengthened the relationship of Christians and Muslims, they have had the equally momentous effect of creating greater suspicion, among Christians, of their Hindu neighbors – something that our conversations suggest has happened in both Odisha and Karnataka.

Christians have also attempted to build alliances and goodwill through efforts that cut across the majority/minority divide. For example, Christian involvement in land rights and antiexploitation movements has increased substantially since the 1990s. As one of our informants put it, "Earlier, Christians were not protesting against the displacement of people due to special economic zones. But now there are active protests. Why? Because, when we are attacked, we need [the] other's support. When somebody else is affected or attacked, they need our support. That realization has come now."[57] For similar reasons, many Christians have become more active in promoting regional languages. The Catholic magazine *Rakno*, for example, promotes the Konkani language, a cause supported not only by Christians and Muslims in the area around Mangalore, but also by the (Hindu) Goud Saraswath Brahmin community.[58]

If the increasing harassment of India's Christians has provoked them to become more active in Indian politics, it has also stirred them to seek and nurture stronger connections with international partners. For example, in addition to its partnerships with international organizations including Christian Solidarity Worldwide (UK) and the Dalit Freedom Network (Australia, Canada, Germany, United Kingdom, and United States), which we have already mentioned, the AICC works closely with Stefanus Alliance International (Norway) and Release International (UK). Christian rights groups have also become increasingly sophisticated in their dissemination of information about attacks on Christians. For example, John Dayal, the general secretary of AICC, and Ajay Singh, director of Odisha Forum for Social Action, played a major role in shaping the report on Freedom of Religion or Belief authored by United Nations special rapporteur Asma Jahangir after her mission to India in the wake of violence in Odisha and Karnataka in 2008. These individuals also subsequently prepared a Joint Stakeholders' Report for the United Nations Human Rights Council for its Universal Periodic Review 2012.[59]

The internationalization of India's religious freedom issues by Indian Christians has had mixed results. On the one hand, many critics of Christianity in India consider it further proof of the "denationalization" and "foreign loyalties" of India's Christians. Detractors see in the intervention of the United Nations and Western Christian and Dalit rights organizations yet another instance of Western (white, Christian) neocolonialism. Nevertheless, the internationalization of these issues has also borne some results. Since India is a signatory to the Universal Declaration of Human Rights and ratified the International Covenant on Civil and Political Rights, it can be pressured and called to account by international bodies with regard to its record on religious freedom and human rights. As Ajay Singh indicates, "International advocacy is naming and shaming; it does not possess any power or legal status. [But] India awakens only when outside people speak about what is happening here."[60]

THE CONTRIBUTION OF CHRISTIANS TO INDIAN CIVIL SOCIETY

It is important to acknowledge, at the outset, that the relationship of Christianity and democratic liberty has historically been an inconsistent one. It cannot be denied, of course, that certain of the ideals of secular, democratic governance, as they emerged in the West, derived in significant ways from Christian ideals. Nevertheless, Christian rulers, institutions, and communities have very often failed to promote these same ideals consistently. Similarly, as Amartya Sen observes, raw materials for the development of civil society – for instance, public debate and dialogue and promotion of tolerance for those with opposing views – were present in non-Western cultures and non-Christian religious traditions such as Buddhism long before they surfaced and became institutionalized in Christianity.[61]

Within the context of India, the inconsistent relationship of Christianity and democratic liberty is also evident. Since the colonial period, European and Indian Christians in India have advocated religious and civil freedoms in a variety of ways. However, during the age of colonialism, the transformative potential of this advocacy was blunted by the perceived-to-be-Christian colonial regime's selective and inconsistent application of the ideals of secular, liberal democracy. British governance was certainly not "democratic" or "secular" in any modern sense. Yet Christianity has long been associated in India with the promotion of freedom, and in particular with the promotion of religious freedom, and today's Indian Christians carry on the tradition in a variety of important ways.

We have already mentioned the role that Christians played in pressing for religious freedom in the Constituent Assembly debates. In addition, Christian magazines, newspapers, and public intellectuals have also been relatively vocal and consistent defenders of religious freedom, and of secular ideals more generally. Christian groups have also been active in promoting tolerance and coexistence among India's different religions, castes, and cultures.[62] Many values education programs in church-run schools include modules on communal harmony and involve learning about different religious traditions.

Christian Contributions to Human Development

While Indian Christians have been strong advocates for secular governance and the rights and freedoms of minorities and the oppressed (including, in many cases, members of their own congregations), their contributions to civil society in the provision and management of health care, education, and poverty-alleviation programs are unparalleled, and totally disproportionate to the actual number of Christians in India. Soon after independence, Prime Minister Jawaharlal Nehru challenged the Catholic Cardinal Valerian Gracias to "involve the Catholic Church in building up a Modern India, focusing on the areas of health, education and socio-economic development."[63] Similarly, Nehru asked the Methodist Bishop J. Waskom Pickett "to initiate a response from the Indian Protestant and Orthodox Churches" to the situation of the grief and agony thousands of Indians faced as a consequence of Partition.[64] Christians were, of course, already heavily involved in these fields and continued to expand their contribution in the decades that followed.

Education

According to the CBCI's 2013 *Directory*, the Catholic Church has a total of 14,148 educational institutions all over India, including 4,079 primary schools, 2,123 middle schools, 3,578 high schools, 1,782 junior colleges, 232 degree colleges, 449 professional colleges, 245 special schools, 979 preprimary schools, and 681 vocational training centers. These schools operate, more often than not, in areas of great need; two-thirds of them are located in rural and tribal areas, according to a survey taken in 2005.[65] In Catholic educational institutions, 54 percent of the students are female, and around a fifth (according to 2005 figures) are from low-caste and tribal communities. It is clear, therefore, that the Catholic Church plays a prominent role in educating not only the urban elite, but also minorities and the downtrodden sectors of Indian society. These educational opportunities provide marginalized groups the opportunity to escape the bondage of ignorance and exploitation and open doors to social, political, and economic mobility.[66]

Catholic educational institutions serve adherents of all Indian religions. In fact, Catholics and non-Catholic Christians constitute fewer than a quarter of the students in Catholic educational institutions. Catholic institutions of education have always implicitly supported secularism and religious tolerance, as they have understood it. However, in the face of mounting antiminority rhetoric and violence, many have made their support more explicit and have resisted governmental attempts to circumscribe their freedom to educate how and whom they see fit.[67]

Health Care

Christians have been rendering remarkable health care service to the people of India for several hundred years. Already in 1527, Catholic Christians in Cochin had established a hospital on Indian soil, and today, India's Catholics manage 5,524 health care facilities.[68] Nearly half of the Catholic medical facilities are located in just four southern states (Andhra Pradesh, Karnataka, Tamil Nadu, and Kerala), and the Catholic Church claims that the "strong presence of the Church in the health care field has had a positive impact on the health indicators of these states."[69] In addition to providing medical therapies, particularly to those who might otherwise have difficulty accessing them, Catholic medical professionals involve themselves in grassroots mobilization efforts. Their initiatives aim at improving the health of communities through educating them and by pressing the government to recognize both citizens' rights and the government's duties and responsibilities related to issues of health and healing.[70]

The Catholic Health Association of India (CHAI), founded in 1943, is the largest and best-known Roman Catholic medical association, catering in particular to the underprivileged populations of India. It boasts the support of six hundred doctor sisters, twenty-five thousand sister-nurses, and more than ten thousand paraprofessionals. CHAI includes 3,410 member institutions, among which are 484 large hospitals and 2,000 medium/small hospitals, diocesan social service societies, nursing schools, and leprosaria. The contribution of CHAI to HIV/AIDS prevention and treatment initiatives has been particularly impressive; CHAI claims to have reached 700,000 people with HIV/AIDS counseling and testing services and more than 2.2 million people with awareness messages. In addition, CHAI provides care for thousands of HIV-positive pregnant women, as well as for the families of HIV/AIDS victims and survivors.[71]

CHAI's Protestant/Orthodox counterpart is the Christian Medical Association of India (CMAI), which was founded in 1905 as the Medical Missionary Association and is related to the NCCI. Today, CMAI allies more than 330 Christian health institutions and more than nine thousand health professionals doing pioneering work in a variety of fields, including the treatment of leprosy, tuberculosis, malaria, and HIV/AIDS. As do its Catholic counterparts, the CMAI engages not only in medical therapeutics, but also in health education and advocacy.[72]

Poverty Alleviation

For good or ill, the destitution of India's masses has frequently been used to encourage and justify foreign evangelistic and imperialistic interventions. Christians are counseled by their scriptures to look sympathetically on the impecunious. Not surprisingly, then, Christians have for many centuries been intimately involved in Indian efforts to ameliorate the plight of the poor. Innumerable are the Christian vocational training institutions, cooperatives, development agencies, land rights organizations, and legal advocacy groups that work on behalf of the poor and disenfranchised in India. Many of these groups operate independently, as the special effort or mission of single Christians, congregations, or groups of congregations. The entrepreneurial charitable activity of the quickly multiplying evangelical, charismatic, and Pentecostal congregations is worthy of special mention in this regard.

As in the case of health care, there are also large Catholic and Protestant/Orthodox associations that focus on improving the lives of India's poor. Among these, the most important, perhaps, are Caritas India, an official body of the CBCI, and the Church's Auxiliary for Social Action (CASA), the social service arm of the Protestant/Orthodox NCCI.

Human Rights

Poverty amelioration efforts blend naturally into human rights advocacy. In fact, Caritas is open about its own historical shift from an early charity model of social service, to a later welfare or needs-based model, to its current rights or empowerment-based model.[73] The present model seeks to promote participation in local, regional, and national political bodies and processes and to educate the marginalized and oppressed about their rights and the resources to which they can lay claim. In so doing, Caritas, and other Christian service organizations like it, contribute significantly to the development of India by transforming mere passive objects of charity into engaged, self-reliant citizens.

Indian Christian involvement in the promotion of human rights has also gained greater prominence as a result of anti-Christian violence, which has prompted Christians to conceive of the infringements upon their own religious rights within a broader, more general context of human rights for all. The AICC, and organizations like Prashant in Gujarat, have been particularly strong proponents of this view, insisting upon linking action on behalf of Christians with action on behalf of other oppressed peoples as well (particularly Dalits, tribals, and women). The circumscription of Christian rights has become, in the view of Christian human rights activists like John Dayal and Ajay Singh, a mere species (rather than the most important example) of the circumscription of fundamental human rights more generally.

CONCLUSION

In conclusion, we would like to highlight two of the points made directly and indirectly in the foregoing analysis. The first point is that the current situation of tension between Christians and Hindus in India is *contingent*, the result of historical trajectories described at the beginning of the chapter and not in any way a necessary state. There may therefore be open paths toward amelioration. There will always be tensions between majorities and minorities, but they need not be as acrimonious as they are in contemporary India.

The susceptibility of certain segments of the Hindu population to Hindu nationalist ideologies and anxieties and the willingness of politicians to exploit this susceptibility for electoral gain are certainly important aspects of the antagonism between Hindus and minorities such as Christianity in India. Hindus themselves have a great deal of social and political control throughout India. Consequently, they bear some responsibility for the current state of affairs.

At the same time, certain aspects of Hindu-Christian antagonism are under Christian control. It is of course impossible for Christians to disentangle themselves completely from the history of European colonialism in India, or from their implication in neocolonial and globalizing processes at work today. India's Christian community undeniably has stronger contacts and relationships with Westerners than most other Indian communities, and they have benefited significantly from those relationships. Nevertheless, it remains possible for India's Christians to continue working steadily toward improving their relationships with contemporary Hindus through greater respect for the piety and devotion of their Hindu neighbors, as well as through social and political projects that are truly interfaith (and not just *interminority*) in scope.

Evangelism will continue to be a sticking point in Christian-Hindu relations until the day, which will not occur soon, when there is greater consensus among

Indians about how and in what context evangelism and conversion should be legal. It seems to us that the current debate often misses the mark and is therefore quite unproductive. "Freedom of religion" or "anticonversion" laws (depending on one's perspective) are clearly sources of social and political conflict, but not because of their actual language. Few Christians would object to the notion that conversion should not come about through force, fraud, or material inducement. What they object to, rather, is the fact that India's judicial system is so easily manipulated, particularly at the local level. In the context of a pliable judiciary, "anticonversion" laws are regularly used to harass Christians who have not engaged in activities that would fall under any prima facie interpretation of the language in the laws. Moreover, Christians object to the fact that terms such as "inducement" or "allurement," if left without a precise definition, could be used to justify the restriction of something so seemingly innocuous as the persuasive power of a preacher's rhetoric. Might there be a way forward, then, in Christians' seeking common ground with Hindus in their concerns about the buying and selling of converts (which, it is important to note, goes on in both directions, to *and* from both Hinduism and Christianity)? Might Christians and Hindus join to condemn conversions and reconversions that result from physical threats and coercion (as they have, most recently, in the wake of the Kandhamal riots), at the same time insisting upon greater precision in the definition and scope of the words used in these laws, and greater safeguards to ensure that they cannot be used to harass innocent Christians?

It may also be the case that interfaith dialogues within India would be more productive if Western politicians, activists, and NGOs were more selective in their interventions. When Western individuals and organizations do intervene on behalf of India's Christians, they play into and perpetuate certain stereotypes about the "foreign loyalties" of India's Christians, and the meddling, neoimperialistic tendencies of Americans and Europeans. This makes it easier for opponents of Indian Christians to portray them as a threatening, denationalized minority. Moreover, in advocating the implementation of an American (or French, or British) brand of secularism in India, many foreigners fail to recognize that secularism has many varieties. Secularism is *not* religiously neutral, and the differences between one secular republic and another quite frequently amount to exactly how far a government is willing to go in regulating religious behavior, that is, in declaring certain kinds of religion illegitimate. European and American secular governments regulate animal sacrifice, the use of psychedelic drugs in worship, marital practices, and even religious clothing and jewelry. When foreign citizens draw a firm line and insist to Indians, without providing sound argumentation, that "real" secular governments cannot and should not regulate evangelism or conversion, they sound, to many Indian observers, rather naïve and jingoistic.

The second point is one adumbrated in the introduction to this chapter, namely, that we must be careful not to assume that the harassment and violence experienced by India's Christians threaten their contribution to Indian civic life. We also must not lose sight of the fact that the nature of Christian influence on Indian society is contestable. Notwithstanding the efforts of Christian institutions in the fields of health care, education, and rights advocacy, many Hindu nationalists claim that the net contributions of the Christian community in India have negatively impacted the country. On this view, Christian tendencies toward expansionism (in the form of evangelism) and Christian activism in civil society constitute a great evil, promoting forms of modernity that undermine Hindu traditional social structures and adulterate the nation's cultural and civil life. Such a suggestion seems disingenuous for a number of reasons but should be taken seriously nonetheless.

Even if we assume that the Christian contribution to Indian society has been significantly more positive than negative, we must still avoid the temptation to assume that an Indian Christian community under rhetorical and physical attack will no longer be able to contribute in the same way. In fact, as we have seen, the attacks by Hindu nationalists on India's Christian community since the 1990s have in many ways *activated* the community politically and provoked them to increase their already substantial contributions to Indian social and political life. Instances of intimidation and violence have also caused the Christian community to refine its contributions – for example, by being more inclusive in their social service, or in their interactions with people of other faiths, and by seeking partners outside their own community – in ways that many Christians consider positive.

This is not to say, of course, that there is no reason for concern. Obviously, a genocidal movement aimed at Christians *would* threaten their contribution. Measures should be taken to defuse the already deadly tension between India's Christians and Hindus. Still, the indications are that acts of large-scale violence will continue to be sporadic and geographically limited in the near-future. Nevertheless, there remain reasons to bemoan the recent experience of India's Christians. Christians in certain parts of India live in constant fear of attack. Others have lost their lives or family members to the violence. Many more, often devastatingly poor Christians, have been made even more destitute by the paroxysms of anti-Christian violence. Still others, particularly women, have suffered sexual assault or been made to feel more vulnerable to sexual violence as a result of the attacks. This is more than reason enough to be concerned about anti-Christian harassment and violence.

The point we are making is simply that we should not presume that this harassment and violence lead also, of necessity, to the loss or retrenchment of the Indian Christian community's contribution to India's social and political spheres. In fact, in what is an otherwise relatively grim and depressing story, the resilience and commitment of India's Christian activists, educators, medical workers, and social workers constitute at least one reason for optimism.

NOTES

1   Both authors would like to thank the Religious Freedom Project of the Berkley Center for Religion, Peace & World Affairs at Georgetown University for its support of this project. Chad M. Bauman would additionally like to thank the Center for Religion and Civic Culture at the University of Southern California and the John Templeton Foundation for a generous grant that supported earlier stages of his research.
2   Todd Johnson and Kenneth Ross, *Atlas of Global Christianity 1910–2010* (Edinburgh: Edinburgh University Press, 2009), 143.
3   Ibid., 143–144; and Jason Mandryk, *Operation World: The Definitive Prayer Guide to Every Nation* (Colorado Springs, CO: Biblica, 2010), 407.
4   The ecumenical Protestant Church of South India (CSI) was established in 1947. Its northern counterpart, the Church of North India (CNI), was founded in 1970.
5   Mandryk, *Operation*, 407–408.
6   Robert Eric Frykenberg, "Christianity in India: From Beginnings to the Present," in *Oxford History of the Christian Church*, ed. Henry Chadwick and Owen Chadwick (Oxford: Oxford University Press, 2008), 102–108.
7   Susan Bayly, *Saints, Goddesses and Kings: Muslims and Christians in South Indian Society 1700–1900* (Cambridge: Cambridge University Press, 1989), 8, 35, 73–74, 247–248, 460.
8   Ibid., 27, 35, 69–70, 275.
9   Ibid., 281–284, 460; and Ajantha Subramanian, *Shorelines: Space and Rights in South India* (Stanford, CA: Stanford University Press, 2009), 73.
10 Bayly, *Saints*, 82–85, 88, 96–98, 252; and Subramanian, *Shorelines*, 74.
11 The status of the St. Thomas Christians has since rebounded, but the same is not true of many other Christian communities.
12 Bayly, *Saints*, 13, 292–293, 300–302; and Subramanian, *Shorelines*, 75.
13 Kim Wagner, *The Great Fear of 1857: Rumours, Conspiracies and the Making of the Indian Uprising* (Oxford: Peter Lang, 2010).
14 Tanika Sarkar, *Hindu Wife, Hindu Nation: Community, Religion, and Cultural Nationalism* (Bloomington: Indiana University Press, 2001).
15 Sandria B. Freitag, *Collective Action and Community: Public Arenas and the Emergence of Communalism in North India* (Berkeley: University of California Press, 1989), 16, 19, 57–78.
16 Prashant Kidambi, *The Making of an Indian Metropolis: Colonial Governance and Public Culture in Bombay, 1890–1920* (Hampshire: Ashgate, 2007), 159.
17 Sanjay Joshi, *Fractured Modernity: Making of a Middle Class in Colonial North India* (New Delhi: Oxford University Press, 2001), 103–104; and Freitag, *Collective Action*, 46, 53–56, 80, 94–96, 125, 284.
18 Joshi, *Fractured*, 2–12.
19 On Bombay, for example, see Kidambi, *Making*, 12–13, 161–166.
20 Ibid., 174–176; and Iris Vandevelde, "Reconversion to Hinduism: A Hindu Nationalist Reaction against Conversion to Christianity and Islam," *South Asia: Journal of South Asian Studies* 34, no. 1 (2011): 34–39.

21 Chad Bauman, *Christian Identity and Dalit Religion in Hindu India, 1868–1947* (Grand Rapids, MI: Eerdmans, 2008), 76–79; and John Zavos, "Conversion and the Assertive Margins," *South Asia: Journal of South Asian Studies* 24, no. 2 (2001): 82.

22 Sumit Sarkar, "Conversion and Politics of Hindu Right," *Economic and Political Weekly* 34, no. 26 (June 26, 1999): 1697; and Zavos, "Conversion," 84; and Christopher Jaffrelot, ed., *Hindu Nationalism: A Reader* (Princeton, NJ: Princeton University Press, 2007).

23 Sebastian C. H. Kim, *In Search of Identity: Debates on Religious Conversion in India* (Oxford: Oxford University Press, 2003), 33; Robert Eric Frykenberg, "Introduction: Dealing with Contested Definitions and Controversial Perspectives," in *Christians and Missionaries in India: Cross-Cultural Communication since 1500*, ed. Robert Eric Frykenberg (Grand Rapids, MI: William B. Eerdmans, 2003), 7–8; and Susan Billington Harper, *In the Shadow of the Mahatma: Bishop V. S. Azariah and the Travails of Christianity in British India* (Grand Rapids, MI: William B. Eerdmans, 2000), 292–345.

24 Robert Ellsberg, ed., *Gandhi on Christianity* (Maryknoll, NY: Orbis Books, 1991), 47.

25 Kim, *In Search*, 51–54.

26 Chad M. Bauman, "Postcolonial Anxiety and Anti-Conversion Sentiment in the *Report of the Christian Missionary Activities Enquiry Committee*," *International Journal of Hindu Studies* 12, no. 2 (2008).

27 Scott Baldauf, "A New Breed of Missionary: A Drive for Conversions, Not Development, Is Stirring Violent Animosity in India," *Christian Science Monitor* (Online), April 1, 2005, accessed June 26, 2008, http://www.csmonitor.com/2005/0401/p01s04-wosc.html

28 Bauman, "Postcolonial Anxiety," 192.

29 Faizan Mustafa and Anurag Sharma, *Conversion: Constitutional and Legal Implications* (New Delhi: Kanishka, 2003), 109–111.

30 See, for example, Joseph DeCaro, "India: Pentecostal Pastors Accused of 'Forced Conversion'," *Worthy News* (Online), September 15, 2011, accessed October 11, 2012, http://www.worthynews.com/10959-india-pentecostal-pastors-accused-of-forced-conversion

31 Kim, *In Search*, 79.

32 Mukul Kesavan, *Secular Common Sense* (New Delhi: Penguin, 2001), 70–72.

33 For more on this violence, see Chad Bauman, "Identity, Conversion and Violence: Dalits, Adivasis and the 2007–2008 Riots in Orissa," in *Margins of Faith: Dalit and Tribal Christianity in India*, ed. Rowena Robinson and Joseph Marianus Kujur (Washington, DC: Sage, 2010).

34 Sushil Aaron, *Christianity and Political Conflict in India: The Case of Gujarat* (Colombo: Regional Centre for Strategic Studies, 2002), 47.

35 Chad M. Bauman and Tamara Leech, "Political Competition, Relative Deprivation, and Perceived Threat: A Research Note on Anti-Christian Violence in India," *Ethnic and Racial Studies* 35, no. 12 (2011).

36 A Maria David, *Beyond Boundaries: Hindu-Christian Relationship and Basic Christian Communities* (Delhi: Indian Society for Promoting Christian Knowledge, 2009), 70–72.

37 National Peoples Tribunal on Kandhamal, *Waiting for Justice: A Report* (New Delhi: Peace & ANHAD, 2010), 9, 28, 37, 105.

38 From the moment they began working in Kandhamal, Sangh Parivar activists found natural allies in the community of mostly caste Hindu Oriya traders who had earlier begun migrating into Kandhamal from the coastal regions of Odisha for business. These Oriyas sought advantageous trading relationships with the local peoples but were often accused by them of exploitation and land grabbing. By allying themselves with the Sangh

Parivar and with willing Kandha leaders, the Oriyas could protect their economic status by deflecting such accusations onto the Christian Pana community, which was also occasionally accused of exploiting the Kandhas as they (the Panas) began to outpace them (the Kandhas) economically, and which had also begun to threaten the Oriya community's trading dominance. See PUCL (Bhubaneswar) and Kashipur Solidarity Group, *Crossed and Crucified: Parivar's War against Minorities in Orissa* (Delhi: PUCL, 2009); and Pralay Kanungo, *RSS's Tryst with Politics: From Hedgewar to Sudarshan* (New Delhi: Manohar, 2003); and National Peoples Tribunal on Kandhamal, *Waiting*.

39 For more on the Kandhamal violence, see Bauman, "Identity, Conversion and Violence: Dalits, Adivasis and the 2007–08 Riots in Orissa."

40 For a statistical exploration of this thesis, see Bauman and Leech, "Political Competition."

41 Aaron, *Christianity*, 44.

42 Zavos, "Conversion," 75.

43 Chad M. Bauman, "Hindu-Christian Conflict in India: Globalization, Conversion, and the Coterminal Castes and Tribes," *Journal of Asian Studies* 72, no. 3 (2013).

44 On the religious effects of anti-Christian riots, see Chad M. Bauman, "The Inter-Religious Riot as a Cultural System: Globalization, Geertz, and Hindu-Christian Conflict," in *Contesting Indian Christianities: Caste, Culture, and Conversion*, ed. Chad M. Bauman and Richard Fox Young (Delhi: Routledge, 2014).

45 National Peoples Tribunal on Kandhamal, *Waiting*, 103.

46 It is important to note that at least some Hindu nationalist authors perceived these efforts as a cynical evangelical ploy more than a sincere attempt to articulate an "Indian" Christianity. See Xavier Gravend-Tirole, "From Christian Ashrams to Dalit Theology – or Beyond: An Examination of the Indigenisation/Inculturation Trend within the Indian Catholic Church," in *Contesting Indian Christianities: Caste, Culture, and Conversion*, ed. Chad M. Bauman and Richard Fox Young (Delhi: Routledge, Forthcoming).

47 Interview with Archbishop Bernard Moras of Bangalore in Bangalore, August 1, 2013.

48 *Dalit* literally means "crushed, broken down," and is used today to refer to the lowest castes, what used to be called "untouchables," what Gandhi called *harijans*, and what official British and Indian bureaucratic parlance calls the "Scheduled Castes."

49 Interview with leaders of Jana Vikas in Nuagaon, May 29, 2013.

50 Interview with Archbishop Bernard Moras of Bangalore in Bangalore, August 1, 2013.

51 Interview with Felix Wilfred in Chennai, August 11, 2013.

52 Interview with Fr. Onil D'Souza in Mangalore, August 4, 2013.

53 Interview with Fr. Lobo in Bangalore, August 2, 2013.

54 For more information, see http://indianchristians.in/news/

55 See http://aicuindia.org/history.html

56 Interview with Advocate M. P. Noronha, President of Christian Lawyers Guild in Mangalore, August 5, 2013.

57 Interview with Fr. Onil D'Souza in Mangalore, August 4, 2013.

58 Interview with Fr. Francis in Mangalore, August 4, 2013.

59 Cf. Odisha Forum for Social Action, *Freedom of Religion in India: A Report to the United Nations Human Rights Council for the Universal Periodic Review 2012* (Bhubaneswar: Odisha Forum for Social Action, 2012).

60 Interview with Ajay Singh in Bhubaneswar, May 28, 2013.

61 Amartya Sen, "The Global Roots of Democracy: Why Democratization Is Not the Same as Westernization," *New Republic*, October 6, 2003.

62 John Fernandez, "Inter-Religious Dialogue Today: Opportunities and Challenges," *Religion and Society* 52, no. 3/4 (2007).

63 Oswald Gracias, "Forward," in *Silent Waves: Contribution of the Catholic Church to Nation Building*, ed. John Chathanatt and Jeya Peter (Bangalore: Claretian, 2012), ix.

64 It is this request that gave birth to the formation of the National Council of Churches Relief Committee, which would later become the Church's Auxiliary for Social Action (CASA) of the National Council of Churches in India (NCCI). Cf. www.casa-india.org

65 Victor Sunderaj, "Educational Institutions of the Catholic Church: A Survey," in *Silent Waves: The Contribution of the Catholic Church to Nation Building*, ed. John Chathanatt and Jeya Peter (Bangalore: Claretian, 2012), 126.

66 Ibid., 128–129.

67 Kuriala Chittattukalam, *Church in India for Nation Building* (New Delhi: CBCI, 2012), 74.

68 Victor Sunderaj and Martina Josephine, "Medical Services of the Catholic Church in India," in *Silent Waves: The Contributions of the Catholic Church to Nation Building*, ed. John Chathanatt and Jeya Peter (Bangalore: Claretian, 2012), 139.

69 CBCI Commission for Health, *Sharing the Fullness of Life: Health Policy of the Catholic Church* (New Delhi: CBCI Commission for Healthcare, 2005), 10. Also, consider the following statistics: percentage of women to receive antenatal checkup in first trimester of pregnancy: these four states' average 77.9, national average 44.9; percentage of safe deliveries: these four states' average 85.5; national average 52.3; prevalence of leprosy – cases per 10,000: these four states' average .43, national average .69. This information can be found at http://cbhidghs.nic.in/writereaddata/mainlinkFile/Health%20Status%20Indicators-2012.pdf, pp. 109–110.

70 Ibid.

71 "The Catholic Health Association of India," last modified 2014, www.chai-india.org

72 For more on CMAI see: http://www.cmai.org

73 H. Beck and Tata Institute of Social Sciences, *Towards Inclusive and Equitable Development: 50 Years Journey of Caritas India, 1962–2012* (Mumbai: Tata Institute of Social Sciences, 2012), 22.

9

Vietnam: Christianity's Contributions to Freedoms and Human Flourishing in Adversity

Reg Reimer

INTRODUCTION

To understand Christianity and its contribution to freedom in Vietnam, one first needs to consider Vietnam's political history, as well as Christianity's intersection with an ancient culture. This chapter examines the interplay between Christianity and the state, and how this affects the human flourishing that accompanies freedom during three main periods: from the inception of Catholic Christianity through the colonial period; then from independence (1954) and the division of Vietnam between a Communist North and a republican South through the Vietnam War; and finally, since the 1975 reunification under Communism.

Today, roughly 10 percent of Vietnam's 90 million people are Christians. Although government census figures for Christians are considerably lower and Christian churches themselves find it very difficult or inconvenient to publish their own figures because of Vietnam's political/social situation, consensus points toward 8 million Catholics and 1.6 million Evangelicals in Vietnam.[1] Rather than discussing Christianity as a whole, the very diverse histories of Catholicism and Evangelicalism[2] in Vietnam require that they be described separately. Catholic missionaries established a continuing presence in Vietnam early in the seventeenth century and Evangelicals early in the twentieth century. The remarkable stories of the growth of the indigenous churches they established, despite adversity, are not widely known.

Social, cultural, and political factors determined that both major Christian traditions often encountered opposition and periods of persecution, sometimes intense. Nevertheless, both traditions took firm root in Vietnamese soil and contributed significantly to the modernization of Vietnam, even though they

I am deeply grateful for five fellow Vietnamese researchers who contributed significantly to this work, and for the many respondents in Vietnam who cooperated with them. It is illuminating of Vietnam's situation that none of them wished to be credited by name for their participation.

sometimes clashed with traditional culture or were at odds with the governments of the day.

The establishment of a Jesuit mission in Faifo in the year 1615, near present-day Danang, began a permanent Catholic presence in Vietnam.[3] In 1624 the missionaries at Faifo were joined by a French Jesuit, Alexandre de Rhodes, who was to outshine them all in influence.[4] The church sent de Rhodes to open a mission in Tonkin in present-day northern Vietnam in 1627, and he baptized sixty-seven hundred believers within three years.

One of the singular accomplishments of de Rhodes was completing an excellent Latinized Vietnamese alphabet, first used in his famous *Eight-Day Catechism* for new believers.[5] This alphabet, called *quốc ngữ*, was eventually employed for common use and became a key tool for Vietnam's modernization. Remembered by Catholics as the beloved apostle of Vietnam, de Rhodes even had his name restored by the Communist regime to a street in Saigon, which itself had been renamed Ho Chi Minh City.

Vietnamese Catholicism suffered serious setbacks from 1670 to 1800 before it resumed steady expansion, though the growth was not as dramatic as in the early years.[6] At times Catholicism was officially proscribed. A main reason for state opposition was that the Confucianism-oriented mandarins feared that the introduction of new loyalties into their ordered society could become subversive. A secondary reason was perceived cultural discontinuity.

In the mid-nineteenth century, the collusion of some of the foreign Catholic hierarchy with French colonial aspirations also motivated the state to oppose Catholicism. But it is a mistake to posit, as Communist histories do, that the chief reason for Catholic growth was the protection of the French colonial impositions from the mid-nineteenth century. The church had taken root and grown for two centuries before French hegemony became real. Graphic trends of Catholic Church growth show little relationship between the projection of French power in the last half of the nineteenth century and an influx of church congregants.[7]

Growth occurred in spite of strong official opposition and waves of brutal persecution in both the eighteenth and nineteenth centuries, leading to martyrdom for many. The severest persecution took place in the nineteenth century under the Nguyen dynasty.[8] Catholic sources estimate that between 130,000 and 300,000 believers died for their faith.[9] Christians were strangled, sawn asunder, tied together in long lines and thrown into a river, killed slowly by slicing or hacked limb by limb with the head being last removed, and tortured with red hot tongs. For sport they were thrown under the feet of elephants, Roman style.[10] When Pope John Paul II canonized 117 Vietnamese and missionary martyrs in 1988, Vietnamese authorities vehemently objected.

Turbulent times for Catholics continued into the twentieth century. The division of Vietnam at the 17th parallel by the 1954 Geneva Accords prompted a mass exodus of Catholics from the North to the South to escape Communism. Eighty percent of the 860,000 refugees were Catholics – almost half of the northern church. Its clergy and laity greatly diminished, the northern Catholic Church struggled for two decades against severe restrictions and persecution. In the southern Republic of Vietnam, the church flourished even as it became the bulwark of anti-Communism, thereby complicating its relations with Vietnam's governments.[11]

The situation for Catholics in post-1975 Vietnam under Communism, after the first difficult years, has been *day* compared to the *night* faced by Catholics who remained in the North after the 1954 division of the country. Post 1975, Catholic leaders, realistic and pragmatic beyond expectation, laid aside their strong anti-communist bias and pledged their church would serve the development of their nation – now unified under Communism.[12] Regrettably, Communist authorities have perpetuated the old Confucian excuse for their skepticism about Christianity, saying that churches promote dangerous, alternate loyalties that compete with and threaten the state. Therefore, they have only grudgingly offered space for this dynamic national resource.

After four centuries of development, Vietnam's Catholic Church is a vibrant and growing community today. Three ecclesiastical provinces or archdioceses, twenty-three dioceses, thousands of churches, and some five thousand religious and diocesan priests provide support for a Catholic population of some 8 million faithful. Vietnam has had three cardinals, and Jean-Baptiste Pham Minh Man presently serves as the acting cardinal. Notably, religious sisters in Vietnam (11,500 in 2003) outnumber male priests, religious and diocesan, by a more than two-to-one margin. Today, after long struggles to reopen them, Catholics have six major seminaries to train clergy in the country.

In Vietnam, any demographic statistics are difficult to verify with precision. However, if we accept the figure of 2.6 million Vietnamese Catholics in 1970[13] and the current estimate of 8 million, the church has added an average of 125,000 people per year over the past four decades. The annual rate of growth (4.8 percent) is particularly impressive if one accounts for the turbulent Vietnam War followed by thirty-eight years of unified Communist rule. The church's growth rate far outstrips Vietnam's slowing annual population growth rate, which was 1.1 percent in 2012. In contrast to their numbers among Evangelicals, ethnic Vietnamese (Kinh) believers constitute a supermajority of the Catholic Church, with ethnic minorities making up only a small percentage of membership.

In spite of lingering accusations to the contrary, after four centuries of inculturation the Vietnamese Catholic Church is well embedded in Vietnamese culture. Jacob Ramsay has convincingly debunked the recurrent myth of Catholicism's discontinuity with Vietnamese culture.[14]

Historically, the Catholic Church's proscription of ancestor worship censured a significant Vietnamese cultural practice. However, Vatican II allowed for the "veneration" of ancestors, and the Vietnamese-born Catholic theologian Peter Phan tells how Vietnamese Catholics have now found a creative solution to this centuries-old Rites Controversy.[15] Though Catholics maintain a distinction between ancestor worship and veneration, at least some state Vietnamese religion scholars accept that Catholic practices in this area fit, if uneasily, into Vietnamese culture.[16]

The Vietnamese Catholic Church had a complicated involvement with Vietnam's two twentieth-century wars of decolonization. The nuances of that story are portrayed in Charles Keith's *Catholic Vietnam: A Church from Empire to Nation* (2012), which includes the Catholic religion as a major factor in the "colonial modernity"[17] of Vietnam. Keith documents how the "decolonization" of the Catholic Church from missionary domination to indigenous leadership and national self-awareness preceded the evolution of the modern Vietnamese state and played a part in the larger dynamic.

After reunification under Communism, Vietnamese authorities cajoled a few individual Catholics to form a "patriotic association" sympathetic to the regime and sometimes introduced the association to foreign visitors as if it represented the church. But, unlike China, they have never denied the church's connection with Rome, nor seriously tried to start an alternate "patriotic church." While there are tensions in Vietnam over government insistence on vetting Vatican-appointed bishops, periodic negotiations between Vietnam and the Vatican have reached the point where Vietnam has approved a papal nuncio, albeit nonresident. It is hoped that this action may be viewed as emerging readiness for the church to play a larger part in Vietnam's development.

EVANGELICAL MISSIONS AND CHURCHES IN VIETNAM: HISTORY, CONTEXTUALIZATION, AND DEMOGRAPHICS

The first permanent Evangelical mission was established in Tourane (present-day Danang) in 1911.[18] The Canadian Robert A. Jaffray, a prominent missionary pioneer and publisher in southern China, had worked for some time to expand the work of his mission, the American/Canadian Christian and Missionary Alliance (C&MA), into French Indochina. The early missionaries faced not only the challenges of communicating the gospel in a new culture, but also the suspicion of the mostly

Catholic colonial authorities and the Catholic Church, which was not eager for competition.

Despite the challenges cited, converts to Evangelicalism increased steadily. Missionaries quickly branched from central Vietnam to northern Hanoi and southern Saigon and from those cities into the countryside. They laid a good foundation early by establishing a clergy training school (1921), translating and publishing the Bible in Vietnamese (1926), and facilitating the formation of the indigenous Evangelical Church of Vietnam (1927). Evangelicals generally ignored the 1928 colonial proscription of Evangelical Christianity in Annam, central Vietnam. By 1929 missionaries had positioned themselves to spread the gospel to the ethnic minority Montagnards near Dalat in Vietnam's Central Highlands.[19]

After the invasion by the Japanese (1941–1945) and the expulsion and internment of missionaries, the young Evangelical church was left without fraternal ties in difficult times, including during the war-caused Great Famine, which starved nearly 2 million people. Churches responded admirably with mutual support.

Inevitably the church became embroiled in the War of Independence that followed Ho Chi Minh's proclamation of the Democratic Republic of Vietnam in Hanoi's Ba Dinh Square on September 2, 1945. Evangelicals, who wanted neither a restoration of French domination nor Communism, tried to take a neutral stance. Summoned to visit Ho Chi Minh, the president of the Evangelical Church of Vietnam, the Reverend Le Van Thai, told the revolutionary leader that many individual Evangelicals were engaged in the independence struggle, but the church, as an organization, would remain neutral.[20] Some individual Evangelicals fought willingly, while others behind Viet Minh lines were pressed to fight or otherwise support the struggle.

As with Catholics, there was virtually no expansion of the Evangelical church during the War of Independence, which ended in 1954 with the division of the country. Many Evangelicals had also joined the exodus to the South, leaving perhaps two thousand members in thirty congregations to face harsh restrictions under Communism for the next twenty years. By 1975 the northern churches had shrunk to ten congregations. The vitality of Evangelical churches in the North further diminished as some leaders appear to have been compromised by Communist pressure.

Meanwhile churches in the South, free to evangelize and engage in helping victims of the Vietnam War (1964–1975), resumed their growth. The C&MA Mission deployed many new missionaries and was joined by several other evangelizing missions in the 1960s as well as by prominent Evangelical relief and development organizations.[21] A 1972 census of Evangelicals in South Vietnam counted 153,000.[22] Adding an estimate for the shrunken northern churches, the total would not exceed

160,000. The vast majority belonged to the dominant Evangelical Church of Vietnam – South (ECVN – S), with fewer than three thousand being adherents of the newer denominations.

The communist victory of 1975 ushered in the "dark decade." Its effects on Evangelical church life and activity were devastating. Many Evangelical Christians whom the communists identified with their vanquished American enemies were too afraid to attend public worship. Virtually all Montagnard pastors and some ethnic Vietnamese ones were imprisoned.[23] Yet even at this time of heightened persecution, many conversions still occurred. After a powerful revival at Pastor Ho Hieu Ha's Tran Cao Van church in Saigon, thousands – including the "Napalm Girl," Phan Thi Kim Phuc – converted. This phenomenon so alarmed authorities that they closed the church, seized the property, and imprisoned Pastor Ha and his coworkers in 1983 and did not release them until 1991.

A watershed event in recent Vietnamese history is Đổi Mới (1986), usually translated as "renovation."[24] Vietnam adopted "socialist-oriented market capitalism" in place of Marxist economics and took the far-reaching decision to integrate with the capitalist world. Besides its positive economic implications, the opening to the world resulting from Đổi Mới allowed for the reconnection of Evangelicals with international church and mission bodies. These unofficial but extensive connections reassured Vietnamese Evangelicals about their fraternal relations, revitalized church life by exposing them to worldwide Christian developments, provided resources for church expansion, and led to the reestablishment of denominational entities that had disappeared.

This new dynamic situation also saw the birth of a house church movement. It began in 1988 when four prominent ECVN-S pastors were pushed out of their churches by a church hierarchy that took exception to some newfound charismatic practices and feared the consequences of their boldness. From this time until the late 1990s, house churches grew dramatically, both in numbers of believers and in organizational expressions.[25] Local growth was bolstered by hundreds of new converts from Hong Kong[26] and by converts among students and guest workers, who had ironically accepted the Christian faith in the crumbling Soviet Union and Eastern Bloc.

There were two other significant, simultaneous "explosions" of Evangelical Christianity in Vietnam.[27] The first was the growth of Evangelicals among Vietnam's Montagnard minorities in the Central Highlands from the late 1980s through the 1990s and to a lesser extent since then. Crushed and disbanded following the 1975 Communist victory, Montagnard churches began to recoalesce when their remaining pastors were released from harsh prison camps in 1981. Today the total number of Montagnard Christians approaches 500,000. Government 2009 census statistics, which Evangelical experts consider very low, show eleven ethnic minorities that are more than 10 percent Evangelicals and four that are more than one-third Evangelicals.[28]

The second explosion was the expansion of Christianity in Vietnam's Northwest Mountainous Region (NMR) among Hmong and some other ethnic minorities.[29] Sparked by Christian radio broadcasts from the Far East Broadcasting Company in Manila, Philippines, Hmong began to communicate their desire for conversion by letters to the Hmong broadcaster the Reverend John Lee in 1988. It was not long before the deluge of Hmong believers formed many congregations, at first under the tutelage of broadcaster Lee and then the Evangelical Church of Vietnam – North (ECVN–N), the historic body of Evangelicals in northern Vietnam, to which Lee directed them. Those closest to the Hmong movement estimate that only twenty-five years after its inception, it numbers more than 400,000. The Hmong Christians have also transmitted their new faith to their ethnic neighbors such as the San Chi, who now have an estimated 10,000 Evangelical believers.

In large part because of these movements, the organizationally diverse Evangelical community in Vietnam has grown from 160,000 at the country's reunification in the mid-1970s to some 1,600,000 today. That tenfold increase in thirty-eight years represents an astounding average annual addition of over thirty-five thousand new believers, or an average annual growth rate of 22 percent based on the starting number. The barrage of new ethnic minority Evangelical believers in hundreds of congregations during the last two decades has dramatically skewed the composition of the Vietnamese Evangelical community. It has grown from about one-third ethnic minority in 1972 to more than three-quarters ethnic minority four decades later. Only 14 percent of Vietnam's population is ethnic minority.

Culturally, Evangelical Christianity is considered more of an outlier than Catholicism by Vietnam's religion scholars and ruling elite. Ramsay suggests Evangelicalism has come to replace Catholicism as culturally anathema to official perspectives on traditional Vietnamese culture.[30] Nevertheless, ethnic Vietnamese Evangelicals, though modest in number, are generally seen in a positive light. And among the ethnic minorities, where they represent a critical mass, the contribution of their religious faith to social and economic uplift is clearly visible. Government officials sometimes note that ethnic Hmong Evangelicals, compared to traditional animists, are more literate, hardworking, and hygienic. They do not use alcohol and thus avoid the debilitating social effects of alcoholism, and their death rituals are more "civilized."[31]

In spite of all government attempts to marginalize, control, regulate, and otherwise manage religious organizations, Vietnam's Catholics and Evangelicals are firmly embedded in the Vietnamese culture and society, to which they have contributed significantly. Nevertheless, the government holds that residual issues remain. In its attitude, Christianity still lacks full recognition within Communism's worldview, is perceived as associated with alleged separatist movements in the Central and Northwest Highlands, is viewed as alien to local culture, and is associated with lingering Western imperialism.

CHRISTIANITY'S CONTRIBUTIONS TO VIETNAM'S MODERNITY

During centuries of history punctuated by waves of discrimination, oppression, and persecution, Christians in Vietnam have nevertheless proven to be a salt-in-society, modernizing, moderating, and liberalizing force. As illustrated later, they have contributed disproportionately to the common good, to social welfare, and to civil society.

ROMAN CATHOLIC CONTRIBUTIONS

The development of *quốc ngữ'*, the near-linguistically perfect Romanized Vietnamese script, by Catholic missionaries in the early seventeenth century, has proven to be an immense and lasting gift to the Vietnamese nation. Obviously it was first used for catechism purposes, but its use eventually expanded until it completely replaced the much more difficult *chữ' nôm*, Vietnam's ancient Chinese character–based script.

The rise in the use of the new script paralleled the French colonial domination of Indochina. After 1860, it was promoted as a useful tool for colonial administration in Cochin China. The Vietnamese intellectuals Truong Vinh Ky and Huynh Tinh Cua, who were in the service of the French, established the first newspaper in *quốc ngữ'* in 1865 and authored, translated, and compiled numerous texts in the script.[32] History has demonstrated that *quốc ngữ'* made a major contribution toward Vietnam's modernity and made possible a very high literacy rate exceeding 95 percent.[33]

Architecture was another Catholic contribution. The early part of the colonial period saw the number of Roman Catholic Church buildings in Vietnam grow from 906 to 4,578, many constructed in the neo-Gothic style.[34] This building boom not only demonstrated growth but also provided the church with *hình thức*, or appearance, an important requirement in Vietnamese thinking for bestowing serious substance on a movement.

From the 1880s, when the majestic cathedrals in Hanoi and Saigon were completed, "missionaries began to found orphanages, hospitals, dispensaries, leper colonies, houses for the elderly and terminally ill, all of which were rare under Nguyen rule."[35] Such institutions introduced to Vietnam the concept of public welfare. These services, freely offered to non-Catholics, played an important part in meeting social needs, ameliorating social ills, and helping people conceptualize a more just and humane society.

While the "colonial civilizing mission" is often considered in the pejorative, especially in the Communist version of history, a more objective reading must acknowledge that it provided many important, long-lasting, and positive contributions to Vietnam's modernity. The role of Catholic schools in Vietnam is a good example. For most of the colonial era, Catholics administered an educational network that rivaled that of the colonial state. In 1922 there were 104,228 students in 2,904 Catholic schools. Some of these were prestigious *lycee* institutions in the main cities. The gender equality found in these schools, which was unusual for the time, was a testament to the religious organizations that ran them.

Catholic involvement in education continued in the postcolonial era but was abruptly stopped by Vietnam's Communist authorities in 1975 – a huge loss to the nation. Today Catholics are allowed very limited public education involvement, primarily at the kindergarten level.

In the area of culture, Catholic musicians through the centuries composed uniquely Vietnamese sacred music and lyrics, adding to the richness of Catholic liturgy. And the Catholic Han Mac Tu (pen name of Nguyen Thong Tri) became a famous Vietnamese poet, whose work ranged from classicist to modernist in style.

It is highly significant that the nationalization process of the Vietnamese Catholic Church preceded Vietnam's independence. Keith suggests that one might date the church's nationalization from the 1930s with the ordination of the first two Vietnamese bishops.[36] The gradual overcoming of French domination in the church clearly contributed to Vietnamese Catholic understanding, sympathy, and support for the wider nationalist project. Catholic clergy were particularly active in helping forge a national identity during the World War II Japanese occupation.[37]

While Vietnamese Catholics were enthusiastic about the aspirations of their countrymen for independence, they drew the line at allying with atheistic Communism. This set the stage for high tension between the church and the independence movement, which early embraced Communism as its main political prop. Later, after the 1954 division of Vietnam at the 17th parallel, and the mass migration of northern Catholics to the South, Catholics became a bulwark of anti-Communism there.[38] However, during the 1960s, a Catholic prime minister, Ngo Dinh Diem, so strongly favored Catholics that he managed to incite such strong sectarian Buddhist opposition that some monks self-immolated. Diem's regime ended in 1963 with his assassination by his own generals and with American collusion.

At the 1975 Communist victory, the diocesan hierarchy courageously took the far-reaching decision to make reasonable accommodation with the new reality. Peter Phan argues convincingly that the Vietnamese Catholic Church has done nothing to threaten Vietnam's national security in the nearly four decades since the

Communist ascendancy. Yet this remained a fear of Vietnam's older generation of leaders.[39]

But ideas are changing. In 2012 a rare article on a government Web site quoted a dozen persons among the who's who of Vietnam's religion scholars citing positive historical and current contributions of religion to Vietnamese society. Catholic contributions were prominently mentioned.[40]

The Catholic Church's vast human resources, its social conscience, its material means augmented by its strong international connections, make it a major resource for Vietnam's national welfare and development. Regrettably, official suspicion still severely limits what the church can offer.

EVANGELICAL CONTRIBUTIONS

Although the first Evangelical missionaries did not arrive in Vietnam until three centuries after the Catholics, Evangelicalism has still had a marked impact on Vietnamese society, in large part because it was early and viably institutionalized. The first indigenous Evangelical clergy were ordained a decade after missionary arrival. An autonomous national church, the Evangelical Church of Vietnam, was formed in 1927.

One of the early goals of Evangelical missionaries was to translate the Bible into Vietnamese. Wisely engaging Phan Khoi, a leading literary figure of the day, they published a fine, complete translation of the Bible by 1926, only fifteen years after their arrival. It contributed to Evangelicals' wide biblical literacy and remains to this day the most popular Bible translation among Evangelicals.[41]

A welcome decade of relative peace in the South from 1954 to 1964 followed the hardships and setbacks of the War of Independence. During that terrible war congregations were disbanded and there were fewer Christians counted in 1954 than in 1946. However, the churches in South Vietnam resumed healthy growth through this peace interval and into the American war. During the Vietnam War aggressive evangelism continued, while both foreign Evangelical missions and indigenous churches increasingly responded with sustained generosity to the massive human needs generated by the conflict. In this they were joined and supported by large Evangelical relief agencies such as World Vision, World Relief, and the pacifist Mennonite Central Committee. Besides providing large-scale relief for the many war-displaced persons, these agencies established schools, clinics, hospitals, and development projects, often in collaboration with the ECVN – S. These good works served the common good, helping to give Evangelical churches significant visibility and recognition.

The reaction of Evangelicals to the dark decade after the Communist victory in 1975 was simply to hunker down and hope for better days. Following the 1986 Đổi

Mó'i renovation policy, there was a relaxation of the oppression of Christians, at least in urban areas. Nevertheless, Communist propaganda continued to taunt Evangelicals by calling their religion the *đạo Mỹ*, the American religion. This was to paint Evangelicals pejoratively as lackeys of the defeated enemy. Catholics had long been accused of being agents of the French, and now Evangelicals were called tools of the Đế Quốc Mỹ, the American Empire, thinking that persists in some quarters to this day. In the minds of Vietnam's ideologically driven leaders, the presumed American-Evangelical connection was clearly illustrated by the explosion of Evangelical Christianity in Vietnam's two main ethnic minority regions.

The implications of these rapid expansions were twofold. First, the government saw these explosions of new Evangelicals as a threat. The many ethnic minority Evangelical converts were no longer fatalistic, easy-to-control animists who lived subserviently in fear of malevolent forces. To quote an old hymn, through the one who "breaks the power of cancelled sin and sets the prisoner free" they had discovered personhood, self-direction, agency, and discipline.[42] Many became literate through use of the Bible. They organized into churches, with clergy and lay leaders, becoming part of a burgeoning worldwide movement.[43]

And they prospered locally. In the 1990s the Canadian Mennonite Jake Buhler, who managed small aid projects for the Canadian Embassy, commissioned a needs assessment in a district dominated by the Stieng minority in southern Binh Phuoc province. The study, done by a local social science survey company, revealed that a significant number of Christians among those surveyed were markedly better off than those who adhered to traditional animism. The survey found they had better houses, valued education and encouraged their children to study more, watched less TV, and were generally more industrious. They did not abuse alcohol and so had more harmonious domestic relationships. The Stiengs' Christian faith translated into productive and happy lives and good citizenship, according to these objective surveyors. This had wide positive economic and social implications. Even the 2009 government census figures, believed by Evangelicals to be low, show that 55 percent of the Stieng are Evangelicals. But instead of applauding their industriousness and social harmony, local government officials have endlessly harassed Stieng Christians. For years they have been threatening to close 161 Stieng churches belonging to the legally recognized ECVN – S. Finally, in response to sustained church advocacy against this threat, the government is considering allowing 45 to remain open.

A significant by-product of the Montagnards' new Christian worldview was their growing awareness of the injustices they were suffering at the hands of the government and of ethnic Vietnamese. Many thousands of the latter migrated from the North, encroaching and settling on traditional Montagnard lands. It was no accident that Christian Montagnards were prominent in the 2001 and 2004 "uprisings" in the

Central Highlands, which protested unjust confiscation of their traditional lands and the oppression of their Christian faith.

In spite of many obstacles and targeted discrimination against Christians in government benefits and education, our respondents reported that this anecdotal Stieng example was frequently replicated throughout the Central Highlands and the NMR. Regrettably, according to Christians' experience, such emerging prosperity sometimes provoked the jealously of lower government functionaries and the resentment of those neighbors who remained animists.

While demonstrating wide social benefits attributable to Christianity, ethnic minority Christians remain special objects of government restrictions, discrimination, and harassment, as well as social hostility, tolerated, if not instigated, by government functionaries. Instead of encouraging a movement that contributes directly to stated government objectives, authorities seem to resist the rise of the "little people" who take positive charge of their own lives.

The second implication of rapid ethnic minority church expansion is an internal church matter. Most denominational leaders are Kinh, or ethnic Vietnamese. It would further strengthen their organizations if the numerically dominant ethnic minorities were more involved in church governance at the highest levels and in the contextualization of Christianity into their minority cultures.

SOURCES OF ADVERSITY AGAINST CHRISTIANITY

As noted, discrimination against Christians remains a critical problem in Vietnam as societal hostilities are frequently reinforced by governmental intolerance. Out of a concern for personal safety, if not fear, neither the researchers engaged for this project nor their many respondents want to be identified by name. Researchers also experienced the direct interference of Vietnam's security forces in communicating research results, complicating the writing of this chapter. These experiences echo findings of the Pew Forum's 2011 and 2012 research: Vietnam is among eight Asian countries that show a recent increase in government restriction and social hostility toward religion.[44]

Fundamental to understanding the Socialist Republic of Vietnam is comprehending that religion, especially Christianity, continues to be categorized as a difficult social problem and a national security threat. The words *Vấn đề tôn giáo*, meaning "the religion problem," regularly appear in official articles and book titles. If this is the official paradigm of religion, it follows that religion warrants scrutiny in the following ways: state sponsored academic study; a national Government Committee on Religious Affairs, which resides in the Ministry of the Interior and operates at all levels of government administration;[45] special religion units of the

Ministry of Public Security; special offices in the Communist Party of Vietnam; and extensive religion ordinances, decrees, and directives to manage religion, even to the point of deciding theological orthodoxy.

The original source of hostility toward religion lay in Marxist ideology, which considered religion as useless superstition distracting the masses from their legitimate social struggle.[46] However, a significant departure from this traditional thinking emerged in 1990. Official Vietnamese Communist Party resolutions recognized that "religion is a need for some people and will exist along with socialism for some time" and that "religion has cultural and moral values in keeping with socialism."[47] Do Quang Hung says that these two resolutions, which heralded a new approach to religion by Vietnam, have been often repeated but, regrettably, rarely implemented.[48]

A second source of hostility has been the officially enhanced version of the collusion of Catholicism with the French colonialists and, more recently, the identification of Evangelicals with the United States of America, Vietnam's recent enemy. It is true that the historic relationship of these nations and these Christian traditions is complicated in Vietnam. But both Catholics and Evangelicals have proven during four decades under Communism that they pose no threat to the state. On the contrary, they offer significant social resources.

But old government suspicions fade slowly. They still find expression in the phrase *Diễn biến hòa bình*, meaning "peaceful evolution" and used by the party and government since the early 1990s. The American Empire, *Đế Quốc Mỹ*, it was reasoned, lost the war of guns and bullets, but it has not given up on dominating Vietnam. The enemy is now employing peaceful evolution, the weapons of which are advocating for human rights, democracy, and religious freedom. In the vanguard of this process are local Evangelicals manipulated by America. It is a false but convenient construct to maintain a needed enemy.

It will be useful here to summarize religion policy and practice since the 1975 reunification of Vietnam to understand the kinds of official adversity Christians have faced.[49] Article 70 of Vietnam's current 1992 constitution states that people have the right "to believe or not to believe." But in the article itself are the seeds of ambiguity. It adds, "No one may take advantage of religious freedom to violate state laws and policies."

Unqualified religious freedom is further diluted by a series of religion decrees. The promises of the decrees for religious believers and organizations have been rarely and selectively fulfilled, and harsh practices toward believers have not even met their low standards. A monograph entitled "Two Distinct and Conflicting Polices" describes the sharp contradictions between the promises of religion decrees and the daily experiences of many Christian believers. Some felt it was a "telephone law," without a paper trail, which allowed the authorities to contravene official public policy regularly.[50]

Evangelical leaders have been intermittently imprisoned since 1975 for alleged infractions of the criminal code such as "disturbing public order" or "plotting against the state" or "harming the great national unity." Ethnic minority Christian communities in the Central Highlands and the NMR were at times invaded by government, police, and paramilitary officials and brutally persuaded to recant, sometimes after being forced to provide lavish meals for the invaders. Persecution of Hmong Evangelicals in the NMR was described as "combatting illegal propagation of religion."[51]

Government pressure ramped up even further in 2001 and 2004 when Christian Montagnards in the Central Highlands were involved in large demonstrations protesting the confiscation of their traditional lands and ongoing religious persecution.[52] Incited by exiled leaders of a former independence movement, FULRO,[53] some radical demonstrators demanded political autonomy. This allowed the authorities to paint all protesters with the brush of ethnoreligious separatism. Vietnam responded to the 2004 Easter uprising with massive military force, occupying some villages for months. Hundreds of participants were jailed with at least seventy-eight, at this writing, known to be still serving long prison sentences.

The explosive growth of Evangelicals among the Hmong, a very large ethnic group among whom Evangelicalism had not previously existed, aroused unusual government scrutiny and strong push back. In 2000 advocates acquired documents concerning the NMR, including some marked "Top-Secret," which detailed the formation of Task Force 184 with plans and budgets aimed at stopping cold or even eradicating (*tiêu diệt*) Evangelicalism.[54] Provincial authorities distributed illustrated propaganda booklets referring to Evangelicals, entitled, for instance, "Don't Follow the Bad People" and "Don't Listen to the Snake Poison Words."[55] The heavy persecution of the 1990s and the early 2000s is illustrated in the life of one Hmong leader. For thirteen years he endured several harsh imprisonments and bouts of cruel physical torture that finally drove him, reluctantly, to flee his homeland.[56]

In May 2011, a spontaneous millennial-type gathering of thousands of Hmong in Muong Nhe district (Dien Bien province) drew a massive security crackdown to the area. The cultic gathering also swept up some orthodox Evangelicals. This underlined the counterproductive nature of Vietnam's policy of severely restricting proper theological education for ethnic minority Christians[57]

Egregious persecution of ethnic minority Christians earned Vietnam a place on the U.S. State Department's "Country of Particular Concern" (CPC) blacklist in 2004. It also placed Vietnam under intense international scrutiny and pressure at the very time it aspired to join the World Trade Organization (WTO). Some breakthroughs would be required. The first was getting off the U.S. CPC blacklist in order to gain Permanent Normal Trading Status. Human rights, especially religious freedom, became major sticking points and provided an opportunity for then–U.S. ambassador-at-large for international religious freedom, John Hanford III, to press for reforms. And press he did.

In 2004 and 2005, Vietnam promulgated three pieces of new religion legislation. The first, which became effective in November 2004, was the "Ordinance on Belief and Religion." This was the highest-level legal framework for religion ever provided by the Socialist Republic of Vietnam. It was followed by "Decree on Religion No. 22" in March 2005, which was to serve as the implementation guideline for the ordinance. At the same time the "Prime Minister's Special Directive No. 1 Concerning Evangelicalism" was published. This was supposed to provide for the rapid registration of local congregations before the complicated registration regime of the new ordinance and decree could be implemented. Focus on the Evangelical minority apparently resulted from Vietnam's belief that it was of special interest to the U.S. government.

The new legislation proposed to increase the legitimacy of congregations and their denominational organizations through registration. Some called it religious freedom by management and control. The future promises of these measures proved enough for the United States to clear the way for Vietnam's accession to the WTO in 2007. Although this new religion legislation did not deliver on its promises to many, it can be said to have marked the end of the "eradication" or "stop cold" paradigm and transition to a "containment" one in regard to the growing Evangelical population. Large government-funded programs to force recantation of faith subsided as Vietnam moved toward the control of religion by registration.

In the near-decade since the new religion legislation, only seven Evangelical denominations that could prove a pre-1975 history have been granted legal recognition at the national level. The constitution of each newly registered denomination was obliged to include an awkward political commitment to the state. No denomination was allowed to retain any organizational structure, such as districts, between a local church and its central headquarters. Doubtless intentional, this provision has greatly handicapped church administration.

None of the dozens of house church organizations begun since 1988 has been granted national legal recognition. A new "Religion Decree No. 92," effective January 2013, which replaced Decree 22, is purported by the government to streamline the registration process. So far it has had no positive effect on registering the roughly half of Protestants who remain unregistered. A requirement for full legal recognition is for churches to demonstrate twenty years of legal, infraction-free operation before applying for recognition. By nature an unregistered group is illegal. The advantages of registration are seen as so dubious that many house churches decline to pursue it. By one common interpretation of Decree 92, it would be twenty-three years, or 2036, before the next church organization might possibly attain legal recognition.[58]

Both Catholics and Evangelicals surveyed in our field research consistently report that they still face opposition and sometimes even persecution when they evangelize and start churches in areas where Christians have not been present before. This is in keeping with the paradigm of containing Christianity. New Christian believers in remote rural areas are still pressured to recant and are often refused public benefits if they do not. New converts to Christianity are often not permitted to register their religion on their ID cards.

Among Vietnam's ethnic minorities, those who convert to Christianity sometimes also experience harsh opposition from their conservative animist fellows. This social hostility plays to the anti-Christian bias of local government officials, who conveniently decline to intervene when the animists destroy the Christians' property or crops, for example. Sometimes hostile officials incite social opposition by hiring thugs to attack Christians, demonstrating a synergy between government opposition and social hostility toward Christianity. Actions against Christians are usually committed with impunity. Violators are almost never brought to justice. In some NMR districts officials brazenly inform Christians who claim their religion rights under national regulations that local officials are not bound by Hanoi's rules.[59]

Where Christians dare to stand up and protest abuses they often attract the full force of state controlled media propaganda. A recent example occurred in My Yen, Nghe An province, in September 2013. Parishioners of the local Catholic Church protested the arrest without charges and detainment for three months of two fellow parishioners. Small protests grew larger when officials reneged on a promise to release the men. The protests were met with overwhelming force and at least a dozen Catholics were seriously injured in the melee that followed. Their bishop who supported them and the parishioners became the object of slanderous official propaganda. A whole alternative narrative accused the Catholics of attacking an official and forcing him to sign a release promise. It included a thinly veiled threat to arrest the bishop. It was then escalated by the government to include the threat that it could reverse gains in government-Vatican relations. On October 26, 2013, the two men who had confronted abuse of police power were sentenced to prison for "disturbing public order."[60]

In contrast to the outright violence cited earlier, Evangelicals in urban Vietnam report that persecution and confrontational opposition have largely been replaced by subtle meddling by religion and security officials. Leaders report being "invited" to pleasant afternoon coffees by suave officials and tempted to compromise in exchange for personal favors. Some leaders have succumbed, sowing suspicion and discord, destroying trust, diminishing unity, and sapping spiritual dynamism.

Another adversity faced by registered groups is interminable delay in getting permissions for what should be routine matters under existing legislation. Permits for constructing or repairing church buildings are one example. Another is theological education. The ECVN – N, registered since 1958, has been allowed to train only two small classes of pastors in the last five decades. And since the supposedly liberalized new religion legislation, it took until 2013 to get permission to open a seminary. Registration applications for 545 of 950 Hmong congregations affiliated with the ECVN – N have been denied or ignored during the same period. Requests to print a Hmong language Bible for the largest Evangelical ethnic minority group have been denied for years.[61]

CHRISTIANS' RESPONSE TO GOVERNMENT RESTRICTIONS, PERSECUTION, AND SOCIAL HOSTILITY

The response of Christians to adversity and harsh periods of persecution through four centuries – including four decades under a unified Communist Vietnam – has been remarkably patient and long-suffering, in keeping with the Christian tradition of "enduring" preached by St. Paul. Several respondents, when describing the hardest days, quoted II Cor. 4:8, 9, "We are hard pressed on every side, but not crushed; perplexed, but not in despair; persecuted, but not abandoned; struck down, but not destroyed."

Vietnam's Christians understand better than many Jesus's prediction that those who followed him would suffer, and so they find themselves living between advocating freedom and justice, on the one hand, and being ready to suffer for Christ's sake, on the other. This has been abundantly demonstrated during the four centuries of Christian history in Vietnam.

It is critical to understand that Christians of both Catholic and Evangelical traditions in Vietnam do not see themselves as mere anthropocentric voluntary organizations sharing religious experience and performing social service. They are both unapologetically evangelistic, witnessing to the historic, orthodox Christian truths, and calling people to faith in Christ and participation in churches. From this basis these communities serve as "salt and light," contributing to the common good as much as they are allowed, and yes, even in adversity.[62]

In the waxing and waning of adversity, this is a time of waning. Strong, overt persecution has been in decline since the mid-2000s. More subtle than in the past, the opposition Vietnamese Christians face can still be very damaging but is not often brutal. Yet, as illustrated, Christians live in far from ideal circumstances. Local officials ignore new national norms, churches regularly encounter a host of time-and-energy-sapping obstacles entrenched in Vietnam's religion-governing system, and they suffer unchecked social hostility in some places.

Through the centuries Christians have responded to pressure and persecution in three main ways. They fled, they resisted, or they quietly endured. Most in

Vietnam's long Christian history have endured. Though a number of Catholics and Evangelicals fled Vietnam at the Communist victory in 1975 and its difficult aftermath, by far the majority stayed in their homeland.

Since the mid-1990s, however, some forty thousand Hmong Evangelicals have fled persecution in their native NMR and "self-migrated," to use a government term, to the Central Highlands. Some members of Vietnam's Christian ethnic minorities still flee abroad. More than three hundred such asylum seekers still languish in Thailand, having difficulty convincing poorly informed UN officials that they have a "well-founded fear of persecution."

Resisting persecution or advocating for its victims remains a risky business in Vietnam. Nevertheless, before Vietnamese Christians were able to speak for themselves, a number of both Catholics and Evangelicals pleaded with international friends to help them "raise our voice in the outside world." At great risk, they cooperated closely with foreign advocates to expose severe abuses of religious freedom. Though the system did not allow and even punished open advocacy for freedom and justice in Vietnam, Christians creatively found ways to make their freedom aspirations known.

To that end, it was a full fifty years after church properties were confiscated that Catholics began publicly to demand the return of some properties in Hanoi. Their advocacy for the return of the Papal Nunciature in Hanoi in 2007 and 2008 scored a partial victory. The valuable property in central Hanoi was not returned to the church, as had been promised, but the international attention attracted by mass prayer vigils forced the government to turn the place into a public library and park, rather than sell it to developers for the personal profit of high officials. Regrettably, Catholics lost the activist Archbishop Ngo Quang Kiet in the fray when under intense government pressure and some believe Vatican complicity, he resigned "for health reasons." The government portrayed it as a victory.[63]

Evangelicals who have dared confront government pressure on their religious activities have been treated harshly. The Mennonite pastor Nguyen Hong Quang, last imprisoned in 2005, is an example. Quang became a marked man when he publicized many cases of religious oppression. When a dustup followed his exposing of government agents staking out his church's center, he and five colleagues were charged and imprisoned for "interfering with an officer doing his duty." Strong international advocacy secured an early release for some, including Ms. Lien, a female church worker, released from the Bien Hoa mental hospital, where she had been abused.

Pastor Quang is an activist outlier to the majority Evangelical community, among whom it is commonly held that churches should confine their concerns to spiritual matters and not be involved in politics. Advocating justice is considered politics. Such a dichotomy between religious faith and concern for social justice domesticates the radical Christian gospel and plays directly into the hands of the Communist rulers who work to silence all criticism.

Catholic and Evangelical activists who became internationally known, such as Father Nguyen Van Ly, the Catholic lawyer Le Quoc Quan, and the Evangelical lawyers Nguyen Van Dai and Le Thi Cong Nhan, clearly underlined the direct relationship between Christian faith and advocacy not only for religious and other freedoms but also for justice. Even more than other activists they were falsely accused and maligned by government propaganda campaigns that portrayed them as enemies of the state.

Without determined local support, even the strongest international advocacy is often not enough.[64] This was demonstrated in early 2013 when two legally registered denominations each experienced cases of egregious persecution of ethnic minority Christians. In Kontum province the homes and farmsteads of four Sodang families, recent Evangelical believers, were destroyed, and they were driven to flee. After four months of determined local advocacy by the denomination's leader, with strong international support, a rare victory was won. The families were given replacement land and promised government support to reestablish their livelihood.

The second case in Dak Nong province involved the murder in police custody of the falsely arrested Hoang Van Ngai, a Hmong community and Evangelical church leader, in March 2013. The police said Mr. Ngai had electrocuted himself in his cell, a fact belied by his brother in the next cell, who heard the beating, and by the battered corpse returned to his family. In this case denominational leaders declined to support the family in demanding an investigation, judging such activity political and off-limits. Strong international advocacy alone accomplished little as authorities unabashedly stood by the police suicide story.

After the family itself pursued this injustice vigorously for a year, however, there is some evidence that high authorities are pressuring local ones to try to make some amends. They offered a cash gift and a verbal apology. The family declined, saying that the police knew who was to blame and that they expected justice. On October 8, 2014, the deputy police chief at the time of the killing, Major Le Manh Nam, was arrested. But by this time the murdered man's family had been so harassed and threatened by officials for their persistent advocacy that they had fled their homes.

In some cases, however, strong Christian leaders, standing on principle and employing effective social and negotiating skills, have been effective. A Montagnard leader in Pleiku, Gia Lai province, exemplifies what morally based yet tough engagement with officials can accomplish. It requires, he reports, willingness to sit many hours in government offices, and sometimes to be humiliated. On one occasion he was hit hard in the face by an angry official but he maintained his cool demeanor. By making strong moral arguments in favor of his people, and by pointing officials to their own regulations, he won concessions and respect. He makes a point of telling officials that in approving reasonable church requests they win too. Exceptional results have included relatively speedy mass church registrations, permission to build several large church buildings, and the holding of large church celebrations.

Evangelicals also demonstrate that their organizations actually practice the democracy the government only talks about. Officials who have inserted themselves into church business meetings have often been surprised to observe free and regular votes for pastors, elders, and denominational leaders.

The Catholic situation has been somewhat easier than that of Evangelicals.[65] The decision of Vietnamese Catholic bishops of South Vietnam after the Communist victory to remain with their people, and to urge the Catholic faithful to participate in effecting the common good in spite of the Communist government, appears to have been courageous and wise.[66] This did not make Catholics' lives problem free, but they were usually spared the harsh persecution that many Evangelicals suffered. Catholic bishops usually remained publicly quiescent, often negotiating successfully behind the scenes. In a division of labor, the main advocacy against government limitations and incidents of persecution has been undertaken by the Catholic religious orders, notably the Redemptorists.[67]

Both Catholic and Evangelical churches fell under special scrutiny in Vietnam with the collapse of European Communism around 1990. The role of churches in that phenomenon was carefully noted by Vietnam's Communist leaders, who vowed it would never happen to them. But the potential of churches' contribution to political liberalization certainly remains a cautionary tale for them.[68]

In 2013 Catholic bishops took a courageous public stand when they responded to a government request for advice on revising the constitution. They asked for the removal of article 4, which enshrines the Vietnam Communist Party's exclusive "leading role" as the only legal political force.[69] This request, made also by others, was rejected.

The unity and size of the Catholic Church are inherent strengths that usually force the government to tread carefully regarding its rights. The fractured nature of the smaller Evangelical movement is a weakness, which invites government disrespect and more cavalier treatment. With no national alliance, with the larger Evangelical groups feeling self-sufficient, and with competing groups and outliers, the Evangelical movement is handicapped in its dealing with the government, which has been quick to exploit this flaw.

In rare interfaith efforts to advocate religious freedom in the country in August and October 2013, some Catholic and Evangelical leaders participated in a group of fifteen leaders of five faiths to raise concerns about the government's policy on religion. They published the highly critical "Statement of Vietnam's Clergies

Concerning the Ordinance on Belief and Religion."[70] A strong theme of their protest was that religious people are still treated as inferior, second-class citizens.

Another response to the situation, particularly for Evangelical groups, has been to forge relationships with international denominations and mission groups. There are, for example, dozens of alliances with international Pentecostal, Baptist, Methodist, and Presbyterian groups. These connections, for the most part illegal under current regulations, nevertheless provide not only financial support but some political cover, they believe. On the other hand, they also feed government suspicions.

Christian charity challenges Vietnamese policy makers with its potential contributions to civil society. Catholics and Evangelicals are quietly helping disadvantaged people with early childhood education, health care, drug addiction, and HIV-AIDS treatment, for example. Several successful drug rehabilitation centers run by Evangelicals in Hanoi have won quiet government admiration from officials who have seen the failures of their own punitive approach to addictions. But some such institutions still experience frustrating obstruction by local authorities.

As civil society activity is scarcely and reluctantly permitted in Vietnam, these fine works are not registered nor widely known. Similar to efforts to promote freedom, such works of charity are often organized by individuals, groups of Christians, or a local church. The government wants charity workers to register and work with local authorities, but this request is often declined because of the lack of integrity and compassion of authorities in many locations. But through the perseverance of Christians in helping the needy and by the visible positive changes of people after their conversion to Christianity, some government policy makers are beginning to see Christian charity as a national resource to help the government care for the poor.[71]

It is widely acknowledged that Vietnam faces an alarming deterioration of morality and hopelessness among young people, even by Vietnam's political leaders. In a counterintuitive development in May 2013, the Buddhist business tycoon Le Phuoc Vu spent U.S. $1.5 million to sponsor Nick Vujicic, the armless and legless Australian evangelist, not to preach Christianity, but to be an uplifting motivational speaker at major stadium events and on national television. His powerful message and example of overcoming adversity took Vietnam by storm. The Christian source of Nick's strength could not be hidden. He may have been seen and heard by a full half of Vietnam's population and became the subject of a wide public conversation. How, people asked, could one with so many handicaps be so positive and happy?[72]

CHOICES FOR THE WAY AHEAD

The long adversarial relationship between the state and the two major Christian traditions documented here does not seem to promise a sudden change to full freedom. But there are reasons to hope. Of the five remaining Communist countries, Vietnam is perhaps the most pragmatic and could conceivably make more room for religious faith and organizations.

The Vietnamese Communist Party (VCP) has already made radical ideological and practical changes, when, in 1986 *Đổi Mới* jettisoned Marxist economics and embraced market principles. The "Market Leninism" that resulted has had rapid and visible positive results for many in Vietnam. If such a fundamental economic reversal was possible, why not a parallel change in religion and civil society?

A significant step in this direction has been taken by party and government resolutions accepting an ongoing need for religion and affirming its value in a socialist society. Already the strategic dial on religion has moved from eradication to containment, from systematic and egregious persecution to much lower levels of harassment and discrimination, in certain provinces. The next turn of the dial could be to minimize the use of the national security lens when viewing religion and perceive it as a social resource for the nation. Such a strategic shift could lead to the release of all religions from the burdensome and costly layers of religion bureaucracy and restrictive rules.

The outlook of some government reformers closely engaged with Christians is changing, in part because of the perseverance and sacrifice of Christians constructively living their faith and promoting the common good with both careful words and strong deeds. The positive results of a new paradigm for religion would be immediate and large for both the religions and the nation. Mere tinkering with current regulations or even trying to draft a proposed be-all-end-all "law on religion" is not the answer. A new operating system is required, not just a few software changes. Could this happen? Optimistic Christians dream and pray for that day! Gradualism, however, is the likely path to change, so, short of achieving that large step at once, what measures could help move toward a better future?

Human rights and religious freedom organizations urge Vietnam to fulfill its commitments incurred by signing international agreements guaranteeing religious freedom.[73] But how? Another frequent suggestion is that the conflicted parties should "build trust." But trust and truth have become very scarce under a system that breeds distrust.

Therefore, as in other highly conflicted and distrustful situations, steps must first be taken by both sides to identify common interests and focus on those. If small successful steps are made in fulfilling mutual interests, there may be a chance to build trust. Failure to engage in such difficult work, however, will leave the parties locked in the legacy demonstrated by nearly a century of very conflicted Christian-Communist coexistence.[74] Fortunately there are players on both sides in Vietnam who acknowledge the need for a better way forward.

Our researchers and respondents suggest the following:

1) Christian communities need to prepare for confident engagement. This will require fresh indigenous theologizing concerning the relationship of churches and the state, of Christian citizens with civil authorities, and the further contextualization of Christian expression in Vietnamese culture. Concerned with survival during much adversity, and deprived of educational opportunity, neither Catholics nor Evangelicals in Vietnam have done theological reflection on these matters very well. Also, Christian scholars, including those trained overseas, need acceptance to join government scholars in academic study of religion issues.[75]

2) It is in Vietnam's interest to facilitate theological training for Christian leaders. Some members of the rapidly growing ethnic minority Evangelical churches, and of Catholic churches, have proven vulnerable to both quasi-Christian cults and calls for radical antigovernment action to right injustices. To resist such sub-Christian tendencies Chris Seiple of the Institute for Global Engagement (IGE) has been making the case with Vietnamese officials for "seminary as security."[76] Catholics, having six seminaries, are in a relatively good position, but Evangelicals are not. It was five decades after legal recognition before the ECVN – N was permitted to open a seminary and almost three decades after the reunification of Vietnam before the ECVN – S was granted permission to do so. Dozens of unregistered church bodies have had no opportunity to train their pastors legally, ever. It is not consistent for authorities to complain about poorly trained pastors and fret over heterodoxy and perceived national security threats of churches and continue to restrict education for church leaders severely.

3) The Christian position would be much strengthened by firm steps toward Evangelical unity, by intentional Catholic-Evangelical collaboration, and by expressions of solidarity for freedom among the Christian traditions and other religions. Herein lies a seedbed for freedom's germination. Some of this is currently beyond the imagination of many Vietnamese Evangelicals and Catholics. It will require visionary and courageous religious leaders willing to confront both internal resistance and government push back.

4) It is imperative that both state officials and church leaders cultivate personal relationships. Both sides have a strong common interest in a respectful dialogue, which is required for adjusting religion policy. A fine example of such a process is the partnership between an American Christian nongovernment organization, IGE, and Vietnamese government organizations.[77] The partnership – having been carefully built and maintained with friendship and trust – has sponsored training

for government officials and faith leaders on international standards and comparative studies on religion and rule of law, church registration issues, Evangelicalism in Vietnam, and conflict resolution skills. These events marked the first face-to-face encounter of some pastors with government officials and an opportunity for dialogue. Using local resources, churches should initiate such events.

5) As the government for some time will likely maintain its position that religion must be controlled by administrative management, the regulations and processes should at least be open, transparent, and consistent. Here are some suggestions:

- The chief guidelines, the 2004 Ordinance on Religion and the 2013 Decree 92, remain ambiguous and arbitrarily implemented. If the government would clarify and abide by its own regulations and cease ignoring churches that try to register, it could open the possibility for trust.
- If the government cannot yet bring itself to throw away the leash on religions, it should at least slacken it. The majority of Christian leaders surveyed say that the religion regulations remain based on the ask-and-receive (*xin cho*) paradigm in which the government retains complete power over every little matter. Authorities have said the latest regulations are more in the report-for-information (*báo cáo*) mode, but many Christian leaders do not yet experience them in this way.
- Our respondents widely agree that the surest sign that the government was sincere about improving its relations with the religious communities would be to prosecute and punish officials who overtly discriminate against, harass, and persecute Christians, and to reprimand openly those who obstruct and fail to meet deadlines set in the regulations. The ongoing impunity of offending officials in a nation that aspires to the rule of law is very harmful for all.

6) The largest and most obvious area of common interest is in the broad area of social welfare, including education, public health, and medicine. The ideological encouragement of Market Leninism to pursue wealth, with the scantest of social conscience, has left many poor and marginalized. Social ills such as drugs and sexual promiscuity have left many thousands of addicts, HIV/AIDS patients, and orphans. Abortions virtually equal live births. A social welfare system has barely been conceived for lack of social conscience and personnel, to say nothing of budget. Catholic and Evangelical churches and agencies stand ready to do much more in these areas. But government announced intentions to expand the possibilities for faith groups' social work are little implemented. Officials may fear that the goodwill that altruism generates could be turned into political activity against an unpopular government. But if Christian charity is outright declined,

unnecessary human suffering will continue and a better quality of life for many will be forfeited.

Having experienced government restrictions and social hostility for four centuries, Christians in Vietnam have nevertheless demonstrated the transcendent strength and the human flourishing and wide social benefits that emerged from their faith and practice. They have contributed to promoting freedom, human dignity and rights, justice, and civil society. The role of Christianity in building moral foundations, in imagining a better future, and in directing policies and actions toward greater justice, freedom, and human flourishing would only increase if the Vietnamese government chose to trust and include the Christian community more fully in national development. This would be a win for everyone.

NOTES

1 "Report on Completed Census Results: The 1/4/2009 Population and Housing Census," Central Population and Housing Census Steering Committee, Hanoi, 2010; the figures given by all religions are markedly higher than government statistics, which themselves vary widely between census figures and those released by the Government Committee on Religious Affairs. Though impossible to verify with complete certainty, figures reported by religions are deemed to be more accurate.

2 The Evangelical tradition dominates Protestant Christianity in Vietnam. The identifying word in Vietnamese is *Tin Lanh*, from the Greek *euanglion*, or "good news/gospel" in English. Vietnamese of this tradition are proud to be historically, popularly, linguistically, and biblically known as Tin Lanh, or Evangelicals. I will respect this self-identification and use "Evangelical" and its variants in this essay. I am aware of the term's problems in some contexts, but it is called for here. The terms "Christian" and "Christianity" will usually indicate both major Christian traditions. It is also noteworthy that since the late 1980s Vietnamese Evangelicals have been considerably influenced by the worldwide Pentecostal/charismatic movement.

3 Phat Huon Phan, *History of the Catholic Church in Vietnam. Tome I. 1533–1960* (Ho Chi Minh City: Vietnam Redemptorist Press, 2002); Piero Gheddo, *The Cross and the Bo-Tree: Catholics and Buddhists in Vietnam* (New York: Sheed & Ward, 1970).

4 Alexandre de Rhodes, *Rhodes of Vietnam*, trans. Solange Hertz (Westminster, MD: Newman Press, 1966). The original work was published in France in 1651.

5 Peter C. Phan, *Mission and Catechesis: Alexandre de Rhodes and Inculturation in Seventeenth Century Vietnam* (New York: Orbis Books, 1998).

6 Reg E. Reimer, "The Protestant Movement in Vietnam: Church Growth in Peace and War among Ethnic Vietnamese" (Master's thesis, Fuller Theological Seminary, 1972), 261–283.

7 Ibid., 273.

8 Nguyen was the last ruling king of Vietnam. Remnants of his dynasty lasted for 143 years, 1802–1945.

9 Gheddo, *The Cross and the Bo-Tree*, 13.

10 John R. Shortland, *The Persecution of Annam: A History of Christianity in Cochinchina and Tonkin* (London: Burns and Oates, 1875).

11 Peter C. Phan, "The Roman Catholic Church in the Socialist Republic of Vietnam, 1989–2005," in *Falling Walls: The Year 1989/90 as a Turning Point in the History of World Christianity*, ed. Klaus Koschorke (Wiesbaden: Harrassowitz Verlag, 2009), 243–257.

12 Lan T. Chu notes the surprising agility of the Catholic hierarchy to maneuver in the constricting political framework of post-1975 Communist Vietnam. See Lan T. Chu, "The Sign of the Cross: Vertical and Horizontal Tensions in Vietnamese Church-State Relations," in *Straddling State and Society: Local Organizations and Urban Governance in East and Southeast Asia*, ed. Benjamin L. Read and Robert Pekkanen (New York: Routledge, 2009)

13 Reimer, "The Protestant Movement in Vietnam," 273.

14 Phillip Taylor, *Modernity and Re-Enchantment: Religion in Post-Revolutionary Vietnam* (Singapore: Utopia Press, 2007) 371–398.

15 Peter C. Phan, *In Our Own Tongues: Perspectives from Asia on Mission and Inculturation* (New York: Orbis Books, 2003), 109–129.

16 Phillip Taylor, *Modernity and Re-Enchantment*, 394.

17 "Colonial modernity" refers to the transformation out of colonialism toward independence and modernity.

18 For a fuller history of Vietnamese Evangelicals, see Le Hoang Phu, "A Short History of the Evangelical Church in Vietnam 1911–1965" (Ph.D. dissertation, New York University, 1972); Reg E. Reimer, "The Protestant Movement in Vietnam"; Reg Reimer, *Vietnam's Christians: A Century of Growth in Adversity* (Pasadena, CA: William Carey Library, 2011).

19 "Montagnards," from French for "mountain people," is the popular collective term for dozens of Mon-Khmer and Malayo-Polynesian ethnic minority groups in Vietnam's Central Highlands.

20 Related in person by the Reverend Thai to the author in 1971.

21 Reimer, *Vietnam's Christians*, 40–42.

22 The author was commissioned to take a census of South Vietnam's Evangelicals for the first Lausanne Congress on World Evangelization in 1974; "South Vietnam: Status of Christianity of Christianity County Profile," Office of Missionary Information, Saigon, 1974.

23 Reimer, *Vietnam's Christians*, 55–62.

24 Đổi Mới is Vietnam's version of *glasnost* (openness) and *perestroika* (reorganization). Vietnam opted for the latter, especially in economics.

25 An undated article on the government's Committee on Religious Affairs Vietnamese-language Web site (accessed November 20, 2014), entitled "Evangelicalism in Vietnam from 1975 to the Present," counts more than eighty denominational groups, including two Christian and Missionary Alliance, fifty Pentecostal, ten Baptist, two Seventh-Day Adventist, two Mennonite, two Presbyterian, two Methodist, and ten miscellaneous.

26 These were boat refugees from Vietnam who made it to Hong Kong but were denied permanent resettlement in third countries and forcibly repatriated. Many accepted Evangelical Christian faith in refugee camps.

27 Internal government documents on the rapid growth of Evangelicalism among ethnic minorities sometimes used the word *bung no* (explosion), but more often used the term *phat trien bat thuong*, meaning unusually rapid development.

28 "Report on Completed Census Results," Central Population and Housing Census Steering Committee, 2010.

29 Reimer, *Vietnam's Christians*, 75–84; James F. Lewis, "The Evangelical Religious Movement among the Hmong of Northern Vietnam and the Government's Response," *Crossroads: An Interdisciplinary Journal of Southeast Asian Studies* 16, no. 2 (2002): 79–112.

30 Phillip Taylor, *Modernity and Re-Enchantment*, 394.

31 This was related to one of our researchers by a ranking government official. See also Nguyen Van Thang, *Giu "Ly Cu" Hay Theo "Ly Moi?"* (Preserve the "Old Way" or Follow the "New Way"?) (M.A. thesis, Hanoi: Nha Xuat Ban Khoa Hoc Xa Hoi, 2009). It is an examination of Hmong reactions to the influence of the Evangelical faith, noting some positive results of adopting Christianity.

32 Charles Keith, *Catholic Vietnam: A Church from Empire to Nation* (Berkeley: University of California Press, 2012), 122.

33 World Bank and other population Web sites put Vietnam's literacy rate at about 20 percentage points higher than that of neighboring Laos and Cambodia.

34 Charles Keith, *Catholic Vietnam*, 30; a notable exception was the famous Phát Diệm cathedral in northern Vietnam, which employed oriental and Buddhist architecture and became a respected example of inculturation.

35 Ibid., 30–31.

36 Ibid., 109.

37 Lan T. Chu on Catholicism in Vietnam, podcast recorded August 10, 2011, accessed November 24, 2014. http://www.researchonreligion.org/player/index.php?episode=RoR_066_Chu_08102011

38 Van Nguyen-Marshall, "Tools of Empire? Vietnamese Catholics in South Vietnam," *Journal of the Canadian Historical Society* 20, no. 2 (2009): 138–159, is a summary of Vietnamese Catholics' social and political contributions in South Vietnam from 1954 to the end of the Vietnam War in 1975.

39 Phan, "The Roman Catholic Church in the Socialist Republic of Vietnam, 1989–2005," 243–257.

40 "New Insights into Religion by Vietnam's Religion Scholars Today." The Government Committee for Religious Affairs (from a seminar hosted by Catholic scholars), http://www.btgcp.gov.vn

41 In "An Overview of Translations of the Bible in Vietnamese," a privately circulated paper, I describe five more recent Evangelical Bible translations. The first whole Catholic Bible, a four-volume Latin-Vietnamese diglot, was published in Hong Kong between 1911 and 1914, three centuries after missionary arrival. Catholics and Evangelicals have recently cooperated in Bible translation and distribution under the United Bible Societies.

42 Charles Taber, "In the Image of God: The Gospel and Human Rights," *International Bulletin of Missionary Research* (2002): 89–102. In a landmark article on the Christian gospel as the basis for human rights, Taber says that the realization that one is made in the image of God is foundational, as are the absolute nondiscriminatory teaching and practice of Jesus Christ.

43 These Vietnam Evangelical movements must be seen as part of the explosion and complete reconfiguration of Christianity toward the Global South since 1970. This shift has been well documented by secular and religious scholars such as Philip Jenkins, Andrew Walls, and Lamin Sanneh, among others.

44 "Rising Tide of Restrictions on Religion," *The Pew Research Religion & Public Life Project*, September 20, 2012, http://www.pewforum.org/2012/09/20/rising-tide-of-restrictions-on-religion-findings/#changes-in-government-restrictions

45 The Government Committee on Religious Affairs is currently led by two former high-ranking members of the Ministry of Public Security.

46 There are indications that Ho Chi Minh, Communist Vietnam's revered founder, at least in 1921, was more accepting of Christianity than this ideology. A highly interesting, heretofore unknown 1921 letter from Ho Chi Minh to a French Protestant pastor, who sought Ho Chi Minh's advice on opening a mission in Vietnam, came to light in 2011. In his letter, Ho Chi Minh cleverly challenges the pastor to think of what the more radical demands of the Christian gospel would say to the French subjugation of Vietnamese people. For a translation of the letter and one analysis, see Pascal Bourdeaux, "Notes on an Unpublished Letter from Ho Chi Minh to a French Pastor" (September 8, 1921) or "The Art of Dissenting Evangelization," *Journal of Vietnamese Studies* 7, no. 2 (2012): 8–28.

47 First passed as Resolution 24 of the Political Branch of the Communist Party of Vietnam on November 26, 1990. But it did not become active policy until it was adopted by the Ministry of Political Affairs on July 2, 1998 as Directive 37-CT/TW under the title "Concerning the Religion Task in the New Situation." It was first made public in the *Nhan Dan* (*Peoples' Daily*) newspaper, the official voice of the Vietnam Communist Party, on July 8, 1998.

48 Do Quang Hung, personal conversation with author in Hanoi, July 19, 2013.

49 Do Quang Hung, leading religion scholar and currently head of the religion section of Vietnam's powerful Fatherland Front, has written many Vietnamese language books on religion policy including *Van De Ton Giao Trong Cach Mang Viet Nam* (2008), translated *The Religion Problem in the Vietnamese Revolution*. In it he describes Vietnam's evolving religion policy, especially since 1990, when it began to be influenced by Vietnam's Doi Moi (renovation policy).

50 Reimer, *Vietnam's Christians*, 97–98.

51 "On the Cruel Edges of the World: The Untold Story of the Persecution of Christians among Vietnam's Minority Peoples," World Evangelical Fellowship Religious Liberty Commission, Bangkok, 1999.

52 An account of the 2001 uprising was published by Human Rights Watch in 2002 under the title *Repression of Montagnards: Conflict over Land and Religion in Vietnam's Central Highlands*.

53 FULRO is the French acronym for the United Front for the Liberation of Oppressed Races, an ethnic minority independence movement that dates back to the 1960s.

54 A collection of internal Vietnamese government documents on religion, including some marked "secret" and "top secret," with English translation was published under the title *Directions for Stopping Religion* by Freedom House in 2000, on the eve of President Clinton's historic visit to Vietnam.

55 These booklets are photocopied and translated in the Freedom House publication cited.

56 Reimer, *Vietnam's Christians*, 78–81.

57 Reg Reimer, "Clash of Cults, Orthodox Christians, Ethnic Minorities and Politics in Dien Bien Province," report, May 17, 2011.

58 "Two Steps Back? Vietnam's Decree on Religion," March 2, 2013, http://www.worldwatchmonitor.org

59 This is particularly true of Dien Bien province.

60 See http://www.asianews.it for news releases on this and other incidents involving Catholics; "Vietnam: My Yen Incident, September 2013," Christian Solidarity Worldwide, http://www.csw.org.uk

61 Even though government departments themselves use the popular missionary-designed Romanized Hmong script to communicate with Hmong, the government keeps on denying its use for printing a Hmong Bible.

62 Andrea P. Dilley, "The World Missionaries Made," *Christianity Today* 58, no. 1 (2014). This article on Robert Woodberry's research shows a remarkable correlation and causation between the work of conversionary Protestant missionaries and the development of democracy.

63 See http://www.asianews.it releases of October 8, 2010, and November 5, 2010.

64 For a description of religious freedom advocacy in Vietnam see Reg Reimer, "Vietnam: Not an Accidental Advocate," in *Sorrow & Blood: Christian Mission in Contexts of Suffering, Persecution, and Martyrdom*, ed. William D. Taylor, Antonia van der Meer, and Reg Reimer (Pasadena, CA: William Carey Library, 2012), 291–298.

65 Peter Hansen, "The Vietnamese State, the Catholic Church and the Law," in *Asian Socialism and Legal Change: The Dynamics of Vietnamese and Chinese Reform*, ed. John Gillespie and Pip Nicholson (Canberra: Asia Pacific Press, 2005), 310–334; Father Peter Hansen makes the case that Catholics reside in the messy middle between all and nothing in regard to religious freedom.

66 Phan, "The Roman Catholic Church in the Socialist Republic of Vietnam, 1989–2005," 243–257.

67 The Redemptorist Father Stephen Chan Tin was a longtime outspoken critic of the regime, until his death in 2012. Other Redemptorists continue advocacy, though in a more discreet way. The Web site www.AsiaNews.it regularly carries news on Vietnamese Catholic conflicts with the state, from reliable in-country sources.

68 Lan T. Chu on Catholicism in Vietnam, podcast recorded August 10, 2011. See also Professor Lan's article "Catholicism vs. Communism in Vietnam" at http://rocknguyen .wordpress.com/2011/04/15/catholicism-vs-communism-in-vietnam/

69 For this and much other information on current Catholic Church matters see the Web site of the Catholic Bishop's Conference of Vietnam at http://www.cbcvietnam.org

70 "Statement of Vietnam's Clergies: Concerning the Ordinance on Religion and Belief of 2004 and the 2012 Decree on Directives and Measures for Implementing the Ordinance on Religion and Belief," Democratic Voice of Vietnam, October 7, 2013, http://dvov.org/2013/10/07/statement-of-vietnams-clergies-concerning-ordinance-on-religion-and-belief

71 This information was obtained directly from a colleague who has worked for a decade in quietly promoting religious freedom among high Vietnamese officials but wishes to remain anonymous.

72 Reg Reimer, "Nick Vujicic in Vietnam – an Evangelist Not Allowed to Preach," privately circulated, June 1, 2013.

73 For example, the Universal Declaration of Human Rights and the International Covenant on Civil and Political Rights.

74 Anyone who doubts the immense challenges involved needs to consult the monumental eight-hundred-page work S. Courtois et al., *The Black Book of Communism: Crimes, Terror, Repression*, trans. M. Kramer and J. Murphy (Cambridge, MA: Harvard University

Press, 1999); see also Johannes Reimer, "Persecution of Christians in the Soviet Union," in *Sorrow and Blood: Christian Mission in Contexts of Suffering, Persecution, and Martyrdom*, ed. William Taylor et al. (Pasadena, CA: William Carey Library, 2012).

75 James Lewis, "Vietnamese Religions, Asian Studies, and the Rule of Law," *The Review of Faith and International Affairs* 11, no. 2 (2013): 55–63.

76 Chris Seiple, "Reflection on Theology, Strategy, and Engagement," *Sorrow and Blood: Christian Mission in Contexts of Suffering, Persecution, and Martyrdom*, ed. William Taylor et al. (Pasadena, CA: William Carey Library, 2012), 437–444.

77 The Institute for Global Engagement has been working on religious freedom with the Vietnamese government since 2004. See http://www.globalengage.org

10

The Challenge and Leaven of Christianity in Pakistan

Sara Singha

INTRODUCTION

In this paper, I discuss the contemporary experience of Christians in Pakistan. In the first section, I describe the role of Christians during the partition of India. This includes the coalition between Christians and the Muslim League in the mid-1940s, which resulted in the migration of many Christians to Pakistan. I argue that this coalition movement was a sign of mutual trust between Christians and Muslims prior to the formation of Pakistan.

Next, I describe the constitutional changes that occurred after Partition – I argue that these changes were fueled by a national anxiety about the relationship between Islam and the state and, in some instances, constricted freedom for religious minorities. In the final section, I describe the multiple challenges facing Christians in the social context, including discrimination, the pressure of religious conversion, and the Blasphemy Law. I also show Christian responses to sociopolitical discrimination through various means and methods, including the formation of political parties and social institutions such as schools, clinics, and hospitals.

DEMOGRAPHY

Most Pakistani Christians are ethnically Punjabi and divided into many denominations. The Protestant Church in Pakistan is the result of low-caste Hindu conversions to Christianity in the nineteenth century.[1] The largest Protestant denomination, with almost 27 percent of the Christian population,[2] is the Church of Pakistan (COP), which was inaugurated in 1970 through a union of Anglicans, Methodists, Lutherans, and Scottish Presbyterians.[3] The next largest denomination is the Presbyterian Church of Pakistan, which was formed in 1990 by the merger of the United Presbyterian Church and the Lahore Church Council. Both the United Presbyterian Church and the Lahore Church Council suffered a schism in 1968 that led to the creation of the Presbyterian Church, which has a sizable following.[4] Other Protestant denominations include the Associate Reformed Presbyterian Church, Baptists, Brethren, Church of Christ, Church of St. Thomas, the Evangelical Church, Eastern Orthodox, Pentecostals, Salvation Army, and Seventh-Day Adventists.

The largest Christian denomination is the Roman Catholic Church, with approximately one-third of the population.[5] In contrast to Protestants, many Catholics are descendants of affluent families from South India or converts from high-caste Hindu backgrounds.[6] There is a sizable Catholic Goanese presence with ancestral connections to Portuguese conversions during the sixteenth century. There is also a small Anglo-Indian community, the result of intermarriage between British Christians and Indians.[7] The majority of Christians reside in the Punjab, and the city of Lahore has the highest Christian presence in the country. The 1981 census reports more than 200,000 Christians in Lahore and large communities in Faisalabad, Sialkot, and Sheikhpura.[8] Christians in Sindh Province reside in Karachi or Hyderabad and almost 80 percent are urbanized.[9] Baluchistan Province has a small Christian presence with 20,000 Christians in the city of Quetta.[10] In Khyber Pakhtunkhwa Province, Christians are also urbanized and live in the city of Peshawar. Records indicate that this community has 50,000 members.[11]

In general, census records are not accurate measures of religious demography in Pakistan. First, the census is not conducted regularly. Second, in rural areas, people often lie about religious membership because of fear of persecution and discrimination.[12] According to the government of Pakistan, Christians compose 2 percent of the total population; these figures are vehemently contested by Christians, who suggest that the government purposely depreciates their numbers for political purposes.[13]

CHRISTIAN POLITICAL HISTORY

Pre-Partition: The Crescent and the Cross

In 1885, Allan Octavian Hume, a British Christian, sympathized with educated Indians and helped form the All India National Congress to encourage civil and political dialogue between Indians and the British.[14] The All India National Congress was the major political voice for Hindus, Muslims, Christians, and other religious communities before independence.[15] However, in 1906, after feeling repeatedly overlooked in their political needs, Muslim leaders separated from the All India Congress Party and formed the All India Muslim League.[16] The formation of the league was fueled by an anxiety that once the British left India, Muslims would be politically ignored and socially disadvantaged under Hindu rule. By the mid-1940s, concern for Muslim safety and equality led the Muslim League to adopt the two-state solution.

The two-state solution promoted by Muhammad Ali Jinnah envisioned India divided along religious lines and the formation of an independent Muslim state.[17] The idea was initially met with suspicion from Muslims and other religious minorities. However, matters changed dramatically with the Jawaharlal Nehru Minority Report in 1928.[18] Among other things, the minority report proposed that independent India would have no official state religion or separate electorates for religious minorities.[19] This emerged as a point of contention because many religious minorities feared that they would lose their political voice in a joint electorate system.

Prior to the minority report, Christians had not seriously considered the partition of India. Many Christian leaders were afraid of dividing the community and did not support the idea of Pakistan. However, the joint electorate system created sociopolitical anxiety among Christians and after the minority report conference, many Christians began to entertain the idea of Pakistan. In response, Jinnah promised Christian leaders "all the rights which have been set up by Islam" and which were guaranteed for Muslims.[20] Anxious for sociopolitical equality, Christian leaders officially supported the Pakistan Resolution.[21] After his success with Christian leaders, Jinnah also approached other minority communities. Jinnah tried to form a coalition with the Sikh leader, Gianni Kirtar Singh, and the Dalit leader, B. R. Ambedkar without success.[22] Without Sikh and Dalit support, the Pakistan movement largely comprised the Muslim and Christian communities.

One of main negotiation points of the Muslim League with the Congress Party was the inclusion of the entire Punjab in Pakistan. The Congress Party did not want the Punjab divided and strongly opposed its inclusion in Pakistan. The Punjab was the primary area of contestation because the region had a large presence of three religious communities: Christians, Muslims, and Sikhs. Without Sikh support, Jinnah relied heavily on Christians to lobby for the inclusion of Punjab in Pakistan. The Joint Christian Board, an umbrella Christian organization formed in 1946, supported Jinnah in this venture.[23] Dewan Bahadur, S. P. Singha the representative of the Joint Christian Board, was so confident in Pakistan that he emphasized the Christian affinity with Muslims instead of Hindus. "Our people have been living with the Muslims a long time and have become Muslimised in culture and outlook."[24] Further, he argued, "Eastern Punjab could rejoin Hindustan if Pakistan really proves to be a non-democratic state. . . . We ourselves have no such apprehensions."[25]

In 1947, the Boundary Commission was established to determine which Indian territories would join Pakistan. Sir Cyril Radcliffe was appointed to lead the proceedings and demarcate the boundaries between non-Muslim and Muslim regions. Christian leaders also played a significant role during these negotiations. Three Christians, C. E. Gibbon, Fazal Elahi, and S. P. Singha, demanded that the Christians of the Punjab be included in the Muslim population in the region.[26] They hoped this would raise the overall population of "Muslims" in Punjab and secure its inclusion in Pakistan. To this end, a Christian lawyer, Chaudhary Chandu Lal, successfully passed the resolution to include the Christian population with the Muslims in the religious demography of Punjab.[27] This increase in population helped to secure the inclusion of part of the Punjab in Pakistan. It was a smart political move and sharply changed the political demarcation of the new state.

On voting day on June 23, 1947, the Punjab Legislative Assembly met to vote on the partition of Punjab. During the vote, the incensed Indian leader Tara Singh raised a slogan, "Whoever demands Pakistan will get a graveyard."[28] To show their solidarity with the Muslim League, the Joint Christian Board raised a counterslogan: "We will die for the establishment of Pakistan."[29] The Christian leaders in the Punjab Legislative Assembly cast their vote in favor of dividing the Punjab and won by a tiny margin: Eighty-eight people voted against the division and ninety-one voted in favor with the help of three Christian votes.[30] With the division of the Punjab, Pakistan was a reality. After this success, Jinnah assured Christian leaders that he would never forget their support and that Pakistan was a democracy with equal rights for all citizens. "We welcome all persons irrespective of caste, colour, or creed as being equal citizens of Pakistan."[31] In an address to the fledging nation, Jinnah stated, "You are free; you are free to go to your temples, you are free to go to your mosques or to any other place or worship in this State of Pakistan. You may belong to any religion or caste or creed – that has nothing to do with the business of the State."[32]

A particularly revealing acknowledgment of Christian leaders and their role in Partition occurred during the presentation of the national flag on August 11, 1947. The flag was dark green with a white vertical bar on the side and a white crescent and a five-point star in the center. While presenting the national flag, Prime Minister Liaquat Ali Khan stated, "Mr. President [Jinnah], the flag is not the flag of any one political party or any one community. The flag is the flag of the Pakistani nation, of the Pakistan State, which has to come into existence on the fourteenth of August, 1947. It will stand for freedom, liberty and equality for those who owe allegiance to this flag."[33] When questioned about the similarity between the Pakistani flag and the Muslim League flag in India, Khan noted that this was not a religious flag and certainly *not* a Muslim flag. Instead, Khan remarked that the designers had given prominence to the color white, which is a combination of seven different colors, in this flag.[34] Khan added, "We want to work in cooperation [with others] and not in opposition."[35]

Jinnah died in September of 1948 before Pakistan could secure its constitutional foundation. His death profoundly affected the Christian community. When Jinnah's death was announced to the fledging nation, the grieving leader of the Christian

Association stated, "Today, the minorities have lost their great leader."[36] Within a few weeks of Jinnah's death, political powers began to shift. S. P. Singha, the leader of the Joint Christian Board, was the speaker of the Punjab Assembly. However, shortly after Jinnah's death, he was replaced by a Muslim.[37] The Christian leader C. E. Gibbon also resigned from the Punjab Assembly. No Christians who were instrumental during Partition are included as "independence leaders" in Pakistan. History books do not mention their contribution to the establishment of the state. With the loss of Jinnah's leadership, Pakistan initiated its turbulent negotiation with Islam. Today, the relationship between Islam and the state remains the most highly contested aspect of Pakistani politics.

CHALLENGES IN THE POLITICAL CONTEXT

Post Partition: Constituting the Crescent

The relationship between Islam and the state in Pakistan was ambiguous from the conception of the two-state solution. Jinnah envisioned a democracy where religion had "nothing to do with the business of the state."[38] However, Jinnah's conception of a secular "Islamic" state was met with consternation from Islamic parties in India including the Tablighi Jamaat (TJ) and the Jamaat-e-Islami (JI). The TJ is an Islamic *deobandi* movement deeply rooted in the South Asian Sufi tradition.[39] The TJ were troubled with Jinnah's vision for Pakistan and did not support a nation where religion had "nothing to do with the state."[40] Instead, they wanted a political state infused with Islamic principles – something they were lacking under British/ Hindu rule in India. In a similar manner, the JI also found Jinnah's vision lacking in Islamic principles. Correspondingly, Maulana Mawdudi, the founder of the JI, was eager to Islamize Pakistan from its formation.[41] For both the TJ and the JI, it was inconceivable that the partition of India should lead to the creation of a "secular" Muslim state. Instead, they thought an Islamic state was a political imperative and a social and moral necessity.

Six months after Jinnah's death, the Objectives Resolution was adopted on March 12, 1949, and was the first articulation of the nature of the Pakistani state. Until the Objectives Resolution, the Constituent Assembly had failed to produce a viable constitution. Hence, until 1956, the date of the first constitution, there were no formal protections for Muslims or religious minorities in Pakistan.[42] The Objectives Resolution determined the "objectives" for the future nation and was soon adopted as the political cornerstone of the constitution. This document invited fierce debate from religious minorities and progressive Muslims because it introduced the role of religion in the nation. For example, the resolution stated that the "sovereignty of the entire Universe belongs to Allah alone."[43] It also stated that "Wherein the

Muslims shall be enabled to order their lives in the individual and collective spheres in accordance with the teachings and requirements of Islam as set out in the Holy Quran and the Sunnah." [quoted in the Objectives Resolution, an official document in the Pakistan Constitution Article 2 (A)][44] However, it guaranteed that "minorities can freely profess and practice their religion."[45] The Objectives Resolution serves as a turning point in the constitutional Islamization of Pakistan. The document was eventually included as a preamble for the constitutions of 1956, 1962, and 1973. It was incorporated into the constitution when the Eighth Amendment of the 1973 constitution was passed in 1985.

The first constitution of Pakistan took almost nine years to formulate – a process that was partially delayed over the negotiation between Islam and the state.[46] Many conservative Muslims disagreed with Jinnah's political vision and the notion that minorities could "freely profess and practice" their faith. The resolution initially echoed Jinnah's sentiments and included safeguards for democracy, freedom, and social justice for all citizens. But the language was amended to include the addendum, "as enunciated by Islam."[47] However, no one attempted to define how democracy, freedom, and social justice are "enunciated by Islam." As such, the Objectives Resolution magnified the struggle between Islam and the state, which was heightened by the sheer diversity of Islamic opinion. The modernists, conservatives, and the ulema could not agree on competing definitions of Islam. While the language "as enunciated by Islam" was purposely vague to appease all parties, it also created space for stringent interpretation.

The first constitution was adopted in 1956 under President Iskander Mirza – a retired military officer from East Pakistan.[48] The original Objectives Resolution survived as the preamble of the 1956 constitution with the proviso that Jinnah *intended* Pakistan to be a democratic state, "based on Islamic principles."[49] This vague statement was also not further clarified. While this constitution named Pakistan an "Islamic Republic," it did not enforce Islam as the state religion. Article II assured religious minorities the right to "profess, practice, and propagate their faith"[50] without conditions. The constitution stated that the president of Pakistan must be Muslim but there were no religious restrictions for the speaker of the National Assembly, who would function as president in absentia. In this way, the 1956 Constitution had little internal cohesion and magnified the tension between Islam and the state. Was Pakistan an Islamic state or a democratic state with "Islamic values"? Were religious minorities equal members of the state or relegated to *dhimmi* status? The 1956 constitution is the first manifestation of these debates that were clarified in subsequent constitutions.

In 1958, without warning, President Iskander Mirza imposed martial law and suspended the constitution and all democratic institutions including parliament.[51] This initiated Pakistan's long battle between democracy and military rule. Mirza was the first president to involve the military in Pakistani politics and appointed his army chief, General Ayub Khan, as the martial law administrator of the country.[52] Within two weeks, General Ayub Khan deposed Mirza in a coup-d'état. General Khan initially appeared to favor a more pluralist Islamic state. He argued, for example, that Islam could not be the only basis of national unity in Pakistan. Hence, pressed for a broader interpretation of national identity that was not connected to religion.[53] In 1962, under General Khan's guidance, a new constitution was drafted and the Objectives Resolution was altered to reveal a more liberal Islamic vision. While the 1956 Constitution required citizens to live according to the Qur'an and Sunna, the new document stated that citizens should simply live according to "the fundamental principles and basic concepts of Islam."[54]

While this new constitution was broader, it retained its ambiguity. What were the "fundamental principles and basic concepts of Islam"? Who was going to define them for the state and how would these principles affect non-Muslims? These questions were heavily debated by the ulema until under pressure from Islamic parties, General Khan created two organizations to help resolve these issues: the Advisory Council of Islamic Ideology and the Islamic Research Institute.[55] These organizations were required to make recommendations to the government to enable Muslims to live according to the "principles of Islam."[56] General Khan hoped that this would appease the ulema. However, the ulema argued that the Advisory Council was too liberal and modernist. Correspondingly, the ulema resumed its pressure on General Khan to Islamize the nation. General Khan took a balanced approach to the ulema. He listened to their critiques but made it clear that their recommendations were *suggestions* and not binding on the government.

In 1969, General Ayub decided to hand over power to the army chief, Yaya Khan. Immediately, Yaya Khan dissolved the national and provincial assemblies and declared martial law. However, General Yaya also held the nation's first free elections, through which the Awami League Party in East Pakistan secured the majority vote. Pressured by Zulfikar Ali Bhutto, whose party secured the most votes in West Pakistan, General Yaya stepped down and handed the presidency to Bhutto. In 1971, Bhutto took office and drafted a new version of the constitution in 1973. Under pressure from conservative Islamic parties, particularly the JI, this constitution declared Islam the state religion and was far more restrictive than its predecessors. The laws for non-Muslims remained fairly unchanged until the last few months of Bhutto's presidency when to appease the ulema, Bhutto instituted a series of stringent Islamic laws. Alcohol was prohibited in the country; bars and discotheques were closed; and the weekend, which was Friday (for Muslims) and Sunday (for Christians), was changed to Friday and Saturday. Bhutto also advocated greater inclusion of sharia in further constitutional amendments.

In 1977, in the third military coup, Bhutto was ousted by his commander in chief, General Zia-ul Haq. Under General Zia, the ambiguity of Pakistan's relationship to Islam was decisively removed. The constitution was reevaluated in 1985 and the Objectives Resolution was stringently altered. Whereas the previous iterations allowed minorities to practice their religion "freely," under General Zia, the word "freely" was omitted. Instead, the new document stated, "Wherein adequate provision shall be made for the minorities to profess and practice their religions and develop their cultures."[57] This created alarm among Christians and other religious minorities with little room for recourse. Other amendments included the requirement for National Assembly members to be "practicing Muslims."[58] Minorities were also limited in their ability to contest any extra seats beyond their reserved quota, which was determined by the population census every ten years. In other words, without governmental proof of an increase in population (through the national census), no additional Parliamentary representation was permitted. Perhaps not surprisingly, demographic statistics for Christians have remained quite static since the late seventies.

General Zia also introduced a series of amendments that had the potential to seriously restrict sociopolitical freedom for both non-Muslims *and* Muslims in the country. For example, a sharia bench was created in the Superior Court for the adjudication of disputes regarding marriage, divorce, and inheritance. Muslims who chose to use civil courts were still accommodated, but were socially pressured to seek legal advice in Islamic courts. The Hudood Ordinances based on punishments mentioned in the Qur'an or Sunnah for sexual misconduct, rape, theft, and prohibition were also introduced and openly embraced by some provinces. The Hudood laws created a great deal of anxiety in Pakistan. Modernist Muslims argued the laws were archaic while conservatives including the JI touted their importance in the moral formation of the state.[59] Christians were no longer allowed to hold the office of prime minister or president, military appointments were harder to secure, and Islamist parties pushed for a separate electorate system for minorities.[60]

Of the constitutional changes during General Zia's regime, separate electorates were the most psychologically and politically damaging for Christians. While some Christians thought separate electorates could politically empower the community, others thought it was an indication that they were "outsiders" in Pakistan and hence, outside the *ummah*. These changes were a sharp contrast to the trust and friendship that inspired the Christian coalition with the Muslim League during Partition. While constitutional restrictions have caused many Christians to migrate from Pakistan, others have moved because of more subtle forms of discrimination. Lack of employment, unequal compensation, poverty, and prejudice have heightened Christian social anxiety. Serious challenges for Christians include social discrimination, the pressure of religious conversion, and false accusations under the Blasphemy Law.

CHALLENGES IN THE SOCIAL CONTEXT

Social Discrimination and Persecution

The Christian community in Pakistan is not monolithic and is replete with socioeconomic and class distinctions. As mentioned earlier, most middle-class Christians are the descendants of affluent families in South India or religious converts among high-caste Hindus during the colonial period. In contrast, most socioeconomically disadvantaged Christians are descendants of "untouchable" Hindu converts during the nineteenth century. While middle-class Christians are largely employed in civil service, education, or in the medical field, low-income Christians are illiterate and hold menial jobs in the sanitation industry or as sweepers. Sanitation work has severe social stigma and many Christians are restricted to this industry because of illiteracy, poverty, and untouchable ancestry. Many Muslims consider sanitation and sweeping "unclean" jobs and will not seek employment in these sectors. Therefore, sanitation work is often interpreted as the traditional employment for Christians and other religious minorities. These types of occupations create stereotypes that Christians are "unclean," exacerbating social discrimination and prejudice.[61] For example, in rural areas, many Muslims practice commensal segregation and often deny Christians service at local restaurants or tea shops because of their occupation in the sanitation industry.[62]

Some Christians argue that the government has several discriminatory policies to keep their community in menial occupations. For example, in July 2013, the Pakistan Tehreek-e-Insaaf (PTI) party created a firestorm when they suggested that in Khyber Pakhtunkhwa Province (KPK), the government would only recruit sanitation workers from the non-Muslim community.[63] Christians were outraged and claimed this was a discriminatory policy aimed at keeping their community in an impoverished socioeconomic position. The PTI argued that they were trying to protect religious minorities from losing jobs in the sanitation industry – a traditional occupation for many Christians. This is because in recent years, the government raised wages for sanitation workers, making the field more appealing to lower-income Muslims. The PTI claims that so many Christians were concerned about losing sanitation jobs that they tried to rectify the situation by limiting recruitment to non-Muslims.[64] However, most Christians were insulted by these comments and responded with anger and resentment.

Other forms of social discrimination emerge in the education sector. In 1979, an Islamization agenda was introduced in government schools.[65] According to the Minorities Concern of Pakistan (MCOP), Christian students in government schools are often the recipients of discrimination from other students and teachers. In some instances, teachers ignore Christian students in the classroom.[66] In other cases, Christian children are forced to study from textbooks and curricula with biased information. For example, some government books interpret Pakistan as an entirely Islamic country and do not acknowledge the presence of minorities. This practice reinforces the notion that Christians are "outsiders" and trespassers in their own country. To this end, many Christian organizations including the Christian Minorities Teachers Association are working to correct these oversights.[67] These Christian activists have had some success in government schools. For example, after many years of Christian pressure, in 2009, the National Educational Policy of Pakistan ruled that Christian students no longer have to study Islamiyaat (compulsory for Muslim students) and can substitute a course in ethics for this class.[68]

Recent years have also witnessed the rise of Islamism in Pakistan. Christian churches and organizations in rural and urban settings are often the recipients of violent attacks. In September 2013, the bombing of a church in Peshawar killed seventy-eight people, including thirty-four women and seven children.[69] Muslim militants have also attacked many rural Christian villages. On February 6, 1997, the village of Shanti Nagur in Punjab was burned by Muslim mobs. In it 785 houses and four churches were destroyed and almost twenty-five hundred Christians had to flee the area.[70] In 2011, the Christian village of Khokarki (Punjab) was attacked for no apparent reason.[71] In May 2013, Khushpur, a Christian village in Faisalabad, was attacked because of an alleged blasphemy charge against a Christian family.[72] Other examples of violence include threats against rural Christians, prompting families to relocate for personal safety. Christian women are often targets of sexual assault, rape, and kidnapping by Muslim men.[73] It should be noted that in rural villages, low-income women of all religious backgrounds are victims of similar sexual violence. However, Christian women are frequent targets of such attacks.[74]

Religious Conversion

A major source of social anxiety for Christians is the pressure for religious conversion, which is often forced. Two Islamic groups that routinely apply pressure on lower-income Christians are the Jamaat-e-Islami (JI) and the Tablighi-Jamaat (TJ), particularly in urban slums and rural villages. The members of the JI and TJ whom I interviewed openly stated that Christians should convert to Islam and find protection under the *ummah*. There is a growing sentiment among Islamist groups including the JI and the TJ that Pakistan is a country for Muslims and non-Muslims are "outsiders." In my discussions with the JI and the TJ, neither group was receiving support from the local or central government to missionize. However, they found legitimacy in a perceived notion that the political state was growing *less* Islamic. For the TJ, this provided the impetus to proselytize non-Muslims. As one TJ member expressed, "If there are not enough Muslims in Pakistan, how will we remain an Islamic society?"[75] This resonates with the anxiety that was a prominent feature in the early history of the nation. After seven decades of independence, the underlying issue remains unchanged: What is the nation's relationship to Islam?

In a similar fashion, the JI is also fearful that Pakistan will lose its Islamic identity. JI leaders I interviewed said that the only way to create unity in Pakistan is through religious conversion. "We can only trust each other if everyone in Pakistan is part of the *ummah*."[76] JI leaders were equally suspicious of other religious minorities including Shi'is. One JI prayer leader was especially critical of the Asif Zardari (PPP) government in 2012 and argued that only a Sunni Muslim should be president of a Sunni country. For the JI, the "ummah" is specifically Sunni and anyone outside the boundary is untrustworthy. This reveals that when certain Islamic parties find government support, for example, under General Zia-ul-Haq's regime, it alleviates their anxiety about the Islamic nature of the state. In contrast, when the government does not actively promote an Islamic agenda, for example, under Zardari, it heightens their apprehension. In the social context, this agitation prompts certain Islamist groups to pressure religious minorities to convert.

The issue of religious conversion, particularly forced conversion, is more prominent among Christians than other religious minorities and is a prevalent feature in rural villages. Christians in rural villages in Baluchistan and Punjab routinely complain about forced conversions, particularly among women.[77] In some villages, Muslim men kidnap Christian women and marry them after forcing them to convert to Islam. In rural areas, there is little legal recourse for these occurrences. Kidnapping is less frequent in urban centers, but there is a still a growing pressure for religious conversion. One trope that is often expressed by Islamic mission groups is that Christians should convert to Islam in order to become authentic members of the *ummah* and "indigenous" sons of the soil. Sometimes Islamic groups reference the untouchable Hindu background of some Christians and accuse them of not being "real Christians." This enables Islamist groups to exert pressure on Christians to become "real" members of a religion by converting to Islam.[78]

Blasphemy Law

The third challenge facing Christians is the abuse of the Blasphemy Law. The law is part of Pakistan's Penal Code and was introduced in 1860 during colonialism, ironically to protect Muslims from the Hindu majority. By 1986, sections 295-B and C of this law were amended to include a clause of life imprisonment for defiling the Holy Qur'an.[79] In 1991, the Federal Sharia Court further revised this amendment in section 295-C and made the death penalty mandatory upon conviction of blasphemy.[80] Anyone charged with blasphemy can be detained by police and arrested without due process. Under the current Blasphemy Law, the only evidence required is the testimony of a reliable Muslim. Judicial proceedings are arduous and can take years to appeal. Many Christians are falsely accused of blasphemy and either are still waiting for a legal conviction or are pressured to leave their homes for safety. During the last decade, at least twenty-five people have been arbitrarily killed by zealots because they were accused of blasphemy.[81]

Although abuses of the Blasphemy Law are more common in rural areas compared to urban centers, it is still a growing concern for Christians. This is partially because Blasphemy Law accusations can emerge from very little evidence. As such, a person can be accused of blasphemy and imprisoned on hearsay. For example, in June 2009, Asia Bibi, a young Christian woman from Sheikhupura, was accused of making derogatory remarks about the Prophet Muhammad. She was convicted of blasphemy by a Pakistani court, and in 2010 she was sentenced to death by hanging. She is currently in jail awaiting her sentence and her case has created international outrage.[82] Many Christians, especially in rural areas, live in fear of blasphemy accusations from which they have little recourse for legal protection.[83] These accusations often invite unofficial punishment leading to violence and murder.[84] However, the Blasphemy Law is heavily contested by both religious minorities and progressive Muslims.

In 2012, Rimsha Masih, a twelve-year-old girl from Mehrabadi, was accused of desecrating the Qur'an. She was arrested by local police and potentially faced the death penalty. Some newspapers claimed that Rimsha suffered from Down syndrome and was unaware of her actions, if she did indeed desecrate the Qur'an. Despite the lack of evidence and news of her mental condition, Rimsha was arrested. Her arrest created furor in Pakistan. Her immediate acquittal was supported by progressive Muslims and the All Pakistan Ulema Council. The chairman of the Ulema Council, Tahir Ashrafi, made a public statement in Rimsha's support and called her a "daughter of the nation."[85] Ashrafi also joined the Pakistan Interfaith League to protest false accusations of blasphemy. In a surprising turn of events, Rimsha's accuser, a local cleric, was found guilty of fabricating evidence leading to her acquittal. However, despite Tahir Ashrafi's influence on the Ulema Council and his public support of Rimsha, her accuser was not arrested. In a press statement, Ashrafi stated that Rimsha's case had "disturbed the entire nation" and that he was "alarmed" that her accuser was acquitted.[86] This particular case highlights the diversity of opinion regarding the Blasphemy Law in Pakistan. However, the law is far from being repealed.

The Blasphemy Law is a cause of deep national anxiety in Pakistan, and even Muslims, both Sunni and Sh'ia, live in fear of false accusations. Of the eighty

blasphemy cases registered under General Zia's regime most were against Shi'is
and Ahmadis.[87] Progressive Muslims who publicly condemn the Blasphemy Law
face threats from Islamist groups and are sometimes the recipients of violence. In
2010, Salman Taseer, the governor of Punjab, expressed solidarity with Asia Bibi
and promised that he would file a mercy petition on her behalf. Taseer visited Asia
Bibi in jail and pledged to safeguard minority rights. After his meeting with Asia,
Taseer noted his support along with the Christian Minority Council to repeal the
Blasphemy Law. On June 4, 2011, shortly after delivering this speech, Taseer was
assassinated by his bodyguard, who shot him twenty-seven times with a submachine
gun.[88] Although his bodyguard was arrested, he was hailed as a hero by many
Islamists, and the judge who sentenced him to jail had to leave the country.[89]

Six months after Taseer's assassination, Shahbaz Bhatti, a Christian politician
and the first federal minister for minority affairs, was assassinated in Islamabad for
denouncing the Blasphemy Law. Bhatti was receiving regular death threats since
2009 after he critiqued the government for their failure to protect Christian villages
from violent attacks. One evening, on his way home, the Tehrik-i-Taliban, a militant
Sunni Muslim group, surrounded Bhatti's car and sprayed his vehicle with bullets.
He died instantly. His death, followed by Taseer's assassination, shook the nation
to its core. Muslims and Christians alike were shocked by the rise of radicalism
and general lack of governance that led to these murders. Neither Taseer's nor
Bhatti's killers have been brought to justice. These assassinations initiated a national
dialogue about civic freedom in Pakistan. The debate has not found resolution but
is raising national consciousness about the state's relationship with Islam.

Discrimination toward Christians in Pakistan is region specific and manifests
in many forms. There are overt forms of persecution such as kidnapping, forced
conversion, and false accusations of blasphemy. In contrast, other forms of
prejudice are more psychologically damaging such as the association of Christians
with "unclean" work including the sanitation industry and corresponding social
segregation. The Christian contribution to the formation of Pakistan is routinely
ignored in government textbooks. Even in the leading Christian schools and
universities, students do not learn the role of Christian leaders in the establishment
of the state.[90] As such, Christians in Pakistan have little social capital and even less
political power. At times, Christian loyalty to Pakistan is questioned by Islamists
because of the unrelenting association of Christianity with the "West." This
"outsider" status of Christianity is also a source of consternation and despair.

CHRISTIAN RESPONSES

Christians in Pakistan are not a cohesive community but are instead replete with
internal divisions. Denominational distinctions and socioeconomic disparities

also play a role in intracommunity discord. Accusations of nepotism and classism abound. Middle-class Christians are often accused by lower-class Christians (particularly those in menial occupations), of promoting their own needs instead of empowering the community as a whole.[91] Christian leaders are accused of securing socioeconomic benefits for just their own families. Impoverished Christians often accuse middle class of ignoring their sociopolitical needs. Such accusations create distrust between middle-class and lower-class Christians. Certainly, there is not much upward mobility among Christians. A small Christian presence dominates in high positions in government and in the private sector and the demography has not altered much since Partition.

In the past decade, many Christians have migrated to Britain, Canada, and the United States, in an effort to escape sociopolitical discrimination in Pakistan. However, few Christians can afford to emigrate. While there is a vibrant middle class, many Christians in the nation are economically disadvantaged compared to Muslims. However, financial constraints are not the only reason many Christians remain in Pakistan. Some Christians are very proud of their heritage and national identity as Pakistanis. These Christians, although grieved by radicalism and sociopolitical discrimination, are actively working to improve conditions in Pakistan through a variety of means and methods, which include the formation of Christian political parties, social organizations, and educational institutions to address minority needs. Through these sociopolitical methods, Christians are not passive recipients of discrimination and prejudice but are actively working to reclaim their voice in the nation.

In the political context, Christians generally shy away from any activity that might invite unwanted attention or discrimination. However, certain events have ignited Christians to seek political redress for social grievances. In 1972, when Christian schools were nationalized, Christians first gathered to protest this injustice. In 1992, when the government proposed including religious membership on national identity cards, Christians organized rallies to protest this law.[92] In February 1996, Christians also rallied to raise awareness of the violence in Shanti Nagur.[93] Christians have also organized marches to protest the Blasphemy Law and the murders of prominent leaders including Shabaz Bhatti. The Christian leader Julius Salik used extreme political means to rally support against injustice toward Christians. He once set fire to his furniture in front of the Punjab Assembly building and gained notoriety by tying himself to a cross.[94] Perhaps the most infamous form of protest was the public suicide of the Catholic Bishop John Joseph, who shot himself on May 6, 1998, inside a courthouse in Sahiwal to protest the Blasphemy Law.[95]

Christians also utilize various forms of media including holding seminars and publishing pamphlets and tracts to raise awareness of sociopolitical discrimination. Christians are successful in attracting Western press and foreign attention to the challenges in Pakistan. For example, Christian campaigns regarding the violence of Shanti Nagur prompted a response from David Smith, the Anglican bishop of Bradford. The bishop wrote a letter in support of Pakistani Christians to the acting Pakistani high commissioner in London. In 1997, the archbishop of Canterbury, George Carey, visited Pakistan to offer his support and encouragement to the community. He spoke firmly about the need for Pakistan to protect Christians and repeal the Blasphemy Law. Christian protest of the Blasphemy Law raised awareness of this issue at the United Nations Commission for Human Rights and among Pakistani Christian expatriates in Britain, Canada, and the United States.

In the social context, Christian religious and secular institutions form an integral part of Pakistan and have a presence in each province. Christian institutions are active in the region since colonialism and continue their service to the nation in the contemporary period. Christian schools and universities are a prominent part of the Pakistani educational system and are highly regarded by Muslims and the Pakistani government. While most Christian schools were nationalized under General Zia, some were returned and many have managed to retain their Christian identity. Catholic nuns and priests form part of the administrative structure of Catholic private schools and universities. Many of these schools incorporate Christian values into curricula and are preferred by Muslim elites because of their moral and educational training.[96] Christian teachers are active participants in the educational community and highly respected by Muslim colleagues.

Christians also operate some of the best orphanages, hospitals, clinics, women's centers, and social work agencies in the nation. Some of these organizations were established by missionaries during the nineteenth century and others are more recent. Christian hospitals and clinics have a presence in each province and offer services in elite neighborhoods, urban slums, and rural villages. Christians of all denominations are active in the medical field. The majority of church run hospitals and clinics are Catholic. These hospitals and clinics offer excellent and cost-effective health care for the underprivileged in Pakistani society. Many Muslims work in these hospitals and medical centers as doctors, social workers, and activists, and the administration is still overwhelmingly Christian. Other noteworthy Christian institutions provide multiple services for underserved communities and are active in the care of widows, drug addicts, mentally handicapped children, orphans, and victims of domestic and sexual abuse. These organizations are highly respected by Muslim citizens and by the government and have been publicly lauded for their commitment to social justice and equality.[97]

CONCLUSION

The negotiation of civic and religious freedom in Pakistan is an evolving process. While the relationship between Islam and the state is often contested by Muslims and religious minorities, no government has escaped the scrutiny and pressure of the ulema and Islamist parties. In the social context, the Christian experience is not homogeneous. The Christian community is splintered through socioeconomic, class, and denominational distinctions. As such, middle-class Christians live a very different life from Christians in urban slums and rural villages. The major challenges facing Christians in modern-day Pakistan include social discrimination, forced conversions, and the Blasphemy Law. Yet, it is significant to note that the Blasphemy Law is also a threat to Muslims who are often victims of false accusations.

While Christians experience discrimination in some regions and in some contexts, they are not marginalized by *all* Muslims. Many Christians hold high positions in education and in the government and are greatly respected by Muslim friends and neighbors. After the devastating church bombing in Peshawar in 2013, Pakistani Muslims, both men and women, organized a protest and formed human chains around churches in Lahore and Karachi to prevent further attacks.[98] Muslim women in all four provinces organized visits to churches to mourn with the Christian community. Muslim social work organizations visited Christians in slums and villages in Peshawar, Karachi, and Lahore to extend condolences. On Facebook, to show solidarity with Christian friends and neighbors, Pakistani Muslims replaced their cover photos with images of churches in Pakistan. Such stories reveal that Islamism and radicalism are heavily contested by both Pakistani Muslims and Christians.

While there are occasions of sociopolitical discrimination, the Pakistani government also publicly lauds Christians for their services to the nation. To show solidarity with Christians, many Muslim government officials attend church on special occasions including Easter and Christmas. In recent years, the media and press are more sensitized to minority rights and actively highlight problems in the Christian community. The media are playing a much-needed role to raise awareness in Pakistani society about social discrimination against minorities, especially in rural areas. Christians are also not passive recipients of discrimination but are active participants in national debates about civic and religious freedom. Through the creation of sociopolitical and educational institutions, Christians are asserting their national identity in many ways. Most importantly, they are engaging the process of social reform in the same way they helped to establish the state of Pakistan – *with* their Muslim neighbors.

NOTES

1 For information on the mass movements to Christianity among low-caste Hindus in the Punjab see, J. Waksom Pickett, *Christian Mass Movements in India* (New York: Abingdon Press, 1933); James Massey, *Panjab: The Movement of the Spirit* (Geneva: World Council of Churches, 1996); and Frederick Stock and Margaret Stock, *People Movements in the Punjab, with Special Reference to the United Presbyterian Church* (South Pasadena, CA: William Carey Library, 1975).

2 David B. Barrett ed., *World Christian Encyclopedia: A Comparative Study of Churches and Religions in the Modern World 1900–2000* (Oxford: Oxford University Press, 1982), 543.

3 Ibid.

4 Ibid., 545.

5 Ibid., 543.

6 Ibid.

7 Wayne McClyntock, "A Sociological Profile of the Christian Minority in Pakistan," *Missiology: An International Review* XX no.3 (July 1992).

8 Ibid.

9 Ibid.

10 Jonathan Addleton, "A Demographic Note on the Distribution of Minorities in Pakistan," *Al Mushir* XXVII, no. I (Spring 1985): 32–45.

11 Lauritus Vemmelund, "The Christian Minority in the North West Frontier Province," *Al Mushir* XV, no. 6 (April–June 1973): 92–202.

12 David Barrett suggests in the *World Christian Encyclopedia* that there are several Christian communities who are "secret believers" and do not publicly profess their faith. David B. Barrett, ed., *World Christian Encyclopedia: A Comparative Study of Churches and Religions in the Modern World 1900–2000* (Oxford: Oxford University Press, 1982), 543.

13 In contrast to government figures which claim Christians compose a mere 1.6 percent of the population, independent church polls report much higher numbers. Pastors in Punjab and Sindh suggest Christians constitute 6 percent of the total population and that the government purposely underreports the Christian population so they are not required to provide extra representation in parliament. In a recent article in the *Pakistani Christian Post*, Nazir S. Bhatti, the president of the Pakistani Christian Congress, a political party, argues that the Christian population is almost 13 percent. Bhatti contends that statistical data collected by fifteen bishop stations in 1978 confirmed the Christian population was 13 million. Bhatti argues these figures are much higher now but are not reflected in the national census because people routinely lie about religious membership. Bhatti suggests that many Christians migrated to Pakistan in 1971 after the creation of Bangladesh and significantly increased the population.

14 S. N. Sen, *History of the Freedom Movement in India (1857–1947)* (New Delhi: New Age International, 2003), 56–57. See also Yasmin Khan, *The Great Partition: The Making of India and Pakistan* (New Haven, CT: Yale University Press, 2008).

15 Ibid.

16 Ian Talbot, *Pakistan: A Modern History* (London: Palgrave Macmillan, 2010).

17 Stephen Philip Cohen, *The Idea of Pakistan* (Washington DC: Brookings Institution Press, 2006).

18 K. S. Padhy, *Indian Political Thought* (New Delhi: PHI Private Learning Press, 2011), 316–317.
19 Ibid.
20 Theodore Gabriel, *Christian Citizens in an Islamic State* (London: Ashgate, 2007).
21 Ibid.
22 Emmanuel Zafar, A *Concise History of Pakistani Christians* (Lahore: Humsookhan Publications, 2008), 32.
23 The Joint Christian Board was a coalition movement formed by the All India Christian Association, Punjab; the All Indian Christian League, Punjab; the All India Anglo-Indian Christian Association, Punjab; and the Catholic Association.
24 Singha, Dewan Bahadur S. P. in "Proceedings of the Punjab Boundary Commission, Lahore 21–32 July 1947," in Mian Sadullah, *The Partition of the Punjab 1947*, Vol. II (Lahore: National Documentation Centre), 225.
25 Ibid., 228.
26 Munir-ul-Anjum "The Role of Christians in the Freedom Movement of Pakistan: An Appraisal," *Pakistan Journal of Social Sciences (PJSS)* 32, no. 2 (2012): 437–443.
27 Ibid.
28 Ibid.
29 "The Christian Association Show Their Support for Jinnah," *Daily Civil and Military Gazette*, June 23, 1947.
30 "The Voting Rally for Pakistan," *Daily Civil and Military Gazette*, June 23, 1947.
31 Ajeet Jawed, *Secular and Nationalist Jinnah* (Oxford: Oxford University Press, 2009), 23.
32 Ibid.
33 "Laiquat Ali's Speech to the Constituent Assembly," http://www.thehindu.com/multimedia/archive/01103/Jinnah_s_Speech_Au_1103506a.pdf
34 Ibid.
35 Ibid.
36 "Pakistan Mourns the Death of the Quaid," *Daily Civil and Military Gazette*, September 11, 1948.
37 Nasir Saeed, "Why Are Christians Missing from Pakistani Textbooks?" *Pakistani Christian Post*, http://www.pakistanchristianpost.com/viewarticles.php?editorialid=1848
38 Patrick Sookhdeo, A *People Betrayed: The Impact of Islamization on the Christian Community in Pakistan* (Fearn, Scotland: Christian Focus and Isaac, 2002), 77.
39 Yoginder Sikand, *Origins and Development of the Tablighi Jama'at (1920–2000): A Cross-Country Comparative Study* (Delhi: Sangam Books, 2002) and Farish A. Noor, *Islam on the Move: The Tablighi Jama'at in Southeast Asia* (Amsterdam: Amsterdam University Press, 2013).
40 Ibid.
41 Seyyad Vali Reza Nasr, *The Vanguard of the Islamic Revolution, The Jama'at-i-Islami of Pakistan* (Berkeley: University of California Press, 1994).
42 Ibid.
43 "Objectives Resolution, [Article 2(A)], Annex 730," *Pakistan Constitution*, http://www.pakistani.org/pakistan/constitution/annex.html
44 Objectives Resolution, [Article 2(A)], Annex 730," *Pakistan Constitution*, http://www.pakistani.org/pakistan/constitution/annex.html
45 Ibid.

46 Patrick Sookhdeo, *A People Betrayed: The Impact of Islamization on the Christian Community in Pakistan* (Fearn, Scotland: Christian Focus and Isaac, 2002), 78.
47 Ibid.
48 Ibid.
49 Ajeet Jawed, *Secular and Nationalist Jinnah* (Oxford: Oxford University Press, 2009), 23; Richard Wheeler, *The Politics of Pakistan: A Constitutional Quest* (Cornell, NY: Cornell University Press, 1970); and Paula J. Newberg, *Judging the State: Courts and Constitutional Politics in Pakistan* (Cambridge: Cambridge University Press, 2002).
50 Ibid.
51 Patrick Sookhdeo, *A People Betrayed: The Impact of Islamization On the Christian Community in Pakistan* (Fearn, Scotland: Christian Focus and Isaac, 2002), 92.
52 Ibid.
53 Ibid.
54 Mohammad Dawood, *The Religious and Political Dilemma of Pakistan* (Lahore: Hasan, 1993).
55 Ishtiaq Ahmed, *Islamic Modernism in India and Pakistan 1857–1968* (Oxford: Oxford University Press, 1967) and Mohammed Amin, *Islamization of Laws in Pakistan* (Lahore: Sang-e-Meel, 1989).
56 Muhammad Asad, *The Principles of Sate and Government in Islam* (Lahore: Dar-al-Andalus Press, 1980); Rafiq M. Butt, *The Constitution of the Islamic Republic of Pakistan* (Lahore: Mansoor Book House, 1991) and Mohammad Dawood, *The Religious and Political Dilemma of Pakistan* (Lahore: Hasan, 1993).
57 Rafiq M. Butt, *The Constitution of the Islamic Republic of Pakistan* (Lahore: Mansoor Book House, 1991).
58 Ibid.
59 The Hudood Ordinances were reformed by General Pervaiz Musharraf in 2006 as the Women's Protection Bill. This bill was still met with anger from liberal Muslims, who argued that it was still discriminatory and did not do enough to protect women's rights in the event of domestic violence and sexual abuse.
60 The separate electorate system for minorities was introduced in 1980 under General Zia and restricted the ability of religious minorities to vote for candidates outside their religious membership. General Zia insisted that this was a form of "affirmative action" that enabled religious minorities to vote for people within their own community. However, religious minorities viewed the system as discriminatory and divisive.
61 Pieter Streefland, *The Sweepers of Slaughterhouse: Conflict and Survival in a Karachi Neighborhood* (Assen, Holland: Van Gorcum Press, 1979), 10–11; Philip Lall S., "Pakistani Christians: Population, Employment and Occupation." *Focus* (Multan) 13, no. 3 (1993): 157; in his article about poor Christians in Pakistan, M. De Vries also argues that the majority of Christians are still employed in low-class positions as *kammis* (laborers) instead of landlords (*zamindars*). M. de Vries, "The Calling of the Church in the Midst of the Rural Poor in Pakistan," *Al-Mushir* (Rawalpindi) XXIII, no.1 (1981): 4–6.
62 Pieter Streefland, *The Sweepers of Slaughterhouse: Conflict and Survival in a Karachi Neighborhood* (Assen, Holland: Van Gorcum Press, 1979), 10–11.
63 "Pakistani Christians Angered by 'Sweeper Comment'" World Watch Monitor, July 24, 2013, https://www.worldwatchmonitor.org/2013/07/2622104/
64 Ibid.

65 Patrick Sookhdeo, A *People Betrayed: The Impact of Islamization on the Christian Community in Pakistan* (Fearn, Scotland: Christian Focus and Isaac, 2002), 225–226.

66 "Pakistan Minorities Teachers Association," *Pakistan Christian Post*, http://www.pakistanchristianpost.com/interviewv.php?editorialid=77. Many students who are frustrated by the lack of attention from teachers tend to drop out of school while others claimed that they were purposely failed in examinations by discriminatory teachers. Christians from "sweeper" families who were engaged in the sanitation industry were recipients of the worst discrimination in government schools. R. A. Butler, "Islamic Resurgence in Pakistan and Church," *Al-Mushir* XXIII, no. 2 (Summer 1981): 51.

67 Ibid.

68 Ibid. However, some Christians interpret this as a form of discrimination as Christians are not allowed to study "Christianity" instead of Islamiyaat. See, for example, J. A. Tebbe, "Separate Curriculum in Religious Education for Christians" in "News from the Country: the Christian Community," *Al-Mushir* XXVII, no. 2 (Summer 1985): 120; J. D. Karaan, "Education in Pakistan" Developments in 1984–1985," *Al-Mushir* XXVII, no. 1 (Spring 1985): 9–10.

69 Ismail Khan and Salman Masoon, "Deadly Attack at Pakistan Church," *New York Times*, http://www.nytimes.com/2013/09/23/world/asia/pakistan-church-bombing.html

70 "Christians of Shanti Nagur Remember the Attack," *AsiaNews.it*, February 8, 2012, http://www.asianews.it/news-en/Christians-of-Shanti-Nagar-remember-the-massacre-of-1997–17569.html

71 Jibran Khan, "Punjab, Muslims Attack a Christian Village," *AsiaNews.it.*, April 16, 2011, http://www.asianews.it/news-en/Punjab,-Muslims-attack-a-Christian-village-21324.html

72 Ibid.

73 "Pakistani Report: 700 Christian Women Kidnapped Yearly, Forced into Muslim Marriages," *Catholic World News*, April 10, 2014, https://www.worldwatchmonitor.org/2014/06/article_3177184.html

74 "Pakistani Muslim NGO Highlights Forced Conversion of Christian Women," *World Watch Monitor*, June 09, 2014, https://www.worldwatchmonitor.org/2014/06/article_3177184.html

75 Jamaat-e-Islami (November 14, 2012), personal interview.

76 Tablighi-Jamaat (November 8, 2012), personal interview.

77 "Immigration and Refugee Board of Canada, *Pakistan: Religious Conversion, Including Treatment of Converts and Forced Conversions (2009–2012)*, January 14, 2013, PAK104258.E, http://www.refworld.org/docid/510f8b832.html

78 Similar pressure to convert to Islam is exerted by Islamist groups on low-caste Hindu converts to Sikhism called "Mazhabi Sikhs" and low-caste Hindu converts to Islam called "Musalli Muslims."

79 Amnesty International, *Pakistan, Time to Take Human Rights Seriously Index ASA 33/12/97* (June 1, 1997), 23. Blasphemy Law accusations are also raised against Muslims. One famous case was raised against the Muslim reformer Dr. Akhtar Hamed Khan by militant Muslims because they disagreed with his interpretation of Islam. For further discussion, see David F. Forte, "Apostasy and Blasphemy in Pakistan" *Connecticut Journal of International Law* (Fall 1994), 57.

80 Patrick Sookhdeo, A *People Betrayed: The Impact of Islamization on the Christian Community in Pakistan* (Fearn, Scotland: Christian Focus and Isaac, 2002), 240. See also,

"Center for Legal Aid Assistance and Settlement Report," http://www.claas.org.uk/right_
   to_the_freedom.aspx

81 Ibid.

82 Cath Martin, "Asia Bibi Death Sentence Appeal," *Mission*, May 26, 2014, http://www
   .christiantoday.com/article/asia.bibi.death.sentence.appeal.fifth.time.lucky.for.christian.
   mother.accused.of.blasphemy/37686.htm

83 Chaudhry Naeem Shakir, "Fundamentalism, Enforcement of Shariah and the Law on
   Blasphemy in Pakistan," *Al-Mushir* 24, no. 4 (1992): 114.

84 Aamer Ahmed Khan, "The Blasphemy Law: The Bigot's Charter," *The Herald* (May
   1994) 46b–50; Peter Jacob Dildar and Alexander Aftab Mughal, *Section 295-C Pakistan
   Penal Code: A Study of the History, Effects and Cases Under Blasphemy Laws in Pakistan*
   (Faisalabad: National Commission for Justice and Peace), 1995, 43–44.

85 "Rimsha Masih Case: Cleric's Acquittal 'Disappointing' Says Tahir Ashrafi," *Tribune*,
   http://tribune.com.pk/story/592117/rimsha-masih-case-clerics-acquittal-disappointing/
   After the recent attack on the church in Peshawar on September 23, 2013, the Council
   for Islamic Ideology has called for the death penalty for anyone who falsely accuses
   another of blasphemy. See "Kate Tracy, "Good News For Pakistan's Christians after
   Deadliest Church Attack Ever," *Christianity Today*, http://www.christianitytoday.com/
   gleanings/2013/september/good-news-pakistan-christians-peshawar-church-attack.html

86 Asian Human Rights Commission, Pakistan: A Historical Overview of Blasphemy Laws,"
   http://www.humanrights.asia/news/ahrc-news/AHRC-STM-090-2013

87 *Asian Human Rights Commission*, "Pakistan: A Historical Overview of Blasphemy Laws"
   The report states, "The known blasphemy cases in Pakistan show that from 1953 to July
   2012, there were 434 offenders of blasphemy laws in Pakistan and among them were,
   258 Muslims (Sunni/Shia), 114 Christians, 57 Ahmadis, and 4 Hindus," http://www
   .humanrights.asia/news/ahrc-news/AHRC-STM-090-2013

88 Since Salman Taseer's assassination, he is considered a martyr by the Christian
   community. See Nazir S. Bhatti, "Pakistani Christiians Pay Tribute to Shaheed Salman
   Taseer," *Pakistani Christian Post*, http://www.pakistanchristianpost.com/vieweditorial
   .php?editorialid=110.

89 Ibid.

90 Pakistani Christians routinely complain about the biases that exist in textbooks that are
   used in government funded schools and universities about religious minorities. The
   textbooks generally contain negative information about conspiratorial Christians who
   tried to destroy Islam or about lack of morality in other religions. See Anjum Paul, "Biased
   Textbooks in Minorities in *Pakistani Christian Post*, http://www.pakistanchristianpost
   .com/viewarticles.php?editorialid=845 However, some provincial governments have
   agreed to make some changes to the curriculum to provide a more balanced view of
   religious minorities including teaching "Ethics" instead of the required Islamiyat classes.
   See Anjum Paul "Pakistan Minorities Teachers Association," *Pakistan Christian Post*,
   http://www.pakistanchristianpost.com/interviewv.php?editorialid=77

91 Muhammed Shan Gul, "Christians versus Christians," *Friday Times*, February 1998, 4.

92 Aamer Ahmed Khan, "Bearing Their Cross" *Herald Annual*, January 1993, 99.

93 Patrick Sookhdeo, *A People Betrayed: The Impact of Islamization on the Christian
   Community in Pakistan* (Fearn, Scotland: Christian Focus and Isaac, 2002), 318.

94 Ibid., 319. Sookhdeo argues that Julius Salik was nominated for the Nobel Prize in peace by Benazir Bhutto, who in her letter of commendation said Salik must be recommended for his "courageous defence of the rights of Pakistani Christians."

95 Linda Walbridge, *Christians of Pakistan: The Passion of Bishop John Joseph* (New York: Routledge Curzon, 2003).

96 Catholic schools and universities are represented in every province of Pakistan. These schools and universities have an excellent reputation and are attended by mostly elite, wealthy Muslim students. There is a reservation system for Christian children but over the years, fewer Christian children attend Christian schools in Pakistan.

97 There are several Christian institutions in Pakistan that have provided social services in the country since independence, for example, Caritas Pakistan, National Commission For Justice and Peace, South Asian Institute of Human Rights Affairs, and Missionaries of Charity. In addition, there are several Christian run and operated hospitals and clinics in the country, including Holy Family Hospital, Memorial Christian Hospital, Christian Children's Hospital and Dar-ul-Sakoon, a home for mentally challenged children.

98 "Muslims Protect Christians from Islamic Extremists," *Christian Post*, http://www .christianpost.com/news/pakistan-muslims-protect-christians-from-islamic-extremists-form-human-chain-around-church-106103/

11

Christianity and the Challenge of Religious Violence in Northern Nigeria

Richard Burgess and Danny McCain

INTRODUCTION

It is 7 September 2001, in Jos, Nigeria. A Muslim is appointed to a controversial political position, traditionally held by Christians. Violence erupts in the streets. This is what we saw.

Richard's story: As I was returning to the Theological College of Northern Nigeria, where I lived and worked, it seemed like a normal Friday afternoon in Jos, apart from the traffic on the road, which was much heavier than usual. When I eventually arrived home it was to rumours that fighting had broken out during Muslim *salat* prayers, precipitating a mass exodus out of the city centre. For the next ten days, until the army intervened, staff and students were confined to the college campus while Muslim and Christian mobs rampaged across the city. As a deterrent to would-be attackers, students armed with machetes took turns to patrol the campus perimeter. Days and nights were disturbed by the sounds of intermittent gunfire, and from the vantage point of a hill overlooking the city we could see smoke rising from multiple locations. A few students ventured out into the neighbouring community, returning with reports of dead bodies on the streets and buildings destroyed.

Danny's story: As I walked through the University of Jos health clinic there were dozens of people sitting and lying around with various kinds of burns and bleeding injuries. Trails of blood crisscrossed each other down the halls and bandage wrappers lay where they had been hastily dropped on the floor. The nurses in their white uniforms looked tired. One doctor was shouting in anger for anyone to hear, "Look at this old woman's arm. What kind of animals will cut an old woman's arm like this? She had nothing to do with this!" The "this" he was referring to was a violent conflict that had started the afternoon before. It was the result of an on-again, off-again appointment of a Muslim man to an office supposedly reserved for the Christian "indigenes" in Nigeria's Plateau State.

We had received word around noon the day before that we should not leave our home on campus because "there is trouble in town." Fortunately we had had a relatively calm night, so the next day I walked to the university clinic. I had heard that there were many casualties and most of the medical personnel could not get there because of the violence. I thought I could help. As I walked around a corner, I saw a lady I recognized. She was the wife of one of my students who pastored the Emmanuel Baptist Church, one of the closest churches to my house. She said, "Doctor, they burned our church and the parsonage. We escaped with this," pointing to a plastic bag. I decided that I might do better helping her and her family than trying to revive my old ambulance skills at the clinic. I invited her to go to my house. As we walked home, more and more of the residents of that community fell behind me, with babies on their backs and bags on their heads. Just as we reached my house a heavy burst of gunfire erupted a short distance away. About thirty people rushed into my house, and another forty joined later that day. They stayed with me for a week.

These events began four days before the well-known American 11 September that forever changed the world. In a similar way, our crisis forever changed our world also. Unfortunately, similar scenes repeated themselves at least four more times over the next ten years. The city of Jos went from being the envy of all in Nigeria, admired for its beautiful climate and cross section of people, to a place where thousands have been killed simply because they were on the other side of the ethno-religious divide. Bodies were buried by the dump truck loads. These included Danny's students, next-door neighbour, university colleagues, painter, mechanic, and relatives of nearly everyone who was close to him. Seven churches and one mosque were burned within a mile of his house.

How have these and similar crises affected religious expression in northern Nigeria? How have Christians responded to such violence? How have government policies and practices helped to inflame or solve these problems? In this chapter, we explore the contemporary contributions of different Christian communities in northern Nigeria to freedom, and their response to the pressures caused by government policies and their encounter with competing and sometimes radical expressions of Islam. The essay focuses on a range of Christian congregations and ministries, including Catholic, mainline Protestant,[1] and Pentecostal churches. It is based on interviews with Christian and Muslim leaders,[2] visits to churches and organizations addressing the issue of ethno-religious violence, and a questionnaire survey.[3] The survey, which was conducted in 2013 among churches in Jos and Kaduna, generated 716 usable questionnaires. The majority of those surveyed attended mainline Protestant congregations (58 percent, compared to 26 percent Pentecostal and 12 percent Catholic). There were slightly more male than female respondents (51 percent compared to 47 percent), and most were aged below forty (71 percent). In each congregation, we adopted a random sampling approach by distributing questionnaires to every fourth person during Sunday worship services.

The main research locations chosen for the study were the cities of Kaduna and Jos and their environs in the Middle Belt, which is roughly the lower half of northern Nigeria. However, the scope of our research also encompasses the core northern states where the violation of Christians' religious freedom is more pronounced. Although all the interviews in Nigeria were conducted in Kaduna and Jos, some of our informants had firsthand experience of visiting or living in the core northern states. We also conducted a number of interviews in London to explore the transnational dimension.

Kaduna and Jos represent contrasting case studies. Both have experienced recurring bouts of ethno-religious violence. Kaduna was the capital of the former northern region and is currently the capital of Kaduna State in the north-western geopolitical zone of Nigeria. Both the city and the state have roughly equal populations of Muslims and Christians, who have coexisted for generations. However, the city has experienced major sectarian riots since the mid-1980s. Jos is the capital of Plateau State, which has become one of the centres of ethno-religious violence in Nigeria over the past decade. Episodes of mass killings and destruction occurred in Jos in 2001, 2002, 2008, and 2010. The violence has also affected rural communities surrounding Jos. In contrast to Kaduna State, Plateau State is a majority Christian state in the north-central geopolitical zone.

The chapter begins with an overview of the Nigerian context and a discussion of the status of Christian communities in central and northern Nigeria. It then examines the causes and consequences of the violence and violation of religious freedom in the region. Finally, it considers the various responses to the pressures and hardships caused by the ongoing conflicts, including Christian contributions to freedom through interfaith dialogue, peace initiatives, advocacy, and social engagement.

POLITICAL AND RELIGIOUS CONTEXTS

Nigeria is Africa's most populous nation with an estimated 167 million people in 2011.[4] The country is evenly divided between Christians and Muslims; estimates of the exact balance vary.[5] The situation is complicated by the geographical distribution of the two faiths. Of the three main ethnic groups, the northern Hausa-Fulani are predominantly Muslim, the eastern Igbo are predominantly Christian, and the western Yoruba are divided between the two faiths. Northern Nigeria as a whole has a majority Muslim population. The Middle Belt has a large number of Christians while the "core north" has only a small percentage of Christians. While both religions have global missionary ambitions, Islamic leaders often state that their objective is to implement sharia, a goal that has created considerable regional tension.

Since the 1970s, there has been a resurgence of Islamic fundamentalist and reformist movements due to increased influences from abroad, which is further facilitated by oil money. These groups tend to be intolerant towards Christianity as well as towards more moderate forms of Islam. At the same time, this Islamic resurgence has coincided with the growth of Pentecostal and charismatic expressions of Christianity. This movement is often characterized by conversion efforts, an antagonistic stance towards other religions, and a growing concern over perceived "Islamic resurgence," which has enhanced religious polarization in Nigeria.[6] However, as Jeff Haynes notes, religion is not necessarily associated with conflict as it can also play a constructive role in building peace. According to Haynes, when successful, religion has a role in resolving conflicts that is a crucial component in helping to achieve human development.[7] As we will see later, some faith-based organisations in Nigeria are responding to ethno-religious conflict in their communities through peace-building initiatives. Another significant development was the formation of ecumenical organisations, such as the Christian Association of Nigeria and the Pentecostal Fellowship of Nigeria, which have enabled evangelicals and Pentecostals to develop a united front in the face of Muslim fundamentalism.[8]

Although the Nigerian Constitution provides for legal protections and extensive rights to all its citizens, including rights to freedom of religion,[9] and Nigeria is a signatory to several international human rights agreements, these rights are not always enjoyed by religious and ethnic minorities in some areas of the country.[10] Two issues in particular affect the status of Christian communities in central and northern Nigeria: first, the concept of "indigeneity," and second, the application of sharia to criminal law. Indigeneity laws in Nigeria declare certain ethnic groups in each state "indigenes," thus preventing members from other groups from formally being considered indigenes. The 1979 Constitution originally introduced the concept of "indigeneity" into public law to guarantee a fair regional distribution of power.[11] However, one consequence is that state governments tend to discriminate against non-indigenes in matters concerning land-ownership, political participation, education, and employment.[12] Currently, sharia has been introduced in twelve northern Nigerian states: Zamfara, Sokoto, Kebbi, Katsina, Kano, Niger, Jigawa, Yobe, Borno, Bauchi, Kaduna, and Gombe.[13] Since its introduction, existing discrimination against indigenous and non-indigenous Christian minorities has increased.

Kaduna State and its capital, Kaduna, have been crucial sites of Christian-Muslim conflict.[14] Northern Kaduna's population is largely Muslim and Hausa-Fulani, while southern Kaduna is home to thirty different, predominantly Christian ethnic groups.

The state capital includes communities from all over the state as well as large populations of non-indigenes from other parts of Nigeria. Prior to independence, the southern minorities suffered repression at the hands of the powerful Hausa Emirate of Zazzau. To an extent, the conversion of southern Kaduna's minority ethnic groups to Christianity was a reaction to the oppression they had suffered under Hausa-Fulani Muslim rule. Today the memory of that history continues to affect relations between northern and southern Kaduna, where hostility persists between Christian and Muslim populations. Thus, intrastate politics are dominated by claims of marginalization and exclusion voiced by many Christian community leaders in southern Kaduna, who maintain that the state government has favoured its Hausa-Fulani population. On several occasions these tensions have incited violence in various parts of the state.[15]

Jos is the state capital of Plateau State, with a population between 800,000 and 1,000,000. According to the 2006 Census, the population of Plateau State is 3.1 million. Accurate percentages of Muslims and Christians are difficult to obtain and are also politically contentious. Estimates are 60/40 or 70/30 percent between Christians and Muslims.[16] Ownership of Jos is hotly contested by the three main indigenous ethnic groups (the Berom, Anaguta, and Afizere), on one side of the fight, and the descendants of Hausa-Fulani settlers (today known as the Jasawa), on the other. Other Plateau ethnic groups migrated to Jos either for commerce or for the tin mining industry. These were joined by people from the South, including the Igbo, Yoruba, Urhobo, Ibibio, and Tiv.

Jos has proved a favourable location for Western and indigenous Christian missions and is regarded as a bastion of Christianity in the North. Initially, it was a base for the evangelization of Plateau peoples, but it has since become the most important missionary centre for all of northern Nigeria. The presence of large southern populations has reinforced its orientation towards Christianity. After the introduction of sharia in some northern states and its attendant crises, the city experienced an influx of people from Kaduna, Kano, Bauchi, and Zamfara states seeking refuge.[17]

CAUSES OF VIOLENCE AND VIOLATION OF RELIGIOUS RIGHTS

In the congregational survey, which was conducted among church members in the Kaduna and Plateau States, 83 percent of respondents said that Christians are free to practice their religion in their state. However, this was at variance with other measures of religious freedom in the survey. For example, 40 percent of respondents said that there have been times when they have not attended church for fear of violence, and 40 percent said that they have attended churches that are now closed or moved because of the violence. A significant minority reported having suffered losses as a result of the violence, ranging from the destruction of property (including church buildings) to the loss of friends and relatives.

General Causes: Sharia, Indigeneity Laws, and Boko Haram

Various factors have heightened Christian-Muslim tensions in the country and contributed to the violation of religious and political freedom. As the survey showed, a large majority (70 percent) said "religion" was the most important cause, compared to 13 percent "politics," 7 percent "tribal/ethnic issues," and 2 percent "injustice." Also, 82 percent said that most of the violence against Christians in the North is religious persecution. In the interviews, most respondents acknowledged the complexity of the problem and the entanglement of religious, political, and ethnic factors within the violence and human rights infringements. In general, a distinction was made between the situation in the core northern states, such as Kano, Borno, Sokoto, and Katsina, where the religious factor is more prominent, and Middle Belt states such as Kaduna and Plateau, where the issue of ethnicity is more starkly in play.

From the interviews, it is possible to identify three inter-related issues that have contributed to escalating violence and violation of religious freedom in northern Nigeria: the imposition of sharia, the indigene-settler issue, and the Boko Haram insurgency. Sharia has existed in Nigeria for many years, but until 1999, it had only been applied to personal and domestic law. Democracy returned to Nigeria on 29 May 1999. In the core northern states, it met a traditional, hierarchical society, which had practiced Islam for hundreds of years. Because these states were overwhelmingly Muslim, they were able democratically to enshrine sharia into state criminal law, a move that was popular among many Muslims but opposed by Christians. Discontent among Christians led to public demonstrations, which were viewed as threatening by Muslims, who then responded with violence. Thus, it can be argued that the re-introduction of democracy, without proper protection of minorities, opened the door to further marginalization of minorities and ultimately to violence.[18] Despite initial assurances that sharia would only apply to Muslims, non-Muslims are regularly subject to its structures. Since its introduction, Christian minorities in the North have endured violence at the hands of Islamic militants, greater restrictions on their rights to own land and establish places of worship, and increased levels of discrimination in employment, education, and access to public services. In some areas, abduction, forced marriage, and conversion of Christian women and girls are relatively frequent occurrences.[19]

In our survey, a large majority (75 percent) of Christians said that Muslims should not be free to establish sharia in Nigeria. In the interviews, respondents referred to the discriminatory nature of sharia in relation to non-Muslims and its undermining of Nigeria's secular status as enshrined in the federal constitution. Several pastors accepted the rights of Muslims to live under sharia but were opposed to its imposition upon non-Muslim populations.[20] Muslim respondents expressed similar sentiments. For example, Ibrahim Hassan, a lecturer in Islamic Studies at the University of Jos, stated: "If you are really talking about religious freedom, not secularism, then Muslims should be allowed to implement sharia for themselves but with the strict condition that in no way should non-Muslims be affected."[21]

The issue of indigeneity is relegating many Nigerians to the status of second-class citizens in states other than their own.[22] Despite the constitutional provisions guaranteeing citizenship rights, many states refuse to employ non-indigenes in their state civil services and deny them access to academic scholarships. Non-indigenes also face other discriminatory practices, such as in admission to state universities, barriers to political participation, and access to basic amenities. Such practices are made more harmful by the increasing levels of poverty throughout Nigeria, which create greater demand for civil service jobs normally not available to non-indigenes. In addition, discriminatory policies have served to aggravate interethnic animosity. The indigeneity issue has combined with other factors such as ethnic tensions, religious extremism, and poverty to push inter-communal relationships towards violence.[23] As we will see later, indigeneity laws have had serious repercussions on Christian-Muslim relations, especially in Plateau State.

Boko Haram is undoubtedly the most significant threat to religious freedom in Nigeria today.[24] Boko Haram (meaning "Western education is forbidden") is a Salafi-jihadi group, which is seeking to eliminate all "western influences" and create a "pure" Islamic state ruled by sharia. As well as attacks on moderate Muslims and government institutions, the group targets Christian communities and churches in northern Nigeria.[25] By 2009, it had set up a headquarters in the Borno State capital, Maiduguri, launching coordinated attacks in Bauchi, Yobe, Kano, and Borno States. Despite claims that its quarrel was with state officials and assurances that Christians would be safe, Boko Haram proceeded to kill several pastors, destroy more than twenty churches and numerous Christian-owned businesses, and hold more than one hundred Christians hostage at its headquarters for use as human shields against federal forces.

One of our respondents spoke to some of the Christian survivors of the siege. During their captivity, male hostages were given the choice to renounce their Christian faith or suffer beheading at the hands of the leader of Boko Haram, Muhammed Yusuf. This was the occasion of the much-publicized "martyrdom" of George Orji, pastor of Good News of Christ Church in Maiduguri. According to an eyewitness, instead of recanting, Pastor Orji preached to his captors and then proceeded to sing Christian songs until he was killed.[26] The message sent by Pastor

Orji through a fellow captive, "Tell my people I died well," was reported widely in the media.[27]

After the destruction of its headquarters and the alleged extrajudicial killing of its leader in July 2009, Boko Haram seemed to disappear. However, an attack in September 2010 on Bauchi prison that freed one hundred alleged members, followed by bomb attacks in northern Nigeria, heralded its return. Since then, northeastern Nigeria in particular has been subjected to a wave of bombings, attacks on church services and Muslim schools, and assassinations of government officials, members of law enforcement agencies, moderate Muslim clerics, and Christians.[28]

Some analysts view Boko Haram primarily as an armed response to government corruption, heavy-handed treatment by security forces, and widening economic disparity, especially in the Muslim North.[29] However, our Christian respondents referred to religious as well as political and economic factors behind the violence.[30] For example, Joseph Maran, a pastor of the Evangelical Church Winning All (ECWA), identified three factors behind the potency of Boko Haram: first, its intention to make Nigeria a "pure" Islamic state governed by sharia; second, the government's failure to address the issue of poverty, which has created a fertile ground for the recruitment of young insurgents; and third, the failure of government security agencies to curb Boko Haram activities.[31] The religious agenda of Boko Haram is reflected in its official name *Jama'atu Ahlis Sunna Lidda'awati Wal-Jihad* (People Committed to the Propagation of the Prophet's Teachings and Jihad), its declaration of jihad against Christians and the federal government, and its alleged links with Somalia's al Shabaab and Al Qaeda in the Islamic Magreb (AQIM).[32] In November 2013, the U.S. government formally designated Boko Haram, and its offshoot Ansaru, as foreign terrorist organizations. This affirmed U.S. support for Nigeria's efforts to address its domestic terrorist threat and its belief that both organizations have links with Al Qaeda in the Islamic Magreb.[33]

Boko Haram has dominated the security discourse in Nigeria since early 2010, creating a climate of fear among both Christians and moderate Muslims throughout the nation but especially in the North. Several respondents referred to the failure of state governments to provide security for non-Muslims, prosecute perpetrators of violence, or compensate victims. For example, Pastor Maran criticized the government for failing to protect Christians in Muslim majority states despite the legal protections and rights to religious freedom specified in the Nigerian Constitution. "The church cannot protect itself," Pastor Maran told us. Consequently, "security must be provided for Christians to worship freely."[34] According to Dr Khataza Gondwe, team leader of Christian Solidarity Worldwide International for Africa and the Middle East, the culture of impunity and injustice that predominates in northern Nigeria, where perpetrators of violence remain unpunished and victims receive no compensation, militates against peaceful resolution and encourages victims to take the law into their own hands.[35] This inability of elected state governments to provide protection for their citizens and recourse to justice for victims of violence is further evidence of how poorly implemented democracy in societies where there is a dominant religion can seriously disenfranchise minority religious and ethnic populations. Furthermore, Boko Haram's efforts to create a "pure" Islamic state by targeting moderate Muslims as well as Christians show how intolerance and persecution of other religions can sometimes lead to intolerance and persecution of sects within the same religion.

Specific Issues in Kaduna and Plateau States

In Kaduna, which has a history of ethno-religious violence stretching back to the 1980s, the proposed introduction of sharia in 2000 generated a fresh wave of inter-religious riots.[36] In view of Kaduna's large Christian population, the introduction of sharia in the state was likely to attract more controversy and protest than in other northern states. Christian concerns emanated, largely, from the perception that their full citizenship rights would be denied. The 2000 crisis was associated with a march on Government House organized by the Christian Association of Nigeria to protest the introduction of sharia. Fighting erupted as marchers clashed with groups of Muslims in the vicinity. The violence spread to poorer areas of the city, resulting in the killing of close to two thousand people and the injuring of many more. A further bout of fighting broke out two years later when Nigeria was to host the Miss World contest, and most recently in the aftermath of the 2011 presidential elections, when, after the defeat of Muhammadu Buhari, supporters of his Congress for Progressive Change party engaged in violent attacks on churches in Kaduna.[37]

Indigeneity laws have also heightened Christian-Muslim tensions, as members of both religious communities have sometimes encountered difficulties obtaining certificates of indigeneship.[38] More recently, Kaduna State has become a prime target for Boko Haram, for two reasons. Firstly, in 2011, a Christian won the gubernatorial elections for the first time in the history of the state. Secondly, in southern Kaduna, where there is a Christian majority, youths retaliated against the April 2011 violence, causing the deaths of a significant number of Hausa-Fulani Muslims.[39]

Christian respondents in Kaduna rated poor governance, political manipulation of religion, and Muslim aspirations to subjugate non-Muslims as the main factors behind ethno-religious violence in their state.[40] For example, Father Anthony Zakka, whose house was burned down in the 2000 riots, blamed the crisis on the political nature of Islam and Muslim ambitions to rule Nigeria after independence.[41] Samuel Salifu, former national secretary of the Christian Association of Nigeria, referred to government discrimination against Christians in relation to access to social amenities and to land for building churches as the main causes for creating tensions between the two communities.[42] For the Pentecostal pastor James Wuye, the main cause of the crisis is the "failure of the state to provide amenities for her citizens," which has caused people to "fall back on God and hold tenaciously to beliefs that are incontestable." According to Pastor Wuye, religious intolerance, combined with competition for scarce resources, lies behind the violent conflicts in his state.[43]

Since the Jos crisis kicked off in September 2001, Plateau State has experienced successive waves of ethno-religious violence, which have caused considerable anxiety and extensive loss of life. In contrast to Kaduna, Plateau is a non-sharia state with a Christian majority. Again the situation is complex as religious, political, and ethnic factors all come into play. Analysts of the crisis have mainly focused on the indigene-settler issue and the politics of participation in government involving the "indigenous" Plateau peoples and the Hausa-Fulani "settlers."[44] In Plateau State, Hausa-Fulani Muslims tend to be defined as "settlers," whereas the mainly Christian Plateau peoples are recognized by the state government as "indigenous."[45] There are also large Christian (mainly Igbo and Yoruba) populations from the South who have been settled in Jos just as long as the Hausa-Fulani and have also been excluded from the benefits of indigeneship. However, unlike the Hausa-Fulani, they are not contesting with the indigenes for political control of Jos. When violence ensues, the Hausa-Fulani often count them with the indigenes, and communities from the South have incurred significant losses as a result.[46] According to Adam Higazi, the indigene-settler issue has served to exclude the Hausa-Fulani from governance.[47]

While this hints at the sense of injustice felt by Hausa-Fulani Muslims in Plateau State, similar injustices have been meted out to Plateau indigenes in some of the core northern sharia states. According to one of our respondents, the indigenous Plateau peoples are not insisting that Hausa-Fulani settlers return to their states of origin. But they are resisting calls for them to be granted indigene status because this is unlikely to be reciprocated in the case of Plateau Christians who have settled in the far North.[48]

The sense of injustice felt by non-Muslim Plateau indigenes partly stems from their experience of colonialism. One of our respondents referred to the system of indirect rule through regional emirs, imposed by British colonialists in northern Nigeria, which relegated non-Muslims to the status of second-class citizens. This created an enduring culture of resentment between Plateau Christians and the Hausa-Fulani.[49] Higazi argues that it is this memory of their minority status that has strengthened the resolve of Plateau indigenes to assert their autonomy from the Muslim North.[50] Increasing ethno-religious tensions can also be traced back to Muslim military rule during the 1980s and 1990s, when Plateau indigenes felt they were being passed over for senior political appointments in favour of Hausa-Fulani Muslims. Again, this memory is fresh in the minds of indigenous

Plateau Christians and can explain their reluctance to allow Hausa-Fulani "settlers" to participate in the political process after the restoration of civilian rule, especially in Jos.[51]

Respondents also referred to contemporary factors behind the crisis, such as competing claims by Plateau Christians and Hausa-Fulani Muslims over "ownership" of Jos, Christian resistance to perceived Muslim ambitions to rule Plateau State, and disputes over land between Muslim Fulani pastoralists and predominantly Christian farmers leading to tit-for-tat killings. The spectre of Boko Haram again looms large. A spate of bomb attacks on churches since 2010, allegedly carried out by Boko Haram militants, has threatened to reignite the long-running conflict in Plateau.

EFFECTS OF VIOLENCE AND REPRESSION

External pressures and hardship caused by ethno-religious violence and violation of religious rights have had a significant impact on Christian communities in relation to family structure, economic status, participation in church activities, and civic engagement. One consequence of the crisis has been the increasing politicization of Christianity in northern Nigeria. Before the 1970s, it was widely believed by the churches that Christianity should distance itself from politics.[52] However, this has changed since the late 1970s as a result of a perception among Christians that Muslims will stop at nothing to establish an Islamic Nigeria. The declaration of sharia following the return to democracy in 1999 was especially instrumental in encouraging Christian political activism.[53] Political competition with Islam has served to unite Christians. Important in this regard are ecumenical organizations such as the Christian Association of Nigeria (CAN) and the Pentecostal Fellowship of Nigeria (PFN), especially in their role as a platform for Christian political engagement.[54] Another consequence is that Christians in northern Nigeria have tended to vote along religious and ethnic lines, preferring to support Christian rather than Muslim candidates as a way of resisting the perceived Islamist agenda in the North. In the remainder of this section, a distinction is made between the experience of those living in core northern and Middle Belt states and inhabitants of sharia and non-sharia states.

Core Northern States: Sharia and Boko Haram

In the core Northern sharia states, Christian minorities experience diverse pressures because of their religious affiliation and ethnic origins including ongoing discrimination in employment and limited access to public services and social amenities. They also face restrictions on access to education due to a lack of government funding for non-Muslim schools and a scarcity of Christian religious education teachers to teach the government-sponsored religious education that is part of the Nigerian primary and secondary school curriculum. Christian children have difficulties obtaining scholarships and sometimes have to change their names to Muslim ones and adopt Islamic practices in order to receive state education.[55] Churches are also denied certificates of occupancy, preventing them from owning land and restricting the construction of church buildings, and existing church buildings are routinely demolished for alleged infractions or when land is seized for "development" projects.[56]

In northeastern Nigeria, Boko Haram is involved in a systematic campaign of "religious cleansing" through suicide bombings, violent attacks on church services, destruction of church buildings, murder of Christian businesspeople, assassinations of church leaders, and house to house killings in Christian surburbs.[57] Despite the government's declaration of a state of emergency in the northeastern states of Borno, Yobe, and Adamawa in May 2013, and an increase in the campaign to defeat Boko Haram, there has been an escalation of the group's activities. While many Christians from southern and eastern ethnic groups have fled to their home areas, the majority of Christians in the North are from indigenous communities and have no other home. To survive, many have been forced to relocate, leaving behind jobs, homes, and ancestral lands. According to the United Nations Office for the Coordination of Humanitarian Assistance (UNOCHA), nearly 300,000 people from Borno, Yobe, and Adamawa States, 70 percent of them women and children, have fled their homes since early 2013, seeking refuge in other Nigerian states or in neighbouring Cameroon, Chad, and Niger.[58] One of our respondents recalled a visit to a group of thirty-three Christian families who had left their ancestral land in Yobe State and relocated to Nassarawa State in the Middle Belt in order to escape the Boko Haram insurgency. Although they acquired land, they had to start from scratch without the benefit of indigeneship status. Presently, they are experiencing a "hunger gap" and are unable to pay their children's school fees. However, despite these privations they prefer to be where they are rather than face the dangers they left behind in Yobe.[59]

Another respondent, an indigene of the majority Christian Chibok local government area of Borno State, told us that Boko Haram militants have killed sixty people of his community, including two of his uncles, and have forced many others to relocate.[60] A third respondent referred to the Gwoza local government area of Borno State, where most of the churches have been wiped out by Boko Haram insurgents.[61] In 2013, a series of orchestrated attacks on Christians in Gwoza resulted in the destruction of forty-six churches and 541 houses, multiple fatalities, and the displacement of more than thirteen thousand indigenes. The suffering of survivors was compounded by the perceived lack of concern of the Muslim state governor, Alhaji Kashim Shettima.[62]

In the first three months of 2014, at least fifteen hundred people were killed in the escalating violence involving Boko Haram insurgents and Nigerian security forces, according to Amnesty International.[63] This compares to twenty-one hundred deaths between 2009 and 2013. Two separate acts of terrorism on 14 April 2014, served as a stark reminder of the continuing potency of Boko Haram. In the capital Abuja, seventy-one people died in bomb blasts at a crowded bus terminal. In addition, in Chibok local government area of Borno State, militants abducted nearly three hundred students of the Government Girls' Secondary School, most of whom were Christian.[64] The abductions by Boko Haram captured international attention as thousands took to the streets of Lagos and Abuja protesting their government's inability to locate and rescue the girls. A social media campaign helped to raise global awareness about the kidnapping, with celebrities and high-profile figures such as the U.S. First Lady Michelle Obama using Twitter to express their concerns. International outrage gathered momentum as it became clear that the girls were being forced to convert to Islam and were at risk of sexual violence. On 17 May, Boko Haram released a propaganda video showing 130 girls in Muslim dress reciting passages from the Quran. Two of them spoke of their conversion from Christianity to Islam.[65]

Under growing criticism for its unsuccessful response to the mass abduction, the Nigerian government finally accepted U.S., British, French, and Chinese offers of assistance to find the girls.[66] A public statement by Nigeria and neighbouring Cameroon, Benin, Chad, and Niger declared "war" on Boko Haram, signalling a change in mood in the West African sub-region.[67] On a local level, a significant development occurred on 14 May, when residents of three villages in the Kala-Balge area of Borno repelled a Boko Haram attack and killed two hundred insurgents.[68] However, Boko Haram insurgents have maintained their assault on towns and villages in northeastern Nigeria. In August 2014, they proclaimed Gwoza town an Islamic Caliphate, introduced sharia, and proceeded to behead Christian men who refused to convert to Islam. In response, the Nigerian army launched an unsuccessful military operation to "liberate" Gwoza from the control of the insurgents.[69] The deadliest massacre to date occurred on 3 January 2015, when the group reportedly killed more than two thousand people in the towns of Baga and Doron Baga close to the border with Chad.[70]

Attacks by Boko Haram on moderate Muslims as well as Christians suggest that one of its aims was to make Nigeria ungovernable in the run-up to the 2015 elections.[71] The effectiveness of this strategy was demonstrated on the 7 February 2015, when Nigeria's electoral commission (INEC) announced the postponement of the elections for six weeks (until 28 March) because the military could not guarantee security in the north-eastern areas of the country.

Kaduna and Plateau States

In our survey of Christian congregations in Kaduna and Jos, 41 percent of respondents said that a relative or friend had been killed as a result of ethno-religious violence; 27 percent said a relative or friend had been injured; 2 percent said they had experienced personal injury; 13 percent reported the destruction of personal property; 22 percent said that their church had been destroyed; 19 percent that church property had suffered damage; and 17 percent said they had to flee because of the violence. These statistics suggest that Christians in Jos and Kaduna have experienced significant violations of their right to religious freedom as a result of the crises.

One consequence of the violence has been the segregation of communities, an indication of deepening polarization in what were once genuinely mixed populations. Michael Adegbola, a Catholic priest in Kaduna, said that people's past experiences of violence have resulted in growing mistrust and spatial segregation in the city between the predominantly Muslim Kaduna North and the predominantly Christian Kaduna South, which are proving detrimental to national unity.[72] The city of Jos has also experienced increasing segregation along religious lines between Jos North, which is predominantly Muslim, and Jos South, which is predominantly Christian. There are now certain parts of the city that are off-limits for members of the "wrong" religion.

One of the effects of the growing levels of distrust, as well as of Christian complicity in acts of violence against Muslims, is the difficulties churches now face in evangelizing their Muslim neighbours. Paradoxically, one respondent reported a rise in Muslim converts to Christianity during the crisis. He explained this in terms of a growing disillusionment with Islam because of its associations with violence against Christians, and the rise of Boko Haram, which targets moderate Muslims as well as Christians.[73]

Meanwhile, church members and pastors have lost houses, cars, and businesses, with severe economic consequences. Families have found it difficult to recover financially, especially when no government compensation has been forthcoming. In Kaduna, post-election violence in April 2011 followed the defeat of the Muslim presidential candidate of the Congress for Progressive Change (CPC), Muhammadu Buhari. This seriously affected Kaduna, as Muslim CPC supporters attacked Christian symbols, alongside offices and homes of ruling People's Democratic Party (PDP) stalwarts (the PDP, like other major political parties in Nigeria, has representatives from all parts of the country, including Christians and Muslims). It is commonly thought that CPC supporters were provoked by pre-election statements by party leaders calling for the North to be made ungovernable and for Muslims not to vote for non-Muslims. Although Buhari's CPC vice-presidential running mate was a Christian from the South, his major following was from the North. As a result of the violence, in some areas of Kaduna, no church was left standing and an estimated five hundred people were killed. While some Christian youth fought back, the number of mosques destroyed was far exceeded by the number of churches. Kaduna has also been a target of Boko Haram attacks on churches.[74] These episodes suggest that in certain areas of Kaduna, some Muslims have engaged in spontaneous campaigns of religious cleansing.

Muslim radicals have also targeted church buildings in Jos. The Baptist pastor Sunday Gomna said that his church has been burned down three times during the various waves of violence. Between 2001 and 2010, they attempted to rebuild in the same location but finally had to relocate.[75] A Pentecostal pastor told us that Muslim militants attacked his church four times in 2011.[76] In February 2012, a suicide bomb attack on the Church of Christ in Nations headquarters killed four people and injured more than sixty others. About twelve hundred people were gathered in the church, including members of the Plateau State government, when it took place.[77] Retrospective accounts focus on God's providential intervention in minimizing the loss of life and damage to the church building. According to one respondent, if it had succeeded, it would have triggered a "chain reaction" of violence across the state, which would have been difficult to control.[78] Significantly, we also came across accounts of local Muslims protecting church buildings from attacks by fellow Muslims from outside. For example, another Pentecostal pastor described how his church in Jos South was protected by Muslim friends during the 2001 crisis.[79]

Nevertheless, the recurrent crises in Plateau State have resulted in thousands of people losing lives and many more injured. Some pastors referred to church members, family members, and friends who had been injured or lost their lives either during Christian-Muslim riots or as a result of attacks by Boko Haram terrorists. Jwan Zhumbes, the Anglican bishop of Bukuru, told us that four members of his church were killed during the 2008 crisis. He also said that five church members were killed when Anglican churches in the rural community of Gyang were attacked by Muslims.[80] The Pentecostal pastor Bamidele Padanu explained how the Christ Apostolic Church headquarters in Kwararafa, Jos North, was burnt down and the pastor killed in 2011 in a reprisal attack by Muslims after indigenous Christians had attacked and killed Muslims in nearby Gada Biyu during their *salat* prayers.[81] His wife, Comfort Padanu, who leads a social ministry for widows in Jos, told us that over the past few years about eight hundred widows have been added to the list of those they assist. Many are young widows whose husbands have been killed during these crises.[82]

Some pastors in Jos reported a significant decline in church attendance due to increased security measures on Sunday mornings, which make travel difficult; the killing of church members; the relocation of members to other parts of the city or to their homes in southern Nigeria; and fear of terrorist attacks. One Pentecostal pastor said that the combination of loss of lives and member relocation had reduced the population of his church from almost 500 members to fewer than 100. The school at his church has also been severely affected, as enrollment has fallen from almost 700 to about 150.[83] The Anglican Bishop of Bukuru reported a drop in attendance in his diocese from about 1,000 in 2007 to around 150 today, largely the result of member relocation.[84]

The attacks by Muslims have often not been unanswered. For example, in response to attacks by Hausa Muslims, some people from Christian communities lashed out against Muslim Fulanis in 2001. In the following years, Fulanis retaliated by raiding predominantly Christian villages and deliberately targeting women and children. The most notorious incident occurred in March 2010 with an attack on the Dogo Nahauwa, Zot, and Ratsat villages, which claimed an estimated 400 lives.[85] This is widely believed to have been an act of retaliation following an attack by Christian mobs in January 2010 on the predominantly Muslim town of Kuru Karama, which killed at least 150 residents.[86] Unfortunately, revenge and retaliation have become regular features of ethno-religious violence in Plateau State. While these attacks are partly motivated by land disputes between Muslim Fulani herdsmen and Christian farmers, some commentators suspect that Islamic extremists from outside Nigeria have aided and incited the Fulani.[87]

RESPONSES AND CONTRIBUTIONS TO FREEDOM

This section examines the responses of Christian communities to pressure caused by ethno-religious conflict and violation of religious freedom. We focus on the efficacy of interfaith dialogue, advocacy, and community organizing initiatives; the use of the media by Christian leaders; the different kinds of Christian social engagement developed in response to the conflict; and the influence of interchurch relations and transnational networks.

Education and Interfaith Dialogue

Some leaders and organizations have responded to the crises by focusing on educating Christians about Islam. One of the leading proponents of this approach was Josiah Idowu-Fearon, former Anglican bishop of Kaduna diocese.[88] Bishop Idowu-Fearon is the co-founder of the Centre for the Study of Christianity and Islam and, until his recent retirement as Bishop of Kaduna diocese, ran educational workshops for Christians. He hoped to dispel ignorance of Islam, which he believed was a major cause of the conflict. He was also involved in teaching Christian-Muslim relations to state government officials.[89] In his capacity as the Anglican bishop of Kaduna, he also spoke out publicly in the media on issues related to ethno-religious conflict.[90] Another example is the ECWA pastor Joseph Maran, founder of Reconciliation Trainers Africa (RETA), which has centres in Plateau, Taraba, and Benue States and in the capital Abuja. RETA works with churches and local communities to educate pastors and community leaders about peace and reconciliation. Apart from running courses at its centres, conducted by Christian and Muslim trainers, it holds peace awareness campaigns for community leaders from both Christian and Muslim communities.[91]

Another approach to conflict prevention is interfaith dialogue.[92] Examples of national bodies engaged in interfaith dialogue include the Nigerian Supreme Council for Islamic Affairs (NSCIA), the Christian Association of Nigeria (CAN), and the Nigerian Inter-Religious Council (NIREC). Most of the pastors we interviewed emphasized the importance of building trust between Muslims and Christians through dialogue and friendships. However, some pastors expressed doubts about the value of dialogue because they felt that Muslims lacked sincerity. This response was quite common among respondents and suggests that deep distrust persists between the two communities. In our survey, only a small minority (22 percent) said they trust most Muslims, while a majority (57 percent) said that most Muslims are hostile to Christians.

Doubts about the efficacy of interfaith dialogue are often based on bitter experience. For example, Father Anthony Zakka described what happened in the aftermath of the 2001 sharia crisis in Kaduna, when the Interfaith Mediation Centre brokered a Muslim-Christian peace accord called the Kaduna Peace Declaration. This was followed three months later by another outbreak of violence associated with the Miss World controversy, which Father Anthony blamed on Muslims.[93] Aaron Ndirmbita, a pastor of Church of Christ in Nations (COCIN) in Jos, expressed similar distrust of Muslims and compared the efficacy of interfaith dialogue in Plateau and Borno States. During his years growing up and working as a civil servant in Borno State, relationships between Muslims and Christians were generally cordial. However, today he finds it difficult to trust Muslims because of their treatment of Christian minorities. In Jos, by contrast, where the balance of power between the two religious communities is more equal, and Muslims have also suffered as a result of the conflict, he believes that interfaith dialogue may be beneficial:

> In cases like Borno where one group is the only one attacking, do you bring the victim and the oppressor together? Dialogue cannot work in those places. The only thing that can work is those people must be stopped. But in places like Jos where people are ready to fight, I think they can be brought together to iron out their differences.[94]

Opinions about the value of dialogue varied among our Muslims respondents. Imam Sani Isah in Kaduna said that interfaith dialogue should be encouraged. In his capacity as a member of staff at the Interfaith Mediation Centre, he has had to defend this approach to conflict resolution before the Kaduna chapter of the Supreme Council for Shari'a In Nigeria and the Council of Ulama.[95] Some Muslims expressed doubts about its value because they believed it seldom leads to positive action and social change. Ibrahim Hassan argued that although people's attitudes might change as a result of dialogue, when conflict occurs, they are still likely to participate in the violence if they are unemployed or unable to further their education. He also said that the degree to which Muslims trust Christians has fallen drastically over the past decade or so, partly because of the recurrent conflicts and Muslim perceptions of Christians as aggressors, but also because Muslims perceive Christianity as a product of the West, which is seeking to dominate the world and "must be sponsoring our contemporary Christian leaders."[96]

Despite the mutual distrust that exists between the two religious communities, there is a willingness on the part of many Christians to engage with Muslims and work proactively with them to bring about peace. In the survey of churches in Kaduna and Jos, the majority of respondents said that Christians should not separate themselves from Muslims (64 percent) or avoid interacting with them (64 percent). Also a significant majority (81 percent) said they were prepared to work with Muslims to bring about peace. A number of pastors we encountered are intentionally seeking to establish friendships with Muslims in their communities. For example, a Pentecostal pastor told us that when he lived in Dadin Kowa, a religiously mixed area of Jos South, which has remained relatively peaceful, he deliberately cultivated friendships with local Muslims by visiting them during their celebrations and engaging in dialogue with Muslim community leaders.[97]

Community Organizing and Peace Initiatives

The Interfaith Mediation Centre in Kaduna and the Young Ambassadors for Community Peace and Inter-Faith Foundation in Jos are two organizations that have moved beyond dialogue to engage in community organizing across the religious divide. The Interfaith Mediation Centre was co-founded in 1995 by two former enemies: the Assemblies of God pastor James Wuye and Imam Muhammed Ashafa. Since its inception, the organization has been involved in mediating religious conflicts in Kaduna, Jos, and Bauchi.[98] The Interfaith Mediation Centre is one of the pioneer peace organizations in Nigeria. One of its aims is to encourage dialogue and promote a culture of mutual respect and acceptance of diversity by drawing on the faith traditions of both religions.[99] According to Talatu Aliyu, communications and monitoring and evaluations officer of the centre, "the faith-based perspective, especially the interfaith perspective, has been vital to our success. We are able to draw participants in by quoting Holy Scriptures from both the Bible and the Qur'an that support peace."[100] Pastor Wuye and Imam Ashafa have faced opposition from some Muslims who regard all peace organizations as supported by Western institutions and therefore untrustworthy. They have also encountered resistance to the interfaith approach to conflict prevention from some Christian leaders. Pastor Wuye acknowledges that there is tension between the need to speak out publicly against violations of Christian rights in the North and the need for conciliatory language to promote peaceful resolution.[101]

The Young Ambassadors for Community Peace and Inter-Faith Foundation was founded by the Assemblies of God pastor Yakubu Pam, who until recently was the pastor of a church located in a Muslim-dominated area close to Jos Central Mosque. When the Jos crisis first erupted in 2001, the Reverend Pam regarded himself as a Christian radical who advocated retaliation as a legitimate response. However, his attitude changed as he developed relationships with Muslim neighbours. In December 2009, Pam even gathered a group of Muslim youth who lived near his church to discuss peace principles.

His efforts were put to the test in January 2010, when a major crisis broke out between Christians and Muslims in Jos. Fortunately, some of the Muslim men he had trained protected his church when other Muslim youth from outside the area tried to destroy it. Soon afterward, he started the Young Ambassadors for Community Peace and Inter-Faith Foundation. Since then, Pam has organized a series of community-wide peace rallies involving Christian and Muslim youth as well as a two-week football competition, called the Jos Peace Cup, in which teams were divided to include both Christians and Muslims. He has also opened a centre in a neutral area of Jos where both Christian and Muslim youth can meet together to watch films, develop friendships, discuss issues related to peace, build conflict resolution and leadership skills, and plan peace programmes in their respective areas. The foundation also sponsored joint Christian-Muslim monitoring teams during the 2011 elections.[102]

Through this foundation, some of the leading perpetrators of the violence have now become advocates of peace and reconciliation. According to Reverend Pam, politicians on both sides of the religious divide are sponsoring the youth for their own political ends. In response, the foundation offers vocational skills training and loans to empower the youth and enable them to start their own businesses, making them less vulnerable to manipulation by unscrupulous politicians. Reverend Pam claims that the strategy of engaging the youth as peace ambassadors has succeeded in reducing levels of ethno-religious violence in Jos; however, his optimism is tempered by concerns over the threat posed by Boko Haram[103]

Retaliation

As previously noted, members of Christian communities in Kaduna and Plateau have sometimes deployed retaliatory and offensive tactics against Muslims. Reprisal attacks by Christians on Muslims have been quite common, especially in Plateau State, where the majority of the population is Christian. However, some of our respondents made a distinction between genuine Christians and so-called cultural or nominal Christians, whose Christian identity is a mark of ethnicity rather than a sign of commitment to the Christian faith. Respondents blamed the latter for instigating revenge attacks.

The congregational survey shows a majority of Christians reject the use of violence as an offensive strategy. For example, 60 percent disagreed with the statement "At times it might be necessary to burn mosques or drive Muslims from Christian areas," while only 13 percent agreed with the statement "The wars of the Old Testament are good examples of how to deal with Muslims" and 17 percent agreed with the statement "To stop Islam advancing southwards, Christians may have to use offensive tactics." The pastors we interviewed said that they would not encourage their church members to retaliate.

Of course, there are certain nuances to this. For instance, a distinction is usually made between retaliation and self-defence. There has been a significant shift in thinking since the 1980s, when Christians were taught to "turn the other cheek." Today, most pastors interviewed opposed the use of violence by Christians except in self-defence. Some pastors said they encourage their members to arm themselves with weapons to defend themselves because the government is failing to protect Christians and provide adequate security. Some churches also employ armed security guards, who are usually church members.

However, the survey shows a majority of Christians reject the use of violence in self-defence. For example, only 23 percent agreed with the statement "Since the government has failed to protect us, we must use arms to defend ourselves," and 13 percent with the statement "It is okay to use violence in defence of one's family." Significantly, our Muslim informants adopted a similar stance, rejecting the use of violence except in self-defence.[104]

Christian responses to ethno-religious violence and infringement of their religious freedom are inspired by a variety of biblical texts and themes, especially from the New Testament. Some referred to Jesus's teaching in Matthew's gospel on loving and praying for one's enemies, a theme that is repeated in Paul's Epistle to the Romans. Several referred to Jesus's own example of non-resistance when confronted by his enemies. The theme of Christian persecution is another strand of biblical teaching and Christian tradition that has proved particularly poignant to Christians suffering the consequences of conflict and discrimination.

Social Responses

Another Christian response focuses on providing practical help to Christians and Muslims affected by the crisis. We identified a variety of social initiatives including relief work, medical projects, ministries to widows and orphans, and microenterprise initiatives that involve making loans available to business entrepreneurs. When asked about the motivating factors behind these initiatives, respondents referred to the Christian imperative to follow the example of Jesus by doing good and loving one's neighbour, and a commitment to demonstrating the holistic nature of the gospel by addressing physical, material, and spiritual needs. Some respondents regarded social engagement as a means of building relationships with Muslims and as a precursor to evangelism.

One initiative engaged in relief work is the Stefanos Foundation, an NGO founded in Jos by the Church of Christ in Nations member Mark Lipdo, which aims to "serve persecuted Christians" and help "victims of violence." The Stefanos Foundation has adopted a multi-strategy approach, which includes relief work and reconstruction of buildings, micro-finance funding of businesses, rehabilitation and trauma counselling, advocacy, and media awareness. According to Mark Lipdo, providing practical relief to Christian victims of the conflict has helped to discourage them from responding aggressively and maintaining the cycle of violence.[105]

Some Christians and churches in Jos and Kaduna have provided charitable relief to Muslims, which has helped them to build interfaith relationships of trust. One example is the Pentecostal pastor Yakubu Pam, who prior to starting the Young Ambassadors foundation encouraged his church to donate foodstuffs to poor Muslim families in the community. He told us that this act of kindness provided the platform for his community organizing activities.[106] Another example is the ECWA pastor Yunisa Nmadu in Kaduna, founder of Christian Solidarity Worldwide (CSW) Nigeria,[107] whose church donated food items to six mosques in August 2012.[108] A former Muslim, Pastor Nmadu has experienced firsthand the effects of the conflict in Kaduna. He told us that his church has been burnt down ten times during successive waves of violence and his life has been threatened on a number of occasions. Like its partner organization CSW International, CSW Nigeria is committed to promoting religious freedom and to mobilizing Christians to pray for those who are persecuted for their Christian faith. Its activities in Nigeria include advocacy initiatives, the use of the media to raise awareness, medical care, capacity building, and research. One outcome of Pastor Nmadu's goodwill gestures was that the local community leader Alhaji Shuai'b Balarbe vowed to protect the churches within his domain from attacks by fellow Muslims.[109]

Some churches are involved in health care initiatives that cater to the needs of Christians and Muslims. One example is the Anglican Diocese of Bukuru in Jos, which runs a medical outreach in its local community. The Anglican bishop of Bukuru, Jwan Zhumbes, said that the rationale behind this initiative is to build a "Muslim-Christian community" through a practical demonstration of the gospel of Christ.[110] Another ministry that caters to both Christians and Muslims is the Comfort Widows Ministry, an interdenominational charity founded by the Pentecostal pastor Comfort Padanu in Jos, which provides food, clothing, medical drugs, skills training, and money for rent and children's school fees. While they encourage the Muslim widows to become Christians, they do not make this a condition of receiving aid.[111]

Ecumenical Organizations and Transnational Networks

Christian responses are also influenced by interchurch relations and transnational networks. Opinion is mixed regarding the role of Christian ecumenical organizations in relation to conflict prevention and promotion of peace. According to the Baptist pastor John Hayab, the Christian Association of Nigeria (CAN) has helped to foster good relationships with Muslim leaders at the national level through its participation in the Nigerian Inter-Religious Council. This is mimicked at the state level in Kaduna, where in his capacity as secretary general for CAN Kaduna State he keeps in constant contact with stakeholders to prevent inter-religious tensions from escalating into violent confrontations.[112] But Pastor James Wuye of the Interfaith Mediation Centre expressed concern about what he perceived as inflammatory public statements by the CAN president, Ayo Oritsejafor, which have sometimes exacerbated tensions between the two religious communities.[113] The former CAN president, the Catholic Archbishop John Onaiyekan, tended to be more conciliatory in his remarks. Several informants commended the organization for its assistance of both Christian and Muslims victims of violence during the 2011 presidential elections, and its advocacy work reminding the government to live up to its responsibilities and counter the perceived bias in the media, which tends to disregard the suffering of Christians.[114] However, some pastors criticized CAN for its partisan support for the government, its unwillingness to challenge government, its failure to provide constructive advice to Christians in crises, and its inability to speak with a single voice on behalf of the Christian community.

There is also a transnational dimension to Christian responses to violence and violation of religious freedom in northern Nigeria. Several of the pastors we encountered have visited the United States and Europe to create awareness among the international community regarding the situation in northern Nigeria. One example is Mark Lipdo, founder of the Stefanos Foundation, which is a partner of the British-based Release International, an advocacy organization self-described as the "voice of persecuted Christians" throughout the world.[115] Another prominent figure is Yunisa Nmadu, founder of CSW (Nigeria), who has visited Britain under the auspices of CSW International and has spoken to British politicians and media representatives about the situation in Nigeria. As a human rights advocacy organization, CSW International campaigns for freedom of religion and belief by documenting and raising awareness of religious persecution around the world. Its mandate for speaking on behalf of persecuted Christians is derived from Proverbs 31:8–9.[116] Its advocacy work is also inspired by the example of Jesus, who "speaks for those who don't have the power or ability to speak for themselves," as well as by the biblical prophets who spoke out for justice and righteousness.[117] Staff members lobby governments and international bodies, including the British and U.S. governments, the European Union, and the United Nations, to ensure that action is taken to alleviate the suffering of those who are persecuted for their religious beliefs. While the focus of its work in Nigeria is on speaking up on behalf of persecuted Christians, CSW International also campaigns on behalf of Muslims subjected to sharia punishments, which are contrary to both the Nigerian Constitution and international statutes. It obtains information on the ground through staff visits and working with reliable local sources.

Nigerian Christians in the diaspora are also seeking to create awareness and mobilize prayer on behalf of victims of violence and human rights violations in northern Nigeria. One example is Love Jos, a London-based organization, which was started by a group of Nigerian Christians concerned about the escalating crisis in Plateau State.[118] Rather than replicate the work of larger organizations such as Open Doors and Release International, Love Jos seeks to mobilize members of the large Nigerian Christian community in Britain and persuade them to lobby their MPs and give charitable donations.[119] To fulfil its objectives, Love Jos organizes conferences and prayer meetings. The theme of its 2011 conference, which was held in the London premises of Matthew Ashimolowo's Kingsway International Christian Centre,[120] was "Stand Up, Speak Out," and featured Christian speakers from Britain, Nigeria, and the Nigerian diaspora.[121] According to a flyer advertising the event, the aim of the conference was to "explore opportunities for advocacy, reconciliation and how practical help might be offered to victims of persecution."[122]

Prayer is integral to the ministry of Love Jos because members believe that persecution has a spiritual dimension and is driven by demonic influences.[123] In January 2012, in collaboration with the Overseas Fellowship of Nigerian Christians, Love Jos organized a prayer vigil outside the Nigerian High Commission in London and presented a letter to the Nigerian high commissioner protesting the Nigerian government's failure to protect Christians in the North. Although it is a small organization, it uses print and electronic media to create awareness and mobilize Nigerian Christians in the diaspora. It also plans to connect with Christians in southern Nigeria, who are sometimes oblivious to what is happening in the North and reluctant to help their fellow Christians.

CONCLUSION

Nigeria continues to be one of the most significant test cases in the modern world of an emerging democracy struggling to find its feet in the floodwaters of surging religious and ethnic competition. This chapter has investigated religious freedom in central and northern Nigeria and the responses of Christians to the pressures caused by government policies and radical expressions of Islam. Our research suggests that poorly implemented democracy in a traditional, hierarchical society where there is a dominant religion can severely disenfranchise minority religions. Despite constitutional provisions regarding religious freedom, twelve states in northern Nigeria were able to pass legislation that violated the human rights of the minority Christian populations. The situation is aggravated by the government's inability to maintain peace and provide security, and its failure to limit the discriminatory effects of state indigeneity laws, which together have resulted in the loss of religious freedom and other basic human rights for both Christians and Muslims. At the time of writing, the government's failure to curb the terrorist activities of the Boko Haram insurgency remains the most significant threat to religious freedom in Nigeria. The fact that Boko Haram has targeted moderate Muslims as well as Christians in its efforts to create a "pure" Islamic state shows how intolerance and persecution of other religions can sometimes lead to intolerance and persecution of sects within the same religion.

The combined effects of ethno-religious violence, the implementation of sharia in some states, and the rise of the Boko Haram insurgency have had a significant impact on Christian communities in relation to economic status, participation in church activities, and civic engagement. Christians have experienced discrimination in employment, restricted access to education and social amenities, barriers to political participation, destruction of churches and personal property, and extensive loss of lives. Christian responses to violence and violation of religious freedom have included interfaith dialogue, peace campaigns, and programs that engage Muslim and Christian youth. Christians are also involved in development projects that cater to both Christian and Muslim victims of violence. Church leaders and ecumenical organizations have also used the media as well as their relationships with international partners to raise awareness of Christian persecution and marginalization. Unfortunately retaliatory attacks on Muslim communities by some members of Christian communities in Kaduna and Plateau States have exacerbated tensions and prolonged the cycle of violence. The case studies discussed in this chapter show how insecurity, the perception of discrimination, and ethnic rivalry can become the breeding grounds for religious intolerance and human rights abuses.

NOTES

1 The main Protestant mainline churches included in the study are Anglican, Baptist, Church of Christ in Nations (COCIN), and Evangelical Church Winning All (ECWA).
2 We interviewed twenty-four Christian pastors and leaders and five Muslim leaders in Jos, Kaduna, and London.
3 We are grateful to the following staff and students at the University of Jos for their assistance in carrying out the fieldwork and statistical analysis for this study: Dr. Katrina Korb, Dr. Ibrahim Hassan, Mr. Cosmas Wule, and Mr. Gideon Yohanna Tambiyi.
4 National Population Commission of Nigeria, "Nigeria over 167 Million Population: Implications and Challenges," accessed 8 August 2013, http://www.population.gov.ng/index.php/84-news/latest/106-nigeria-over-167-million-population-implications-and-challenges. This figure is a projection from the last national census (2006), when the estimated population was 140 million.
5 John N Paden, *Faith and Politics in Nigeria: Nigeria as a Pivotal State in the Muslim World* (Washington, DC: United States Institute of Peace, 2008).
6 Matthews Ojo, "Pentecostal Movements, Islam and the Contest for Public Space in Northern Nigeria," *Islam and Christian-Muslim Relations* 18, no. 2 (2007): 175–188; Asonzeh Ukah, "Contesting God: Nigerian Pentecostals and their Relations with Islam and Muslims," in *Global Pentecostalism: Encounters with Other Religious Traditions*, ed. David Westerlund (London: I. B. Tauris, 2009), 92–114.
7 Jeffrey Haynes, *Development Studies* (Cambridge: Polity, 2008).
8 The Christian Association of Nigeria (CAN) consists of five groupings: the Catholic Secretariat of Nigeria (CSN), the Christian Council of Nigeria (CCN), the Organisation of African Instituted Churches (OAIC), the Pentecostal Fellowship of Nigeria (PFN), and Tareyar Ekklisiyar Krista a Nigeria (Fellowship of Churches of Christ in Nigeria)/Evangelical Church Winning All (TEKAN/ECWA). The second group (CCN) consists of most mainline Protestant denominations. The fifth group (TEKAN/ECWA) consists of those Protestant denominations started by the Sudan United Mission and the Sudan Interior Mission.
9 The Nigerian Constitution includes a strong statement about freedom of religion: "Every person shall be entitled to freedom of thought, conscience and religion, including freedom to change his religion or belief, and freedom (either alone or in community with others, and in public or in private) to manifest and propagate his religion or belief in worship, teaching, practice and observance." Federal Republic of Nigeria Constitution of 1999," chapter iv, section 38, accessed 14 April 2014, http://www.nigeria-law.org/ConstitutionOfTheFederalRepublicOfNigeria.htm
10 Nigeria is a signatory to the following international human rights agreements: the International Covenant on Civil and Political Rights, the African Charter on Human and Peoples Rights, and the Convention on the Rights of the Child. Christian Solidarity Worldwide, "Universal Periodic Review: Federal Republic of Nigeria" (stakeholder submission, Christian Solidarity Worldwide and Stefanus Alliance 17th Session, March 2013), http://www.stefanus.no/filestore/Rapporter_notater_blader_etc/NigeriaCSWreport2013.pdf
11 Centre for Democracy & Development, "Nigeria: Country Report Based on Research and Dialogue with Political Parties" (Stockholm: International Institute for Democracy and Electoral Assistance, 2006).
12 Human Rights Watch, "'They Do Not Own This Place': Government Discrimination against 'Non-Indigenes' in Nigeria," *Human Rights Watch* 18, no. 3 (2006): 1–64.

13 Nine states have instituted full sharia. Three states (Kaduna, Niger and Gombe) have instituted sharia in areas with large Muslim populations.

14 H. B. Yusuf, "Managing Muslim-Christian Conflicts in Northern Nigeria: A Case Study of Kaduna State," *Islam and Christian-Muslim Relations* 18, no. 2 (2007): 252–255.

15 Human Rights Watch, "They Do Not Own This Place."

16 The 1963 Census found it to be 26 percent Muslim, 23 percent Christian, and 51 percent "Other." Since then, most of the "Others" have become either Muslims or Christians. One basis for estimation is the number of Muslim elected officials in local government, which in March 2011 was 16 percent. See Philip Ostien, "A Survey of the Muslims of Nigeria's North Central Geo-political Zone" (Working Paper no. 1, Nigeria Research Network, Oxford Department of International Development January 2012).

17 Adam Higazi, "The Jos Crisis: A Recurrent Nigerian Tragedy," Discussion Paper 2 (Abuja: Friedrich-Ebert-Stiftung, 2011), 6, http://library.fes.de/pdf-files/bueros/nigeria/07812.pdf

18 Though no state in Nigeria has introduced any legislation that would enthrone Christianity or the Bible as part of the legal framework, Muslims who live in areas where Christians are in the majority such as Jos often complain that they are also marginalized.

19 Cyril Imo, "Evangelicals, Muslims, and Democracy: With Particular Reference to the Declaration of Shari'a in Northern Nigeria," in *Evangelical Christianity and Democracy in Africa*, ed. Terence O. Ranger (Oxford: Oxford University Press, 2008), pp. 43–44; United States Commission on International Religious Freedom, *USCIRF Annual Report 2010 Countries of Particular Concern: Nigeria*," 29 April 2010, accessed 25 October 2012, http://www.unhcr.org/refworld/docid/4be2840c6.html; USCIRF 2010; Christian Solidarity Worldwide, "Nigeria: Religious Freedom," Unpublished Report, May 2011.

20 Interview, Yunisa Nmadu, Kaduna, Nigeria, 3 July 2013.

21 Interview, Ibrahim Hassan, Jos, Nigeria, 1 July 2013.

22 John Boye Ejobowah, "Ethnic Conflict and Cooperation: Assessing Citizenship in Nigerian Federalism," *Publius* 43, no. 4 (2013): 728–747.

23 Human Rights Watch, "They Do Not Own This Place."

24 Abimbola Adesoji, "The Boko Haram Uprising and Islamic Revivalism in Nigeria," *Africa Spectrum* 45 (2010): 95–108; Andrew Walker, "What Is Boko Haram?" (Special Report 308, United States Institute of Peace, June 2012); James J. F. Forest, "Confronting the Terrorism of Boko Haram in Nigeria," *JSOU Report* 12-5 (MacDill Air Force Base, Florida: JSOU Press, 2012); David Cook, "Boko Haram: A Prognosis" (Houston: James A. Baker III Institute for Public Policy, 2011), http://bakerinstitute.org/media/files/news/c90b9ac8/REL-pub-CookBokoHaram-121611.pdf

25 Boko Haram originally gained prominence in 2003, claiming inspiration from the Taliban in Afghanistan. In late 2003, it began an armed uprising in Yobe State in northeastern Nigeria, causing havoc in several towns and villages and the displacement of around ten thousand people.

26 Interview, Dr. Khataza Gondwe, London, 16 July 2013.

27 Sam Eyoboka, "How Pastor Orji and I Were Captured by Boko Haram Operatives: Survivor," *Vanguard*, 4 September 2009, accessed 14 April 2014, http://www.vanguardngr.com/2009/09/how-pastor-orji-and-i-were-captured-by-boko-haram-operatives-survivor/; Naira Forum, "Tell My Brothers, I Died Well': Slain Borno Pastor," *Nairaland Forum*, 7 August 2009, accessed 19 April 2014, http://www.nairaland.com/306644/tell-brothers-died-well-slain; Maria Mackay, "Jesus Can Transform Hearts of Persecutors,

Says Pastor," *Christian Today*, 11 September 2009, http://www.christiantoday.com/article/christians.remember.victims.of.nigerian. islamic.sect/24173.htm; Rupert Shortt, *Christianophobia: A Faith Under Attack* (Reading: Rider, 2013): 121.

28 Christian Solidarity Worldwide, "Nigeria: Religious Freedom."

29 Mohammed Aly Sergie and Tony Johnson, "Boko Haram," *Council on Foreign Relations*, 26 February 2014, accessed 15 April 2014, http://www.cfr.org/nigeria/boko-haram/p25739; John Campbell, "Escaping Nigeria's Cycle of Violence," *Council on Foreign Relations*, 15 May 2013, accessed 18 March 2014, http://www.cfr.org/nigeria/escaping-nigerias-cycle-violence/p30714

30 Interview, Bamidele Padanu, Jos, 22 June 2013; interview, Joseph Maran, London, 30 July 2012; interview, Pauline Lere, Jos, 20 June 2013.

31 Interview, Joseph Maran, London, 30 July 2013.

32 "Boko Haram Seen Linked to Other African Terror Groups," *VOA News*, 26 December 2011, accessed 18 April 2014, http://www.voanews.com/english/news/africa/west/Boko-Haram-Seen-Linked-to-Other-African-Terror-Groups–136260858.html; Jide Ajani, "Al-Qaeda Takes Over Boko Haram," *Vanguard*, 9 March 2014, accessed 18 April 2014, http://www.vanguardngr.com/2014/03/ al-qaeda-takes-boko-haram/. Boko Haram's change of strategy, more organized style of attacks, and use of sophisticated weaponry have prompted some analysts to suggest that group members have received training from Al Qaeda in the Magreb in the period between its seeming disappearance and re-emergence.

33 U.S. Department of State, "Terrorist Designations of Boko Haram and Ansaru," 13 November 2013, accessed 18 April 2014, http://www.state.gov/r/pa/prs/ps/2013/11/217509.htm

34 Interview, Joseph Maran, London, 30 July 2013.

35 Interview, Khataze Gondwe, London, 16 July 2013.

36 Colette Harris, "Transformative Education in Violent Contexts: Working with Muslim and Christian Youth in Kaduna, Nigeria," *IDS Bulletin* 40, no. 3 (May 2009): 34–40.

37 Human Rights Watch, "'They Do Not Own This Place"; Collete Harris, "Gender and Religion in Conflict and Post Conflicts: The Cases of Tajikistan, Northern Uganda, Northern Nigeria" (Paper presented at the DSA-EADI Joint Conference "Rethinking Development in an Age of Scarcity and Uncertainty: New Values, Voices and Alliances for Increased Resilience," University of York, 20 September 2011).

38 Human Rights Watch, "They Do Not Own This Place."

39 Christian Solidarity Worldwide, "Nigeria Assignment: 10–21 February 2012," Unpublished Report (March 2012).

40 Interview, Joshua Mallam, Kaduna, 4 July 2013.

41 Interview, Anthony Zakka, Kaduna, 5 July 2013. Father Zakka is the assistant director of the Catholic Media Centre in Kaduna.

42 Interview, Samuel Salifu, Kaduna, 3 July 2013.

43 Interview, James Wuye, Kaduna, 4 July 2013.

44 Higazi, "Jos Crisis"; Philip Ostien, "Jonah Jang and the Jasawa: Ethno-Religious Conflict in Jos, Nigeria," *Muslim-Christian Relations in Africa* (August 2009): 1–42; Human Rights Watch, "They Do Not Own This Place."

45 Some Hausa-Fulanis contend that they settled in Jos long before the Beroms. Also most do not consider themselves "settlers" as the Igbos and Yorubas do.

46 Ostien, "Jonah Jang," 10–11.

47 Higazi, "Jos Crisis," 9.

48 Interview, Joseph Maran, London, 30 July 2013.

49 Interview, Yusufu Turaki, Jos, 22 June 2013.

50 Higazi, "Jos Crisis," 3.

51 Interview, Kefas Tangan, London, 17 July 2013.

52 Toyin Falola, *Violence in Nigeria: The Crisis of Religious Politics and Secular Ideologies* (Rochester, NY: University of Rochester Press, 1998), 15; Imo, "Evangelicals," 45.

53 Imo, "Evangelicals," 60.

54 Richard Burgess, *Nigeria's Christian Revolution: The Civil War Revival and Its Pentecostal Progeny (1967–2004)* (Carlisle: Regnum/Paternoster, 2008), 272–273; Falola, *Violence,* 107–114.

55 Christian Solidarity Worldwide, "Universal Periodic Review – 17th Session, CSW (Joint Submission) – Stakeholder Submission, Federal Republic of Nigeria" (March 2013): 1–8.

56 Interview, Kefas Tangan, London, 17 July 2013; interview, Dr. Khataza Gondwe, London, 16 July 2013.

57 Christian Solidarity Worldwide, "Universal Periodic Review"; interview, Kefas Tangan, London, 17 July 2013.

58 "Nigeria: Boko Haram Attacks Cause Humanitarian Crisis," *Human Rights Watch,* 14 March 2014, accessed 15 April 2014, http://www.hrw.org/news/2014/03/14/nigeria-boko-haram-attacks-cause-humanitarian-crisis

59 Interview, Khataza Gondwe, London, 16 July 2013.

60 Interview, Aaron Ndirmbita, Jos, 18 June 2013.

61 Interview, Kefas Tangan, London, 17 July 2013.

62 Ayuba J. Bassa, "Plight of Christians in Gwoza, Borno State," An Open Letter to Borno State Governor, Alhaji Kashim Shettima, 12 November 2013, accessed 7 April 2014, http://www.nigeriavillagesquare.com/press-releases/an-open-letter-to-borno-state-governor-his-excellency-alh-kashim-shettima-on-the-deliberate-lack-of-concern-over-the-plights-of-christians-in-gwoza-local-government-area-in-the-wake-of-sponsored-annihilation-of-its-membe.html; "Nigeria: Christian Village Attacked by Insurgents and Abandoned by Nigerian Security Forces," *Voice of the Persecuted,* 22 January 2014, https://voiceofthepersecuted.wordpress.com/tag/borno-state/

63 Heather Murdock, "Amnesty International: 1,500 Nigerians Killed in Boko Haram Violence in 2014," *VOA News,* 30 March 2014, accessed 18 April 2014, http://www.voanews.com/content/amnesty-international-1500-nigerians-killed-in-boko-haram-violence-in-2014/1882683.html. See also Tunde Ajaja, "Terrorism: Over 2,596 Nigerian Killed in Three Months," *Punch* (Lagos), 19 April 2014, accessed 21 April 2014, http://www.punchng.com/feature/terrorism-over-2596-nigerians-killed-in-three-months/

64 Simon Allison, "Boko Haram Will Keep Killing, and Nigeria's Leaders Are Powerless," *Guardian Africa Network,* 17 April 2014, accessed 18 April 2014, http://www.theguardian.com/world/2014/ apr/17/boko-haram-will-keep-killing-and-nigerias-leaders-are-powerless; Will Ross, "Nigerians Reel From Multiplying Attacks," *BBC News,* 18 April 2014, accessed 18 April 2014, http://www.bbc.co.uk/news/world-africa-27080722; "Chibok Abductions in Nigeria: 'More Than 230 Seized'," *BBC News,* 21 April 2014, accessed 22 April 2014, http://www.bbc.co.uk/news/world-africa-27101714. According to the Christian Association of Nigeria, 90 percent of the abducted girls were Christian (see Friday Olokor, "Boko Haram Holding 165 Chibok Christian girls – CAN," *Punch Nigeria,* 4 May 2014, accessed 23 June 2014, http://www.punchng.com/news/boko-haram-holding-165-chibok-christian-girls-can/).

65 "Nigeria Kidnapped Girls 'Shown' in New Boko Haram Video," *BBC News*, 12 May 2014, accessed 22 May 2014, http://www.bbc.co.uk/news/world-africa-27370041

66 Harriet Sherwood, "Boko Haram Abduction: US and UK Step Up Military Effort to Find Girls," *Guardian*, 14 May 2014, accessed 23 May 2014, http://www.theguardian.com/world/2014/ may/13/boko-haram-abduction-us-uk-military-effort-find-girls

67 Martin Williams, "African Leaders Pledge 'Total War' on Boko Haram after Nigeria Kidnap," *Guardian*, 17 May 2014, accessed 23 May 2014, http://www.theguardian.com/world/2014/may/ 17/west-african-countries-must-unite-fight-boko-haram-nigeria

68 Aminu Abu Bakr, "Nigerian Villagers Fight Off Attacks by Boko Haram," *CNN*, 16 May 2014, accessed 22 May 2014, http://edition.cnn.com/2014/05/15/world/africa/nigeria-girls-abducted/

69 "Boko Haram Militants Appoint Emir for Captured Gwoza as Women Bury Their Dead," *Sahara Reporters*, 12 August 2014, accessed 6 September 2014, http://saharareporters.com/2014/08/12/boko-haram-militants-appoint-emir-captured-gwoza-women-bury-their-dead; Maina, "Boko Haram Declares Full Sharia; Beheads Christian Men, Forces Women to Marry in Gwoza, Madagali," *Daily Post*, 28 August 2014, accessed 9 September 2014, http://dailypost.ng/2014/08/28/boko-haram-declare-full-sharia-beheads-christian-men-forces-women-marry-gwoza-madagali/; "Military Operation Underway to Reclaim Gwoza from Boko Haram," *Information Nigeria*, 31 August 2014, accessed 6 September 2014, http://www.informationng.com/2014/08/military-operation-underway-to-reclaim-gwoza-from-boko-haram.html

70 Thomas Fessy, "Boko Haram Attack: What Happened in Baga?" *BBC News*, 2 February 2015, accessed 20 February 2015, http://www.bbc.co.uk/news/world-africa-30987043; Monica Mark, "Boko Haram's 'Deadliest Massacre': 2000 Feared Dead in Nigeria," *Guardian*, 10 January 2015, accessed 20 February 2015, http://www.theguardian.com/world/2015/jan/09/boko-haram-deadliest-massacre-baga-nigeria

71 Kiran Moodley, "Boko Haram Leader Vows to Disrupt Nigerian Elections," *Independent*, 18 February 2015, accessed 22 February 2015, http://www.independent.co.uk/news/world/africa/boko-haram-leader-vows-to-disrupt-nigerian-elections-10054271.html; "Nigeria Unrest: 'Boko Haram' Gunmen Kill 44 at Mosque," *BBC News Africa*, 13 August 2013, accessed 1 November 2013, http://www.bbc.co.uk/news/world-africa-23676872; "Boko Haram Has Killed 13 of My District Heads, Two Council Members, Says Shehu of Borno," *This Day Live*, 19 July 2013, accessed 1 November 2013, http://www.thisdaylive.com/articles/boko-haram-has-killed-13-of-my-district-heads-two-council-members-says-shehu-of-borno/153769/. There are claims that more Muslims than Christians have been killed by Boko Haram; this assertion is difficult to prove and is disputed by the Christian Association of Nigeria.

72 Interview, Michael Adegbola, Kaduna, 5 July 2013.

73 Interview, Kefas Tangan, London, 17 July 2013.

74 Christian Solidarity Worldwide Report, "Nigeria: Religious Freedom"; Christian Solidarity Worldwide Report, "Nigeria Assignment."

75 Interview, Sunday Gomna, Jos, 20 June 2013.

76 Interview, Felix Oluwatayo, Jos, 10 May 2012.

77 Interview, Aaron Ndirmbita, Jos, 18 June 2013.

78 Interview, Kefas Tangan, London, 17 July 2013.

79 Interview, Kenneth Amadi, Jos, 30 June 2013.

80 Interview, Jwan Zhumbes, Jos, 15 June 2013.
81 Interview, Bamidele Padanu, Jos, 22 June 2013.
82 Interview, Comfort Padanu, Jos, 22 June 2013.
83 Interview, Kenneth Amadi, Jos, 30 June 2013.
84 Interview, Bishop Jwan Zhumbes, Jos, 15 June 2013.
85 "Nigeria: Investigate Massacre, Step Up Patrols: Hundreds Killed by Mobs in Villages in Central Nigeria," *Human Rights Watch*, 8 March 2010, accessed 2 November 2013, http://www.hrw.org/ news/2010/03/08/nigeria-investigate-massacre-step-patrols
86 "Nigeria: Protect Survivors, Fully Investigate Massacre Reports," *Human Rights Watch*, 24 January 2010, accessed 2 November 2013, http://www.hrw.org/news/2010/01/22/nigeria-protect-survivors-fully-investigate-massacre-reports; Nafata Bamaguje, "Jos Crisis: When Christians Go Beserk," *Nigerian Voice*, 17 February 2010, accessed 2 November 2013, http://www.thenigerianvoice.com/nvnews/11319/1/jos-crisis-when-christians-go-beserk.html
87 Interview, Dr Khataza Gondwe, London, 16 July 2013.
88 Bishop Fearon is from the evangelical wing of the Church of Nigeria and has a master's degree in Islamic Theology from the University of Birmingham. He is a former president of the Network for Inter-Faith Concerns of the Anglican Communion and a member of the Nigerian Inter-Religious Council (NIREC).
89 Christopher O'Connor, "A Discussion with Bishop Josiah Fearon of Kaduna," *Berkeley Center for Religion, Peace & World Affairs*, 1 July 2010, accessed 16 October 2013, http://repository.berkleycenter.georgetown.edu/PInterviewJuly2010-BishopFearon.pdf
90 "Bishop Idowu-Fearon Asks: Murder in the Name of Which God?" *Vanguard* (Nigeria), 6 May 2012, accessed 12 September 2014, http://www.vanguardngr.com/2012/05/bishop-idowu-fearon-asks-murder-in-the-name-of-which-god/; "Nigerian Will Not Break Up – Bishop Fearon," *Anglican Communion News Service*, 13 January 2014, accessed 12 September 2014, http://www.anglicannews.org/news/2014/01/nigeria-will-not-break-up-bishop-fearon.aspx
91 Interview, Joseph Maran, London, 30 July 2013.
92 Matthews Ojo and Folaranmi T. Lateju, "Christian-Muslim Conflicts and Interfaith Bridge-Building Efforts in Nigeria," *The Review of Faith & International Affairs* 8, no. 1 (2010): 31–38.
93 Interview, Anthony Zakka, Kaduna, 3 July 2013.
94 Interview, Aaron Ndirmbita, Jos, 18 June 2013.
95 Interview, Imam Sani Isah, Kaduna, 4 July 2013.
96 Interview, Ibrahim Hassan, Jos, 21 June 2013.
97 Interview, Declain Onyebuchi, Jos, 20 June 2013.
98 Ray Ikechukwu Jacob and Suhana Saad, "Ethnic Conflict in Nigeria: Constitutional Law and the Dilemma of Decision-Making," *Malaysia Journal of Society and Space* 7, no. 2 (2011): 28–36; Rosalind I. J. Hackett, "Religious Freedom and Religious Conflict in Africa," in *Religion on the News Agenda*, ed. Mark Silk (Hartford, CT: Leonard E. Greenberg Center for the Study of Religion in Public Life, 2000): 102–119.
99 Interview, James Wuye, Kaduna, 4 July 2013.
100 Christopher O'Connor, "A Discussion with Talatu Aliyu of Interfaith Mediation Centre," *Berkeley Center for Religion, Peace & World Affairs*, 1 July 2010, accessed 30 October 2013, http://repository.berkleycenter.georgetown.edu/PInterviewJuly2010-Talatu.pdf

101 Katherine Marshall, "A Discussion with Pastor James Wuye and Imam Muhammad Ashafa," *Berkeley Center for Religion, Peace & World Affairs*, 31 October 2011, accessed 3 April 2013, http://berkleycenter.georgetown.edu/interviews/a-discussion-with-pastor-james-wuye-and-imam-muhammad-ashafa. Pastor Wuye and Imam Ashafa have received several international awards for their work. Especially influential is the film *The Imam and the Pastor*, which has been shown around the world. The IMC is affiliated to several national networks, including the Nigerian Supreme Council for Islamic Affairs, the Christian Association of Nigeria, and the Jama'atu Nasril Islam.

102 Interview, Yakubu Pam, Jos, 8 May 2012; Yakubu Pam and Katrina Korb, *Fighting for Peace: Learning from the Peace Heroes among Us* (Jos: FAB Educational Books, 2011). Danny McCain, Musa Gaiya, and Katrina Korb, "Salt and Light or Salt and Pepper: Views on Ethno-Religious Violence and Peace among Pentecostals in Nigeria," *Pneuma* 36 (2014): 100–102.

103 Interview, Yakubu Pam, Jos, 8 May 2012.

104 Interview, Sale Hassan, Jos, 1 July 2013.

105 Interview, Mark Lipdo, Jos, 20 May 2012.

106 Interview, Yakubu Pam, Jos, 8 May 2012.

107 Pastor Nmadu started CSW Nigeria after a brief work attachment to CSW's international headquarters in London as part of a twelve-week programme on conflict resolution at the University of York. After his return to Kaduna, CSW Nigeria was inaugurated in November 2008. Members of its Board of Trustees include Engineer S. Salifu of All Nations Christian Assembly, Bishop Benjamin Kwashi (Anglican Bishop of Jos), the Reverend Danjuma Bom from ECWA, and Wilson Badejo (General Overseer of Foursquare Gospel Church).

108 "Nigeria: Church in Kaduna Donates Food to Local Mosques in Ramadan Goodwill Gesture," *Christian Solidarity Worldwide*, 11 August 2012, accessed 24 July 2013, http://dynamic.csw.org.uk/article.asp?t=press&id=1413

109 "Govt. Apparatus Is Used against Christians," Christian Solidarity Worldwide, accessed 17 July 2013, http://cswng.org/govt-apparatus-is-used-against-christians/

110 Interview, Bishop Jwan Zhumbes, Jos, 15 June 2013.

111 Interview, Comfort Padanu, Jos, 22 June 2013.

112 Christopher O'Connor, "A Discussion with Pastor John Joseph Hayab, Christian Association of Nigeria," *Berkeley Center for Religion, Peace & World Affairs*, 1 July 2010, accessed 16 October 2013, http://berkleycenter.georgetown.edu/interviews/a-discussion-with-pastor-john-joseph-hayab-christian-association-of-nigeria

113 Interview, James Wuye, Kaduna, 4 July 2013.

114 Interview, Joshua Mallam, Kaduna, 4 July 2013; interview, Aaron Ndirmbita, Jos, 18 June 2013.

115 *Release Magazine*, Issue 74 (July/August 2013), http://www.releaseinternational.org/media/ download_gallery/RELEASE%20MAG%20R74%20linked.pdf

116 Proverbs 31:8–9: "Speak up for those who cannot speak for themselves, for the rights of all who are destitute. Speak up and judge fairly; defend the rights of the poor and needy" (NIV).

117 Interview, Dr Khataza Gondwe, London, 16 July 2013.

118 One of the founders of Love Jos is Fred Williams, who was formerly a pastor in Jos.

119 Interview, Tade Agbewanwa, London, 2 July 2013.

120 Kingsway International Christian Centre is the largest single congregation in Western Europe. It was founded by the Nigerian Pentecostal Matthew Ashimolowo in 1992.

121 Speakers included Baroness Caroline Cox (a former president of Christian Solidarity Worldwide), Matthew Ashimolowo, Anglican Bishop Michael Nazir-Ali, and Mark Lipdo (Stefanos Foundation).

122 Flyer advertising the Love Jos Conference "Stand Up, Speak Out," 24 September 2011.

123 Interview, Tade Agbewanwa, London, 2 July 2013.

12

Copts of Egypt: Defiance, Compliance, and Continuity

Mariz Tadros

INTRODUCTION, BACKGROUND, AND METHODOLOGY

The Copts of Egypt represent the largest Christian community in an Arab state, comprising 10–15 percent of an 84 million population.[1] The Coptic Orthodox Church of Egypt is one of the oldest indigenous churches in the world, believed to date back to 48 AD. The trajectory of the Copts has been the subject of extensive study, with much focus on their status and role as a religious minority in a Muslim majority context. This paper seeks to contribute to the literature on the positioning of Copts in relation to state, society, and church by examining

(i) the role of the Christian communities in promoting particular aspects of freedom and analysing what will be lost for state and society if the Christian community is marginalised;

(ii) the sources and severity of encroachment on freedoms affecting Copts as members of a religious group;

(iii) the coping strategies that citizens have individually and collectively espoused, including compliance, defiance, and subversion.

This chapter has two objectives. First, it examines religious diversity not only as a source of conflict, but also as a safeguard against totalitarian political and societal forces that are intolerant of pluralism and difference. In the case of Egypt, the struggle for an egalitarian political order and society by Christians via civil society activism and political parties – and in some instances the Coptic Christian churches – serves to promote freedoms not only for non-Muslim minorities, but also for minorities within Islam such as the Sufis and Shi'is, who also feel threatened by ultra-radical Islamist forces. However, in celebrating the value of religious diversity, the intention is not to conceal or negate ways in which unequal power relations have influenced citizens' relations with the state and in society.

The second objective of the chapter is to dispel some of the prevailing myths regarding the status and position of Copts in the broader political and historical context. These myths include that the Copts are a "happy" minority, and that any discrimination or persecution is not religiously mediated but is primarily an expression of the broader structural inequalities in society. While these myths are discussed in the context of Egypt, they also permeate the narratives of Christian minorities in the region more broadly.

The first part of this chapter succinctly describes the history of Christianity in Egypt and provides an overview of the key Christian churches, the factors influencing demographic shifts in the country, the emergence of strong diasporas overseas, and the multi-vocal nature of Christian communities in the country.

The second part highlights ways in which the role of the Coptic churches, movements, activists, scholars, and businesses have enriched the political, civil, and economic life of the nation. It argues that the strength of the broad based national civil movement, which emerged to reject theocracy, would have been severely weakened if it were not for the role of the Coptic civil movements. Their role in the revolutions in January 2011 and June 2013 is part and parcel of the broader struggle by the Egyptian people against dictatorial rule.

The third part of chapter describes the changing nature of Muslim-Christian relations, with a particular focus on the period between two regime ruptures (January 2011 and June 2013) and their aftermaths. This exceptional revolution witnessed one of the worst backlashes against Copts in the modern history of Egypt, as well as episodes of the highest levels of solidarity between citizens of different religious affiliations. Sectarian relations among ordinary citizens changed significantly and will be discussed.

Fourth, I will analyse different ways in which Copts have engaged with the rise of sectarianism, both collectively and individually. A discussion of people's practices of compliance and defiance in their daily lives in their communities is followed by an examination of collective forms of mobilization around citizen rights that sought to influence state policy. Finally, the fifth part highlights my key findings and the emerging policy messages for external stakeholders.

Two key epistemological approaches inform this study. The constructivist approach underpins the representation of the historical narrative of the Copts' trajectory across different eras. It is premised on privileging the viewpoint of Coptic historians and analysts in view of the fact that their narratives have often been side-lined by more mainstream historical accounts. The emphasis on capturing voices of Copts also informs the study of the founders and activists in Coptic coalitions, movements, political parties, and non-governmental organizations, as well as ordinary women and men. The focus on representing multiple voices does not in any way suggest that it is possible to draw generalisations for a highly diverse citizenry, especially since religious affiliation is but one of many identity qualifiers (gender, age, class, geographic origin, profession, political orientation being among the many others). However, in purposely privileging the voices of Coptic citizens, I seek to capture their constructions and interpretations of changing realities, in view of the absence of such voices from scholarly research in political science on the subject. In privileging different voices and experiences of Coptic citizens, I seek to position them as subjects in a struggle, rather than as objects lacking in agency.

The second approach is an empirical one, displacing some widely held myths by inductively developing theoretical arguments from the experiences on the ground. The research methodology relied on a mixed data approach, combining qualitative and quantitative analysis of contemporary phenomena. Quantitative data on incidents of sectarian assault, whether verbal or physical, were collected for the period between 2008 and 2013. While by no means conclusive, they point to important patterns and trends on the nature of sectarian encroachments on Christians (see the section Sources and Severity of Pressure on the Christian Community). An ethnographic approach using focus groups and observation was used to capture the nuanced perceptions of ordinary Coptic women and men. Eight focus groups were organized between December 2012 and August 2013 in the Upper Egyptian governorate of Minya, 260 kilometres south of Cairo.

Minya was selected because it has a long history of being the governorate with the highest incidence of sectarian violence against Copts. It was also the worst hit governorate in terms of churches and property burnt in August 2013 (see the section Sources and Severity of Pressure on the Christian Community). Two communities were chosen, the urban town of Abou Qorqas and the rural village of Al Amoudein. Abou Qorqas, which has a large Christian population, has been the site of two very bloody sectarian incidents in the past twenty years. Throughout the 1990s, there was a spate of attacks on Christians and their property, including one on 12th September 1997, when radical Islamists entered a church and fired shotguns on worshippers, leaving ten dead. In April 2011, Abou Qorqas also witnessed one of the worst sectarian assaults on Christians after a dispute over a road hump (a curve in the road intended to make cars slow down; in this case it was constructed by people rather than the road authorities)between a Muslim man riding a microbus and the guard of a Christian-owned villa ended with gunshots being fired. Two Muslim men died, allegedly by bullets fired by Christians. Though there was no evidence for this, members of the community collectively mobilised the population to launch an attack on Copts, their homes, and their property in the town. The security forces did not intervene.

Like Abou Qorqas, the village of Al Amoudein has a large proportion of Christians. Most of the inhabitants work in agriculture. The village is about sixteen kilometres from the city centre of Minya governorate. Relations between Christians and

Muslims in Al Amoudein have by and large been peaceful, though social cohesion has been occasionally under strain in recent years. Christian inhabitants also began to complain of attacks by Muslim thugs from outside the village after 2011 (see the section Sources and Severity of Pressure on the Christian Community).

Two in-depth focus groups were organised in Abou Qorqas in December 2012, one with young women (between twenty and twenty-six years old) who were either university students, publicly employed, or engaged in unpaid care at home. The same group of women participated in another focus group in October 2013. Similarly, two focus groups in the same time frame were organized with young men (between twenty and thirty-five years old), also mostly university students and white-collar professionals. In Al Amoudein, working women and housewives (between thirty and fifty-five years old) also participated in two focus groups. Likewise, men who were unemployed, day labourers in the fields, and public servants (between twenty and fifty-five years old) participated in two focus groups in the same time frame as those in Abou Qorqas. The purpose of having two sets of focus groups at different intervals was to allow for a longitudinal study of how the same people were responding to rapid socio-political changes around them and to decipher whether their interpretations of actors and events had changed accordingly.[2]

Qualitative methods, such as open-ended interviews and case studies, were used in order to understand sectarian violence as was experienced by Copts from different backgrounds and the kind of multiple strategies of engagement pursued. Open-ended interviews were also undertaken with founding members of different Coptic initiatives (ten interviews) to see whether they described themselves as coalitions, movements, or alliances. These represented collective forms of resistance and defiance from the ground up that sought to influence macro-policy.[3]

HISTORY AND COMPOSITION OF CHRISTIAN COMMUNITIES IN EGYPT

Christians today are estimated to compose around 10 percent of the wider population – although some estimates put it at 20 percent.[4] Of the 10 percent, it is estimated that about 9 percent follow the Coptic Orthodox faith, with the remaining 1 percent following the Protestant and Catholic faiths. Over the past sixty years, Christians have witnessed several periods of emigration, first in the 1960s, then in the 1970s, and more recently, since the Egyptian Revolution of 2011. Coptic emigration has been driven by aspirations for a better life economically, as well as subjection to discrimination and, in some instances, persecution. Since the Egyptian Revolution of 2011, feelings of insecurity towards the future have increased among Copts, who feared the political ascendency of Islamists and the increasing failures of one government after another to secure rule of law. One estimate suggests that some 350,000 Copts left Egypt in 2011.[5] Dennis Ross of the Washington Institute for Near

East Policy estimates that no fewer than 100,000 Coptic Christians emigrated after the Brotherhood rose to power in 2012.[6] Prior to the 2011–2013 surge of emigration, it was estimated that there are about 2 million Copts living in the diaspora.[7]

Another important demographic change, which is possibly occurring on a scale that is far greater than meets the eye, is the internal migration of Copts from areas where they are a minute minority (i.e., a handful of families living in a majority Muslim area) to where they constitute larger communities, even if they still represent a minority within the larger municipality or town. Internal migration has been occurring over the course of many decades; however, it has been mostly individual cases rather than a collective phenomenon.[8]

This section briefly traces the historical roots of the Christian population in Egypt, with reference to the different denominations and their churches. The history of the Copts of Egypt is presented as spanning five historical phases.[9]

First Phase: From the Conversion of the Egyptians to Christianity to the Arab Conquest (48–641 AD)

It is believed that St. Mark the Evangelist took the Christian faith to Egypt in 48 AD, a date that marks the formation of the indigenous church. The Coptic era is considered to have commenced in the second century with the invention of the Coptic alphabet and the flourishing of Coptic art, music, and language. Coptic Christianity also acquired an international standing on account of its internationally renowned Catechetical School of Alexandria. Copt Christians experienced two periods of intense persecution, first under the Romans (fourth century) and then by the Melkitesin in the Byzantine era (311–641).

Second Phase: From the Arab Conquest to the End of the Ikhidids (641–969)

The year 641 marked the conquest of Egypt by Amr ibn al-'As of Egypt, who established a new covenant with the Christian Egyptians (the covenant of *dhimmitude*)[10] and instated Patriarch Benjamin, the pope of the Coptic Orthodox Church, who had been exiled by the former rulers. The Copts did not resist the Arab conquest and believed it would produce religious enfranchisement from the Melkites.

While a certain degree of religious tolerance was accorded, Christians were given a choice of converting to Islam or paying the *jizya* (poll tax). Between 739 and 773, there were five rebellions by Christians against the growing financial burdens being imposed upon them. In some instances, Muslims joined forces with the Copts, as they too were suffering from the predatory economic policies of the rulers. These rebellions and others ended with bloody repressions, the most famous being the Bashmuric uprising of 829–830.

Third Phase: The Fatimids and Abbasids (969–1250)

The Fatimid caliphs invaded Egypt from Tunisia in 969 and held it until 1171.[11] While Copts and Egyptians more generally were favourably treated under the first two rulers, the rule of Caliph al-Hakim (985–1021) marked the beginning of a thirty-six-year rule that was considered one of the worst in Egyptian history, in particular for Christians and Jews, who were subject to intense religious persecution.

Fourth Phase: The Mamluks and the Ottomans (1261–1805)

Egypt continued to experience economic, political, and social decline under the Mamluks, who represented yet another dark chapter in the history of the country. Persecution of religious minorities continued, and the Crusades released a backlash against local Christian communities. Later, Egypt became one of a number of satellite states within the Ottoman Empire in 1517. The millet system was instituted, giving the Coptic Church hierarchy substantial freedom to govern its followers. However, this was also a period when heavy taxes were levied upon Copts.

Fifth Phase: From the Rule of Mohamed Ali to Today (1805–Present)

The era of Muhammad Ali has often been described as the beginning of the formation of the modern Egyptian state: Particular attention was given to modernising the country's agricultural base, raising standards of health and education, and putting an end to the predatory relationship that existed between Egypt and the Sublime Porte. Against this backdrop, Copts witnessed a renaissance largely due to the shift in their status from one of *dhimmitude* to citizenship: The *jizya* was dropped, conscription in the army was allowed in 1855, and full participation was secured in the newly opened parliament in 1866. Muhammad Ali's grand modernisation project also entailed the building of strong political and commercial relations with Europeans; through this process, European missionaries entered Egypt through Catholic and Protestant missions that began to gain ground in 1852 and 1854, respectively.

Gradually, Egypt drifted away from being a satellite in an Islamic caliphate ruled by the Ottomans towards a nation-state espousing the concept of citizenship. In 1919, Egyptians revolted against British colonial rule in a widely publicised display of national unity between the crescent and the cross, and while relations waxed and waned in the decades that followed, Copts championed political movements that endorsed secular nationalism.

From 1950 up to 2010, Egypt was ruled by three military dictatorships (Abd el Nasser, Sadat, and Mubarak), during which Copts experienced periodic phases of increased sectarian violence. Under Sadat's Islamisation of state and society policy,

Copts experienced increased sectarian violence in the 1980s, and this continued into the first part of Mubarak's rule (up to the mid-1990s). In the early 2000s, there was a resurgence of sectarian violence against Christians, which escalated until Mubarak was ousted in 2010. Generally, the state security investigation apparatus regulated sectarian affairs, sometimes being responsible for exacerbating conflict as a strategy of divide and rule, and sometimes acting as the mediator of conflict, thus maintaining its power over communities.[12]

There are two overarching themes running through the history of Copts in Egypt. First, there is a clear congruence between the wider predicaments of the country and that of the Copts. In other words, the status of the Copts serves as one of the ways of capturing the pulse of the wider polity and the state of the country more generally. It is important to note, however, that the existence of such synergies does not mean that any decline in the status of Copts is simply a projection of the state of the rest of the country. One cannot be blind to the religion-specific nature of discrimination that affects Christians.

The second theme relates to modern Egypt: From the 1900s up to the present time, there has been an ideological and political struggle over the country's identity, which has had a direct impact on the status, positioning, and role of Copts. While complex and diverse, the struggle has essentially been between two camps: on the one hand, those who identify Egypt with secularism and nation-bound citizenship, and, on the other, those who see the country as part of a broader Islamic nation (*Ummah*) and endorse the revival of the Islamic caliphate. From historical experience (the shift from *dhimmitude* to citizenship) and their experiences with Islamist movements, the Copts have by and large been some of the staunchest supporters of the concept of a "civil" state as distinct from any theocratic institution.

The Role of the Christian Community in Promoting Aspects of Freedom

Across the centuries, Copts have enriched the country in several ways. While recognising the socio-cultural and economic roles they have played, this chapter will focus on their contributions to politics in particular.

Economically, Copts have contributed to the development of the private sector and have been responsible for the transfer of large remittances to Egypt by those living in the diaspora. Leading Coptic figures, such as the business tycoon Naguib Sawiris, are among the biggest private sector employers in Egypt. Sawiris's Orascam group of companies provide more than 100,000 Egyptians with jobs. Furthermore, in April 2011, when the Egyptian exchange risked suffering downturn due to the volatile political situation, Sawiris injected $82 million through stock purchase[13] in order to prevent it from spiralling downwards further.[14]

It is in the realm of advancing Egyptian nationalism, secular political thought, and the concept of citizenship that Copts have made their greatest contribution. In nineteenth-century Egypt, there emerged a new stratum within the Coptic citizenry: the intelligentsia. Their power did not emanate from their wealth, as with the existing land-owning Copts, nor from assuming positions of leadership in the clergy. Rather, it stemmed from their education.

The Copts who became associated with the Egyptian intelligentsia greatly contributed to indigenous conceptions of secular political thought, which in turn deeply influenced ideas of modern citizenship, the separation of religion and state, and the delineation of an Egyptian identity. The founding members of this intellectual class include personalities such as George Henein, Fawzy Habashy, Ramsis Yunan, and Anwar Kamel. Examples from the generation that followed include Salama Moussa, Abou Seif Youssef, Youssef Karam, and Anwar Abd al-Malik – all renowned thinkers who played an influential role in the leftist movement. Copts have also contributed to the formation and leadership of political parties, social movements, and non-profit organizations, both in the nineteenth century and since the demise of Hosni Mubarak.

With respect to political parties, while there were a number of attempts by Coptic activists to form political parties to represent and defend the rights of Copts, their appeal within the larger population of Coptic followers has been very minimal. The overwhelming trend has been for Copts to seek participation and representation in liberal political parties that believe in the secular state and endorse full citizenship for all.[15] Many of the principal non-Islamist political parties that were established after the demise of Mubarak's regime included leading Coptic figures, as well as founding members such as in the Egyptian Democratic Party, the Free Egyptians Party, and the popular Socialist Front Party.

Moreover, Coptic Christians played an active role in resistance movements against Mubarak's regime. George Ishak, a Coptic Catholic, was for many years the co-ordinator of the Kefaya (meaning "Enough!"), the first movement in Egypt to challenge openly the inheritance plans of Mubarak to turn the country to his son. Kefaya opened the floodgates for the emergence of other movements and groups that pressed for a democratic order.

Copts have played a key role in emancipatory revolutions in modern Egyptian history, such as in the revolt against British colonialism in 1919, in the revolt against authoritarianism in January 2011, and in the largest Egyptian Revolution so far in June 2013 against Islamist theocratic rule.

The 1919 Revolution mobilised Christians and Muslims to join ranks to rid the country of colonialism. Almost a century later, a similar show of unity was witnessed on January 25, 2011, when Egyptians rose against the authoritarianism of Mubarak's regime. It is impossible to capture the numbers of Copts who participated, since the great majority were keen to emphasise that their participation was as Egyptians defending the homeland.[16] The participation of Copts dispelled two myths: first, that they are a "cocoonized" minority not interested in participating in the political affairs of the country; and second, that their interests lie in preserving authoritarian rule.

Coptic Citizens' Activism in the 30th of June 2013 Revolution

The political weight of Copts' participation in emancipatory revolutionary struggles was positioned even more at the fore in the 30th of June 2013 Revolution. It can be argued that the participation of Copts was crucial for the successful mobilisation of a mass revolt. It is impossible to determine the number of people who participated in the revolution, with estimates ranging from 17 to 33 million, making it one of the largest peaceful protests in the region's contemporary history.[17] The numbers far surpassed those of participants in the 25th of January Revolution of 2011. Large-scale dissatisfaction with poor governance and increasing economic hardship (in particular electricity blackouts and severe shortages of petrol) had their toll on a population that was promised better living under a "godly" president. A youth group, Tamarod (meaning "Rebel"), called upon the population to rise against the president, demanding that he either call an early presidential election or step down. In relative terms, Copts represent sections of the Egyptian population who had not participated in the January 25th revolution but took part in the June 30, 2013, demonstrations.

What is striking about many of the accounts of the youth from Abou Qorqas who participated in the June 30th uprisings is the use of a narrative similar to that of the Copts who participated in the January revolution. Both narratives speak of being driven by a desire to reclaim their country, to rise against forces of oppression, and to make a sacrifice for a country worth dying for. These narratives speak of mobilisation along national allegiance rather than religious or sectarian interests.

The Revolutionary Role of the Evangelical Church in Kasr el Doubara

The Evangelical Church popularly known as "Kasr el Doubara" Church is situated in close proximity to Tahrir Square. The Kasr el Doubara Church was one of the first Christian institutions that publicly endorsed the Egyptian Revolution. The leaders of three churches in Egypt (Orthodox, Catholic, and Protestant) had, at the outset of the revolution, announced their rejection of the youths' call to revolt. Yet many Christian youths defied their orders and took to the streets. The Evangelical Church in Kasr el Doubara took a stance in favour of the revolution on the basis of the biblical principle of fighting injustice and speaking up for the oppressed. It became iconic of the Christian stance in favour of dignity, freedom, and rights.

Since the Egyptian Revolution of 2011, the Evangelical Church of Kasr el Doubara has played a pioneering role in joining Muslims and Christians to pray for peace and prosperity in Egypt. On New Year's Eve in 2012, they organised a public prayer event in Tahrir Square, with hymns and spiritual songs about Egypt sung under candlelight. The Kasr el Doubara Church's circulation of the hymn "Barek ya Rab Beladi" (Bless O' Lord My Country) was widely sung by a large number of Muslims and Christians alike. Giving Christian songs a broad-based appeal across a Muslim majority population attending these events went beyond promoting tolerance. In those instances when all Egyptians sang Christian hymns, the terms of engagement had changed. It was no longer a case of simply acknowledging and respecting religious difference; it was a case of celebrating the value of religious diversity.

While transient, this is no small achievement. In both revolutions (2011 and 2013), Christians would often participate with Muslims in chanting the Islamic declaration of faith *Allahu Akbar* (God Is Great). However, it would have been inconceivable, even for the most open-minded Muslims to chant any religious slogans or idioms that are associated with Christianity. To do so would have stirred too many popular sensibilities. The chanting of Christian hymns under candlelight by thousands of Muslims and Christians represented an embracing of the positive contributions that a Christian faith can offer to a religiously heterogeneous community. It is not surprising, therefore, that the ultra-radical Islamist Salafi groups found this display of solidarity so threatening as to send threats against the convening of these candlelight prayers for New Year's Eve in 2013.[18]

In addition to these candlelight prayers, the Kasr el Doubara Church is renowned for converting its backyard into a makeshift hospital to receive those who were injured or suffocating from the effects of tear gas. As the political violence heightened in 2011–2013, the fighting was sometimes just metres away from the church. Volunteers, including doctors, were organised into shifts that would sometimes be sustained for days on end. Maged Adel, the media spokesperson for the church, reflected: "We decided that we needed to help – we have a safe, clean place and volunteers. This was a humanitarian and not a political act, it was a ministry of mercy that we provided for anyone who came to us – revolutionaries, army, or police."[19]

SOURCES AND SEVERITY OF PRESSURE ON CHRISTIAN COMMUNITY

Many of the narratives around sectarian violence in Egypt have been characterised by the politics of denial. There is sometimes a denial of both the nature of the problem (that it is sometimes religiously mediated) as well as a denial of agency (accountability and complicity).

An analysis of the incidents of sectarian violence as reported in the mainstream press was systematically pursued for the period from 2008 to present (Table 12.1). Since incidents of sectarian assault are severely under-reported, this study does not present the full scale of the phenomenon. Rather, its purpose is strictly *indicative*: It points to patterns or trends of growth/decrease, causes of the conflict, demographic characteristics, and how it is handled by various stakeholders, including the government, religious authorities, the media, and human rights organizations.[20]

Frequency of Sectarian Incidents

It is clear from Table 12.1 that there was a dramatic increase in sectarian violence recorded in the press in 2011 and then again in 2012. This is not due to increased press freedom but a rise in the frequency of incidents. This is also corroborated with evidence collected in focus groups with men and women in Minya, Cairo, and Fayoum,[21] in which they described their exposure to higher levels of verbal and physical assault on account of being perceived as *kufar* (infidels). The Egyptian population at large experienced a dramatic increase in levels of crime after the January 2011 revolution due to security laxity, sudden surge in the availability of weapons, and increasing economic pressures. It was also a time of increased political violence as a consequence of the confrontations between the army (the Supreme Council of Armed Forces that ruled Egypt between February 2011 and June 2012) and the youth revolutionary forces, and then again between the latter and the ruling Muslim Brotherhood from July 2012 to June 2013. While recognising the need to situate sectarian violence in the broader context of a suffering population, it is still important to note, however, that many Copts felt they became the target of assault, not only as part of the general citizenry, but as Christians.

Undoubtedly, the percentage of sectarian assaults continued to rise in 2013. When Minister of Defence General el Sissi stepped in to oust President Morsi after the three-day mass revolt, pro-Morsi supporters initiated a large-scale assault on all property associated with Christians. The largest of such acts occurred on August 14th when in the space of twelve hours there were sixty-four assaults on Christian churches (sixteen of which were burnt to the ground), schools, civic associations, and private property in eight governorates across the entire country. Within the space of forty-eight hours, twenty-one churches were burnt to the ground.

By the end of 2013, the record amounted to more than two hundred incidents of sectarian assault. This represents almost a fivefold increase in the levels of sectarian violence from 2008 to 2013. Many hoped that incidents of sectarian violence would gradually diminish, as a consequence of the security clampdown on pro-Morsi supporters. However, so far, sectarian violence against Copts has continued.

TABLE 12.1. *Incidents recorded in the press and verified, 2008–2012*

	Year 2008	Year 2009	Year 2010	Year 2011	Year 2012	TOTAL	Percentage
Escalation of small disputes/fights	11	14	1	11	24	61	20.89
Building/expansion of churches or related to its registration/license[a]	1	8	10	15	12	46	15.75
Muslim/Christian gender relations *and disappearance of women and girls*	4	7	9	13	13	46	15.75
Reasons related to Coptic converts to Islam	3	0	13	6	7	29	9.93
Property disputes	7	2	3	3	5	20	6.85
Attacks on Christian protesters	0	0	1	4	0	5	1.71
News/rumours of defamation of Islam	2	0	1	1	7	11	3.77
Alleged Christian evangelical activities	1	0	2	0	0	3	1.03
Other reasons	4	1	2	1	4	**12**	**4.11**
Untriggered – no reason	0	0	3	16	40	59	20.21
Total number of incidents	**33**	**32**	**45**	**70**	**112**	**292**	**100.00**

[a] Please note that the parts in italics were not applied to the original analysis for 2008–2010 but were added later as a consequence of the widening scope of the nature of the trigger.

349

Triggered and Untriggered Forms of Sectarian Violence

As noted from the table for the years 2008, 2009, and 2010, the three most frequent triggers of violence were associated with church construction/expansion, gender matters, and the escalation of small fights into major sectarian crises. An archaic set of legal regulations that has created restrictions on the construction, extension, and repair of churches entrenched the unequal status of Christian places of worship in relation to their Muslim counterparts. There has also been no legal redress for perpetrators of violence against Christian places of worship; nor have the security forces been held accountable for failure to protect Christian places of worship from attacks.

The gendered dimension of sectarian conflict is highly complex; at its essence lies the question of whether Coptic women who disappear and/or convert to Islam do so of their full free will or under coercion or duress. Until institutional mechanisms are re-instated for guaranteeing transparency in such matters, the phenomenon of the missing Coptic women will be a source of acute sectarian tensions. Accusations by Christians of the kidnapping of women for conversion to Islam will be countered with accusations by Islamist leaders of Christian intolerance towards freedom of religion.

In addition, the escalation of petty fights between citizens that are completely unrelated to religious affiliation into communal violence raises alarm, since it cannot be treated by legal or institutional reform. Rather, it requires a systemic exploration of why and how ruptures in social cohesion occur so rapidly and spontaneously.

Finally, from 2011 to 2013 there was a perplexing rise in "untriggered" assaults: incidents that do not fit under the causes/triggers identified in 2008–2010. These include attempted annexation of buildings belonging to churches, the imposition of levies on Copts, and the sudden prohibition of worshippers from visiting a church if they were from outside the village/town.

Changes in the Intensity of Incidents of Assault

New forms of violence specific to religious identity began to emerge in the past three years, such as the cutting of women's hair in public transport, the cutting of a Coptic man's ear, the killing of a Coptic student in a classroom in the presence of his teacher, and the murder of an elderly lady leaving church. The assaults were becoming more brutal and were in some cases afflicting not only individuals but entire villages as well, such as in the villages of Badraman and Deir Mawas in Minya.

Geographic Coverage

The geographic distribution of sectarian incidents shows that all but one governorate (Damietta) has been violence-free, possibly because there are hardly any Christians living there. The geographic distribution of sectarian incidents points to two disturbing trends. The first is that governorates that were hotspots of sectarian assault on Christians in the 1980s and 1990s have witnessed a dramatic increase in number of incidents. These include Minya and Asiut in Upper Egypt and Giza in greater Cairo. These governorates are some of the poorest in Egypt (in terms of Human Development Index) and have historically been the strongholds of Islamist movements such as the Muslim Brotherhood and Gama'aat Islamiyya. They also happen to be governorates with the greatest concentration of Christians.

The governorate of Minya reported the highest percentage of incidents of violence throughout the 2008–2012 period and the highest number of church burnings in 2013. What is most unfortunate is that some of the acts of assault that occurred, especially those of August 2013, could have been averted had the authorities responded to warnings. In other words, in view of the high-alert situation in a governorate such as Minya and its particular historical/political trajectory, there was security complicity in failing to prevent a pre-orchestrated, systematic assault on churches and faith-based institutions.

The second observable trend is that of governorates that did not experience any incidents of sectarian violence in 2008–2010 and that recorded new sectarian tensions in 2011 and 2012. Aswan and Ismailiya governorates, known to be tourist resorts (the former for foreign tourists, the latter for middle-class Egyptians), had generally enjoyed low levels of communal tension. Yet, the first incidents in five years were documented in 2011. Similarly, Al Sharqia, New Valley, and New Sea governorates also recorded no such incidents between 2008 and 2013, but new incidents were reported in 2012. Of the twenty-seven governorates, the only two governorates that had no incidents of sectarian violence recorded at all during the five-year period are Damietta and South Sinai. These cases of positive deviance are worthy of further examination.

Grassroots Perspectives on Sectarianism

Findings from the focus groups organised in the town of Abou Qorqas and the village of Al Amoudein suggest that the three key preoccupations that affected people's lives in the period 2011–2013 were (1) the security breakdown/laxity, (2) economic decline, and (3) rising sectarian violence. The first two preoccupations are likely to characterise the experiences of Egyptians across class, gender, religion, and geographic location, while the third is more likely to be cited by ordinary men and women of religious minorities.

In the first four sets of focus groups taken in December 2012, participants mentioned that security laxity, economic decline, and sectarianism were all intrinsically connected. A nationwide security breakdown and no rule of law made Christians vulnerable to two kinds of assaults: economic predatory behaviour by criminals and gangs, and ideologically motivated attacks by Islamist groups. These played out in the lives of ordinary men and women in different ways. In a focus group with young women (twenty to thirty-five) who were working or studying at university and living in the urban context of Abou Qorqas, it was the intersection of gender and religious identity that had the greatest impact on their lives.

While sexual harassment was on the rise before the revolution, it assumed far greater proportions thereafter, both in terms of its prevalence and in the forms that it took (i.e., high levels of physical molestation). This affected all Egyptian women irrespective of religious affiliation, geographic location, or class. However, women were exposed to different levels of harassment. In Abou Qorqas, young Coptic women in the focus group expressed anguish that they were exposed to discriminatory behaviour; they felt pressured by pedestrians unknown to them, men and women, to cover their hair and dress in long flowing robes on the street. They also spoke of increasing pressure from members of ultra-radical Islamist groups and even from colleagues at work to don some sort of headcover. While there are no ethnic differences in the appearances of Christian and Muslim women, the one distinguishing marker is that most Muslim women in Egypt (though not all) wear the veil and Coptic women do not.

As it did with many Egyptian women exposed to harassment, this affected every aspect of their lives: They felt that their presence in public space was always threatened, and that they had to make some critical changes in their daily lives. For example, some restricted their mobility to their neighbourhood and refrained from going out at night unless they were chaperoned. As Coptic women, they also were targeted with religious slurs about how Christian women were immodest, immoral, and indecently dressed, which were often linked with statements about being infidels.

Young men in my focus group, also living in the urban context of Abou Qorqas, pointed to ways in which the increasing Islamisation of society was also affecting them. They spoke about how relationships with good friends had been ruptured as tensions had risen, how violence had increased in their communities, and how public discourses against Christianity conveyed in public transport or at work were becoming common.

The most dramatic change that both men and women mentioned in the focus groups in Al Amoudein was their exposure for the first time to economically motivated assaults on their village. Organised gangs and thugs from surrounding villages have been launching assaults on their village, kidnapping men for a ransom or occupying land and insisting on a levy to leave it. While the men in the focus groups conceded that these gangs were not affiliated with religious leaders/movements, the gang members have nonetheless been specifically targeting Copts on the basis of their religious denomination and have not been attacking Muslims living in the same village. The participants in the focus groups complained that the security forces turned a blind eye. Regrettably, the kidnapping of Copts for a ransom is a post-revolution type of sectarian violence against Christians that has continued even after the ousting of the Muslim Brotherhood regime.

However, it is important to note that the Copts in the village of Al Amoudein are divided along class lines, with some very wealthy land-owning families and others who are landless day labourers living well below the poverty line. Many of the poorer labourers in the focus group insisted that the lack of collective action is partly to blame for their increasing vulnerability to attacks and is due to a lack of solidarity between the wealthier and poorer Copts in the village. They contrasted the situation in Al Amoudein with that in a nearby village that also has a large Christian population, and where a sense of collective solidarity enabled them to cope far better in resisting such assaults.

In the second set of focus groups that took place in October 2013, three months after the end of the Muslim Brotherhood–led government, participants spoke of a sense of triumph at having ousted the Morsi regime. In both Abou Qorqas and Al Amoudein, the narrative was about "Egyptians winning the country back." The sense of relief at not having to live in the shadow of the Brothers was more psychological than anything else. Women and men in Al Amoudein and Abou Qorqas said that communal relations by and large had changed for the better. The Islamists' discourse of teaching the Copts a lesson for rejecting Morsi in the presidential elections, which was so prevalent when the Brothers were in power, had dissipated, as they were no longer in a position to flex their muscles. Instead of society's being polarised on the basis of Christians versus Muslims, on religious grounds, a new polarisation based on political orientation took precedence: between supporters of Morsi versus opponents of Morsi, both comprising Muslims. While a slight improvement in the presence of security forces has been cited by participants in both Abou Qorqas and Al Amoudein as making them feel slightly safer, the security complacency in dealing with the continued pattern of kidnapping Christians for a ransom was still a source of insecurity.

COPING STRATEGIES OF COMPLIANCE AND DEFIANCE

In the two communities in which focus groups were held, people spoke of multiple strategies of engaging with a politically volatile context characterised by unpredictable political outcomes, high levels of violence, and uncertainty regarding their role and position in a new Egypt. By and large, demographic determinants are important for understanding variations in coping strategies of Christians in both communities. In Al Amoudein women and men sought to insulate themselves from the increasing sectarian violence by remaining within the vicinity of the village and limiting their interactions with the world outside. For example, to offset the harassment of girls and young women in public transport to and from secondary school (which lies outside the village), the church hired microbuses to take them to and from school. When young men were subjected to bullying and religious slurring in their secondary school, some families removed them from school and enrolled them in long-distance education (i.e., a through system of remote learning). When Coptic women found that merchants were treating them differently than Muslim buyers, they quietly took their business to Christian sellers, even when the prices were higher.

In Abou Qorqas, women spoke more of strategies of open resistance than accommodation, though the age factor may have also played a role. When some of their family members and a couple of parish priests suggested that they should cover their hair to appease the Islamists, they objected. One young female teacher said she even resisted her (Muslim) colleagues' suggestion at school that she should tie her hair back and not let it loose. She felt that though this would have been a small gesture, she refused to comply with or accede to the kind of coercion she was being subjected to because it felt like an affront on her identity.

Young men in Abou Qorqas spoke of using multiple strategies of coping with the new realities. At times, their reaction was one of defiance, in particular when they were faced with an inflammatory speech about Christians being infidels. They openly expressed their objection in public transport, at religious institutions, or at work. At other times they used strategies of subversion by seeking quietly to mobilise discontent against the regime by engaging in conversations with their peers and passengers in public transport. At times, youths described themselves as pacifists, avoiding conversations with radical Islamists so as not to enter into disputes. Others spoke of how some of their families were becoming more defensive: Some men, for the first time ever, have purchased guns and stored weapons to protect their households. In a context where there is no rule of law, some of the men in the focus group said they feared that should disputes escalate into sectarian assaults on Christians, Abou Qorqas could potentially turn into a civil war zone.

One striking response was that of two young men active in church services. They said that the response of Christians is sometimes neither defiance nor compliance, but love. As volunteers who regularly make their rounds in public hospitals to visit the sick, they make a point of stopping by each patient, irrespective of his/her religion, to offer moral, financial, and in-kind support. On one of their rounds, their actions caught the attention of a radical Salafi sheikh, who was so moved by their pastoral care that he made a significant financial donation to them on the spot, saying how touched he was by their sincerity and often sustained financial support.

The strategies of engagement cited are by and large individual responses. However, there were also collective responses to the increasing encroachment on spaces and freedoms, the most important of which was the revolution of June 30, 2013. Many women and men from Abou Qorqas participated. The villagers of Al Amoudein said that while they welcomed the uprising against the regime, they did not participate in the revolts because they feared the bloodshed.

Many of the youth spoke of the liberating experience of participating in these mass demonstrations. One young doctor explained that he and his family were possessed by a strong patriotic desire to participate in the protests to save Egypt. "We thought to ourselves we may die today, but if we don't [participate in the protests] we will die anyway. Perhaps if I die [in these protests] my son will have a chance to live, and this gave me the impetus to go and join [the protests] in spite of all the threats."

The stakes for Coptic women to participate in these protests were particularly high, not only on account of their anti-Morsi political orientation and their Christian religion, but also on account of their gender.[22] One young woman, Sally, travelled to Minya city with her girlfriend to join the protest on June 30th despite the opposition of family. "This was for our country; it was out of the question, we had to take part!" she explained. Feeling that the probability of her not returning home were high, Sally wrote a letter containing a personal message to her family an hour before she left home. She called another friend and told her to tell her family of the letter should she not return, and she even wrote a message on her Facebook page that she might not return. When she arrived in the city centre in Minya, she and her girlfriend joined the protests. "I felt everyone shared one goal, all bound by one heart, one hand working together." This stirred her hope in the power of the collective across religious affiliation. Sally says she went home feeling very happy to have taken part. "I felt I will always carry this memory in my heart and one day I will tell my children that I took part in making history."

In Al Amoudein, people did not join the protests, citing all kinds of reasons. They feared the situation would turn bloody and lives would be lost, there was pessimism that the protests would amount to nothing, the village was situated in an area far from the Minya city centre where the protests were held, and there was no leadership on a village level mobilising them to join en masse. However, participants in the focus group also spoke of how the Muslims in their village gathered and offered to protect the premises of the churches when news of the torching and destruction of the churches in the rest of the governorate began to circulate. Participants from the focus group described how Muslims came by to tell them that they were ready to protect the church and would form a defence line if they were asked. This gesture on the part of the Muslim members of the village bears tremendous symbolic power far greater than the actual physical act of shielding the church from possible attacks.

In the previous section, we examined strategies of engagement on a micro-level in the governorate of Minya. In the next section, we examine responses on a macro-level, with a particular focus on a new form of political agency among Copts, who played a powerful role in challenging the status quo in 2011–2013.

Copts' Defiance through Civil Society Activism

In nineteenth-century Egypt, there was a boom in the number of Coptic civil society associations whose raison d'être included charity, education, cultural heritage, and advocacy for Coptic rights.[23] The Nasserite regime that gained power in the 1950s repressed civil society, including Coptic civic associations. An entente between President Nasser and Pope Kyrollos II also meant the patriarch of the Coptic Orthodox Church became the sole political spokesperson for the Copts. Over the course of those sixty years from 1950 to 2010, there were few signs of an independent Coptic civil society able to advocate effectively for the citizenship rights of Copts, as Kyrollos's successor, Pope Shenouda, also assumed the role of political spokesman for the Copts in negotiating with the regimes of President Sadat and later Mubarak.[24]

In 2010, a government attack on a church in the poor district of Al Ameriyya in Giza propelled thousands of Coptic youths to take to the streets in protest, in defiance of state and church, and many were arrested. On New Year's Eve of 2011, a bomb exploded inside a church in Alexandria, leaving at least twenty-one dead and ninety-six wounded. Again Coptic youth, joined by many Muslims, took to the streets in protest, openly attacking the minister of interior and the government for the rising incidence of sectarian violence in Egypt. According to Bishoy Tamri, one of the founders of the Maspero youth movement, there were a number of attempts during those last years of Mubarak's rule to form initiatives that would advocate equal citizenship, such as Aqbat min ajl Misr (Copts for Egypt) and Gabhet al Shabab el Qibti (the Coptic Youth Front). These initiatives had a twofold aim: first, to present a lay front to press for the rights of Coptic citizens "because we believed that the position of the church on incidents of sectarian violence was one of the principal reasons for the violation of Coptic citizens' rights," explained Tamri. The second reason for the formation of these movements was to encourage Coptic youth to engage in the political, social, and economic life of the nation and express their voices for themselves (as opposed to relying on the church to mediate their demands to the state and society).[25]

After 25 January 2011, revolution the Coptic youth activists dissolved these initiatives, convinced that there would be no need for a movement to advocate Coptic rights in the light of the unity that was displayed in the revolt to oust Mubarak. Yet in response to the growing pattern of sectarian assaults on Christians perpetrated by the Supreme Council of Armed Forces, the security forces, Islamist groups, and thugs, the youth realised that they needed to organise into a movement. Immediately after the Egyptian Revolution, there was an explosion of political activism in Egypt, which made people responsive to calls for collective action for demanding entitlements. Some of the Copts who had participated in the revolution, as well as those who did not, experienced a new political consciousness and formed and joined political parties and movements working on general liberties and democratic rights. Others established and joined movements and coalitions that specifically championed the rights of Coptic Christians in Egypt, and most became active on both fronts.

The Maspero movement (see Appendix) organised its first sit-in in March 2011 in response to the burning of a church in Atfeeh,[26] Giza, and the expulsion of Coptic families. They demanded the opening of the churches that were previously closed by the state security, the issuance of a unified church law, and the holding to account of the perpetrators of violence. A delegation of youth from the Maspero movement were invited to meet with members of the Supreme Council of Armed Forces (SCAF) and the prime minister to negotiate. The outcome was that SCAF rebuilt the church and the families who were evicted were returned to their homes. In May 2011, there was another incident involving the burning of churches in Imbaba, Cairo, and the Maspero youth movement and other Coptic movements went back to the streets to protest. When the Coptic Church leadership pressed them to stop their demonstrations, they refused until some of their demands were met: a commitment to the rebuilding of the burnt churches and the arrest of some of the known perpetrators.

A number of Coptic movements began to sprint out of the Maspero youth movement such as the Free Copts, Copts for Egypt, and the Coptic Union. A number of observations can be made regarding these coalitions and movements that emerged in the period 2011–2013.

First, all of the collective movements and initiatives cited in the following emerged in reaction to a perceived increase in violence and injustice to Copts as Egyptian citizens. In other words, they represent a collective response of defiance against increased violations of citizen rights. They did not emerge to make claims for a privileged position or to demand new rights for Copts in the post-Mubarak Egypt.

Second, all the actors perceive the rights of Copts as indivisible from the rights of Egyptian citizens and argue that rights can only be secured in a civil state, which is usually defined in their discourses as being of a non-religious character.

Third, all of the actors discussed in the following emphasise at length that they are autonomous from the church and strongly believe that the role of the Coptic lay movements is essential for the advancement of the rights of Christians. Some of these movements such as the Maspero youth movement have priests in their ranks who they insist should participate as citizens rather than church representatives.

Fourth, with the exception of a few collective actors (such as al Tahalof al Qibty al Misry) most of the movements have been engaged in street politics: organising sit-ins, marches, demonstrations, and candlelight memorial services. Their mode of activism reflects the political juncture at the time of their establishment: a country in the throes of an intense revolutionary struggle. In fact, many of the activists who participate in these Coptic movements are also active in broader political movements that are pressing for a democratic form of governance in Egypt.

Fifth, all of these actors adopted an ideological position opposed to the reign of the Muslim Brotherhood and strongly believed that in order to defend the rights of full citizenship for all, irrespective of religious affiliation, they needed to develop a collective front together with other Egyptians against the rule of the Islamists.

Sixth, the majority of these actors (exceptions are Al Tahalof Al Qibty Al Misry) were led by youth, and their membership comprised large numbers of youth. Though Coptic women were poorly represented in leadership positions (for the most part), these movements sought to build a broad-based constituency.

Seventh, many of these collective actors are still at a nascent phase of development. Their ability to act collectively in a sustained manner has been hampered by limited experience with mobilization, internal power struggles, poor resources, and weak leadership. Most of these movements have leaders who play musical chairs: A leader emerges in one movement and then exits to forge another movement or rotates from one initiative to the other simultaneously. There is still a need for broadening both the leadership circles as well as the membership base; otherwise, many of these nascent collective actors will be reduced to a closed circle of a group of friends.

However, the very presence of Coptic-based actors committed to responding to violations against Christians is critically important as they work to expose injustices, openly hold state and non-state actors accountable, and use a variety of mechanisms (such as legal redress, open protest, and outreach) to press for more rights. Equally important is the way in which they advocate their agenda, which involves coalition and alliance building with sympathetic allies, be they the youth revolutionary movements or the leaders of the Sufi orders. Such cross-cutting collective action has obstructed the image that they are only interested in advancing the rights of members who share their faith and has contributed to the emergence of a broad-based counter-coalition against perceived sources of injustice.

Coptic movements have also played a critical role in keeping a check on the political actions of Coptic churches, so that they would not be co-opted by the ruling powers. The Coptic protest movements together with leading Coptic figures played an incisive role in convincing the Coptic Orthodox Church to withdraw from the constituent assembly delegated by the Muslim Brotherhood–led government to draw Egypt's new constitution.

The acting pope, Bishop Pachomious, responded to the growing discontent felt by the Coptic movements by organising a meeting to which seventy-six representatives from Coptic movements and civil society activists, media persons, and legal experts were invited. Georgette Kalini, a legal expert and former MP, explained in an interview that in the meeting she urged the church leadership to withdraw from the constituent assembly. "I was warmly applauded from among those present and there was voting on three options for whether the church should withdraw, to freeze or to continue its representation in the constituent assembly. Sixty-seven voted for withdrawal, three for freezing the membership and three to continue," she recounts. Bishop Pachomious responded to the pulse of the wide prevailing sentiment among Coptic activists by deciding to withdraw the Coptic Orthodox Church from the constituent assembly.

Similar sentiments characterised followers of the Catholic and Protestant faiths, who also pressed their leaders to withdraw from the constituent assembly. The three churches united ranks and announced a joint position of withdrawing from the constituent assembly on the basis of a non-consensual decision-making process and the introduction of articles in the constitution that undermine inclusive citizenship for all. Their withdrawal had a ripple effect: Many non-Islamist figures and political party representatives followed suit and announced their resignation from the constituent assembly. The withdrawals led by the churches delegitimised the constitution in terms of both process and outcome. This success was due in large part to the mobilization work of the Coptic civil society, as well as the responsiveness of the church and their alliance building across the three denominations.

BROADER LESSONS FOR EXTERNAL ACTORS

For international policy-makers:

- At the time of writing, many in Egypt harbored an intensely anti-Western (in particular anti-American) sentiment on account of a perception that foreign governments endorsed the Muslim Brotherhood and rejected the June 2013 revolution as "a coup." Copts believed that the United States government only pursues its own interests and has no genuine commitment to human rights, including the rights of Christians. The contrast in the Western reactions to the assault on the Muslim Brotherhood and the assault on the Christians in the aftermath of the June 30th revolution greatly contributed to this impression. A deep mistrust among Copts towards the West has arisen, and there need to be measures to help people differentiate between government policy and a wide array of international civil society actors.

- It is vital that the lessons from Egypt's experience inform other countries currently in transition in order to safeguard the position of Christians there, in particular Libya and Syria, where attacks against Christians have been acute. The Egyptian experience has shown that while sectarianism is an outcome of decades of entrenched egalitarian policies and practices, the political ascendency of the Islamists in 2011 and assumption of governance in 2012 were major factors in creating the environment for increased persecution of Christians.
- It is important to work with local allies who have played a pioneering role in exposing, naming, and shaming those who have contributed to instigating sectarian hatred towards Christians. Such allies include persons in the media, political party representatives, and some youth revolutionary movements and coalitions.

For the research community:

- It is important to document thoroughly, meticulously, and systematically the deteriorating sectarian situation on the ground. This requires the institutionalisation of mechanisms supporting local efforts at documentation and wide documentary dissemination in both Arabic and English. A rigorous nationwide system of collecting quantitative and qualitative data does not exist to date.
- It is important to pursue an approach that is both sensitive to the intersectionality of identities and how these affect power configurations on the ground. For example, the intersection of class and religion makes poor and rich Christians vulnerable to different kinds of discrimination (one socio-cultural, one economic). Another example is the intersection of gender and religion, with Coptic women being victims of both misogyny and religious fanaticism at the hands of the religious conservatives in Egypt.
- It is important to adopt a contextually grounded approach to research that is cognizant of the wider forms of inequalities and repressions inherent in the current political order. For example, the judiciary, independent media, and

youth revolutionary movements are exposed to a process of political cleansing at the hands of the current regime, which tends to be very ruthless towards them. To focus exclusively on Christians without consideration for their embeddedness in a political system where other groups are also suffering is very dangerous for the framing of any research on minorities.

- Since the Egyptian Revolution, Egypt has witnessed an impressive and rich proliferation of artistic and cultural expression of voice and agency. This has manifested itself in graffiti, songs, films, and poetry. It would be worthwhile to capture both the contribution of Copts to this cultural wave as well as representations of Christians and Christian-Muslim relations in such media.
- It is critical that the transformations occurring within the Coptic Christian churches are also researched, in terms of shifts in their positioning, standpoints, and engagements with the state, as well as how their spirituality affects and is affected by the changing political context. For example, the move towards reconciliation across churches in Egypt has certainly been facilitated by the change in leadership of the Coptic Orthodox Church. However, it has also been driven by the sense of common danger facing all Christian faiths in the country.

CONCLUSION

The standpoint adopted in this chapter simultaneously privileges Coptic narratives of history and change and recognises the diversity of Coptic voices and agency. This is critical in order to prevent representing Copts in the person of the pope, a bishop, or a Coptic political figure. To do so would be highly reductionist of the diversity in political standpoints, age, gender, class, and geographic location. As with any population, agency and identity are multiple and fluid; for example, thousands of Coptic youths joined the protests composing the 25th of January revolution despite the fact that Pope Shenouda stood against it. In that instance, they rebelled against the authoritarian regime, parental authority, and the political stance of the Coptic Church.

The primary focus of this chapter has been on the contribution of Copts in civil society to the political life of the nation, exemplified in their participation in national struggles for liberation from authoritarian rule; in the formation of coalitions and movements that endorse full citizenship rights; in their support for revolutionary movements that have pressed for the fulfilment of the January 25th revolution's aims of bread, freedom, and dignity well after; and in their alliances with other religiously marginalised groups such as the Sufis. The unified Coptic Church's refusal to give its approval to any constitution that paves the way for encroachment on religious freedoms is also a powerful testament to how, withstanding all social and political pressures, the Christian churches can play a positive role in supporting a more inclusive social contract.

This is not to suggest that the Christians' advancement of religious freedom is necessarily always part of a broader human rights agenda that recognizes the indivisibility of rights. The record of Coptic political thought or civil activism (and especially that of the Coptic Orthodox Church) in advancing the rights of women or the poor has so far been disappointing. However, the outcome of struggles for the state recognising full citizenship rights for Egyptians irrespective of their religious affiliation is likely to have far-reaching benefits, even for those who are not Christian.

In order to understand the Copts' quest for equality in Egypt, this chapter has sought to dispel some of the common myths associated with the nature of religion-inspired discrimination and violence. It has argued that the scope, intensity, and geographic coverage of sectarian violence are worrisome. Over the past sixty years, the Egyptian state has played a central role in institutionalising discriminatory policies, practices, and decrees.

However, it is also important to recognise the ideological struggle over Egypt's identity and how it affects experiences of citizenship. The Islamist movements' project of instating an Islamist state in Egypt has demonstrated in practice a failure to show respect for religious diversity, whether within religion (in Islam) or across religions (with respect to Christians and other minorities). What this chapter has sought to show is that the large-scale participation of Copts in the June 30, 2013, revolution was a revolt against not only deteriorating living standards but also the rising levels of intolerance that they experienced on account of their religious difference. However, the overthrow of the Muslim Brotherhood will not automatically pave the way for an inclusive political or social order. The instatement of a democratic system and economic development are key to advancing citizen rights, but they will need to be complemented with specific measures that tackle religious discrimination in laws, state institutions, and public discourses.

If the current trend of large-scale Coptic emigration continues, the losses for religious diversity on a regional and national level will be immense. If the physical presence of the largest Christian community in the Arab world weakens, this would make some Christians living in other parts of the region question whether there is a place for them as minorities, where numerically and politically they have a weaker presence.

In Egypt, the marginalisation or emigration of Copts will severely undermine their political weight and prospects of influence of the secular liberal political parties, movements, and civil society. Coptic citizens have contributed to the development of ideas and practices around Egyptian citizenship. Fady Youssef, a Coptic activist, concedes that while the struggle against the Islamisation of Egyptian identity is attributable to collective action involving partnerships with liberal political parties and forces, "Copts represent the biggest power and the biggest line of defence for protecting the Egyptian identity."

If Copts continue to emigrate in large numbers, the mobilizing capacity of non-religious political forces to engage with the people will dramatically shrink. The Copts represent a political constituency whose power emanates from its size. What is critically important to note, however, is that they belong neither to a political party nor to the church. Instead, they have been a political constituency against the Brotherhood regime and are likely to act as such against any regime that marginalises them. While the Copts are not a monolithic entity, they have nonetheless been demonstrating a growing collective self-awareness due to attacks against them based on religious grounds. While such awareness has not produced a unified political group, there is nonetheless a constituency that is capable of rising en bloc. In the Egyptian context, in which opposition parties have struggled to forge a constituency, there is no doubt that any marginalisation of Copts will negatively affect local politics.[27]

Coptic civil society movements would also suffer if marginalisation of Coptic citizens continued. Coptic civil society movements have been extremely important in advancing human rights and democratic freedoms on three fronts: first, as coalition partners with democratic parties and movements in holding the government accountable for its performance; second, in exposing human rights violations against Coptic Christians and in serving as a pressure group on the government; and, third, for holding the Coptic churches' powers in check so that they will not forge alliances with the authorities that would harm the Coptic citizens. If Copts leave Egypt in large droves, their ability in particular to hold the church in check will be severely undermined. This will increase the lack of accountability of the church to its Coptic citizens. The economy will also suffer, as the closure of enterprises and economic activities will negatively affect the employment opportunities for the poor. Culturally, political movements that are interested in homogenising Egypt's religious identity would be deeply strengthened, and in the long run the culture of tolerance and respect for individual choice would be undermined.

APPENDIX

Name of initiative	Objective	Set up	Activities	Establishment	Founder	Distinctive attributes
1. Maspero	To defend the rights of citizens, in particular Copts	A political bureau for strategy and policy, a media spokesperson, a committee for training	Sit-ins, protests, issuance of reports	Formally in March 2011 when they protested against the sectarian violence in Atfeeh	Formed by revolutionary youth such as Ramy Kamel	Has been the largest, most renowned and in some cases most influential movement yet formed
2. Copts of Egypt coalition	Defence of the rights of all Egyptian citizens, in particular all groups that are marginalised in Egypt, including all kinds of religious minorities (such as Baha'is) and those politically excluded such as women	Founder, consultative committees, 16 branches of the coalition	Holding sit-ins when the people of Dahshour were evicted from their homes and sending a fact finding mission Having a protest with other movements against the first constituent committee and protests in the case of Abou Qorqas	Established on the first anniversary of Egyptian Revolution, January 2012	Fady Youssef, 28, founder	Membership open to all Egyptians, encouragement of people from different religious denominations to join; at one time headed by a Muslim who was elected Founders include bishops Bishoy & Paula, and Bishoy and Sheikh Saber

3. Free Copts	The civility of the state (non-religion, non-military), Participating in monitoring the elections to identify problems faced by Coptic citizens	Low level of institutionalisation	Participate in protests demanding rights of Copts	Founders were friends who had participated in the 25th of January Revolution, and were then interested in apolitical activities such as cleaning up the square, assisting senior citizens with mobility; in March 2013, Muslim Brotherhood invited them to meeting with Prime Minister Essam Sharaf; a they then formed the movement to have a collective representation	Walaa Aziz, 29	50 members	"Our greatest ambition is to go back to the military state"
4. Copts without Qoyoud	To defend the rights of Coptic citizens as indivisible from the rights of the rest of Egyptian citizens	Movement does not seem to have mobilised a constituency, and seems organisationally weak	Marches, protests, candlelit sit-ins, issuance of condemnatory statements after events	Established out of the protests that began in Maspero by Copts in March 2011	Nine founders including Sherif Ramzy, Ibram Louis, Mina Magdy, George Noshy, Haytham Kameel	Has been very responsive in speedy issuance of statements to condemn most forms of assault on rights of Copts, including Coptic Orthodox Church; however, founders (at the time of writing) now limited to 4, as a consequence of people exiting to form their own movements/initiatives; without a consistuency base, fate is unclear	

(continued)

Name of initiative	Objective	Set up	Activities	Establishment	Founder	Distinctive attributes
5. Al tahalof al Qipty al Misry Coptic Egyptian coalition	Defence of rights of Copts, endorsement of citizenship	Dr Mona Makram Ebeid is the head of board of directors, Tharwat Bekheet secretary general, board of 15 members; decisions by voting when disagreement arises	Activities include formation of legal defence team to endorse the rights of Copts in major lawsuits the initiation of lawsuits themselves where infringements have materialised Monitoring and documenting abuses	Realised that despite high Coptic participation in January 2011 Revolution, still excluded from new political parties and movements	Hany Bahna, Ihab Ramzy (later to become MP), Adel Roshdy, Tharwat Bakheet, Kamal Sedrak	Unlike other initiatives established post January Revolution, collective action does not engage in street politics, not led by youth revolutionary activists, but by high-ranking Coptic members of society
6. Egyptian Sufi-Coptic Alliance	To act as counter force against radical Islamist movements and forces To promote minority rights To engage in joint serve activities to help communities	Sheikh Alaa Abou el Aza'em head of the alliance, Ihab Ramzy e secretary general, clergy representatives from different Christian denominations, and representatives from 15 Sufi Ways[a]	Organization of several conferences to counter radical Islamist threat, including one to announce joint rejection of constitution	Movement formed after "Kandahar Friday," which convinced them of the need for forces between the Sufi Way and the Copts[b]	Alaa Ramzy, Sheikh Alaa Abou el Aza'em	Represents strong form of Muslim-Christian co-operation *from below*; organised by religious and lay persons across the spectrum; Christian Sufi followers large bloc of substantial political weigh.

		Intends to register as NGO	Organized mass demonstration with theme "in the love of Egypt" to counter "Kandahar Friday" Organised march to Coptic cathedral after assault on it Has contributed to building of hospital in impoverished area Bani Mazar		Important to note that Sufi orders have also seen assault on their shrines, making them keen to collaborate in collective front against extremism
7. Alliance for the victims of kidnapping and forced disappearance	To assist Coptic girls and women who have disappeared and wish to return to families To provide legal assistance and psychological support for families of girls who have disappeared	Comprises 20 activists and lawyers Considering registering as NGO	Documentation of cases of missing girls and women Awareness-raising seminars among families via churches Provision of legal aid for families on how to file lawsuit for missing girls Sit-ins to demand return of missing girls/women	Established in 2010 after disappearance of Magdalene Essam, alleged to have converted to Islam Ibram Louis, 24; George Noshy, Gehan Atta	Alliance established at the same time as "New Muslims" composed of members of various Islamist groups, to defend rights of women they believe converted to Islam and held against their will by Coptic Church Alliance has sought to collaborate with Salafis to identify whereabouts of absent women; occasionally successful

(continued)

Name of initiative	Objective	Set up	Activities	Establishment	Founder	Distinctive attributes
8. Coptic Youth Front (Gabhet al Shabab al Qibty)	To defend rights of Copts through independent platform	Saeed Fayez, co-ordinator, is opposed to institutionalisation of movement; 8–12 core members	Fact finding missions and documentation in two key incidents of assaults on Copts (Al Ameriyya Church, All Saints Church)	Established in 2010 after attack on church in al Ameriyya, Giza.	Saeed Fayez, late Mina Daniel, Ramy Kamel	Saeed refers to the Coptic youth front as "wave" – a time bound initiative that energised the Coptic scene, generated new Coptic youth leaders, who then led other more sustained movements

[a] Including renowned public religious figures such as Sameh Maurice, pastor of the Evangelical Church in Cairo, and Bishop Yohanna Kolta of the Catholic Church.
[b] Kandahar Friday refers to the mass demonstrations organised by the Muslim Brotherhood in alliance with the ultra-radical Salafis and other Islamist movements on August 29, 2011, to demand the instatement of an Islamist state and the implementation of the sharia.

NOTES

1 There is considerable dispute about the Coptic Christian percentage of the population in Egypt. The Pew Research Center estimates that Christians make up about 5 percent of the population, but this figure is based on the Egyptian government census (CAPMAS), which tends to undercount the Coptic population (See "Global Christianity – A Report on the Size and Distribution of the World's Christian Population," Pew Research Center, December 2011, http://www.pewforum.org/files/2011/12/Christianity-fullreport-web.pdf). On the other hand, Coptic Church sources, based on recorded baptisms across the diocese, put the figure at nearly 23 percent, a figure, however, that includes some in the diaspora ("The Number of Copts in Egypt," *Akhir Sa'a*, 18 June 2012). Mohamed Hassanein Heikal, a renowned historian and political figure, said that a more realistic estimate of the Coptic population is 10 percent: Mohamed Haikal, *Autumn of Fury* (London: Andre Deutsch, 1983).

2 I facilitated the four focus groups in December 2012 with the very capable assistance of the local researcher and development practitioner Mina Wagdy. I am grateful for Mina's facilitation of all four focus groups in August 2013 since because of the high-risk security situation and the halting of the national railways between Cairo and Minya, I was unable to be there in person.

3 I am extremely grateful for the very capable research assistance rendered by Nader Shoukry, one of the most prolific and competent journalists in Egypt covering sectarian violence against Christians. Nader identified the founders of the different movements and undertook the interviews with them in Cairo between December and March 2012. Nader also interviewed prominent political figures such as Georgette Kallini, who shared her analysis of the political struggles occurring at the time.

4 This is a deeply controversial question because the national census has not released population figures disaggregated along religious affiliation since 1986. The state and Islamists have tended to deflate the percentage while the Coptic Church has tended to inflate the figure. Tharwat Bassily, a former member of the Majlis al-Milli (a lay consultative body to the Coptic Church), said in an interview in January 2012 that the total population of Copts was 18,565,484 as of January 2012. Given that CAPMAS's official figure for the total population is 81,395,000, this would suggest that Copts represent 22.81 percent of the population ("Number of Copts in Egypt," *Akhir Sa'a*).

5 Gamal Nkrumah, "Hail the Holy Synod," *Al-Ahram Weekly*, 22 March 2012, http://weekly.ahram.org.eg/2012/1090/eg20.htm

6 Michael Adel, "The Copts Flee Egypt," *Al Ahram Weekly*, 4 April 2013, accessed on 10 November 2013, http://weekly.ahram.org.eg/News/2402/24/The-Copts-flee-Egypt.aspx

7 Abdel Rahman Youssef, "Egyptian Copts, It's All in the Number," *Al Akhbar English*, 30 September 2012, accessed 10 November 2013, http://english.al-akhbar.com/content/egyptian-copts-its-all-number

8 This section relied on ethnographic observations in urban squatter settlements and rural communities in Minya and interviews with informants and members of the communities there. It is therefore difficult to generalise for the entire country, and there have been no studies published documenting such processes.

9 This section is an abridged version of parts of chapter 1 of M. Tadros, *Copts at the Crossroads: The Challenge of Building Inclusive Democracy in Egypt* (Cairo: American University in Cairo Press, 2013).

10 The word "dhimmitude" is from *dhimmi*, an Arabic word meaning "protected." *Dhimmi* was the name applied by the Arab-Muslim conquerors to indigenous non-Muslim populations who surrendered by a treaty (*dhimma*) to Muslim domination. "The Status of Non-Muslim Minorities under Islamic Rule," Dhimmitude, http://www.dhimmitude.org/.

11 See Atiya 1968: 87 in Tadros, *Copts at the Crossroads*.

12 See chapters 3 and 4 in Tadros, *Copts at the Crossroads* for further details on sectarian violence under Mubarak.

13 Michael Georgy and Yasmine Saleh, "Tycoon Sawiris to Invest in Egypt, Fears Economic Collapse," *Reuters*, 14 November 2013, accessed 15 November 2013, http://news.yahoo.com/tycoon-sawiris-invest-egypt-fears-economic-collapse-085740993.html

14 Al Shark Al Awsat, "Sawiris: I Intervened to Purchase Stock from Orascom Not with the Purpose of Profit," *Ahmed Abou el Wafa*, 5 April 2011, accessed 5 October 2013, http://www.aawsat.com/details.asp?section=6&article=615773&issueno=11816#.UoV-YOI7nKd

15 The word "liberal" here does not refer to economic orders but political orientations.; it refers to leftist, left of center, and right of centre political ideologies that can all be distinguished from more right-leaning political parties that use political Islam as an ideological framework for their political projection.

16 A nuanced analysis of Coptic participation in the 25 January revolution suggests that while they participated as Egyptians, some of the grievances that led to their "tipping over" were associated with the sectarian policies of the Mubarak regime and the rising violence that they have been subjected to, which they believed occurred with government complicity.

17 Abby Ohlheiser, "Here's What Today's Massive Anti-Morsi Protests in Egypt Looked Like," *Wire*, 30 June 2013, accessed 4 July 2013, http://www.theatlanticwire.com/global/2013/06/heres-what-todays-massive-anti-morsi-protests-egypt-looked/66728/

18 For security reasons, Kasr el Doubara Church cancelled holding the event in Tahrir Square and instead held it in one of Cairo's northern suburbs. However, the event was attended by a large number of Muslims in addition to Christians from different denominations, though the church could not accommodate the kinds of numbers that would have convened in Tahrir Square.

19 Sarah Carr, "Beyond the Walls of the Church," *Egypt Independent*, 1 April 2012, http://www.egyptindependent.com/news/beyond-walls-church

20 This is based on analysis of data collected through a grant from the Swiss Development Cooperation (SDC) to IDS.

21 This refers to two sets of focus groups, one set undertaken in May 2011 in Cairo, Minya, and Fayoum for an SDC-Egypt assignment and the other undertaken in Minya for Georgetown's Religious Freedom Project.

22 Many women were subjected to sexual assault in protest spaces between 2012 and 2013.

23 This section covers the movements and coalitions that were established to protest state discriminatory policy towards Copts; however, there are many other initiatives that have been established in recent years that were for other purposes such as the Coptic lay movement (formed in 2006 to promote internal church reform, transparency, and accountability) and "Group 38," a Coptic lobby group demanding the reform of Coptic personal status law to allow for divorce under the conditions set out in the church decree of 1938, which was later abrogated.

24 See M. Tadros, "Vicissitudes in the Coptic Church-State Entente in Egypt," *International Journal of Middle East Studies* 41, no. 2 (2009): 269–287.

25 Please see the Appendix for a table of the key Coptic movements to have emerged in the period around the Egyptian Revolution of 2011.

26 For a detailed discussion of the sectarian assaults witnessed in 2011 after the Revolution, see chapter 6 of Tadros, *Copts at the Crossroads*.

27 M. Tadros, "The Brothers and the Copts," *Middle East Institute*, 12 August 2013, http://www.mei.edu/content/backlash-after-demise-brothers-and-copts

13

Between the Hammer and the Anvil: Indigenous Palestinian Christianity in the West Bank

Duane Alexander Miller and Philip Sumpter

INTRODUCTION

The indigenous Christian population of the West Bank is a shrinking, historically fragmented community whose contribution to civil society outweighs its small size. The theme of this essay is these Christians' unique contribution in a context that nevertheless seems set to squeeze them increasingly out of their homeland. We say "squeeze," as the major sources of pressure arise from two directions, both Jewish and Muslim. From the Jewish side, the challenge arises from the consequences of the Israeli occupation of the West Bank. From the Muslim side, the challenge arises from the growing influence of the radical Islamic movements. Corruption within the Palestinian Authority (PA) also appears to have created an economic and social situation in the country that many Palestinian Christians refuse to tolerate, choosing instead to vote with their feet.

Much has been written on this topic, and it is not our purpose to provide a synthesis of the secondary literature. Within the framework of Georgetown's Christianity and Freedom Project, our mandate is to provide fresh fieldwork on the current situation, situated within a broader grasp of the contemporary scenario.

As such, the paper is set out as follows: A brief introduction by Phil Sumpter will provide the historical, social, and political context. The next section, authored by Duane Miller, will describe the findings of our fieldwork, which is the prime focus of this essay.[1] This fieldwork is based on a two-week sojourn in the West Bank, where we interviewed representatives of the various traditional churches about the challenges their communities face and the responses that are being provided. In both sections, the authors have been in dialogue with one another so that our ideas have been mutually influential.

OVERVIEW: INDIGENOUS CHRISTIANITY IN THE
CONTEMPORARY WEST BANK

Historical Overview

The decisive event that has shaped the contemporary context is the war of 1948, called the War of Independence by (Jewish) Israelis and the Catastrophe (al Nakba) by Palestinians. In short, the General Assembly of the United Nations had adopted a proposal for the political future of the region in 1947, which envisioned the existence of two states side by side, an Arab state and a Jewish one (the Jews were to receive some 55 percent of the country [much of the allotted area being desert] and the Arabs about 40 percent).[2] Jerusalem and the Bethlehem area were to be a *corpus separatum* under an international regime due to their unique multireligious significance.

The Jews eventually accepted the decision and declared the State of Israel upon the withdrawal of the British on May 14, 1948. The Arabs rejected the decision and invaded. The result was that Israeli forces occupied more territory than originally stipulated in the UN proposal (78 percent of the territory constituting former Mandatory Palestine), and the land was divided into three regions: Jordan annexed the West Bank, along with East Jerusalem; Egypt occupied Gaza; and Israel gained control of the rest (the Golan Heights remained in Syrian hands until the Six Day War in 1967).

The impact was traumatic for all the local Arabs, regardless of religion (although the Israeli historian Benny Morris does note that Christians and Druze, who were less involved in anti-Zionist militancy, at times received less aggressive treatment than Muslims).[3] Many fled to neighboring countries for a number of complex and interconnected reasons, such as the general hostilities, breakdown of the economy and law and order, encouragement by Arab forces, expulsion by Jewish forces, flight of the Arab elite inspiring the Arab poor to leave, and others.[4] Many expected to return, but after the war Israel closed its doors (an exception was Israel's Reunion of Families Scheme).[5] In time, a physical return was made progressively impossible, as many of the villages were either bulldozed or resettled with incoming Jewish immigrants.[6] The Palestinian sociologist Bernard Sabella claims that 7 percent of the 714,000 Palestinian refugees were Christian (i.e., 50,000 people) – 35 percent of the total Christian population.[7]

In 1967, Israel launched what became known as the Six Day War, a preemptive attack that successfully gained control of the Golan Heights from Syria, the West Bank and East Jerusalem from Jordan, and Gaza/Sinai from Egypt. The Sinai

Peninsula was eventually returned to Egypt in 1977 after the two signed a peace treaty, the Golan Heights and East Jerusalem were annexed, and the West Bank remained under Israeli military occupation.[8]

After the Six Day War, the Arab-Israeli conflict underwent a process of "Palestinization," as indigenous Arabs organized themselves politically to take matters into their own hands rather than depend on other Arab states. This new form of national consciousness also spread to the Arabs in Israel, particularly Christians, who up until that point had largely identified with Israel's mixed Arab-Jewish Communist Parties. In 1974, the Palestinian Liberation Organization (PLO) was recognized by the Arab League as the official representative of the Palestinian people rather than Jordan, which finally rescinded its claims in 1988. In addition to providing a political voice and identity, a primary purpose of the new organization was the armed liberation of the whole of Israel-Palestine, a goal it sought to achieve using violent means that many defined as terrorist.

Since the establishment of the PLO, Christians have distinguished themselves in the organization mainly as spokespersons and theoreticians, and they have been less involved in the military arms of the organization.[9]

A major milestone in the Palestinian national cause was the First Intifada (1987–1993), a spontaneous uprising against harsh Israeli rule that was initially nonviolent in nature. Indeed, many Christians played a role in preaching nonviolent civil disobedience. Mubarak Awad, for example, established the Palestinian Center for Non-Violence in 1985. In the late 1980s, the largely Christian town of Beit Sahour launched the "taxes revolt," in which they refused to pay taxes, suffering heavy penalties as a result. Beit Sahour was to win several international prizes for its nonviolent struggle.[10]

This conflict ended in 1993 with the Oslo Peace Accords. The PLO promised to recognize the State of Israel and cease armed conflict, while Israel promised a gradual disengagement from the territories and the facilitation of the creation of an independent Palestinian state. The process failed, and a Second Intifada (2000–2005) started, this time far more violent than the first, particularly because of the increased involvement of Islamic groups such as Hamas.

Since then, the Palestinian leader Yasser Arafat has died, and Hamas was voted into power. In fact, many Christians voted for Hamas as an act of protest against the Palestinian Authority, though in hindsight many regret this decision, given Hamas's sharia-based approach to governance (this reaction has been communicated to us both directly and indirectly in numerous conversations). Conflict then broke out between Hamas and members of Arafat's more secular Fatah Party, with the result that Hamas now rules Gaza, while Fatah controls the West Bank. Hamas is religiously obliged to seek the destruction of Israel; Fatah is largely committed to secularism and has recently renounced the use of violence.

On the Israeli side, there has been a marked growth in antipathy toward Arabs and an erosion of hope for the possibility of peace. The most recent response to the violence by the government has been to cordon off both Gaza and the West Bank by constructing huge separation barriers. For the West Bank, it roughly follows the 1949 armistice treaty line (the so-called Green Line), though much of it is built inside Palestinian land – sometimes up to six kilometers – and around many of the still-expanding illegal Jewish settlements. Although it has been highly effective in reducing the number of suicide bombings in Israel, it is suffocating the Palestinian economy, has cordoned off the Palestinian people from important medical and economic resources, has hindered free movement within the territories, and is threatening a de facto annexation of further Palestinian land (the Israeli authorities claim that the barrier is not permanent).

These dire conditions affect all Palestinians in the West Bank equally, regardless of religious affiliation. However, in recent years Christians have been having markedly more success in getting entry permits to Israel than Muslims, an issue raised in our interviews. Another recent development is the so-called price tag attacks perpetrated by more radical elements within the Jewish settlement movement, in which Christian and Muslim religious symbols and institutions are desecrated in retaliation for any action taken against their settlement enterprise – even if that action is taken by the Israeli government itself.[11]

General Characteristics of West Bank Christians under the Palestinian Authority and Israel

There are perhaps four significant features of indigenous Palestinian Christians that affect their status and ability to respond to their environment: 1) They are historically fragmented along denominational lines yet recently united – at least among the leadership – along political lines; 2) they often have powerful international advocates by virtue of their denominational affiliation; 3) they tend to be highly educated; and 4) they are shrinking as a community at an alarming rate.

1) Concerning fragmentation, a region of such theological significance as the Holy Land has obviously attracted a large array of denominations, each wanting to maintain some kind of contact with the holy places. Historically, the Greek Orthodox have been the primary indigenous denomination, though missionary activity by both Catholics and Protestants has reduced that majority and further contributed to denominational diversity. For instance, one Catholic strategy has been to set up churches, such as the Greek Catholic Church, that maintain local, non-Latin traditions and have their own hierarchy but are under the pope in Rome.[12]

Despite this historical diversity, however, there has been a growing rapprochement among Church leaders that coincides with the "Arabization" of the clergy. The initially largely foreign clergy remained neutral concerning political developments in the early phase of Israel's history, but their gradual Arabization from the late 1960s onward, climaxing in the appointment of Michael Sabbah as Latin patriarch in Jerusalem in the 1980s, led to a sea change in the churches' attitudes to politics and even to each other (the Greek Orthodox Church has retained the hegemony of the Greeks). Politically, leaders now openly speak out against Israeli policies, and church leaders worked together in a previously unheard-of manner.

In addition, the higher and more Western education of the clergy has enabled them to mediate between the Palestinians and the West. One prominent example was the publication in 1987 of a strongly worded joint statement signed by all "Heads of the Christian Communities in Jerusalem" – including the ethnically Greek Orthodox patriarch – describing the suffering of the Palestinians and protesting the activities of the Israeli authorities. It was addressed to the international community and called upon the UN to take action. Another significant document is the so-called Kairos for Palestine (2009). Modeled on the 1985 South African Kairos document, this ecumenical statement decries Israeli policies as well as Christian Zionist interpretations of the Bible, repeatedly advocates nonviolent resistance, and calls for the international community to boycott Israel.[13] Since then, other institutes have been set up in order to make Christian theology and practice relevant to the Palestinian national cause. These are the Tantur Ecumenical Institute for Theological Studies, the Al-Liqa' Center, and the Sabeel Institute, which have become venues for the development of a "contextual Palestinian theology."[14] A major theme of public statements, publications, and even theological content has been the oneness of the Palestinian people – Christian and Muslim – and the attempt to articulate and endorse a unity that transcends these religious divides.

A major impetus toward uniting these two religious groups has been the Palestinian experience of a common enemy: Israel. As one Bethlehemite stated in an interview with Bowman in 1990, "We forget our religion; we forget our political groups. The bullets do not differentiate between Christian and Muslim, PLO, DFLP, etc."[15] Yet despite efforts by Christians and many secular-leaning Muslims to advance a single Palestinian *ethnic* rather than *religious* identity, lived experience has often proved disappointing, with many scholars noting a growing fragmentation of Palestinian identity along sectarian lines.[16] Part of the source of the tension appears to be related to unequal distributions of power within the Occupied Territories, in which religious identity is only tangential to the persecution. At times there appears to be a growing radicalization of Islamic elements among Palestinian society.

The issue of the distribution of power has been treated in a recent article by Baard Kaartveit. He argues that during the first ten years following the signing of the Oslo Accords, "Palestinian institutions were ridden with corruption, incompetence, and a systematic misuse of economic funds and human resources. For a long time ...

the Palestinian Authority failed to establish a functioning legal system and a rule of law in the occupied territories."[17] Limitations placed upon the coercive power of the authority by the terms of the accords did not help matters. As a result, the PA enjoyed little trust and legitimacy among local Palestinians, who thus turned to more traditional institutions to regulate matters of justice.

One of these institutions is the patrilineal family clan, which can provide individual and family security. With the collapse of PA institutions during the Second Intifada, this process has been accelerated. This arrangement, however, is disadvantageous to Christians, for they are a minority with a less developed clan system. Their ability, therefore, to attain justice in a range of cases (murder, manslaughter, rape, and theft of land using forged documents) is severely curtailed.[18] Kaartveit tentatively suggests that religion is not the primary motivator in these crimes, placing the blame instead on human greed and the failures of the legal system.

A number of scholars have, however, also pointed out the growth in religiously motivated violence directed toward Christians.[19] Examples are vandalism of Christian institutions, public displays of disrespect, coercion to live according to Islamic mores (such as not smoking during Ramadan and wearing headscarves), graffiti threatening the extermination of Christians once the Jewish problem has been solved, and unjust treatment by the police force. Often the persecution takes the form of continuous doubt about the authenticity of Christian commitment to the "Arab" cause, the assumption being that as a "Western religion" Christians can only be secret Zionists or sympathizers with colonialism. (Palestinian Christians often point out the irony of this accusation, made in the Holy Land, of all places.) Two ethnographies by Bowman and Lybarger document the gradual drift of Palestinians back into a more religiously, rather than nationalistically, defined sense of identity as a response, as well as their sense of betrayal by many of their Muslim compatriots, who they feel are becoming more radicalized. Significantly, these sentiments are often only mentioned in private conversation and hardly addressed publicly.

This tension between political dream and lived reality as well as differing interpretations of that experience are major themes of our fieldwork.

2) The names of the various churches listed previously reveal the second significant feature: their international character. The center of power and influence for each denomination lies outside the country.[20] The Latin Church obviously submits to Rome, but the prelates of the new churches that have submitted to Rome are also located outside the country.

For example, the archbishop of the most numerous church in Israel-Palestine, the Greek Catholics, is located in Damascus, Syria, as is the head of the Syriac Orthodox Church. The Syriac Catholic archbishop resides in Beirut, Lebanon. The dominant Greek Orthodox Church is closely affiliated with Greece, to such a degree that local Arab Orthodox consider it a foreign "occupier," more concerned with serving Hellenic interests than those of local Arab Christians. In our fieldwork, we will see how this international connection has helped local churches create work on the ground.[21]

3) The third factor is the above-average educational levels of Palestinian Christians compared to their non-Christian counterparts. According to Sabella, for example, "the percentage of Christians with a secondary certificate, or higher qualification, is almost twice the percentage in the general population, while the percentage of Christians with an academic degree is close to three times the general percentage."[22] An initial reason is the activity of Western missionaries, who, since the nineteenth century, have built not only hospitals and orphanages in the region but also numerous schools. These schools remain the best in the region, attracting many of the Muslim elite. They have also opened Palestinians up to a more secular, Western worldview, making it easier for them to act as intermediaries between the Islamic elements of Palestinian society and the West. A prominent example is the Anglican politician Hanan Ashrawi, who has served as the PA's spokeswoman to the West for many years.[23] Our fieldwork reveals how local Christians interpret the meaning of this contribution to Palestinian society as a whole. It also reveals an unintended drawback: its ability to facilitate Christian emigration and thus contribute to the diminishing of the local community.

4) This takes us to the final point: Palestinian Christians are a shrinking minority. In 1922, for example, 11 percent of the Arab population of Mandatory Palestine was Christian, whereas in 1946 this number had sunk to 8 percent.[24] Within the State of Israel in the 1990s, they constituted 2.6 percent of the entire population, with Arabs constituting 14 percent.[25] In the West Bank, East Jerusalem, and Gaza during the same period, they may have constituted 1.5 percent of the total population.[26]

This trend in fact started during the Ottoman Empire as Christians fled abroad to seek economic and religious freedom from Turkish-Muslim oppression, though the events of recent history have accelerated the trend. According to Lybarger, the primary factors for this "implosion" of the Christian population include "declining fertility rates; persistent political upheaval, especially the wars of 1948 and 1967; and the concomitant loss of educational and job opportunities."[27] The ability of Christians to emigrate is enhanced by their Western-style education and the already expansive Palestinian-Christian diaspora. As our fieldwork revealed, this final characteristic of indigenous Christianity tended to be the most pressing issue in the minds of our informants.

Having provided a brief overview of the historical, political, and economic context in which Christians live along with some of the salient features of the contemporary community, we now turn to our own fieldwork in the West Bank.

A POISED EXISTENCE: CHRISTIANS IN THE WEST BANK (2013)

Research Question and Methodology

We carried out two weeks of field research in the West Bank.[28] Insights and experiences from previous fieldwork in the Arab world were likewise included.[29] This section will focus on material procured in the West Bank *within* the boundaries of the separation barrier because Jerusalem's status is complex and problematic. This research was carried out in Bethlehem, Jericho, Nablus, Rafidia, Ramallah, Taybeh, and Zebabdah. These locales are both small and large, traditionally Christian or not. We intentionally spoke with women as well as men and laity as well as clergy. Some interesting information resulted from casual conversations rather than structured interviews. Interviews were carried out in Arabic, English, or Spanish. All interviewees were informed that this was for a project on Christianity and freedom in relation to their communities (*tawaa'if*) in the West Bank (research in Gaza was not possible because of security issues). Notes were recorded by hand and then transcribed to Microsoft Word or recorded using an audio recorder and then transcribed to Microsoft Word.

A stereotype of the Palestinian Christian living under the Israeli occupation of the West Bank is one of powerlessness and victimhood. This section explores how some Christians are exercising agency for the sake of maintaining their position as a small minority in Palestinian society. "Agency" refers to exercise of power for the sake of accomplishing a goal in order to further one's interests. This agency-centered approach to research leads to a further question: What are the interests of the Palestinian Christians, and are they in fact engaged in the activity of discerning their own interests?

Counteracting Emigration

Housing

Our research suggested that one primary interest or concern of Christians in the West Bank is their continued existence in their land. Since continued existence is a prerequisite of any action and nonaction for and against freedom, and since substantial agency was deployed for the sake of avoiding the extinction of Palestinian Christianity, this must be explored.

When asked about the main difficulties and challenges that Christian Palestinians face, the two most common answers were closely related: the economy and Christian emigration. Another, but less frequent, concern was restricted freedom of movement, especially in relation to international travel. The latter refers to the well-documented Israel Defense Forces checkpoints and other travel restrictions.[30]

Interviewees related economic difficulties to differing extents in relation to the occupation, however. One said that if the occupation ended tomorrow, the economy would still not improve; another said that it might improve, but that there were "other problems," namely, corruption in the PA; and one said that everything would be great. In all, there were differing opinions on the relationship between the economy and occupation, and the interviewees were aware of the economic difficulties in nearby countries not under occupation, such as Jordan and Egypt. One interviewee noted that Palestine (Gaza included) has few natural resources.

The economic situation was problematic, in part, because of what it caused – emigration of Christians. While Muslims emigrate, too, their continued existence in the West Bank is not perceived as imperiled by the people with whom we spoke, whereas the continued existence of Christians is. Here is where we find clear examples of agency. Young Christians emigrate, even though the interest of the larger Christian community is that they not do so. They emigrate because they cannot find jobs, or if they find jobs, they do not have the funds to procure a home, marry, and have children.

A solution is to construct affordable housing. In this area the Latin Church excelled, though other churches also made their contributions. We found completed buildings or planned building projects around Bethlehem, Jerusalem, Rafidia, Taybeh, and Nazareth (an Arab city in Israel). In terms of our own limited fieldwork, we perceived that the primary interest of Palestinian Christians is simply survival, or avoiding extinction by emigration. The construction of affordable housing for young families represents a concrete attempt to avoid that.

Employment

But even with housing, there remains the question of work. Throughout the entire West Bank, unemployment was reported to be a big problem, for both Muslims and Christians, with one recent estimate placing it at 16.5 percent, though several respondents alleged it was higher.[31] The secretary of the Orthodox bishop of Bethlehem lamented that Christians finished university and approached the diocese for jobs, jobs that the diocese could not provide. Father Jack, a Greek Catholic priest in Taybeh, explained how he tried to teach his people to be self-dependent and not to look to the church for money or work. One of his main concerns is self-sufficiency. While the church *may* provide housing or (rarely) a job, the people must not develop a mentality of dependency on their church. He referred to this mental attitude as "the inner occupation."

This is a source of tension for the churches in the West Bank: How can they improve the economic situation of their people while not fostering a sense of dependence and patronage? The question was not resolved on a general level, as far as we could tell. But we did note that there was not only an awareness that dependency was undesirable, but also that creating jobs or helping people to gain profitable skills was desirable. Father Jack's own response was to communicate in sermons and in his pastoral ministry that Christians bear responsibility and may live in hope. In doing this, the priest was drawing on his pastoral, biblical, and ecclesiastical resources as a pastor, preacher, and teacher of the local community, reminding us that not all resources that lead to change are immediately related to political, military, or financial power.

While catering to tourists and pilgrims has long provided employment to some Palestinians, both Muslim and Christian, the flow of tourists and pilgrims in a volatile region such as the Middle East is often erratic. Outbreaks of violence between Palestinians and Jews lead to a slump in visitors, but even conflagrations in foreign countries including Lebanon and Egypt can cause the number of visitors to plummet from one week to the next.[32] While tourism and pilgrimage are and will continue to be important sources of income for Christians in particular and the PA in general, the sector as it exists presently clearly does not provide enough jobs, and so Christians have explored ways to address this problem.[33]

The desire to create work manifested itself in several manners. Sometimes the jobs were specifically for Christians, sometimes not. Sometimes the efforts were initiatives of foreigners and sometimes of the indigenous Christians. An example of a foreign initiative was that of the Salesians in Bethlehem, where they had an arts center for training locals in olive wood carving. During an interview with a Roman Catholic laywoman from Rome, she explained that the craftsmanship of carving olive wood had been largely lost. People had learned to make only a few stock figures, rather than master the authentic craft itself. Paradoxically, she mentioned that the ongoing construction of the separation wall (of which she was very critical) had led to a fall in prices for olive wood, as so many olive trees were being uprooted to make way for it, and other countries in the Middle East did not have abundant supplies. She felt that the supply of raw material might well be in danger soon. Nonetheless, this is an example of an endeavor originating and funded from outside the region that not only promotes the revival of an indigenous craft but provides people with a marketable skill.[34]

An example of an indigenous effort to create work can be found in the small and once predominantly Christian town of Zebabdah near Jenin. After reviving a moribund parish, the local Greek Catholic priest started partnering with Western Christians who arrive on short-term missions and help to rebuild/expand the church facility. It is one example of ecumenical partnership (many of the Americans are Presbyterians, he says). Once the separation wall had gone up, people in the town were limited in terms of selling their olives. He had a man who knew how to make olive oil soap teach his skills to the locals. Now that soap is sold abroad. Other projects had been undertaken: hand stitching things for women at home and then selling them via his international allies, and a future project to construct a building in which the lower floors would be rented as shops and the upper levels would function as residences.

These are but two examples that demonstrate the diversity in approaches of such projects.[35] Neither of them could have been completed without assistance from abroad. One initiative was local, the other foreign. Both relied on local natural resources coupled with honing the skills of locals. One was focused mostly on Christians, the other equally on both Muslim and Christians.[36]

Education

When asked how the West Bank would be different if all the Christians were gone, one recurring answer involved education. One Arab Latin nun felt that the educational services provided by Christians to both Christian and Muslim students were highly appreciated. Many respondents felt that Christian education had a kind of leavening effect on society in that it inculcated an ethic of peacemaking and tolerance among students. According to Madanat and Twal, inculcating tolerance and unity is an explicit policy in the Latin Patriarchate's educational endeavors. As they put it:

> The philosophy of the Latin Patriarchate Schools (LPS) concentrates on bringing Muslims and Christians together. Accordingly the schools are places to facilitate interfaith understanding among the Muslim and Christian students and teachers in them. . . . Moreover the schools' philosophy reinforces a spirit of unity and resists any spirit of dissimilarity or discrimination.[37]

In reference to education, the Latin Church, while not large in terms of indigenous membership, was a clear leader. As of 2012, the Latin Patriarchate and various Catholic religious orders, most notably the Franciscans, supervised thirteen schools in Palestine, while having only twelve parishes or congregations there. This commitment to education spreads beyond Palestine to Israel (five schools) and Jordan (twenty-three schools).[38] These educational institutions serve all ages, from small children through the university level, and include one of the most important universities in the West Bank, namely, Bethlehem University.

While the Latin Christians are the most significant educational Christian presence in Palestine, other communities have made contributions. A few examples are the Ramallah Friends Schools, two Quaker schools in Ramallah; the Christian National Kindergarten of the Episcopal Church in Nablus; and the Talitha Kumi Evangelical

Lutheran School in Beit Jala. Even in Hebron, which has a tiny Christian population, there is an Arab Evangelical School. Christians have also been key players in higher education; Birzeit University was founded by the Naser family, who are Palestinian Christians, a fact that the history section of their Web site does not mention.[39] It is within this context of a robust educational program sponsored by various churches and denominations in the West Bank that our fieldwork took place. The Orthodox Church has far more members than the Roman Catholic Church, but far fewer educational institutes, a circumstance that was noted unhappily by some of the Orthodox Christians we interviewed.

Given the rise of "extremist" and "fundamentalist" Muslims in the Arab world and in the West Bank in particular, where they appear to be less powerful, this topic of education, which intentionally includes Muslim students, seemed of particular importance. An Orthodox layman with the Orthodox Society of Bethlehem mentioned that Christians faced "social" problems, including "fundamentalism." When asked to give some example he said, "You know them," and pointed to Syria and Egypt, implying that the rise of "extremist" or "fundamentalist" Islam in those countries was also taking place in the West Bank. Rami,[40] from Bethlehem as well, made an observation that appeared to be connected – that the struggle for Palestinian statehood had shifted from a nationalist movement (Palestinians against Israelis) to a religious struggle (Muslims versus Jews).

We noted that usually when Christians spoke positively of Muslims, without qualifying that word in some way, they were referring to tolerant and/or secular-leaning Muslims. When they wanted to refer to "extremist" or "radical" Muslims they spoke of *al mutatarrifiin*. Almost all the Christians interviewed felt that they could live under an Islamic government, as long as it was oriented toward secularism. One person contrasted this to the rule of Hamas in Gaza and said, "If a party like Hamas took power here ... that would be hard."[41] Whether Hamas or Fatah controls the PA and specifically the Ministry of Education is directly relevant to the continued functioning and existence of Christian schools in the West Bank.

We read the educational role of the Christians as being, possibly, a way of making themselves important for Palestinian (Muslim) society. Some of the Christians involved in Christian education seemed to be aware that through such education, while making converts was forbidden or not even considered, there was a real value in teaching their Muslim students Christian *ethics*, if not Christian doctrine. The Lutheran-sponsored Diyar Institute in Bethlehem is an excellent example of this. In an interview, a spokesperson for Diyar emphasized that while they teach Christian values to all their students, both Muslim and Christian, they would never help a Muslim to convert to Christianity. In relation to freedom, either Christians do not have the freedom to teach their religion to Muslim students, or the exercise of that freedom is not considered to be valuable, or is considered too risky.

In sum, schools counteract emigration and create jobs for Christians, as one Syrian Catholic told us in Jericho. Furthermore, they attempt to inculcate Christian values (but not Christianity itself) in their Muslim students. These values emphasize tolerance and so counteract other powerful voices in society, namely, what many Christians view as a sometimes intolerant and increasingly powerful discourse of some Muslims.

Double-level Discourse: One Palestinian Family, or Muslim Intolerance toward Christians?

How Do You Relate to the Local Muslims?

Some of the questions asked in interviews were the following: How are your relationships with the other churches? How are your relationships with the government? How are your relationships with Muslims? It was not possible to ask about their relationships to Jews as Jews are now forbidden by the Israeli government to enter the areas we visited, though many older informants spoke without animosity about the times when Israelis would go shopping in their towns and when they would go to the settlements. This section seeks to explore Christian-Muslim relations in the context of the West Bank based on our limited field research and thus should not be interpreted as representative of all Palestinian Christians.

A veteran journalist told me how he once interviewed a wealthy and influential Christian man in Bethlehem who said that the Palestinians are all one people and that Muslims and Christians are brothers and live in harmonious conviviality. During the interview, the interviewee's wife was speaking with the journalist's driver (both Arabs), and she told him, "Don't believe what my husband is saying at all. The Muslims stole our land, and we sent our daughters to the USA for schooling." This perception was shared by Father Jack of Taybeh, who talked of the intentional "Islamification" of the West Bank by Muslims buying up land at high prices.[42]

This led us to entertain the possibility that there are two different levels of rhetoric – one public, which portrays the idea of "one people" regardless of religion, and the other private, which reports that Christians are sometimes the victims of the intolerance and coercion by Muslims. The remainder of this chapter explores our hypothesis.

Clerics Presenting the "One People" Rhetoric

Archimandrite Galactios of Ramallah is an Arab monk,[43] and in an interview he offered an excellent example of this sort of discourse. During the interview, he clearly said, some three times, that in Palestine all citizens have the same rights, obligations, and privileges. He mentioned (correctly) that Christians can serve in the police, security, and political areas, and that historically Christian towns are guaranteed a certain proportion of Christian representatives on the council or as mayor. He emphasized the discourse of human rights in relation to freedom of religion: that God created each person and each person had freedom (from God) to choose his or her own religion.

However, Galactios's discourse was difficult to understand fully. His authoritative tone in answering questions indicated that he was accustomed to acting as a spokesperson for his church. Was he describing the way conditions actually were, or was he making a public statement about how conditions are *ideally*? Or is it possible that as a male figure of authority in the relatively cosmopolitan (and formerly Christian) city of Ramallah, he is not aware of or subject to intolerant or coercive treatment?

The archimandrite's claims about Christians being able to serve in most official government positions is correct, at least when the secular-leaning Fatah Party is in power. Professor Vera Baboun was elected to the mayoralty of Bethlehem in October of 2012, thus maintaining the tradition of Bethlehem's having a Christian mayor, while also becoming the city's first woman ever elected to the office.[44] However, since her election Baboun has allegedly faced a smear campaign and had her vehicle vandalized because she allegedly forbade female pupils at her Catholic school to recite a poem containing the phrase "Islam is our religion." The smear campaign was allegedly carried out by Al Aqsa Martyrs Brigade, the armed wing of her own political party, Fatah.[45] The example illustrates that even within the framework of Fatah, Christians lead a poised existence. Vera Baboun was elected to be mayor of what has now become a Muslim majority city, Bethlehem, but she also has been marginalized and maligned because she allegedly offended the sensitivities of some Muslims.

The mayor of Ramallah is also a Christian woman, Janet Mikhael. It is worth noting that Mikhael was a headmistress of a school before becoming mayor. In an interview she listed the challenges she was facing as mayor:

I have faced many challenges, namely: 1. Tremendous pressure to relinquish the mayor's seat or share it with other parties, but I refused out of respect for voters. 2. Intimidation and threats. 3. Traditions undermining the role of women in society and declaring their inability to be in public positions. This position was adopted by a restricted group, but I ignored these attempts as I was confident and ambitious. 4. Israeli occupation limits our ability to implement our plans. 5. Political instability which posed a challenge, but today the situation is much better.[46]

Christians, including these two Christian women, are able to and do hold positions of authority and significance within the government of the Palestinian Authority. In other words, there is solid evidence to back up the claim of Galactios about Christian participation in public life. On the other hand, it is clear from both examples that there are powerful groups who appear actively to oppose people who take part in said public life. It is unclear whether this opposition occurs because they are female or Christian, though it is likely that both factors are significant.

Returning to our interviews, one Greek Catholic priest in the same city understood his entire ministry as revolving around the concept of Arabness ('*uruuba*). In doing this he was maintaining a tradition advocated by Arab Christians since the late nineteenth century, wherein national belonging (Arabness) was emphasized over religious affiliation (see the discussion of fragmentation and unity in the Overview).[47] He taught both Christians and Muslims about their Arabness. As such, he claims to be "a priest and father to *all* people." When asked about Arabophone people such as Copts and Syriacs who may emphasize that they are distinct from Arabs, he answered that they were indeed Arabs, because they had an Arab mentality.

The reason that such people wanted to differentiate themselves from Arabs was the influence of Zionism. He explained that Christians should be thankful for the rise of Islam because Islam had a certain power to it that forged an Arab unity, which the church, for whatever reason, had not been able to achieve. He emphasized that he always accepted invitations to nonchurch events so he could embody and proclaim this Arabness. He also explained that before the rise of Zionism, there were Arab Jews, presumably referring to Mizrahi Jews, who for centuries lived in what are today the countries of Yemen, Egypt, Tunisia, and Morocco.

Interestingly, when asked whether those Arab inhabitants of Ramallah who were Baptists were Arabs, he said, "No! They are just a front for Americanism." When asked about intolerant actions by Muslims against Christians, he explained that this was something new, "rejecting those who are not like me," and strangely, this made Islamic fundamentalism like Zionism. According to the priest, the source of this divisive fundamentalism, however, was not the Arabs themselves but began *ab extra* under the influence of those non-Arabs who wished to "divide and conquer" the Arab nation (in a similar vein, he said that the current conflict in Syria was simply the product of the machinations of Mossad).

The Reality of Intolerance and Coercion

I asked a layperson in Bethlehem why the senior clergy and bishops do not denounce the mistreatment of Christians at the hands of some Muslims, and he answered that it was not in their interest. That is, their power and status could only be maintained insofar as they did not recognize the reality of intolerance and anti-Christian violence. Their positions of power, in his thinking, required them to maintain the façade that "we are all brothers." The implication is that there are limits to the power of these visible Christian figures, and publicly calling attention to abuse by Muslims would lead to retaliation.

On the other hand, our Palestinian Israeli contacts said that Palestinians in the Territories "have to" say such things because the backlash against them personally would be violent. Kaartveit felt that the interpretation of potential sectarian discrimination in terms of more accidental phenomena (the distribution of power) functions to stave off growing sectarianism in the community as a whole.[48] In an interview with a Bethlehemite, Bowman was told that Palestinians say such things to foreigners because the future is so uncertain they do not know what else they should say.[49] Perhaps we should also entertain the possibility that "one Arab family" advocates such as our Greek Catholic contact in Ramallah truly do believe in the power of ethnic identity to contain and control religious differences.

Worry about the ascent of intolerant Islam (*tatarruf*) in Palestine and the Middle East as a whole was widespread. The rise of the Brotherhood in Egypt, Hamas in Gaza, and Jabhat al Nusra in Syria were specifically cited. (This research was carried out prior to the rise of the Islamic State.) Christians we spoke with are aware that since they assisted in toppling Mubarak, the security of Copts has plummeted. They are also aware that Christians under Assad in Syria are accorded a measure of freedom, security, and stability that will end if his regime is toppled. Finally, they are also aware that Christians in Hamas's Gaza are on the verge of extinction.[50] A physical reminder of the dire situation in Syria was seen at the Orthodox church in Ramallah, where there was a poster of the two bishops who had been kidnapped in Syria.

A cleric in Nablus described how since the beginning of the Syrian civil war his church had been vandalized. I asked whether the police did anything about it. He said, "No, they are afraid to go into the refugee camps." In the mind of this priest, the Christians had been identified as allies of Assad, and some Sunni Muslims from a refugee camp, who identify themselves with the Islamist element of the anti-Assad forces, had vandalized his church. There was, moreover, no interest among the police in finding the perpetrator, for Christians who are denied justice will do nothing, but venturing into a refugee camp is, in itself, a dangerous activity, to say nothing of arresting a Muslim there.[51]

This is the sort of event that someone like Rami would say is grounds for action and advocacy. But according to him, many local clergy believe that such activity would be more harmful than helpful, possibly leading to retaliation by some Muslims. I recall the description of the journalist I met on my first day of field research in Jerusalem: "The Christians in the West Bank live *a poised existence*." In terms of agency, these clerics did indeed have power, but either they did not realize they possessed it, or they decided (not consciously, perhaps) that exercising their power would not further their interests. On the other hand, on a personal level, there is an exercise of agency among a few of the interviewees: They are Christians, we (the researchers) are Christians (albeit Protestants), and we have access to resources and an audience that they (think they) do not have access to: you, the reader.

The reality of discrimination and even violence against Christians, however, cannot be denied. A young Christian woman in Bethlehem said that she sometimes did not even want to leave her home because of the way some Muslim men look at her. An old woman told us, "The Muslims don't like us, and we don't like them." Others mentioned how the Muslims call them "unbelievers" (*kuffaar*). This opposition did not, it appears, originate with the government itself. When informants were asked about building permits, for instance, no discrimination was reported.[52]

A good example of the narrative of one, united Palestinian people is the Kairos document, *A Moment of Truth*, signed by many important Christian leaders in Israel-Palestine (see the discussion of fragmentation and unity in the Overview). The document denounces the injustice of the occupation while also criticizing Christian Zionism (§2.2.2), the inaction of the international community and the Arab world (§1.2), and the silence of Palestinian Christian leaders (§5.2). The document claims that Palestinian Christians "must resist evil of whatever kind" (§4.2). But in sixteen pages of single-spaced print, *there is not a single mention of the intolerance and even violence that Christians in Palestine experience at the hands of some Muslims.*[53]

During an interview with a Palestinian Christian human rights activist and well-connected journalist, Rami (not his real name), I mentioned that many Christian leaders claim that there is one Palestinian family wherein Christians and Muslims are brethren. This well-informed person responded by referring to the Kairos document (which we had not discussed) and saying that it only contained part of the truth. He had been asked to sign the document but declined. This was because while the document rightly denounced the occupation, it did not denounce the discrimination and abuse that Christians suffer at the hands of some Muslims. He said the signers of the Kairos document would say that denouncing abuses by some Muslims would be used against them by their enemies (Israel). Rami, however, would include Muslim abuses of Christians in a document like that "even if Satan himself were to use it" and then referenced John 8:32: "And then you will know the truth, and the truth will set you free." "Truth cannot be partitioned," he concluded.

Rami is a vocal advocate for the rights of Christians. When I first met him it was outside a courthouse where he had filed charges against a young man for making derogatory comments on Facebook about Christians, saying, "They are drunkards, they fuck their sisters." This sort of activism on his part sometimes led to opposition by some local Christians, who told him to be quiet and not make waves. The implication is that when Christians stand up to the occupation, it is acceptable, but when they stand up against Muslim abuses of their own rights, it compromises the safety of the community.

One final question related to the reality of intolerance and coercion is this: Is it possible to identify more or less coercion in specific locales? Intolerance and coercion are, as we have argued, already concealed, minimized, or ignored to various extents by different people at different times. This makes answering such a question very challenging. Our sources sometimes contradicted each other on this matter: A man from Ramallah said, "It is peaceful here in Ramallah, not like in Bethlehem," while a source in Bethlehem claimed that Muslim-Christian relations there were generally good, unlike in "other cities."

It is possible to make one observation: There is a general sense among the people with whom we spoke that Ramallah is the cosmopolitan "mixing pot" of the West Bank. As the economic and de facto political capital of the West Bank, it attracts people from the whole region. This appears to lead to a greater acceptance of people with different traditions and backgrounds, including Christians. We thus suggest that Ramallah is relatively more tolerant than other cities in the West Bank toward Christians. This is only a hypothesis, however, and requires further research.

Interpreting the Findings

It is at this point possible to suggest a hypothesis that requires testing and further research. First, we hypothesize that in private there is often a different narrative than in public; and second, that leaders with visibility tend to give the "one family" answer, while laity are more likely to discuss the tense, disadvantageous relationship that Christians have with Muslims. The journalist from Jerusalem agreed that Christians in the West Bank have inferior rights to Muslims. He described their existence as "poised" and "living in an environment of fear." He said that over the years Christian girls were abducted, raped, and sometimes murdered. When asked why this was not reported on he responded with one word: "Fashion." By this, he meant that it is not fashionable in the press and academia today to report heinous crimes committed by Muslims, regardless of truth. This is something he claims to know on the basis of his years of experience in journalism in the region.

An old Orthodox priest told me one of these heinous stories, which concerned the death of his daughter. She was driving on the highway, and a man who was driving an ambulance ran into her. She died, and her sister was disabled. A small amount of blood money was offered, but he was told that Christians should not get blood money at all. The police officer had to draw up a report on the car accident immediately – but in fact he did not do that until five days after the accident. Ultimately, he blamed the girls for the accident.

This was an instance of corruption, but even the PA's anticorruption office did nothing to resolve the matter. This was in spite of the fact that the man who caused the accident, a Muslim, did not even have a license to drive the ambulance and had already been told not to drive. The matter was then taken to the president's counselor for Christian affairs, who likewise did nothing. According to the priest, none of this would have happened if they were Muslims, but because they were Christians, they were denied justice.

It is on the basis of these interviews and others that we propose two levels of discourse. One is more often provided by quotable leaders with visibility, and it claims that there is one Palestinian people, in which religious affiliation is less important than "ethnic" affiliation. To what extent the people saying these things *really believed* them cannot be known, of course. But in terms of agency and maintaining freedom, this strategy seeks, it appears, to maintain a strong solidarity among all Palestinians in the face of the occupation that will have the fortunate consequence of ensuring the secure well-being of the Christian minority vis-à-vis their Muslim neighbors.

Aimed at local Palestinian Christians, it seeks to remind them of this "solidarity," whether real or imagined. Aimed at the press and researchers like us, it seeks to paint the picture of one, harmonious, tolerant, and united family. Aimed at Muslims, it seeks to remind them that in spite of the sharia, Christians should be accorded rights and freedoms roughly equal to those of Muslims. The other level of discourse is generally presented in private by laity who understand the "one family" narrative to be inauthentic and inaccurate, if not downright deceitful.

It appears to us that the "one family" narrative has built into it a defense mechanism whereby the intolerance and discrimination suffered by Christians at the hands of some Muslims could be explained away or justified in a couple of manners. One was to say that these points of view originated outside the West Bank, so even if the claims were being made by indigenous Palestinians, they were somehow not authentic. A second was to say that religious freedom in the Middle East is not the same as religious freedom in the West, meaning that there were unspoken rules about what Christians could and could not say about Islam, the Qur'an, and the Prophet. Christians were expected, in public speech, to engage in self-censorship regarding these topics. In private, though, they might speak of them. A third defensive mechanism explained that while there may be problems between Muslims and Christians from time to time, they are certainly not attributable to religion, but must be reducible to some other cause, such as money or pride.

These matters imply deep questions about identity, or specifically, how identity is *portrayed* – is one a Palestinian, and only then a Christian or a Muslim? Or is one a Muslim or Christian, and *then* a Palestinian? We do not pretend to have resolved these issues here. Nor do we claim that our findings from our admittedly brief period of fieldwork are representative or authoritative. We do believe, however, that our hypothesis of a two-level discourse is worthy of further research and testing in the field.

CONCLUSION

Trying to tie these many observations together, one metaphor emerges as especially appropriate: being between the hammer and the anvil. We propose the following approximate outline for further research: The fundamental and central concerns of Palestinian Christians are economic difficulties and emigration. The two are related to each other. The occupation is universally considered an injustice, but the poor state of Christians who have exerted agency to replace regimes (as in Egypt) does not encourage large numbers of Christians to upend the present political order. Violent opposition to the occupation is considered to be incompatible with Christian ethics or ineffective or both and is thus, presently, discarded as a real possibility. Nonetheless, the Christian communities have opted for other forms of agency. To counteract emigration, we find the construction of housing for young couples and the provision of job training, which draws heavily on foreign support.

The "poised existence" of Christians makes them aware that projects to protect their existence must be deployed. Education is one such project, as it both makes Christians useful to Muslims *and* offers them the chance to inculcate in Muslim pupils tolerance and charity – values that, if adopted by Muslims, will safeguard (they suppose) their continued presence. Public and visible ecclesiastical figures are aware of their "poised existence" and tend to deploy a specific rhetoric that appears to reinforce the opinion that all Palestinians, regardless of religion, belong to one, tolerant, peaceful community. Whether or not anyone actually believes this is impossible to establish, but such rhetoric might perpetuate itself with the goal (we hypothesize) of establishing the idealistic (but in fact fictitious) order of society enunciated. It holds the Muslims accountable to live up to their proclaimed values and their allegation that Islam is tolerant, peaceful, and compatible with human rights. This deployment of the rhetoric of "one family" (not our phrase) would be an instance of agency with the goal of, we think, the maintenance of the precarious and "poised" existence of the Christians in the West Bank. Multiple rhetorical devices exist to counteract rhetoric that counteracts the "one family" narrative. This rhetoric negates or dodges any allegation that some Palestinian Muslims, because of their Islam, actually exercise power unjustly and coercively against Palestinian Christians. For such a reality would call into question the discourse of "one family" and thus endanger their project of self-preservation.

We further hypothesize that there exists another level of discourse – personal, laical, enunciated more often by women than men – that resists the former rhetoric. It reports experiences of some Muslims being intolerant and violent to Christians. It often attributes this violence to the essence of Islam itself, rather than to other sociological and economic problems.[54] While deeply "politically incorrect" in suspecting that Islam, rightly practiced, is intolerant, it represents an exercise of agency: the powerless (and this means powerless in relation to other Christian Palestinians, who at least have the power of an audience) engaging in a secret rhetoric that may, perhaps, be passed on to those who have power. The researcher is a possible patron here, and imparting the forbidden gnosis of Muslim intolerance is nothing less than an effort to change matters.

And power, let us remember, is nothing other than the ability to change situations – even if exercised mediatorially. This is, we think, a cogent hypothetical model that accounts for the information we received during our field research. It is commended to the Palestinians for further reflection, and to scholars for testing and further research.

NOTES

1 In addition to this fieldwork, it is worth noting that Miller's experience in the Middle East includes several months of fieldwork studying a community of Arabophone evangelical Christians, including a number of Christians from a Muslim background and a series of interviews with all the Episcopal clergy of Jordan. These prior periods of fieldwork resulted in "Living among the Breakage: Contextual Theology-making and Ex-Muslim Christians" (Ph.D. thesis, University of Edinburgh, 2014) and "The Episcopal Church in Jordan: Identity, Liturgy, and Mission," *Journal of Anglican Studies* 9, no. 2 (2011). Participation-observation among indigenous Christians in Amman, Cairo, Jerusalem, and Nazareth has resulted in a number of minor articles appearing in *Anglican and Episcopal History* and *St. Francis Magazine*.

2 For a succinct summary of the conflict and ensuing refugee problem, see Benny Morris, *The Birth of the Palestinian Refugee Problem Revisited* (Cambridge: Cambridge University Press, 2004).

3 Morris, *Refugee Problem Revisited*, 491.

4 For a summary, see Morris's "Conclusion" in *Refugee Problem Revisited*.

5 Abu El-Assal reports the difficulties his family experienced with this scheme in *Caught in Between: The Story of an Arab Palestinian Christian Israeli* (London: SPCK, 1999).

6 Recounting these experiences for a Western audience has been one of the strategies used by Palestinian Christians to further the cause of the Palestinian people as a whole. One successful example is the Greek Catholic bishop Elias Chacour's highly poeticized biographical account of the destruction of his rural village in the Galilee (Bir'am) and attempt to rebuild the Arab community in Israel (*Blood Brothers: The Dramatic Story of a Palestinian Christian Working for Peace in Israel*, 2nd, enl. ed. [Grand Rapids, MI: Chosen Books, 2003]). See also Naim Ateek's biographical sketch of his deportation from Beisan in *Justice and Only Justice: A Palestinian Theology of Liberation* (Maryknoll, NY: Orbis Books, 1989) and Atallah Mansour's memories in *Narrow Gate Churches: The Christian Presence in the Holy Land under Muslim and Jewish Rule* (Pasadena, CA: Hope Publishing House, 2004).

7 Bernard Sabella, "Socio-economic Characteristics and Challenges to Palestinian Christians in the Holy Land," in *Palestinian Christians: Religion, Politics and Society in the Holy Land*, ed. A. O'Mahony (London: Melisende, 1999), 84.

8 Morris's detailed analysis of the events of 1948 (*Palestinian Refugee Problem*), specifically in relation to the Palestinian refugee problem, indicates that Christians and Druze tended to receive better treatment than Muslims. Among other reasons this was primarily due to their general lack of militant anti-Zionism. The IDF, however, had no fixed policy of discrimination, so decisions varied from region to region (references are scattered throughout the book; see, for example, p. 476 as well as the conclusion).

9 Daphne Tsimhoni, "Palestinian Christians and the Peace Process: The Dilemma of a Minority," in *The Middle East Peace Process: Interdisciplinary Perspectives*, ed. Ilan Peleg (New York: State University of New York, 1998), 143. Morris's account of the 1948 war (*Refugee Problem*) also highlights the nonviolent nature of indigenous Christian responses to Zionism. Leading Palestinian Christian theologians have consistently advocated a nonviolent approach to Israel (e.g., Elias Chacour, Naim Ateek, Mitri Raheb). For details, see the excellent analysis of "contextual Palestinian theology" by Uwe Gräbe, *Kontextuelle palästinensische Theologie: Streitbare und umstrittene Beiträge zum ökumenischen und interreligiösen Gespräch*. Missionswissenschaftliche Forschungen. New Series 9 (Erlangen: Erlanger Verlag für Mission und Ökumene, 1999). When Christians do opt for militancy, they favour extreme left-wing parties such as the National Front for the Liberation of Palestine, a Marxist-Leninist group that joined the PLO. It was founded by the secular Orthodox Christian George Habash, and a number of countries consider it to be a terrorist organization.

10 Tsimhoni, "Palestinian Christians," 145.

11 Sabella, "Socio-economic Conditions." For a report on the impact of the barrier, see *The Impact of Israel's Separation Barrier on Affected West Bank Communities: Report of the Mission to the Humanitarian and Emergency Policy Group (HEPG) of the Local Aid Coordination Committee (LACC)*, May 4, 2003, http://www.ochaopt.org/documents/HEPG_Report_on_Israels_Separation_Barrier_July03.pdf. For a more recent report, see Sorcha O'Callaghan, Susanne Jaspars, and Sara Pavanello, "Losing Ground: Protection and Livelihoods in the Occupied Palestinian Territory," *HPG Working Papers*, July 2009, http://www.odi.org.uk/sites/odi.org.uk/files/odi-assets/publications-opinion-files/4616.pdf

12 Lybarger provides the following statistics for the various denominations in East Jerusalem, the West Bank, and Gaza: Greek Orthodox, 52.6 percent, Roman Catholic, 30.1 percent, Greek Catholic, 5.7 percent, Protestants, 4.8 percent, Syrian Orthodox, 3.0 percent, Armenians, 3.0 percent Copts, 0.5 percent, Ethiopians, 0.1 percent, Maronites, 0.2 percent. Miller's research on Muslim-background converts to a form of evangelical Christianity numbers them at around 500 and he reckons that this is by far the fastest growing denomination in the region. See L. D. Lybarger, "For Church or Nation? Islamism, Secular-Nationalism, and the Transformation of Christian Identities in Palestine," *Journal of the American Academy of Religion* 75, no. 4 (2007): 787. Miller, *Living among the Breakage*, appendix A.

13 For a sympathetic interpretation of this contested document see Muriel Schmid, "From the Church of the Nativity to the Churches of the World: Palestinian Christians and Their 'Cry of Hope'," *Theology Today* 69, no. 4 (2013): 428–440.

14 See Gräbe, *Kontextuelle palästinensische Theologie*. Much less sympathetic Zionist responses can be found in Ehrlich, "Attitudes" and Gershon Nerel, *Anti-Zionism in the "Electronic Church" of Palestinian Christianity*, Analysis of Current Trends in Antisemitism 27 (Jerusalem: SICSA, 2006). Briefer summaries can be found in

Tsimhoni, "Palestinian Christians" and Daphne Tsimhoni, *Christian Communities in Jerusalem and the West Bank since 1948: An Historical, Social and Political Study* (Westport, CT: Praeger, 1993).

15 Glenn Bowman, "Nationalizing and De-Nationalizing the Sacred: Shrines and Shifting Identities in the Israeli-occupied Territories," in *Sacred Space in Israel and Palestine: Religion and Politics*, ed. Marshall J. Breger, Yitzhak Reiter, and Leonard Hammer (London: Routledge, 2012), 209. See also Bernard Sabella, "Socio-economic Characteristics."

16 See, for example, Lybarger, "Church or Nation?" Bowman, "Nationalizing and De-Nationalizing," 195–227; Tsimhoni, "Palestinian Christians."

17 Baard Helge Kaartveit, "The Christians of Palestine: Strength, Vulnerability, and Self-restraint within a Multi-sectarian Community," *Middle Eastern Studies* 49, no. 5 (2013): 738.

18 See Kaartveit, "Christians of Palestine," for details. Justus Reid Weiner has a catalog of crimes against Palestinian Christians under the PA in *Human Rights of Christians in Palestinian Society* (Jerusalem: Jerusalem Center for Public Affairs, 2005, http://www.jcpa .org/text/Christian-Persecution-Weiner.pdf). However, concerns have been expressed that his approach is overly politicized in favor of Israel. Although many of his data ring true with our own experience, his overall interpretive framework lacks the nuances found in Kaartveit's article.

19 Lybarger, "Church or Nation?" Weiner, *Human Rights*; Tsimhoni, "Palestinian Christians"; Tsimhoni, *Christian Communities in Jerusalem*.

20 Saul Colbi's historical overview of Christianity in the Holy Land reveals how international Christianity in the region has always been in *A Short History of Christianity in the Holy Land* (Jerusalem: Am Hassefer, 1965).

21 For a detailed treatment of the struggle between indigenous Arab Orthodox and their Greek clergy, see Tsimhoni, *Christian Communities*. Another significant drawback of the fractured nature of Christianity in the region is that it has enabled the Israeli government to relate to the churches in a "divide and conquer" and "stick and carrot" manner, negotiating with each denomination on its own and distributing desired "goods" (such as visas and tax exemptions) on the basis of criteria that suit Israel's purposes (e.g., degree of Arabization, willingness to let land, relative power of each denomination's international backers). See Michael Dumper, "Faith and Statecraft: Church-state Relations in Jerusalem After 1948," in *Palestinian Christians: Religion, Politics and Society in the Holy Land*, ed. A. O'Mahony (London: Melisende, 1999), 56–81; Amnon Ramon, נצרות ונוצרים במדינת היהודים: המדיניות הישראלית הכנסיות והקהילות הנוצריות (1948) (*Christians and Christianity in the Jewish State: Israeli Policy towards the Churches and the Christian Communities [1948–2010]*), JIIS Studies Series 420 (Jerusalem: Jerusalem Institute for Israel Studies, 2012). A detailed English-language synopsis can be found online at this address, http://www.jiis.org.il/.upload/christianspdf-eng%20abstract .pdf (accessed October 25, 2013); Merav Mack, "Christian Palestinian Communities in Israel: Tensions between Laity, Clergy, and State," in *Sacred Space*: 292–295.

22 Sabella, "Socio-economic Characteristics," 87.

23 In *Caught in Between* Abu El Assal states that Arab Protestants in particular have been particularly well placed to contribute to national life in a modern world because of the traditional dedication of the Protestant missionaries to critical thought and high levels of education.

24 Lybarger, "Church or Nation?" 789.
25 Sabella, "Socio-economic Characteristics," 94.
26 Lybarger, "Church or Nation?" 787.
27 Lybarger, "Church or Nation?" 790. See also Sabella, "Socio-economic Characteristics."
28 The first week was carried out by Miller alone, the second by Miller and Sumpter.
29 Additional details on that fieldwork are included in the Introduction section of this essay.
30 For more on this topic see, for instance, Abeer Ayyoub, "Travel Restrictions Take Toll on Palestinian Relationships," *Al Monitor*, June 11, 2013, accessed March 3, 2014, http://www.al-monitor.com/pulse/originals/2013/06/israel-palestine-travel-restrictions-relationships.html
31 Akiva Eldar, "Another Israeli Summer of Occupation, Apathy," *Al Monitor*, July 1, 2013, accessed March 3, 2014, http://www.al-monitor.com/pulse/originals/2013/07/israeli-summer-occupation-apathy.html
32 Jafar Subhi Hardan Suleiman and Badaruddin Mohamed, "Factors Impact on Religious Tourism Market: The Case of the Palestinian Territories," *International Journal of Business and Management* 6 (2011): 256.
33 For research on how Palestinian Christian discourse in Bethlehem interprets the separation wall to visiting Christian pilgrims see Jackie Feldman, "Abraham the Settler, Jesus the Refugee: Contemporary Conflict and Christianity on the Road to Bethlehem," *History & Memory* 23 (2011).
34 Some conservative Muslims believe that making the representation of any human (aside from dolls for children) is to tempt humans to worship something other than God, and thus forbidden.
35 For more information on how the ongoing construction of the separation wall has recently adversely affected freedom of movement and the ability to work, see Danny Rubinstein, "The Economic Breach in the Security Fence," *Al Monitor*, February 11, 2014, accessed March 3, 2014, http://www.al-monitor.com/pulse/business/2014/02/separation-fence-israel-palestine-economy-vat-shared-customs.html
36 A further complication in relation to work is this: Should Palestinians (regardless of religion) work for the state of Israel, settlements, or Israeli businesses? While we did not encounter anyone who specifically mentioned this challenge, more information can be found in Jodi Rudoren, "In West Bank Settlements, Israeli Jobs Are Double-Edged Sword," *New York Times*, February 11, 2014, A1.
37 Hanan Madanat and Imad Twal, "'Communion and Witness': The Contribution of Latin Patriarchate Schools to Better Muslim-Christian Relations in the Holy Land," *International Studies in Catholic Education* 4 (2012): 35.
38 Ibid., 38.
39 "History," Birzeit University, accessed March 29, 2014, http://www.birzeit.edu/history. Indeed, in the lengthy history page neither "Christian" nor "Muslim" appears a single time.
40 In reference to this particular individual a pseudonym has been used.
41 The different approaches of Hamas and Fatah to religion can be seen in a recent move made by the Fatah-ruled PA to remove the person's religion from his ID card. This move was a surprise and was lauded by human rights advocates, and criticized by Hamas. Additional details are in Adnan Abu Amer, "Hamas Slams PA for Removing Religion from ID Cards," *Al Monitor*, February 2, 2014, accessed March 4, 2014, http://www.al-monitor.com/pulse/originals/2014/02/palestinian-authority-hamas-national-id-religion.html

42 "Throughout the last two decades theft of private property and manipulation of land documents have become serious problems in the West Bank. Christian landowners in Bethlehem appeared to be disproportionately targeted, creating suspicion that these crimes were the work of Muslim extremists motivated by sectarian hostility" (Kaartveit, "Christians of Palestine," 733).

43 This is significant because in the Jerusalemite Orthodox Church (as with all Orthodox Churches) only monks can become bishops. Most of the Orthodox priests in the Patriarchate are Arabs who are married and as such cannot become bishops.

44 Daoud Kuttab, "Bethlehem Has New Female Mayor, Yet Same Old Problems," *Al Monitor*, December 23, 2012, accessed March 29, 2014, http://www.al-monitor.com/pulse/originals/2012/al-monitor/christmas-bethlehem-palestine.html

45 Khaled Abu Toameh, "Bethlehem's Female Mayor Faces Smear, Threat," *GateStone Institute*, May 30, 2013, accessed March 29, 2014, http://www.gatestoneinstitute.org/3738/bethlehem-mayor-vera-baboun

46 "Interview with Janet Mikhael, Mayor of Ramallah," *National Women's Council of Ireland*, October 6, 2010, accessed March 29, 2014, http://www.nwci.ie/?/news/article/palestine_west_bank_interview_with_janet_mikhael_mayor_of_ramallah. (Note: Numbers in list were added for clarity by author.)

47 Anthony O'Mahony, "Palestinian Christians," 9–55; Arab Educational Institute, *Bethlehem Community Book* (Bethlehem: AEI, 1999), 59; Bernard Lewis, *Islam and the West* (Oxford: Oxford University Press 1993), 143.

48 Kaartveit, "Christians of Palestine," 733.

49 Bowman, "Nationalizing and De-Nationalizing," 218–219.

50 A recent article suggests a number of fifteen hundred Christians in Gaza as of December of 2013 (Asmaa al-Ghoul, "Gaza Christians Yearn for Bethlehem," *Al Monitor*, December 24, 2013, accessed April 8, 2014, http://www.al-monitor.com/pulse/originals/2013/12/gaza-christians-christmas-restrictions.html#). An article from 2012 contains an estimate of twenty-five hundred and reports that Christians are under pressure to convert to Islam (Nidal al-Mughrabi, "Gaza Christians Sense Pressure to Convert to Islam," *Reuters*, July 26, 2012, accessed March 3, 2014, http://www.reuters.com/article/2012/07/26/us-palestinians-christians-conversion-idUSBRE86P0J420120726).

51 Kaartveit, "Christians of Palestine," describes a similar situation.

52 This is a good example of why Palestinian Jerusalem does not fit in with the larger West Bank for this study. The dynamics of landownership and construction there were totally different, and much more onerous, than in cities such as Bethlehem and Ramallah.

53 The single hint in the entire document that not all is well between Muslims and Christians is §5.4.1, which encourages Muslims to "reject fanaticism and extremism."

54 Lybarger, in "Church or Nation?" also describes how some of her interviewees would cite the relevant anti-Christian verses from the Qur'an by heart. It is worth noting that in our fieldwork, carried out more than a decade after Lybarger's, we likewise encountered such opinions of Islam and the Qur'an.

14

Christians in the State of Israel: Between Integration and Emigration

Daphne Tsimhoni

INTRODUCTION

Christians in the State of Israel form a small minority of approximately 2 percent of the total population. Yet, their significance exceeds by far their small proportion of the population. Their unique position has been due first and foremost to their presence in the Holy Land in the vicinity of the Christian holy places, but also to their forming a minority within a minority in the Jewish state and living in the midst of the Israeli-Palestinian conflict.

This paper discusses the Christian communities within the territory of the State of Israel including East Jerusalem but excluding the West Bank and the Gaza Strip, which have never been officially annexed to the state. It focuses on the social, cultural, and political aspects of the Christian communities rather than the Christian churches and their theologies and hierarchies. The paper starts with a historical overview of the Christians in the Holy Land. It continues with their demographic features and trends, viewing the concerns about their future existence. It then discusses the position of Christians in Israel – in theory and in practice: the promise for equality and religious freedom, its limits and deterioration. It continues with the collapse of intercommunal balance among Christians, Muslims, and Druze in the north of Israel. It discusses the restrictions put on Christians as part of the Palestinian Arab minority with the deepening of the Israeli-Palestinian conflict, most obviously in Jerusalem. Finally it discusses the position of Christians in Jerusalem and in Haifa as two different paradigms of Jewish-Arab relations.

HISTORICAL AND DEMOGRAPHIC PERSPECTIVES

The Holy Land is the birthplace of Christianity. But from the fourth century onward, since the discovery of the holy sites by Queen Helena, the mother of Emperor Constantine, and the establishment of Christianity as the official

397

religion of the Byzantine Empire, Christians in the Holy Land became marginal in the Christian world. The major center of theologian intellectual activity was shifted to Asia Minor and to Europe, where the major schisms within Christianity took place and created the Orthodox, non-Chalcedonies (Monophysite), and Uniate Catholic Churches. During the nineteenth century Protestant churches established centers in the Holy Land. Hence, no fewer than fourteen Christian communities exist in the Holy Land maintaining their church headquarters or representation in Jerusalem.

From the seventh century, under the rule of Islam, Christians gradually became a minority in the country. They became *dhimmis* (protected by the Muslim rulers but in an inferior position to the Muslims) similarly to the Jews. Their position under the Muslim rulers had its ups and downs, suffering occasional persecutions. It somewhat stabilized under the Muslim Ottoman empire from the sixteenth century. The Christians' position in Palestine deteriorated over the several decades leading to World War I with the attempts of the Young Turks to convert the empire into a Turkish nation state and force conscription to the Turkish army on all of its citizens including Christians and Jews. Both were relieved with Palestine's occupation by the British forces toward the end of World War I.

A new phase in the development of Palestinian Christians began with the activities of the European churches in the Holy Land during the nineteenth century, as part of the growing interest of the European powers in Palestine. The churches established Western-style schools, hospitals, and welfare institutions among the centers of indigenous Christians. Hence, the process of modernization and Westernization started among Palestinian Christians already during the nineteenth century, earlier than among their Muslim countrymen.[1]

Christians began emigrating from Ottoman Palestine during the late nineteenth century, both in search of better economic opportunities and as an escape from harsh Ottoman treatment, and conscription to the Turkish army, on the eve of World War I. The Christians' concentration in towns and their education in European missionary schools facilitated their migration and settlement abroad. The emigrant communities have kept strong family, community, and village links with their homeland. For example, Christians from Jerusalem often headed either to Australia or to North America; the people of Ramallah tended to relocate to North America, while families from Bethlehem headed to South America. According to local Christian sources, the daughter communities in North and South America had already outnumbered their mother communities by 1948.[2]

Within Palestine, Christians migrated during the nineteenth century to localities around holy sites that enjoyed European educational, commercial, and welfare activities: Jerusalem, Bethlehem and Ramallah in the center of Palestine, and Nazareth in the north. Christians were also attracted to the coastal towns of Acre,

Haifa, and Jaffa, where they constituted a considerable part of the Palestinian Arab middle class.

The British Mandatory rule of Palestine (1918–1948) was the heyday of Christians in Palestine, as enhanced security measures, new working opportunities, and the expansion of church educational and medical institutions improved their position. By 1944, 77 percent of Christians had become urbanized, as compared with only 28 percent of Muslims, and 90 percent of the Christian children were attending schools, the same percentage as that of the Jewish children (compared with only 25 percent of Muslim children).[3] Hence, Palestinian Christians formed a link between the foreign European rule and the local Muslim population. Enjoying new opportunities and a stronger sense of freedom, the size of the local Christian communities expanded in absolute figures but decreased in proportion from 20 percent of the Palestinian Arab population at the beginning of the British Mandate to only 11 percent at its end. This was due to the Christians' lower birth rate and higher emigration rate as compared with their Muslim countrymen.

Christians took part in the Palestinian Arab national movement from its emergence during the 1920s, often as spokespersons, but rarely participated in acts of violence. Prominent in the Palestinian Arab national movement were first and foremost members of the Arab laity of the Greek Orthodox Patriarchate as well as the small but important Protestant communities.[4]

The 1948 war formed a major crossroad in the life of Palestinian Christians. Many escaped or were banished from their homes in the territory of the State of Israel, but in a smaller proportion than their Muslim countrymen. Hence, their proportion increased in 1949 to 21 percent of the Palestinian Arabs who remained within the boundaries of the State of Israel after the 1948 war. Since then, the proportion of Christians in the Arab population in Israel has gradually decreased, falling to 13.1 percent by 1990, 11.7 percent by 1997, and further declining to 8.0 percent in 2012. This trend has mainly been due to the higher birth rate of Muslims and to the continuous emigration of Christians, while Palestinian Christian immigration into the State of Israel has been negligible. However, together with the Christian decline in proportion of the Arab population there has been a continual moderate growth of the Christian population in Israel in absolute figures. Furthermore, Palestinian Arab Christians in Israel form proportionally one of the largest Christian minorities and certainly the safest within Arab populations in the Middle East, particularly in view of the disastrous effects of the "Arab Spring" in Iraq and Syria.

A recent publication of the Israeli Central Bureau of Statistics shows that the emigration rate of Christian citizens of the State of Israel is the highest among the population groups in the state, although just slightly higher than that of Jews. The emigration rates of all groups diminished in recent years.[5] While Israeli Jewish emigration is compensated by immigration of Jews, Christian immigration to Israel

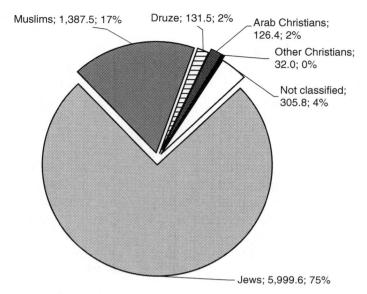

FIGURE 14.1. Population of Israel by religion 2012 (in thousands and percentages). *Source*: State of Israel, Central Bureau of Statistics, *Statistical Abstract of Israel 2013* Table 2.13: *Sources of population growth, by district, population group, and religion(figures for end of 2012 in thousands; total population 7,984.5).*

hardly exists. Church heads and community leaders have expressed concern that continuous Christian emigration is liable to turn the churches into places of worship only, stone buildings without living communities. The findings of this paper show that with the exception of some small communities in East Jerusalem (discussed later in this chapter), this is not occurring.

The religious groups in Israel at the end of 2012, according to the Israeli Central Bureau of Statistics (CBS) data, are shown in Figure 14.1. Christians numbered approximately 158,400. Of these, 126,400 were ethnic Arabs and 32,000 were defined as non-Arab Christians. The majority of this latter group immigrated to Israel together with their Jewish family members during the mass immigration of the 1990s from the former Soviet Union (FSU) states and to a smaller extent from Ethiopia.

Another group, which today amounts to approximately 300,000 (or 4 percent of the total population), is defined by the CBS as "others," or religiously unclassified. According to the estimate of Bishop Dr. David Neuhaus, the Latin (Roman Catholic) patriarch deputy in charge of the Hebrew speaking Catholic community, about a quarter of the "religion unclassified" group are Christians. However, members of this group, regardless of their official classification, largely consider themselves as part of the Israeli Jewish majority. They attend Hebrew-speaking schools and celebrate Jewish holidays; they also celebrate Christmas, Sylvester (New Years' Eve), and the New Year. They maintain familial, cultural, and social contacts with Jews beyond their (usually Russian-speaking) closest family circles. The Israeli Jewish identity among the second generation of this group is even stronger. This group therefore is not discussed in this paper.

The major geographical centers of Christians in the State of Israel are Galilee in the north, the coastal towns, and – since 1967 – East Jerusalem as well. Today, only six villages in Galilee have retained a Christian majority. Estimates based on the 1995 census of the CBS show that Nazareth is the largest Christian center as well as the major Arab town in Israel. Even though numbering approximately 20,000, Christians lost their majority in Nazareth, forming about 40 percent of the town's population. The second most populous Christian-Arab center is the coastal town of Haifa, where 15,500 Christians constitute about 50 percent of the local Arab population altogether, making up about 10 percent of Haifa's total population. The 14,800 Christians in Jerusalem represent just a remnant of what was the largest Christian community in Mandatory Palestine. Socially and economically, they form part of the Palestinian Christians in the West Bank rather than the Christians in the State of Israel, as will be discussed later in this chapter.

Socially, economically, and culturally, the Christian Arabs in Israel are closer to the Jewish majority than to the Muslim Arabs in the state. This finds expression in similar urbanization rates, similar rates of high schooling and university graduates, and, above all, similar lifestyle to that of the Jews in mixed towns, particularly regarding the position of women. Hence, Christian Arabs are the most integrated group in Jewish majority towns. Indeed, Christian presence in universities and in white-collar professions in general is higher than that of the total Arabs. Christians have reached top positions such as hospital managers, supreme court judge, scientists at research institutes, theater and film actors, and political activists.

The Establishing of Christians' Position during the First Decades of the State of Israel

Whereas British Mandatory rule provided numerous benefits to the Christian population in Palestine, the political transition to the State of Israel brought about many challenges for this group.

The Declaration of Independence of the State of Israel (May 14, 1948) represented the ideals and high aims of the founders of Israel to establish a liberal-democratic nation state. The Declaration still serves as the constitution for the state of Israel, and its fifth chapter reads:

> It [the State of Israel] will foster the development of the country for the benefit of all its inhabitants; it will be based on freedom, justice and peace as envisaged by the prophets of Israel; it will ensure complete equality of social and political rights to all its inhabitants irrespective of religion, race or sex; it will guarantee freedom of religion, conscience, language, education and culture; it will safeguard the Holy Places of all religions; and it will be faithful to the principles of the Charter of the United Nations.

The morning after this declaration took place, the bloody war of 1948 started with the incursion of the armies of the Arab states into the newly established State of Israel. The war brought about the flight and banishment of many Palestinian Arabs and the creation of the Palestinian refugee problem. In Galilee in the north of Israel, the major center of the Christian Arabs, the Israeli Defense Forces (IDF) showed preference to Christians in some localities. Except for places with strategic significance or on the cease-fire lines with Lebanon, such as the villages Bir'am and Iqrit, or Beisan in the Jordan Valley, Christians were allowed to stay or were forced to leave their homes in smaller numbers than neighboring Muslims. Residents of the Christian town of Nazareth and its neighboring villages were generally allowed to stay. Christians received this favorable treatment for their limited involvement in acts of violence against Jews and the friendly relations that a number of Christian villages maintained with their Jewish neighbors. The intervention of European church heads, particularly the Vatican, in support of their indigenous church members helped too. For example, the Catholic Christian inhabitants of the Galilee village of Eilabun were initially expelled from their homes in 1948 by Israeli soldiers, who suspected that they had cooperated with the Syrian invading forces. They were allowed to return after Vatican intervention on their behalf. Shortly after the war, Israeli authorities demonstrated a greater openness regarding the return of Christian refugees and the unification of Christian families than they did regarding the fate of Muslim refugees.[6]

Autonomy and Religious Freedom

The Israeli authorities adopted British Mandatory legislation regarding the religious communal autonomy that had been based on the Ottoman *millet* system. Accordingly, churches were allowed the freedom of worship and full autonomy in managing their affairs. This included the maintenance of church property; management of all communal institutions, including schools and hospitals; and religious courts to deal with matters of personal status. Communal autonomy and freedom of worship were consistent with the United Nations and international commitments that the young State of Israel undertook, desiring to establish itself as part of the Western democratic bloc. Hence, the church and communal schools were allowed to teach a curriculum of their choice in any language including Arabic or European languages. The Israeli Ministry of Foreign Affairs was well aware of the possible pressures that Christian church headquarters in the West, particularly the Vatican, might bring to bear on the state in light of what might appear as harassment of the churches in the Holy Land. Hence, the Israeli authorities abstained as much as possible from confiscating church properties, particularly if they were registered in the name of Western churches or European clergymen. They were less cautious regarding local and Eastern churches.[7]

Whereas the communal autonomy of Christians and Jews was expanded by the British Mandate, the administration of Muslim endowments (*waqfs*) and properties remained under the supervision of the British Mandatory government.[8] The Israeli government further limited the authority of Islamic institutions, most obviously the religious courts. Unlike the Christian churches' properties, a large proportion of the Muslim endowments became absentee properties and were assigned to the direct administration of the Israeli authorities.[9] This is one of the major reasons why the Muslims have not developed educational and other communal welfare institutions of their own and often apply to Christian ones.

The State of Israel did not invest sufficient funds in the development of the periphery, particularly the rural areas of the Arab minority, in order to bridge the gap between Jewish and Arab educational and socioeconomic institutions. Hence, Christian educational and medical institutions have made a great contribution to improving the position of the Christian Arabs and the Arab minority at large. Still today, the majority of the Arabic-speaking secondary schools, certainly the premier ones in town, are Christian.

Unlike the Christian churches, individual Christian Arabs have been treated by the Israeli authorities similarly to Muslim Arabs in matters such as the confiscation of lands, most obviously during the 1950s and 1960s, when large tracts of land were confiscated from the Arab citizens of the state, regardless of their religious-ethnic affiliation, in order to enable the establishment of new Jewish agricultural settlements and to absorb the influx of Jewish immigrants from Europe and the Arab states. The Israeli government further implemented the British Mandatory emergency regulations to impose military administration on the Arabs – including Christians, Muslims, and Druze – which limited their movements to their areas of residence and required special permits to travel outside these areas. The military administration was finally abolished in 1966.

The Israeli government never formulated a policy or guideline regarding the Christian citizens in the state. It left the decisions to be made ad hoc by civil servants. The attitudes of many of them toward the churches and the local Christians have not been empathic because of the Jewish collective memory of European anti-Semitism, persecutions, and perceptions that the Holocaust originated in ancient Christian theology. The active role that Christians played in the Palestinian Arab national movement has caused resentment and suspicion as well, even though such Christian participation was usually nonviolent and on the intellectual level.

The Department for the Christian Communities, the administrative unit dealing with the government's relationships with Christian groups, was centered in the Ministry for Religious Affairs, one of the first ministries established in the State of Israel. Church heads were treated with dignity as a result of the non-Arab ethnicity of most of them as well as the affiliation of the local churches (particularly the Catholic and Protestant ones) with their headquarters in Europe. The heads of the State of Israel were aware of the importance of maintaining good contacts with the European states in which church headquarters were located, above all with the Vatican, which was far from recognizing the State of Israel. The Israeli government took into consideration public opinion in Europe and its concern for the local Christians. Furthermore, the heads and personnel of the Christian Communities Department during the early years of the state had a scholarly background regarding Christianity and included personalities such as Dr. Jacob Herzog, Haim Vardi, and Saul Colbi.

During the late 1990s, the Department for the Christian Communities declined in influence, and a number of its experts left or retired. During 2001–2002 the Ministry of Religious Affairs was disbanded, and the Department for Christian Communities was transferred to the Ministry of Interior. These changes followed the rise to power of Ariel Sharon's right-wing government, which ruled in coalition with the secularist Shinuy Party. The latter had demanded the disbanding of the Ministry of Religious Affairs. These administrative changes were initially designed to place Christian citizens on an equal footing with all other citizens, Jews and non-Jews alike. In actual fact, these transformations divided the government treatment of Christian communities among a number of government agencies and consultants, each pursuing a different end. The effect of the new arrangement has been most obvious in the government's dealings with the Christian communities in Jerusalem, as discussed later.

POLITICAL CONFIGURATION AND ACTIVITIES

The noted historian of eastern Mediterranean Christians Robert Haddad observed that "the power [of the marginal community] to influence and shape is greatest at those junctures when the characteristic institutions of the dominant community are in the process of formation, radical modification, or destruction."[10] This statement well defines the influence of Christians on the political activity of the Arab minority in Israel during the first decades of the state. The Christians filled the gap caused by the exodus of prominent Palestinian Muslim families and political leadership as the result of the 1948 war.

During those formative years, Christian Arab representation and activities in the Knesset (Israeli parliament) exceeded by far their numerical strength and proportion in the Arab population. This phenomenon was due to several reasons: the doubling of the Christian proportion within the Arab population, their higher education, and their forming a large proportion of the Arab urban population. As Knesset protocols demonstrate, from the first to the seventh Knessets (1949–1973), Christian Knesset members numbered two to four members, constituting 40–50 percent of the total Arab Knesset members. The Christian Knesset members considered themselves and acted as representatives of the whole Arab minority. Attempts for separate independent Christian representation failed. As all Arab Knesset members were, Christian Knesset members were elected in three parties: the Communist Party in its various manifestations (Maki, Rakah, Hadash); the Zionist left-wing Mapam Party; and the Labor Party (Mapai, Avoda, Ma'arakh). Forming the major government coalition until the mid-1970s, the Labor Party established adjunct Arab parties for the purpose of boosting votes among the various Arab sectors: the Muslims, Christians, Druze, and Bedouins. The candidates of these adjunct parties were accordingly selected on a communal-sectorial basis and included one Christian, Muslim, Druze, and Bedouin candidate to represent each of the ethnoreligious groups.

During the 1950s and 1960s the Communist Party was the only legitimate party that spoke for the national aspirations of the Arabs in Israel. Christians, in particular members of the Arab Orthodox community, have been prominent activists in this party since its inception in 1940s Mandatory Palestine. For many years Tawfiq Tubi (1949–1992) and Emile Habibi (1951–1973) were prominent representatives of the Communist Party in the Knesset and led the struggle for civil rights and equality for the Arabs in Israel. From the late 1970s the number of Christian Knesset members dropped to one or two, while the total number of Arab Knesset members rose. The decline of the Christian Knesset members in both absolute figures and proportion of the Arab representation was the outcome of several processes: the proportional demographic decline of Christians within the Arab population, the rising generation of educated Muslims, and the abolition of the Labor Party's adjunct Arab parties, together with their secured communal representation."

The growing number of Muslim Arab Knesset members is connected with the strengthening of the Arab national parties since the early 1990s, a process that accelerated in the 1999 elections, when nine of the thirteen Arab Knesset members represented the Arab parties. These elections marked the political success of Ra'am (United Arab Party), in which the moderate branch of the Islamic movement in

Israel participates but no Christian has. This party became the strongest Arab party in most of the Knessets. Christian support and representation have been obvious in the Communist Hadash Party, but there too they have declined.

Established as an Arab-Jewish party, the Communist Hadash Party has been leaning largely on Arab votes and has adopted, since the early 1990s, an unofficial policy of reserving the first seat for a Muslim, the second for a Christian, and the third for a Jew. The Communist Party, which was considered by the Zionist establishment during the 1950s–1960s as extremely anti-Zionist, has become since the early 1990s the center of moderate Arabs who advocate the establishment of a Palestinian Arab state alongside Israel together with the demand for equal rights for all Palestinian Arab citizens of Israel.

In 1995 the Balad Party (National Democratic Alignment) was established by Azmi Bishara. Balad ran together with Hadash in the 1996 Knesset elections and decided to run separately in the 1999 elections. These elections marked a shift of votes from the Communist Party (Hadash) to Balad. The drop in Hadash's appeal indicated the decline of the Christians' influence within the party and paralleled the decline of Communist ideology. The success of Balad was first and foremost due to the charisma of its leader, Azmi Bishara, a Knesset member from 1996, the main figure behind the new party's constitution and agenda. A prominent Arab Christian intellectual, Bishara offered a secular nationalist and uncompromisingly anti-Zionist ideology without the Communist tinge of Hadash, which was resented by many Arab Christians and Muslims. Born to a Greek Catholic family in Galilee – thus into the Arab indigenous Christian community that has identified itself as the Christian Arab community par excellence – Bishara appealed to young educated students and intellectuals, among whom the Christian percentage has been relatively high. He desired to end his double marginality as a Christian within Muslim Arab society and as a member of the Arab minority in the Jewish state. Promoting in his public appearances Arab secular nationalism while portraying Judaism as religion only, he confronted the Jewish majority of the state and challenged the basic idea of Israel's being the nation-state of the Jewish people. Instead, he preached for a completely secular state "of all its citizens." The sharp and often aggressive manner in which he promoted his ideas irritated many Israeli Jews, who took Bishara's vocal speeches as aiming at the abolition of the Jewishness of the State of Israel to be replaced by an Arab entity in which the Jews would become a minority. Hence Bishara contributed to his becoming identified in the eyes of many Jews with all the Christian Arabs in Israel, conceiving them all as adversaries of the State of Israel. Many Arab public figures, both Muslims and Christians, expressed their reservations about Bishara's public utterances, apprehensive of the hostile reactions that he might bring about from Jews. This became most obvious after the First Intifada and particularly during the Second Lebanon War in summer 2006. Bishara was accused of making open calls to the Muslim fundamentalist organization Hamas to attack Israel. During the bombardments of Haifa in the Second Lebanon War Bishara was suspected by the Israeli secret services of providing Hamas with targets for bombing. Whether that was true or not, Bishara left Israel for Qatar and Jordan in 2007 while still a member of the Knesset. Fearing arrest, he never returned. Based in Qatar Bishara has become a prominent intellectual promoting secular pan-Arabism in the Arab media. Since Bishara left Israel and the Knesset, no Arab public figure, either Christian or Muslim, has replaced him as a charismatic Arab leader advocating secular Arab nationalism.

In Bishara's absence, several Christian Arab Knesset members and public figures have been trying to present the issues of the Arab minority in Israel less vocally and in a way that would appeal to the Jewish liberal audience. Noteworthy among these was Nadia Hilou (1953–2015), who represented the Zionist socialist Labor Party in the seventeenth Knesset (2006–2009), the first Arab Christian woman elected to the Knesset. A native of the mixed Jewish-Arab town of Jaffa, Hilou gained a reputation as a prominent activist for family services and rights of children, both Arab and Israeli in general. On several occasions she pushed to the fore acts of discrimination against Arabs such as humiliating security checks at the Ben Gurion International Airport. In summer 2014 she denounced calls for boycotting Arab businesses that, she felt, were inspired by some right-wing government members during the Protective Edge operation.[12]

Another noteworthy Christian Arab Knesset member was Dr. Hanna Sweid (Swaid). A native of the Christian village Eilabun in Galilee, he studied at the Technion in Haifa, where he received his Ph.D. in civil engineering and town planning. Having fulfilled several public positions including as the mayor of Eilabun and the director of the Arab Center for Alternative Planning, he represented the Hadash Party at the Knesset during 2006–2015. Sweid defines his political agenda as supporting the establishment of a Palestinian state to the side of Israel and promoting equality for all the citizens of Israel regardless of ethnicity. A civil engineer, Sweid has preferred to concentrate his efforts on repairing the town planning bills for the benefit of his voters. Sweid has been active in promoting the building of a new Arab town in Israel as well as the urban planning of Galilee for Jews and Arabs alike.

Sweid made precedent when he officially requested that the speaker of the Knesset in December 2013 post a Christmas tree at the entrance of the Knesset. He explained his request as a gesture to the Christians in Israel and worldwide in response to "price-tag" vandalism in churches as well as the strengthening multiculturalism of Israel. The speaker of the Knesset, Yuli Edelstein, turned down the request, explaining, "It is not appropriate for the Knesset to have a Christmas tree in the official space of the Knesset." However, Edelstein added, "there is nothing stopping

Sweid from putting a tree in his office or for Hadash to set one up in its faction room."[13] Sweid was disappointed but his effort might bear fruit in the future.

THE COLLAPSE OF INTERCOMMUNAL BALANCE AND GROWING CHRISTIAN VULNERABILITY

The decline of Christian prominence in politics since the 1980s was the inevitable outcome of their demographic decline and the social change among Israeli Arabs. Further processes have damaged the sense of security of Christians in Israel. These include the rise of the Islamic movement; the undermining of the intercommunal balance within the Arab minority, particularly in Galilee; and the dismantling of the Soviet Union together with the decline of Communism.[14] These processes pushed the Christians in Israel from the forefront of political leadership into a marginalized, defensive position.

The mountains of Galilee in the north of Israel form the largest Christian population center in Israel, where, as explained earlier, the majority of Christians have lived for generations as a minority within mixed Muslim-Druze-Christian villages. Christians have been the most prosperous group among the Arabs of Galilee but at the same time the most vulnerable one, depending on the Muslim majority in their vicinity and requiring government protection. Since the 1980s the delicate balance among Muslims, Christians, and Druze has been dismantled as a result of growing interference of external forces. The balance between Christians and Druze was undermined first. These two communities have lived and cooperated together for hundreds of years as an extension of their cohabitation in the south of Lebanon. Unlike the Christians, the Druze have been a cohesive warrior community whose leadership knew how to accommodate rulers wherever they live whether in Lebanon, Syria, or Israel. In 1956 the Druze religious leadership in Israel decided on compulsory service of Druze men in the Israeli army (IDF) equivalent to that of the Jews. This decision gave the Druze military careers, easier access to the Israeli administration, and above all readier access to arms. On the other hand, Druze became jealous of the better economic conditions and higher education that their Christian neighbors achieved during the three years of Druze compulsory army service. The Druze have also been frustrated viewing the fact that their army service did not bring about the complete equality and integration within the Jewish state they expected for fulfilling their duties to the state.

Furthermore, during the First Lebanon War Druze soldiers in the IDF found themselves involved in Druze–Christian feuds in south Lebanon and sometimes confronted Christian armed groups. Hence, Christian–Druze tensions in Lebanon were imported to Galilee and became additional cause for the deterioration of Druze–Christian relations; Druze usually had the upper hand in these feuds. Such was the attack of Druze from Yarka on Christians in the neighboring village Kafr Yasif after a squabble over a football match in 1981. Several were killed or wounded and property of Christians was looted; it ended with a forced reconciliation by the police. Druze–Christian clashes took place near the Christian village of Eilabun during 2004–2009 and in the Druze majority village Mughar in 2005. Less severe clashes between Druze and Christians took place also in Rameh in 2003, Abu Snan in 2005, and the town of Shefa'amr in 2009.

Feuds between extended families (*hamulas*) due to local personal affairs are common in Arab villages. Since the early 1990s, they have intensified, particularly prior to local or general elections; the skirmishes reflect an increasingly violent atmosphere in Israel. Whenever such feuds occur between Christians and Muslims, socioreligious dimensions aggravate them. Similarly to feuds with the Druze, the Christian side is often the weaker party, which requires the protection of the police, who do not always respond in time.

Muslim-Christian feuds have intensified since 1996 in several villages in Galilee, most violently in the village of Tur'an in the vicinity of Nazareth, demonstrating the growing vulnerability of Christians in Muslim vicinities.[15]

The major causes for the growing sense of insecurity among Christians have been the rise of the Islamic movement in Israel and the growing impact of fundamentalist Islam in many Muslim localities. The official declarations of the movement in Israel are cautiously phrased, speaking of a common fate with "our Christians brethren" as well as the need for cooperation with them in "the common national struggle." No public discourse has taken place regarding the position of the Christians in the future Islamic state. But nobody is misled regarding the Christians' place in such a state, bearing in mind the traditional *dhimmi* position of the Christians and Jews in Islam.

Since the early 1990s, a growing number of verbal incitements against Christians and Jews have been proclaimed in the mosques and printed in the newspapers of the Islamic movement. Christians have answered these attacks in the local Arabic press. Though cautiously phrased and appealing to reason, they have been unable to put an end to the Muslim attacks. Occasionally, Christians are called on to prove their Arab nationalism, and they must tolerate the Islamist attacks for the sake of a "united front" in their national struggle. In these circumstances local Christians have generally abstained from any initiative of political organization on the basis of religious community, and many go further and denounce any discussion or academic study connected with Christians lest they be blamed with betraying the Palestinian Arab national unity.

Growing Islamic influence can be noticed in many Muslim neighborhoods. The observance of the fast of Ramadan in public has become commonplace, and more girls are clothed in Islamist dress, including head covers, even though this phenomenon is still less evident than in neighboring Arab countries. Loudspeakers calling for prayers and reading chapters of the Qur'an broadcast for hours at a time, reminding Christians that they live in a Muslim society. The general atmosphere in the Arab Muslim dominated street denounces a Western lifestyle as "Israelization" and the maintenance of social contacts with Jews as "collaboration." Many of those blamed for these "faults" are Christians.

The culmination of Christian–Islamist feuds was the Shihab al-Din affair, which agitated Nazareth during 1997–2003. It erupted from the intrusion of a group of Islamists into a government-owned square in front of the Basilica of the Annunciation. The group demanded to build a huge mosque that would overshadow the basilica. The hostilities extended far beyond a local conflict over a piece of land and signified the triangle of Muslim–Christian, Jewish–Christian, and Jewish–Muslim relations in Israel and above all the treatment of the Arab citizens by the Israeli–Jewish government. The events further demonstrated the significance of Nazareth, the Basilica of the Annunciation, and other holy sites to worldwide Christianity along with the ability of the international community to put pressure on the Israeli government's decision making regarding the Christian holy places. It was only after the American President George W. Bush interfered that the building of the mosque was stopped.[16] Since the solution of this problem, life in Nazareth has returned to normal. Nazareth has prospered economically with the development of tourism. However, it has been losing its Christian atmosphere. The election of a Muslim though secular mayor in 2013 signified to many Christians the end of the Christian chapter of Nazareth.

RESTRICTIONS ON RESIDENCE

Christians all over Israel and most obviously in Jerusalem have been greatly affected by new regulations regarding the entry and residence of non-Jews in Israel intended to limit their presence in the state. These regulations were enacted against the backdrop of the outburst of the Palestinian Second Intifada in 2000, which provoked two major concerns: national security and the declining Jewish majority in Israel. Suicide bomb attacks on Israeli cities raised demands to close the borders with the PA territories in the West Bank so to prevent the entry of potential Palestinian terrorists into Israel. Another factor was the growing apprehension about the decline of the Jewish majority in Israel. Publications of the central Bureau of Statistics heated up the debate over the future of Israel as a Jewish democratic state. According to the Statistical Abstract of Israel 2003, the Jews constituted 76 percent of the total population of Israel (excluding the Occupied Territories) at the end of 2002. Statisticians projected that by 2020 the Jewish majority will decline to between 65 and 70 percent of the total population of the state.[17]

How far the predictions of the decline of the Jewish majority in Israel are going to materialize is beyond the discussion of this paper. However, the public concern about the Jewish majority induced the Ariel Sharon right-wing government (in coalition with the Shinuy center secularist party) to take legal steps. It enacted various regulations in order to restrict the stay of non-Jews in Israel and above all to prevent Palestinian Arab immigration both Muslim and Christian into the State of Israel, first and foremost to Jerusalem. Another set of regulations intended to limit the stay of foreign clergy in the state.

In July 2003 the Knesset enacted for one year The Citizenship and Entry into Israel Law (temporary provisions) 2003. According to the law (sec. 2), "the Minister of Interior shall not grant the inhabitant of an area (i.e. Judea and Samaria, and the Gaza Strip) citizenship on the basis of the Citizenship Law, and shall not give him a license to reside in Israel on the basis of the Entry into Israel Law." The law enables the interior minister to grant licenses to reside in Israel for a cumulative period of no more than six months on the basis of his consideration of the applicant's special medical or working needs (reservation 3.1) as well as to grant citizenship "if he [the interior minister] is convinced that he [the applicant] identifies with the State of Israel and its goals, ... or performed a significant act to promote the security, economy or some other important matter of the State" (reservation 3.2).

The provisional law froze for one year all requests by Palestinian Arabs for citizenship, including for the purpose of family unification. It was widely criticized in Israel for its discriminatory application to Palestinian Arabs only. In July 2004 the Knesset, after a hot debate, extended the provisional law for another six months rather than one year as a compromise with the opposition to the law raised by Interior Minister Avraham Poraz and other members of the secular Shinuy Party.[18] It was extended since then several more times, and as of August 2015 it is still in force.

This regulation has caused great human suffering to all Palestinian Arab citizens of the State of Israel. But it has had a particularly severe effect on the Palestinian Christians of East Jerusalem. First and foremost, it has affected marriages of community members in Jerusalem with those in the West Bank. Spouses have not been allowed to settle down in Jerusalem or in Israel at large. It also separates the elderly and their children and damages the close-knit family relationships so essential in small communities. In 2004 Israeli decision making officials seemed unaware of or simply lacked empathy regarding the effects of the law on Palestinian Arab residents and on Christian communities in particular in East Jerusalem.[19]

In 2015 consultants to several ministries and local executive level officials, some of whom are Christians, have been aware of the effect of the regulation. They have been trying their best to mitigate it but admit that they cannot do much. Hence, the lack of consideration for Christians and the Palestinian middle class, in general, is likely to exacerbate the decline of these groups further, particularly in Jerusalem.

VISAS FOR CLERICS AND CHURCH STAFF

Whereas the restrictions on entry and naturalization of Arabs from the West Bank and the neighboring Arab states applied to Palestinians in general, new restrictions on visas for clerics and church staff targeted the churches specifically. The idea behind them was to limit the number of church staff settling in Israel for life and to preclude the possible expansion of numerous new churches in Israel.

From the establishment of the State of Israel until the late 1990s the Department for Christian Communities at the Ministry of Religious Affairs maintained the procedure of issuing and renewing visas for clerics and church staff. Clergy visas include two categories:

- A3: this cleric visa lasts a maximum of three years and can be renewed within Israel an unlimited number of times.
- A5: this permanent citizen visa may be applied for by clergy staying in the country for more than fifteen years. It enables people to work and enjoy all government social and medical benefits.

Other relevant visas are the A2 student visa, the B1 volunteer visa, and the B2 tourist visa. These are issued for a limited period and can be renewed in the country of origin of the applicant only. Their renewal is limited to a specified number of times, and the visa holders are not entitled to receive government social and medical benefits.

Until the late 1990s the Department for Christian Communities would recommend, and the Ministry of Interior would issue, an A3 clergy visa for all persons involved in long-term religious service in recognized institutions. This included a wide spectrum of Christian personnel: pastors, administrators, priests, nuns, and laity with special skills such as teachers, nurses, and doctors. The whole procedure normally took no more than several weeks and was appreciated by the churches as fair.[20]

Daniel Rosing, who headed the department during the 1980s, explained the reasoning for expanding the scope of those entitled to A3 cleric visa by the department's desire to facilitate the life and activities of the various churches and their institutions. Hence, the department broadly interpreted the term "religious personality" to include laity who fulfilled central functions in the church even if they were not ordained clergy. For instance, within the Protestant Church many positions such as school headmasters are filled by lay people rather than by ordained priests as in the Catholic Church. "We were aware that the law did not cover everything and that there were issues that could not be solved within the context of the existing law. Flexibility and common sense are essential in the application of laws."[21]

With the disbanding of the Ministry of Religious Affairs and the inclusion of the Christian Communities Department in the Interior Ministry, the main procedure of issuing the A3 visas was transmitted from the Christian Communities Department to the main section of Population Administration in the Ministry of Interior. The new head of the Population Administration in 2004, Herzl Gedge, a tough former army officer affiliated to the Likud right-wing party and a close friend of Prime Minister Sharon, decided to apply the very narrow formal definition of the law to the procedure of granting all visas and stay permits. His aim was to limit as much as possible illegal stay in Israel of any kind: foreign workers, non-Jewish family members of new immigrants, and, above all, Palestinians.[22]

Accordingly, a new narrow interpretation of the visa regulations was contemplated by leading officials at the Ministry of Interior. According to their new interpretation, persons entitled to receive the A3 visa were to be only ordained clergy who functioned as priests in charge of their local communities in Israel. As a result of the new policy, many of the staff of churches and Christian institutions were denied their A3 visas and were offered other types of visas: volunteer, student, foreign worker, or tourist. These types of visa were granted for a short period and for a limited number of renewals. New applications and renewals would need to be done in the applicants' country.[23]

Severe restrictions have been put on the entry of clerics from the Arab states. Applicants from these states whether in the status of clergy, students, or tourists need to go through special security checks and interrogations by a special security committee before referring their application to the Ministry of Interior. Given the severity of these restrictions, clerics complain, hardly anyone can pass through them. On top of the general atmosphere of mistrust, suspicions of the security authorities regarding Christian clergy from Arab countries extend back to 1974, when the Greek Catholic vicar in Jerusalem, Hilarion Kapucci, was imprisoned for smuggling ammunitions on behalf of the Palestine Liberation Organization (PLO). However, hardly any Christians have been involved in such activities since then.

Suspending the entry of clergy from the Arab states has had a serious effect, particularly on smaller Christian communities: Orthodox and Catholic Syrians, Copts, and Maronites. They do not consider themselves Palestinian Arabs and have been maintaining friendly relations with the Israeli authorities. Their church centers are in the Arab states, and they have no power or organization in the West that can mediate on their behalf with the Israeli authorities. Because of the newly restrictive policy of the A3 visa, along with enhanced security measures, these small communities face enormous difficulties gaining entry for foreign clergy into the State of Israel. This has impaired the conduct of their religious ceremonies and communal life. For instance, the Coptic Church in Jerusalem has had great difficulties in getting visas for deacons because of the new policy of the Ministry of Interior. Deacons have an essential role in conducting the prayers in the Coptic Church, a function that does not exist in the Western churches and therefore has not been recognized by the Ministry of Interior. The absence of deacons has impaired the conduct of their ceremonies.[24]

The new restrictions on issuing and renewing A3 visas were implemented without sufficient preparation and explanation and without any guideline. They aroused a wave of protests from the churches both inside and outside Israel. As of 2015, government officials dealing with visas for foreign clergy maintained that "the regulations work well." Foreign clergy comply with the A3 visa regulations. As one of the consultants put it to me, "This is a regulation issued by the Israeli government and even the Pope in his visit to Israel in 2009 did not manage to abolish it."

HATE CRIMES AND "PRICE TAG" VERSUS INITIATIVES TO CONSCRIPT CHRISTIANS TO THE IDF

The second, third, and fourth terms of Benjamin Netanyahu's right-wing government (2009–today) have witnessed the deterioration of public security and the growing impact of the extreme ultra-Orthodox right-wing settlers in the West Bank on the Israeli government. This includes anti-Arab incitements and legislation aimed at the marginalization of the Arab minority in Israel. The culmination of this trend has been the unprecedented wave of hate crimes against Arabs, Muslims, Christians, and Druze alike particularly in May 2014 and after. It has found expression in the desecration of mosques, churches, holy sites, as well as vandalizing private properties including houses and cars and properties most often along with attacks on Palestinian olive groves in the West Bank. The settlers' attacks on their Palestinian neighbors were initially dismissed by the police and government circles as "marginal" acts by some "urchins." These "price tag" acts intensified in Jerusalem and have expanded to the north of Israel. It was not until early May of 2014 that government circles admitted the seriousness of this wave of hostility and the dangers involved, particularly with preparations for the visit of the pope in Israel on May 25. Former security services and army commanders such as Carmi Gilon and Gadi Shamni heavily criticized the government and Prime Minister Netanyahu, in particular, for refraining from declaring the initiators of these crimes as terrorist organizations and for not treating them forcefully as such.

At the same time, a renewed initiative to conscript Christians to the Israel Defense Forces (IDF) has been taking place. Initiatives to conscript Christian Arab citizens began during the 1948 war in Galilee but did not result in an agreement for a compulsory conscription similar to the one with the Druze. Unlike the Druze, who are known for cohesiveness and famously as brave fighters, the Christians are divided into numerous somewhat rival denominations dependent on their Muslim and Druze vicinity for their security.

Throughout the years Israeli government consultants on Arab affairs attempted in vain to achieve an agreement with Christian leaders for a compulsory conscription to the IDF similar to that of the Druze. Fuad Farah, who was the chair of the Nazareth Orthodox Arab communal council and the chair of the Arab Orthodox Congress in Israel, recalls several meetings during the 1970s and 1980s toward that end with Israeli consultants on Arab affairs, Samuel Toledano and Moshe Arens. Farah recalls refusing the request, pointing out the precarious position of the Christians and their vulnerability; he expressed apprehension regarding Muslim responses to Christians' conscription into the IDF, including fear of the possibility that Christian Arabs might be forced to fight against their brethren and family members across the border.[25] Still, a number of Christian Arabs volunteered with the IDF in past years, and some continue to do so.

The present initiative for conscription started in August 2012 with the establishment of the Forum for the Conscription of Christians to the IDF by retired IDF Christian officers in order to encourage Christians to join the army. The forum has been supported by the extreme right nationalist organization Im Tirzu (If You Wish) and by nationalist Jewish right-wing politicians. The spiritual leader of the forum is Gabriel Naddaf, who served as a priest in several Orthodox Arab communities in Nazareth and its vicinity. He was deposed from his position by the Orthodox Arab Community Council of Nazareth when he became involved in the conscription forum. In a conference organized by the forum in early May 2014 Naddaf declared, "we are not Arabs; we are Israelis and desire to serve our state and become integrated in it."[26]

This call for conscription has appealed to some marginal Christian groups, but no church head or leader has declared support for it. Some proponents of Christian conscription are Maronites who, like their brethren in Lebanon, do not identify as Arabs but rather as members of the Maronite "nation" centered in Lebanon. The conscription initiative also appeals to some Christians in Haifa and Galilee who live among Jews and desire to become fully integrated into the Israeli society and state hoping to end their marginal position and discrimination against them in the State of Israel.

Some descendants of the Maronite and Greek Catholic villages of Iqrit and Bir'am express their hope that by serving in the IDF and by becoming fully accepted as Israelis they will have a strong basis to demand their full rights and be allowed to return to the villages that their fathers had been forced to leave during the 1948 war. Others from mixed Druze–Muslim–Christian villages in Galilee express the desire to gain access to arms similar to that of the Druze to overcome their inferior position and weakness in possible future interethnic feuds. Still others realize the significance of having arms in view of the persecution of Christians in the neighboring Arab states in the wake of the "Arab Spring."

The initiative for conscription reached its peak with the declaration of Defense Minister Moshe Ya'alon in early May 2014 that all Christians reaching the age of seventeen will receive official invitations from the Defense Ministry to join the army as volunteers. Ironically, the campaign for the conscription of Christians has coincided with an unprecedented wave of hate crimes apparently perpetrated by Jewish extremists. About the time of Ya'alon's declaration a price tag attack occurred in the village of Jish, where quite a number of potential Christian volunteers reside. More than fifty cars were damaged and hateful inscriptions were smeared on the walls. More ironic is the fact that almost none of the perpetrators of these hate crimes has been caught and taken to the court.

Another problematic issue is the support that this conscription initiative gains from the extreme-right-wing government and coalition members whose declared support is likely to offend and incite the Muslim Arab citizens of the state. In an interview in early 2014, Yariv Levin, the chair of the government coalition, explained government support for the initiative to Shalom Yerushalmi of the *Ma'ariv* daily paper: "We [Israeli Jews] have a lot in common with the Christians. They are our natural allies against the Muslims who wish to eliminate the state from inside .... They [the Christians] are neither Muslim nor Arab. They are Christian and can identify with the state."[27] Levin further declared his intention to initiate regulations that would distinguish between Christians and Muslim Arabs in all walks of life.

As expected, the forum's declarations have aroused a lot of opposition in the Arab sector, among Christians and Muslims alike. Many opponents of the forum recalled that Christian Arabs were among the initiators of the Palestinian Arab national movement. Demonstrations against the forum's initiative took place in April and May 2014 at university campuses. A demonstration at the Hebrew University campus degenerated into violence between the right-wing Im Tirtzu and Communist Hadash demonstrators.[28] Open government support in the forum has not alleviated the opposition to the conscription calls; nor have the "price tag" attacks on Arabs in Israel.

CHRISTIANS IN JERUSALEM: A MINORITY AT RISK

As of 2012 Christians in Jerusalem numbered 14,830, 11,890 of whom were Arab Christians.[29] Forming a small minority of less than 2 percent of the total population of Jerusalem they have significance far beyond their proportion of the population due to their unique religious, cultural, and social features. Yet, they form the indigenous Christian minority whose position is the most precarious and their future within the state of Israel is at stake. As the site where Jesus spent his last days and where he was buried, nearly every Christian church has representation in the Holy City. The Christian communities in Jerusalem thus form a microcosm of worldwide Christianity in the Holy City.

Jerusalem is the residence of the three major patriarchs: the Greek Orthodox, the Armenian Orthodox, and the Latin (Roman Catholic), as well as the representative bishoprics of major Western churches such as the Anglican (Evangelical Episcopal) Church and the Lutheran Church. The majority of the laity of the bigger communities, the Latin and Greek Orthodox, is Palestinian Arab. The smaller communities – the Armenians, Copts, Syrians, and Ethiopians – are indigenous but not Palestinian Arab.

The churches own about 29 percent of the real estate of the Old City, including approximately 133 churches and educational and medical institutions that cater to the whole of the local Arab population.[30] They maintain research institutions, theological seminaries, branches of Western universities, and hostels all over Jerusalem, which contribute to its unique spiritual and cultural atmosphere.

Jerusalem became, from the nineteenth century, a target of internal Christian migration from the countryside and the traditional inland towns such as Bethlehem and Nablus. Having become the center of activity of the Western churches and the capital of Mandatory Palestine, Jerusalem offered better opportunities for education and work and a greater degree of security. As a result, the Christian population in Jerusalem more than doubled by the end of the British Mandate, and the city became the largest Christian center in Palestine. Nevertheless, the Christians lost their majority within the Arab population of the city owing to the Muslims' higher birth rate and wider immigration into the city.

The severe hostilities and political consequences of the 1948 war brought about fundamental changes in Jerusalem, which was divided into two cities: The new western suburbs became Israeli-Jewish, while the Old City and the eastern suburbs became Jordanian-Arab. The events of 1948 and this division greatly affected the Christian inhabitants of Jerusalem. Nearly half of them, who had resided in the well-to-do western suburbs of the city, were dispossessed of their properties. Many sought refuge in the Old City in monasteries and church institutions. Jordanian East Jerusalem, like the rest of the West Bank, stagnated economically throughout the 1950s, as indicated by a high rate of unemployment and a shortage of suitable accommodation. This situation particularly affected the middle class, to which the majority of Christians belonged. The troubled economy led to large-scale Christian emigration to Amman, the capital of Jordan, and abroad that dramatically reduced the size of the Christian population of Jerusalem, from 29,350 (49 percent of the total Arab population) in 1944 to 10,982 (18 percent) in 1961. The higher birth rate of the Muslims and their smaller scale of emigration, as well as the expansion of Jerusalem's municipal boundaries by the Jordanian government to include the

Muslim village of Silwan, nearly doubled the Muslim population of East Jerusalem by 1967.

The 1967 war spurred a second wave of Christian emigration, though much smaller than that of 1948, resulting largely from the wish of Christians to unite with family and community members who had already established themselves in Jordan or in the Arab states. Although Israel officially united Jerusalem, annexing the Old City and the eastern suburbs in 1967, East Jerusalem has remained economically and socially distinct from West Jerusalem; it has largely remained part of the West Bank, as have its Palestinian Christian inhabitants.

Under Israeli rule after 1967, Jerusalem's Christians further decreased, both absolutely and proportionately, because of a combination of the following: a further expansion of the boundaries of the municipality of Jerusalem to include several villages with a Muslim majority, a lower Christian birth rate, and higher emigration rates. Since 1967 the ongoing Palestinian-Israeli conflict and the lack of a foreseeable long-term political solution for East Jerusalem have added new incentives to those that already encouraged Christian migration from Jerusalem. The motivation for leaving has been particularly strong among the small communities of the Armenians and Syrians, who harbor the memory of the Turkish massacre of World War I and wish to avoid being caught up in national clashes. The loss of the Christian atmosphere and the diminishing size of these communities, impairing their communal life, form a further incentive for Christian emigration, particularly for the youth of the small communities.[31]

Furthermore, the higher cost of living, the deterioration of the economic position of the urban middle class to which the majority of Christians belong, the lack of proper employment for university graduates, and the shortage of affordable accommodation have further induced emigration from Jerusalem. Similar economic incentives have caused the emigration of Muslim members of the middle class as well, but, unlike for the Christian emigration, their higher birth rate and their migration from rural districts into Jerusalem have compensated for the Muslim emigration.

MAIN CHALLENGES FACING CHRISTIANS IN JERUSALEM

One of the major issues facing the Christians in Jerusalem has been their treatment by the Israeli authorities. The dissolution of the Department of the Christian Communities in 2001 and the intensification of problems involving Christians in Jerusalem brought about the involvement of various government authorities in attempts to solve Jerusalem's affairs. No fewer than nine consultants from several ministries, the Jerusalem police, the municipality of Jerusalem, and the Israeli army are involved in the issues of the Christian communities and churches in Jerusalem.

Today, no influential body exists to initiate a sensible government policy toward Christian communities and their headquarters in Jerusalem. All the government officials with whom I spoke cited this as a serious limitation of the government's relations with the Christian churches. The decision-making level has been too influenced by emotional reactions to events and by sectarian and party interests. As stated by one of the consultants: "There is no landlord here. There isn't even a reliable data center on the Christians." Consultants and officials expressed considerable empathy and goodwill in assisting the churches to find their way in the maze of bureaucracy. However, the core problems run far deeper than administrative structure; they emanate from the struggle for Jerusalem and are discussed in the highest political levels of the government decision making.[32]

Israeli officials agree on the need to preserve a vast Jewish majority within the expanded boundaries of Jerusalem as part of the struggle against the Palestinian Authority over the rule of East Jerusalem. Indeed, a general concern with the so-called demographic problem has been dominating Israeli politics and public debate since the 1990s. This debate has found its utmost expression in the demography of Jerusalem. The expansion of the boundaries of Jerusalem and the Palestinian, mostly Muslim, immigration from the West Bank to East Jerusalem since 1967 have created a large minority of Palestinian Arabs – representing 38 percent of the population compared to 62 percent of Jews in the city as of 2012.[33]

The annexation of East Jerusalem by the State of Israel soon after the 1967 war has not been officially recognized by most world states, despite Israeli efforts to gain such international recognition, but rather aroused international condemnation. When the Israeli Knesset issued a special law confirming that united Jerusalem is the capital of Israel in 1980, it aroused an international protest and the relocation of thirteen embassies from Jerusalem to Tel Aviv. Only two foreign embassies remained in Jerusalem,[34] those of Costa Rica and El Salvador, and they also moved to Tel Aviv in 2006.

The main struggle between Israelis and Palestinians over East Jerusalem has found expression in legal ownership and the control of lands and buildings. In order to prevent any possibility of partition of Jerusalem in the future, the Israeli government confiscated numerous tracts of land and began to build new neighborhoods for Jewish inhabitants in the territories surrounding the city from the north, the east, and the south. Hence, vast areas were purchased or confiscated in the vicinity of Mar Elias monastery (known in Hebrew as Har Homa) south of Jerusalem, thus blocking the city from the Bethlehem area.[35] The various Israeli authorities have not differentiated between Christians and Muslims in confiscating lands and buildings in and surrounding Jerusalem. Hence, 50 percent of the lands confiscated during 1995 in order to build the Har Homa (Mar Elias) project were from the Christian town of Beit Sahur. Furthermore, no consideration has been given to the housing needs of Arab citizens of East Jerusalem, Christians and Muslims alike; no housing plans were allocated for them in the Har Homa projects built on their confiscated lands.[36]

Since the 1990s, during and after the First Intifada, several buildings were purchased through a third party in the Old City by Jewish ultra-Orthodox associations, a move discreetly supported by the Israeli government. Such was the case of the St. John Hospice in the vicinity of the Church of the Holy Sepulchre, which was leased from the Greek Orthodox Patriarchate through a third party. This move was widely denounced by both Palestinians and Israelis, who appealed to the court sceptical of the legality of the deal, and the case is still pending in the courts.[37] For the same purpose of "Judaization" of Jerusalem, additional properties have been purchased or leased from the churches in the Old City, in many cases by putting pressure on them to sell.

As far as the Christians in East Jerusalem are concerned, the term of Teddy Kollek, the acclaimed mayor of Jerusalem (1965–1993), represented the high point of Israeli attention to their needs. A man of the world, Kollek understood the significance of the Christian churches and communities for making Jerusalem the flourishing capital of Israel and achieving the international community's recognition of Jerusalem as such. He realized the importance of developing Christian educational institutions, pilgrim sites, and archaeological excavations in Jerusalem as part of the city's Christian and world heritage at large. Experienced in Israel's foreign relations, he also grasped the importance of developing good contacts with the various local churches for Israel's relations with the Christian world and above all with the Vatican, which in those days was far from recognizing the State of Israel.

At the same time according to the testimony of Teddy Kollek and Amir Heshin, his consultant on Arab affairs (1984–1993), the municipality of Jerusalem maintained a deliberate policy of discrimination in urban planning and educational, medical, and social services as well as building accommodations for the Arab population in East Jerusalem. This policy was meant to ensure that the Arab proportion of the city's population, 28.8 percent in 1967, would not exceed that level. At the end of his term, Kollek acknowledged his discriminatory attitude toward East Jerusalem, deplored it, and suggested self-rule in East Jerusalem.[38] As East Jerusalem was on a much lower level of municipal services when it was annexed in 1967, special funds were needed in order to fill the gap in services, and the Israeli government did not allot these.[39] Hence, Christian medical, educational, and cultural social services have been catering to the Palestinian population in East Jerusalem and have somewhat compensated for the lack of sufficient municipality and government services.

Since the loss of Kollek in the municipal elections of 1993 to the Likud candidate Ehud Olmert, Jerusalem has been governed by right-wing and Orthodox religious mayors. This brought about a change in the municipality's empathic attitude toward the local Christians. Furthermore, the open support expressed by the Jerusalemite church heads for the First Intifada has influenced Israeli officials to consider them as supporters of the Palestinian Authority (PA), and therefore as enemies of the State of Israel.[40] Rather than attempting to create a more measured attitude toward the churches, the Israeli treatment of the Christians in Jerusalem has been marked by spontaneous emotional reactions to events and declarations. One of the major concerns of the Israeli officials has been to reassert Israel's hold over the Old City and the Holy Places and to eliminate the presence of the PA administration and security forces from East Jerusalem.

In the absence of clear authority, there have been a number of cases of encroachment of the Muslim *waqf* into Christian property, in which the Israeli government abstained from taking action. The Christian churches in the Old City have been trying to "walk on a narrow rope" in an attempt to maintain good contacts with both the Israeli government and the Palestinian Muslim society in which they live. In several cases the government abstained from interfering in local conflicts between Christians and Muslims, explaining that the Israeli law requires an official complaint with specific details and names in order to make the police act, as a number of consultants to the mayor of Jerusalem explained to me. According to them, Christians seldom complain about Palestinian Muslims to the Israeli authorities in a manner that would enable the authorities to take action.[41] The Christians' reticence can be explained by their doubts whether the Israeli government would take efficient action to prevent violence.

Law enforcement as a political instrument rather than as the government's duty was obvious in the affair of the Khanqah (al-Khanqah al-Salahiyya) mosque adjacent to the Church of the Holy Sepulchre. In April 1997 members of the Muslim *waqf* intruded into the Greek Orthodox part of the Holy Sepulchre adjacent to the wall and annexed to the mosque two rooms belonging to the patriarchate. After an urgent appeal on April 24, 1997, to Prime Minister Netanyahu by the Greek Orthodox, Latin, and Armenian patriarchs of Jerusalem, Netanyahu declared Israel's commitment to maintain the status quo. Accordingly, the Jerusalem court issued a decree to stop the work at the Khanqah. The *waqf* ignored it, and the police refrained from enforcing the decree. Intervention by Jordan, the Greek government, and Yasser Arafat to convince the *waqf* to knock down the illegal wall failed. The Israeli authorities decided in consultation with the security authorities not to intervene by force.[42] As a result, the illegal annex of the Muslim *waqf* is still standing.

The lesson of the Khanqah affair for the Christian communities has been that they cannot rely on Israeli protection of their properties and that they need to conduct their affairs cautiously, walking a tightrope between the Israelis and the PA.

From the early 2000s Christians in the Old City of Jerusalem have been harassed by ultra-Orthodox and settler Jews. As Israeli governments have been almost exclusively right-wing ones, the "Jewdization" of Jerusalem has become an official open policy particularly under Prime Minister Benjamin Netanyahu. This has been obvious in the Old City of Jerusalem, where the presence of Christian churches and communities has been significant.

A new phenomenon emerged with the harassment of church people and Christians wearing the cross. In March 2004, the Interior minister in charge of the Department for Christian Communities, Avraham Poraz, visited the Old City and met with priests and church dignitaries, who complained to him about harassment by ultra-Orthodox Jews: "They spit on us and sometime harm us." The minister promised to study the issue and transmit the matter to the police in charge of security in the Old City. The police reaction was that Christian religious ceremonies and processions would receive police security guards, but "the police was unable to provide an escort to each individual clergyman."[43]

This downplaying or toleration of attacks by ultra-Orthodox Jews on Christians in Jerusalem has been occurring for years now and serves as the background of the recent wave of hate crimes all over Israel. Since 2009 more than forty Muslim and Christian holy sites have been desecrated. It has become clear that this is a national issue rather than a minor local one. Yet, hardly any of the attackers has been caught and punished. Prime Minister Netanyahu has been criticized for not denouncing the offenders strongly enough and for not taking special measures to put an end to these harassments.

THE SEPARATION BETWEEN JERUSALEM AND THE PA/WEST BANK

The connection between Jerusalem and the Bethlehem area is of particular significance for the smaller communities in the Bethlehem district as well as in Jerusalem. Closing the borders and separating Jerusalem from the rest of the West Bank, above all the Bethlehem district, have been serious blows for Christians on both sides.

When Israel officially annexed East Jerusalem in 1967 the Christian enclaves of the Bethlehem area remained in the status of occupied territories along with the rest of the West Bank. Free access between Jerusalem and the Christian enclaves continued until the outburst of the First Palestinian Intifada in 1987 despite their different legal status. The temporary prosperity of East Jerusalem and Bethlehem that followed the 1967 war, particularly in tourism and commerce, in which Christians excelled, contributed to their feeling of greater security under Israeli rule than under Jordanian governance during the 1960s. Indicative of this feeling was a petition to the Israeli government on July 3, 1967, signed by 550 dignitaries, mostly Christians of the Bethlehem area, calling for the annexation of their town to the State of Israel. They explained their request, "We are deeply connected with the city of Jerusalem and if you unite the city with Israel, include us within it as well.[44] The appeal was indicative of the essentiality of free connection between Jerusalem and the West Bank for Christians on both sides. It did not indicate, however, support for Israeli occupation as such.

The separation between Christians of Jerusalem and those in the West Bank, above all the Bethlehem area, was carried out in practice with the Israeli-Palestinian peace accord in 1993. With an eye to a comprehensive peace settlement with open borders, the Israeli government negotiated for Bethlehem to be included within full Palestinian rule (Zone A) without giving any consideration to securing free connection between the Christians of the area with East Jerusalem. In the optimistic atmosphere of those days it was not contemplated that the temporary legal separation would become an absolute and permanent one.[45]

Until the outburst of al-Aqsa Second Intifada in autumn 2000, the roads between Jerusalem and the Christian enclaves in the PA territory were open and the movement of clergy and church leaders between their centers in Jerusalem and their flock in the West Bank was regular. The Aqsa Intifada drastically deteriorated the situation. After suicide bombings in Israeli towns, Israel blocked the roads between Jerusalem and the West Bank and has been constructing a separation wall between them on Palestinian territory. Getting in and out of Jerusalem to Bethlehem in the south and to Ramallah in the north is only possible through gates and army checkpoints. The wall and checkpoints have harmed the well-being of Palestinians, Christians, and Muslims alike.

Israeli consultants say that in building the wall, Israeli planners took into consideration the Christian institutions and tried as much as possible to prevent damage to their property. In one case, that of the Rosary Sisters educational institution in the north of Jerusalem, the wall was shifted a bit after negotiations with this Christian order. An arrangement was set up so that the students who reside on the other side of the wall would be able to pass through a gate to the school. The daily management of these passages is in the hands of the army, whose major consideration is security. Local students and their families complain of frequent delays in these passages, sometimes for hours. Ad hoc local arrangements cannot compensate for the overall damage caused to the communal life and the activity of educational and medical institutions in East Jerusalem separating family and community members on opposite sides of the wall as well as dividing East Jerusalem from the Ramallah and Bethlehem districts.

All the officials dealing with Christian affairs in Jerusalem with whom I spoke were aware of the misery and the disastrous effect of the wall on the Palestinian inhabitants of East Jerusalem and on Christians in particular. However, they maintain that it is beyond their power to do more than what has been done. Security considerations are foremost. The wall, they maintain, has proved its utility in dramatically reducing the number of car and suicide bombs. The municipality of Jerusalem has been trying to intervene in order to ameliorate the position of Christian citizens in East Jerusalem and to enable municipal services to reach the neighborhoods close to the wall but has not been very successful.

The sieges and roadblocks have been widely criticized by human rights organizations and the media in Jerusalem, but this has not brought about improvements in the treatment of the Palestinian population and Palestinian Christians in particular. In early 2015, after nine years of legal battle, the Israeli Supreme Court took its decision against the construction of the separation wall in the Cremisan valley that would expropriate vast lands of 57 families in the Bethlehem–Beit Jala area and separate two monasteries in the valley. It suggested to the Defence Ministry to reconsider an alternative less harmful rout. Nevertheless, the Defence Ministry restarted works in August 2015 causing enormous local and international protests.[46] A special problem has been the passage of church dignitaries and clerics through the army checkpoints. The young, untrained soldiers manning the checkpoints have not been given clear instructions of how to treat religious dignitaries with due respect. Together with the Citizenship and Entry to Israel laws, the separation wall is likely to inflict further serious damage on the diminishing Christian communities in Jerusalem and the West Bank.

CHRISTIANS IN HAIFA – A DIFFERENT MODEL OF JEWISH-ARAB RELATIONS

Haifa presents a different model of the Christian position and Jewish-Arab relations from that of Jerusalem as a result of the different historical, social, ethnoreligious, as well as economic settings of the two cities.

Holiness versus Secularism

Jerusalem is not only the capital of Israel but one of the most venerated cities in the world, if not the holiest. It bears the mark of interreligious and intercommunal rivalries and competition over the holy sites of the three monotheistic religions as well as a considerable degree of communal segregation. Haifa is the largest coastal town in the north of Israel. It has hardly any significant holy sites in it and religious competition over them barely exists. It has a hard core of secular middle class who have relatively free intercommunal relations.

Historical Development

In contrast to the historical religious significance of Jerusalem, Haifa developed into a town relatively late, at the turn of the nineteenth century and the beginning of the twentieth century. Furthermore, Haifa's major development took place during the British Mandate, destined to become the biggest deep water harbor in the eastern Mediterranean and the major British army base in Palestine. Haifa and its bay became under the British Mandate the largest center of heavy industry, including the oil refineries, the railways headquarters, as well as industries catering to the British army. As such it attracted Jewish entrepreneurs, blue-collar workers, and white-collar professionals. Haifa also attracted many Arabs, among whom Christians were prominent in search of economic opportunities and open lifestyle were prominent. Jews and Arabs partnered and worked together in many commercial and professional firms. For years the mayor of Haifa was a Muslim Arab and the mayor's deputy was a Jew. The two cooperated for the development of the town. On the eve of the 1948 war, the heads of the Jewish leadership of Haifa called the Arab leadership to remain in town and not to leave. After the war the good relations between Jews and Arabs resumed.

Communal Establishment and Institutions

The Jewish establishment, part of the Christian one, and some Muslim Arab dignitaries of the British Mandatory period remained in or returned to Haifa after the 1948 war. However, Haifa has had no old established traditional religious or ethnocommunal leadership equivalent to that of Jerusalem. The religious leadership of all communities in Haifa has had no significant influence on the town's public life. In contrast, Jerusalem is dominated by the holy sites and the communal rivalry over them; religious communities are highly segregated and religious leaders control not only their segregated communities but also the public sphere.

Majority-Minority Relationship

The fact that since 1948 a large proportion of Haifa's Arab population has been Christian explains the relatively smooth relationship between Jews and Arabs in this town. Christian Arabs have been closer to the Jews than to Muslim Arabs in their family lifestyle, education, and position of women. Furthermore, the Arab population of Haifa forms approximately 10 percent of the town's total population and therefore is not in any way a menace in the eyes of the Jewish majority. In contrast, the Arab population of East Jerusalem is approximately 30–40 percent and is conceived as a menace by many of the Jewish majority of the city. Whereas Jerusalem suffers from the decline of its Christian citizens, Haifa attracts migration of Arabs, largely Christians, mainly from the north of the country.

More than in any other town in Israel, Christians in Haifa are prominent in white-collar professions as hospital doctors, nurses, academics, lawyers and judges, engineers, and pharmacists. With quite a number of Arab largely Christian actors in the Haifa Theater, one of the first Arabic theaters was established in the town. Hence, Haifa competes with Nazareth as the premier center of Arab cultural and leisure activities.

Perhaps the zenith of multiculturalism in Haifa is the annual festival of "The Holiday of the Holidays" that has been taking place during December for the last twenty years. The festival celebrates the holidays of the three monotheistic religions but focuses on Christmas and New Year celebrations. Centered in Wadi Nisnas and the German Colony, the downtown Arab commercial marketplace and restaurants area in the vicinity of the Christian Arab neighborhoods of Haifa, the celebrations include Christmas parades by various scouting groups, lightings and singings, street theater and dances, food vendors, gift shops, and an indoor antiques market. In recent years the festival has expanded to include new exhibitions in the neighboring museums and art galleries as well as liturgical and classical music concerts in the local churches.

Many Jewish visitors go to this festival from all parts of Israel to enjoy its cheerful multicultural atmosphere. The spirit of the festival is symbolized by the huge ecological Christmas tree, made of recycled materials, that the Haifa municipality builds at the bottom of the German Colony facing the magnificent Baha'i gardens on the slope of Mount Carmel. The festival opens each year with an official ceremony chaired by the mayor of Haifa in the presence of Christian and other communal dignitaries. Haifa is the third-largest town in Israel and its open multiculturalism can serve as a model in sharp contrast to the extremism and violence that threaten Jerusalem and its vicinity.

SUMMARY

After hundreds of years of marginalization, Western powers and churches brought about the improvement of the position of indigenous Christians in nineteenth-century Palestine. The most significant contribution was the establishment of Western style schooling systems in which local Christians acquired education that enabled them to become the link between the local Muslims and the European powers; they maintained that capacity under the British Mandatory rule in Palestine 1918–1948, which made this period the heyday of the local Christians in Palestine.

The transformation from the British Mandate to the newly established State of Israel in 1948 presented many challenges to Palestinian Christians. Established as the nation-state of the Jewish people, Israel declared freedom and equality for all of its citizens regardless of religion, ethnicity, and gender. During its war of independence against its neighboring Arab states in 1948, Israel enabled its Arab citizens including the Christian ones to take part in the elections to its parliament, the Knesset, as in the political arena. Christian Knesset members played a conspicuous role in representing the Arab minority during the formative years of the state. However, they were marginalized to a large extent by their identification with Communist ideology and the Soviet Union and were conceived by many Jews as adversaries of the state.

The numbers and proportion of Christian Knesset members have declined since the 1980s, but they have still remained prominent. Such was Azmi Bishara, an Arab nationalist intellectual from Galilee who maintained a vocal campaign for the abolition of Israel as the nation-state of the Jewish people. Against the background of the right-wing governments and the intensifying Palestinian Israeli conflict, Bishara's speeches and activities harmed the Jewish-Christian as well as Jewish-Arab fragile relations in Israel and unjustly stigmatized the Christian Arab citizens of the state as anti-Israeli. Since Bishara left Israel, Christian Knesset members such as Nadia Hilou and Hanna Sweid have taken a more settled line, targeting economic and social issues of the Arab sector that apply to the Israeli public at large. They have met some success and opened the way to more understanding in the Israeli public of the problems of the Christians and the Arab minority at large.

The mountains of Galilee in the north of Israel form the largest center of the Christian Arabs in Israel. Residing often in mixed villages of Muslim, Christian, and Druze, the Christians have been the most prosperous element as a result of their easier access to Western and higher education. At the same time they have been the most vulnerable community vis-à-vis their Muslim and Druze neighbors. The 1980s marked the undermining of the intercommunal balance among Muslims, Christians, and Druze in Galilee. The relations with the Druze were damaged as a result of the First Lebanon War, in which the Druze soldiers of the IDF sometimes fought against Christians of south Lebanon. The relations with the Muslims were impaired by the rise of the Islamist movement and its growing influence on Arab localities. Hence intercommunal feuds have occurred between Christians and Druze as well as between Christians and Muslims in which the Christians have often been the losers. Police intervention was often insufficient and late.

The deepening Israeli-Palestinian conflict has had a worsening effect on the position of the Christians and the Arab minority at large most obviously since the 2000 Second Palestinian Intifada. In order to combat terror attacks and suicide bombs in Israeli cities and above all in Jerusalem, the Israeli government made regulations to block the entry of Palestinians into Israel. It also intended to preserve the Jewish majority in the state of Israel and to this end made steps to limit the entry and stay of church workers. These regulations have caused great damage to Christian communities in Jerusalem, in particular to the smaller ones, as well as to church institutions. Christians in other parts of Israel have been integrated to varying extents in the state; many of them have reached senior professional positions despite government discrimination. An obvious example of integration of Christians is Haifa, a coastal town with a strong core of secular middle class.

The treatment of minorities and in particular Christians is a touchstone of Israeli democracy; it has flaws but nevertheless Israel is still a haven for Christians compared to their status in other parts of the Middle East. Emigration of Christians from Israel has taken place since the nineteenth century and increased during times of crisis. At present, the Christian emigration rate is just a little higher than that of the Jews and does not pose an existential danger except for several small communities in East Jerusalem. Integration is stronger than emigration.

NOTES

This paper was written at the Harry S. Truman Institute for the Advancement of Peace, the Hebrew University of Jerusalem. Thanks are due to the assistance given.

1   On the Anglican and Protestant activities in Palestine in the nineteenth century see A. L. Tibawi, *British Interests in Palestine 1800–1901* (Oxford: Oxford University Press, 1961). On the Catholic activity, see P. Medebielle, *the Diocese of the Latin Patriarchate of Jerusalem* (Jerusalem, 1963).

2   Daphne Tsimhoni, *Christian Communities in Jerusalem and the West Bank since 1948: An Historical, Social and Political Study* (Westport, CT: Praeger, 1993); Daphne Tsimhoni, "The Christians in Israel and the Territories – Disappearance," *Middle East Quarterly* (Rutgers University) 8, no.1 (2001): 31–42.

3   *Statistical Abstract of Palestine, 1944–1945.*

4   Daphne Tsimhoni, "The Greek Orthodox Patriarchate of Jerusalem during the Formative Years of the British Mandate in Palestine," *Asian and African Studies* (*Journal of the Israel Oriental Society, University of Haifa*) 12, no. 1 (1978): 77–121; Daphne Tsimhoni, "The Arab Christians and the Palestinian Arab National Movement during the Formative Stage," in *The Palestinians and the Middle East Conflict*, ed. G. Ben-Dor (Ramat Gan: Turtledove, 1978), 73–98.

5   State of Israel, Central Bureau of Statistics, *Features of Israeli Citizens Who Departed Israel for More Than One Year and Came Back between 1996–2009*, publication no. 1558 published 24.4.2014, tables 2 and 7. Accessible at http://www.cbs.gov.il

6   Benny Morris, *The Birth of the Palestinian Refugee Problem, 1947–1949* (Hebrew edition) (Tel Aviv: Am Oved, 1997), 268–272, 317–318, 321–322, 392–393.

7   Uri Bialer, "Horse Trading: Israel and the Greek Orthodox Ecclesiastical Property, 1948–1952," *Journal of Israeli History* 24, no. 2 (2005): 203–213.

8   U. M. Kupferschmidt, *The Supreme Muslim Council: Islam under the British Mandate for Palestine* (Leiden: Brill, 1987); Daphne Tsimhoni, "The British Mandatory Government and the Status of the Religious Communities in Palestine," *Kathedra* no. 80 (1996): 150–174 (in Hebrew).

9   Aharon Layish, "The Communal Organization of the Muslims" in *The Arabs in Israel: Continuity and Change*, ed. Aharon Layish (Jerusalem: Magnes University Press, 1981), 104–122 (in Hebrew).

10 Robert M. Haddad, *Syrian Christians in Muslim Society, and Interpretation* (Princeton, NJ: Princeton University Press, 1970), 3.
11 Daphne Tsimhoni, "The Political Configuration of the Christians in Israel," *Hamizrah Hehadash* 32 (1989): 139–164 (in Hebrew).
12 See, for instance, her article in *I24 News* August 4, 2014 "Boycott of Israel's Arabs Is Guaranteed to Backfire," accessed October 15, 2014, http://www.i24news.tv/en/opinion/ 39262-140805-boycott-of-israel-s-arabs-is-guaranteed-to-backfire
13 *Times of Israel*, December 19, 2013, accessed October 14, 2014, http://www.timesofisrael .com/christian-mk-calls-for-knesset-christmas-tree/; *Jerusalem Post*, December 22, 2013.
14 Daphne Tsimhoni, "The Christians in Israel: Between Religion and Politics," in *The Arabs in Israeli Politics: Dilemmas of Identity*, ed. Elie Rekhes (Tel Aviv: Tel Aviv University, 1998), 66–68 (in Hebrew).
15 *Ha'aretz*, June 14, 1999.
16 Daphne Tsimhoni, "The Shihab Al-Din Mosque Affair in Nazareth: A Case Study of Muslim-Christian-Jewish Relations in the State of Israel," in *Holy Places in the Israeli-Palestinian Conflict*, ed. Marshall J. Breger, Yitzhak Reiter, and Leonard Hammer (London: Routledge, 2010), 192–230.
17 State of Israel, Central Bureau of Statistics, *Statistical Abstract of Israel* no. 54, 2003 (Jerusalem, 2003), tables 2.2, 2.27, http://www.cbs.gov.il
18 The Citizenship and Entry into Israel Law (Temporary Provision), Israel Code 5763 (2003), http://www.knesset.gov.il/laws/special/eng/citizenship_law.htm
19 Eli Varon, senior consultant to the minister of the interior on population administration, interview by Daphne Tsimhoni, July 29, 2004.
20 Daphne Tsimhoni, "Christians in Jerusalem: A Minority at Risk," *Journal of Human Rights* 4(2005): 406–407.
21 Daniel Rosing, interview by Daphne Tsimhoni, August 5, 2004.
22 Tsimhoni, "Christians in Jerusalem," 407.
23 Jacob Salama, head of the Religious (Non-Jewish) Communities section, interview by Daphne Tsimhoni, July 27, 2004; Yossi Hershler and Gadi Golan, head of the Religious Affairs Bureau in the Israeli Foreign Ministry, interview by Daphne Tsimhoni, August 5, 2004.
24 Daniel Rosing, Gadi Golan, Yossi Hershler, legal consultant to the Religious (non-Jewish) Section, Ministry of the Interior, interviews by Daphne Tsimhoni, August 5, 2004; Shmuel Evyatar, consultant to the mayor of Jerusalem on Christian affairs, interview by Daphne Tsimhoni, July 28, 2004; Eli Varon, interview by Daphne Tsimhoni, July 29, 2004.
25 Fuad Farah, interview by Daphne Tsimhoni, April 20, 2014.
26 Riad Ali's reportage about Naddaf and the conscription forum, *Friday Evening News*, Israeli TV Channel 1, May 2, 2014.
27 Yariv Levin, interview by Shalom Yerushalmi, January 8, 2014, *Ma'ariv* http://www.nrg .co.il/online/1/ART2/538/036.html
28 For reporting about the events see the Communist Party of Israel Web site, April 30, 2014, http://maki.org.il/en/?p=3031, visited October 28, 2014.
29 Jerusalem Institute for Israel Studies, *Statistical Yearbook of Jerusalem*, 2014 edition (Jerusalem, 2014) table III/10 – Population of Jerusalem, by Age, Religion and Geographical Spreading, 2012, http://jiis.org/?cmd=statistic.503
30 For a list of these institutions, see Ruth Lapidoth, *The Old City of Jerusalem* (Jerusalem: Jerusalem Institute for Israel Studies, 2002), 41, 151–158 (in Hebrew).

31　For a detailed discussion see Tsimhoni, "Christians in Jerusalem," 391–394.

32　Tsimhoni, "Christians in Jerusalem," 394–399.

33　Jerusalem Institute for Israel Studies, *Statistical Yearbook of Jerusalem* 2014 edition (Jerusalem, 2014) Table III/10 – Population of Jerusalem, by Age, Religion and Geographical Spreading, 2012, http://jiis.org/?cmd=statistic.503

34　Shmuel Berkovits, *The Battle for the Holy Places* (Or Yehuda: Hed Arzi, 2000), 58–60, 174–176 (in Hebrew).

35　Berkovits, *Battle for the Holy Places*, 63–64, 177.

36　Berkovits, *Battle for the Holy Places*, 199–202.

37　Tsimhoni, *Christian Communities*, 176–180; Berkovits, *Battle for the Holy Places*, 180–183.

38　Amir Cheshin, Bill Hutman, and Avi Melamed, *Separate and Unequal, the Inside Story of Israeli Rule in East Jerusalem* (Cambridge, MA: Harvard University Press, 1999), 32, 236–238, 241–242.

39　Berkovits, *Battle for the Holy Places*, 183–190.

40　Tsimhoni, *Christian Communities*, 167–202.

41　Tsimhoni, "Christians in Jerusalem," 398–403.

42　Tsimhoni, "Christians in Jerusalem," 399–401; Berkovits, *Battle for the Holy Places*, 165–167.

43　Reports in *Haaretz*, March 2004; Shmuel Evyatar, interview by Daphne Tsimhoni, July 28, 2004.

44　Tsimhoni, *Christian Communities*, 11.

45　According to several Israeli officials who maintained contacts with the population of Bethlehem during the early 1990s, Christian dignitaries appealed discreetly and privately to Israeli officials to annex the Bethlehem area to Jerusalem or at least not to transfer it to the PA's full authority (zone A). The then-Israeli foreign minister, Shimon Peres, refused to take any action in that direction.

46　*Haaretz*, August 5 & 9, 2004 and in particular the public challenge of the chief of staff by Shmuel Toledano, the former consultant to the prime minister on Arab affairs; *Haaretz*, August 18, 2015.

15

Arab Muslim Attitudes toward Religious Minorities

Michael Hoffman and Amaney A. Jamal

INTRODUCTION

Recent developments in the Arab world have shattered the feeble equilibrium that once existed. Uprisings in Egypt, Libya, Syria, and elsewhere have undermined long-established dictators and created an ever-present threat of violence in many parts of the region. In many cases, religious minorities are particularly endangered. The conflict in Syria has taken an increasingly sectarian tone in lockstep with its increasing level of violence. Conditions have become so severe that some Arab Christian observers outside Syria believe that this conflict "will likely be the final blow for Syria's embattled Christians."[1] Electoral victories for Islamist parties in Tunisia and Egypt (albeit a short-lived victory in the latter case) have certainly not comforted Christians and other non-Muslims in the Arab world. It seems that the birthplace of several of the world's largest faith traditions is still a hotbed of conflict between religious groups, and the outcome remains as uncertain as ever.

The growing uncertainty in the region – particularly for religious minorities – creates a vital need for understanding the social forces that shape relations between the faiths in these countries. If the Arab Spring revolutions were to bring about a more "popular" form of government, in contrast to the dictatorships that preceded them, then it is crucial to examine what popular demands might be. Popular rule does not necessarily mean tolerance. As Tocqueville famously warned, rule by the majority can result in highly unequal treatment of minority groups.[2] There is thus no logical necessity that elections, however free and fair, will lead to improved conditions for non-Muslims in the Arab world; in fact, many observers have predicted just the opposite.

This chapter remedies some of the uncertainty regarding Arab attitudes toward religious minorities and religious freedom. Using recent original data from the Arab

Department of Politics, Princeton University. The authors thank Ravonne Nevels for outstanding research support.

Barometer, it examines the attitudes of Arab citizens toward religious minorities through a number of different religious and political lenses. Furthermore, it considers the origins of these attitudes. Views about non-Muslims (and political policies relevant to them) were collected in ten Arab societies, providing valuable insight into the minds of everyday citizens in this important part of the world. In order to understand the plight of Christians and other religious minorities in the Arab world, we must consider the beliefs and attitudes of the Muslim citizens who make up the majority of the population in these countries.

HISTORICAL BACKGROUND

Relations between Christians and Muslims in the Arab world have, since the establishment of Islam in the region, consisted of a complex mixture of coexistence and conflict. Hourani observes that after the spread of Islam, Muslims and Christians generally managed to live side by side, though "there remained a gulf of ignorance and prejudice between them."[3] Mitri characterizes this persistent arrangement as "hierarchical pluralism."[4]

The history of Muslim-Christian interactions in the Middle East is one that begins from the very inception of Islam, which has theological ties to Christianity. As the scholar of Islam John Esposito writes in his book *Islam: The Straight Path*, "The monotheistic message of the Qur'an and the preaching of Muhammad did not occur in a vacuum. Monotheism had been flourishing in Semitic and Iranian cultures for centuries preceding Muhammad's ministry."[5] This monotheistic message, grounded in the belief of the God of Abraham, was the starting marker for both Christian and Islamic belief. Islam, in its dawning after the inception of Christianity, sees itself as the completed continuation of Christian message. In Islam, Muhammad is God's final prophet and the Qur'an is God's final revelation. For many Muslims, Christianity is therefore mistaken in thinking not only that Jesus was God, but that the revelation ended in him. As Sidney Griffith writes, "Arabic speaking Jews and Christians were no doubt in the audience to whom the Qur'an first addressed the word of God.... Just a brief acquaintance with the text of the Qur'an is sufficient to convince any reader that it presumes in its audience a ready familiarity with ... the Old and New Testaments"[6] – or, as Albert Hourani alternatively describes it, "for those who accepted the message, the familiar world was made anew."[7]

Islam cannot be completely separated from Christianity theologically, and technically Arab Christians were among the religious plurality that Islam was trying to convert. Thus the questions of what it means theologically and practically to be a tolerant Muslim when there are professing Christians around, and to be a tolerant Christian when there are professing Muslims around, is a question that began in seventh-century Arabia and continues to this day.[8] This is especially evident considering the two groups' somewhat competing views of completed revelation and, historically, their competing grabs for power.[9]

A fundamental way that Muslims, during the inception of Islam and throughout the early period, thought of Christians was through the concepts of People of the Book and *dhimmi* status. *Ahl al-kitaab*, or "People of the Book," is a term the Qur'an uses to signify the adherents of Judaism and Christianity and sometimes Sabaeans or Zoroastrians.[10] Their "books," although seen as "inaccurate" in some ways, still hold a position of value within Islamic thought because the Qur'an is considered to be their completed continuation;[11] thus, "like their books," Christians were seen as being misled by the New Testament and belief in a triune God, but at the same time as still deserving due respect from Muslims because of their monotheistic tradition and belief in the divine.[12]

During Islam's early days, Christians and Jews were called *dhimmis*, followers of religions that were protected by the Qur'anic mandate to tolerate "People of the Book." While tolerated, these subjects were not considered equal to Muslims and were required to pay a special tax (*jizyah*) and placed under various restrictions.[13] However, as Cleveland notes, this arrangement was "unusually tolerant" for the period.[14]

This vague quality of due respect was a part of the concept of the *dhimmi*. As Esposito notes, during the early Islamic conquests, People of the Book were allowed legal protections under Islamic rule, including religious freedom,[15] the right to practice and worship in their own churches, and the right to govern their own affairs, so long as they paid a tax.[16] It should also be noted that "*dhimmis* were not permitted to publicize or proselytize their faiths."[17] Christians suffered other forms of marginalization and discrimination. For example, they were not allowed to marry Muslim women, they often could not launch legal disputes against Muslims, and they were excluded from positions of power.[18] Nevertheless, Esposito notes, "while by modern standards this treatment amounted to second-class citizenship, in premodern times, it was very advanced. No such tolerance existed in Christendom, where Jews, Muslims, and Christians (those who did not accept the authority of the pope) were subjected to forced conversion, persecution, or expulsion."[19] The concept of the *dhimmi*, though, has generally become unfashionable and irrelevant in modern times, especially considering its discriminatory features and notion of second-class citizenship. The latter idea is particularly ill suited to modern politics given the establishment of modern, Western-style nation-states – where usually one either is or is not a citizen.[20]

During the Middle Ages, an important development in Christian and Muslim relations was the spread of Islamic civilization, and the eleventh-century Christian Crusades that emerged in response. Hourani notes that the period of the seventh and eighth centuries was the time when Islamic armies, under the caliphate, made massive inroads into Christian territory – including Syria, Jerusalem, Egypt, North Africa, Spain, and Sicily – leaving masses of conversions in their wake.[21] Esposito writes, "While conversions were initially slow, by the eleventh century large numbers of Christians living under Muslim rule were converting to Islam through force or choice. Even those who had remained Christian were becoming 'Arabized,' adopting Arabic language and manners. The European Christian response was, with few exceptions, hostile, intolerant, and belligerent."[22] He also writes, "By the eleventh century, Christendom's response to Islam took two forms: the struggle to reconquer (the *Reconquista*) Spain (1000–1492) and Italy and Sicily (1061), and the undertaking of another series of Christian holy wars – the Crusades (1095–1143)."[23] It should be noted that even during these very hostile times, Muslims and Christians still traded,[24] the Islamic and Arabic intellectual traditions were still greatly influenced by the growth of European intellectual development,[25] and Muslims still "tolerated the practice of Christianity."[26] Thus, it has been said that "the Middle Ages presented many apparent contradictions in Christian-Muslim relations."[27]

The Ottoman Empire (1299–1922) organized religious minorities within its borders into relatively autonomous communities called *millets*. Under this system, Christians (along with Jews) were given religious freedom and allowed to maintain separate religious educational and legal systems.[28] This arrangement is commonly cited as the predecessor of systems of "personal status" in such countries as Lebanon, where religious rather than civil courts have jurisdiction over matters such as inheritance and marriage law. With the formation of contemporary states in the Arab region were introduced a variety of different institutional arrangements regarding matters of religion and state, an issue to which we will turn shortly.

During the Ottoman Empire, the *millet* system was conceptually very similar to the *dhimmi* system.[29] In it, the Ottoman sultanate legally protected non-Muslim religious leadership – particularly those of "Greek Orthodox, Armenian Gregorian, and Jewish"[30] religious persuasion – especially in their rights to religious freedom by allowing them to govern their own affairs as long as they collected taxes.[31] During this period, Christian and Muslim relations, at least legally, were positive, and Christians generally retained the freedom to practice their own religion under Islamic rule.

In its dealings with Europeans, the Ottoman Empire engaged in the practice of giving out capitulations, which were "commercial privileges ... granted by Muslim states ... to Christian Europe states desiring to carry on trade in what was technically enemy territory ... these capitulations set custom rates, established security of life, property, and religion, and set up channels for dealing with problems and legal disputes."[32] Although this system at face value seemed to be an excellent force for Christian and Muslim relations, in actuality it was part of the basis for the downfall of the Ottoman Empire. European powers used capitulations to further their economic stature, leading to imperial ambitions.[33]

Although the basic *dhimmi* and *millet* systems are no longer a modern feature of Islamic societies, there are small minorities today that seek to implement something like them in Islamic states – while there are those who desire only to look to these systems as a paradigm of the tolerance of pluralism within Islam.[34] Yet the question of how Muslims and Christians should, on a grand scale, relate to each other in Islamic societies has not ended. This question has not been resolved by the contentious relationship between Muslim and Western societies in recent years.[35] Certainly, the rise of militant Islam, especially after the September 11 attacks, and other instances of fringe militant Islamic aggression, have elevated Christian concerns and worries about Islam and the future of pluralism in the Middle East.[36] In order to help answer basic questions about the other faith, as well as to practice interreligious pluralism, Muslim-Christian interreligious dialogue and understanding groups are slowly becoming a prominent feature of current Muslim-Christian relations.[37]

RELATIONSHIPS AND PATTERNS TODAY

It is no secret that many Arab countries lag behind world averages in terms of formal religious freedom. Both formal policies and political discourse move between expressions of tolerance and repression of heterodoxy with remarkable fluidity; Egypt's Muslim Brotherhood is a clear example. While the Brotherhood's agenda is clearly Islamist in nature, one of its most important former leaders, Abdel Moneim Aboul Fatouh, stated that "nobody should interfere if a Christian decides to convert to Islam or a Muslim decides to leave Islam and become a Christian."[38] In elite discourse, certain levels of religious tolerance are usually present, but explicit support for complete religious freedom is rare.

Perhaps unsurprisingly, studies of religious freedom and tolerance in the Arab world are mixed. Fox and Sandler find that while Arab countries, on average, integrate religion and state more than Western democracies, Western countries combine religion and politics more than is commonly believed.[39] Their data suggest that within the region of the Middle East and North Africa (MENA), an overwhelming majority of countries have dietary laws, religious inheritance laws, restrictions on conversion away from Islam, restrictions on interfaith marriages, and censorship laws that suppress materials deemed antireligious.[40] Further, close to 90 percent of these countries restrict proselytization among minority religions. However, the majority of MENA countries do *not* restrict public observance, access to places of worship, production or dissemination of religious materials, or ordination of clergy, and barely 20 percent of countries in the region require religious minorities to observe Islamic religious laws.[41]

A more severe picture emerges in the findings of the Pew Global Restrictions reports. The MENA region records the highest levels of both government restrictions on religion and social hostilities involving religion. Indeed, the median scores of the MENA countries on these two measures – 5.8 and 4.3, respectively – are outliers compared to those of other regions in the world (the next highest region, Asian-Pacific, records scores of 3.4 and 2.2, respectively).[42] We elaborate on these findings later.

Many Christians in the Arab World have reacted fearfully to these sometimes repressive or hostile state policies. Kattan writes, "It is also well known that Christians in the Middle East today are extremely anxious about their steadily diminishing numbers and feel threatened by an ascending Islamic extremism."[43] While acknowledging the threats facing the Arab Christian community, Mitri argues that the major problems for Arab Christians also affect Arab Muslims in the same countries.[44] At the same time, it is clear that the considerable amount of formal religious discrimination faced by Christians in most Arab countries does not affect Muslim religious freedoms in the same way. In some cases, the Arab Spring has only heightened Christian fears. Pope Francis recently told leaders of Arab Christian churches that the Vatican "will not resign itself to a Middle East without Christians."[45] In late 2011, the Maronite Christian Patriarch Bechara Rai vocally expressed his concern about the potential removal of the Assad regime in Syria, suggesting that its likely successor was a Sunni fundamentalist regime that would threaten Christian minorities in the country.[46] Other Christian leaders have made similar observations, implying that a brutal authoritarian regime, whatever its faults, might nevertheless provide essential protection for religious minorities (and Christians particularly). Without these protections, some elites fear that successor states will pursue policies akin to the more repressive practices found in other Arab states, or perhaps enact even more severe laws.

Of course, it is important to distinguish between formal policies and individual attitudes, since the actions of the regime may not reflect the personal convictions of citizens in any meaningful way. Arzt writes that "it must be borne in mind that the repressive policies of militant Islamic regimes today have been imposed top-down, by the unelected (even where they claim to be 'the elect').[47] They are not by any means a reflection of the will of the Muslim people." Religious discrimination in the Arab world may exist to serve the political purposes of incumbent regimes rather than constitute a response to the will of the citizenry. To this end, we must turn to individual-level data regarding attitudes toward members of other faiths.

In addition to the new realities and fears that have been exacerbated by the possible limitations on minority rights posed by Islamists winning greater political influence after the Arab Spring, there remain other concerns as well. Primarily, Christians in the Middle East and North Africa have by and large been a minority population. While many Christian groups have managed to integrate very successfully, and in fact many Christian groups outperform their Muslim counterparts socioeconomically, they nevertheless retain minority status across the region. While Christian standing varies from country to country, our chapter examines in further detail the ways in which Muslim populations assess minority rights across the Arab world.

SURVEY EVIDENCE

Tolerance of members of other religions can be measured in a variety of ways. The second wave of the Arab Barometer, conducted in 2010 and 2011 in ten Arab countries, includes several items that can be used to assess the level of religious tolerance across the region. Perhaps the most useful item asks, "Which of the following groups would you not like to have members of as neighbors?" Respondents were then prompted with "Followers of other religions" and allowed to answer either "I do not want them to be my neighbors" or "I do not object."

Figure 15.1 displays the proportion of respondents in each country who responded that they would not object to having members of other religions as neighbors. As this figure demonstrates, a solid majority of Arab citizens express a willingness to live near members of other faiths; however, the proportion falling into this category

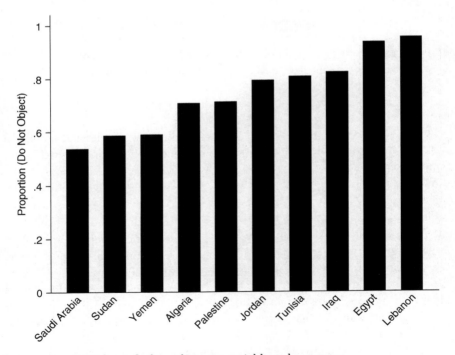

FIGURE 15.1. Members of other religions as neighbors, by country.
Do you object to having members of other religions as neighbors?

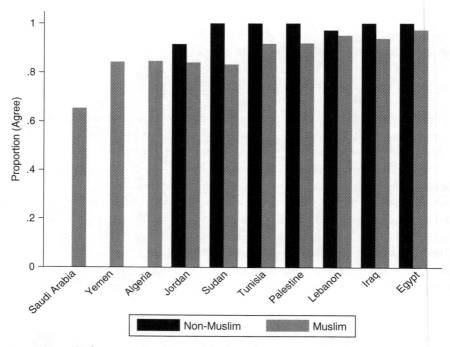

FIGURE 15.2. Right to practice for non-Muslims, by country and religion.
Religious minorities have the right to practice their religion freely [Agree/Disagree].

varies widely across countries. In Lebanon and Egypt, virtually all respondents
responded that they did not object, while barely half of Saudi Arabian respondents
expressed this sentiment. Less than 60 percent of respondents from Sudan and
Yemen reported tolerance according to this measure.

Another possible way to measure tolerance relates to religious practice more
directly.

Figure 15.2 displays the proportions of respondents in each country (divided
into Muslims and non-Muslims where applicable) who agreed with the statement
"Religious minorities have the right to practice their religion freely." Unsurprisingly,
in each country for which Christian respondents are available, Christians are more
likely than Muslims to support this statement.[48] Nevertheless, most respondents of
either faith support the right of non-Muslims to practice their faith. The proportion
of Muslims supporting religious freedom according to this measurement exceeds
60 percent in all countries and exceeds 80 percent in every country except Saudi
Arabia. The fact that support for this proposition remains so high even in Saudi
Arabia is surprising given the kingdom's policies on religious freedom: The U.S.

State Department's 2012 report on religious freedom in Saudi Arabia begins with the following statement: "Freedom of religion is neither recognized nor protected under the law and the government severely restricted it in practice."[49] It is evident that Saudi citizens express support for these freedoms even though their own government expressly denies them. In this sense, it is perhaps surprising that Saudi Arabia does *not* diverge from the general trend in a more noticeable way. In every country in our sample, a solid majority supports religious rights of non-Muslims. Thus, the evidence suggests that Arab Muslims widely support freedom of religious practice for religious minorities.

The Arab Barometer also asked respondents a question about the *political* rights of non-Muslims in their countries. This item asked respondents the extent to which they agreed with the following statement: "In a Muslim country, non-Muslims should enjoy less political rights than Muslims." This measure provided much more variation in responses than the previous item, as shown in Figure 15.3. As expected, Christians were far less likely to support this statement than were Muslims (the sole exception being Tunisia, where the small number of Christian respondents makes it impossible to draw conclusions about the Christian population). What is more noticeable, however, is the wide range of opinions on this issue across countries. In countries with sizable Christian populations such as Lebanon and Egypt, agreement with this claim was fairly rare (less than 10 percent among Lebanese Muslims and below 25 percent among Egyptian Muslims). More homogenously Muslim countries such as Sudan and Saudi Arabia had higher levels of agreement, between 40 and 50 percent. Still, it is notable that in no country did a majority of respondents agree either weakly or strongly with this statement. While on average Arab Muslims appear to be more supportive of the *religious* rights of non-Muslims, a majority in every country rejects the idea of non-Muslims being politically inferior, even in a Muslim country.

Figure 15.4 depicts the responses to a question asking about the relationship between religious and political values. In this question, respondents were asked the extent to which they agree with the statement "Religious or denominational difference should not be a reason for doubting the patriotism of any individual." On this item, a few trends stand out. First, Christians are not necessarily more likely than Muslims to agree with this statement. In Lebanon, where more than five hundred Christians were surveyed, Christians are actually slightly *less* likely to agree. Second, overall agreement with this statement is quite high: Arab citizens, whether Muslim or Christian, overwhelmingly agree that religious differences are *not* a reason to doubt another person's patriotism. Third, Saudi Arabia is once again the country demonstrating the lowest average level of support for religious tolerance, though this difference is fairly slim in this case. By and large, Arab citizens do not view religious denomination as a criterion for judging someone's patriotism.

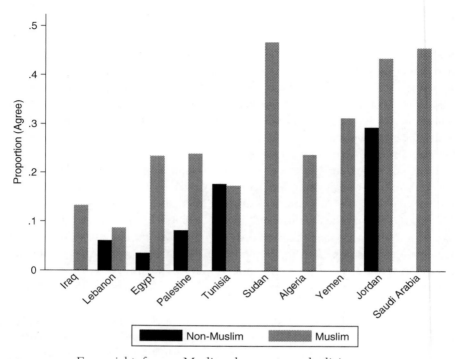

FIGURE 15.3. Fewer rights for non-Muslims, by country and religion.
In a Muslim country, non-Muslims should enjoy less political rights than Muslims [Agree/
Disagree].

It is worth considering the extent to which religious tolerance varies according to levels of religious behavior. We examine differences in religious tolerance (as measured by willingness to have a member of another religion as a neighbor) according to frequency of mosque attendance. For this question, respondents were asked how often they attended Friday prayers at the mosque: We divided respondents into a "yes" category (those who responded "always" or "most of the time") and a "no" category (all others). Mosque attendance is a useful measure of religious behavior; Jamal (2005) finds that in the United States, mosque attendance enhances group consciousness. In the Arab context, it is plausible that enhanced Muslim group consciousness may decrease religious tolerance. Figure 15.5 compares attenders and non-attenders according to our first measure of tolerance. In six of the ten countries (Yemen, Sudan, Algeria, Palestine, Jordan, and Iraq), attenders are indeed less tolerant than non-attenders, though these differences are only larger than a few percentage points in Sudan and Algeria. In the remaining countries (Saudi Arabia, Tunisia, Egypt, and Lebanon), attenders are *more* likely to express tolerance than are

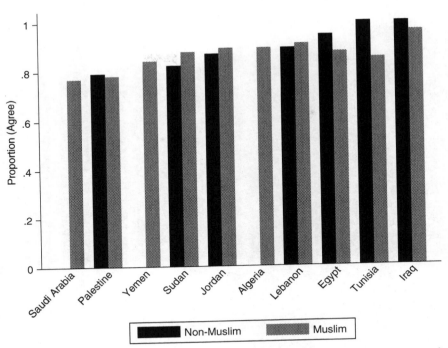

FIGURE 15.4. Religious differences not a reason to doubt someone's patriotism, by country and religion.
Religious or denominational difference should not be a reason for doubting the patriotism of any individual [Agree/Disagree].

non-attenders, although these differences are not sizable in any case. What is clear is that mosque attendance does *not* seem to promote religious intolerance across the board. While in a few countries, attenders may be markedly less tolerant than non-attenders, in almost half of the countries we examine, attenders are actually *more* tolerant than non-attenders on average.

One important limitation of the questions examined is that they ask about religious minorities or members of other faiths in a general sense rather than asking about members of particular groups. Specifically, the Arab Barometer does not ask respondents about their attitudes toward *Christians* as a precise group (though in most Arab countries, the term "religious minorities" would tend to imply Christians). To remedy this shortcoming, we analyze data from the Pew Forum's global survey of Islam, collected between 2008 and 2012. This survey covers several Arab countries and asked respondents a number of items regarding their attitudes toward Christians specifically.

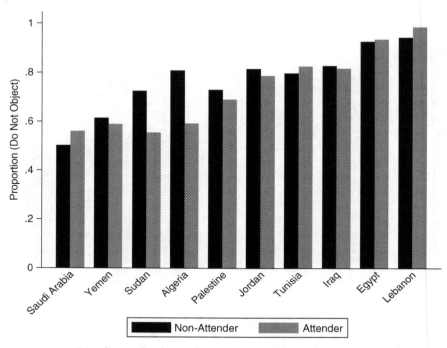

FIGURE 15.5. Members of other religions as neighbors, by country and mosque attendance (Muslims only).
Do you object to having members of other religions as neighbors?

The Pew survey asked respondents a number of questions that are quite different from anything found in the Arab Barometer, providing valuable insights into how Arab Muslims perceive Christianity. A particularly interesting item asks respondents whether or not they think Christianity and Islam "have a lot in common" or "are very different."

Figure 15.6 displays the relative frequencies of these responses by country and religious denomination. As this figure demonstrates, considerable variation exists among the countries in this sample. In general, however, more Arab Muslims believe that Islam and Christianity are very different. For the most part, Christians are more likely than Muslims in their respective countries to perceive similarities between the faiths; the lone exception is in Egypt, where Christians were somewhat less likely to agree that Islam and Christianity have a lot in common. Perhaps surprisingly, Iraq is the country where the highest percentage of respondents perceived such similarities (Palestinian Christians accounted for only eight respondents, so their striking result should be interpreted with caution).

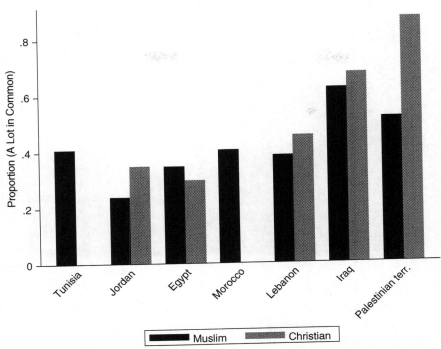

FIGURE 15.6. Islam and Christianity have a lot in common, by country and religion. From what you know, do you think that the Muslim religion and the Christian religion have a lot in common, or do you think that the Muslim religion and the Christian religion are very different?

It is worth asking, however, how much the Muslims in this sample actually *know* (or believe they know) about Christianity; to the extent that they perceive differences between the faiths, they may simply possess a lack of information about the Christian religion. Fortunately, the Pew survey asks respondents a question that captures self-perceived knowledge of Christianity. This question asks respondents how much they know about the Christian religion and its practices. Figure 15.7 displays the proportion of respondents in each country who believe that they know "a great deal" or "some" about Christianity, with the remainder of respondents knowing "not very much" or "nothing at all." The distribution of responses to this question is astonishing. In no country did more than 7 percent of respondents report that they know a great deal, and a clear majority in every country responded with "not very much" or "nothing at all." In countries with relatively larger Christian populations (Egypt, Jordan, and especially Lebanon), respondents were more willing to claim that they knew "some" about Christianity. Nevertheless, on the whole, knowledge

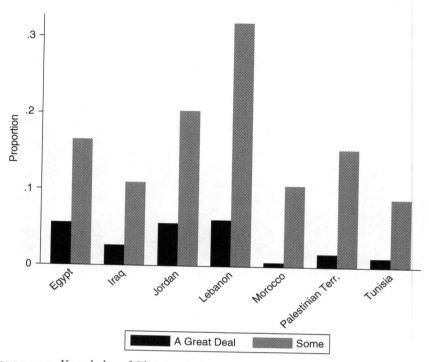

FIGURE 15.7. Knowledge of Christianity, by country.
How much would you say you know about the Christian religion and its practices – a great deal, some, not very much or nothing at all?

about the Christian faith – even *self-reported* knowledge – appears to be very low among Muslims in the Arab world and may be an important determinant of Muslim attitudes toward Christians in the region.

The Pew questionnaire also asks respondents about certain social attitudes relating to Christianity. Specifically, Muslim respondents were asked, "How comfortable would you be if a son [daughter] of yours someday married a Christian?" Figure 15.8 displays the proportion of respondents in each country who said that they would be "very" or "somewhat" comfortable with such an arrangement. Several important patterns stand out. First, less than a third of respondents in any country would be comfortable with their son's marrying a Christian, with several countries containing levels of support closer to 15 percent. Second, respondents in every country are even less supportive of their daughter's marrying a Christian; this difference is sizable in every country. Particularly worth noting is the Egyptian case; the "daughter" bar for Egypt is not missing; *not a single Egyptian respondent reported being comfortable*

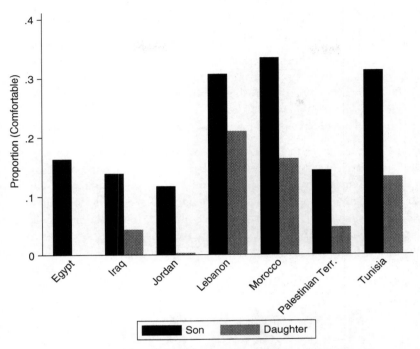

FIGURE 15.8. Comfort with son/daughter marrying Christian, by country.
How comfortable would you be if a son [daughter] of yours someday married a Christian?
Would you be very comfortable, somewhat comfortable, not too comfortable or not at all
comfortable?

with their daughter's marrying a Christian. Thus, while in general Arab Muslims
are tolerant of religious minorities and support their religious and political rights,
traditional religious boundaries remain strong in the area of social relations.

In order to obtain a more fine-grained understanding of the patterns of tolerance
toward Christians (and other religious minorities), the authors added several items
relevant to these topics to an original, nationally representative survey in Lebanon.
The case of Lebanon is of particular importance to this analysis as Lebanon is
the Arab country with the largest Christian population (though this population is
decreasing in relative terms, and certainly no longer constitutes the majority that it
once did). As a highly divided sectarian society with political institutions that revolve
around differences in religious denomination, Lebanon represents an ideal case
for specific analysis in this chapter; the fact that Syria's ongoing (and increasingly
sectarian) conflict has spilled over into Lebanon only heightens the importance
of this case. In this survey, respondents were asked four questions about religious

tolerance; in each case, they were presented with a prompt and asked to agree (weakly or strongly) or disagree (weakly or strongly):

1) Christians should be free to practice their religion throughout the Arab world.
2) A democracy must protect complete freedom of religion.
3) Discrimination against Christians and other religious minorities is a major problem in the Arab world today.
4) Most Lebanese citizens are tolerant of members of other religious groups.

Figure 15.9 displays the proportions of respondents who agreed with each of these statements, separated by sect. As this figure demonstrates, reported support for religious freedom is overwhelmingly high in Lebanon, even among non-Christians. Virtually all Shiites supported Christian religious freedom throughout the Arab world; somewhat fewer, though still more than 80 percent, of Sunnis agreed with this statement. A similar pattern was present for the question asking whether democracy requires complete freedom of religion, though in this case Sunnis were

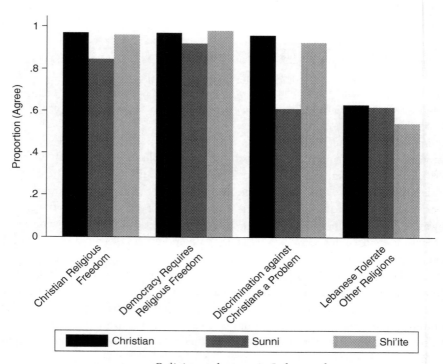

FIGURE 15.9. Religious tolerance in Lebanon, by sect.

close to unanimous as well in their support of this statement. The question regarding religious discrimination against Christians in the Arab world demonstrated the largest sectarian difference. While nearly all Christians and Shiites agreed with the statement, only about 60 percent of Sunnis did so. It is conceivable that the reasons for these differences may be largely demographic. Since these questions usually asked about the Arab world in general, where Sunnis constitute an overwhelming majority, Christians and Shiites would be likely to be more concerned about religious freedoms, even when they were not asked about their own sect explicitly. The final question asked respondents whether or not they believed that Lebanese were mostly tolerant of members of other religious groups. Christians and Sunnis were similar in their responses to this question, with a majority (though not overwhelming at just above 60 percent in each case) agreeing with the statement. Shiites were somewhat less optimistic about this claim, with a little more than half of respondents agreeing with the claim. For the most part, reported religious tolerance is high in Lebanon, though perhaps less so among Sunnis.

The results presented so far suggest a puzzling trend: While the Arab world is well known for its relatively repressive policies in the area of religion, ordinary citizens overwhelmingly express support for more tolerant policies. We suspect that the reason for this gap relates to the region's generally highly authoritarian regimes; religious freedom is hardly the only area in which public policies do not match public opinion in the Arab world (or in other places as well). Still, it is useful to consider the extent to which (average) public opinion is correlated with policies regarding religion in these countries. Using the seven cases from the Pew survey described, we compare the average level of belief that Islam and Christianity have a lot in common to the Pew Government Restrictions Index (GRI), which measures the extent to which governments restrict religion; higher scores indicate tighter restrictions. Figure 15.10 presents a scatterplot and linear fit of the countries' GRI scores and the proportion who believe that Islam and Christianity have a lot in common. As this figure demonstrates, the relationship is weak at best. While the linear fit slopes slightly downward, the slope is very small (-0.022) and nowhere close to statistical significance (p value $= 0.504$). It appears, therefore, that there is no clear correlation between public opinions on religious tolerance and government policies.

While bivariate comparisons by country are very useful for sketching patterns of attitudes across the Arab world, it is also helpful to consider these patterns in a multivariate setting. To that end, we estimated logistic regressions for each of the religious tolerance/knowledge variables from the Pew data as described earlier. Each model controls for standard covariates (gender, age, Internet usage, and rural residence) and includes country fixed effects, meaning that the estimated

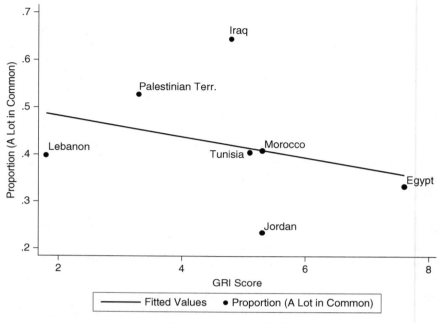

FIGURE 15.10. A lot in common and GRI, by country.

effects are for *within-country* variation rather than variation across countries. Our key independent variables of interest are weekly attendance at religious services and importance of religion. Table 15.1 presents the results of these models. A few interesting patterns stand out. First, weekly attendance is an extremely robust predictor of attitudes regarding Christianity, but not always in the same direction. While weekly attenders are much more likely to oppose the idea of their children's marrying a Christian and are much less likely to believe that Christianity and Islam have a lot in common, they are also substantially more likely to report that they know a great deal about the Christian faith. Importance of religion demonstrates similar (though even stronger) effects for the marriage items, but has no discernable effect on knowledge of Christianity or belief that Christianity and Islam are similar. Thus, different types of religious beliefs and behaviors appear to influence attitudes toward Christians on matters related to intermarriage across the faiths. Communal religious practice, as measured by weekly attendance, appears to play an especially strong role in predicting attitudes toward Christians; interestingly, weekly attendance increases self-reported knowledge about Christianity, but reduces pro-Christian attitudes.

TABLE 15.1. *Logistic regression results, PEW data*

	(1) Know a great deal	(2) A lot in common	(3) Son marry Christian OK	(4) Daughter marry Christian OK
Weekly attendance	0.51***	−0.21***	−0.43***	−0.35***
	(0.18)	(0.06)	(0.07)	(0.12)
Religion very important	0.02	−0.04	−0.82***	−1.07***
	(0.18)	(0.08)	(0.08)	(0.12)
Female	−0.08	−0.22***	−0.11	0.03
	(0.15)	(0.06)	(0.07)	(0.11)
Age	0.01*	0.00	−0.01***	−0.02***
	(0.01)	(0.00)	(0.00)	(0.00)
Uses Internet	0.24	0.19***	0.03	0.17
	(0.16)	(0.06)	(0.07)	(0.12)
Rural	0.11	−0.09	−0.14*	−0.16
	(0.17)	(0.07)	(0.07)	(0.12)
Constant	−3.78***	−0.39***	−0.29**	−0.32
	(0.34)	(0.13)	(0.15)	(0.22)
Country fixed effects	Y	Y	Y	Y
Observations	8147	6512	8161	6408
Pseudo-R-squared	0.066	0.036	0.078	0.151
AIC	2158.36	8509.82	7785.53	3434.30

Note: Standard errors in parentheses.
*$p < 0.10$, ** $p < 0.05$, *** $p < 0.01$.

CONCLUSION

In total, many patterns are evident in public opinion data regarding Arab attitudes toward religious minorities, and Christians in particular, but it is difficult to provide a singular account of these attitudes without paying attention to national differences and differences between citizens of various levels of piety. Still, a few general conclusions can be drawn.

First, cross-national differences in attitudes toward Christians and other religious minorities are often sizable. These differences do not necessarily correspond to state policies (or any monolithic Islamic negative agenda) toward non-Muslims, highlighting the importance of recognizing the difference between state behavior and individual attitudes. Second, support for the religious and political rights of non-Muslims is high in virtually every Arab country, even those where such rights are not formally recognized by political institutions. Arab citizens, regardless of their national origin, tend to support religious liberty and reject placing non-Muslims on a lower political tier.

At the same time, however, the high level of support for political and religious rights for non-Muslims does not necessarily translate into completely pluralistic attitudes about religion. Throughout the Arab world, Muslims report low levels of knowledge about Christianity and are uncomfortable with the idea of their sons' or daughters' marrying Christians. In most Arab countries, only a minority of Muslim respondents reported that Islam and Christianity have a lot in common. For the most part, the average Arab Muslim remains fairly conservative and rather insular when it comes to the more personal dimensions of religion.

The evidence in this chapter suggests, therefore, an interesting coexistence: On the one hand, Arab Muslims overwhelmingly support religious and political freedoms for Christians and other religious minorities; at the same time, however, they remain somewhat uncomfortable with Christianity on a personal level. It is unclear exactly how this peculiar equilibrium may serve to reinforce or undermine existing social structures during this period of profound change in the region. What is clear, however is that *tolerance* does not require total comfort. Arab Muslims overwhelmingly demonstrate tolerance for Christians and simultaneously report a lack of knowledge and comfort with Christianity in their personal lives. As has become typical of behavioral studies of this region, generalizations present a challenge – but the empirical evidence suggests that this simultaneous tolerance and discomfort are widespread.

NOTES

1 Joseph Amar, "The Loss of Syria: New Violence Threatens Christianity's Ancient Roots," *Commonweal*, September 19, 2012.
2 Alexis Tocqueville, *Democracy in America* (Chicago: University of Chicago Press, 2000 [1835]).
3 Albert Hourani, *A History of the Arab Peoples* (Cambridge, MA: Harvard University Press, 1991).
4 Tarek Mitri, "Christians in the Arab World: Minority Attitudes and Citizenship," *Ecumenical Review* 64, no. 1 (2012): 43–49.
5 John L. Esposito, *Islam: The Straight Path* (New York: Oxford University Press, 1991).
6 Sidney H. Griffith, *The Church in the Shadow of the Mosque: Christians and Muslims in the World of Islam* (Princeton, NJ: Princeton University Press, 2008).
7 Hourani, *History of the Arab Peoples*, 21.

8 John L. Esposito, *What Everyone Needs to Know about Islam* (Oxford: Oxford University Press, 2002), 81.
9 Ibid., 82.
10 *Oxford Encyclopedia of the Islamic World*, s.v., "People of the Book."
11 Ibid.
12 Ibid.
13 Anh Nga Longva, "From the *Dhimma* to the Capitulations: Memory and Experience of Protection in Lebanon." In *Religious Minorities in the Middle East: Domination, Self-Empowerment, Accommodation*, ed. Anh Nga Longva and Anne Sofie Roald (Leiden: Brill, 2012), 47–70, 48–49.
14 William L. Cleveland, A *History of the Modern Middle East* (Boulder, CO: Westview, 2004), 14.
15 By "religious freedom," we refer to the right to practice one's religion.
16 Esposito, *What Everyone Needs to Know about Islam*, 71.
17 *Oxford Encyclopedia of the Islamic World*, s.v., "Dhimmi."
18 Hourani, *History of the Arab Peoples*, 47.
19 Esposito, *What Everyone Needs to Know about Islam*, 71.
20 *Oxford Encyclopedia of the Islamic World*, s.v., "Dhimmi."
21 Albert Hourani, *Islam in European Thought* (Cambridge: Cambridge University Press, 1991), 7.
22 Esposito, *Islam: The Straight Path*, 59.
23 Ibid.
24 Hourani, *Islam in European Thought*, 7.
25 *Oxford Encyclopedia of the Islamic World*, s.v., "Christianity and Islam."
26 Esposito, *What Everyone Needs to Know about Islam*, 84.
27 *Oxford Encyclopedia of the Islamic World*, s.v., "Christianity and Islam."
28 Cleveland, *History of the Modern Middle East*, 49.
29 Esposito, *Islam: The Straight Path*, 64.
30 Esposito, *What Everyone Needs to Know about Islam*, 84.
31 Esposito, *Islam: The Straight Path*, 64.
32 *Oxford Encyclopedia of the Islamic World*, s.v., "Capitulations."
33 Hourani, *History of the Arab Peoples*, 274.
34 Esposito, *What Everyone Needs to Know about Islam*, 85–86.
35 *Oxford Encyclopedia of the Islamic World*, s.v., "Christianity and Islam."
36 Ibid.
37 *Oxford Encyclopedia of the Islamic World*, s.v., "Muslim-Christian Dialogue."
38 Quoted in Olivier Roy, "The Transformation of the Arab World," *Journal of Democracy* 23, no. 3 (2012): 5–18; 12.
39 Jonathan Fox and Shmuel Sandler, "Separation of Religion and State in the Twenty-First Century: Comparing the Middle East and Western Democracies." *Comparative Politics* 37, no. 3 (2005): 317–335.
40 Fox and Sandler, "Separation of Religion and State," 325.
41 Ibid., 324.
42 "Rising Tide of Restrictions on Religion," *Pew Research Center's Forum on Religion & Public Life*, September 2012.
43 Assaad Elias Kattan, "Christians in the Arab World: Beyond Role Syndrome." *Ecumenical Review* 64, no. 1 (2012): 50–53, 51.

44 Mitri, "Christians in the Arab World."

45 BBC News, "Pope Bemoans Plight of Mid-East Christians."

46 Doreen Khoury, "Is It Winter or Spring for Christians in Syria?" Heinrich-Böll-Stiftung Middle East Office, 2011.

47 Donna E. Arzt, "Religious Human Rights in Muslim States of the Middle East and North Africa." *Emory International Law Review* 10 (1996): 139–161, 143.

48 It should be noted, however, that for several countries in our sample, the number of Christians surveyed was small enough to prevent clear inferences from being made. In total, our sample contains 71 Christians in Egypt, 6 in Iraq, 39 in Jordan, 576 in Lebanon, 31 in Palestine, 4 in Sudan, 4 in Tunisia, and 0 elsewhere.

49 United States Department of State, 2012 *Report on International Religious Freedom – Saudi Arabia*, May 20, 2013, http://www.refworld.org/docid/519dd491e.html

16

They That Remain: Syrian and Iraqi Christian Communities amid the Syria Conflict and the Rise of the Islamic State

Matthew Barber

The past decade has inaugurated a devastating new reality for the Christian minorities of Iraq and Syria. The survival of these vulnerable communities has been jeopardized by a deadly triad composed of the security vacuum resulting from the U.S.-led War in Iraq, Islamist violence, and the consequences of despotic power. This chapter presents the current status of Christian communities in Iraq and Syria, providing brief historical background and then focusing on the seismic events that transpired from 2011 through 2014.[1]

Christian communities in these two countries identify according to a number of ethnic labels, such as Assyrian, Chaldean, Armenian, Arab, Syriac, and even Kurdish. Christians are further distributed among various Orthodox, Catholic, and Protestant denominational affiliations, some of which correspond exclusively to ethnicity. To speak of "Christians" broadly across both Syria and Iraq necessarily means reducing an expansive diversity to an oversimplified generality; however, for the purpose of this chapter, which is to consider the overall welfare of Christian communities in these two countries, it will be possible to speak of certain trends about which nearly all Christian communities have shared concerns.

This chapter consists of seven sections. First, historical context is provided in separate sections for Iraqi and Syrian Christian communities. In the third section, the experience of Christians in the current Syria conflict is presented, before moving to the origins of the Islamic State jihadist organization in the fourth section. The fifth section describes the situation for Christians under Islamic state control in Syria and Iraq and narrates the expulsion of Mosul's Christian population. The sixth section investigates why Christians in Mosul did not perceive *jizya* as a viable option, followed by a conclusion that considers political questions and trends of militarization.

THE CONTEXT FOR IRAQI CHRISTIANS: MORE THAN
A CENTURY OF INSECURITY

The Armenians of Anatolia were not the only Christians who suffered during the final days of the Ottomans. The transition from empire to nation-state was also calamitous for Assyrian Christians, who, along with the Armenians, had been convinced by the Allies to fight against the Turks during World War I.[2] Ottoman forces responded with such widespread massacres of Christian civilians that the word "genocide" was coined to describe the massive slaughter that began in 1915. Survivors were expelled and many Armenians settled in Arab countries. Thousands of Assyrians fled to Iran, where subsequent massacres perpetrated by Kurdish tribes resulted in continued flight.[3] Many eventually joined other Christian communities in the northern part of what would soon become the modern state of Iraq. The violence of the era greatly reduced the numbers of the indigenous Assyro-Chaldean-Syriac[4] and Armenian Christians and redrew the demographic landscape as their communities were displaced and relocated, in many cases multiple times. The advent of the Iraqi state did not spell relief for Christians, who became subject to violence carried out by national forces.

In August of 1933, the year after the British Mandate had ended, Iraqi troops carried out a systematic massacre of several thousand Assyrians after disproportionate Assyrian participation in the British Levies had fueled anti-Assyrian animosities and had been framed by Arab nationalists as an "Assyrian force created against the Iraqi people."[5] The majority of those killed were in the village of Simele, where Assyrians fleeing Ottoman violence had settled. During the genocidal cleansing, neighboring Kurdish and Arab tribes looted Assyrian villages and conducted killings from Amedi to Sheikhan.[6] Serving to crush any competing expression of nationalism that might vie with the state, the operation was a way to extinguish Assyrian ambitions for autonomy.[7] The Simele massacre has carried an ominous significance for Assyrians: Occurring soon after Iraqi independence, it was a bloody initiation into a nation state that would continue to exclude and oppress them.

A renewal of oppression followed the rise of Ba'thism. Between 1974 and 1989, hundreds of Christian villages were destroyed during campaigns of forced assimilation that occurred as part of a larger Arabization program.[8] In 1977, this included a prohibition of Assyrian identity – Christians were required to register as Arab or Kurdish[9] – and in the same period, Neo-Aramaic language schools were made illegal. Though famous for its genocidal assault against the Kurds, Saddam Hussein's Anfal campaign (1988) targeted some Iraqi Christian communities as well.[10] Christians also suffered alongside the Kurds during Saddam's reprisals for the Kurdish uprising following the 1990 Gulf War.[11] Saddam sometimes placed token

Christians in visible leadership positions, such as Tariq Aziz, who embraced Baʻthism and held several ministerial positions as a member of Saddam's inner circle.

The Iraq War Years

Though Christians had already weathered a long legacy of persecution and violence, the Iraq War of 2003 unleashed an unprecedented existential threat to the Christian communities of Iraq. The United States–led overthrow of Saddam Hussein effected the breakdown of the state and created a security vacuum in which extreme Islamist groups were able to proliferate and operate extensively, using terrorism to target an array of ethnic and religious communities perceived as ideological or political rivals.

Attacks on Christians occurred across the entire breadth of the country, from Basra to Mosul. Christians were routinely terrorized with bombings of churches, targeted vandalism of Christian businesses, bomb and mortar attacks on Christian houses, and frequent instances of kidnapping and rape. Christians were killed inside their homes, while on their way to school, and while working in their shops.[12] Christians employed by U.S. companies, including women, were specifically targeted, often while traveling to work.

Attacks at churches were a regular occurrence throughout the Iraq War. Simultaneous attacks on multiple churches (as many as seven on the same day) began in 2004. In late 2008, a widespread campaign of violence targeted Mosul's Christians; dozens were killed and thousands were terrorized into fleeing the area.[13] One of the worst attacks occurred on October 31, 2010, when fifty-eight parishioners were massacred at a Chaldean Catholic church in Baghdad.[14] One source counted more than sixty attacks on churches in major cities across the country between 2004 and 2013.[15]

Throughout this decade of turmoil, Christian clergy were specifically targeted; the kidnapping and murder of priests, nuns, and bishops were common. Some kidnappings were part of targeted killings; others were ostensibly for ransoms (and many Christian families paid thousands to secure the release of family members), yet abductees were often killed – by shooting, beheading, and even starvation – both in cases when ransoms were paid and when they could not be paid.

Though Iraqis of all backgrounds took positions as U.S. military translators or jobs with private reconstruction contractors, minorities were often targeted as a whole for "aiding the occupiers." Christian condemnation of the American invasion of Iraq[16] notwithstanding, extremists framed Christians as collaborators en bloc, and the maligning of Christians reached even more irrational levels, as Christians were associated with the West itself.[17] Much of this violence was carried out by al-Qaida in Iraq and related groups of the jihadist milieu that in 2006 launched the "Islamic State of Iraq" (ISI) in areas where jihadists had influence.

Persecution of Christians was not solely the purview of terrorist groups, but a wider social phenomenon in which students in universities harassed Christian students, Iraqi police participated in oppressive action, Christian women were pressured to wear the hijab, and local imams incited congregations to boycott Christians so that they would leave the country and relinquish their wealth. Terror groups and local extremists frequently targeted women, who were assaulted and killed for not conforming to certain dress norms.[18]

The terrorizing of Iraqi Christians resulted in repeated waves of internal displacement, and a large percentage of the community opted for emigration, permanently leaving their country. Nevertheless, many had stayed, and despite the ongoing violence, a future for Christians in the country was not out of the question. However, the effects of the Syria conflict would later link the fate of Christians in both countries and prove even more seismic for some Iraqi Christian communities than the violence of the Iraq War era.

THE CONTEXT FOR SYRIAN CHRISTIANS: PRIVILEGE, COMPETITION, AND ACCOMMODATION

Christians in Syria have long held an important place of influence in society and culture. Their intellectuals were an important element in the Arab *nahḍa* ("renaissance"), beginning in the late nineteenth century, and this role continued in the twentieth century. Enjoying better access to missionary schools and instruction in the colonial language, Syrian Christians maintained a strong public presence and a healthy level of government participation from the inception of the Syrian state under the French Mandate. The French had previously intervened on behalf of Christians in Lebanon after a bloody war in 1860 that spilled over into Syria, resulting in the plunder and massacre of thousands of Christians in Damascus.[19] This legacy influenced Christian perceptions of the French, and an important relationship would develop between them during the mandate period, which began in 1920.

In 1925, the Great Syrian Revolt was triggered by increasing resentment of French rule. Anti-Christian violence was an aspect of a number of the rebellions around the country. With the memory of 1860 still alive, Christians were inclined to support the French, and the latter had exploited this dynamic, using the Christians as a tool of influence. After the French used Christian forces against participants of the revolt, Sunni newspapers in Hama printed pledges to massacre Christians.[20] As the British in Iraq were to turn the recently cleansed Assyrians into a weapon, the French employed the displaced Armenians – recent survivors of genocide – as muscle in Syria. Animosity against Armenians mushroomed after the harsh manner employed by these troops during the French conflict with the revolting nationalists.[21]

To be sure, some Christians were disaffected with colonial administration. But the fraternization with the French, Muslim resentment at the growing ascendency of Christians, and local frustrations about the influx of Christian refugees from Turkey (both Syriac and Armenian),[22] all contributed to a hostility that would prove damaging to Christians during the revolt. In Hama and the Hauran this materialized in the boycotting of Christian businesses, the looting of Christian shops, and the plunder and destruction of Christian villages.[23]

Despite this sometimes rocky road, the overall position of Christians in Syria remained a fairly privileged one through the initial decades of the state, as many Christians belonged to the urban elite class. A Christian, Faris al-Khuri, even served as prime minister briefly in the 1940s. The brief period of Nasser's Arabism and the United Arab Republic (UAR) (a union between Egypt and Syria established in 1958) disturbed this atmosphere as Christians were purged from the military and other positions of influence. Many fled the country.[24] As Nasser's pan-Arabism (which contained a strong component of Islamic identity) overcame prior ideologies of Syrian nationalism, so the UAR only lasted a few years before its ideology was likewise supplanted by the Arabism of the Ba'th Party, which emphasized secularism in greater degree.

An Armenian informant recounted to me a traumatic memory from his childhood in Aleppo during this period when men in trucks with *Lā 'ilāha 'illā Allah*[25] painted on the sides terrorized Armenian neighborhoods with threats that they would kill the inhabitants, shouting the taunt *Yā Arman maskīn, taḥta al-sikkīn!* ("Poor Armenians, under the knife!"). This Armenian credited the rise of Hafez al-Asad, who helped the Ba'th take power in the early 1960s and later seized full control in 1970, with ending the persecution of Christians, describing how Hafez "criminalized insults on the basis of religion, such as cursing the cross." This anecdote exemplifies the Syrian Christian attitude toward the Asad legacy (and the brutal suppression of sectarianism so characteristic of Asad rule), which many saw as having put an end to expressions of anti-Christian hostility and refusing to tolerate deviation from a forcefully maintained secular atmosphere. Christians had advanced from being massacred in the streets of Damascus a century earlier to feeling protected by the state from religious insults. As the dominant clique of the Asad regime itself comprised minority Alawites, it was important for the regime to accommodate other minority populations, such as the Christians, whose predominantly middle- and upper-class privilege was preserved, even while elite Sunnis were co-opted to ensure the regime's durability.

Though Syria does contain small communities of Syriac-Assyrian-Chaldean Christians (whose children may grow up speaking a Neo-Aramaic language and whose liturgies are performed in Syriac), most Syrian Christians identify as Arab. Whereas Ba'thist Arabism was alienating for the non-Arab Iraqi Christian communities,[26] Arabism could be embraced by the Arab Christian communities of Syria as a solution to religiously inflected politics. Indeed, one of the founders of the Ba'th Party, Michel Aflaq, was himself a Syrian Christian intellectual.

One of the hallmarks of the Asad regime (and its particular method of commandeering Ba'thism) has been the forced preservation of an environment conducive to coexistence for all groups.[27] However, maintaining the ascendency of the Alawite-dominated regime has necessitated capitulation to certain Muslim majority interests, which is played out in such arenas as public education, where a narrative that describes Islam as the superior religion is included in the standard curriculum. This narrative is damaging to minorities, whose religions are presented as incomplete and "more primitive."[28] The label "secular" for Syria (and Iraq) is also problematic on more systemic levels: That Christians and Muslims are held to separate, religiously derived personal status laws[29] reflects an order that is necessarily damaging to the Christian minorities. The implementation of the traditional Islamic position that Muslim men may marry non-Muslim women, but non-Muslim men are only allowed to marry Muslim women if they first convert to Islam, threatens Christian communities with gradual shrinkage since, in Arab culture, children are automatically ascribed the religion of their father.

Other Muslim-Christian competitions have been similarly unopposed by the minoritarian regime vested in placating the religious segment of its Sunni constituency. Despite the constant recitation of nationalist mantras about "Syrian unity," Syrian Christians will frequently disclose that they perceive the building of new mosques in Christian areas or near churches as an aggressively competitive gesture conveying a sense of Muslim dominance and muting the expression of Christian presence in public life.[30] Many Christians believe that traditionally Christian majority villages, from Saidnaya to those of the region of Wadi al-Nasara, are being deliberately targeted by projects to settle Muslims within their communities, with the longer-term objective of demographic change whereby no areas will retain a predominantly Christian character.[31]

CHRISTIANS AND THE SYRIA CONFLICT

The beginning of 2011 saw the outbreak of an unprecedented popular uprising in Syria, as a large segment of the population demanded that President Bashar al-Asad relinquish power. The Arab Spring was already in full swing and major uprisings had spread through Tunisia, Egypt, Libya, and Yemen before the momentum reached Syria. The initial period of uprising can only be described as hesitant, as large segments of the Syrian population avoided involvement or supported the Syrian regime.

Proponents of the uprising and regime supporters alike resented the suggestion that religion had any relation to one's political alignment regarding the uprising. The Syrian regime and those who stood with it parroted a mantra-like narrative of all Syrians being united against "terrorism," while members of the opposition likewise promoted the view that their movement was made up of a representative distribution of Syrians from all sects. Taking a "sectarian view" of the situation was deplored by some observers as "neo-orientalist."

When the conflict began, however, it was immediately clear to me that sectarian affiliation had great bearing on where Syrians stood in the uprising, and the claim that the sectarian dimension emerged later is mistaken. My assertion is not that the uprising was sectarian in *its motivations*; it was sectarian in *the demographic makeup of its participants*. Many revolutionaries were not driven by an anti-Alawite animosity but by a genuine desire for new freedoms and the increased economic well-being of the country. But the sectarian character of the uprising was apparent in light of the demographics of those who chose to support versus reject the revolution. It was impossible for the uprising not to have had this sectarian character, because the regime itself had always been a sectarian one, disproportionately privileging members of the Alawite community.

Nevertheless, historical relationships with the Syrian regime were far more complex than a neat division between a privileged ruling sect and an oppressed rival sect. Though dominated by powerful Alawite figures, the Syrian regime's heavy hand was felt by all, including minorities and even Alawite rivals who may have posed a challenge to the hegemony of the Asad circle. Mutual regime-Christian affections are sometimes overstated,[32] and Syria's long-stifled opposition movement had a legacy of minority members, including such dissenting figures as Michel Kilo and George Sabra, both Christians.[33] In the uprising, many Sunnis (usually of privileged backgrounds) could also be found among regime supporters and it was possible to find some Christians and even an occasional Alawite among the ranks of the opposition. Whether or not Christians have participated in opposition protests depends on locality; some towns and villages have seen political unity among Christians and Muslims in revolutionary activity.[34]

Despite these exceptions, the unavoidable reality was that the vast majority of Syrians participating in the revolution/uprising were Sunni, and the vast majority of minority populations stood with the regime. The uprising quickly heightened the visibility and awareness of sectarian boundaries, and the speed with which Syrian society polarized was remarkable. I was struck when observing minority families who had adverse histories with the regime – some had family members who had been imprisoned and tortured, even for years – undergo an uncanny and sudden transformation into born-again believers in Asad. Much of this loyalist segment was not enamored with the president and his ruling clique, but was defending a certain definition of the country, where many enjoyed the degree of openness that originated with the secularism of the regime. Paradoxically, this sense of openness existed uncomfortably alongside the suffocating surveillance, intimidation, and mafia-like control of the state and its economy. Though many Christians had no love for the Asad leadership or for a regime infamous for its brutality and torture, in their final calculation, the trade-off of repression for secular society was deemed preferable to the dangers posed by regime change. Already enjoying middle-class status, they stood to gain little by braving the many risks of uprising, and this feeling was only reinforced as the conflict grew into a civil war.

Syria's Christians were hounded by several fears – of the regime itself and the potential repercussions for betraying it, of Islamist violence, of chaos. The widespread violence that proliferated in the security vacuum following the interruption of state authority in Iraq served as a frightening precedent for Christians, who were not convinced by revolutionaries' assurances that "Syria would be different." When I mentioned to one Syrian Christian that extremists only made up a small percentage of the opposition fighters, the man responded: "Look, we don't care if the extreme Islamists are only a 'small fraction' of the total opposition forces. If only 2% of the rebels are extremists they will be enough to eliminate all the Christians from Syria."

Minorities and the secularly minded were also concerned about undesirable social change, fearing the loss of "their Syria," a Syria where religion did not figure into the foreground and where tolerance was strictly – though often brutally – enforced. The fear was not of a new set of leaders, but of a change in the nature of power that defines Syrian culture and inevitably sets the tone for public life. Christians noted that every country that underwent an Arab Spring upheaval experienced a popular movement strengthening the position of Islamist actors within the political order. Even if a "soft Islamism" were to become dominant in Syria, it would be seen by Christians as an inimical transformation, for whom a greater degree of shari'a-informed rulings would be discriminatory.

Syrian Christians therefore did not "choose Asad" only after Islamist groups emerged with growing prominence; the mere possibility that the uprising would produce an instability within which extremist Islamist groups might proliferate was enough to prompt the majority of Christians to reject any expression of revolution, from the earliest days of unrest.

The Asad regime also worked to exploit these fears, exaggerating the actual level of hostility toward minorities[35] and refusing to acknowledge that the uprising was composed of ordinary Syrians, instead attributing it entirely to invading foreign saboteurs. However, the regime did not have to work hard to stoke the fears of the Christian community, whose concerns were largely preexistent, and over the course of the conflict, these fears were borne out[36] amid frequent abuses and a trend toward

Islamism that remained constant among the Syrian rebels. Raqqa, the first Syrian governorate to be conquered by opposition forces (early March 2013), was taken by Islamist rebels. This event represented more than a changing of the guard; it was a change in the culture of authority that could be expected to dominate a post-Asad Syria. The visible shift to Islamism was troubling for many Syrians.

The Syrian civil war has resulted in the almost complete disappearance of Christian populations in areas taken over by the opposition or where high levels of fighting have occurred. Initially, most Christians fled conditions of war rather than persecution. Most rebel groups were focused on fighting the regime and did not harbor an anti-Christian agenda. However, Christians experienced rebel control uncomfortably, and as the conflict developed, a climate that was specifically hostile to Christians developed. Acts of violence against Christians increased, often fueled by perceptions of Christians as regime loyalists.[37] The city of Qusayr was one example where Christians were caught in the middle as the regime and opposition forces battled over the town in early 2012, both sides demanding loyalty. Some Christians did side with the regime, but rebels branded all Christians as loyalists. In addition to numerous killings, Christians were expelled from the city when threatening demands that they leave were broadcast via the loudspeakers of Qusayr's mosques.[38] Christians also emptied out of cities such as Homs and Deir ez-Zor, fleeing the war, evicted by jihadists, or feeling threatened among their neighbors.[39]

On September 4, 2013, Syrian rebels attacked the majority Christian town of Maloula (Ma'lūlā), prompting the flight of its residents. Maloula is a phenomenal example of Syria's cultural heritage, as home to some of the oldest monasteries in the country and the last area where Western Neo-Aramaic is spoken. Attacking the town may have done more to damage the rebels' public image in the West than any other act up to that point. As had many minority-inhabited communities, Maloula had avoided participation in the conflict, hoping to remain on the sidelines. The town was not a source of revolutionary energies; any rebel presence was uninvited and unwanted, and taking the fight to the vulnerable community was highly irresponsible. Though churches and religious sites were not initially targeted for destruction, the fact that the assault was led by the al-Qaida wing Jabhat al-Nusra terrorized the locals. Fighting over the city continued between regime and rebels, and in December, al-Nusra kidnapped thirteen nuns from one of the town's monasteries and kept them as hostages until their release was negotiated in March 2014. The regime eventually retook control of the town in April, leading to a restored calm, but recent reports suggest that only about a third of Maloula residents have returned to the town.[40] After the recapture, it was found that the churches and monasteries had been desecrated or burned, their contents (altars, frescoes, crosses) smashed, their items of value (icons, woodwork, ancient church bells) stolen, and statues of Christ and Mary blown up with explosives.[41]

Plenty of Christian communities, both urban and rural, experienced similar fates: Yabroud's churches underwent the defacement of their icons and holy objects;[42] an Armenian church in Aleppo was burned October 2012;[43] two churches were looted in Latakia governorate December 2012;[44] an important Maronite church north of Aleppo was attacked late 2013;[45] several churches in Deir ez-Zor were completely destroyed;[46] Kessab, which was taken over by rebels in March 2014, had its churches burned and their contents demolished;[47] al-Nusra destroyed an Orthodox church in al-Thawrah;[48] the Um al-Zinar church in Homs was destroyed;[49] and in a gesture of twisted cruelty, jihadists of the Islamic State of Iraq and ash-Sham (ISIS) destroyed the Armenian Genocide Memorial Church – on the very day that the anniversary of the Armenian Genocide is commemorated, September 21, 2014.[50] Less commonly, regime bombings have also inadvertently damaged Christian sites and churches.[51]

Though some accounts of religious cleansing of Christians were exaggerations,[52] numerous targeted killings occurred and at least one massacre was conducted by Islamist rebels, when the Christian village of Sadad was invaded by al-Nusra, ISIS, and other rebels in October 2013.[53]

Anti-Christian animosity has also resulted in vandalism or looting of many Christian sites including a monastery in Saidnaya, the Deir Mar Musa monastery in the mountains near Nabak, and countless other holy places. The criminality that has proliferated in the security vacuum has also resulted in frequent kidnappings for ransom. In cases of looting and kidnapping, distinguishing between rebel groups and criminal opportunists as actors is challenging.

Christian clergy in particular have been targeted with violence or kidnappings for ransom during the Syria conflict. Fady al-Haddad, a Greek Orthodox priest, was abducted and killed in late 2012 for unknown reasons.[54] A high-profile attack occurred on April 22, 2013, when two archbishops – Yohanna Ibrahim (Syriac Orthodox) and Boulos Yaziji (Greek Orthodox) – were kidnapped and the deacon traveling with them murdered near Aleppo. Neither has resurfaced and their fate remains unknown. In June 2013, the Catholic priest Francois Murad was shot and killed inside his church, reportedly for resisting when Islamist rebels ransacked it.[55] Around the same time, a video circulated of another man, wearing a priest's or monk's clothing, being brutally beheaded by Chechen jihadists while a crowd, including young children, looked on.

Non-Syrian priests working in the country have also been targeted. The Italian priest Paolo Dall'Oglio, who for years ran the Deir Mar Musa monastery and conducted interfaith dialogue conferences in the country, was kidnapped by ISIS in Raqqa in July 2013.[56] Frans van der Lugt, a Dutch priest who had lived and served in Homs for many years, was shot and killed in his monastery in April 2014.[57] The

Syrian al-Qaida organization Jabhat al-Nusra abducted a Franciscan priest, Hanna Jallouf, along with twenty of his parishioners, in October 2014, accusing them of collaboration with the Syrian regime. They were later released.[58]

Though the vast majority of hostile acts against Christians have originated with groups or individuals aligned with the "opposition side" (such a dichotomy is somewhat artificial), I have received reports from Christians of opportunistic actors affiliated with the *mukhābarāt* or politically aligned with the "regime side" exploiting the chaotic environment of lawlessness and chaos to kidnap Christians for ransom.

As the conflict encroached upon urban centers, Christian neighborhoods in cities became subjected to bombardment. On March 17, 2012, a large bomb was detonated beside the Damascus Christian neighborhood of Qasaʿ.[59] The target was a local *mukhābarāt* headquarters, but because it was located in the heart of a Christian area, the Christian population was terrorized and the bomb damaged many nearby homes. On October 21, 2012, a car bomb was detonated in Bab Tuma, the Christian area of the Old City.[60] Incidents of smaller bombings occurred in the Christian Old City, often targeting police stations. The mixed Druze-Christian neighborhood of Jaramana that adjoins Damascus saw scores of civilians killed during 2012 and 2013 in repeated car bombings punishing the community, which had refused to grant access to rebels.[61] In 2013, the Damascene Christian community came under increasing literal fire as rebels besieging Damascus stepped up attacks on the eastern side of the city. Just west of rebel lines lay the majority of Damascus's Christian population centers, in the neighborhoods of Qaṣur, ʿAbasiyyin, Qasaʿ, Bab Tuma, and Dweilaʿ. For an extended period spanning much of 2013 and 2014, rebels assaulted civilian areas of Damascus with indiscriminate mortar fire that rained down daily. During peak periods, Damascus could be subjected to as many as forty mortar attacks per day, the majority of which fell in these Christian neighborhoods, often hitting homes and businesses. Civilians were frequently killed by this random shelling. Attacks would sometimes occur during Sunday church services and numerous churches were damaged by mortar fire. Christians of all ages have been killed by projectiles striking hospitals, elementary schools, and school buses.[62] These examples have dealt with Damascus, but the Aleppo experience was even more devastating, with much of the city destroyed and made uninhabitable.

Christians, like all Syrians, have throughout the country been caught in the crossfire, inadvertently killed by car bombings, mortar attacks, or gunfire – expected in a context of war. More irresponsible is the indiscriminate shelling of civilian areas that are known to be Christian. Beyond these forms of action, Christians and their places of worship have been deliberately targeted by bombings, and Christian towns have been invaded by Islamist forces, opening the door to further violence and destruction of churches.[63] Though the rebel violence directed at Christians pales in comparison with the brutality levied against the Sunni civilian population by regime assaults, it has not been insignificant.[64]

The Outcome as of 2015

The few examples cataloged previously illustrate the climate of terror that has driven many Syrian Christians to flee their areas or leave the country altogether.

Well into the third year of the uprising, a one-sided narrative remained dominant in Western media that understood the "regime side" as all-villain and the "opposition side" as all-hero, though Damascene Christians were enduring a much different reality. It was difficult at that time to find articles discussing the rationale behind Christian support for the regime, and international media largely ignored the uncomfortable experience of Christians whose neighborhoods were being shelled by rebels. Now entering the fifth year of conflict, the irony is that since the spread of the Islamic State (IS), the narrative has flipped so dramatically that it similarly risks losing balanced perspective. Some Western voices have even begun calling for cooperation with the regime against IS, a course that would be ethically questionable, to say the least. Though the regime's resources are stretched to the breaking point, this juncture represents a remarkable victory for it in terms of international public perceptions of what this conflict now represents.

THE RISE OF THE SELF-DECLARED ISLAMIC STATE

The roots of the Islamic State organization stretch back before the Iraq War. The earliest incarnation of the group that would someday become IS was formed in 1999 by Abu Musab al-Zarqawi. Called Jama'at al-Tawhid wa-l-Jihad, the organization operated alongside al-Qaida and the Taliban in Afghanistan before relocating to Iraq prior to the Iraq War. Zarqawi declared allegiance to al-Qaida in 2004 and his organization became known as al-Qaida in Iraq (AQI), though ideological differences divided Zarqawi and bin Laden.[65] In 2006, AQI and several other Iraqi jihadist groups joined to form the Mujahidin Shura Council; Zarqawi was killed shortly thereafter. Ibrahim Awad Ibrahim al-Badri, more commonly known as Abu Bakr al-Baghdadi, was a leader within one of the groups absorbed into this al-Qaida-led coalition. In the same year, the jihadist umbrella group declared itself an Islamic state and began to identify as the Islamic State of Iraq (ISI).[66] In 2010, Abu Bakr al-Baghdadi became the leader of ISI, and in the following year (the first year of the Syrian uprising) began developing an extension of the organization inside Syria. On April 8, 2013, al-Baghdadi announced that the organization's name was changed to the Islamic State in Iraq and ash-Sham (ISIS), reflecting its expanded area of operation.

From this point on, serious tensions began to develop between Ayman al-Zawahiri, the head of al-Qaida internationally, and Abu Bakr al-Baghdadi, whose agenda to rapidly create utopian Islamic governance had begun to outgrow Zawahiri's vision. Unable to resolve their disputes over organization and leadership, in February of 2014 al-Zawahiri formally declared that no relationship existed between ISIS and al-Qaida.[67] Al-Qaida's dissociation had little effect on ISIS, which continued to achieve success in Syria, eventually becoming the most powerful rebel group operating in the country and replacing al-Qaida as the most relevant champion of jihadism in the two countries.[68]

As one among several thousand oppositional rebel groups operating within Syria, ISIS followed a strategy of avoiding regular engagement with the Syrian regime, focusing instead on consolidating control over territories that had fallen to other rebels, whom they would then defeat and absorb. Whereas al-Qaida had always been forced to operate solely as an underground network limited to hidden cells and exclusively using terrorism as its method, ISIS employed forms of conventional warfare in its conquests and was able to actualize the jihadist dream in transitioning to a public organization that imposed its theologically derived system of rule on populations.

After having achieved a sufficient level of strength and organization inside Syria, the ISIS leadership (composed primarily of Iraqi former Ba'thists) turned their gaze back upon Iraq, where Fallujah was taken in early 2014. On June 5, 2014, ISIS forces began a large campaign to conquer vast territories in Iraq, initially focusing on areas that were primarily inhabited by Sunni Arabs, among whom ISIS could find varying measures of local support. The most important area captured in Iraq was Mosul, which fell to the group on June 10.[69]

After gaining control of Mosul, ISIS announced on June 29, 2014, that it was declaring itself a caliphate, designating its leader, Abu Bakr al-Baghdadi, as the new caliph. It also modified its name at this point to reflect its global aspirations, dropping the "in Iraq and ash-Sham" to be simply "the Islamic State" (IS).[70]

THE EXPERIENCE OF CHRISTIANS UNDER ISIS/IS: RAQQA AND MOSUL

The Syrian city of Raqqa fell to a coalition of Islamist rebels in March 2013, but ISIS was not a dominant force in the city until mid-May, when it wrested control from the groups that had conquered the city.[71] The case of Raqqa is unique for several reasons: 1) It fell to rebel forces quickly without a great deal of violence or a long period of warfare; 2) unlike in other Syrian cities, the absence of a lengthy siege meant that much of its Christian population was still intact when rebels took the city; 3) the larger governorate of Raqqa was the first to fall to the rebel opposition;

4) the city of Raqqa served as the first "capital" for ISIS, prior to their capture of Mosul; 5) that Raqqa was ISIS's first capital, and that it retained a Christian presence, resulted in its being the first place where ISIS imposed a *dhimmī* framework on a Christian population.

After ISIS took control of the city the situation deteriorated with murder, possible forced conversion, vandalism of churches, and replacement of church crosses with ISIS flags.[72] Two churches in the city of Raqqa were desecrated in September and the interior of the Holy Cross Armenian Orthodox church in Tel Abyad was burned by ISIS members in October.[73] ISIS set up operations inside the Sayyida al-Bashara church in the city of Raqqa, which they transformed into their *daʿwa* ("missions" or "proselytism") office.[74]

In February of 2014, ISIS made the payment of *jizya* (a tributary head tax for non-Muslim minorities with roots in the practice of the early Islamic community but conceptualized differently in different historical contexts) mandatory for Christians as part of a framework of *dhimmī* status imposed on the local Christian population.[75] The framework required Christians to apportion to ISIS an amount of gold that varies according to income level. The annual amount due could exceed thirteen hundred dollars for those with higher incomes, and more than three hundred dollars annually is expected from "the poor," an onerous challenge for Christians.[76]

The *dhimmī* contract also dictated other requirements: Christians must not build any new churches or repair existing ones; Christians must not allow Muslims to hear the recitation of Christian scriptures or the sound of church bells; they must follow ISIS dress norms; they may not display the cross; they may not engage in any public worship outside a church.

Though brutal public punishments and executions (such as beatings, mutilations, beheadings, and crucifixions) have often targeted members of the majority Muslim population, the environment has likewise been menacing for Christians. The majority of Raqqa's Christians have opted to leave, entrusting their possessions to Muslim neighbors so that they will not be seized by ISIS. An exceedingly small remnant of Christians has remained in the city under ISIS (now IS) control and has paid *jizya*.[77]

Whereas Raqqa had no history of Islamist harassment, Mosul's Christians had been bullied by Islamist elements, including al-Qaida and ISIS's previous incarnation, ISI, since 2003. The takeover of Mosul therefore proved far more traumatic for its Christian inhabitants.

A little more than a month after Mosul's June 10 takeover by ISIS (subsequently renamed IS), the city lost the presence of its historic Christian community. On the evening of Thursday, July 17, IS announced an ultimatum giving Christians in Mosul until noon on Saturday to do one of the following: 1) convert to Islam; 2) pay *jizya*; 3) be killed "by the sword." In addition, the statement issued by IS gave

Christians who did not wish to select one of these choices the option to leave Mosul; otherwise they would be killed.[78]

The accounts I collected from Christians who fled Mosul differed widely. A few had seen or heard the ultimatum firsthand; some had only heard about it; many were not sure what was happening but were warned by Muslim neighbors that they should flee the city. Christians reported that in some areas the announcement was broadcasted via the loudspeakers on minarets. In some Christian neighborhoods, vehicles equipped with loudspeakers drove around broadcasting the message, along with such statements as "the period of the Christians has ended."[79]

Just prior to the announcement, IS had demanded that church leaders meet with them in order to discuss the "status" of Christians. No bishops would attend this meeting and after their absence, IS issued the three-option ultimatum. Some churches sent text messages to the cell phones of parishioners notifying them that they should depart the city immediately.

On Friday, July 18, families piled what valuables they could into their cars, took whatever savings they had in cash, and began the drive north to the nearby Kurdistan Region. Upon reaching the checkpoints that controlled the entrances of the city, every fleeing Christian family or individual was compelled by the IS fighters manning the checkpoints to give up their cars and everything they were carrying.

Women showed me lines on their fingers where their wedding rings used to be, before IS gunmen pulled them off. Cell phones hidden inside bras were pulled out, bank cards and wallets taken away – everything except the clothes on their backs was taken. Many lost their life savings. A number of families reported that when IS fighters suspected that they were not giving up all jewelry or cash that they had hidden on their persons, they would threaten to take away their children.[80]

The experience was deeply humiliating for the Christian community. This was exacerbated by cruel treatment by the IS fighters. One man described to me how, in front of his family, a fighter placed a pistol barrel against his temple and said, "Convert to Islam now, or you will die."[81] The man replied, "You can kill me, but I will not leave my religion." It was an empty threat – perhaps the fighter was merely toying with him – and the gun was put away. More than one elderly person recounted how they begged the fighters to allow them to keep medicine that they depended on, but the fighters would open the medicine bottles and pour it on the ground. The same happened to parents begging to be allowed to keep some water for their small children, for the long walk ahead, but the fighters would pour their water on the ground in front of them. After being robbed, each family was dropped at a halfway point some distance from the city, where they had to walk until reaching the Kurdish lines.

This event marks the first time in Mosul's history since the introduction of Christianity for it to be without a Christian presence and represents the unhappy end of a long and painful saga for the community.

Further Christian Displacement

On August 3, 2014, IS attacked the Yazidi homeland of Sinjar. Abandoned by the Kurdish forces responsible for Sinjar's security,[82] more than 300,000 Yazidis were displaced and a still-unknown number were massacred.[83] Nothing to which the Christian community had been subjected compared to the atrocities done to the Yazidis,[84] who were targeted with a planned strategy of ethnic cleansing and mass enslavement that involved abducting thousands of Yazidi women and girls, who are now being sold and distributed among IS jihadists as concubines.[85]

After the August 3 attack on Sinjar, IS continued assaults on the Nineveh Plain and Kurdistan Region, capturing the Mosul Dam and the nearby town of Wana, taking Tel Kayf, pushing northward toward the city of Dohuk and reaching as far as Telesquf, and launching an assault eastward toward Erbil. This unchecked advance was finally halted when President Obama ordered air strikes on August 7,[86] but many villages of the Nineveh Plain were not retaken by Kurdish forces in the following months and remained under IS control. Demonstrating how the fate of Christians is linked with that of other minorities, these mixed villages are important homelands for Yazidis and Christians. Their populations fled into the Kurdistan Region.[87] On August 6–7, an attack was made on Qaraqosh, the largest Christian city in Iraq.[88] As many as 100,000 fled their homes in a single day, exacerbating Kurdistan's refugee crisis, which already included Mosul's Christians, Sinjar's Yazidis, the minorities of the Nineveh Plain, refugees from several years of civil war in Syria, and internally displaced Iraqis from the Iraq War years.

WHY DID THE CHRISTIANS NOT SIMPLY PAY *JIZYA* AND REMAIN IN MOSUL?

Why did Christians in Mosul not make *jizya* payments to IS and remain in their city, as some Christians of Raqqa had opted to do? However objectionable a practice of discriminatory taxation may be, compliance with it would seem preferable to the loss of one's home. Though Christians were uncomfortable after IS jihadists took over Mosul, there was no campaign of mass killing that targeted them before their exodus, and many had already weathered the reality of sporadic violence for years. In my interviews with Christians, I endeavored to understand what was unique about this case.

Pro-IS voices portrayed this incident as the voluntary departure of Christians who rejected a reasonable offer to protect the Christian minority in exchange for reasonable taxation. The reality was that several factors, including the behavior of ISIS/IS after taking control of the city, created an environment of intimidation that eroded any potential trust that Christians could have had.

The Jihadist Legacy and the Association of Violence with Iraq War Era Jizya Demands

Much of the ISI violence targeting Iraqi Christians during the Iraq War years was part of a financial extortion strategy that continued to function even after the withdrawal of U.S. troops. In 2007 the Baghdad neighborhood of Dora underwent a sectarian cleansing of Christians and Shi'a. Hundreds of Christian families were driven out after a fatwa was distributed demanding that Christians convert to Islam or pay *jizya*, or else be killed. In conditions bearing striking resemblance to the 2014 plunder of Christians that would transpire in Mosul, Christians in Dora who chose to leave were required to leave behind their possessions.[89] Christian residents of Mosul had also paid *jizya* to jihadists for "protection" during the Iraq War years (after al-Qaida threatened death for those who did not pay). Thus, the IS membership had inherited a familiarity with projects of cleansing for plunder, and the Mosul crisis of 2014 was not the first scenario of its kind.

The many kidnappings and assassinations of priests throughout Iraq during the war contributed to the unwillingness of Mosul's clergy to deal with IS. One of the highest-profile killings had occurred in Mosul itself when the Chaldean archbishop, Paulus Faraj Raho, was kidnapped and killed in 2008, shortly after speaking out about the persecution of Christians.[90] He had previously made *jizya* payments to jihadists in Mosul in order to protect his congregation.[91]

The ISIS organization that conquered Mosul in 2014 was simply a later incarnation of the same ISI group that had conducted targeting killings and financial extortion of Christians throughout the Iraq War years. That its leadership was composed of many of the same people was enough to dissuade Christian clerics from further dealings with jihadists, hence the refusal of bishops to attend the meeting that IS had requested before the July 17 ultimatum. While al-Qaida/ISI violence had been conducted from the underground, ISIS was now the acting "government" of the city. In other words, Christians now saw themselves ruled by the same entity that had been committing atrocities against them for years. Further, the prior experience of Iraqi Christians had already created, for them, an association between the institution of *jizya* and violence.

The Precedent That ISIS/IS Set with Other Minorities after the Takeover of Mosul

Upon the ISIS takeover of Mosul, thousands of members of jittery minority groups fled the city. ISIS immediately began an effort to woo minorities back to the city through friendly gestures and promises of security. It then, however, betrayed these overtures of goodwill.

After large numbers of Yazidis working in Mosul's police and security forces fled to their home villages in Sinjar,[92] ISIS members approached Yazidis and encouraged them to keep working in the city, telling them that they were welcome to remain. Many started returning, but a program of systematic kidnapping, which constituted a scheme to obtain profit through ransoms, began. Scores were kidnapped and nearly $1.5 million was acquired in ransoms from Yazidi families. The Shabak (an ethnoreligious minority with distinct beliefs and practices but generally perceived by others as divided between Shi'i and Sunni factions) received the same initial reassurances; however, a pattern of betrayal began almost immediately. Eleven of Mosul's "Shi'i Shabak" villages were attacked, beginning on June 12, with the explicit purpose of plunder. ISIS gunmen arrived in convoys, entered homes and looted their contents, stole cars, and seized the villages' sheep and cattle – thousands of animals. The meat from these stolen flocks was later distributed among Mosul's poor as a gesture of Ramadan charity: ISIS pillaged one people to purchase the favor of another. Rampant killing accompanied these raids and by late July the Shabak claimed they were missing more than 135 people.[93]

Violence toward Yazidis and the destruction of the Shabak communities, after pledges of protection, set a precedent of dishonesty and deceit in ISIS's dealings with the vulnerable, which influenced the decision of Christians to abandon their homes when the time arrived.

Discriminatory Economic Policies Implemented to Damage Minorities

Virtually absent from the media coverage of the situation, my interviews with Christians revealed that a widespread strategy to deprive minorities of their incomes was conducted in the weeks before the final exodus. This scheme was executed in at least three ways.

First, ISIS informed governmental, civil, and administrative agencies to freeze the salaries of Christian, Yazidi, Shabak, Mandean-Sabean, and Shi'i employees. Christians commonly held positions as teachers, doctors, or workers at public utilities, and the new policy affected many with whom I spoke. ISIS/IS followed a practice used by the Syrian regime, which would place *mukhābarāt*[94] agents inside hospitals, hotels, and other facilities, to monitor goings on and the movement of funds that could be skimmed. IS similarly began to install operatives within institutions to enforce their rulings and monitor the environment. These individuals could look at an employee roster and discern from the names which individuals belonged to non-Muslim communities. ISIS/IS instructed institutions to redirect the salaries of non-Muslims to IS. The pattern was that one day a Christian employee would arrive at the workplace to pick up his or her pay, and the manager would take the person aside and regretfully inform him or her that he was not allowed to pay the salary.

The second economic measure was an ISIS mandate that Muslim renters no longer pay rent to non-Muslim landlords. In the accounts I gathered, this affected owners of both residential and commercial property. ISIS would first determine which property was owned by Christians and would then approach the tenants and order them to pay their rent to ISIS directly, instead of to the landlord. Some accounts related that ISIS would tell the tenants that they themselves would portion out the rent to the landlords. This never happened; ISIS would keep all of the "confiscated" rent.[95] Some businesses were shut down, as well. One Christian woman I spoke with was the owner of a hair salon, which became dangerous to operate after ISIS judged that such establishments were not to function in the city.

The third measure of economic oppression was to prevent Mosul's poorer Christians from participating in the government-run ration card system. This program was similar to food stamps, a way for poorer members of the city to obtain food. The cards were taken away from Christians who had them.

An irony is that while demanding *jizya*, on the one hand, IS simultaneously sabotaged the income of the community that was expected to produce it, thereby creating the conditions under which Christians were more likely to leave. In light of the economic measures outlined here, a picture begins to form of the IS state-building effort in Mosul as a project supported, partially, through the pilfering of the wealth of specific communities, in order to make possible their project of establishing governance over the majority population. IS set up a win-win scenario for itself: If Christians opted to remain in the city, they would be required to serve as an ongoing revenue source in the form of *jizya*; if they chose to leave, IS would benefit even more by appropriating the community's wealth – a practice they believe they are entitled to perform against all those who forsake the "Islamic State."

The Behavior of ISIS/IS toward Christians

On June 27, two Chaldean nuns and three orphans in their care were kidnapped by ISIS (two days before the group renamed themselves IS and declared the caliphate) and held for seventeen days. They were released without ransom and were not harmed while being held, but their unexplained disappearance was unnerving for the Christian population.

I interviewed one of the nuns,[96] who described how, on the night before their release, one of their captors handed over a cell phone and demanded that they "call somebody we can talk to." They called one of the local bishops and the IS fighter gave him options for Christians that he was to convey to the Christian community. This was the evening of July 13, four days before the ultimatum issued to Christians on Thursday July 17, and the options given over the phone differed from those issued later. They were told to become Muslim or pay *jizya* and accept the *shurūṭ ʿUmar*, a set of strictures for Christian behavior attributed to an early agreement between conquered Christians and the caliph 'Umar that involve markers of subservience to Muslims and the abstention from any public display of Christian religious practice.[97]

By trying to convey this message to the larger Christian community by simply having the nuns call a bishop who was not even a leading figure of the local Christian community, the jihadists gave the impression that they did not know whom to deal with in the Christian community. This reflects the larger picture of how IS, while establishing themselves as the new law and government, failed to engage the Christian community.

The nuns reported that a Tunisian jihadist who guarded them seemed to have never had contact with Christians previously and could not comprehend their "choice to be wrong;" he verbally harassed the nuns, attacked their beliefs, and tried to coerce them to convert, but an Iraqi jihadist who had more familiarity with Christians (and understood what a nun was) shielded them from this to a degree.

This underscores the fact that much of IS was culturally alien to Mosul's inhabitants, who – Christian and Muslim alike – were disturbed to suddenly have outsiders patrolling their streets. Families related that they encountered Afghans, Saudis, Lebanese, and Chechens roaming their area. Many Christians related that they did not know who was in charge or whom they could contact when needing to deal with problems. Prior to the final ultimatum, many families were not even aware of the meeting that IS had demanded with church leaders. If any Christians had wanted to pay *jizya*, most would not have known how such a transaction was expected to be conducted, or through what official body.

Several other incidents terrorized Christians after the ISIS takeover, such as the occupation of churches by fighters, the destruction of a statue of the Virgin Mary at one church,[98] and the replacing of crosses atop churches with the ISIS flag. Shortly before the July 17 ultimatum was issued, IS personnel began marking Christian properties with the Arabic letter *nūn* (ن), which stood for the Arabic word for "Nazarene," a term that has been used historically to refer to Christians.[99] Having the emblem conspicuously spray-painted in red on the sides of homes served to expose the residences of Christians, who had typically endeavored to maintain low profiles. After Christians fled, the *nūn* served to designate properties that IS felt entitled to appropriate. After the events of mid-July, the *nūn* became an international symbol of solidarity with Iraq's Christian community and was widely displayed in demonstrations and social media as a show of support.

The Result

ISIS did not make the effort to seek out and build relationship with church leaders. If they had been serious about creating trust and fulfilling their self-declared role as protectors, they would have taken measures to make Christians feel safe.

Instead, their takeovers of churches, kidnappings of nuns, violence toward other minorities, and targeted economic punishments accomplished the opposite: sowing terror and eliminating any chance for engagement. Had their intention been to protect the vulnerable, they would never have conducted or allowed the systematic plundering of minorities. Instead, a clear pattern emerged of ISIS plundering each minority in turn, after using deceit and false promises of security. Beyond the factors detailed above, the coercive nature of the *jizya* demand – with its attached threat of death – did the most to strike fear into the hearts of local Christians. Already feeling vulnerable, having vehicles drive through their neighborhoods with loudspeakers announcing that "the period of the Christians has ended" was merely the final straw.

THEY THAT REMAIN

Militarization: The Other Cheek Is Worn Out

By 2013 it was likely that only about half to a third of Iraq's pre-2003 Christian population remained in the country;[100] but the severe damage done by IS in 2014 has no doubt further reduced the Christian population. In Syria there is no official figure, but the Christian population could be less than 8% of the population. At present, a pattern is emerging in many parts of these two countries suggesting that Christians are only able to remain in contexts where their communities militarize.[101] In areas of Syria that have fallen out of state control, and in areas of Iraq where both the central government and the Kurdistan Regional Government (KRG) have been incapable of or unwilling to do what is necessary to protect Christians, Christian populations have either abandoned their communities (becoming internally displaced or seeking asylum abroad), or have remained in their villages where the creation and maintenance of local militias has been a possibility.[102] In both Syria and Iraq, the ability of Christians to maintain their own militias has largely depended on their proximity to Kurdish populations with whose militias or forces they can cooperate.

Even in areas of Syria where the regime maintains control, the formation of local Christian militias is increasing. Syria is experiencing a trend of "militiafication"[103] in which those forces that represent the "regime side" of the civil war are not necessarily under regime control but are increasingly fragmented, corresponding to smaller, local environments; minority interest groups, such as militarized Christians,[104] Alawites, or Druze;[105] or political groups such as the Syrian Social Nationalist Party that are ideologically competitive with the Ba'thist regime but stand on its side in opposition to insurgent movements that represent or facilitate the rise of Islamist power. The SSNP has also attracted a significant level of Christian participation.[106] The militarization of Christians in Iraq can also be seen as part of the larger trend of militiafication, but Christians in either country will never be powerful enough to sufficiently protect themselves apart from a larger sponsor such as the Syrian regime or Kurdish forces.[107]

During the Syria conflict, the Christian community of Saidnaya developed a local militia that has become something of a model of success for Syrian Christians. A good number of Christians from Saidnaya were kidnapped and killed while traveling through Sunni areas to and from the village, and the population felt that they had to produce an organized response to their vulnerability. Equipped with winter gear to make possible the surviving of very low temperatures in its mountainous area, militia members work in organized shifts and have successfully defended their village throughout the conflict. The village has been attacked by rebel forces several times, but they have not been able to take the village. However, this defense has not succeeded apart from sponsorship; government troops have also worked alongside the militia to protect the village.

Whereas some militarized rural villages, if positioned with sufficient proximity to allied communities, may be able to maintain effective defenses, most armed communities are still unlikely to have sufficient experience or weaponry to prove a match for the battle-hardened forces of IS. At the end of February 2015, IS jihadists overran several Christian villages near Hasakah, kidnapping at least 250 Christians, overwhelming the ability of local militias to defend. (Some or all of the kidnapped Christians were released in the first week of March, allegedly after ransoms were paid.)[108]

The collective sense of vulnerability and the need to militarize are fostering region-wide cooperation among Christian communities who are attempting to find strategies that can strengthen their positions, and Lebanese Christians have visited Iraqi Christians who solicited their "expertise" on how to proceed.[109]

The Political Ambitions of Iraqi Christians

One cannot read about Iraqi Christians without encountering the ubiquitous calls for a "safe zone." The basic idea of this agenda is to create a semiautonomous area in the Nineveh Plain with a distinct security environment where the local Christian communities can enjoy better protection than what the state offers. However, being related to Assyrian nationalist aspirations, the idea is more relevant for Christians of northern Iraq that those of, for example, Baghdad. Despite the prevalence of this demand, it is difficult to find nuanced articulations of how the zone would be defined and administered. Would the international community maintain a troop presence to enforce the defense of the zone? Would the UN establish a permanent peacekeeping presence? Would the local Christian communities be provided sufficient arms to form an army? Would the zone constitute a unique autonomous entity (*'iqlīm*) under Iraq's constitution (like Kurdistan Region) or would it be a governorate (*muḥāfiẓa*)?

If the latter, would the governorate be directly under central Iraqi administration, or would it become a new governorate belonging to Kurdistan Region?[110]

The idea of a safe zone runs counter to the U.S. goal of a "united Iraq," but the widespread lack of security and ongoing destruction calls the U.S. position into question: in the view of many minorities, a united Iraq is non-existent. The invasion of IS has underscored the absence of the state. Difficult choices regarding the policies toward these areas now beset decision makers. Increased minority autonomy inescapably means arming local militias. The lessons of the mandate period as to the dangers of arming sectarian and ethnic groups may explain the reluctance of the U.S. administration to pursue such an option. Though militiafication runs counter to the united Iraq policy, it is already taking place and is the inevitable reaction to the IS threat. Further, without some form of the often-invoked "safe zone," what future can there be for minority communities that remain unprotected by their governments? The political message of the Yazidi community has now come to mirror that of the Christians, in calling for a safe zone to include Sinjar as well as the Nineveh Plain. Local people have stopped waiting for governments to act and Western civilians have begun volunteering to aid Christians in forming their own military forces.[111]

The Kurdish Option

Christian communities have had an ugly and bloody history with Kurdish tribes, stretching back to the mid-nineteenth century Bedr Khan massacres in Anatolia, and continuing with the early twentieth century conflicts with Kurds in Iran and Iraq. Though today's context is different, competitions remain salient, and Iraqi minorities have very ambivalent feelings regarding Kurdistan.

Today, the Kurdistan Regional Government (KRG) promotes a narrative championing itself as the protector of minorities, and it has been largely successful in selling this image of itself to the international community. There is some truth in this narrative, in that the Kurdistan Region remains one of the last places in Iraq where persecuted minority communities can take refuge. However, several areas of intrigue belie this picture.

The KRG has pursued a strategy to increase, as much as possible, the territory of a future Kurdistan, which has translated into an endeavor to consolidate control over the Nineveh Plain and Sinjar, both of which are heavily populated with minority communities. The KRG's approach toward minorities has been to accept their presence and even at times promote their well-being, but at the price of their acceptance of the ruling Kurdistan Democratic Party (KDP)'s dominant national narrative. The KRG has invested sizable funds to develop services for Christian communities, to upkeep churches, and so forth. Yet Christians are divided in their attitudes toward these gestures. Some are appreciative, while others see this as part of a political game of cooptation, where loyalties are bought.[112] Many Christians and Yazidis feel that the imposition of Kurdish-defined identities (whether political or ethnic) are reminiscent of Saddam's Arabization schemes, and both speak of a history of "Kurdification."[113] Intimidation and violence have also been directed at those resisting KRG agendas.[114]

Competition over land remains a more serious problem. The KRG has reportedly seized Christian-owned lands following instances of Christian displacement that occurred from the Saddam era through the Iraq War years.[115] Assyrians complain that the KRG has failed to return much of this Christian property to its owners. Ongoing political marginalization remains a problem for Christians and other minorities, including cases where the KDP prevented Christians from voting.[116]

Despite the often widespread submission of minority communities to the expanding KRG authority, many have been tragically failed by the KRG when protection was most needed, creating the impression that they are not considered equal or valued citizens when defending them would require effort. Though advancing to capture new ground at Kirkuk and fighting tenaciously to hold it, Peshmerga forces quickly withdrew from many Christian and Yazidi areas when IS attacked in August 2014, producing widespread emotions of betrayal and abandonment.

Though many Christians and other minorities have preferred Kurdish authority over absent Iraqi security, it remains uncertain whether Kurdistan can provide a long-term solution to the problem of Christian vulnerability.

Final Observations

The causes underlying the persecution and pressures experienced by Christians over the last century and a half are not all of the same nature. Christians have experienced violence stemming from tribal competitions, ethnic cleansing during nationalization efforts, the oppression of megalomaniacal despots, the crossfire of war, and Islamist terrorism. Regardless of the many factors behind the violence, the net effect is singular: numbers of Christians in the region have been undergoing a trend of steady decline to the point of existential crisis.[117]

Christians in the Middle East have long participated in historical endeavors to work out political frameworks and cultural identities that can satisfy the need for security and inclusivity. Though none of these attempts has proven sufficient to solve the problems that continue to plague Middle Eastern polities, Christians have contributed vitality to an ongoing conversation; their disappearance from the region would therefore constitute a profound setback for other minorities who contend with similar dilemmas. Likewise, the Christian exodus represents a loss to the majority

Muslim communities who are enriched by the diversity that the Christian presence provides.

As the despotic rulers who previously enforced the partially-secular nationalist orders of the region are removed or weakened, state-sovereignty is being rendered meaningless and authority is being sequestered by non-state actors in an increasingly fragmented environment. As traditional state-structures fail, religiously-inflected nationalism appears to be the only sufficiently compelling alternative embraced by large numbers of the population. Often characterized by a high level of Salafi Islamist influence, the religion-dominated landscape has proven unviable for Christian survival.[118] The emerging reality indicates that continued Christian presence in the absence of a strong, secular ruler may depend upon the ability of Christians to militarize and self-protect. However, the history of early twentieth century violence as a result of competitions between armed ethnic groups and minorities casts doubt on the potential of this trend to serve as a solution, and influential international players, such as the United States, have shown great reluctance to pursue a strategy of arming minority populations. Without the ability to self-protect, and in the absence of security furnished by the state, the future of Christians in the region remains a grim portrait of uncertainty.

NOTES

1 I lived in Syria during the advent of the 2011 Syrian uprising and was later in northern Iraq when Mosul and Nineveh's Christian communities fled the group self-identifying as the Islamic State in 2014. The field research component of this chapter is therefore based on extensive contact with members of Christian populations in both countries during these key events. My gratitude is extended to Daniel Brown and the Institute for the Study of Religion in the Middle East for supporting my work in Iraq where it was possible to observe the events that befell the Christian community in 2014. For their comments I am also grateful to Syria analysts Aron Lund and Aymenn Jawad al-Tamimi, Prof. Orit Bashkin of the University of Chicago, and Joel Veldkamp who worked among Christians in Syria.

2 Frederick A. Aprim, *Assyrians: From Bedr Khan to Saddam Hussein* (Bloomington, IN: Xlibris, 2006), 50.

3 Joseph Yacoub, *The Assyrian Question* (Chicago: Alpha Graphic, 1986), see 58–118. See also Aprim, *Assyrians*, 61–106.

4 Some scholars and Iraq Christians use these terms interchangeably; others use "Assyrian" to refer to Iraqi Christians generally. Whether the terms "Assyrian" and "Chaldean" demarcate an ethnic, religious, or "cultural" boundary can be muddled by identity politics. I will use the term "Christian" where the generality will suffice and "Assyrian" when referring to events concerning Neo-Aramaic speaking Iraqi Christians that have specifically adopted that label. On the label "Chaldean" and identity issues, see Yasmeen S. Hanoosh, "The Politics of Minority: Chaldeans between Iraq and America" (PhD diss., University of Michigan, 2008), 7–10 and chapter 2.

5 Aprim, *Assyrians*, 155–158.

6 See Sargon George Donabed, "Iraq and the Assyrian Unimagining: Illuminating Scaled Suffering and a Hierarchy of Genocide from Simele to Anfal." PhD diss., University of Toronto, 2010, 61–73.

7 Charles Tripp, *A History of Iraq*, 2nd ed. (Cambridge: Cambridge University Press, 2002), 80.

8 Sargon Donabed and Shamiran Mako, "Between Denial and Existence: Situating Assyrians within the Discourse on Cultural Genocide," in *The Assyrian Heritage: Threads of Continuity and Influence*, ed. Önver A. Cetrez, Sargon G. Donabed, and Aryo Makko (Sweden: Elanders Sverige, 2012), 287.

9 Donabed and Mako, "Denial and Existence," 288.

10 Donabed, "Assyrian Unimagining," 185–252.

11 Aprim, "Assyrians," 239–241.

12 Amnesty International, *Human Rights Briefing* (London: Amnesty International, 2010); Human Rights Watch, *On Vulnerable Ground: Violence against Minority Communities in Nineveh Province's Disputed Territories* (2009), 35.

13 HRW, *On Vulnerable Ground*, 32.

14 Martin Chulov, "Baghdad Church Survivors Speak of Taunts, Killings, and Explosions," *The Guardian*, November 1, 2010, http://www.theguardian.com/world/2010/nov/01/baghdad-church-siege-survivors-speak; see also "The Massacre of Assyrians at Our Lady of Deliverance Church in Baghdad," *AINA*, December 3, 2010, http://www.aina.org/releases/20101203154244.htm

15 "Church Bombings in Iraq since 2004," *AINA*, January 7, 2008 (updated periodically), accessed February 3, 2015, http://www.aina.org/news/20080107163014.htm. The version of this periodically-updated list accessed as of this writing describes the 45 churches of Mosul as "destroyed," which is not correct, though they have been seized by IS.

16 Joseph Yacoub, "Christian Minorities of the Countries of the Middle East: A Glimpse to the Present Situation and Future Perspectives," in *Syriac Churches Encountering Islam: Past Experiences and Future Perspectives*, ed. Dietmar W. Winkler (Piscataway, NJ: Gorgias Press, 2010), 189.

17 During the Iraq War years, Iraqi Christian communities were sometimes punished with revenge attacks for perceived Western insults to Islam. International Crisis Group, *Iraq's New Battlefront: The Struggle over Ninewa*, Middle East Report no. 90 (September 28, 2009), 25 n. 151.

18 U.S. Department of State, Bureau of Democracy, Human Rights and Labor, *International Religious Freedom Report for 2009*; Some of the numbers in this report are inflated, such as the claim that 45 churches were destroyed in Mosul in 2014, which comes from the AINA article reporting the same. This report nevertheless represents a useful compilation of information on the experience of the Iraqi Christian community since 2003, including many photographs: Peter BetBasoo, *Incipient Genocide: The Ethnic Cleansing of the Assyrians of Iraq* (AINA: June 12, 2007, updated Sept. 3, 2014), 21–27; U.S. Commission on International Religious Freedom, *Annual Report: Iraq Chapter* (2009), 45; ICG, *Iraq's New Battlefront*, 25, 25 n. 151.

19 Ezel Kay Shaw and Stanford J. Shaw, *History of the Ottoman Empire and Modern Turkey. Vol. 2. Reform, Revolution, and Republic* (Cambridge: Cambridge University Press, 1977), 143. Amid the violence, some Christians were protected by Muslim neighbors in several areas, a famous example being the Algerian Abd el-Kader who lived in the city's citadel.

20 N. E. Bou-Nacklie, "Tumult in Syria's Hama in 1925: The Failure of a Revolt," *Journal of Contemporary History* 33, no. 2 (1998): 277–278, 278 n. 12.

21 Ellen Marie Lust-Okar, "Failure of Collaboration: Armenian Refugees in Syria," *Middle Eastern Studies* 32, no. 1 (1996): 61.
22 Bou-Nacklie, "Tumult," 276; Lust-Okar, "Failure of Collaboration," 58.
23 Bou-Nacklie, "Tumult," 288; Philip S. Khoury, *Syria and the French Mandate: the Politics of Arab Nationalism, 1920–1945* (Princeton, NJ: Princeton University Press, 1987), 151.
24 Aprim, "Assyrians," 268–269.
25 The *shahāda*, a creedal declaration of faith in Islam.
26 Donabed and Mako, "Denial and Existence," 286.
27 This perception is legitimate in some respects, but it is incorrect to assume that only the Sunni majority has been constrained under Asad power and that minorities have not also had to tread carefully under the state's heavy hand.
28 Joshua Landis, "Syria: Secularism, Arabism, and Sunni Orthodoxy," in *Teaching Islam: Textbooks and religion in the Middle East*, ed. Eleanor Abdella Doumato and Gregory Starrett (Boulder: Lynne Rienner, 2007), 184–185.
29 Personal status law is a legal convention in most Arab states where an area of the law dealing with many issues that involve gender (such as what is expected of marriage partners, who qualifies for divorce, and how inheritance is distributed) is reserved for derivation from shari'a rulings. For an understanding of this institution, see: George N. Sfeir, *Modernization of the Law in Arab States: An Investigation into Current Civil, Criminal, and Constitutional Law in the Arab World* (San Francisco: Austin & Winfield, 1998), chapter 2.
30 I have frequently encountered such sentiments among Syrian Christians. One ethnographer who has recently focused on these issues is Andreas Bandak: "Of Refrains and Rhythms in Contemporary Damascus: Urban Space and Christian-Muslim Coexistence," *Current Anthropology* 55, no. S10 (2014): S254–S256.
31 In 2010, I was told by Syrian Christians that a particular village was the last Christian village in Syria to not have a mosque, and that plans to build a mosque there were underway. Whether or not this is the case, the statement reflected a prevalent sense of vulnerability. The Christians did not seem to begrudge the building of mosques where the needs of local Muslim populations called for it, but felt that their communities were targeted in ways where there was no reciprocal equivalent to assert a Christian presence – new churches in majority-Muslim areas not appearing.
32 Phillip Smyth, "Syria's 31 Percenters: How Bashar al-Asad Built Minority Alliances and Countered Minority Foes," *Gloria Center: Global Research in International Affairs* 16, no. 1 (2012), http://www.gloria-center.org/2012/04/syria%E2%80%99s-31-percenters-how-bashar-al-asad-built-minority-alliances-and-countered-minority-foes/; Aymenn Jawad al-Tamimi, "Syria's Assyrians, Caught in the Middle," *Daily Star*, December 7, 2012, http://www.aymennjawad.org/12643/syria-assyrians
33 Syrian Christians have also disliked the fact that the constitution bars them from the presidency: Sami Moubayed, "Why Syria's Christians Are Angry," CNN, February 28, 2012, http://edition.cnn.com/2012/02/28/opinion/moubayed-syria-christians/index.html
34 "Try to Stay Peaceful," *The Economist*, May 5, 2012, http://www.economist.com/node/21554224. Minorities belonging to liberal circles of artists and intellectuals often opposed the repressive control of the Syrian regime, a prime example being the famous television star Fares Helou, who during the uprising vocally supported the Syrian opposition, and had to flee with his family to France. Fares' commitment to the values of the revolution engendered the animosity of many of his own relatives, who remained pro-regime and shared with me their sense of outrage that he would "stir up trouble." For

an earlier interview with Fares that sheds light on the relationship between artists and the regime, see Lawrence Wright, "Captured on Film," *The New Yorker*, May 15, 2006, http:// www.newyorker.com/magazine/2006/05/15/captured-on-film

35 Aryn Baker, "Eyewitness from Homs: An Alawite Refugee Warns of Sectarian War in Syria," *Time*, March 1, 2012, http://world.time.com/2012/03/01/eyewitness-from-homs-an-alawite-refugee-warns-of-sectarian-war-in-syria/

36 In early 2012 an armed group invaded a mixed Sunni-Christian area at the southern end of the Christian region of al-Wadi al-Nasara. The villages of this area were already filled with Alawite and Christian (and some Sunni) refugees whose neighborhoods in Homs had been bombarded by rebel shelling. The militants erected makeshift checkpoints in an attempt to intercept Alawite families passing through the area (in similar fashion to the Syrian mukhābarāt who were frequently committing violence in Homs against those deemed to be oppositional at similar roadblocks). Several Christians were killed by the group before government forces restored order, but in the meantime, thousands of the refugees were terrorized, prompting a second surge of fleeing, this time into the mountainous area to the north. The incident was not reported in major media; I received the reports from Christians in the area. Though far less serious than the more violent situations that would unfold as the war moved to various Christian areas later on, this event illustrated the uncomfortable paradox of Syria at that point: the forces of the regime would crack down violently on dissent, yet conversely were the only source of protection and stability for most of the country. While the government reacted harshly in Homs to crush the resistance threatening its authority, it simultaneously intervened in other areas to maintain security.

37 Ulrike Putz, "We're Too Frightened to Talk: Christians Flee from Radical Rebels in Syria," *Der Spiegel*, July 25, 2012, http://www.spiegel.de/international/world/christians-flee-from-radical-rebels-in-syria-a-846180.html

38 This happened twice, in both February and June. Hugh Macleod and Annasofie Flamand, "Inside Syria: Aleppo's Christians Arm against Islamists," *Global Post*, July 31, 2012, http://www.globalpost.com/dispatch/news/regions/middle-east/syria/120731/aleppo-christians-islamists-jihadis-al-qaeda-iraq-sectarian-conflict; Sam Dagher, "Syrian Conflict Draws in Christians," *Wall Street Journal*, July 23, 2012, http://www.wsj.com/articles/SB10001424052702303644004577524653025270434

39 Kim Sengupta, "The Plight of Syria's Christians," *The Independent*, November 2, 2012, http://www.independent.co.uk/news/world/middle-east/the-plight-of-syrias-christians-we-left-homs-because-they-were-trying-to-kill-us-8274710.html; Jose Rodriguez, "Syrian Christians Dream of Life Without Assad or Radical Islamists," *Agence France Press*, March 13, 2013, http://www.businessinsider.com/syrian-christians-dream-of-life-without-assad-or-radical-islamists-2013-3. A resident of Homs described to me how her three elderly Christian neighbors had decided not to leave their homes in the Old City when most Christians fled, but were later turned out into the street in their pajamas by fighters, without being allowed to take any of their money or gold.

40 Kinda Jayoush, "In Maaloula, a Christian Community Struggles to Survive and Keep the Language of Jesus Alive," *Syria Deeply*, December 25, 2014, http://www.syriadeeply.org/articles/2014/12/6544/maaloula-christian-community-struggles-survive-language-jesus-alive/

41 "Syrian Government Says Maaloula's Sites Sacked by Rebels," *al-Monitor*, May 5, 2014, http://www.al-monitor.com/pulse/security/2014/05/syria-maaloula-damage-christian-sites.html

42 "The Churches of Yabroud in Ruins," *al-Akhbar*, n.d., http://english.al-akhbar.com/photoblogs/churches-yabrud-ruins

43 "Armenian Church Reportedly Burned Down in Aleppo," *ArmeniaNow*, October 30, 2012, http://armenianow.com/news/40665/armenian_st_gevorg_church_aleppo

44 "Syria: Attacks on Religious Sites Raise Tensions," *Human Rights Watch*, January 23, 2013, http://www.hrw.org/news/2013/01/23/syria-attacks-religious-sites-raise-tensions

45 "Armed Rebels Attack Ancient Village, Church in Northern Syria," *Xinhua News*, February 11, 2013, http://news.xinhuanet.com/english/world/2013-02/11/c_132164734.htm

46 Waleed Abu al-Khair, "Al-Qaeda-linked Groups Desecrate Churches in Syria," *Al Shorfa*, archived January 10, 2014 by AINA, http://www.aina.org/news/20140110112609.htm

47 Ruth Sherlock, "Dispatch: Syria Rebels 'Burned down Churches and Destroyed Christian Graves," *The Telegraph*, January 3, 2015, http://www.telegraph.co.uk/news/worldnews/middleeast/syria/11323109/Dispatch-Syria-rebels-burned-down-churches-and-destroyed-Christian-graves.html

48 "Syrian Rebels Destroy Orthodox Church in Al-Thawrah," *AINA*, August 9, 2013, http://www.aina.org/news/2013089111228.htm

49 Alan Taylor, "Syria's City of Homs, Shattered by War," *The Atlantic*, May 14, 2014, http://www.theatlantic.com/photo/2014/05/syrias-city-of-homs-shattered-by-war/100735/

50 Sam Hardy, "ISIS Have Destroyed the Armenian Genocide Memorial Church in Deir ez-Zor," *Conflict Antiquities*, September 27, 2014, https://conflictantiquities.wordpress.com/2014/09/27/iraq-syria-islamic-state-destruction-deir-ez-zor-armenian-genocide-memorial-church/; "US Officials and Armenians Condemn Destruction of Armenian Church and Genocide Memorial at Deir Zor, Syria," *The Armenian Mirror-Spectator*, October 3, 2014, http://www.mirrorspectator.com/2014/10/03/us-officials-and-armenians-condemn-destruction-of-armenian-church-and-genocide-memorial-at-deir-zor-syria/. The above has merely been a short list of such examples; by the end of 2013 alone, Patriarch Gregory III Laham released a list counting 88 churches that had been damaged or destroyed in Syria thus far: "Updated List of Churches and Monasteries and Shrines Damaged in the Syrian Crisis," *Byzantine Catholic Church in America*, December 22, 2013, http://byzcath.org/index.php/news-mainmenu-49/3862-updated-list-of-churches-and-monasteries-and-shrines-damaged-in-the-syrian-crisis-22-dec-2013

51 al-Tamimi, "Caught in the Middle."

52 Aymenn Jawad al-Tamimi, *Christians in Syria: Separating Fact from Fiction* (London: The Henry Jackson Society, 2012), http://henryjacksonsociety.org/wp-content/uploads/2012/11/HJS-Christians-in-Syria-Report.pdf

53 Forty-six Christians were reported killed, mostly civilians including women and children; others were used as human shields; 30 bodies were dumped in mass graves; the bodies of an entire family, including elderly and children, were thrown down a well; and churches were wrecked. "Syria: Opposition Abuses during Ground Offensive," *Human Rights Watch*, November 19, 2013, http://www.hrw.org/news/2013/11/19/syria-opposition-abuses-during-ground-offensive. On the fact that such cases have often involved an array of rebel groups, and not just ISIS, Aymenn al-Tamimi commented: "In Tabqa [Thawrah] ... desecration and looting of Christian property, with the destruction of local churches, began in earnest once rebels including Jabhat al-Nusra took over the city. This happened, it should be noted, *before* the announcement of ISIS. In any event, Jabhat al-Nusra was also a participant in the Sadad massacre of Christians, and is accused by the Syriac Military Council of being behind the burning down a specific church in

Qamishli countryside. Simply blaming any abuses that happen against Christians on ISIS – typically characterized as a foreign-dominated group – is a distortion of the record that diverts attention from the rebels who abetted the rise of the jihadi groups." "Christian Militia and Political Dynamics in Syria," *Syria Comment*, February 24, 2014, http://www.joshualandis.com/blog/christian-militia-political-dynamics-syria/

54 "Priest Who Negotiated Syria Hostage Releases Slain," *al-Arabiya*, October 25, 2012, http://english.alarabiya.net/articles/2012/10/25/245933.html

55 Ruth Sherlock, "Priest 'Beheaded' in Syria Video Actually 'Shot Dead,'" *The Telegraph*, July 1, 2013, http://www.telegraph.co.uk/news/worldnews/middleeast/syria/10153954/Priest-beheaded-in-Syria-video-actually-shot-dead.html

56 A staunch supporter of the revolution, Father Paolo was expelled from Syria by the regime, and was later kidnapped after traveling to rebel-controlled Syria to meet with Islamist rebels to attempt dialogue with them about their chosen methods and goals; he has not reemerged from captivity and may have been killed. Neil MacFarquhar, "Syria Expels Jesuit Priest Who Spoke for Change," *New York Times*, June 20, 2012, http://www.nytimes.com/2012/06/21/world/middleeast/syria-expels-activist-roman-catholic-priest.html; Khaled Oweis, "Al Qaida Group Kidnaps Italian Jesuit Paolo Dall'Oglio in Syria," *Reuters*, July 29, 2013, http://blogs.reuters.com/faithworld/2013/07/29/al-qaeda-group-kidnaps-italian-jesuit-paolo-dalloglio-in-syria-activists/

57 "Syria: Dutch Priest Fr van der Lugt Shot Dead in Homs," *BBC*, April 7, 2014, http://www.bbc.com/news/world-middle-east-26927068

58 "Nusra Front Frees Priest, Other Christians in Syira," *al-Arabiya*, October 10, 2014, http://english.alarabiya.net/en/News/middle-east/2014/10/10/Nusra-Front-frees-priest-other-Christians-in-Syria.html; The problem may have followed al-Nusra's demand that the Christian hand over part of their harvest: Julia A. Seymour, "Militants in Syria Free Kidnapped Franciscan Priest," WORLD, October 20, 2014, http://www.worldmag.com/2014/10/militants_in_syria_free_kidnapped_franciscan_priest

59 Anne Barnard, "Two Blasts Strike Near Security Agencies in Syria," *New York Times*, March 17, 2012, http://www.nytimes.com/2012/03/18/world/middleeast/damascus-syria-two-large-explosions-reported.html

60 Most of the victims of this particular bomb happened to be Muslims. "Car Bomb Kills 13 in Syrian Captial," *Associated Press*, October 21, 2012, http://newsok.com/car-bomb-kills-13-in-syrian-capital/article/feed/450671

61 Ruth Sherlock, "50 Dead in Damascus Car Bomb Attacks," *The Telegraph*, November 28, 2012, http://www.telegraph.co.uk/news/worldnews/middleeast/syria/9709945/Syria-50-dead-in-Damascus-car-bomb-attacks.html; Patrick J. McDonnell, "In Syria, Pro-Assad Damascus Suburb Feels Targeted," August 13, 2013, http://articles.latimes.com/2013/aug/13/world/la-fg-syria-violence-jaramana-20130814

62 Example reports on mortar attacks on civilian areas: "Jets Bomb Homs as Mortar Fire Rocks Damascus," *Daily Star*, March 12, 2013, http://www.dailystar.com.lb/News/Middle-East/2013/Mar-12/209729-jets-bomb-homs-as-mortar-fire-rocks-damascus.ashx; "One Child Killed, Dozens Wounded in Damascus School Attack," *Xinhua News*, April 15, 2014, http://news.xinhuanet.com/english/world/2014-04/15/c_133264573.htm; "Damascus Mortar Attack Kills Eight," *AFP*, October 6, 2013, https://uk.news.yahoo.com/damascus-mortar-attack-kills-eight-state-media-133004830.html; "Ten Civilians Injured in Mortar Attacks in Damascus, Its Countryside, and Hama," *SANA*, Sept. 15, 2014,

http://107.6.182.27/en/?p=13145; "Mortar Shells on the Center of Damascus: Children, Civilians, and Churches Affected," *Vatican Network*, n.d., http://www.news.va/en/news/asiasyria-mortar-shells-on-the-center-of-damascus-; "Funerals of 4 Slain Syrian Kids Held in Damascus," *Xinhua News*, November 12, 2013, http://www.globaltimes.cn/content/824370 .shtml; "Shelling Kills Nine Children in Damascus," *al-Akhbar*, November 11, 2013, http://english.al-akhbar.com/node/17570; "U.N. Denounces Mortar Attacks on Schools in the Syrian Capital," *LA Times*, November 12, 2013, http://articles.latimes.com/2013/nov/12/world/la-fg-wn-un-syria-mortar-attacks-schools-20131112. Syrian state media has been the source for the majority of the reports of deaths occurring inside Damascus, and many Western analysts have questioned its credibility as a vested belligerent in the conflict; however, I have corroborated most of these attacks in conversations with local Christians. On March 28, 2013 a projectile hit the architecture department of Damascus University, killing between 15 and 20 graduate students and injuring 30: Oliver Holmes and Hamdi Istanbullu, "Mortar Kills 15 at Damascus University," *Reuters*, March 28, 2013, http://www.reuters.com/article/2013/03/28/us-syria-crisis-idUSBRE92R0TV20130328

63 When Alawites of Adra, an industrial town north of Damascus, were massacred in December 2013, Christian families were among those kidnapped and taken from Adra to Douma. I was informed by sources who helped care for Christian survivors of Adra that Christian families had been kidnapped. "Islamists Kill 15 Alawite and Druze Civilians in Syria," *Reuters*, December 12, 2013, http://www.reuters.com/article/2013/12/12/us-syria-crisis-adra-idUSBRE9BB0PM20131212; "Syrian Troops Launch Offensive after Dozens Killed," *Associated Press*, December 13, 2013, http://news.yahoo.com/syrian-troops-launch-offensive-dozens-killed-154525456.html

64 Though as a vulnerable minority the Christian population risks shrinkage and eventual disappearance, in terms of overall suffering during the conflict, Christians have fared better than their average Sunni counterparts, due to better social positioning, strong networks of support, access to aid, and greater ease in emigrating to the West.

65 Aaron Y. Zelin, *The War between ISIS and al-Qaeda for Supremacy of the Global Jihadist Movement*, Research Notes no. 20 (Washington, DC: WINEP, 2014), 2–3.

66 Whether ISI remained part of al-Qaida until the disputes of early 2014 or had ceased to be officially affiliated in 2006 is a complicated question. See Zelin, *War between ISIS and al-Qaeda*, 3–4; Aron Lund, "A Public Service Announcement from Al-Qaeda," *Carnegie: Syria in Crisis*, February 3, 2014; Romain Caillet, "The Islamic State: Leaving al-Qaeda Behind," *Carnegie: Syria in Crisis*, December 27, 2013.

67 Charles Lister, *Profiling the Islamic State*, Brookings Doha Center Analysis Paper no. 13 (Brookings Institute: November 2014), 13.

68 Jean-Pierre Filiu, "Al-Qaida Is Dead, Long Live Al-Qaida," *Carnegie: Syria in Crisis*, April 22, 2014, http://carnegieendowment.org/syriaincrisis/?fa=55401

69 "How Can Militants Take Over Iraqi Cities?" *BBC*, June 11, 2014, http://www.bbc.co.uk/news/world-middle-east-25588623

70 "Sunni Rebels Declare New 'Islamic Caliphate,'" *al-Jazeera*, June 30, 2014, http://www.aljazeera.com/news/middleeast/2014/06/isil-declares-new-islamic-caliphate-201462917326669749.html

71 Chris Looney, "Al-Qaeda's Governance Strategy in Raqqa," *Syria Comment*, December 8, 2013, http://www.joshualandis.com/blog/al-qaedas-governance-strategy-raqqa-chris-looney/

72 Firas al-Hakkar, "The Mysterious Fall of Raqqa, Syria's Kandahar," *al-Akhbar*, November 8, 2013, http://english.al-akhbar.com/node/17550; Richard Spencer, "Militant Islamic group in Syria Orders Christians to Pay Tax for Their Protection," *The Telegraph*, February 27, 2014, http://www.telegraph.co.uk/news/10666204/Militant-Islamist-group-in-Syria-orders-Christians-to-pay-tax-for-their-protection.html

73 Alison Tahmizian Meuse, "In Show of Supremacy, Syria al-Qaida Branch Torches Church," *Syria Deeply*, October 30, 2013, archived here: http://www.aymennjawad.org/14010/in-show-of-supremacy-syria-al-qaida-branch

74 Kamal Shekho, "Christians Leave Raqqa, the Capital of the Islamic State," *All4Syria/ The Syrian Observer*, July 16, 2014, http://syrianobserver.com/Features/Features/Where+Are+the+Christians+of+Raqqa+After+It+Became+the+Capital+of+the+Islamic+Caliphate. Establishing a *da'wa* office in a requisitioned church was a symbolical gesture of triumphalism.

75 An image of the *dhimmī* agreement was posted online here, showing signatures of local Christians who signed it: http://justpaste.it/ejur. Aymenn Jawad al-Tamimi has provided a partial translation with commentary, here: "The Islamic State of Iraq and ash-Sham's Dhimmi Pact for the Christians of Raqqa Province," *Syria Comment*, February 26, 2014, http://www.joshualandis.com/blog/islamic-state-iraq-ash-shams-dhimmi-pact-christians-raqqa-province/

76 Aryn Baker, "Al-Qaeda Rebels in Syria Tell Christians to Pay Up or Die," *Time*, February 28, 2014, http://world.time.com/2014/02/28/al-qaeda-in-syria-extorts-christians/

77 Kamal Shekho, "Christians Leave Raqqa."

78 A translation of the document is available in Aymenn Jawad al-Tamimi, "Archive of Islamic State Administrative Documents" (Specimen S, "Ultimatum for the Christians of Mosul"), *AymennJawad.org*, January 27, 2015, http://www.aymennjawad.org/2015/01/archive-of-islamic-state-administrative-documents

79 This was not the first time this method had been employed to publically pressure Christians to depart: HRW, *On Vulnerable Ground*, 33.

80 This was not the work of opportunistic local actors but an official policy handed down to the fighters that day, when IS realized that Christians were leaving *en masse*. During the period following the takeover of Mosul, Christians were not prevented from transporting their valuables out of the city. Many Christians had immediately fled upon the jihadist invasion, but had returned to their homes in the following weeks when the situation seemed somewhat stable. Some planned to remain. Others decided to leave and had already relocated their families before the exodus of July 18. Those Christians who left the city even within the days immediately preceding the 18th were able to do so without having their belongings confiscated.

81 Conversion to Islam is performed by reciting a short affirmation that can be uttered in a few seconds.

82 Christine van den Toorn, "How the U.S.-Favored Kurds Abandoned the Yazidis When ISIS Attacked," *Daily Beast*, August 17, 2014, http://www.thedailybeast.com/articles/2014/08/17/how-the-u-s-favored-kurds-abandoned-the-yazidis-when-isis-attacked.html

83 "Yazidi Man Tells of Family Wiped Out by Islamic State 'Massacre' in Kocho," *The Telegraph*, August 17, 2014, http://www.telegraph.co.uk/news/worldnews/middleeast/iraq/11039575/Yazidi-man-tells-of-family-wiped-out-by-Islamic-State-massacre-in-Kocho.html

84 Though rejected by many mainstream Muslims as misguided, IS' approach to each minority community is determined by a theologically-derived criteria. Though IS

dispossessed Mosul's entire Christian community, they did not massacre them or conduct a widespread female enslavement project. IS' approach to Yazidis has been different. They believe that as a non *'ahl al-kitāb* ("people of the book") minority, Yazidis should not exist in "Muslim lands." IS targeted the Yazidi community not as *kuffār* (infidels), but as *mushrikīn* (polytheists); whereas Christians were given the *jizya* option in addition to conversion or "the sword," Yazidis were told to convert to Islam or be killed. See the collection of fatwas by Muslim clerics condemning IS practices: "Open Letter to Dr. Ibrahim Awwad al-Badri, Alias 'Abu Bakr al-Baghdadi,'" September 19, 2014, http://www.lettertobaghdadi.com/

85 Amnesty International, *Escape from Hell: Torture and Sexual Slavery in Islamic State Captivity in Iraq* (2014). Following initial denials from IS supporters that the enslavement phenomenon was taking place, IS published its own manifesto, publically revealing that they were conducting a slavery revival program: "The Revival of Slavery before the Hour," *Dabiq* no. 4, October 2014, 14–17.

86 The airstrikes began on August 8: "Statement by the President," White House, Office of the Press Secretary, August 7, 2014.

87 Towns such as Ba'shiqa saw all of the Yazidi shrines destroyed, as had occurred in Sinjar.

88 "Iraq Christians Flee as Islamic State Takes Qaraqosh," *BBC*, August 7, 2014, http://www .bbc.com/news/world-middle-east-28686998

89 Liz Sly, "Baghdad Christian District Besieged," *Chicago Tribune*, May 9, 2007, http://articles.chicagotribune.com/2007-05-09/news/0705090173_1_sunni-shiites-insurgents-and-militias; A *Documentary History of Modern Iraq*, ed. Stacy Holden (Gainesville: University Press of Florida, 2012), 326; Richard Spencer, "Iraq Crisis: The Last Christians of Dora," *The Telegraph*, December 22, 2014, http://www.telegraph.co.uk/news/worldnews/middleeast/iraq/11307515/Iraq-crisis-The-last-Christians-of-Dora.html

90 Erica Goode, "Kidnapped Iraqi Archbishop Is Dead," *New York Times*, March 14, 2008, http://www.nytimes.com/2008/03/14/world/middleeast/14iraq.html; HRW, *On Vulnerable Ground*, 31. Other Mosul clergy members had been previously killed.

91 ICG, *Iraq's New Battlefront*, 25. Mosul residents were divided about who may have been responsible, but an al-Qaida leader was tried and convicted for murder. Iraqi church leaders subsequently opposed his death sentence, calling instead for reconciliation: "Violence should not call for more violence ... We are on the side of justice, not the death penalty," "Iraqi Bishop Assails Execution of Prelate's Abductor," *Zenit*, May 20, 2008, http://www .zenit.org/en/articles/iraqi-bishop-assails-execution-of-prelate-s-abductor

92 Yazidis were particularly wary of Islamist groups, having experienced devastating levels of violence. An operation involving four coordinated car bombings in August 2007 killed almost 800 Yazidis and wounded over 1,500 – the single deadliest terror attack of the entire Iraq War period.

93 The information in this paragraph is based on unpublished findings provided to me by Khidher Domle, a Dohuk-based Yazidi volunteer who monitors human rights violations in northern Iraq.

94 Secret police who are charged with the country's security but regularly commit extortion.

95 Some suggested that ISIS believed they had an Islamic basis for doing this, to the effect that Christians should not be in a position of property ownership, receiving rents from Muslims. Whether or not this was the case, what is interesting is that ISIS viewed Christian income as a legitimate booty, something they could snatch up at will.

96 Matthew Barber, "The Account of the Kidnapped Nuns," *Syria Comment*, August 2, 2014, http://www.joshualandis.com/blog/expulsion-mosuls-christians-part-1-account-kidnapped-nuns/

97 That IS invokes the provisions of this early treaty can explain aspects of their approach to Christians. (It should be noted that this set of conditions may have evolved later and been falsely attributed to 'Umar, or may have been initiated by him and then expanded to include more conditions later.) IS occupied some Christian churches during the Mosul takeover; this may have been in response to the *shurūṭ's* requirement that Christians give Muslims lodging upon request. The *shurūṭ* also stipulate that Christians may not display the cross, which can be understood as IS' basis for always removing the cross. The *shurūṭ* do not call for the destruction of churches (and a Mosul bishop I interviewed related that all accusations that churches had been destroyed in Mosul following the takeover were rumors), but they stipulate that Christians may not repair churches or build new ones. Though the *shurūṭ* were followed at times in early Islamic history, it is clear that they were later disregarded, as Christians have maintained or built churches since the coming of Islam, and displayed the cross on them. IS' fixation with this document probably stems from the fact that Ibn Taymiyya, a Medieval jurist frequently referenced by Salafi-Jihadists, considered the *shurūṭ* to be authentic and binding. See Norman A. Stillman, "Dhimma." In *Medieval Islamic Civilization: An Encyclopedia*. Vol. 1. A-K, ed. Josef W. Meri (New York: Routledge, 2006), 205–207; Vincent Cornell, "Religious Orthodoxy and Religious Rights in Medieval Islam: A Reality Check on the Road to Religious Toleration," in *Justice and Rights: Christian and Muslim Perspectives*, ed. Michael Ipgrave (Washington, Georgetown University Press: 2009), 58. It is significant that IS has ignored another treaty, also attributed to 'Umar (its authenticity also under question), in English termed "'Umar's Assurance," which was purportedly made with the Christians of Jerusalem when the city was first conquered by Muslims, and which extended to Christians the right to display the cross on churches and to "leave with the Byzantines" taking their property with them (rather than having it plundered as IS has done). If the treaty contains authentic elements, IS may have acted contrary to the practice of 'Umar. The treaty has been used historically: Mahar Y. Abu-Munshar, *Islamic Jerusalem and Its Christians: A History of Tolerance and Tensions* (London: I. B. Tauris, 2007), 81–117. IS has destroyed churches in Iraq since the summer of 2014: David D. Kirkpatrick, "Iraq: Militants Destroy Historic Church," *New York Times*, September 24, 2014, http://www.nytimes.com/2014/09/25/world/middleeast/iraq-militants-destroy-historic-church.html

98 Cathy Otten, "Last remaining Christians flee Iraq's Mosul," *al-Jazeera*, July 22, 2014, http://www.aljazeera.com/news/middleeast/2014/07/last-remaining-christians-flee-iraq-mosul-201472118235739663.html

99 In more recent times the term often carries a derogatory connotation, as most Middle Eastern Christians prefer to identify as *mesīḥiyyin*.

100 U.S. Commission on International Religious Freedom, *Annual Report: Iraq Chapter* (2013), 5. There are no reliable figures for the breakdown of religious populations for Iraq or Syria. For a useful comment on the numbers of Iraqi Christians – the pre-2003 figure being often inflated – see ICG, "Iraq's New Battlefront," 24 n. 143.

101 Sofia Barbarani, "Meet the Christian Soldiers Fighting for Their Lives against ISIS," *Haaretz*, December 16, 2014, http://www.haaretz.com/news/middle-east/1.631927

102 Jack Moore, "'4,000-Strong' Christian Militia Formed to Fight ISIS in Northern Iraq," *Newsweek*, February 4, 2015, http://www.newsweek.com/4000-strong-christian-militia-formed-fight-isis-northern-iraq-304371

103 Aron Lund, "Gangs of Latakia: The Militiafication of the Assad Regime," *Syria Comment*, July 23, 2013, http://www.joshualandis.com/blog/the-militiafication-of-the-assad-regime/

104 Jihad al-Zein, "Christians Taking Up Fight in Syria," *al-Monitor*, March 10, 2014, www .al-monitor.com/pulse/security/2014/03/syria-conflict-threat-to-christians-take-up-arms .html

105 Aymenn Jawad al-Tamimi, "The Druze Militias of Southern Syria," *Syria Comment*, November 13, 2014, http://www.joshualandis.com/blog/druze-militias-southern-syria/; For more on the dynamics of the Druze in the Syria conflict, see Tobias Lang, "Druze Sheikhs Protest in Sweida," *Carnegie: Syria in Crisis*, April 16, 2014, http:// carnegieendowment.org/syriaincrisis/?fa=55356

106 Joel Veldkamp, "Resurgence of the SSNP in Syria: An Ideological Opponent of the Regime Gets a Boost from the Conflict," *Syria Comment*, December 19, 2014, http:// www.joshualandis.com/blog/resurgence-of-the-ssnp-in-syria-an-ideological-opponent-of-the-regime-gets-a-boost-from-the-conflict/; The party has also clashed with regime forces: Lauren Williams, "Fighting among Pro-Assad Groups Points to Factional Future," *Daily Star*, May 17, 2014, http://www.dailystar.com.lb/News/Middle-East/2014/May-17/256755-fighting-among-pro-assad-groups-points-to-factional-future.ashx

107 For one of the most comprehensive overviews of Christian militias in Syria, see Aymenn Jawad al-Tamimi, "Christian Militia and Political Dynamics in Syria," *Syria Comment*, February 24, 2014, http://www.joshualandis.com/blog/christian-militia-political-dynamics-syria/. Despite the current cooperation between Kurdish and Christian forces against IS in northeastern Syria, tensions between the communities have been notable in recent memory: Salim Abraham, "Assyrians, the Indigenous People of the Middle East, Leave Home," *Ground Report*, July 7, 2008, archived here as "The Christians Are Leaving:" http://www.joshualandis.com/blog/the-christians-are-leaving-by-salim-abraham/

108 Martin Chulov and Kareem Shaheen, "Christian Militia in Syria Defends Ancient Settlements against Isis," *The Guardian*, March 3, 2015, http://www.theguardian .com/world/2015/mar/03/christian-militia-syria-defends-ancient-settlements-isis; Gianluca Mezzofiore, "Syria: Isis 'frees all Assyrian Christian hostages,'" *International Business Times*, March 17, 2015, http://www.ibtimes.co.uk/syria-isis-frees-all-assyrian-christian-hostages-1490798

109 Rania Abouzeid, "Iraqi Christians Weigh Taking Up Arms against the Islamic State," *National Geographic*, August 27, 2014, http://news.nationalgeographic.com/news/2014/08/140827-iraq-dahuk-islamic-state-assyrian-christians-peshmerga-nineveh-kurdistan/

110 At present, the Nineveh Plain is a disputed territory claimed by both the Iraqi government and the KRG and its administration has already been *de facto* divided between the two. This is further complicated by the IS conquest of much of it.

111 Michael Pizzi, "Assyrian Christians Crowdfund An Army to Reclaim Homeland from ISIL," *al-Jazeera America*, February 26, 2015, http://america.aljazeera.com/articles/2015/2/26/on-the-brink-of-extinction-assyrian-christians-crowd-fund-an-army. html; "Meet the Christian Soldiers Fighting for Their Lives against ISIS," *SINA*, December 16, 2014, http://www.syriacsnews.com/meet-christian-soldiers-fighting-lives-isis/

112 "To consolidate their grip on Nineveh and to facilitate its incorporation into the Kurdistan Region, Kurdish authorities have embarked on a two-pronged strategy: they

have offered minorities inducements while simultaneously wielding repression in order to keep them in tow." HRW, *On Vulnerable Ground*, 9, 25–26.

113 Aprim, "Assyrians," 287; Preti Taneja, *Assimilation, Exodus, Eradication: Iraq's Minority Communities Since 2003* (Minority Rights Group International: 2007), 20.

114 HRW, *On Vulnerable Ground*, 44–47.

115 U.S. Commission on International Religious Freedom, *Annual Report: Iraq Chapter* (2007); Donabed and Mako, "Denial and Existence," 291–292.

116 Taneja, *Assimilation*, 21.

117 Philippe Fargues explains that though Christians underwent tremendous decline in the first millennium following the coming of Islam, this trend reversed under the Ottomans with the percentage of the Christian population tripling during the period. A trend of decline resumed in the twentieth century. "The Arab Christians of the Middle East: A Demographic Perspective," in *Christian Communities in the Arab Middle East: The Challenge of the Future*, ed. Andrea Pacini (Oxford: Oxford University Press, 1998), 48–66. In the same volume, see also the discussion of emigration by Bernard Sabella, "The Emigration of Christian Arabs: Dimensions and Causes of the Phenomenon." Additionally, the efforts of Western Protestants to missionize eastern Christians have contributed to the reduction of the Christian population. Having "transmitted a cultural discourse permeated with a foreign vision," Western missionaries have helped alienate Christians from their own traditions and context, have incurred Muslim suspicions that Christians collude with Western powers, and have inadvertently promoted trends of emigration. Yacoub, "Christian Minorities," 217. In 2010 Syria conducted a crackdown on Protestant Evangelicals, at the behest of Orthodox and Catholic churches who resented losing congregants to the newer churches. "Don't Try Too Hard: Protestant Christians Are under Rare Fire," *The Economist*, November 18, 2010, http://www.economist.com/node/17528080

118 In response, some Christians are embracing similarly religiously-defined nationalisms: Hussain abdul-Hussain, "The Case for a Christian Lebanon," *NOW News*, November 10, 2014, https://now.mmedia.me/lb/en/commentaryanalysis/564377-the-case-for-a-christian-lebanon

Index

Abou Qorqas (Egypt): coping strategies of people in, 354; Muslim-Christian relations in, 353, 354, 355; sectarian violence in, 340; sexual harassment of women in, 352

Adegbola, Michael, 319

Adel, Maged, 347

Adventist Relief and Development Agency, 134, 136, 149

Advocates International, 154

Afghanistan: persecution of Christians in, 71, 72. *See also* Muslim majority states

Aflaq, Michel, 458

Africa: Christianity in, 15, 21, 61; Pentecostalism in, 90. *See also* Eritrea; Ethiopia; Nigeria; Somalia; Sudan

agnostics. *See* atheists/agnostics

Ahmadiyah, 207, 210, 215, 296

AIDS. *See* HIV/AIDS

Akerlof, George, 124

Akhil Bharatiya Vanvasi Kalyan Ashram (ABVKA), 226

Al Amoudein (Egypt): coping strategies of people in, 354; Muslim-Christian relations in, 340–341, 353, 354–356; sectarian violence in, 353

Al Aqsa Martyrs Brigade, 395, 422

al-Baghdadi, Abu Bakr, 464, 465

Algeria: persecution of Christians in, 71. *See also* Muslim majority states

al-Hakim, Caliph, 343

Ali, Suryadharma, 204

Aliyu, Talatu, 323–324

Allen, John, 2

Al-Liqa' Center, 376

All India Catholic Union (AICU), 240, 241

All India Christian Council (AICC), 240–241, 243, 247

All-India Hindu Mahasabha, 226

All India Muslim League, 285–286, 287

All India National Congress, 285

Alnemeh, Archbishop Selwanos Boutros, 59

Al-Qaeda in Iraq (AQI), 62, 464–465

Al Qaeda in the Islamic Magreb (AQIM), 313

Al-Shabab, 70–71, 72, 313

Al Tahalof Al Qibty Al Misry, 358

Ambedkar, B. R., 237, 286

American Friends Service Committee, 136, 146

American/Canadian Christian and Missionary Alliance (C&MA), 257, 258

Amity Foundation, 184

Amnesty International, 318

Amr ibn al-'As, 342

Anderson, Allan, 88

Anglicans: persecution of, 52, 53

Annis, Sheldon, 110

apostasy laws: in Pakistan, 7–8

Aqbat min ajl Misr (Copts for Egypt), 356

Arab Barometer (survey) 437–442

Arab countries: Christian communities in, 9–10; religious discrimination in, 436; religious freedom in, 435–436. *See also* Coptic Christians; Middle-East and North Africa; survey of religious attitudes in the Middle East West Bank; *and names of specific Arab countries*

Arab Evangelical School, 383

Arab-Israeli tensions, 373–375, 411, 416; as manifested in the Knesset, 405–407. *See also* Israel, State of; West Bank

Arab League, 374

Arabness, concept of, 386

Arab Spring, 431

Arafat, Yasser, 374, 421

Arbow, Batula Ali, 70–71

489

Seiple, Chris, 153, 276
Sen, Amartya, 126, 243
Seventh Day Adventist Church, 134
sex trafficking. *See* human trafficking
Seymour, William J., 87
Shah, Rebecca S., 5; essay by, 107–132
Shah, Timothy, 144
Shamni, Gadi, 414
Shanti Nagur (Pakistan): violence against
Christians in, 293, 297, 298
sharia law, 36; in Indonesia, 194, 195, 211–212;
in Nigeria, 8, 309, 311–312, 313; in Pakistan,
290, 291
Sharon, Ariel, 404, 411
Shea, Nina, 1, 2, 28, 154
Shenouda, Pope, 356
Shettima, Alhaji Kashim, 317
Shi'i/Shiites: in Indonesia 207, 210, 215; in
Pakistan, 296
Shihab al-Din affair, 410
Shinuy Party (Israel), 404, 411
Shortt, Rupert, 2
Shouwang Church (Beijing), 78, 177–178
Sikhs: in Pakistan, 286
Simonian, Artur, 101, 102
Sinai Peninsula, 373–374
Singh, Ajay, 243, 247
Singh, Gianni Kirtar, 286
Singh, Tara, 287
Singha, Sara, 7–8; essay by, 284–305
Sissi, Abdel Fattah el, 348
Six Day War (1967), 373–374
slavery, modern. *See* human trafficking
Smith, Bishop David, 298
Sobat KBB, 215–216
Society for Religious Freedom
(China), 175
Soeharto, Muhammad, 194, 199, 204–205,
213; ouster of, 195, 199–200
Somalia: religious persecution in, 70–71, 72.
See also Muslim majority states
Song Jong-nam, 142
South Africa: Pentecostalism in, 90
South Asian religious nationalist states:
persecution of Christians in, 29, 58,
65, 68–70; religious conflict in, 69–70;
religious demographics of, 36, 37, 38, 44,
45. *See also* India; Nepal; Pakistan
Southern Hemisphere. *See* Global South
Southern People's Liberation Army (SPLA)
(South Sudan), 148, 149, 150
South Korea: Pentecostalism in, 88

South Sudan: as independent state, 147–148, 149;
ongoing conflict in, 148–150
Soviet Union, collapse of: and religious freedom,
66, 67–68, 73
speaking in tongues: and Pentecostalism,
87–88, 92
spiritual capital, 111, 116. *See also* human
development
Sri Lanka, 69; persecution of Christians in, 70.
See also South Asian religious nationalist states
Stanislaus vs. The State of Madhya Pradesh,
229–230
Stark, Rodney, 185
Stefanos Foundation (Nigeria), 326, 327
Stefanus Alliance International, 243
Stepan, Alfred, 151
Strotz, Robert, 116
Sudan: in conflict with South Sudan, 147–150;
persecution of Christians in, 71. *See also*
Muslim majority states
Sudan Council of Churches, 148–149
Sudan Peace Act, 147, 149
Sufis, 207, 210
Suharto. *See* Soeharto, Muhammad
Sukarno (Soekarno), President (of Indonesia),
207, 213
Sumpter, Philip, 9; essay by, 372–396
Sun Zhongshan (Sun Yat-sen), 174
Supreme Council of Armed Forces (SCAF)
(Egypt), 357
survey of religious attitudes in the Middle East:
and knowledge of Christianity, 443–444; and
mosque attendance as measure of religious
behavior, 440–441, 448; and religious
denomination as criterion for patriotism, 439;
religious tolerance as measured by, 437–439,
447–448, 449–450; and social attitudes toward
Christians, 444–445
Sweden: religious freedom in, 76
Sweid, Hanna, 407–408, 427
Syria: Alawites in, 457, 459; Armenians in,
457; Ba'th Party in, 457; Christian militias
in, 473; Christian minorities in, 10, 387,
453, 456–458; French conflict with,
456–457; Islamic State's involvement
in, 464; Muslim-Christian relations in,
458; persecution of Christians in, 59,
72; sectarian conflict in, 431, 459–464;
tolerance of Christians in, 457–458;
uprising in, 458–459. *See also* Muslim
majority states; Syrian Christians; Syrian
civil war

Printed in the United States
By Bookmasters